UNITED STATES ARMY IN WORLD WAR II

The War in the Pacific

VICTORY IN PAPUA

by

Samuel Milner

MILITARY INSTRVCTION

CENTER OF MILITARY HISTORY
UNITED STATES ARMY
WASHINGTON, D.C., 1989

Library of Congress Catalog Card Number: 56–60004

First Printed 1957—CMH Pub 5–4

Special commemorative edition by the National Historical Society
6405 Flank Drive, Harrisburg, PA 17112
1993
Printed in the United States of America

UNITED STATES ARMY IN WORLD WAR II

Kent Roberts Greenfield, General Editor

Advisory Committee
(As of 30 March 1955)

James P. Baxter
President, Williams College

Samuel Flagg Bemis
Yale University

Gordon A. Craig
Princeton University

Elmer Ellis
University of Missouri

William T. Hutchinson
University of Chicago

Brig. Gen. Samuel G. Conley
Continental Army Command

Brig. Gen. Thomas W. Dunn
Army War College

Brig. Gen. Charles E. Beauchamp
Command and General Staff College

Brig. Gen. Urban Niblo
Industrial College of the Armed Forces

Col. Thomas D. Stamps
United States Military Academy

Charles H. Taylor
Harvard University

Office of the Chief of Military History
Maj. Gen. Albert C. Smith, Chief

Chief Historian
Chief, War Histories Division
Chief, Editorial and Publication Division
Chief, Editorial Branch
Chief, Cartographic Branch
Chief, Photographic Branch

Kent Roberts Greenfield
Col. Ridgway P. Smith, Jr.
Col. William H. Francis
Joseph R. Friedman
Maj. James P. Holly
Margaret E. Tackley

. . . to Those Who Served

Foreword

This is a companion volume to the one on *Guadalcanal* in the series on the war in the Pacific. Both record the operations designed to halt the advance of the enemy toward the vital transpacific line of communications with Australia and secure Australia as a base. Success in Papua and Guadalcanal, achieved in February 1943, put the Allied forces in a position to neutralize Rabaul and, this accomplished, to advance to the Philippines.

The present volume concentrates on the action of one United States Army division. In telling the story of a comparatively limited number of troops, the author has been able to present the combat experience of small units in sharper focus than has been possible in most of the other full-scale campaign volumes.

The campaign abounds in lessons. Of these one of the most vital is the frequent necessity for all commanders to evaluate their own actions by asking themselves this question: "How could I have helped, how should I have helped, how can I help my subordinates to accomplish their assigned tasks?"

Washington, D. C.   A. C. SMITH
15 March 1955   Maj. Gen., U. S. A.
                                                                Chief of Military History

The Author

Mr. Samuel Milner holds a graduate degree in history from the University of Alberta and has done further graduate work in political science at the University of Minnesota. During World War II, he served in Australia and New Guinea as a historian with the Air Transport Command, Army Air Forces. Upon completing *Victory in Papua* he left the Office, Chief of Military History, to become historian of the Air Weather Service, U.S. Air Force.

Preface

The strategic significance of the Papuan Campaign can be briefly stated. In addition to blunting the Japanese thrust toward Australia and the transpacific line of communications, it put General MacArthur's forces in a favorable position to take the offensive. But this little known campaign is significant for still another reason. It was the battle test of a large hitherto-inexperienced U. S. Army force and its commanders under the conditions which were to attend much of the ground fighting in the Pacific. Costly in casualties and suffering, it taught lessons that the Army had to learn if it was to cope with the Japanese under conditions of tropical warfare.

Since the official records of this early campaign were quite poor, the task of portraying American ground action in it accurately required that a great deal of essential information be found elsewhere. This supplementary information was secured in large part from participants whose names are to be found in the Bibliographical Note at the end of the volume All of them have my thanks, and certain of them who went to great lengths to help me have my special thanks. The following (ranks as of February 1952 when the manuscript was completed) are in the latter category: Lt. Gen. Robert L. Eichelberger, Maj. Gen. Clovis E. Byers, Maj. Gen. Jens A. Doe, Maj. Gen. Edwin F. Harding, Maj. Gen. Clarence A. Martin, Maj. Gen. Albert W. Waldron, Col. Bernd G. Baetcke, Col. Charles R. Dawley, Col. John E. Grose, Col. Alexander J. MacNab, Col. Kelsie E. Miller, Col. Herbert A. Smith, Col. Clarence M. Tomlinson, Lt. Col. Peter L. Dal Ponte, Lt. Col. Herbert M. Smith, Lt. Col. Bert Zeeff, and Maj. Robert H. Odell. A true picture of conditions as they existed at the time could not have been given without their help.

To tell the Australian side of the story adequately also required more information than was to be found in the available sources. That I never lacked for such information was due principally to Gavin Long, the Official Australian War Historian and to two members of his staff, John Balfour and Dudley McCarthy. McCarthy's draft chapters on Australian action on the Sanananda front were invaluable in helping me to round out the picture of the fighting that went on on that front. Lt. Col. Peter S. Teesdale-Smith, a participant in the campaign and a member of the Australian Military Mission in Washington during the time that this book was in preparation, helped me greatly in making Australian action come alive.

While the information thus given me has been of the greatest assistance, the responsibility both for the way it was used and for any errors that may have resulted is, of course, my own.

In the Office of the Chief of Military History, I wish to express my gratitude to Dr. Kent Roberts Greenfield, Chief Historian, for his careful reading of the manuscript and his excellent suggestions for its improvement. Particular thanks are due to Mr. Joseph R. Friedman, Chief of the Editorial Branch, for his extremely fine work in editing the manuscript. It was a pleasure to work with him. Thanks are also due to Mr. Wsevelod Aglaimoff, now Cartographic Adviser to the Chief Historian, who prepared the layouts for the maps and supervised their production; to Maj. James F. Holly, Chief of the Cartographic Branch, who carried out the detailed research for the maps; and to Miss Margaret E. Tackley, Chief of the Photographic Branch, who selected the illustrations. My special thanks go to Miss Valerie K. Stubbs of the General Reference Section for checking the numerous Distinguished Service Cross citations referred to in the book. This was no mean task since, in addition to the two Medals of Honor awarded in the campaign, more than a hundred Distinguished Service Crosses were also awarded.

Washington, D. C.   SAMUEL MILNER
15 March 1955

Contents

Maps

Illustrations

The illustrations on pages 19 and 85 are Australian War Memorial photographs; those on pages 295 and 326 are *Life* photographs taken by Strock. All other illustrations are from the files of the Department of Defense.

CHAPTER I

The Japanese Threaten Australia

In mid–1942, the Japanese made two attempts to take Port Moresby, a key Australian base in southeast New Guinea. These efforts were part of a plan to isolate Australia lest it be used for counteroffensives against them. Port Moresby was an inviting target, for it stood guard over Australia's vital Melbourne–Brisbane coastal belt, the Commonwealth's most thickly populated and most highly industrialized area. The first attempt was turned back by the U.S. Pacific Fleet at the Battle of the Coral Sea; the second resulted in the Papuan Campaign, one of the longest and most bitterly fought campaigns of the Pacific War. The fight ostensibly was for Port Moresby, but it was Australia, no less than Port Moresby, which was in danger.

The Danger

Australia's Plight

Since late 1939 when they first began sending troops to the Middle East, the Australians had relied upon the British forces in Malaya, the base at Singapore, and the British Eastern Fleet to hold the Japanese enemy from their shores should he attack. They had sent troops, ships, and planes to Malaya before the Japanese struck; and, in mid-January 1942, with the Japanese mov-

ing forward rapidly in Burma, Malaya, and the Netherlands Indies, and the bulk of Gen. Douglas MacArthur's command in the Philippines already cut off on Bataan, their government had joined with other Allied governments in the Far East in the establishment of the American, British, Dutch, Australian Command (ABDACOM). Gen. Sir Archibald P. Wavell of the British Army, and then Commander-in-Chief, India, was put in supreme command.[1] Named as his deputy was Lt. Gen. George H. Brett, at the time Commanding General, United States Army Forces in Australia (USAFIA). USAFIA, a small hastily improvised service command a few weeks old, was engaged, on the one hand, in largely barren attempts to get supplies through to the Philippines by blockade runner and, on the other, in providing for the supply of American air units striking at the enemy from Darwin and advance bases in the Netherlands Indies.[2]

General Wavell was given as his principal

---

[1] *Despatch by the Supreme Commander of the ABDA Area to the Combined Chiefs of Staff* (London, 1948); Gavin Long, Australia in the Second World War, Part Seven, Ch. XXVII, pp. 389–95, in C. Hartley Grattan, ed., *Australia* (Berkeley, 1947); Winston S. Churchill, *The Hinge of Fate* (Boston, 1950), p. 14.

mission the task of holding the Malay Barrier, a defensive line which included the Malay Peninsula, Sumatra, Java, and Timor and extended eastward from Timor to the coastal waters of northwestern Australia. Australia (specifically excluded from the ABDA Area at the time) was to be used as "an essential supporting position." [3]

As the Allied plan of operations called for the build-up at top speed in Australia of a strong U.S. air force to strike at the enemy from forward bases in Java, USAFIA became in effect a supply echelon of ABDACOM, charged primarily with the logistical support of U.S. air operations in Java. United States aircraft and supplies would be rushed to Australia by way of the newly opened South Pacific ferry route whose island bases—Hawaii, Christmas Island, Canton Island, Samoa, Fiji, and New Cale-

donia—formed steppingstones all the way from the west coast of the United States to the east coast of Australia. Upon arrival the planes and matériel would be assigned to General Wavell for defense of the Barrier. [4] The Australians were left to defend the island continent's eastern and northeastern approaches as best they could using their own resources, the assumption at the time being that Australia was safe as long as the Barrier held.

The trouble was that Australia was, if anything, even more exposed from the northeast than from the northwest. What was more, it had heavy obligations there, being responsible for the defense of territories in New Guinea, the Bismarck Archipelago, and the Solomon Islands. Its two territories in New Guinea—Papua, a territory of the Commonwealth, and North East New Guinea, a part of its New Guinea Mandate—together made up the eastern half of that immense island, the rest being controlled by the Dutch. Its mandated territory also included New Britain and New Ireland in the Bismarck Archipelago and Buka and Bougainville in the northern Solomons. It was, in addition, responsible for the defense of the British, or southern, Solomons, the whole New Guinea–Bismarcks–Solomons defense zone being known as the Northeast Area.

The means available to the Australians for the defense of this vast area and of

---

[2] Msg, CG AAF to Gen Brett, No. 59, 2 Jan 42, copy in AG 381 (1–1–42) Misc, DRB HRS, AGO; Msg, Gen Brett to Gen George C. Marshall, No. CR 0139, CM–IN 30, 23 Jan 42; Maj Gen Julian F. Barnes, Rpt of Orgn and Activities USAFIA, copy in OCMH files. The command had been established on 22 December as the United States Forces in Australia (USFIA) upon the arrival at Brisbane of the *Pensacola* convoy, a 4,600-man movement of air corps and field artillery troops originally destined for Manila and diverted to Australia upon the outbreak of hostilities with Japan. General Brett, a noted air corps officer, and then a major general, reached Australia by air from Chungking on 31 December and took command, becoming commander of United States Army Forces in Australia (USAFIA) when USFIA took that name on 5 January. For a full account of the contemporary operations of the United States Army Forces in the Far East (USAFFE), General MacArthur's command in the Philippines, and of the blockade-running activity, see Louis Morton, *The Fall of the Philippines,* UNITED STATES ARMY IN WORLD WAR II (Washington, 1953).

[3] CCS Dir to Supreme Comdr ABDA Area, 2 Jan 42, copy in ABDACOM Msg File, OPD Exec File.

[4] Msg, Gen Brett to Gen Marshall, No. CR 0139, CM–IN 30, 23 Jan 42; Msgs, Gen Marshall to Gen MacArthur, No. 879, 24 Dec 42, No. 885, 26 Dec 41, in AG 381 (12–25–41), Sec 1; Msg, Gen Marshall to Gen Brett, No. 41, 25 Dec 41, in same file; Msg, Marshall to Brett, No. 25, 16 Jan 42, in WPD 4639–19; Memo, Brig Gen Leonard T. Gerow, ACofS, for Gen Marshall, 27 Jan 42, sub: Messages from Australia, in WPD 4628–24.

Australia itself were very limited. By late 1941 Australia, a country of only a little over seven million people, had already been at war for more than two years. Loyally joining the mother country in the fight against the European Axis, the Australians had dispersed their land, sea, and air strength around the world. When the Japanese struck, nine squadrons of the Royal Australian Air Force (RAAF) were serving with the British in the United Kingdom, the Middle East, and Malaya. Some 8,800 Australians were with the Royal Air Force (RAF). Major units of the Royal Australian Navy (RAN), which then consisted principally of two heavy and three light cruisers, had just reached home waters after months of service with the Royal Navy in the Mediterranean Sea and Indian Ocean.

Australia's only trained and equipped troops, four divisions of the Australian Imperial Forces (AIF), the overseas volunteer force, were nearly all abroad. The 8th Australian Infantry Division, less one brigade, was in Malaya. The remaining three divisions, the 6th, 7th, and 9th, were in the Middle East. By agreement with Mr. Winston S. Churchill, the British Prime Minister, the 6th and 7th Divisions' six brigades, with corps and service troops, had been ordered to Malaya on 8 December, but their leading elements were not due to arrive there until early March. Two of the remaining three battalions of the 8th Division had been sent to the Netherlands Indies to reinforce the Dutch garrisons at Amboina and Timor. The last battalion was at Rabaul in New Britain, the main Australian base in the Bismarck Archipelago, and a few hundred troops, part of an independent (Commando) company, were scattered through the islands north and south of Rabaul. The defense of the mainland and

of its main outpost in New Guinea, Port Moresby, was left to the militia.[5]

Australia's home defenses were in a desperate state. Most of the 165 combat aircraft which it had in the Pacific when the Japanese struck were in Malaya. The total bombing force available for Australia's defense consisted of twenty-nine Hudson medium bombers and fourteen Catalina flying boats, forty-three aircraft in all. Inasmuch as Australia's only fighter-type planes, obsolete Brewster Buffaloes, were in Malaya, RAAF units defending the homeland had no choice but to employ in lieu of fighter planes the Australian-built Wirraway, a type of advance trainer virtually useless in aerial combat.[6]

The ground forces were not much better off. Except for training cadres and an Australian Imperial Forces armored division without tanks, there were virtually no trained soldiers left in Australia. The bulk of those at hand were militia troops who would need months of training before they would be ready for combat.

The Australian home defense organization, the Australian Military Forces (AMF) had two components: the Permanent Forces or regular army (28,000 men in September 1939), and the Citizen Military

---

[5] Msg, Prime Minister of Australia to Prime Minister of United Kingdom, 21 Feb 42, in OPD Exec Off File, Bk 4; WD, Survey of Australia, 25 Feb 42, pp. 95–97, copy in OCMH files; Rpt on Australia for the CinC Allied Forces, 14 Mar 42, in G–3 Jnl GHQ SWPA; Long, Australia in the Second World War, pp. 391, 396; Churchill, The Hinge of Fate, p. 10.

[6] AAF, The Army Air Forces in the War Against Japan, 1941–1942 (Washington, 1945), p. 62; USSBS, The Campaigns of the Pacific War (Washington, 1946), p. 53; E. Roland Walker, The Australian Economy in War and Reconstruction (New York, 1947), p. 57.

Forces (CMF), the conscripted home defense force then liable for service only in Australia and Papua. The AMF was poorly armed. It was deficient in field equipment and, until February 1942, when the full mobilization of the CMF was finally completed, did not have even its minimum quota of small arms. It was organized into seven militia divisions, but these were at best only training units, which had just begun to train their personnel on a full-time basis.

It had been planned to keep the militia force at a constant strength of 250,000 men, but during 1941 only half that number had been in the training camps at any one time. The basis of call, three months in camp and three months at home, had insured that Australia's overtaxed war industry would not be robbed of men it could ill afford to lose, but it had not done much to further the training of the troops, most of whom were scarcely beyond the recruit stage when full-time training began.

An organized reserve of about 50,000 men, the Volunteer Defence Corps (VDC), was also available for defense of the mainland. Made up principally of veterans of World War I, who served in their home districts on a part-time basis without pay, the VDC at the outset had to use whatever weapons were at hand, including in some cases shotguns and antiquated fowling pieces.[7]

The Australian Chiefs of Staff, the staff officers charged with the security of Australia, were faced with the problem of how best to use their inadequate forces in its defense. To begin with, they had to decide whether to make the principal defense effort in Australia or on its periphery, in the Northeast Area.

After pondering the situation, the Chiefs of Staff came to the conclusion that, with untrained, ill-equipped troops, a critical lack of aircraft, and insufficient naval forces, an effective defense of the forward bases to the northeast, especially the base at Rabaul, was out of the question. Additional troops committed to their reinforcement would probably be lost, and the only result would be to reduce by that much the forces available for the final defense of the mainland. On 15 December 1941 they therefore recommended to the Australian war cabinet that the existing garrison at Rabaul, and lesser garrisons in its vicinity, be neither withdrawn nor increased, but that the garrison at Port Moresby (which in their opinion had some chance of survival because of its more favorable geographical position) be increased from a battalion to a brigade group, the largest force that could be maintained there out of Australia's slender resources.[8] The rest of Australia's available manpower and resources would be con-

---

[7] Memo, Brig Gen Raymond E. Lee for ACofS WPD, 9 Jan 42, in SWPA–MacArthur File, OPD Exec File; Ltr, Gavin Long, Official War Historian, Australia, to Maj Gen Orlando Ward, Chief of Military History, USA, 7 Mar 51, in OCMH files; WD, Survey of Australia, pp. 95–100; Long, Australia in the Second World War, pp. 395–97.

[8] Memo, Lt Gen V. A. H. Sturdee, CGS AMF, and Lt Gen Sydney F. Rowell, VCGS AMF, for author, 16 Dec 47, in OCMH files. Generals Sturdee and Rowell, respectively Chief and Deputy Chief of the General Staff, AMF, in December 1941, and the last remaining members of the Chief of Staff organization of that day to be still serving in 1947, graciously wrote this memorandum for the author to present the point of view of the Australian Chiefs of Staff during the opening months of the war.

centrated on the mainland, the assumption being that as matters stood there was no choice but to make the fight for Australia in Australia itself.

The war cabinet accepted these recommendations, and the available troops were deployed accordingly. Because of Australia's vast area, its 12,000-mile coast line, and the slowness and general inadequacy at the time of its road and rail communications, a relatively static local defense of the country's most vital areas was adopted. Provision was made, however, for a mobile reserve in each military district or command in order to give the defense as much flexibility as possible. The main concentration of forces was in the Brisbane–Newcastle–Sydney–Melbourne area, the industrial and agricultural heart of Australia. Smaller forces were deployed in South Australia, Western Australia, and Tasmania, and independent garrisons were established at Darwin, Townsville, Cairns, and Thursday Island. A reinforced battalion was sent to Port Moresby, and the garrisons at Rabaul and in the rest of the Northeast Area were left to fend for themselves.[9]

The situation to the northeast was exceedingly grave. Except for Port Moresby, the Northeast Area was held by only token forces, and even Port Moresby was in no position to defend itself successfully. Its strength, with the arrival of the promised reinforcements in January, was 3,000 men, but the troops were only partially trained, and their support—a 6-inch coastal battery, a 3.7-inch antiaircraft battery, a few antitank guns, and a handful of Catalinas and Hudsons—was scarcely such as to give any

confidence that the place could be held against a full-scale Japanese attack.[10]

To the northwest of Port Moresby, high in the mountains of North East New Guinea, there was another, much smaller, force. It consisted of a single platoon of the 1st Australian Independent Company, AIF, and a few hundred men of the New Guinea Volunteer Rifles (NGVR), a local militia recruited in Papua and territories of the Mandate. This force held the 3,000-foot-high Bulolo Valley, an area famous in prewar days for its gold mining activity. The valley, which boasted a small mountain airfield at Wau, was most strategically situated. Airplanes based at Wau were within easy flying distance of the great bight known as the Huon Gulf, and a series of native trails connected the valley with Lae and Salamaua, the two most important points on the gulf. Too weak even to attempt to hold Lae and Salamaua, the NGVR and AIF troops based themselves principally in the valley intending, when the Japanese came, to harass them from there and, later on when greater strength was available, to drive them out.[11]

Rabaul, a fine seaport at the northeast tip of New Britain, had two good airfields and a small coastal fort. Its 1,400-man garrison consisted of the 2/22 Infantry Battalion, AIF, a 100-man formation of the NGVR, a small detachment of the RAAF,

<hr>

[9] Rpt on Australia for CinC Allied Forces, 14 Mar 42; WD, Survey of Australia, p. 96.

[10] Rpt on Australia for CinC Allied Forces, 14 Mar 42; OCE SWPA, Draft Engr Rpt 1942, 31 Dec 42, in AFPAC Engr File; Memo, Long for Hist Div, SSUSA, n. d. Jan 48, sub: Answers to Questions by the Historical Division, in OCMH files; George H. Johnson, *The Toughest Fighting in the World* (New York, 1943), pp. 15, 43, 45; Osmar White, *Green Armor* (New York, 1945), pp. 43, 44, 52.

[11] Memo, Long for Hist Div, SSUSA, n. d. Jan 48; Australian Military Forces, *The Battle of Wau* (Canberra, 1943), *passim;* White, *Green Armor,* pp. 89–148.

and a few officers of the RAN. In support were two discarded 6-inch naval guns, two 3-inch antiaircraft guns, seven Wirraways, and a few Hudsons.[12]

The rest of the Northeast Area was held by the 1st Australian Independent Company, AIF (less the platoon in the Bulolo Valley), a force of about three hundred men. Detachments of the company were stationed at Lorengau in the Admiralties, at Kavieng in New Ireland, and at Buka and Tanambogo in the Solomons where there were also a few RAAF Catalinas and some RAAF personnel. In addition, a part of the company's strength was to be found at Vila, in the New Hebrides.[13]

Also stationed at strategic points in the Northeast Area was a small band of picked observers known as the Coast Watchers. Usually long-time residents of the area which they were to keep under surveillance, they had the duty of remaining behind when the Japanese came and reporting on their movements by radio.[14] The Coast Watchers, who had long prepared themselves for the task, did not have long to wait.

The Fall of Rabaul

By the end of December, the Japanese had thoroughly reconnoitered the Bismarck

Archipelago and the Lae–Salamaua area. Beginning on 4 January, four-engine flying boats and carrier aircraft bombed Rabaul repeatedly, forcing the Hudsons to withdraw to Australia. On 20 January all the Wirraways were shot down in a raid by one hundred carrier planes. A day later carrier-based dive bombers literally blasted both coastal guns out of the ground.[15] The stage was set for the conquest of Rabaul.

The Japanese force chosen to take Rabaul was the same force that had taken Guam. It was to be the main force also in the Japanese attempt to take Port Moresby. Known as the *South Seas Detachment,* or *Nankai Shitai,* it had been detached on 8 December 1941 from the year-old *55th Infantry Division,* then stationed on the island of Shikoku, Japan. The detachment was roughly five thousand strong. It consisted of the *144th Infantry Regiment* and supporting divisional troops and was under the command of Maj. Gen. Tomitaro Horii, an experienced general officer who had previously been in command of the *55th Division Infantry Group,* from whose headquarters his staff had been drawn.[16]

On 4 January 1942, *Imperial General Headquarters* ordered General Horii, then still stationed at Guam, to proceed as soon

[12] Rpt on Australia for CinC Allied Forces, 14 Mar. 42; USSBS, *The Allied Campaign Against Rabaul* (Washington, 1946), p. 6; Comdr Eric A. Feldt, RAN, *The Coast Watchers* (Melbourne, 1947), p. 39; Johnson, *The Toughest Fighting in the World,* p. 28; White, *Green Armor,* pp. 32–33. The prefix "2/" in front of the 22 in 2/22 Battalion indicates that this was the second time that the 22d Battalion was constituted an AIF unit.

[13] Rpt on Australia for CinC Allied Forces, 14 Mar 42; Memo, G–3 SWPA for CofS SWPA, 19 Sep 42, sub: Australian Independent Companies, in G–3 Jnl, GHQ SWPA; Memo, Long for Hist Div, SSUSA, n. d. Jan 48; Feldt, *The Coast Watchers,* pp. 31, 35, 47, 53.

[14] Feldt, *The Coast Watchers, passim.*

[15] Statement, Lt Col H. H. Carr, CO 2/22 Bn, AIF, 13 Jun 42, in Allied Geographic Section, Terrain Study No. 22, Area Study of Gazelle Peninsula and Rabaul, App A–1, pp. 50, 51; USSBS, *The Allied Campaign Against Rabaul,* p. 6; Feldt, *The Coast Watchers,* pp. 39–42; White, *Green Armor,* pp. 33–34.

[16] 1st Demob Bur, Hist Sec G–2, GHQ FEC, *South Seas Det* Opns 1941–42, Japanese Studies in World War II, No. 55, pp. 1–3; 1st Demob Bur, Hist Sec G–2, GHQ FEC, Central Pacific Opns I, Japanese Studies in World War II, No. 36, pp. 1, 2. Both in OCMH files. SEATIC, Hist Bul No. 243, Hist of the Japanese *28th Army,* 1 Oct 46; ATIS SWPA, Biographical Sketch, Gen Tomitaro Horii, 27 Aug 42. Both in ACofS G–2 WDGS Files.

as possible with the capture of Rabaul. The commander in chief of the *4th Fleet*, Vice Adm. Shigeyoshi Inouye, was ordered to support General Horii in the Rabaul operation and, simultaneously with the capture of Rabaul, to use his naval troops to take Kavieng. On 8 January (after having in the meantime flown to Truk and concluded an agreement with Admiral Inouye as to the fleet's part in the operation), General Horii issued orders for the capture of Rabaul. D Day was to be 23 January, and the landings were to begin at approximately 0100.

The *South Seas Detachment* left Guam for Rabaul on 16 January. The transports were escorted by units of the *4th Fleet*, and by the two fast carriers, *Kaga* and *Akagi,* detached for the operation from Admiral Chuichi Nagumo's *Special Striking Force,* the same carrier force that had attacked Pearl Harbor. The convoy was joined off Truk by the naval task force which was to take Kavieng, and the combined force headed from Truk directly for the Bismarcks.[17]

The naval landing forces detailed to take Kavieng and points in its immediate vicinity met with no opposition. The small Kavieng garrison, which sought at the last moment to escape in a schooner, was captured intact when the vessel came under the guns of a Japanese destroyer.[18]

The main body of the invasion convoy arrived off Rabaul on the night of 22–23 January and, a few minutes after midnight, began landing at Karavia and Simpson Harbor. Landings at Raluana Point and Vulcan Island followed. The Australians, who had only mortars, machine guns, and rifles, resisted stoutly from prepared positions and, though almost completely surrounded, continued to fight through the night and early morning: By 1000 the situation was seen to be hopeless, and the order was given to withdraw. Some of the Australian troops held their positions and fought to the death; the rest took to the hills with Japanese patrols in pursuit. Many of the fleeing Australians were caught and massacred, but four hundred of them managed to elude the Japanese and, after a harrowing march that tested their every ounce of endurance, reached the south and north coasts of New Britain more dead than alive. There other Australians, who had reached the scene from New Guinea, searched them out and took them to safety in small boats.[19]

With the fall of Rabaul, the forward defense of the Northeast Area crumbled. All that was left of it was the garrison at Port Moresby, the troops in the Bulolo Valley, and a handful of commandos in the Admiralties and the Solomons who were prepared to leave or "go bush" at a moment's notice.

The damage had been done. The Japanese were now in position to move at a

[17] Walton L. Robinson, "AKAGI, Famous Japanese Carrier," in *United States Naval Institute Proceedings,* May 1948, p. 581; *South Seas Det* Opns, pp. 3, 5, 6; 1st Demob Bur, Hist Sec G–2, GHQ FEC, *South Seas Det* Opns, 2d ed., Japanese Studies in World War II, No. 109, pp. 4–6, in OCMH files; SEATIC, Hist *28th Army;* USSBS, *The Allied Campaign Against Rabaul,* pp. 6, 83, 14; Samuel Eliot Morison, *History of United States Naval Operations in World War II,* Vol. III, *The Rising Sun in the Pacific* (Boston, 1948), pp. 59–60.

[18] Msg, U. S. Mil Attaché, Melbourne, to Gen Marshall, No. 46, CM–IN 53, 26 Jan 42; Feldt, *The Coast Watchers,* pp. 44–45.

[19] Statement, Col Carr, 13 Jun 42; *South Seas Det* Opns, pp. 7, 8; *South Seas Det* Opns, 2d ed. pp. 6–8; USSBS, *The Allied Campaign Against Rabaul,* pp. 6, 83, 114; Feldt, *The Coast Watchers* pp. 42–43, 54–65; White, *Green Armor,* pp. 32–42

bound into North East New Guinea and the Solomons. Port Moresby and the Allied communications line to Australia, three of whose main bases—New Caledonia, Fiji, and Samoa—were within striking distance of the southern Solomons, were in danger.

The Collapse of the ABDA Area

The Combined Chiefs of Staff, aware by this time of Australia's perilous position, began making the best provision they could to strengthen its defenses. On 24 January at the request of the Australian Prime Minister, Mr. John Curtin, they ordered that Darwin and its environs be incorporated in the ABDA Area; five days later they took their first measures in defense of Port Moresby and Australia's vital east coast. To meet Mr. Curtin's insistent demand for fighter planes for Port Moresby, the Combined Chiefs gave General Wavell the alternatives of either providing the place with fighter aircraft or taking over its defense himself. Then, in a measure designed to throw a protecting naval cordon around Port Moresby and the east coast, they established the ANZAC Area, a new strategic command covering principally the ocean areas to the east and northeast of Australia, in which a combined Australian-American force, ANZAC Force, was to operate with the support of the U.S. Pacific Fleet.[20]

ANZAC Force—the Australian cruisers *Australia, Canberra,* and *Hobart,* the U.S. cruiser *Chicago,* four destroyers, and a few

corvettes—under command of Vice Adm. Herbert F. Leary, USN, was in operation by 7 February. To assist him in the discharge of his mission, Admiral Leary was assigned a squadron of B–17's from Hawaii. The bombers reached Townsville, Australia, on 17–18 February and several days later bombed Rabaul, the first U.S. bombers to do so.[21]

But if Port Moresby now had a modicum of protection from the sea, its garrison continued as before without fighter planes. The direction from the Combined Chiefs to the contrary, General Wavell was able neither to provide it with aircraft nor to take over its defense.[22] Indeed, so badly had things gone in Wavell's area that he soon found himself unable to hold the Barrier with the means at hand.

The strong U.S. air force which was to have retrieved the tactical situation on the Barrier failed to reach Java in time. Of some 260 fighter planes allotted to the project, only thirty-six actually reached Java. While forty-nine heavy bombers got there, a portion arrived too late to affect the issue, and the rest, because of a critical lack of fighter protection, antiaircraft, and maintenance personnel, were soon reduced to a state approaching impotence. By the third week in February the ABDA Air Force (which had

[20] CCS 8, Inclusion of Port Darwin in the ABDA Area, 24 Jan 42; CCS 15, Institution of the ANZAC Area, 24 Jan 42. Both in ABC 323.31 (1–29–42), Sec 1a. Msg, CCS to ABDACOM, No. 1231, CM–IN 25, 29 Jan 42.

[21] Msg, Gen Marshall to Gen Brett, No. 166, 2 Feb 42, copy in AG 381 (11–27–41), Sec 2c; Hi 19th Bomb Gp (H), 8 Dec 41–31 Dec 41; AA The AAF in Australia to the Summer of 1942. Bo in USAF Hist Off. Morison, *The Rising Sun in t Pacific,* p. 261.

[22] Msg, Gen Wavell to CCS, ABDA No. 0064 1 Feb 42; Msg, CCS to Gen Marshall, DBA No. 3 Feb 42. Both in ABDACOM Msg File, OPD Ex File. Msg, Gen Marshall to Gen Wavell, No. 8 CM–IN 18, 6 Feb 42; Msg, COMANZACFOR COMINCH, n.n., CM–IN 96, 13 Feb 42.

never been able to put more than fifteen heavy bombers in the air at any one time) had, in all, ten heavy bombers, seven dive bombers, and thirteen fighter planes in operative condition.[23]

Malaya, against which the Japanese marshaled their strongest force, was the first to go. On 15 February the Malay Campaign came to an end with the surrender of Singapore. More than 64,000 troops (15,375 of them Australians), their guns, transport, and equipment were surrendered that day to the Japanese, in what Mr. Churchill has called "the worst disaster and greatest capitulation of British History." [24]

The Japanese by this time had invaded Borneo and the Celebes, taken Amboina, and landed in Sumatra. Now they could concentrate on the reduction of the Indies. On 19 February they bombed Darwin into rubble, and the next day began landing on Timor, Darwin's closest neighbor in the Indies.[25] Opposition on the island was quickly overcome, except for an Australian independent company in the hills of Portuguese Timor, most of whose men were out of reach of the Japanese when the landings began. Swollen by fugitives from the fighting elsewhere on the island, the company was to operate guerrilla-fashion from the hills for more than a year thereafter, scourging the Japanese garrison with hit-and-run raids,

but scarcely threatening its control of the island.[26]

The Barrier was now completely breached. With no further reason for being, ABDACOM was dissolved on 25 February. General Wavell returned at once to India, and General Brett to Australia, where each resumed his former command.[27] The defense of Java fell to the Dutch, who, disregarding the odds, chose to fight on, though the struggle by this time was clearly hopeless and the early fall of the island was a foregone conclusion.

With the Japanese about to overrun the Indies, northwest Australia, and especially the Darwin area, lay open to invasion. But whether the Japanese would find it profitable to stage an invasion there was another matter. The area, mostly desert and very sparsely settled, possessed only the most

---

[23] Wesley F. Craven and James L. Cate, eds., *The Army Air Forces in World War II: Vol. I, Plans and Early Operations January 1939 to August 1942* (Chicago, 1948), p. 400; AAF, *The AAF in the War Against Japan 1941–1942*, pp. 52, 53, 57.

[24] WD, *The World at War* (Washington, 1945), p. 123; Hugh Buggy, *Pacific Victory* (Melbourne, 1945), pp. 60, 61, 63; Churchill, *The Hinge of Fate*, p. 92.

[25] WD, *The World at War*, p. 123; Buggy, *Pacific Victory*, pp. 51, 52, 111–16.

[26] Memo, Australian Dept of External Affairs for the Minister, 30 Aug 42, sub: Summary Report on Portuguese Timor during the period December 1941 to June 1942, by Mr. David Ross, Australian Consul at Dili, who arrived in Darwin from Timor on 10 July 1942, copy in G–3 Jnl, GHQ SWPA; Buggy, *Pacific Victory*, pp. 51–59.

[27] Msg, Gen Marshall to Gen MacArthur, No. 1083, 24 Feb 42; Msg, Gen Wavell to Gen MacArthur, No. 1088, 25 Feb 42. Both in AG 381, Sec 2c. *Despatch Supreme Commander ABDA Area* (London, 1948), p. 16; Gen Barnes, Rpt of Orgn and Activities, USAFIA. Upon General Brett's resumption of command, General Barnes, who since 25 January had served as Commanding General, USAFIA, became Deputy Commander. Col. Stephen J. Chamberlin, who had served as chief of staff under Barnes since the latter's assumption of command, continued as chief of staff under General Brett. Barnes, who had reached Australia on 22 December in the *Pensacola* convoy as a brigadier general, had also served briefly as commanding general of the predecessor command, USFIA. Colonel Chamberlin, who had reached Australia by air on 9 January directly from Washington, had for a time been its G–4.

tenuous of communications and, by the only available road, was more than a thousand miles from Australia's developed and inhabited areas on the other side of the continent. Even though the Japanese could, if they wished, take Darwin, it was clear that they would have to think long and carefully before they undertook operations in Australia's parched and inhospitable Northern Territory.

The Occupation of Lae and Salamaua

Things had gone well for the enemy. He had thus far triumphed everywhere and was now ready for his first move onto the New Guinea mainland. On 2 February *Imperial General Headquarters* ordered the *4th Fleet* and the *South Seas Detachment* to take Lae and Salamaua, and at the proper time Port Moresby. Tulagi in the southern Solomons was also to be occupied, on a date as yet unspecified, in order, as the instructions put it, "to bring further pressure on Australia." [28]

On 16 February, after some preliminary discussions, General Horii and Admiral Inouye concluded an agreement for joint operations against Lae and Salamaua, under the terms of which Navy troops were to take Lae and Army troops Salamaua. The landings were to be made before the end of the month, and the Navy was to supply the permanent garrison for both points when their seizure had been completed. [29]

The landings were delayed. The U.S. aircraft carrier *Lexington* and a protecting force of four heavy cruisers and ten destroyers had moved into the area on 20 February with orders to break up the gathering Japa-

nese concentrations at Rabaul in concert with the ANZAC B–17's at Townsville. Japanese reconnaissance detected the *Lexington* force while it was still some 350 miles from Rabaul. After a running fight which cost the Japanese eighteen bombers, the carrier force ran short of oil and withdrew. The clash with the *Lexington* force upset the Japanese timetable for the Lae–Salamaua operation, which, as a result, was postponed to 8 March. [30]

The forces chosen to make the landings were the *2d Battalion, 144th Infantry*, a unit of the *South Seas Detachment* which was to take Salamaua, a battalion of the *Maizuru 2d Special Naval Landing Force* accompanied by a naval construction unit of 400 men, and a naval base unit about 1,500 strong which with the *Maizuru* troops was to constitute the garrison force. The *144th Infantry* troops would return to Rabaul as soon as the area was secured. [31]

The landings were preceded by heavy air attacks on Lae, Salamaua, Wau, Bulolo, and Port Moresby, beginning 2 March. The invasion convoy of three cruisers, eight destroyers, a seaplane tender, and several transports and cargo ships left Rabaul on the night of 5 March and made for New Guinea along the south coast of New Brit-

---

[28] *South Seas Det* Opns, pp. 8–9.

[29] Army and Navy Agreement, 16 Feb 42, quoted in *South Seas Det* Opns, p. 9.

---

[30] ONI, Early Raids in the Pacific Ocean, pp. 35, 38, 40, copy in OCMH files; *South Seas Det* Opns, pp. 9, 10.

[31] *South Seas Det* Opns, pp. 10, 11; 1st Demob Bur, G–2 Hist Sec, GHQ FEC, Naval Account, Japanese Invasion Eastern New Guinea, Japanese Studies in World War II, No. 100, pp. 5–9; 1st Demob Bur, G–2 Hist Sec, GHQ FEC, *18th Army* Opns, I, Japanese Studies in World War II, No. 41, p. 4; AMF, Interr of Lt Gen Hatazo Adachi, formerly CG *18th Army*, and members of his staff, by O/C 5th Mil Hist Fld Team, AMF, Rabaul. All in OCMH files. ALF, History of the Lae–Salamaua Garrison (Japanese), 1 Apr 44, copy in DRB HRS, AGO.

ain. Its progress was uncontested, and the convoy reached the Huon Gulf shortly before midnight, 7 March. At 0100, 8 March, the *2d Battalion, 144th Infantry,* made an unopposed night landing at Salamaua, and completed the occupation within the hour. At 0230 the *Maizuru* troops occupied Lae, eighteen miles to the north. They too met no opposition, for the NGVR, after putting both Lae and Salamaua to the torch, withdrew its few troops to the Bulolo Valley, leaving only light patrols behind.[32]

On 9 March, the day that the Java garrison finally surrendered,[33] a flight of AN-ZAC B–17's from Townsville tried to prevent the Japanese from consolidating their newly won positions on the Huon Gulf. The attack was unsuccessful, but the enemy landing forces were not to go unscathed. After the abortive attempt of the *Lexington* to raid Rabaul in late February, a larger carrier force, comprising the *Lexington* and *Yorktown,* supported by eight heavy cruisers and fourteen destroyers, including cruisers and destroyers from ANZAC Force, was assembled in early March to complete the mission. The Japanese landings, which the carrier forces might have prevented had they struck earlier, caused an immediate change in plan. On 10 March 104 carrier planes

took off from the *Lexington* and the *Yorktown,* which were then in the Gulf of Papua, flew through a pass in the Owen Stanley Mountains, and struck at enemy concentrations on the Huon Gulf.

The bombing was effective, and eight ANZAC B–17's and six RAAF Hudsons attacked when the carrier strike was over and finished the job. In addition to sinking three ships and damaging four, the Allied planes killed 130 Japanese troops and wounded 245. The ANZAC B–17's attacked again the next day and did heavy damage to buildings, runways, and piers at both Lae and Salamaua.[34]

Though the Allied air attacks of 10 and 11 March were unusually successful, they did not seriously disturb the efforts of the Japanese to establish themselves on the Huon Gulf. Work had been begun at once to improve the airfields, the first fighter planes from Rabaul arriving there 10 March, just after the main carrier attack. By 13 March the area was considered secure. The Navy troops took over, and the *2d Battalion, 144th Infantry,* left for Rabaul, reaching it safely on the 15th.[35]

The Plan To Isolate Australia

Allied headquarters during early March was alive with conjecture as to what the

---

[32] Msgs, Gen Brett to Gen Marshall, No. 511, CM–IN 106, 5 Mar 42, No. 582, CM–IN 9, 9 Mar 42; *South Seas Det Opns,* pp. 11, 12; *18th Army Opns,* I, 4; Naval Account, Japanese Invasion Eastern New Guinea, pp. 6–8; ALF, History of the Lae–Salamaua Garrison (Japanese); AMF, Interr Gen Adachi *et al.;* Feldt, *The Coast Watchers,* pp. 49, 52; Johnson, *The Toughest Fighting in the World,* pp. 44–45; White, *Green Armor,* pp. 64, 66–67.

[33] The garrison included, in addition to some 5,500 Britishers and 2,500 Australians, the 541 officers and men of the 2d Battalion, 131st U. S. Field Artillery Regiment, who had reached Soerabaja in January. USAFIA Check List, 11 Jul 42, in G–3 Jnl, GHQ SWPA; *Despatch by the Supreme Commander ABDA Area,* p. 16.

[34] Msg, Lt Gen Delos Emmons, CG Haw Dept, to Gen Marshall, No. 2740, CM–IN 26, 12 Mar 42; Ltr, Gen George C. Kenney to Gen Ward, 26 Feb 51, in OCMH files; *South Seas Det Opns,* pp. 11, 12; Naval Account, Japanese Invasion Eastern New Guinea, pp. 6–9; ALF, History of the Lae-Salamaua Garrison (Japanese); ONI, Early Raids in the Pacific Ocean, February 1 to March 10, 1942, pp. 57–68; Morison, *The Rising Sun in the Pacific,* p. 389.

[35] *South Seas Det Opns,* pp. 11, 12; *18th Army Opns,* I, 4; Naval Account, Japanese Invasion of Eastern New Guinea, pp. 7–9.

Japanese planned to do next. There were profound differences of opinion. General Brett (who had resumed command of USAFIA upon his return from the Indies) was convinced that the Japanese would invade Australia from the northwest, since they had large concentrations of troops, planes, and naval task forces in the Java area and could, if they chose, turn them against Darwin at a moment's notice.[36] The Australian Chiefs of Staff took a contrary view. In an estimate of the situation of 5 March, prepared by Maj. Gen. Sydney F. Rowell, Deputy Chief of the General Staff, they concluded that the real threat lay elsewhere.[37]

The Chiefs of Staff reasoned that if the Japanese bothered to take Darwin at all their aim would be to prevent its use by the Allies as a "spring-board" from which to attack them, rather than to use it as a "stepping stone" for the invasion of Australia. As the Australians saw it, the main object of the Japanese was "to cut the air and shipping lines of communication between United States and Australia with a view to preventing the development of Australia as a base for eventual offensive operations." They thought that the Japanese could best achieve this aim by occupying New Caledonia and Fiji. Nevertheless, since Port Moresby threatened Japanese lines of communication, the Australians believed it only natural that the enemy would act to eliminate that threat first. They could see no reason why the Japanese should not attack Port Moresby immediately, provided they were prepared to run the risk of meeting the naval units of ANZAC Force and units

available to it from the U.S. Pacific Fleet. Should the Japanese choose to attack New Caledonia first, their lines of communication would be longer, and their risk of encountering ANZAC units and reinforcements from the Pacific Fleet would be correspondingly greater; furthermore, Port Moresby would be left as a hostile base on their flank. For that reason the Australian Chiefs thought Port Moresby would be attacked first, and New Caledonia four to six weeks afterward.[38]

Though he did not know it at the time, General Rowell had guessed the enemy's intent exactly. In the orders of 2 February for the landings at Lae and Salamaua, *Imperial General Headquarters* had spoken of moves against Port Moresby and Tulagi but had issued no specific orders pertaining to those operations. On 9 March the *4th Fleet*, in a companion move to the landings on the Huon Gulf, sent a landing party to Buka, in the northern Solomons;[39] on the 15th the *Army* and *Navy Sections* of *Imperial General Headquarters* met to decide on some definitive line of action with regard to Australia.

The representatives of the *Navy Section* pointed to an ominous increase in air and sea activity between the United States and Australia as evidence that Australia was to be used as a base for counterattacks against them. They urged therefore that Australia be seized whatever the cost. The representatives of the *Army Section,* though equally perturbed by the prospect that Australia might be used as a base from which attacks

---

[36] Msg, Gen Brett to Gen Marshall, No. 490, CM–IN 48, 4 Mar 42.

[37] Ltr, Gen Rowell, DCGS AMF, to author, 16 May 49, in OCMH files.

[38] Appreciation of the Australian Chiefs of Staff, 5 Mar 42, sub: Probable Immediate Japanese Moves in Proposed ANZAC Area, in G–3 Jnl, GHQ SWPA.

[39] Ltr, Maj Gen Charles A. Willoughby, ACofS G–2, GHQ FEC, to Gen Ward, 12 Apr 51, in OCMH files; *South Seas Det Opns*, p. 8; Feldt, *The Coast Watchers,* p. 108.

would be launched against them, were strongly opposed to the invasion. It would require ten or more divisions to take and hold Australia, they pointed out, and they did not have at the time "the munitions, the reinforcements, or the ships," for such an operation. The Army gained its point. Instead of approving an operation against the Australian mainland, the Japanese agreed to seize Port Moresby as planned and then, with the parallel occupation of the southern Solomons, "to isolate Australia" by seizing Fiji, Samoa, and New Caledonia.[40]

The plan said nothing about invading Australia; it did not have to. If everything went well and all objectives were taken, there would be time enough to begin planning for the invasion of the Australian mainland. Meanwhile, it would be possible to squeeze Australia and render it harmless without invasion and at much less cost.

It was clear from the circumstances that the Japanese had not given up the idea of invading Australia. They had merely laid it aside in favor of measures that, if successful, would make invasion—in the event they

found it necessary later on—a comparatively easy matter. The immediate object was to isolate Australia, and the plan for doing so was ready to go into effect. Japanese naval aviation was now within 170 air miles of Port Moresby, close fighter distance. The *4th Fleet* was spreading rapidly through the northern Solomons, with the southern Solomons next. The final step, after Port Moresby was taken, would be to seize New Caledonia, Fiji, and Samoa, thereby severing the line of communications between the United States and Australia.

The Japanese had already taken Singapore and the Indies and, with General MacArthur's main force hopeless and starving on Bataan, would soon complete the reduction of the Philippines. Their success thus far had been astounding, and now after only three months of operations they were threatening Australia, the last major position still left to the Allies in the southwest Pacific. The danger to the Commonwealth was immediate. If it was to be organized as a base for Allied offensive operations, it could not be permitted to succumb to the Japanese, whatever their designs upon it. The Allied high command, seeing the danger, already had under consideration measures that sought both to strengthen Australia's defense and to organize it for future offensive action.

---

[40] 1st Demob Bur, G–2 Hist Sec, GHQ FEC, Hist Rec *Army Section Imperial General Headquarters,* Japanese Studies in World War II, No. 72, pp. 48, 50, 51. The following are to the same effect: *South Seas Det* Opns, pp. 12, 14; *18th Army* Opns, I, 5, 7.

CHAPTER II

Preparing the Defense

The declared policy of the War Department during January and early February on troop movements to Australia had been to restrict them to air corps, antiaircraft, and service troops—to such troops, in short, as would be of direct value to the support of air operations. This policy had been adopted in the hope that, if everything was concentrated on the air build-up of the Indies, it might still be possible for General Wavell to hold the Barrier. The hope had proved vain. By mid-February, the debacle was at hand. Not only was the ABDA Area on the point of collapse, but Australia itself was in danger. Faced with this situation, the War Department, in a swift reversal of policy, ordered the first U.S. ground forces to Australia.[1]

The High Command Acts

Reinforcing the Australian Base

The first unit ordered to go was the 41st U.S. Infantry Division, then in training at Fort Lewis, Washington. On 17 February, Gen. George C. Marshall ordered its transfer to Australia. The main body, less one regiment, was to go immediately; the remaining regiment would leave later when additional shipping became available. Upon arrival, the division's mission would be to protect Australia's ports and air bases and to provide garrisons for the defense of its eastern and northeastern coasts.[2]

While the War Department was thus preparing to send U.S. ground troops to Australia for use in its defense, the question came up of what to do with the Australian corps which was then en route to the Southwest Pacific from the Middle East. Inasmuch as it was clear by this time that the corps would arrive too late to be of use in the defense of the ABDA Area, General Wavell proposed on 18 February that it be diverted to Burma where the enemy was advancing unchecked on Rangoon. President Roosevelt and Mr. Churchill took substantially the same position. Pointing out that the leading elements of the corps (which was then in the Indian Ocean) were the only troops that could intervene in time to save Burma, each asked Mr. Curtin on the 20th that he permit the temporary diversion to that country's defense of at least the leading division.[3]

---

[1] Memo, WPD for TAG, 8 Jan 42, sub: Personnel and Supply Policy in Australia, in WPD 4630–28; Memo, WPD for ACofS G–3 WDGS, 17 Feb 42, sub: Movement of Troops to SUMAC, in WPD 4630 66.

[2] Memo, WPD for ACofS G–3 WDGS, 17 Feb 42, sub: Movement of Troops to SUMAC; Msg, Gen Marshall to Gen Brett, No. 479, 1 Mar 42, in AG 381, Sec. 2c.

[3] Msg, Gen Brett to TAG, No. 27, CM–IN 833, 17 Feb 42; Msg, Mr. Curtin to Mr. Churchill, 21 Feb 42, in OPD Exec Off File, Bk 4; General Staff, India, *ABDACOM: An Official Account of Events in the Southwest Pacific Command, January–February 1942* (New Delhi, 1942), pp. 71–72, 83; Churchill, *The Hinge of Fate*, pp. 155–59.

Feeling, as he was to put it later, that his "primary obligation" was "to save Australia," Mr. Curtin flatly refused to sanction the diversion.[4] Moreover, in addition to demanding the immediate return to Australia of the 6th and 7th Divisions (the two divisions en route) he demanded the return of the 9th Division, the one Australian division still in the Middle East.[5]

Little exception could be taken to the transfer home of the 6th and 7th Divisions, especially since the Australian Government agreed to the temporary diversion of two brigades of the 6th Division to Ceylon, which was then believed to be in imminent danger of invasion. The case of the 9th Division was another matter. To pull it out of the Middle East without replacement could conceivably so weaken the British line in the western desert that disaster might result. The United States, at Mr. Churchill's suggestion, therefore offered to send a second division to Australia if the Australian Government would temporarily leave the 9th Division in the Middle East. The Australian Government gave its consent to this arrangement,[6] and the 32d U.S. Infantry Division, then at Fort Devens, Massachusetts, where it had been preparing for early shipment to Northern Ireland, was immediately ordered to Australia.[7] The leading elements of the AIF began debarking in Aus-

tralia in mid-March, and with the 41st Division due to arrive in April, and the 32d Division in May, a rapid concentration of ground forces in Australia was assured.[8]

The U.S. Air Force in Australia, at low ebb after the Indies campaign, was strengthened, and immediate steps were taken to bring it up to authorized strength—two heavy and two medium bombardment groups, one light bombardment group, and three pursuit groups.[9] The island bases in the South Pacific were secured. By early February there were garrisons at Palmyra, Christmas Island, Canton Island, Bora Bora, Samoa, and the Fiji Islands. On 26 February the garrison for New Caledonia, a force of 17,500 men, reached Australia, and on 12 March it was redeployed to its destination without incident.[10]

As a crowning touch to this defensive deployment, new bases were being established at Tongatabu in the Tonga Islands and at Efate in the New Hebrides. The establishment of these bases had more than merely a defensive intent. As Admiral Ernest J. King pointed out to the President, when these and the existing bases at Samoa, the Fijis, New Caledonia, and Bora Bora were "made reasonably secure, we shall not only be able to cover the lines of communication to Australia and New Zealand, but given the naval forces, air units and amphibious forces,

[4] Msg, Curtin to Churchill, 23 Feb 42, quoted in Churchill, *The Hinge of Fate*, pp. 163–64.
[5] Msg, Curtin to Churchill, 21 Feb 42.
[6] Ltr, Mr. Churchill to Mr. Roosevelt, No. 37, 4 Mar 42, in CCS 56, ABC 311.5 (1–30–42); CPS 7th Mtg, 6 Mar 42, in CCS 56/1; Msg, Gen Marshall to CG USAFFE, No. 739, 18 Mar 42, in SWPA–MacArthur File, OPD Exec File; Long, Australia in the Second World War, p. 396; Churchill, *The Hinge of Fate*, pp. 163–66, 173, 174.
[7] Memo, Lt Col Henry I. Hodes for Brig Gen Robert W. Crawford, 17 Apr 42, in OPD 400 Australia.

[8] *Ibid.;* Msg, Gen Marshall to Gen Brett, No. 626, 10 Mar 42, in WPD 381 Aust (3–8–42).
[9] Msg, Gen Marshall to Gen Brett, No. 479, 1 Mar 42; Msgs, Gen Brett to Gen Marshall, No. 490, CM–IN 48, 4 Mar 42, No. 505, CM–IN 99, 5 Mar 42. The original allotment had been four, not three, pursuit groups, but an undertaking by the United States to maintain one Australian pursuit group at full strength had cut down U.S. pursuit strength by one group.
[10] Msg, Gen Marshall to CG USAFFE, No. 1024, 8 Feb 42; Msg, Gen Marshall to Gen Brett, No. 351, 18 Feb 42. Both in AG 381, Sec. 2c.

we can drive northwestward from the New Hebrides into the Solomons and the Bismarck Archipelago after the same fashion of step by step advances that the Japanese used in the South China Sea." [11]

Reorganizing the Pacific Theater

These reinforcing moves were accompanied by a reorganization of the Pacific Theater to fill the void left by the collapse of ABDACOM. After sounding out the British and finding them agreeable, the President proposed on 9 March that the world be divided into spheres or areas of strategic responsibility and that the United States, as the power best fitted to do so, assume responsibility for operations in the Pacific.[12]

With British approval of the plan a foregone conclusion, the Joint Chiefs had meanwhile been considering how the Pacific Theater was to be organized. They had heard from the Australian and New Zealand Governments in connection with the matter on the 8th. After a four-day conference at Melbourne, attended by their Chiefs of Staff, the responsible ministers, and General Brett, the Australian and New Zealand Governments had agreed that the new area should have an American supreme commander; that it should include Australia, New Zealand, Timor, Amboina, and New Guinea; and

that it should be under the strategic direction of the Combined Chiefs of Staff.[13]

The Joint Chiefs objected to these proposals on two main grounds. They had already agreed that the Supreme Commander would operate directly under them, not the Combined Chiefs of Staff; and they did not like the idea of having Australia and New Zealand in one area, for the reason that the two did not constitute a strategic entity.[14] As Admiral King was to explain the matter to the President:

Marshall and I are in complete agreement on subdividing the Pacific. We believe Australia proper and the New Zealand line of communication area are two strategic entities. The defense of Australia is primarily a land-air problem for which the best possible naval support is a fleet free to maneuver without restrictions imposed by local conditions. New Zealand, on the other hand, is the key point for Pacific lines of communication which is a naval responsibility. New Zealand has no relation to the defense of Australia in these circumstances.[15]

By the following day, 9 March, the Joint Chiefs of Staff had worked out the main lines that the organization in the Pacific was to take. It was decided that the ABDA and ANZAC Areas would be abolished; that

---

[11] Memo, Admiral Ernest J. King for the President, 5 Mar 42, in OPD Exec Off File, Bk 4.

[12] Msg, Roosevelt to Churchill, No. 115, 9 Mar 42, in CCS 56/1 ABC 311.5 (1-30-42). The full proposal was that there be three theaters: the Pacific Theater, the Indian Ocean–Middle East Theater, and the European–Atlantic Theater. The Pacific Theater as a responsibility of the United States would be under the Joint Chiefs of Staff; the Indian Ocean–Middle East Theater would be under the British Chiefs of Staff; and the European–Atlantic Theater would be a joint responsibility.

[13] Appreciation by the Australian and New Zealand Chiefs of Staff, 26 Feb 42, sub: Future Policy and Strategy for Conduct of War in the Pacific—Australia and New Zealand, in 314.7 MacArthur File, Rec Sec Files, GHQ SWPA; Msgs, Gen Brett to Gen Marshall, No. 81, 27 Feb 42, in OPD Exec Off File, Bk 4, No. 390, CM–IN 1458, 28 Feb 42, No. 467, CM–IN 30, 3 Mar 42; Msg, British Chiefs of Staff to Joint Staff Mission, No. W–109, 7 Mar 42, in CCS 57, ABC 323.31, POA (1–29–42), Sec. 1a.

[14] JCS 5th Mtg, Item No. 1, 9 Mar 42, sub: Governmental and Stategical Control and Commands in the ANZAC Area–Demarcation of New Strategic Areas in the Japanese War Zone.

[15] Memo, Admiral King for the President, 5 Apr 42, in CCS 57/2, ABC 323.31, POA (1–29–42) Sec. 2.

Australia and New Zealand would be in separate areas; and that the Pacific Theater would be divided into two main areas: the Pacific Ocean Area, including the North, Central, and South Pacific Areas; and the Southwest Pacific Area, including Australia, the Philippines, a portion of the Netherlands Indies, and Australia's land and sea approaches, north and northeast. Australia, the Netherlands Indies, and the United States, as the governments participating in defense of the latter area, would select a Supreme Commander, whose directive would be prepared by the Joint Chiefs of Staff in collaboration with the governments concerned.[16]

Because the Pacific Ocean Area covered principally the ocean areas already under command of Admiral Chester W. Nimitz, Commander in Chief of the U.S. Pacific Fleet, it became obvious that Nimitz would be its commander. Nor was the identity of the Supreme Commander of the Southwest Pacific Area to be long in doubt; he was already preparing to leave for Australia.

General MacArthur's Arrival

As early as 4 February, General Marshall had radioed General MacArthur that, with the situation on Bataan what it was, there might be more pressing need for his services elsewhere, and that there was therefore a likelihood that the President might order

his withdrawal with such a purpose in view.[17] The orders from the President came on 22 February. In them, General MacArthur was directed to proceed as quickly as possible to Mindanao, and from Mindanao to Australia. "It is the intention of the President," the dispatch continued, "to arrange with the Australian and British Governments for their acceptance of you as commander of the reconstituted ABDA Area."[18]

General MacArthur, fifteen members of his staff, two naval officers, his wife and child, and the child's nurse left Corregidor by motor torpedo boat on 11 March, and arrived safely at Mindanao two days later. To take them the rest of the way, General Brett had sent four B-17's to Mindanao— "beat-up" veterans of the fighting in Java but the best he had. Three of the B-17's failed to arrive because of mechanical difficulties, and the fourth was found to be in such poor condition upon arrival that General Brett had to ask Admiral Leary for the loan of three of his comparatively new ANZAC B-17's. Leary's bombers reached Mindanao on 16 March, picked up their passengers, and landed them safely at Darwin the next day.[19]

General Brett, who had been ordered to keep MacArthur's coming a matter "of profound secrecy" until the actual moment of

---

[16] JCS 18, Governmental and Strategical Control and Command in the ANZAC Area, 8 Mar 42, in ABC 323.31, POA (1-22-42), Sec. 1a; JCS 18/2, Creation of Southwest Pacific Area, 9 Mar 42, in ABC 323.31, POA (1-29-42), Sec. 2; JCS 5th Mtg, 9 Mar 42. In addition to the Southwest Pacific Area and the Pacific Ocean Area, the Pacific Theater included the Southeast Pacific Area—a broad band of ocean facing the western coasts of Central and South America, well outside the combat zone.

[17] Memo, WPD for Officer in Charge, Code Room, 4 Feb 42, WDCSA 370.05 Philippines (3-17-42), in DRB HRS, AGO.

[18] Msg, Gen Marshall to Gen MacArthur, No. 1678, 22 Feb 42, WDCSA 370.05 Philippines (3-17-42).

[19] Msg, Gen MacArthur to Gen Brett, No. 58, 13 Mar 42; Msg, Gen MacArthur to Gen Marshall, No. 482, 14 Mar 42; Msgs, Gen Brett to Gen MacArthur, No. CG 1179, 14 Mar 42, No. 79, 15 Mar 42; Msg, Gen Brett to Gen Marshall, No. 736, 17 Mar 42. All in 384-1, MacArthur File, G-3 Files, GHQ SWPA. Lt. Gen. George H. Brett, "The MacArthur I Knew," *True,* October 1947, p. 140.

his arrival,[20] at once called Mr. Curtin by
telephone and told him the news. Then, in
accordance with prior instructions from the
President and speaking in the President's
name, he proposed that the Australian Government nominate General MacArthur as
the Supreme Commander of the Southwest
Pacific Area. It was a matter of regret to
the President, Mr. Curtin was told, that it
had not been possible to inform the Australian Government "in advance of General
MacArthur's pending arrival," but such a
course had been necessary "because safety
during the voyage from the Philippines required the highest order of secrecy."[21]

Mr. Curtin, who had had no prior intimation that General MacArthur was coming, was (as the President reported to Mr.
Churchill) extremely "enthusiastic" at this
turn of events and at once nominated General MacArthur as his government's choice
for Supreme Commander.[22]

A joint press release was issued on 17
March at Melbourne and Washington, an-
nouncing that General MacArthur had ar-
rived in Australia and would be Supreme
Commander of the forces there and in the
Philippines. To forestall Axis propaganda
which might make capital of General Mac-
Arthur's departure from the Philippines, the

release at Washington contained the additional statement (later cleared with the Australians) that his arrival had been "in accordance with the request of the Australian
Government."[23]

A great feeling of relief swept the Australian people when they learned that General MacArthur had arrived to take charge
of their country's defense. The Australians
had good cause to be enthusiastic over Mac-
Arthur's coming. One of the most renowned
soldiers of his time, a divisional commander
in World War I, a former Chief of Staff
of the United States Army, a field marshal
in the Philippine Army, and, as Commanding General of the United States Army
Forces in the Far East, the leader of the
heroic defense of the Philippines, MacArthur had shown himself to be possessed of
exceptional gifts as a commander. There was
every reason to believe that Australia's defense would be safe in his hands.

The Interim Period

The Initial Problems

On 18 March, the day after his arrival
in Australia, General MacArthur, who was
then still operating as Commanding General, United States Army Forces in the Far
East, was told by General Marshall that in
accordance with the ABDA precedent he
would as Supreme Commander be ineligible
to command a national force. General Brett
would therefore have to continue temporarily at least, as commander of USAFIA,

[20] Msg, Gen Marshall to Gen Brett, No. 613, 10
Mar 42, in 384–1, MacArthur File, G–3 Files, GHQ
SWPA.
[21] Tel Msg, Gen Brett to Mr. Curtin, 17 Mar 42,
in 384–1, MacArthur File, G–3 Files, GHQ
SWPA. The message, which had been prepared in
advance, was read over the phone to Mr. Curtin at
1615 that day, and a confirmation was sent by mail
later the same day.
[22] Msg, President Roosevelt to Former Naval Person, 17 Mar 42, in Item No. 10, Exec No. 10, Col
Gailey's File, OPD Exec File; Msg, Gen Brett to
Gen Marshall, No. 736, 17 Mar 42, in 384–1,
MacArthur File, G–3 Files, GHQ SWPA.

[23] WPD Press Release, 17 Mar 42, copy in OCMH
files; Msg, President Roosevelt to Former Naval
Person, 17 Mar 42; Msg, Gen Marshall to Gen
Brett, No. 716, 17 Mar 42. Both in Item No. 10,
Exec No. 10, Col Gailey's File, OPD Exec File.

GENERAL MacARTHUR ARRIV-
ING IN SYDNEY *is met by the Australian Prime Minister, Mr. Curtin.*

though it was intended that he would ultimately command the combined air forces
of the area; Admiral Leary, the naval
forces; and an Australian, the ground
forces.[24]

Three days later, with the approval of the
Australians, General MacArthur, and the
War Department, General Brett became
Allied Air Commander, with Maj. Gen.
Julian F. Barnes, Deputy Commander of
USAFIA, slated to take Brett's place as its

commander.[25] This at once brought up the
problem of the command of the American
ground forces. General MacArthur proposed that this command go to General
Barnes when he became commander of
USAFIA. General Marshall strongly opposed the suggestion and pointed out that,
with the bulk of the ground forces in the
area Australian, both the American and
Australian ground forces should be under
an Australian commander, "in accordance
with the policy developed for combined
commands." [26]

Acting on this suggestion, General Mac-
Arthur at once worked out the ground force
organization which was subsequently
adopted. As outlined to General Marshall
on 24 March, its basic feature was that all
ground combat forces, Australian and
American, would be under command of
"the appropriate Australian general." The
Australian and American ground forces
would, however, continue as before with
separate service organizations. The existing
Australian supply organization would continue to operate through established Australian channels while USAFIA, its American counterpart, would have only supply
and administrative functions, and its commander, General Barnes, would operate, as
General MacArthur put it, "under policies
established by me." In this way, General
MacArthur felt, he would "free the combat

[21] Msg, Gen Marshall to Gen MacArthur, Melbourne, No. 79, 18 Mar 42, copy in OPD Exec Off
File, Bk 4.

[25] Ltr, Mr. Curtin to Gen Brett, 17 Mar 42, in
314.7 MacArthur File, Rec Sec Files, GHQ SWPA.
Msg, Gen Brett to Gen Marshall, No. 792, 21 Mar
42; Msg, Gen Marshall to Gen MacArthur, No. 3,
21 Mar 42. Both in SWPA–MacArthur File, OPD
Exec File.

[26] Msg, Gen MacArthur to Gen Marshall, No. 3,
21 Mar 42; Msg, Gen Marshall to Gen MacArthur,
No. 810, 22 Mar 42. Both in SWPA–MacArthur
File, OPD Exec File.

echelons of all administrative, supply, and political considerations, permitting uninterrupted concentration on combat." [27]

Since General MacArthur was not at the time Supreme Commander of the Southwest Pacific Area and could not be until the area was formally established and he assumed command, it became necessary that he act in the interim as if he had already become Supreme Commander. With the good will and enthusiastic support of the Australians, the transition was successfully negotiated. By the end of the month, General MacArthur was able to report that he was enjoying extremely cordial relations with the Australian authorities, that all his suggestions were being adopted without reservation, and that every possible step within the means available was being taken "to place the area in a posture of secure defense." [28]

The Joint Directives of 30 March

On 18 March, Prime Minister Churchill replied favorably to the President's proposal of nine days before that the world be divided into areas of strategic responsibility, with the United States responsible for the conduct of the war in the Pacific.[29] On 24 March, the Combined Chiefs of Staff formally established the Pacific Theater as an area of U.S. responsibility.[30] By 30 March the directives

to General MacArthur as Supreme Commander of the Southwest Pacific Area, and to Admiral Nimitz as Commander in Chief, Pacific Ocean Area, were ready, and the President approved them the next day.[31]

The Southwest Pacific Area, as set forth in the directive to General MacArthur, included Australia, the Philippines, New Guinea, the Bismarck Archipelago, the Solomons, and, except for Sumatra, the Netherlands Indies. As Supreme Commander, General MacArthur was to hold Australia as a base for future offensive action against Japan; sustain the U.S. position in the Philippines; support the operations of friendly forces in the Pacific Ocean Area and Indian Ocean; and "prepare to take the initiative." [32]

The Pacific Ocean Area, Admiral Nimitz's command, was to be divided into three component parts: the Central Pacific, North Pacific, and South Pacific Areas. The first two would be under Admiral Nimitz's direct command; the third, the South Pacific Area, the area immediately adjoining the Southwest Pacific,[33] would be under a naval officer of flag rank, who would be appointed by Nimitz and operate under his direction.

---

[27] Msg, Gen MacArthur to Gen Marshall, No. 19, 24 Mar 42, copy in SWPA–MacArthur File, OPD Exec file.

[28] Msg, Gen MacArthur to Gen Marshall, No. 56, CM–IN 0013, 1 Apr 42.

[29] Msg, Prime Minister Churchill to President Roosevelt, No. 46, 18 Mar 42, in JCS 19/1, ABC 271 (3–5–42).

[30] CCS 57/2, Strategic Responsibility of the U.K. and the U.S., 24 Mar 42, in ABC 323.31, POA (1–29–42), Sec. 2.

[31] JCS Directive to the Supreme Commander in the Southwest Pacific Area, 30 Mar 42; JCS Directive to the CinC Pacific Ocean Area, 30 Mar 42. Both in CCS 57/1. Memo, Brig Gen W. B. Smith, U.S. Secy CCS, for Gen Marshall and Admiral King, 1 Apr 42, in ABC 323.31, POA (1–29–42), Sec. 2.

[32] JCS Directive to the Supreme Commander, Southwest Pacific Area, 30 Mar 42.

[33] It should be noted that the South Pacific Area included everything south of the equator between 160° east longitude and 110° west longitude, except for the Solomon Islands, which were then in the Southwest Pacific Area, and Canton Island, which was in the Central Pacific Area. Fiji, Samoa, New Caledonia, and New Zealand were thus in the South Pacific Area, as were the New Hebrides and the Santa Cruz Islands.

GENERAL HEADQUARTERS
SOUTHWEST PACIFIC AREA

General Orders)   Melbourne, Vic.,
No.   1)   18 April, 1942.

  1. By agreement among the Governments of Australia, the United Kingdom,
the Netherlands and the United States there has been constituted, effective
1400 GMT, 18 April, 1942, the Southwest Pacific Area, with boundaries as
defined in Annex 1.

  2. By virtue of the same authority, the undersigned hereby assumes
command.

  3. The following commands are hereby created with commanders as indicated,
composed of forces assigned to the Southwest Pacific Area by the respective
Governments, and assigned to specific commands by this headquarters, initially
as provided in Annex 1.

    <u>a</u>. Allied Land Forces, Southwest Pacific Area.

        Commander: General Sir THOMAS BLAMEY, K.C.B.,
                    C.M.G., D.S.O., Australian Army.

    <u>b</u>. Allied Air Forces, Southwest Pacific Area.

        Commander: Lieutenant General GEORGE H. BRETT,
                    United States Army.

    <u>c</u>. Allied Naval Forces, Southwest Pacific Area.

        Commander: Vice Admiral HERBERT F. LEARY,
                    United States Navy.

    <u>d</u>. United States Forces in the Philippines.

        Commander: Lieutenant General JONATHAN M.
                    WAINWRIGHT, United States Army.

    <u>e</u>. United States Army Forces in Australia.

        Commander: Major General JULIAN F. BARNES,
                    United States Army.

                                    DOUGLAS MacARTHUR,
                                    General, United States Army,
                                    Commander-in-Chief.

As CINCPOA, Admiral Nimitz was to hold the island positions between the United States and the Southwest Pacific Area; support the operations of the Southwest Pacific Area; protect essential sea and air communications in his area; and "prepare for the execution of major amphibious offensives against positions held by Japan, the initial offensives to be launched from the South Pacific Area and the Southwest Pacific Area." [34]

The Assumption of Command

Approval of General MacArthur's directive by the participating governments was delayed. The Australian Government—the last to give its approval—only did so on 14 April, after certain questions relating to the movement of its troops out of Australian territory, and the right of its local commanders to communicate freely with their government, had been settled to its satisfaction.[35] On 18 April, a month almost to the day after his arrival in Australia, General MacArthur assumed command of the Southwest Pacific Area.[36] All combat echelons of the Australian forces, naval, ground, and air, were assigned to his command as of that date, and the Australian commanders concerned were notified that orders issued by him as Supreme Commander Southwest Pacific Area were to be considered "as

emanating from the Commonwealth Government." [37]

General MacArthur, who chose to designate himself as Commander in Chief Southwest Pacific Area rather than as Supreme Commander,[38] formally established the Allied Land Forces, Allied Air Forces, and Allied Naval Forces the same day. General Sir Thomas Blamey, Commander in Chief, Australian Military Forces, who had just arrived from the Middle East, became Commander Allied Land Forces; General Brett became commander of the Allied Air Forces; and Admiral Leary took over command of the Allied Naval Forces. Also incorporated into the command structure of the area that day were two previously established U.S. commands—the United States Army Forces in Australia, under General Barnes, and the United States Army Forces in the Philippines, under Lt. Gen. Jonathan M. Wainwright, then only eighteen days away from surrender and dissolution.[39]

In the matter of his staff, General Marshall had recommended to General MacArthur that all the participating governments be represented as had been done in the case of ABDACOM. Marshall suggested to MacArthur that this arrangement would be particularly desirable in his area since the Supreme Commander of the area,

---

[34] JCS Directive to the CinC Pacific Ocean Area, 30 Mar 42.

[35] Msg, Mr. Curtin to Dr. H. V. Evatt, No. 31, 7 Apr 42; Ltr, Admiral King to Dr. Evatt, 10 Apr 42; Ltr, Dr. Evatt to Admiral King, 14 Apr 42. All in ABC 323.31 POA (1–29–42), Sec. 2. Msg, Gen Marshall to Gen MacArthur, 14 Apr 42, in SWPA–MacArthur File, OPD Exec File.

[36] GHQ SWPA GO No. 1, 18 Apr 42.

[37] Ltr, Mr. Curtin, to Gen MacArthur, 17 Apr 42, in G–3 Jnl, GHQ SWPA.

[38] Ltr, Gen MacArthur to Mr. F. G. Shedden, Minister for Defence Coordination, Commonwealth of Australia, 13 Apr 42, copy in 314.7, MacArthur File, Rec Sec Files, GHQ SWPA.

[39] GHQ SWPA GO No. 1, 18 Apr 42; Msgs, Gen MacArthur to Gen Marshall, No. AG 381, CM–IN 5422, 20 Apr 42, No. AG 415, 20 Apr 42, copy in SWPA–MacArthur File, OPD Exec File, No. AG 441, CM–IN 2601, 25 Apr 42; Allied Air Forces GO No. 2, 27 Apr 42.

his chief of staff, and the air and naval commanders would be Americans, and the President had stated it as his wish that "a number of the higher positions" on the staff go to Dutch and Australian officers, and particularly to Australians.[40]

The staff of General Headquarters was named on 19 April, the day after General MacArthur assumed command. Its members were Maj. Gen. Richard K. Sutherland, Chief of Staff; Brig. Gen. Richard J. Marshall, Deputy Chief of Staff; Col. Charles P. Stivers, G–1; Col. Charles A. Willoughby, G–2; Brig. Gen. Stephen J. Chamberlin, G–3; Col. Lester J. Whitlock, G–4; Brig. Gen. Spencer B. Akin, Signal Officer; Brig. Gen. Hugh J. Casey, Engineer Officer; Brig. Gen. William F. Marquat, Antiaircraft Officer; Col. Burdette M. Fitch, Adjutant General; and Col. LeGrande A. Diller, Aide-de-Camp and Public Relations Officer.[41]

General Chamberlin, Colonel Whitlock, and Colonel Fitch had served on the staff of USAFIA, and the other members of the staff had come out of the Philippines with General MacArthur and served on his staff there. All the heads of staff sections were Americans; such Dutch and Australian officers as were assigned to General Headquarters Southwest Pacific Area served under them as members of the staff sections.

Though General Marshall again pressed him on the point, General MacArthur did not then or later assign a Dutchman or an Australian as a senior member of his staff. The reason for his failure to do so, as he stated it to General Marshall in June, was that there were no "qualified Dutch officers" present in Australia, and that the Austra-

lians, with a rapidly expanding army, did not have nearly enough staff officers to meet their own needs, let alone to serve on his staff. "There is no prospect," he told Marshall flatly, "of obtaining qualified senior staff officers from the Australians." [42]

The Defensive Problem

General MacArthur's Decision

General MacArthur arrived in Australia to find that the Australian Chiefs of Staff, feeling that they could not hope to hold Port Moresby without proper naval and air support, had based their strategy for the defense of Australia on continental defense, the defense, that is, of the mainland rather than of the approaches. They had considered the reinforcement of Port Moresby a few weeks before and decided that "it was out of the question since we have inadequate forces for defense of the east coast . . . the only area from which reinforcements can be drawn." Since to withdraw the garrison was also out of the question, they concluded that they would have to hold Port Moresby "as long as possible, and exact heavy toll from the enemy should he attack it." [43]

Though they were thus committed to continental defense, the Australian Chiefs of Staff were well aware of the difficulty of attempting to defend a country so vast in area and so poor in communications without adequate naval and air support. "Until such time as adequate naval and air forces are available," they noted, "it is estimated

[40] Msg, Gen Marshall to Gen MacArthur, No. 1178, CM–OUT 1495, 9 Apr 42.
[41] GHQ SWPA GO No. 2, 19 Apr 42.
[42] Msg, Gen MacArthur to Gen Marshall, No. AG 994, CM–IN 4634, 15 Jun 42.
[43] Appreciation by the [Australian] Chiefs of Staff—February 1942, 27 Feb 42, in G–3 Jnl, GHQ SWPA.

that it would require a minimum of 25 divisions [to hold Australia] against the scale of attack which is possible." "This would mean," they added, "that 10 fully equipped divisions would have to be supplied by our Allies" [44]—an impossible figure, as they well knew, since neither the British nor the United States between them were in any position at the time to supply them with that many ground troops.

In March 1943, a year after his arrival, General MacArthur publicly revealed that he had no sooner reached Australia than he concluded that the key to its defense lay not on the mainland but in New Guinea. Although his available means were extremely meager,[45] he assumed as a matter of course that he would be given sufficient naval and air support to ensure a successful defense of the continent at its approaches,[46] an assumption that the Australian Chiefs were then in no position to make, especially

after what had happened to their ground forces in Malaya, Amboina, and Timor.

MacArthur's position, as he explained it a year after the event, was essentially that it was too much to expect that naval and air support on a scale sufficient to defend the vast reaches of the continent successfully either would or could be made available. He told Mr. Curtin (who understood it to be the main point of difference between him and "our Chiefs of Staff earlier appreciations") that even twenty-five divisions would probably be insufficient to hold the mainland without such support.[47] He was reasonably sure, however, that it could be held with such forces as were likely to be made available if the main defensive effort was made not in Australia itself but in New Guinea. The strategic principle as he conceived it at the time, and as he stated it later on, was that the successful defense of Australia required that the battle "be waged on outer perimeter territories rather than within the territory to be defended." [48] The fight for Australia, in short, would be waged not on the mainland but in New Guinea. As events turned out, both the defense and the offense—when offense became possible—were pivoted on Port Moresby.

That General MacArthur had conceived such a strategy upon his arrival was questioned by the Australians. Mr. Curtin's impression of the matter was, for instance, that it was not until some considerable time later that MacArthur was able to transform his strategy "from a defensive one on

---

[44] *Ibid.*

[45] The order of arrival from the Middle East of AIF brigades at Fremantle was as follows: the 25th on 4 March, the 21st on 15 March, the 18th on 20 March (these three units comprising the 7th Australian Infantry Division); and the 19th Brigade of the 6th Australian Infantry Division on 20 March. United States troops in Australia numbered less than 25,000—about half of them air force personnel and the rest, field artillery, antiaircraft, and service troops. The Air Corps had planes enough only for one heavy bombardment squadron, one light bombardment squadron, and six pursuit squadrons. Admiral Leary's command consisted of a few cruisers and destroyers, and the squadron of B–17's assigned to him for operations against Rabaul. Msgs, Gen Brett to Gen Marshall, No. 510, CM–IN 115, 8 Mar 42, n. n., CM–IN 108, 12 Mar 42, No. 727, CM–IN 59, 17 Mar 42; CPS 9th Mtg, 9 Mar 42, sub: Defense of Australia, in ABC 381 Australia (11–23–42); Msg, COMINCH to COMANZACFOR, 11 Mar 42, in OPD Exec Off File, Bk 4; Craven and Cate, *The Army Air Forces in World War II*, I, 411.

[46] Ltr, Mr. Curtin to Gen MacArthur, 8 May 42, in 314.7 MacArthur File, Rec Sec Files, GHQ SWPA; Frazier Hunt, *MacArthur and the War Against Japan* (New York, 1944), pp. 82, 83.

[47] Ltr, Mr. Curtin to Gen MacArthur, 16 May 42, in 314.7 MacArthur File, Rec Sec Files, GHQ SWPA. In this letter, Mr. Curtin summarizes for General MacArthur and the record his understanding of a previous conversation with MacArthur.

[48] Ltr, Gen MacArthur to Mr. Curtin, 6 Oct 42, in 314.7, MacArthur File, Rec Sec Files, GHQ SWPA. See also Hunt, *MacArthur and the War Against Japan*, pp. 82, 83.

the mainland, to a defense of the mainland from the line of the Owen Stanley Range." But General MacArthur insisted that he had held this view from the start. "It was never my intention," he told Mr. Curtin, "to defend Australia on the mainland of Australia. That was the plan when I arrived, but to which I never subscribed, and which I immediately changed to a plan to defend Australia in New Guinea." [49]

Putting the Strategy into Effect

On 4 April, the Australian Chiefs of Staff, in conjunction with General MacArthur's headquarters, prepared a joint estimate of the situation. The estimate noted that the enemy had virtually undisputed control of both sea and air in the South and Southwest Pacific and could be expected to undertake an offensive in great strength "against Australia's supply line and against Australia itself," in the very near future. The one part of Australia "essential to the prosecution of the war," the estimate continued, was on the southeast and east coasts in the general area between Melbourne and Brisbane. The "critical point" which controlled this area was Port Moresby, against which a major offensive could be expected almost any time, for the enemy was known to be massing heavy forces at Rabaul for a possible thrust against it. Darwin and Fremantle, isolated points on the north and southwest coasts far from the vital centers of the country, were also open to attack, but their defense presented no great problem if they were to be suitably reinforced, for their position was such that they could be held as outposts. The

real danger was at Port Foresby. If Port Moresby fell to the Japanese, its loss would put in immediate jeopardy the safety of Australia's "all important area"—the Brisbane–Melbourne coastal belt.

Such being the case, a maximum effort would have to be made to provide additional air and sea power for the defense of Port Moresby and the other threatened areas. A successful defense would require several aircraft carriers and at least 675 land-based aircraft, including seventy B–17's. Both staffs were agreed that, if such a force was provided, it would be possible to defend Australia successfully and ultimately mount an offensive to the northeast of it, aimed at Rabaul.[50]

The means with which to begin putting this strategy into effect were at hand. The 7th Australian Infantry Division, and Headquarters, 1st Australian Corps, reached Adelaide from the Middle East at the end of March. The main body of the 41st U.S. Infantry Division docked at Melbourne on 6 April; a few days later, the 32d U.S. Infantry Division and the rest of the 41st Division were put on orders for early departure to Australia.[51] The Air Force was brought up to strength during April, except for one heavy bombardment group and one medium bombardment group, neither of which had as yet any planes.[52] Admiral Leary's command was substantially reinforced and soon came to include three heavy cruisers, three light cruisers, fifteen destroyers, twenty modern submarines, eleven old

[49] Ltr, Gen MacArthur to Mr. Curtin, 6 Nov 43, in 314.7, MacArthur File, Rec Sec Files, GHQ SWPA; Ltr, Mr. Curtin to Gen Blamey, 16 Nov 43; Ltr, Gen Blamey to Mr. Curtin, 28 Jan 44. Copies of both in OCMH files.

[50] Msg, Gen MacArthur to Gen Marshall, No. 70, CM–IN 1069, 4 Apr 42.
[51] Prov Opns Rpt, Australian Army, 3 Apr 42, in G–3 Jnl, GHQ SWPA; Msg, Gen Marshall to Gen Brett, No. 1167, 7 Apr 42, copy in OPD 320.2, Australia; Barnes Rpt.
[52] Allied Air Forces Opns Rpt, 20 Apr 42; G–3 Opns Rpt, 27 Apr 42. Both in G–3 Jnl, GHQ SWPA.

submarines, six or seven sloops, and some smaller craft. One of the light cruisers was Dutch; two of the heavy cruisers, one of the light cruisers, and four of the destroyers were Australian; and one heavy cruiser, two light cruisers, eleven destroyers, and all the submarines were American.[53]

Though the Dutch also provided a fusilier company and a completely equipped medium bombardment squadron (B–25's), their greatest contribution was a merchant marine, a part of the *Koninklijke Paktevaart Maatschappij*, better known as the K.P.M. Line, which had operated a far-flung inter-island service in the Netherlands Indies before the war. After the fall of Java, most of the K.P.M. ships escaped to Australia and India. A portion of those which reached India were rerouted to Australia. In all, twenty-nine ships, displacing from 500 to 6,000 tons, reached Australia where they were to play a major role in the supply and reinforcement of the Southwest Pacific Area's outlying positions.[54]

The reinforcement of Port Moresby and the more isolated garrisons in Australia itself began in early April. The 19th Brigade Group and U.S. antiaircraft and engineer troops were sent to Darwin; a squadron of U.S. heavy bomber planes and a U.S. antiaircraft regiment were ordered to the Perth–Fremantle area; a U.S. antiaircraft regiment and an additional Australian infantry brigade to Townsville. The rest of the U.S. antiaircraft troops were concentrated in the Brisbane area, and the bulk of the remaining land forces, including the 7th Australian Division and the 41st U.S. Division, were deployed in the Melbourne–Brisbane area.[55] The Air Force concentrated most of its striking forces in the Townsville–Cloncurry region, where by this time airfields (which had been begun in January) were ready for their reception.[56] The Allied Naval Forces, with the addition of more ships, expanded their operations; and the submarines began operating against the enemy from Fremantle and Brisbane—the new type of submarines from Fremantle, the old types from Brisbane.[57]

The reinforcement of Port Moresby was no easy matter. Its supply line from Australia across the Gulf of Papua was exposed to enemy action. Its port facilities were inadequate; its two existing airfields were small and poorly built; and, except for one field at Horn Island in Torres Strait, there were no intermediate air bases between it and the concentration area in the Townsville–Cloncurry region, 700 miles away.

After a thorough reconnaissance of Port Moresby, General Casey, General MacArthur's engineer officer, began drawing plans for its conversion into a first-class

[53] JCS 9th Mtg, 6 Apr 42; Msg, Gen MacArthur to Gen Marshall, No. AG 460, CM–IN 6648, 25 Apr 42; Hist of U.S. Naval Admin in World War II, Comdr U.S. Naval Forces Southwest Pacific, pp. 7, 8, copy in the Office of Naval History.

[54] Msgs, Gen MacArthur to Gen Marshall, No. AG 441, CM–IN 2601, 25 Apr 42, No. AG 506, CM–IN 7516, 28 Apr 42; The *Koninklijke Paktevaart Maatschappij* (K.P.M. Line) and the War in the Southwest Pacific Area, copy in the Office of Naval History. The K.P.M. ships, with Dutch masters and crews, were under charter to the British Ministry of Transport, which had allocated them to the U.S. Army. They were thus under direct control of USAFIA, rather than (as might be imagined) of Allied Naval Forces.

[55] Prov Opns Rpt, Australian Army, 3 Apr 42; Allied Air Forces Opns Rpts, 10 Apr 42, 20 Apr 42; G–3 Opns Rpts No. 3, 11 Apr 42, No. 5, 12 Apr 42, No. 7, 15 Apr 42, No. 10, 17 Apr 42, No. 19, 27 Apr 42; Opns Rpt USAFIA, 20 Apr 42. All in G–3 Jnl, GHQ SWPA.

[56] Allied Air Forces Opns Rpt, 10 Apr 42; G–3 Opns Rpt No. 35, 13 May 42. Both in G–3 Jnl, GHQ SWPA. OCE SWPA, Draft Engr Rpt, 1942; Hist Base Sec 2, Townsville, in AFPAC Engr File.

[57] JCS 9th Mtg, 6 Apr 42; ANF Daily Opns Rpt, 16 May 42, in G–3 Jnl, GHQ SWPA.

operational base. The port and the two existing airfields were to be improved, and three new airfields were to be built in the general Port Moresby area. It was also planned to improve the existing field at Horn Island and to begin the construction of new fields northward from Townsville along the Cape York Peninsula, principally at Mareeba (southwest of Cairns), Cooktown, and Coen. When completed, these fields would permit the rapid staging of all types of aircraft to Port Moresby. They would not only make it possible for the Air Force to provide cover for Torres Strait and the supply line to Port Moresby, but would give the Air Force greater flexibility in both offensive and defensive operations.[58]

Work began at once on the bases in the Cape York Peninsula; and, in late April, the first U.S. engineer troops were ordered to Port Moresby. The first to go were Company E, 43d Engineer Regiment (GS), and two Negro units, the 96th Engineer Battalion (less two companies) and the Dump Truck Section of the 576th Engineer Company. The 101st Coast Artillery Battalion (AA), the first U.S. antiaircraft unit to be ordered to Port Moresby, followed hard on their heels and arrived there only a short while after.[59] Two other moves were to be made as soon as possible: the troops in the Bulolo Valley were to be reinforced with an Australian Independent Company, and the Port Moresby garrison with an additional infantry brigade.[60]

Air activity at Port Moresby, meanwhile, had been greatly intensified. By late April, B–17's, B–25's, and B–26's were using it regularly as a jump-off point for attacks on Lae, Salamaua, and Rabaul; and air units based there, in addition to Australian P–40's, Catalinas, and Hudsons, included two American air groups, one equipped with A–24's, and the other with P–39's.[61]

A good beginning had been made in the defense of Australia and its advance base, Port Moresby, but it was only a beginning. General MacArthur, who had counted on greater support than he was receiving, felt very strongly that the allotted means were insufficient for the task in hand and began at once to press for additional forces.

The Sufficiency of the Means

CINCSWPA Asks for More

General MacArthur was to have no easy time in his attempt to secure greater means than had already been allotted to his area. In late December, the President of the United States and the Prime Minister of Great Britain, meeting at Washington with

[58] Interv with Lt Gen Stephen J. Chamberlin, 14 Jan 50, in OCMH files; OCE SWPA, Draft Engr Rpt, 1942; Hist Base Sec 2, Townsville; Hunt, *MacArthur and the War Against Japan*, pp. 82, 84, 85, 86. Unless otherwise indicated, all interviews were conducted by the author in Washington.

[59] Memo, Maj Gen Richard K. Sutherland, CofS, for CG USAFIA, 18 Apr 42, sub: Movement of Co E, 43d Engrs and the 96th Engr Bn (Cld), less two companies, and the attached Dump Truck Section of the 576th Engr Co; Memo, Gen Sutherland for CG USAFIA, 22 Apr 42, sub: Movement of One Separate Battalion Coast Artillery, Automatic Weapons; G–3 Opns Rpts No. 18, 26 Apr 42, No. 19, 27 Apr 42, No. 20, 28 Apr 42. All in G–3 Jnl, GHQ SWPA. OCE SWPA, Draft Engr Rpt, 1942.

[60] NGF OI, No. 7, 23 Apr 42; Ltr, Gen MacArthur to Gen Blamey, 1 May 42; Ltr, Gen Blamey to Gen MacArthur, 2 May 42. All in 385, G–3 Files, GHQ SWPA. Memo, Gen MacArthur for Comdr ALF et al., 13 May 42, in G–3 Jnl, GHQ SWPA.

[61] AAF, The AAF in Australia to the Summer of 1942, pp. 21, 23; Craven and Cate, *The Army Air Forces in World War II*, I, 425. The A–24's, the first U. S. planes to be based at Port Moresby, reached it in late March. The P–39's arrived in late April.

their military advisers, had decided that the Atlantic–European area would be the decisive theater of operations. They had also agreed as a corollary to that decision that until Germany was defeated operations in the Pacific would have to be primarily defensive in nature.[62] On 16 March, the matter came up before the Joint Chiefs of Staff. After considering a paper submitted to them by the Joint Staff Planners listing the alternatives open to the United States in its conduct of the two-ocean war, the Joint Chiefs decided that they could maintain a strong defensive in the Pacific with the forces already allotted to that theater and still build up forces in the United Kingdom for an early offensive against Germany.[63]

The decision having been reached, General MacArthur was given prompt intimation that his means would be limited. On 18 March, the day after he arrived in Australia, he was advised by General Marshall that because of serious shipping shortages and critical situations elsewhere it had become necessary to fix definite limits on United States commitments in the Southwest Pacific. United States ground forces, other than field artillery and antiaircraft units already in Australia or en route, would be limited to the two divisions already allotted to the Southwest Pacific Area. United States air units in Australia would be brought up to full strength as soon as possible, and MacArthur's lines of communication with the United States would be secured. Six weeks later, in response to a request for an aircraft carrier to increase the effectiveness of his naval force, he was

told that all the carriers were being employed on indispensable tasks.[64]

General MacArthur did not take this as the final word on the subject. Two days later, in a meeting with Mr. Curtin, he expressed himself as being "bitterly disappointed" with the meager assistance promised him by Washington. After going on to say that the forces allotted to him were "entirely inadequate" for the performance of the tasks imposed upon him by his directive, he agreed, upon Mr. Curtin's query, that the latter would do well to ask the British Prime Minister not only for an aircraft carrier, and the temporary diversion to Australia of two British divisions then on their way to India, but also for a substantial increase in the number of British ships allocated to the United States–Australia run. Mr. Curtin communicated these requests to Mr. Churchill the next day, stating that he was doing so at General MacArthur's request.[65]

Surprised that General MacArthur should have apparently cut through channels in this way, Mr. Churchill passed the message on to the President with the remark that he was quite unable to meet these demands. "I should be glad to know," he

---

[64] Msgs, Gen Marshall to Gen MacArthur, No. 739, 18 Mar 42, No. 1499, 26 Apr 42, in SWPA–MacArthur File, OPD Exec File; Msgs, Gen MacArthur to Gen Marshall, No. AG 453, CM–IN 6430, 24 Apr 42, No. AG 470, CM–IN 6643, 25 Apr 42.

[65] Ltr, Mr. Curtin to Gen MacArthur, 28 Apr 42, in 314.7, MacArthur File, Rec Sec Files, GHQ SWPA; Msg, Mr. Churchill to Mr. Roosevelt, No. 73, 29 Apr 42, in OPD Exec Off File, Bk 10; Msg, Gen MacArthur to Gen Marshall, CM–IN 0667, 3 May 42. General MacArthur's quoted statements are from Mr. Curtin's letter to MacArthur, which is devoted principally to the text of a cablegram which Mr. Curtin sent that day to his Minister for External Affairs, Dr. H. V. Evatt, who was then in Washington, telling Evatt what MacArthur had said in the course of this meeting.

---

[62] American–British Grand Strategy, ABC 4/CS–1, 31 Dec 41, ARCADIA Proceedings, in ABC 337 ARCADIA (24 Dec 41).

[63] JCS 6th Mtg, 16 Mar 42.

added, "whether these requirements have been approved by you . . ., and whether General MacArthur has any authority from the United States for taking such a line." [66]

Taken to task in the matter by General Marshall the next day, MacArthur, who had just sent Marshall a message complaining about the general inadequacy of his forces,[67] replied on 3 May that he should not be held responsible for the use to which Mr. Curtin had put his remarks. He had made them, he said, at Mr. Curtin's request, and purely as he thought for the Australian's personal information. His position was, MacArthur pointed out, a delicate one. Mr. Curtin expected him to advise the Australian Government on all matters relating to Australia's defense, and if he was to continue as Supreme Commander, and hold the confidence of the Australian Government, he had no choice but to do so. The preoccupation of the Australian Government with the security of its country was well known. The difficulty was that the Australians, both in government and out, were fearful that insufficient forces had been allotted to the defense of their country, a view in which he in his professional military capacity could not help but concur.[68] The issue was joined; the next move was General Marshall's.

By this time, the decision of the Joint Chiefs of Staff on 16 March to build up forces in the United Kingdom for an early offensive against Germany had found expression in the BOLERO plan. Proposed by General Marshall and accepted by the British Chiefs of Staff and the British Government on 14 April, the plan called for the reception and maintenance of an American force in the United Kingdom which, in concert with the British, would launch an air offensive against western Europe and ultimately invade it.[69] Since it was clear that BOLERO would either have to be suspended or appreciably delayed if further reinforcements were sent to the Pacific, General Marshall asked the President what his desires were. Mr. Roosevelt replied at once that he felt that further reinforcement of the Pacific would be inadvisable inasmuch as he did not want BOLERO slowed down.[70]

The President went further and, in a personal message to General MacArthur, explained why it had been decided not to increase the existing allocation in his area. He wrote that he found it difficult to get away from the fact that the armies of the USSR were, at that time, "killing more Axis personnel and destroying more Axis materiel than all the other twenty-five United Nations put together." It seemed logical therefore to try to support the Russian effort "in every way that we possibly can, and also to develop plans aimed at diverting German land and air forces from the Russian front." MacArthur was assured that despite this emphasis on European operations, his needs would not be lost sight of, and he was promised all the air strength that could possibly be spared.

[66] Msg, Mr. Churchill to Mr. Roosevelt, No. 73, 29 Apr 42.

[67] Msg, Gen Marshall to Gen MacArthur, No. 8, CM–OUT 6034, 30 Apr 42; Msg, Gen MacArthur to Gen Marshall, No. AG 588, CM–IN 0186, 1 May 42.

[68] Msg, Gen MacArthur to Gen Marshall, No. 151, CM–IN 0667, 3 May 42.

[69] The matter is fully discussed in Gordon Harrison, Cross-Channel Attack (Washington, 1951), a volume in this series.

[70] Memo, Gen Marshall for the President, 6 May 42, sub: The Pacific Theater versus BOLERO, in JCS 48, ABC 381, Pacific Bases (1–22–42), Sec 2; Memo, President Roosevelt for Gen Marshall, 6 May 42, in SWPA–MacArthur File, OPD Exec File.

The President told General MacArthur that the difficulty of his position was appreciated, and the fact understood that he had "to be an ambassador as well as Supreme Commander." "I see no reason," Mr. Roosevelt said, "why you should not continue discussing military matters with the Australian Prime Minister, but I hope you will try to have him treat them as confidential matters, and not use them as appeals to Churchill and me." [71]

General MacArthur replied two days later, urging that he be provided at once with additional means in order to secure Australia properly and that, when the country was secured, a full-scale offensive be launched in the Pacific. Such an offensive, he said, besides having "the enthusiastic psychological support of the entire American nation," would serve not only to secure Australia and India, but would also open up a "second front" which would be of incalculable aid to Russia. The first step was to secure Australia, and to do that properly, he said, required at least two aircraft carriers, an increase of U.S. air strength in Australia from 500 to 1,000 planes, and the assignment to his command of a U.S. Army corps of three first-class divisions "capable of executing an offensive maneuver." [72]

The same day that he dispatched this message to the President, General MacArthur told Mr. Curtin (who at once passed on the information to Dr. H. V. Evatt, his Minister for External Affairs) that he was "determined to seek a clarification in regard to the precise terms of his directive, and the forces which were to be made available to

him to enable him to fulfill it." "He would not be content," he said, "to be left with a directive which sounds grand but has no backing behind it." [73]

Mr. Churchill had neither a surplus aircraft carrier nor additional shipping to allocate to General MacArthur's area, nor did he take kindly to Mr. Curtin's request that two British divisions be diverted from the defense of India to that of Australia. In a letter to Mr. Curtin on 4 May, he recalled that, while it was true that he had promised to divert British divisions to Australia if the Japanese gave signs of an intention to invade it with eight or ten divisions, there was no sign that the Japanese had in mind a major attack on Australia. That being the case, he questioned the wisdom of sending the divisions to Australia instead of India, especially because India had already been invaded, and the switch, if it went through, "would involve the maximum expenditure and dislocation of shipping." [74]

Four days later, Dr. Evatt, who was then in London conferring with the British authorities, was assured personally by Mr. Churchill that, should Australia be invaded, he would "at once divert at least two divisions including an armored division, as they pass around the Cape"; and that he would, in addition, "throw everything possible into the defence of Australia preferring it to the defence of India." [75]

[71] Msg, Gen Marshall to Gen MacArthur, No. 31, CM–OUT 1131, 6 May 42.
[72] Msg, Gen MacArthur to Gen Marshall No. 176, CM–IN 2333, 8 May 42.

[73] Ltr, Mr. Curtin to Gen MacArthur, 8 May 42, in 314.7 MacArthur File, Rec Sec Files, GHQ SWPA. This letter contains the full text of Mr. Curtin's cable to Dr. Evatt. The material quoted above is to be found in that cable.
[74] Ltr, Mr. Curtin to Gen MacArthur, 4 May 42, in 314.7 MacArthur File, Rec Sec Files, GHQ SWPA.
[75] Ltr, Mr. Curtin to Gen MacArthur, 8 May 42, in 314.7, MacArthur File, Rec Sec Files, GHQ SWPA.

The President Has the Last Word

General MacArthur was still not satisfied. On 12 May he presented Mr. Curtin with an estimate of the situation which read in part as follows:

I cannot too strongly emphasize the need for haste in the development of this defensive bastion. The territory to be defended is vast; the means of communications are poor; the defensive forces are few in number and only partially trained. The enemy, on the other hand, if supported by major elements of his fleet, can exercise control of the sea lanes, and consequently can strike with a preponderance of force on any chosen objective. We have present therefore in this theater at the present time all of the elements that have produced disaster in the Western Pacific since the beginning of the war.[76]

Aroused, Mr. Curtin dispatched a message to the Australian Legation in Washington on 14 May with the request that its contents be communicated to the President through the appropriate channels. Repeating General MacArthur's request for additional forces, including aircraft carriers, the message went on to say that the Australian Government would continue to "argue" the matter, until such time as General MacArthur was satisfied that he had at least the minimum forces needed for the proper discharge of his mission.[77]

The message reached Field Marshal Sir John Dill, head of the British Joint Staff Mission in Washington, on the 16th. Dill at once referred the matter to General Marshall, who replied on 18 May that the planned strength of U.S. Forces in Aus-

tralia was 100,000 men, including two infantry divisions and considerable numbers of antiaircraft and auxiliary troops. First-line air strength to be provided by the United States was, he added, 535 planes, and both troops and planes were either already in Australia or on the way.[78]

Four days later, General Marshall wrote to Sir John again. Noting that Australian ground strength in Australia would total 400,000 men by June, he told Dill that, with the shipping situation what it was, there seemed to be little justification for the dispatch of additional U.S. ground forces to Australia. Ground and air forces projected for Australia, General Marshall continued, were believed to be sufficient for such operations as were immediately visualized for the area, especially since full-scale invasion of Australia did not appear to be imminent and the British had obligated themselves to send both troops and naval forces from the Indian Ocean if it was.

General Marshall agreed that aircraft carriers for the Southwest Pacific Area would be extremely useful, but pointed out that they were simply not to be had. The Chief of Staff concluded his analysis of the situation in these words:

The directive to General MacArthur definitely assigns a defensive mission with the task of preparing an offensive. This conforms to our basic strategy. To be able to take positive action in any theater, it is necessary to hold forces in defensive theaters to a minimum, and, in doing so, to recognize the acceptance of certain calculated risks. The measures General MacArthur advocates would be highly desirable if we were at war with Japan only. In our opinion the Pacific should not be the principal theater.[79]

---

[76] Ltr, Gen MacArthur to Mr. Curtin, 12 May 42, in 314.7, MacArthur File, Rec Sec Files, GHQ SWPA.

[77] Ltr, Mr. Curtin to Gen MacArthur, 16 May 42, in 314.7, MacArthur File, Rec Sec Files, GHQ SWPA.

[78] Ltr, Gen Marshall to Field Marshal Sir John Dill, 18 May 42, in OPD Exec Off File, Bk 5.

[79] Ltr, Gen Marshall to Field Marshal Dill, 22 May 42, in OPD Exec Off File, Bk 5.

The President, who still had to answer Mr. Curtin personally, did so the next day. Taking up where General Marshall left off, he told the Australian Prime Minister that while he too was concerned about the possibility of a Japanese invasion of Australia from New Guinea, and recognized the serious threat to its communications if the enemy should attack New Caledonia, Fiji, and Samoa, he nevertheless "could not lose sight of the fact that Australia could not be supported, nor could her lines of communication be kept open unless Hawaii was securely held." Mr. Roosevelt conceded that the naval and air resources available to the United Nations in the Pacific were insufficient as yet to hold at all threatened points, but he assured Mr. Curtin that the available resources would be used wisely, and "in accordance with the most thorough and careful consideration of the potentialities, known dispositions and intentions of the enemy as they can be deduced or otherwise discovered." [80]

The matter was settled. If the primary effort in Europe was not to be hamstrung, General MacArthur would have to make the best shift he could with what he had.

---

[80] The President's message in paraphrase is in Ltr, Mr. Curtin to Gen MacArthur, 23 May 42, in 314.7, MacArthur File, Rec Sec Files, GHQ SWPA.

CHAPTER III

The Thwarted Landing

To the great relief of the weak and dis-pirited Port Moresby garrison, the occupa-tion of Lae and Salamaua was not immedi-ately followed by a move on Port Moresby. Fortunately for its defenders, the Japanese left the Port Moresby operation temporarily in abeyance and sent their carrier striking force into the Indian Ocean instead to raid the British. This was to prove a fatal mis-take. For when the Japanese finally under-took to land troops at Port Moresby, it was to find that carriers of the U.S. Pacific Fleet stood in their way, and they had sent too little and moved too late.

Frustration at Jomard Passage

Carrier Division 5 *Leaves for Truk*

The Port Moresby landing had to wait because the Japanese had decided to com-mit Admiral Nagumo's entire striking force to the raid in the Indian Ocean. They made this decision because they were after a more glittering prize—the British Eastern Fleet. They hoped that Nagumo would be able to surprise and destroy the fleet, which was then based at Ceylon, in the same way that only three months before he had surprised most of the U.S. Pacific Fleet at Pearl Har-bor. For such a strike, he would require all of his available carriers. Only when the raid was over would carrier strength be detached for the Port Moresby mission.

When operations in the Indian Ocean were over, the large carrier *Kaga* would go on to Truk to support the Port Moresby landing. The rest of Admiral Nagumo's force, which had been months at sea, would be sent home for refitting. On hearing of the U.S. carrier strikes at Lae and Salamaua on 10 March, the Japanese began to have doubts that one large carrier would be enough and decided to send two. Admiral Nagumo, with an eye to his training needs after the Indian Ocean operation, sent the *Kaga* back to Japan and chose the two large carriers, *Shokaku* and *Zuikaku* (*Car-rier Division 5*), then undergoing minor repair in Japan, for the Port Moresby operation.

On 24 March the *Shokaku* and the *Zui-kaku* reached Kendari in the Celebes, where the striking force was then based. Two days later Nagumo left Kendari for the Indian Ocean with five fast carriers under his com-mand. He raided Colombo and Trincoma-lee, main British bases in Ceylon, on 5 and 9 April, but without catching the British Eastern Fleet at anchor as he had hoped. He did run into portions of the fleet at sea and, while other Japanese naval units op-erating in the area sank more than a score of Allied merchantmen, dealt it a stagger-ing blow by sinking in quick succession an aircraft carrier, two heavy cruisers, a de-stroyer, a corvette, and a fleet auxiliary.

By mid-April, the raid was over. The

striking force left the Indian Ocean and,
after a final rendezvous off Formosa, split
into two. The main body, under Admiral
Nagumo, made for Japan, and *Carrier Division 5* and its escort, for Truk. The date
was 20 April.[1]

The Orders of 29 April

At Rabaul, meanwhile, the *South Seas
Detachment* was on the alert, waiting for
orders to land at Port Moresby. There had
been a Japanese landing at Lorengau in the
Admiralties on 6 April by a small naval
force from Truk. A larger force from the
Netherlands Indies had begun a series of
landings along the coast of Netherlands
New Guinea earlier the same week.[2] But no
orders had been received to move on Port
Moresby. General Horii, who had expected
to receive them immediately after Lae and
Salamaua were taken, inquired of *Imperial
General Headquarters* on 15 April why
there had been no action in the matter.
Tokyo's reply was received three days later.
In addition to ordering Horii to begin im-

mediate preparations for the Port Moresby
landing, it alerted him to the fact that he
would soon receive orders for the seizure of
New Caledonia. This operation and that
against Fiji and Samoa would follow the
capture of Port Moresby.[3]

On 28 April, ten days later, at the instance of Admiral Isoroku Yamamoto,
Commander in Chief of the *Combined
Fleet, Imperial General Headquarters,*
sanctioned operations against Midway and
the Aleutians. It was agreed that these operations would follow the Port Moresby
landing, and would be followed in turn by
the scheduled operations against New Caledonia, Fiji, and Samoa.[4]

The decision of 28 April did not affect
preparations for the Port Moresby landing.
By this time they were so far advanced that
General Horii was able to issue his first
orders for the operation the next day, 29
April—a particularly auspicious date, Horii
felt, since it was the emperor's birthday.
The orders provided that the *Detachment*
would leave Rabaul on 4 May, under escort of the *4th Fleet,* and at dawn on 10
May would make a landing at Port
Moresby with the support of units of the
Kure 3d Special Naval Landing Force. The
main body of the *Detachment* was to land
on a beach seven and a half miles northwest of Port Moresby, and the *1st Battalion,
144th Infantry,* and the naval landing parties, were to land on another beach to the
southeast of the town. The two forces would
launch a converging attack and in short

---

[1] Ltr, Gen Willoughby to Gen Ward, 12 Apr 51;
Southeast Area Naval Opns I, 5; Robinson,
"AKAGI, Famous Japanese Carrier," in *United
States Naval Institute Proceedings,* May 48, pp.
582–86; ONI, *Japanese Story of the Battle of Mid-
way* (Washington, 1947), p. 6; Morison, *The Rising
Sun in the Pacific,* pp. 382–86.
[2] Tactical Summary, 8 April, in G–3 Jnl, GHQ
SWPA; Feldt, *The Coast Watchers,* p. 17; 1st
Demob Bur, G–2 Hist Sec GHQ FEC, Japanese
Studies in World War II, No. 35, Japanese Naval
Activities in Mopping-up Operations, p. 5, in
OCMH files. Lorengau's garrison of a dozen or
so AIF troops, warned in time that the Japanese
were coming, took off safely in a small schooner just
before the enemy landed. Between 12 and 20
April the Japanese landed successively at Fakfak,
Babo, Sorong, Manokwari, Momi, Nabire, Seroei,
Hollandia, and Sarmi. Except at Manokwari, where
there was a slight skirmish, all the landings were
unopposed.

[3] *South Seas Det* Opns, p. 12; *South Seas Det*
Opns, 2d ed., pp. 14, 15; *18th Army* Opns I, 5.
[4] USSBS, *Interrogation of Japanese Officials,* II,
525–526; Hist Rec, *Army Section Imperial General
Headquarters,* pp. 51–52; *17th Army* Opns I, 3;
Samuel Eliot Morison, *Coral Sea, Midway and Submarine Actions* (Boston, 1949), pp. 6, 75.

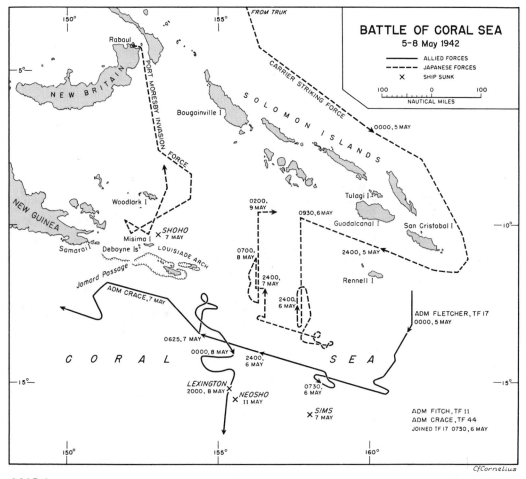

Map legend:

BATTLE OF CORAL SEA
5–8 May 1942

———— ALLIED FORCES
– – – – JAPANESE FORCES
× SHIP SUNK

100   0   100
NAUTICAL MILES

MAP 1

order take all their objectives—the harbor, the town, and Kila Kila airdrome immediately outside the town.[5]

Moving Out for the Landing

The *4th Fleet* had made careful preparations for the landing, and Admiral Inouye

himself came to Rabaul from Truk to take personal charge of the operation. The occupation force, seven destroyers, five transports, and several seaplane tenders, was to have the support of the small carrier *Shoho*, which in turn would be screened by a force of four heavy cruisers, two light cruisers, and a squadron of submarines. *Carrier Division 5*, which had arrived at Truk toward the end of the month with its screen *Cruiser Division 5*—three heavy cruisers, a light cruiser, six destroyers, and an oiler—was to

[5] *Kure 3d SNLF* Orders [29 April 42], copy in G–3 Jnl, GHQ SWPA; *South Seas Det* Opns, p. 14; *South Seas Det* Opns, 2d ed., p. 16; *Hist Rec Army Section Imperial General Headquarters*, pp. 51–52; *18th Army* Opns I, 7; *Southeast Area* Naval Opns I, 5.

THE BATTLE OF THE CORAL SEA, *8 May 1942. The Japanese fast aircraft carrier,* Shokaku, *is heavily damaged by Navy torpedo planes.*

serve as the attack force. It was to destroy Allied sea and air units seeking to attack the occupation force, cover the landings, and raid Townsville in order to immobilize Allied attempts to interfere with the landing from Australia.[6]

Because the invasion plan also called for flying boats to operate out of Tulagi in support of the operation, the Japanese at once sent a force to that point to prepare it for its appointed role. On 2 May, the small RAAF detachment at Tulagi and other Australian forces in its immediate vicinity learned of the Japanese approach. They set demolitions and made for Vila in the New Hebrides, where there was part of an Australian Independent Company, reaching it safely a few days later. The next day, 3 May, the Japanese landed a small force at Tulagi and began to convert it into a seaplane base.[7]

The *South Seas Detachment* began to embark at Rabaul for Port Moresby on 2 May. On 4 May, the scheduled date of departure, the transports left the harbor. The convoy met the *Shoho* force at a rendezvous point off Buin, Bougainville. Shortly thereafter, the *Shokaku* and *Zuikaku* and their escort rounded San Cristobal Island at the south-

---

[6] *Southeast Area* Naval Opns, p. 5; *18th Army* Opns, I, 5; USSBS, *The Campaigns of the Pacific War*, pp. 52–54; USSBS, *Interrogations of Japanese Officials*, I, 29–31, 53–55.

[7] Allied Air Forces DOI, Brief Appreciation of the Coral Sea Battle, 5–8 May 42; Periodical G–2 Msg Summary, 5 May 42. Both in G–3 Jnl, GHQ SWPA. *Southeast Area* Naval Opns, p. 5; *18th Army* Opns I, 5.

THE BATTLE OF THE CORAL SEA, *8 May 1942. Aircraft carrier USS* Lexington, *seriously damaged by the Japanese, is abandoned.*

ern tip of the Solomons and took up a supporting position to the eastward of the invasion convoy. By 7 May, the *Shoho* force was assembling in the area between Deboyne and Misima Island in the Louisiade Archipelago preparatory to passing through Jomard Passage, a channel which would bring them safely through the reefs of the Archipelago into Port Moresby's home waters. The transports, at Admiral Inouye's orders, were standing on the western side of Woodlark Island. The *Shokaku* and *Zuikaku* lay in open water to the southeast.[8] (*Map 1*)

_____

[8] *Southeast Area* Naval Opns I, p. 5; *South Seas Det* Opns, p. 14; ONI, The Battle of the Coral Sea, pp. 11, 13, 16; USSBS, *The Campaigns of the Pacific War*, p. 52; USSBS, *Interrogations of Japanese Officials*, I, 54, Plate 10–A.

The Battle of the Coral Sea

This time the Allies were prepared. The concentration of naval forces in the Mandates and at Rabaul, and a sudden increase of air strength in the Lae–Salamaua–New Britain–Solomons area, had given warning that the long-expected thrust at Port Moresby was at hand. To meet the danger, the Southwest Pacific Area made the best preparations it could. The Allied Air Forces, under General Brett, by this time based mainly on the newly built airfields in the Townsville–Cloncurry area, intensified their reconnaissance of New Britain, Bougainville, and the Louisiade Archipelago. Allied ground forces in northeast Australia and at Port Moresby were put on the alert. Three cruisers of the Allied Naval Forces, the *Australia,* the *Chicago,* and the *Hobart,* under Rear Adm. J. G. Crace, RN, were sent to the Coral Sea to reinforce elements of the U.S. Pacific Fleet, which were gathering there preparatory to closing with the enemy.[9]

The Pacific Fleet, anticipating a Japanese thrust against Port Moresby, had made suitable provision for countering it. After the strikes at Lae–Salamaua on 10 March, the *Yorktown* had remained in the Coral Sea. On 1 May, it was rejoined there by the *Lexington,* and the combined force—two carriers, seven heavy cruisers, a light cruiser, thirteen destroyers, two oilers, and a seaplane tender—came under command of Rear Adm. Frank J. Fletcher the same day.

Late on 3 May Admiral Fletcher learned of the Japanese landing at Tulagi. Fletcher, who was on the *Yorktown* and out of touch with the *Lexington,* struck at Tulagi early on the 4th. Results were disappointing, for there were no important targets in the harbor. Early the next morning, the *Yorktown* rejoined the *Lexington* at a rendezvous point a few hundred miles south of Rennell Island, and the combined force moved out to the northwest, its search planes looking for the enemy.

Early on 6 May, after a great deal of search by carrier-based planes had failed to locate the enemy, Allied Air Force B–17's reported a large force west of Misima Island moving in the direction of Jomard Passage. Admiral Fletcher, who was then fueling at a point roughly 700 miles southeast of Rabaul, at once ordered the tanker *Neosho* and its escort, the destroyer *Sims,* to move south to a fueling rendezvous point believed to be out of the enemy's way. The rest of the fleet moved northwestward in the direction of the Louisiade Archipelago. The next morning, as the Louisiades came within range, a task force of cruisers and destroyers was given the mission of blocking the southern end of Jomard Passage, and the main force prepared to engage the enemy.[10]

Ironically, the rendezvous point of the fueling group, chosen because it was believed to be out of harm's way, brought the *Neosho* and the *Sims* within easy range of the positions the *Shokaku* and *Zuikaku* had taken in order to cover the movement of the occupation force through Jomard Passage. Early on the 7th, a Japanese search plane sighted the tanker and its escort and reported them to the Japanese carrier commander, Rear Adm. Tadaichi Hara, as a carrier and a cruiser. Hara at once ordered out all his planes for the kill. The Japanese carrier pilots made short work of the two ships. The *Sims* sank at once, and the *Neosho* was left in a sinking condition.

Just before noon the same day, search planes from the *Yorktown* discovered the *Shoho* and a part of its screen off Misima Island. Planes from both the *Lexington* and the *Yorktown* immediately closed in. The carrier and a light cruiser, which was escorting it, were hit, and they sank immedi-

---

[9] GHQ SWPA OIs No. 2, 24 Apr 42, No. 5, 7 May 42; Allied Air Forces DOI, Brief Appreciation of the Coral Sea Battle, 5–8 May 42; Msg, Gen MacArthur to Gen Marshall, No. AG 719, 13 May 42, in Pac Strat File, OPD Exec File; ONI, The Battle of the Coral Sea, pp. 9–10; Craven and Cate, *The Army Air Forces in World War II,* I, 447; Morison, *Coral Sea, Midway and Submarine Actions,* pp. 19–20.

[10] ONI, The Battle of the Coral Sea, pp. 2, 10–12, and map facing p. 60; Craven and Cate, *The Army Air Forces in World War II,* I, 448; USSBS, *The Campaigns of the Pacific,* pp. 52, 53, 56; Morison, *Coral Sea, Midway and Submarine Actions,* pp. 26, 27.

ately. There the day's action ended. Despite feverish search activity on both sides, neither side had thus far succeeded in definitely locating the main body of the other.

The opposing carrier forces finally located each other in the early morning of 8 May and their planes joined battle at once. On the Allied side both the *Lexington* and the *Yorktown* were damaged, the *Lexington* seriously. On the Japanese side the *Shokaku* was heavily damaged, though the damage was by no means fatal; and the *Zuikaku,* though undamaged, lost most of its planes. With the *Shoho* gone and the *Shokaku* in no condition to continue the fight, Admiral Inouye, whose oil was running low, broke off the engagement and withdrew to the north. Admiral Fletcher, who had the problem on his hands of saving the *Lexington,* its planes, and its crew, withdrew in turn to the south. The *Shokaku* got back safely to Truk, and the transports carrying the *South Seas Detachment* reached Rabaul, but the *Lexington* developed uncontrollable gasoline fires and had to be abandoned and sunk.

The battle was over. The Allies had suffered heavier losses than the Japanese, but the fact that the latter had been turned back from Port Moresby left the victory, strategically at least, with the Pacific Fleet.[11] On 9 May, *Imperial General Headquar-*

ters advised General Horii that because of the action at the Coral Sea the invasion of Port Moresby would have to be temporarily suspended. He was assured, however, that he would not have long to wait for a resumption, for it had been definitely decided that the operation would be carried out sometime in July.[12]

The landing had miscarried completely. Thanks to the U.S. Pacific Fleet, the Southwest Pacific Area now had a respite in which to continue with the barely begun task of reinforcing Australia's approaches.

Securing the Approaches

GHQ Authorizes BOSTON

Believing that the Japanese would strike at Port Moresby again with at least a division of troops and carrier- and land-based aircraft "any time after June 10," [13] General MacArthur and his staff at once set themselves to secure the area to the maximum extent that the available means would allow.

The means were growing. On 14 May the 32d U.S. Infantry Division, under command of Maj. Gen. Edwin F. Harding, arrived in Australia with the rest of the 41st Division. A day later, the 14th Australian Infantry Brigade Group, 3,400 strong, began moving to Port Moresby with 700 attached Australian antiaircraft troops.[14]

---

[11] *Southeast Area* Naval Opns, I, p. 5; *South Seas Det* Opns, p. 15; ONI, The Battle of the Coral Sea, pp. 11, 21–35; USSBS, *The Campaigns of the Pacific War,* pp. 52, 53, 55; USSBS, *Interrogation of Japanese Officials,* I, 29, 53–54. The Allied Air Forces, except for reconnaissance, proved remarkably ineffective during the battle. In forty-five sorties against enemy shipping with B–17's, B–26's, B–25's and a Hudson, it scored no hits whatever on the enemy, and actually bombed Allied ships by mistake. For a full discussion of the matter, see Craven and Cate, *The Army Air Forces in World War II,* I, 449–50.

[12] *South Seas Det* Opns, p. 15.

[13] Memo, CINCSWPA for Comdr ALF, *et al.,* 20 May 42, sub: Reinforcement of Combat Means in Northeast Australia, in G–3 Jnl, GHQ SWPA.

[14] Memo, CINCSWPA for Comdr ALF, *et al.,* 13 May 42; G–3 Opns Rpt No. 38, 14–15 May 42; Memo, Gen Sturdee, COGS Dept of the Army, ALF, for GHQ SWPA, 16 May 42, sub: Opns Rpt for Australian Army; Memo, Comdr ANF for Comdr ALF, *et al.,* 22 May 42. All in G–3 Jnl, GHQ SWPA. The 32d Division, which went into camp near Adelaide, was assigned to the operational control of Allied Land Forces, effective 1 June 1942, per GO 7, GHQ SWPA, 30 May 42.

One of the lessons of the Coral Sea had been that to cover Port Moresby's eastern approaches effectively the Air Force would have to have a base at or near the southeastern tip of New Guinea. A base in the low-lying regions in that area would do more than provide protection for Port Moresby's uncovered flank. It would give the Air Force a new staging point for attacks on Japanese bases to the north and northwest and one, furthermore, that was not subject to the turbulences and other operational hazards that beset flight over the Owen Stanleys. Ultimately it would provide a point of departure for an advance along the southeast coast.[15]

These considerations were not lost on General MacArthur. In a letter to General Blamey on 14 May, he wrote that a careful study of weather and operating conditions along the southeast coast of Papua had resulted in a decision to establish new airdromes there for use against Lae, Salamaua, and Rabaul. Noting that suitable sites appeared to be available in the coastal strip between Abau and Samarai near the southeast tip of Papua, he asked Blamey if he had the necessary ground troops and antiaircraft units to protect these bases. When General Blamey replied that he had the troops, General MacArthur authorized the construction of a landing strip 50 feet by 1,500 feet at BOSTON, the code name for Abau-Mullins Harbor area, a wild and largely unexplored coastal area requiring an immense amount of development. The new field (so the orders read) was to be built "in a location susceptible of improvement later on to a heavy bombardment airdrome."[16]

The Plan of Reinforcement

On 20 May, the same day that he authorized the construction of an airfield at BOSTON, General MacArthur issued a comprehensive plan to his commanders for the "reinforcement of combat means" in northeast Australia and New Guinea. Under terms of this plan, the Air Force would bring its existing pursuit squadrons at Port Moresby up to full strength, and U. S. antiaircraft troops at Brisbane would be transferred to Townsville, Horn Island, and Mareeba, Cooktown, and Coen, the bases in the Cape York Peninsula. These bases, Port Moresby, and the new base at BOSTON were to be fully stocked with aviation supplies, bombs, and ammunition, so that when an emergency arose the Air Force would be able to use them for the interdiction of enemy "movements through the Louisiades and along the southeast coast of New Guinea." The construction or improvement of the airfields in northeast Australia and in New Guinea was to be accelerated, and the transport to them of reinforcements and supplies was to be arranged by USAFIA, in consultation with Allied Land Forces.[17]

When completed, the new air bases in northeast Australia and the York Peninsula would advance the forward bomber line by as much as 500 miles. They would bring the bombers as close to Port Moresby as it was physically possible to get them without

---

[15] Interv with Gen Chamberlin, 14 Jan 50.

[16] Ltr, Gen MacArthur to Gen Blamey, 14 May 42, in G–3 Jnl, GHQ SWPA; Ltr, Gen Blamey to

[15] Gen MacArthur, 16 May 42, in 314.7, MacArthur File, Rec Sec Files, GHQ SWPA; Memo, CINCSWPA for Comdr ALF, *et al.*, 20 May 42, sub: Location and Construction of an Airfield, Southeast Coast of New Guinea, in 385, FALL RIVER File, G–3 Files, GHQ SWPA.

[17] Memo, CINCSWPA for Comdr ALF *et al.*, 20 May 1942, sub: Reinforcement of Combat Means in Northeast Australia.

actually basing them there, and would place them in position for active defensive and offensive action. The new fields and dispersal areas at Port Moresby would not only facilitate the progress of the bombers as they staged through it in their tramontane attacks upon the Japanese bases in North East New Guinea and New Britain but would also permit more fighters and light bombers to be based there. The field at BOSTON, in addition to providing its offensive possibilities, would help to thwart any further Japanese attempt to take Port Moresby from the sea.

On 24 May Allied Land Forces picked the garrison for BOSTON and assigned it its mission. Being apparently in some doubt that BOSTON could be held, Land Force Headquarters instructed the troops chosen that they would be responsible for ground defense of the area against only minor attacks. If the enemy launched a major attack against them, they were to withdraw, making sure before they did so that they had destroyed "all weapons, supplies, and material of value to the enemy." [18]

Milne Bay

The field at BOSTON was never built. When an aerial reconnaissance of the eastern tip of New Guinea was ordered on 22 May,[19] it was discovered that there were better sites in the Milne Bay area. On 8 June, a twelve-man party, three Americans and nine Australians, under Lt. Col. Lev-

erett G. Yoder, Commanding Officer, 96th U.S. Engineer Battalion, left Port Moresby for Milne Bay in a Catalina flying boat to reconnoiter the area further. A good site suitable for several airfields was found in a coconut plantation at the head of the bay. Developed by Lever Brothers before the war, the plantation had a number of buildings, a road net, a small landing field, and several small jetties already in place. Impressed by the terrain and the existing facilities, Colonel Yoder turned in a favorable report on the project the next day.[20]

Colonel Yoder's report was at once recognized at GHQ to be of the greatest significance. Here at last was a base which if properly garrisoned could probably be held, and GHQ lost no time ordering it to be developed. Construction of the field at BOSTON was canceled on 11 June. The following day, GHQ authorized construction of an airfield with the necessary dispersal strips at the head of Milne Bay. A landing strip suitable for pursuit aviation was to be built immediately, and a heavy bomber field was to be developed later on.[21]

On 22 June, GHQ authorized a small airfield development at Merauke, a point on the south coast of Netherlands New Guinea, in order to give further protection to Port Moresby's western flank.[22] On the

[18] Memo, COGS Dept of the Army, ALF, for NGF, 24 May 42, sub: BOSTON Opns, in 385, FALL RIVER File, G-3 Files, GHQ SWPA.

[19] Memo, Brig Gen Hugh J. Casey, Chief Engr SWPA, for Engr USAFIA, 22 May 42, sub: Instructions for Reconnaissance, New Guinea Airfield, in 686, New Guinea No. 2, G-3 Files, GHQ SWPA.

[20] Rpt, Lt Col Leverett G. Yoder, CO 96th Engr Bn, Port Moresby, 9 Jun 42, in 385, FALL RIVER File, G-3 files, GHQ SWPA.

[21] Memo, CINCSWPA for Comdr ALF et al., 11 June 42, sub: Suspension of Instructions Relating to the Movement of Certain Troops to BOSTON; Memo, CINCSWPA for Comdr ALF et al., 12 Jun 42, sub: Location and Construction of Airfield, Southeast Tip of New Guinea. Both in 385, FALL RIVER File, G-3 Files, GHQ, SWPA.

[22] Memo, CINCSWPA for Comdr ALF et al., 22 June 42, sub: Plan for Occupation and Construction of An Advanced Airfield at Merauke, New Guinea, in G-3 Jnl, GHQ SWPA.

same day, Milne Bay's initial garrison—two companies and a machine gun platoon on loan from the 14th Australian Infantry Brigade at Port Moresby—left Port Moresby for Milne Bay in the K. P. M. ship *Karsik*, and early on 25 June the troops disembarked safely at Milne Bay. Four days later, the K. P. M. ship *Bontekoe* came into Milne Bay with a shipload of engineering equipment, and Company E, 46th U.S. Engineers. The new contingent immediately began working on the base.

The 7th Australian Infantry Brigade, one of the better-trained militia units, was ordered to Milne Bay from Townsville on 2 July. The brigade commander and advance elements of the brigade left by sea within the week, arriving at Milne Bay several days later. The rest of the brigade arrived shortly thereafter, and a squadron of RAAF P–40's came in toward the end of the month.[23] Port Moresby's vulnerable eastern flank was no longer uncovered.

The Bulolo Valley

Reinforcement of the troops in the Bulolo Valley, held up in late April when the threat to Port Moresby was at its height, was resumed when the 5th Australian Independent Company, the reinforcing unit, again became available for use in the Bulolo Valley. The company and an attached mortar

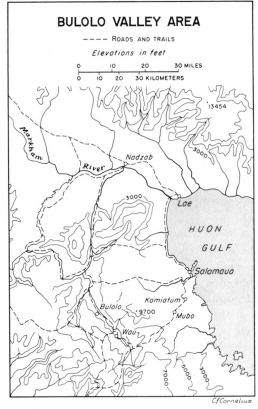

MAP 2

platoon were flown to Wau on 26 May; and the troops in the valley, by this time known as KANGA Force, began preparing for the long-delayed attacks on Lae and Salamaua.[24] (*Map 2*)

The attacks were meant to be purely defensive—to delay the enemy and throw him off stride. Should KANGA Force succeed in seizing Lae and Salamaua, it was planned to base pursuit planes immediately at Lae and to send further reinforcements to the area by sea. To hold the area for two or

[23] Ltr, Maj Gen G. A. Vasey, ALF, to GHQ SWPA, sub: Fall River Operation, 23 June 42; Msg, NGF to ALF, No. G–283, 26 June 42; Memo, GHQ SWPA for Comdr ALF *et al.*, 2 July 42; Msg, Col Albert G. Matthews to Brig Gen S. J. Chamberlin, G–3, GHQ SWPA, No. 2797, 7 July 42. All in 385, FALL RIVER File, G–3 Files, GHQ SWPA. Allied Air Force Opns Rpt, 6 July 42; ALF Daily Opns Rpt, 10 July 42; LHQ OI No. 27, 18 July 42. All in G–3 Jnl, GHQ SWPA. Annual Rpt, OCE SWPA, 1942.

[24] NGF OI No. 7, 23 Apr 42; Ltr, Gen Blamey to Gen MacArthur, 2 May 42. Both in 385, G–3 Files, GHQ SWPA. Allied Air Force Opns Rpt, 25–26 May 42, in G–3 Jnl, GHQ SWPA.

three weeks, it was hoped, would greatly delay the enemy and cause him to postpone further major action against Port Moresby.[25]

The operation ran into difficulties. Learning from the natives that the Japanese were planning a major attack on the Bulolo Valley, the commander of KANGA Force had to split his troops and put part of them on the defensive. The first attack of KANGA Force, made with only a part of the unit's strength, was launched on Salamaua in late June. Sixty Japanese were killed and considerable damage was done, but the approach of enemy reinforcements from Lae caused the attackers to withdraw. A raid on Lae several days later had the same result. Forty Japanese were killed, but KANGA Force had to withdraw again in the face of superior numbers.[26]

The diversion had failed. KANGA Force obviously was not strong enough to dislodge the enemy, even for a few days.

Kokoda

One further loophole in Port Moresby's scheme of defense remained. From Buna, a point on the northeast coast of Papua, a difficult and little-known trail led over the Owen Stanleys to Port Moresby via Kokoda, a small plateau in the foothills of the range on which there was a small mountain airfield. General MacArthur's headquarters realized that an enemy force landing at Buna could quickly invest Kokoda and move on Port Moresby through a nearby 6,000-foot mountain pass known as the Gap. (*Map I*)* An inquiry was made into the matter during the first week in June, and it was discovered that Maj. Gen. Basil Morris, who, as GOC, New Guinea Force, was in command of the Port Moresby area, had thus far made no move to send a force to defend it.[27]

Alive to the danger, General MacArthur wrote to General Blamey on 9 June:

There is increasing evidence that the Japanese are displaying interest in the development of a route from Buna on the north coast of southern New Guinea through Kokoda to Port Moresby. From studies made in this headquarters it appears that minor forces may attempt to utilize this route for either attack on Port Moresby or for supply of forces [attacking] by the sea route through the Louisiade Archipelago. Whatever the Japanese plan may be, it is of vital importance that the route from Kokoda westward be controlled by Allied Forces, particularly the Kokoda area.

"Will you please advise me," he concluded, "of the plan of the Commander, New Guinea Force, for the protection of this route and of the vital Kokoda area." [28]

General Morris, who was also head of the Australia-New Guinea Administrative Unit (ANGAU), the military government of Papau and the territories of the Mandate, replied several days later, but the reply was scarcely reassuring. There were, Land Forces was told, several ANGAU officers in

*Maps numbered in Roman numerals are placed in inverse order inside the back cover.

---

[25] Ltr, Gen Blamey to Gen MacArthur, 2 May 42; Safehand Msg, G–3, GHQ SWPA to MilComd, Moresby. Both in 385, G–3 Files, GHQ SWPA.

[26] G–2 Daily Msg Summary, 12 Jun 42, 20 Jun 42; Msgs, NGF to ALF, No. G–2953, 14 Jun 42, No. 2140, 30 Jun 42; Msg, Air Intel, Moresby, to Air Intel, Melbourne, 30 Jun 42; ALF Daily Opns Rpts, 1 Jul 42 and 2 Jul 42. All in G–3 Jnl, GHQ SWPA. White, *Green Armor*, pp. 143, 144.

[27] G–2 Periodic Msg Summary, 3 Jun 42; Ltr, Gen MacArthur to Gen Blamey, 9 Jun 42. Both in G–3 Jnl, GHQ SWPA. Msg, ALF to NGF, No. G–27411, 20 Jun 42, in 385, New Guinea, G–3 Files, GHQ SWPA.

[28] Memo, Gen MacArthur for Gen Blamey, 9 Jun 42, sub: Defense of the Buna–Kokoda–Port Moresby Trail, in 385, New Guinea, G–3 Files, GHQ SWPA.

the area with radio sets; native constables were to be found in all the villages; and two platoons of the Papuan Infantry Battalion (PIB), a light reconnaissance unit made up principally of natives, were constantly patrolling the area. The PIB was being reinforced, the report continued, and a company of infantry at Port Moresby was being readied for movement to Kokoda on short notice. It was considered "most unlikely," the report concluded, that "any untoward incident" could occur in the area without the knowledge of the district officer.[29]

General Chamberlin made it clear to Land Forces that he did not consider these measures adequate provision for Kokoda's security. But he decided to take no further action in the matter when he learned that General Blamey's headquarters had sent a radio message to General Morris ordering him "to take all necessary steps to prevent a Japanese surprise landing along the coast, north and south of Buna, to deny the enemy the grasslands in that area for an airdrome, and to assure that we command the pass at Kokoda."[30]

In the radio General Morris was told that, as matters stood, enemy troops that landed at Buna could reach the vital passes in the Kokoda area before reinforcements from Port Moresby could get there. He was reminded that the forces in the Kokoda area were "entirely native, very weak, and probably not staunch," and was ordered to take immediate steps "to secure the vital section of the route with Australian infantry," and "to prepare to oppose the enemy on lines of advance from the coast."[31]

Five days later, General Morris established a new unit, MAROUBRA Force, and gave it the mission of holding Kokoda. The new force included the 39th Australian Infantry Battalion (less one company) from the 30th Brigade, and the PIB—280 natives and twenty whites. One company of the battalion, Company B, was ordered to Kokoda on 26 June, but did not leave until 7 July, eleven days later. The rest of the battalion, on orders of General Morris, remained on the Port Moresby side of the range, training and improving communications at the southern end of the trail.[32]

---

[29] Ltr, Gen Vasey, DCofS ALF, to GHQ SWPA, 15 Jun 42, sub: New Guinea–Protection on Route, Buna–Kokoda, in 385, New Guinea, G–3 Files, GHQ SWPA.
[30] R&R, Col J. D. Rogers, G–3 Sec GHQ, to Gen Chamberlin, 20 Jun 42; R&R, Gen Chamberlin to Gen Sutherland, 20 Jun 42. Both in 385, New Guinea, G–3 Files, GHQ SWPA.

[31] Msg, ALF to NGF, No. G–27411, 20 Jun 42, in 385, New Guinea, G–3 Files, GHQ SWPA.
[32] NGF OI No. 18, 25 Jun 42; Brig S. H. Porter, Rpt on Part Played by 30th Aust Inf Bde Hq in Owen Stanleys, copy in OCMH files.

CHAPTER IV

PROVIDENCE Forestalled

The Joint Directive of 30 March 1942 had visualized a defensive phase followed by "major amphibious operations," which would be launched from the Southwest Pacific and South Pacific Areas. The idea of an offensive of any kind in the Pacific seemed wildly optimistic in March and early April, but the establishment by Admiral King on 29 April of a South Pacific Amphibious Force made up principally of the amphibiously trained and equipped 1st Marine Division was at least a step in that direction.[1] While the assignment of this force laid the foundation for an eventual offensive from the South Pacific Area, it was clear that as long as the Japanese enjoyed overwhelming naval superiority in the Pacific, especially in carriers, the offensive would have to wait and the striking forces of both areas would have to remain dispersed and on the defensive. Should it become possible, however, to destroy a substantial portion of Japan's carrier strength, the way would be open for offensive action in the Pacific with the available means, limited though they were. The opportunity to inflict such a blow upon the Japanese Fleet came in early June, and the Pacific Fleet, which had long waited for the chance, exploited it to the full.

Moving to the Offensive

The Battle of Midway

On 5 May Admiral Yamamoto was ordered to seize Midway and the Aleutians immediately after the capture of Port Moresby. The reverse at the Coral Sea caused the Port Moresby operation to be postponed, and Midway and the Aleutians went into top place on the Japanese operational schedule. On 18 May Yamamoto was further instructed that when he had taken Midway and the Aleutians he was to cooperate with the *17th Army,* which had been established that day, in the capture of New Caledonia, Fiji, and Samoa, and in the seizure as well of Port Moresby. Though New Caledonia, Fiji, and Samoa were to be taken first, the seizure of all four objectives was, as far as possible, to be accomplished in one continuous thrust.[2]

The commander of the *17th Army,* Lt. Gen. Haruyoshi Hyakutake, was ordered to attack New Caledonia, Fiji, Samoa, and Port Moresby in order "to cut off communications between America and Australia." He lost no time in alerting the elements of

---

[1] Ltr, COMINCH to CINCPAC *et al.,* 29 Apr 42, sub: Basic Plan for the Establishment of the South Pacific Amphibious Force, in G-3 Jnl, GHQ SWPA.

[2] *Navy Staff Section, Imperial General Headquarters* Orders No. 18, 5 May 42, and No. 19, 18 May 42; ATIS SCAP Doc No. 14016B, in OCMH files; Ltr, Gen Willoughby to Gen Ward, 12 Apr 51; Hist Rec, *Army Section Imperial General Headquarters,* pp. 51–53.

his newly formed command—the *South Seas Detachment* at Rabaul, the *Kawaguchi Detachment* at Palau, and the *Yazawa* and *Aoba Detachments* at Davao—to their part in the forthcoming operations. Hyakutake parceled out the objectives as follows: the *South Seas Detachment* (the *144th Infantry* reinforced) was to take New Caledonia; the *Kawaguchi Detachment* (the *124th Infantry* reinforced) and an element of the *Yazawa Detachment* (the *41st Infantry*) were to move against Samoa; and the *Aoba Detachment* (the *4th Infantry* reinforced) was to land at Port Moresby. All units were to be in instant readiness for action as soon as the Midway–Aleutians victory was won.[3]

Admiral Yamamoto had meanwhile detailed an immense force to capture Midway including the four large fast carriers *Kaga*, *Akagi*, *Hiryu*, and *Soryu*. The remainder of Admiral Nagumo's command, the *Shokaku* and *Zuikaku*, were not able to participate because of the action at the Coral Sea.

Admiral Nagumo's carrier force left Japan for Midway on 27 May, the same day that the transports left Saipan and the cruisers and destroyers, which were to cover them, left Guam. The main body of the fleet, with Admiral Yamamoto in command, left from various Japanese ports a day later.[4]

The U.S. Pacific Fleet had learned ahead of time of Yamamoto's intentions. Three aircraft carriers, the *Enterprise, Hornet,* and *Yorktown,* lay in wait for the enemy a couple of hundred miles north of Midway. The first sightings of the Japanese force were made on 3 June, and the issue was decided the next morning after a massive attack on Midway by enemy carrier planes.

The last enemy plane had scarcely left Midway when three of the enemy carriers—the *Akagi, Kaga,* and *Soryu*—all closely bunched together, were hit fatally by the dive-bomber squadrons of the *Enterprise* and the *Yorktown*. The *Kaga* and *Soryu* went down late that afternoon; the *Akagi*, with uncontrollable fires raging aboard, took longer to succumb but was finally scuttled by its own crew that evening. The *Hiryu*, which had been a considerable distance ahead of the main carrier force, succeeded in knocking out the *Yorktown* before it too was set afire by dive bombers from the *Enterprise* and *Hornet*. Burning fiercely, the *Hiryu* was scuttled by its crew the next morning.

The loss of the carriers forced Yamamoto to break off the engagement and to withdraw his fleet to the north and west with U.S. naval units in pursuit. The Pacific Fleet had lost a carrier, a destroyer, 150 aircraft, and 300 men, but it had broken the back of the Japanese Fleet and gained one of the greatest naval triumphs in history.[5]

With the *Combined Fleet* routed, and its main striking force destroyed, the Allies were at last in a position to seize the initiative. The time had come to counterattack.

The 2 July Directive

The magnitude of the Japanese disaster at Midway was immediately realized. Offensive plans to exploit the new situation

---

[3] *17th Army* Opns I, 1, 4, 6, 7, 9.

[4] ONI, *The Japanese Story of the Battle of Midway*, p. 6; USSBS, *The Campaigns of the Pacific War*, pp. 74–76.

[5] ONI, The Battle of Midway, pp. 9–27; ONI, *The Japanese Story of the Battle of Midway*, pp. 8–10; USSBS, *The Campaigns of the Pacific War*, pp. 58–70; Morison, *The Coral Sea, Midway and Submarine Actions*, pp. 117–37.

USS *YORKTOWN* UNDER JAPANESE FIRE *during the Battle of Midway.*

and add further to the enemy's discomfiture were quickly evolved and presented to the Joint Chiefs of Staffs for consideration.

General MacArthur, who assumed as a matter of course that he would be in command from start to finish since all the objectives lay in his area, had proposed that the operation be an uninterrupted thrust through New Guinea and the Solomons, with Rabaul as the final objective. The Navy, standing for a more gradual approach, insisted that Tulagi would have to be taken and secured before the final attack on Rabaul was mounted. In addition, it had raised strong objections to having General MacArthur in command of the operation, at least in its first, purely amphibious, stages.

General Marshall found it difficult to secure agreement on these issues, but succeeded finally on the basis of a draft directive that divided the operation into three tasks. Task One, the seizure of the Tulagi area, was to be under Vice Adm. Robert L. Ghormley, Commander of the South Pacific Area, while Tasks Two and Three would be under General MacArthur.[6]

Agreement on the final form of the directive was reached on 2 July. After stating that offensive operations would be conducted with the ultimate objective of seizing and occupying the New Britain–New Ireland–

---

[6] The matter is fully discussed in John Miller, jr., *Guadalcanal: The First Offensive* (Washington, 1949), pp. 8–17, a volume in this series.

New Guinea area, the directive laid down the following tasks:

    a. *Task One*. Seizure and occupation of the Santa Cruz Islands, Tulagi, and adjacent positions.
    b. *Task Two*. Seizure and occupation of the remainder of the Solomon Islands, of Lae, Salamaua, and the northeast coast of New Guinea.
    c. *Task Three*. Seizure and occupation of Rabaul and adjacent positions in the New Guinea–New Ireland area.

Task One, under Admiral Ghormley, was given a target date of 1 August. Mac-Arthur would not only supply naval reinforcements and land-based air in support of Task One but would also provide for the interdiction of enemy air and naval activities westward of the operating areas. To remove the objection that Admiral Ghormley would exercise command in General MacArthur's area, the boundary between the Southwest Pacific Area and South Pacific Area would, as of 1 August, be changed to 159° East Longitude, thereby bringing Tulagi and adjacent positions into the South Pacific Area.[7] (*Map 3*)

The SWPA Prepares

Girding for Action

General MacArthur now had a twofold responsibility. His responsibility under Task One was to lend the South Pacific Area the fullest support possible with his aircraft, submarines, and naval striking force. His responsibility under the succeeding tasks was to prepare his command for early offensive action, and this he lost no time in doing.

A change was made in the command of

the Allied Air Forces. On 13 July, Maj. Gen. George C. Kenney, then commanding general of the Fourth Air Force at San Francisco, was ordered to take over command of the Allied Air Forces. General Brett was to remain temporarily in command until Kenney's arrival.[8]

The U.S. Army services of supply were reorganized. The United States Army in Australia (USAFIA), which was essentially a supply echelon, and not, as its name suggested, an administrative headquarters for U.S. troops in Australia, was discontinued on 20 July. The United States Army Services of Supply, Southwest Pacific Area (USASOS SWPA), with General MacArthur's deputy chief of staff, Brig. Gen. Richard J. Marshall, in command, was established the same day. General Barnes, like General Brett, was ordered back to the United States for reassignment.[9]

To achieve more effective control over operations, General Headquarters, Southwest Pacific Area (familiarly known as GHQ), and subordinate Allied land, air, and naval headquarters were moved from Melbourne to Brisbane. The move was completed on 20 July,[10] and brought the highest headquarters in the area 800 miles closer to

---

[7] Joint Directive for Offensive Operations in the Southwest Pacific agreed upon by the Joint Chiefs of Staff, 2 July 42, copy in 381, OPD SWPA, Sec 2.

[8] Msg, Gen MacArthur to Gen Marshall, No. AG 24, CM–IN 8604, 26 Jun 42; Msg, Gen Marshall to Gen MacArthur, No. 390, CM–OUT 3429, 13 Jul 42; Gen George C. Kenney, *General Kenney Reports* (New York, 1949), pp. 9–11.
[9] Msg, Gen MacArthur to Gen Marshall, No. C–62, 10 Jul 42; USAFIA GO 78, 18 Jul 42; GHQ SWPA GO 17, 20 Jul 42; USASOS SWPA GO 1, 20 Jul 42. All in G–3 Jnl, GHQ SWPA.
[10] GHQ SWPA OI No. 11, 14 Jul 42; Msg, Gen MacArthur to Gen Marshall, No. C–107, CM–IN 5468, 16 Jul 42. The original intention had been to move GHQ to Townsville, in order to be that much closer to New Guinea. A critical lack of communications facilities at Townsville resulted in the decision to move to Brisbane. Ltr, Gen Sutherland to Gen Ward, 27 Feb 51.

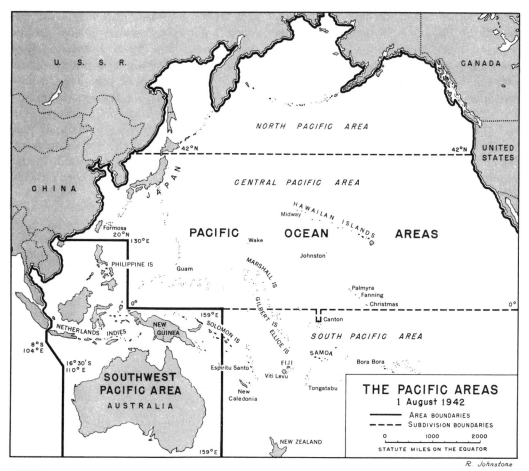

MAP 3

R. Johnstone

the combat zone and in position to make a further forward move should one be required by the trend of operations.

United States antiaircraft units at Perth, which were obviously no longer needed there, were transferred to Townsville, and the 32d and 41st Divisions were ordered to new camps in Queensland, where they were to be assigned to a corps and given training in jungle warfare.[11] The 41st Division, then in training near Melbourne, began to move to Rockhampton on 12 July. A day later, the 32d Division began to move from Adelaide to a camp near Brisbane.[12]

[11] Msg, Gen MacArthur to Gen Marshall, No. 12, CM–IN 0586, 2 Jul 42.

[12] Ibid.; Memo, Col. S. E. Anderson for CG AGF, 6 Jul 42, sub: Remarks by Commanding General, Southwest Pacific Area; Memo, Maj Gen Robert C. Richardson, Jr., for Gen Marshall, 9 Jul 42, sub: Report No. 5. Both memos in Special Collections File, OPD Exec File. ALF Daily Opns Rpts, 12 Jul 42 and 13 Jul 42; G–3 Opns Rpt, No. 96, 13 Jul 42. All in G–3 Jnl, GHQ SWPA.

The corps command had been given initially to Maj. Gen. Robert C. Richardson, Jr., then Commanding General, VII Corps. However, when it was found that General Richardson (who had reached Australia in early July, in the course of a tour of inspection for General Marshall) had strong objections to serving under Australian command, the assignment went to Maj. Gen. Robert L. Eichelberger, Commanding General, I Corps, a classmate at West Point of both Generals Harding and Fuller of the 32d and 41st Divisions, which were to make up his corps.[13]

Airfield construction in the forward areas was accelerated. By early July, the airfields in the York Peninsula–Horn Island area were well along, and air force units were occupying them as rapidly as they became ready for use.[14] At Port Moresby, seven fields were projected, and work was progressing on four. At Milne Bay, three fields were under way, and one strip was expected to be in full operation by the end of the month.[15]

These heavy construction commitments made it necessary to send more U.S. engi-

neer troops to New Guinea to assist the American and Australian engineers already there. The 808th Engineer Aviation Battalion, then at Darwin, was put on orders for Port Moresby on 21 July. The 2d Battalion of the 43d U.S. Engineers (less Company E, which was at Port Moresby) was ordered to Milne Bay the same day to join with the company of the 46th Engineers, which was already on the ground, in the construction of the crucially needed airfields there.[16]

Buna and the Theater Plan

The theater plan of operations, the TULSA plan, was revised in the light of the 2 July directive. It had previously merely pointed to the need of a major airfield in the Buna area if Lae and Salamaua were attacked. As revised, it now provided for the immediate establishment of a field in that area in order that it might be available for support of operations against Lae and Salamaua as prescribed by Task Two.[17]

The problem was how to meet this requirement. There was a small neglected emergency strip just southeast of Buna about which little was known except that it seemed to be too wet and too low lying to be exploited profitably for military use. On 9 July GHQ ordered a reconnaissance of the Buna area. The object of the reconnaissance was to ascertain whether the existing strip had any military value and, if not, to find an all-weather site elsewhere in the area which the military could use.

[13] Msgs, Gen Marshall to Gen MacArthur, No. 353, CM–OUT 1779, 7 Jul 42, No. 367, CM–OUT 2303, 9 Jul 42, No. 332, CM–OUT 8821, 30 Jul 42, No. 440, CM–OUT 7373, 2 Aug 42; Msg, Gen MacArthur to Gen Marshall, No. C–182, CM–IN 0155, 1 Aug 42; *Official Army Register*, 1942, pp. 260, 305, 368. All three generals were born in the year 1886. Two of them, Eichelberger and Harding, were appointed to the academy from Ohio. Fuller, who was from South Dakota, had been an appointee at large.

[14] Msg, Gen MacArthur to Gen Marshall, No. Q–147, CM–IN 1067, 2 Aug 42; Memo, Gen Chamberlin for Gen Sutherland, 21 Aug 42, in 385–9, G–3 Files, GHQ SWPA.

[15] Msg, U. S. Mil Comd (Moresby) to GOC NGF, No. C–28613, 26 Jun 42, in 385, FALL RIVER File, G–3 Files, GHQ SWPA; Msg, Gen MacArthur to Gen Marshall, No. C–301, CM–IN 7017, 19 Aug 42; Ltr, Gen Casey to Gen Chamberlin, 21 Aug 42, sub: Engineer Annex for Tulsa Plan; Annual Rpt OCE SWPA, 1942. Both in AFPAC Engr File.

[16] Ltr, GHQ SWPA to Comdr ALF, *et al.*, 6 Jul 42, sub: Employment of Engineers at Fall River, in 686, New Guinea, G–3 Files, GHQ SWPA; ALF Daily Opns Rpt, 21 Jul 42, in G–3 Jnl, GHQ SWPA; Annual Rpt OCE SWPA, 1942.

[17] TULSA IIA, Joint Basic Plan for the Occupation of the Area New Britain–New Ireland–Admiralty Islands [n. d. Jul 42], abstract in OCMH files.

The PROVIDENCE Operation

The Reconnaissance

The reconnaissance was made on 10 and 11 July by a party of six officers from Port Moresby, who reached the area in a Catalina flying boat. The party was headed by Lt. Col. Bernard L. Robinson, a ranking U.S. engineer officer at Port Moresby, and included three Australian officers who had personal knowledge of the area, Lt. Col. Boyd D. Wagner, U.S. fighter group commander at Port Moresby, and Colonel Yoder. Carefully examining the terrain of the entire area, the six officers found that, while the existing strip was virtually useless for military purposes, the grass plains area at Dobodura fifteen miles south of Buna was an excellent site suitable for large-scale air operations, even in the rainy season which was then only a few months away.

In a special report to General Casey, Colonel Robinson recommended that the existing site not be developed, except perhaps as an emergency landing field for fighter aircraft. The site at Dobodura, on the other hand, he thought almost ideal for large-scale military use. Drainage was good; stone, gravel, and timber in adequate amounts were to be found in the area; and considerable native labor was available locally for the construction of the field. The site would provide ample room for proper aircraft dispersal, and with only light clearing and grading would provide an excellent landing field, 7,000 feet long and more than 300 feet wide, lying in the direction of the prevailing wind.[18]

The Plan To Occupy Buna

When the news was received at GHQ that Dobodura was an all-weather site, it was decided to establish an airfield there with all possible speed. On 13 July General Chamberlin called a meeting of the representatives of the Allied Land Forces, the Allied Air Forces, the Antiaircraft Command, and the supply services to discuss in a preliminary way the part each could expect to play in the operation. A second meeting was called the next day in which the matter was discussed in greater detail and a general scheme of maneuver for the occupation of Buna was worked out.[19]

The plan was ready on the 15th, and instructions to the commanders concerned went out the same day. The operation, which was given the code name PROVIDENCE, provided for the establishment of a special unit, Buna Force, with the primary mission of preparing and defending an airfield to be established in the Buna area. At first the airfield would consist only of a strip suitable for the operation of two pursuit squadrons, but it was eventually to be developed into a base capable of accommodating three squadrons of pursuit and two of heavy bombardment.

Brig. Gen. Robert H. Van Volkenburgh, commanding general of the 40th Artillery Brigade (AA) at Port Moresby, was to be task force commander with control of the troops while they were moving to Buna. An Australian brigadier would take command at Buna itself.

The movements of Buna Force to the target area would be in four echelons or serials,

---

[18] Memo, Lt Col Bernard L. Robinson, CE, for Gen Casey, 13 Jul 42, sub: Rpt on Airdrome Site in the Vicinity of Buna, New Guinea, in AFPAC Engr File.

[19] Memo, Lt Col Elvin R. Heiberg, CE, for Gen Casey, 15 Jul 42, sub: Conference on Buna Airdrome, in 337, Conf Rpts, in AFPAC Engr File.

covered by aviation from Milne Bay and Port Moresby to the maximum extent possible. Defining D Day as the day that Buna would first be invested, the orders provided that Serial One, four Australian infantry companies and a small party of U.S. engineers, would leave Port Moresby on foot on D minus 11. These troops were scheduled to arrive at Buna, via the Kokoda Trail, on D minus 1, at which time they would secure the area and prepare it for the arrival of the succeeding serials.

Serial Two, 250 men, mostly Americans, including an engineer party, a radar and communications detachment, some port maintenance personnel, and a .50-caliber antiaircraft battery, would arrive at Buna in two small ships on the morning of D Day. The incoming troops would combine with those already there and, in addition to helping secure the area, would provide it with antiaircraft defense.

Serial Three, the main serial, would include the Australian brigadier who was to take command at Buna, an Australian infantry battalion, a RAAF radar and communications detachment, the ground elements of two pursuit squadrons, an American port detachment, and other supporting American troops. This serial was due at Buna on D plus 1, in an escorted convoy of light coastwise vessels, bringing its heavy stores and thirty days' subsistence for the garrison.

The fourth serial would consist of a company of American engineers and the remaining ground elements of the two pursuit squadrons that were to be stationed in the area. It would reach Buna from Townsville by sea on D plus 14, accompanied by further stores of all kinds for the operation of the base.

The attention of hostile forces would be diverted from the Buna area, both before and during the operation, by attacks upon Lae and Salamaua by KANGA Force and the Allied Air Forces. Since the "essence" of the plan was "to take possession of this area, provide immediate antiaircraft defense, and to unload supplies prior to discovery," no steps were to be taken to prepare the airdrome at Dobodura until Serial Three had been unloaded, lest the enemy's attention be prematurely attracted to it.[20]

Colonel Robinson, who was to be in charge of the construction of the airfield, was cautioned that no clearing or other work was to be started at Dobodura until the engineers and protective troops had disembarked and the ships had been unloaded. Lt. Col. David Larr, General Chamberlin's deputy, who had been detailed to assist General Van Volkenburgh in co-ordinating the operation, made it clear to all concerned that its success depended upon secrecy in preparation and execution. Every precaution was to be taken to conceal the movement, its destination, and its intent. Above all, the existence of the airdrome was to be concealed from the Japanese as long as possible.[21]

Movement orders for the first three serials were issued on 17 July. Serial One was to leave Port Moresby at the end of the month, 31 July. It would arrive at Buna on 10–12 August, a few days after the Guadalcanal

[20] Ltr, Gen Sutherland to Comdr ALF, et al., 15 Jul 42, sub: Occupation and Construction of Airdrome in Vicinity of Buna Bay, Southeastern Peninsula of New Guinea, in G–3 Jnl, GHQ SWPA.
[21] Msg, Gen Casey to Col Robinson, 15 Jul 42, copy in AFPAC Engr File; Ltr, Gen Sutherland to Gen Van Volkenburgh, 15 Jul 42, sub: Instructions, in 385, G–3 Files, GHQ SWPA; Lt Col David Larr, G–3 Sec, GHQ SWPA, Scheme of Maneuver for the Occupation of Buna, 15 Jul 42, in G–3 Jnl, GHQ SWPA.

landing, which, by this time, had been advanced to 7 August.[22]

The Japanese Get There First

Colonel Larr Sounds the Alarm

General Van Volkenburgh and Colonel Larr had scarcely begun to make their first preparations for the operation when they received the disturbing intelligence on 18 July that the Japanese also appeared to have designs on Buna. Twenty-four ships, some of them very large, had been seen in Rabaul harbor on 17 July, and a number of what appeared to be trawlers or fishing boats loaded with troops had been reported off Talasea (New Britain). The troops, estimated as at least a regiment, were obviously from Rabaul,[23] and to General Van Volkenburgh and Colonel Larr, who talked the matter over, it added up to just one thing— that the Japanese were moving on Buna.

Colonel Larr, then at Townsville, at once got General Sutherland on the telephone. Speaking both for himself and General Van Volkenburgh, he noted that Serial One, which was not to begin moving till the end of the month, might reach Buna too late. He proposed therefore that forces be immediately dispatched to Buna by flying boat in order to forestall a possible Japanese landing there. He urged that an antiaircraft battery be dispatched by flying boat to Buna at least

by 21 July, and that the PBY's then go on to Moresby to fly in as many troops of Serial One as possible. The whole schedule of PROVIDENCE, he said, had to be accelerated. Serials Two and Three would have to arrive together; and the occupying force would, if necessary, have to be supplied entirely by air.

Larr went on to say that he knew that the Air Force could not possibly move more than a hundred men into Buna by flying boat at one time. He urged that immediate action be taken nevertheless to accelerate PROVIDENCE, for both he and General Van Volkenburgh felt that the element of surprise had already been lost. He concluded his call with these words: "We may be able to hold Buna if we get there first." [24]

General Chamberlin answered for General Sutherland the next day. The troop concentrations at Rabaul and Talasea, General Chamberlin radioed, did not necessarily mean that the Japanese intended a hostile move against Buna. Nor was it by any means certain that the element of surprise had been lost. The suggested plan to occupy Buna immediately was likely to defeat itself because it lacked strength. The danger was that it would serve only to attract the enemy's attention, and perhaps bring on an enemy landing—the very thing that was feared. For that reason, the original plan would have to be adhered to substantially as drawn. General Van Volkenburgh and Colonel Larr were assured that the dispatch of Serial One to Kokoda would be hastened and that every effort would be made to get it there at the earliest possible moment.[25] It was clear however that even

[22] USAFIA Movement Dir No. 174, 17 Jul 42, in AFPAC Engr File; LHQ OI No. 26, 17 Jul 42, in G–3 Jnl, GHQ SWPA. Ltr, Gen Sutherland to Gen Blamey *et al.*, 17 Jul 42, sub: Occupation and Construction of Airdrome "PROVIDENCE," in 385, New Guinea, G–3 Files, GHQ SWPA.
[23] Rad SIO, Townsville to DNI, Melbourne, No. 4299, 18 Jul 42; G–2 Daily Summary Enemy Intel, No. 117, 18 Jul 42; Transcript Tel Msg, Col Larr to Gen Sutherland, Brisbane, 18 Jul 42. All in G–3 Jnl, GHQ SWPA. See below, Ch. V, n. 8.

[24] Transcript Tel Msg, Col Larr to Gen Sutherland, 18 Jul 42.
[25] Rad, Gen Chamberlin to Gen Van Volkenburgh (through ACH, Townsville), 19 Jul 42, in 385, G–3 File, GHQ SWPA.

if there was an acceleration it would be slight. D Day would still have to follow the Guadalcanal landing.

The Enemy Crashes Through

The Air Force had meanwhile been striking at Rabaul as frequently as it was able. The bombing had been sporadic at best; and because the B–17's in use were badly worn, and the bomber crews manning them (veterans, like their planes, of Java and the Philippines) were tired and dispirited, the results were far from gratifying.[26] Thinking to give the men a rest and to gain time in which to put "all equipment in the best possible condition," General Brett (who continued as air commander, pending General Kenney's arrival) suspended all bombing missions on 18 July.[27] Except for a nuisance raid on Kieta on Bougainville Island by an LB–30 from Townsville, no combat missions were flown on either the 18th or 19th. A single Hudson sent from Port Moresby on the 19th to reconnoiter Talasea and Cape Gloucester (on the northwest tip of New Britain) for some further sign of the troop-laden trawlers which had so disturbed General Van Volkenburgh and Colonel Larr reported no sightings whatever in the area.[28]

The next morning the picture changed completely. A B–17, staging from Port Moresby, sighted two warships and five other vessels thought to be warships about seventy-five nautical miles due north of Talasea. Two merchantmen, which could have been transports, were sighted just north of Rabaul moving in a westerly direction as if to join the ships off Talasea.[29]

What followed was a study in frustration. Bad weather set in; there was a heavy mist; and visibility went down to virtually nothing. The air force though on the alert, and with an unusually large number of aircraft in condition to attack, could find no trace of the convoy until 0820 on the morning of 21 July, when a cruiser, five destroyers, and several transports were glimpsed fleetingly ninety miles due east of Salamaua. The convoy, which was seen to be without air cover, was sighted again at 1515 off Ambasi, a point forty miles northwest of Buna. A single B–17 followed by five B–26's located and attacked it there, but without result. Darkness set in, and, although the Japanese gave away their position by shelling Gona and Buna from the sea at 1800 and 1830, all further attempts to locate the convoy that night proved fruitless.[30]

The Landing

At 0635 the following morning, the invasion convoy was discovered just off Gona

---

[26] Allied Air Force Opns Rpts, 1–2 Jun through 17–18 Jul 42, in G–3 Jnl, GHQ SWPA; Craven and Cate, *The Army Air Forces in World War II*, I, 482; Kenney, *General Kenney Reports*, pp. 35, 36, 42.

[27] Allied Air Forces Opns Rpt, 18, 19 Jul 42; Gen Brett, "The MacArthur I Knew," in *True*, October 47, p. 148.

[28] Allied Air Forces Opns Rpt, 19 Jul 42, with incl Allied Air Recon Rpt, 19 Jul 42.

[29] Allied Air Forces Opns Rpt, 20 Jul 42, with incl Allied Air Recon Rpt, 20 Jul 42; Rad, Port Moresby to ACH, Townsville, No. A–51, 20 Jul 42. Both in G–3 Jnl, GHQ SWPA.

[30] Allied Air Forces Opns Rpt, 21 Jul 42, with incl Allied Air Recon Rpt, 21 Jul 42; Rad, Port Moresby to ACH, Townsville, No. A–392, 21 Jul 42; G–2 Daily Summary Enemy Intel No. 121, 22 Jul 42; COIC Sitrep No. 3012, 22 Jul 42. All in G–3 Jnl, GHQ SWPA. ALF, Summary of Opns in New Guinea, Owen Stanley–Buna–Gona areas, 21 Jul 42–22 Jan 43, in OCMH files. The landing actually began at 1800 on 21 July. Intel Rpt No. 3, *17th Army*, Rabaul, 30 Jul 42, in ATIS EP No. 28.

by an RAAF Hudson.[31] The exact point was Basabua, about one and one-half miles south of Gona and about nine miles northwest of Buna. At the moment of discovery, landing operations, though far advanced, were not yet complete. Landing barges were still moving from ship to shore, and supplies, which were being rapidly moved into the surrounding jungle, still littered the beach. Antiaircraft had already been set up ashore, but there were no Japanese aircraft overhead [32] despite the fact that Lae was only 160 miles away, and the Japanese, who had air superiority in the region, were suffering from no dearth of aircraft at the time. Fortunately for the Japanese ashore, a heavy haze hung over the area and made effective attack from the air extremely difficult. The Air Force made 81 sorties that morning, dropped 48 tons of bombs, and used up more than 15,000 rounds of ammunition in

strafing the area,[33] but the results were disappointing.

One transport was hit and went up in flames. A landing barge with personnel aboard was strafed and sunk; a float plane (probably from the Japanese cruiser that had escorted the convoy) was shot down; landing barges, tents, supplies, and antiaircraft installations were bombed and strafed; and a hit was claimed on one of the destroyers. By 0915, all the vessels with the exception of the burning transport, had cleared the area safely and were heading north.[34]

The Japanese in the landing force lost no time in clearing their supplies from the beach. Shielded by the luxuriant jungle and the deepening haze, they quickly made good their landing. The implications of its success for the Southwest Pacific Area were all too clear. The PROVIDENCE operation had been forestalled by almost three weeks. Plans for the early inception of Task Two had been frustrated. The Papuan Campaign had begun.

---

[31] Allied Air Forces Opns Rpt, 22 Jul 42; G–2 Daily Summary Enemy Intel No. 121, 22 Jul 42. Both in G–3 Jnl, GHQ SWPA.

[32] Ibid.; Fld Log Sakigawa Tai, Jul–Aug 42, in ATIS EP No. 27; Intel Rpt No. 3, 17th Army Hq, Rabaul, 30 Jul 42, in ATIS EP No. 28; ATIS Bul No. 183, Items 17, 18, in ATIS CT 25; Rad, ACH, Townsville, to CWR, No. A–470, 22 Jul 42; G–2 Daily Summary Enemy Intel, No. 122, 22–23 Jul 42; Allied Air Forces DOI, Weekly Review Air Activities, 25 Jul. Last three in G–3 Jnl, GHQ SWPA.

[33] Allied Air Forces Opns Rpt, 22 Jul 42; G–2 Daily Summary Enemy Intel, No. 122, 23 Jul 42. The planes involved were B–17's, B–25's, B–26's, P–39's, P–40E's, P–400's, and the Hudson that had made the first sighting.

[34] Ibid.; Fld Log Sakigawa Tai, Jul–Aug 42; Interr, Gen Adachi et al.; ALF, Summary of Operations in New Guinea, Owen Stanley–Buna–Gona Areas, 21 Jul 42–22 Jan 43, in OCMH files.

CHAPTER V

Kokoda Thrust

The landing at Basabua on the night of 21–22 July was a direct outgrowth of the naval reverses the Japanese had suffered at the Coral Sea and Midway. After the Battle of the Coral Sea, they had temporarily postponed the Port Moresby operation with the understanding that they would return to it as soon as succeeding operations against Midway and the Aleutians had been completed. The loss of their first-line carriers at Midway had disrupted these plans. Not only were the Japanese forced to postpone indefinitely the projected operations against the South Pacific island bases, but they had to abandon the idea of taking Port Moresby by amphibious assault. They realized that to use the few remaining carriers for support of a second amphibious thrust against Port Moresby would probably be to lose them to superior carrier forces of the U. S. Pacific Fleet, a risk that they were not prepared to take. Since they were agreed that Port Moresby, which flanked Rabaul, would have to be taken at the earliest possible moment, the problem became one of taking it without carrier support. The successful landing in the Buna–Gona area was the first indication of the manner in which they had chosen to solve that problem.[1]

---

[1] Hist Rec *Army Section Imperial General Headquarters*, pp. 53, 60; *Southeast Area* Naval Opns, p. 7; *17th Army* Opns I, 7, 8; USSBS, *Interrogations of Japanese Officials*, II, 524, 525.

Planning the Overland Attack

The Operations Area

The die was cast. The fighting was to be in the Papuan Peninsula, or, as the Japanese insisted on calling it, eastern New Guinea. The peninsula, part of the Territory of Papua, a lush, tropical area, most of it still in a state of nature, lies at the southeast end of New Guinea, forming the tail, so to speak, of that vast, bird-shaped island. Occupying an area of 90,540 square miles, Papua is an Australian possession, annexed by the British in 1884, and turned over to the Australians in 1901. The natives, of Melanesian stock, are at a primitive stage of development; and the fact that their hair is generally frizzly rather than woolly has given Papua its name—*Papuwa* being the Malay for frizzly or frizzled.

The Japanese could scarcely have chosen a more dismal place in which to conduct a campaign. The rainfall at many points in the peninsula is torrential. It often runs as high as 150, 200, and even 300 inches per year, and, during the rainy season, daily falls of eight or ten inches are not uncommon. The terrain, as varied as it is difficult, is a military nightmare. Towering saw-toothed mountains, densely covered by mountain forest and rain forest, alternate with flat malarial, coastal areas made up of matted jungle, reeking swamp, and broad

patches of knife-edged kunai grass four to seven feet high. The heat and humidity in the coastal areas are well-nigh unbearable, and in the mountains there is biting cold at altitudes over 5,000 feet. The mountains are drained by turbulent rivers and creeks, which become slow and sluggish as they reach the sea. Along the streams, the fringes of the forest become interwoven from ground to treetop level with vines and creepers to form an almost solid mat of vegetation which has to be cut by the machete or the bolo before progress is possible. The vegetation in the mountains is almost as luxuriant; leeches abound everywhere; and the trees are often so overgrown with creepers and moss that the sunlight can scarcely filter through to the muddy tracks below.

The Owen Stanley Mountains, whose peaks rise to heights of more than 13,000 feet, overshadow the entire Papuan Peninsula, running down its center to Milne Bay like an immense spine. On the northeast, or Buna, side the foothills of the range slope gently to the sea. On the southwest or Port Moresby side, the picture is startlingly different. Sharp ridges which rise abruptly from the southwest coast connect with the main range to produce a geographical obstacle of such formidable proportions that overland crossing is possible only by means of tortuous native footpaths or tracks that lead from one native village to the other, often at dizzy heights.

The Kokoda Trail

The best overland route to Port Moresby passed through Kokoda, a point about fifty miles from Buna and more than one hundred miles from Port Moresby. (*Maps II and 4*) At Wairopi, about thirty miles

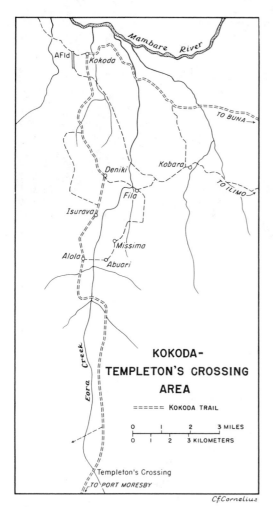

KOKODA-
TEMPLETON'S CROSSING
AREA

===== KOKODA TRAIL

0   1   2   3 MILES
0   1   2   3 KILOMETERS

Templeton's Crossing
TO PORT MORESBY

Cf.Cornelius

MAP 4

southwest of Buna, a wire-rope bridge, from which the place took its name, spanned the immense gorge of the Kumusi River, a broad turbulent stream subject to dangerous undertows and flash floods. Between Buna and Wairopi the country is gentle and rolling. Past Wairopi it suddenly becomes steep and rocky. Kokoda itself is set on a little plateau between the foothills of the Ajura Kijala and Owen Stanley Ranges. On this plateau, which is about 1,200 feet above sea level, there was a small airfield, suitable only for use by light commercial planes and the smaller types of military transport aircraft.

From Kokoda, the trail leads southward along the western side of a huge canyon or chasm, the so-called Eora Creek Gorge. It passes through the native villages of Deniki and Isurava to a trail junction at Alola, where a cross-country trail from Ilimo, a point southwest of Wairopi, joins the main track via Kobara, Fila, Missima, and Abuari, a short-cut which makes it possible to bypass Kokoda. From Alola, the trail crosses to the eastern side of Eora Creek and climbs to Templeton's Crossing, where the immense spurs of the main range are met for the first time at an elevation of 7,000 feet.

Just past Templeton's Crossing is the Gap, the mountain pass that leads across the range. The Gap, which is only twenty miles south of Kokoda, is a broken, jungle-covered saddle in the main range, about 7,500 feet high at its central point. The saddle is about five miles wide, with high mountains on either side. The trail runs about six miles through the Gap over a rocky, broken track, on which there is not enough level space to pitch a tent, and room enough for only one man to pass. From the Gap, the trail plunges downward to Myola, Kagi, Efogi, Menari, Nauro,

JUNGLED MOUNTAIN RIDGES NEAR THE GAP *in the Owen Stanleys. (Photo-graph taken November 1943.)*

Ioribaiwa, the Imita Range, and Uberi, traversing in its course mountain peaks 5,000 and 6,000 feet high, and sharp, east-west ridges whose altitude is from 3,000 to 4,000 feet. The southern edge of the range is at Koitaki, about thirty miles from Port Moresby by road, where the elevation is 2,000 feet.

From Kokoda to Templeton's Crossing the trail climbs 6,000 feet in less than twenty miles as it crosses a series of knife-edged ridges. The peaks in the area rise as high as 9,000 feet, and the valleys, whose sides slope as much as 60 percent from the horizontal, descend as low as 1,000 feet. Ridges rising from creeks and river beds are 1,500 to 2,000 feet high, and the soil in the valleys has up to thirty feet of humus and leaf mold. The area is perpetually wet, the rainfall at 3,000 feet being 200 and 300 inches a year.

The situation is only slightly better between Myola and Uberi. There are still knife-edges and razorbacks, but now they are not as precipitous as before. The gorges, though deeper and with denser under-growth, are less frequent, but they are still extremely hard to cross. Not till the trail reaches Koitaki does the going moderate. It was a moot point whether a large, fully equipped force could complete the difficult march from Kokoda to Koitaki, in the face of determined opposition, and still be in condition to launch an effective attack on Port Moresby when it got there. Yet it was by an advance over this trail that the Japanese proposed to take Port Moresby.[2]

The Enemy Plans a Reconnaissance

The Japanese did not act recklessly in their attempt to send troops over the Owen Stanley Range. On 14 June, six days after Midway, General Hyakutake, commander of the *17th Army*, was told to prepare for an overland attack on Port Moresby. General Hyakutake, then on his way to Davao, was specifically cautioned not to order major forces under his command to New Guinea until the trail had been thoroughly reconnoitered, and the operation found to be feasible. He was told that his forces were to be held in readiness for instant action should the reconnaissance have a favorable result. General Horii, commander of the *Nankai Shitai*, was to have the immediate responsibility for the operation. The *15th Independent Engineer Regiment*, a highly trained and well-equipped combat engineer unit stationed at Davao, which had distinguished itself in combat in Malaya, would be assigned to General Horii to perform the reconnaissance.[3]

On 29 June the engineer regiment, with supporting antiaircraft, communications, medical, and service troops, was ordered to Rabaul, and General Horii flew to Davao on the 30th to receive his orders from General Hyakutake for the reconnaissance. Hyakutake issued the orders the next day, 1 July. They provided that the force making the reconnaissance was to consist of the engineer regiment, an infantry battalion of the *Nankai Shitai*, the *47th Field Antiaircraft Artillery Battalion*, and supporting troops. The force was to be under command of Col. Yosuke Yokoyama, commander of the engineer regiment. Yokoyama's mission was to land in the Buna area, advance rapidly to Kokoda and "the mountain pass south of Kokoda," and reconnoiter the trail leading from it to Port Moresby. He was to report to General Horii as quickly as possible on the state of the Buna–Kokoda "road" and on all possible routes of advance from Kokoda to Port Moresby. Horii, in turn, was to pass on the information to higher headquarters with an indorsement setting forth his views on the feasibility of the proposed operation.[4]

On 11 July, with Colonel Yokoyama on his way from Davao to Rabaul, the *Army Section* of *Imperial General Headquarters* gave General Hyakutake the go-ahead signal for the reconnaissance. Hyakutake passed the orders on to General Horii, who at once worked out an agreement with the Navy and the naval air force at Rabaul for the escort and support of Colonel Yokoyama's force. The latter force reached Ra-

[2] G–2 Daily Summary Enemy Intel No. 123, 24 Jul 42, in G–3 Jnl, GHQ SWPA; Osmar White, Notes on Owen Stanley Fighting in New Guinea, 15 Sep 42, copy in OCMH files; ALF Rpt on New Guinea Opns Buna–Ioribaiwa; NGF, Notes on Opns in New Guinea, Ser 3; AGS, SWPA, Terrain Study No. 28, Main Routes Across New Guinea, 18 Oct 42, in OCMH files; Survey Northeast New Guinea and Papua, 15 Jul 43, in G–2 WDGS Files.

[3] AMF, Interr Gen Adachi *et al.*; SEATIC Hist Bul No. 243, 1 Oct 46, Hist Japanese *28th Army*; *17th Army* Opns, I, 10–12; *18th Army*, Opns, I, 8–9; *Southeast Area* Naval Opns, I, 7. *Nankai Shitai* was the Japanese name for *South Seas Detachment*.

[4] *15th Indep Engr Regt* Opns Orders No. A–124, 24 Jun 42, in ATIS CT 21, No. 276; *17th Army* Opns Orders, n. n., 1 Jul 42, quoted in *17th Army* Opns, I, 12–13.

baul on the 14th, and two days later Horii ordered Yokoyama to "carry out a landing near Basabua, and quickly occupy a strategic line south of Kokoda in order to reconnoiter the route over which it is intended to advance." If he found it out of the question to advance beyond Kokoda, he was to occupy and hold the area from the coast westward to the Owen Stanley Range. Yokoyama was specifically ordered to put the "road" east of the Owen Stanley Range in condition to handle motor traffic, and to prepare the "roads" in the mountains for the use, if not of vehicles, at least of pack horses.[5]

On 18 July, on the eve of the departure of the *Yokoyama Force* for Buna, General Hyakutake prepared a plan looking to the capture not only of Port Moresby but also of a flanking position at Samarai, a small island just off the southeast tip of New Guinea. Samarai had an excellent harbor and in prewar days had been a trading center of considerable importance. The Japanese, who as yet knew nothing of what was going on at Milne Bay, wanted Samarai (where they believed there was a small Allied garrison) in order to establish a seaplane base there for use in the attack on Port Moresby. The plan provided that the entire strength of the *17th Army*—the *South Seas Detachment* at Rabaul, the *Aoba* and *Yazawa Detachments* at Davao, and the *Kawaguchi Detachment* at Palau—would be committed to these operations. The *South Seas Detachment*, with the support of the *Yazawa Detachment*, would take Port Moresby by an advance over the mountains, and the Navy, aided by the *Kawaguchi Detachment*, would seize Samarai. The *Aoba Detachment* would remain in army reserve.[6]

The Japanese apparently were no longer interested in a thorough reconnaissance of the Kokoda Trail. The mission of the *Yokoyama Force* had changed. Instead of being primarily a reconnaissance force, it had become an advance echelon. Its mission was not so much reconnaissance as to secure a firm foothold in the Buna–Kokoda area. When that was done, the main force would arrive and do the rest.

The Japanese Strike Inland

The Yokoyama Force *Departs*

The *Yokoyama Force* was quickly in readiness for the operation. Its troop list included the *1st Battalion, 144th Infantry,* the *15th Independent Engineer Regiment* (less one company and two platoons), a detachment of the *10th Independent Engineers,* a company of the *55th Mountain Artillery,* a company of *Sasebo 5th Special Naval Landing Force,* the *47th Field Antiaircraft Artillery Battalion* (less two companies), several signal units, a field hospital section, and a service unit that included supply, transport, water-purification, and port battalion troops. Attached to this force of about 1,800 men were 100 naval laborers from Formosa, 52 horses, and 1,200 Rabaul natives im-

[5] *Nankai Shitai* (Horii) Opns Orders No. A–85, 13 Jul 42; *Yokoyama Adv Tai* Opns Orders No. A–2, 16 Jul 42. Both in ATIS CT 29, No. 131. *17th Army Opns,* I, 13, 20, 21.

[6] Ltr, Gen Willoughby to Gen Ward, 12 Apr 51; *17th Army* Opns Orders, 18 Jul 42, quoted in *17th Army Opns,* I, 15–16, and dated in error 18 Jun.

pressed by the Japanese to act as porters and laborers.[7]

The *Yokoyama Force* received its instructions on 16 July and left for Buna four days later with an advance unit of the *Sasebo 5th Special Naval Landing Force,* in three heavily escorted transports.[8] Effective diversions were mounted in support of the *Yokoyama Force.* As the convoy sped to its target, Japanese naval troops massed at Lae and Salamaua launched heavy raids upon Mubo and Komiatum in the Bulolo Valley, the two most forward outposts of KANGA Force. In addition, Japanese submarines, which had been operating off the east coast of Australia since early June, stepped up their activity

and sank four Allied merchantmen the very day of the landing.[9]

The landing cost the Japanese one ship, the transport *Ayatozan Maru,* which Allied air units caught and sank as it was unloading off Gona. Forty men and a number of vehicles were lost with the ship. The other two transports, whose cargo had already been unloaded when the air attack began, managed to escape without damage, as did their escort.[10]

It had been agreed that Buna would be a naval installation, and the advance unit of the *Sasebo Naval Landing Force* was sent there immediately on landing. Colonel Yokoyama chose Giruwa, about three and a half miles east of the anchorage, as the site of the Army base and immediately ordered all Army troops there. The evening of the landing an advance force under Lt. Col. Hatsuo Tsukamoto, commander of the infantry battalion, was organized at Giruwa and sent southward. The force was composed of the infantry battalion, an attached regimental signal unit, and a company of the *15th Independent Engineers.* Tsukamoto, whose orders were "to push on night

---

[7] Annex No. 3, 17 Jul 42, to Horii Opns Order No. A–85, 13 Jul 42; *Yokoyama Adv Force* Orders No. 1, 16 Jul 42, in ATIS CT 4, No. 103; No. A–3, 17 Jul 42; No. A–5, 18 Jul 42. Both in ATIS CT 29, No. 131. Rad, CofS *17th Army* to CO *Yazawa Det,* 30 Jul 42; *17th Army* Intel Summary No. 5, 7 Aug 42. Both in ATIS EP No. 28. AMF, Interr General Adachi *et al.; 17th Army* Opns, I, 20–21. There is no authoritative figure for the total strength of the *Yokoyama Force.* Troop strength, less the infantry battalion, is known to have been 1,115 men. Allowing 700 men for the battalion would bring the total strength to 1,800, the figure given.

[8] *Yokoyama Adv Tai* Orders No. 2, 16 Jul 42, in ATIS CT 4, No. 103; No. A–3, 17 Jul 42, in ATIS CT 29, No. 131; Fld Log *Sakigawa Tai,* 16 Jul–7 Aug 42. It will be recalled that several transports had been glimpsed that day—the 20th—by Allied reconnaissance leaving Rabaul at approximately the same time that a naval force of cruisers and destroyers had been sighted standing due north of Talasea. Oddly enough, the troops seen three days earlier on the trawlers at Talasea, whose presence there had led Colonel Larr and General Van Volkenburgh to conclude that a landing in the Buna area was imminent, did not figure in the landing at all. Why the troops were in the Talasea area is unknown. The only conjecture which seems to fit the circumstances is that a portion of the *South Seas Detachment* may have been practicing amphibious landings in the Talasea area at the time.

[9] Msg, Airintel, Port Moresby, to Airintel, NE Area, 9 Jul 42; Msg, NGF to ALF, Melbourne, No. G–3095, 17 Jul 42; Msg, Port Moresby to ACH, Townsville, No. 4167, 18 Jul 42; GHQ Sitrep No. 312, 21 Jul 42; Msg, ACH, Townsville, to COIC, Brisbane, No. 4638, 22 Jul 42; G–2 Daily Summary Enemy Intel No. 122, 22–23 Jul 42. All in G–3 Jnl, GHQ SWPA.

[10] Fld Log *Sakigawa Tai,* Jul–Aug 42; AMF Interr Gen Adachi *et al.; 17th Army* Intel Rpt No. 3, 30 Jul 42; *17th Army* Opns, I, 21; Naval Account, Japanese Invasion Eastern New Guinea, pp. 16–17. The hulk of the sunken ship, which came to be known familiarly as "the Gona wreck," was subsequently investigated by Allied patrols and "definitely identified as the *Ayatozan Maru.*" ALF Daily Opns Rpt No. 294, 2 Feb 43.

and day to the line of the mountain range," appears to have taken them literally. The attacking force, about 900 men, made its first bivouac that night just outside of Soputa, a point about seven miles inland, and by the following afternoon was approaching Wairopi.[11]

The Onset

Only light opposition faced the Japanese. MAROUBRA Force, the Australian force charged with the defense of Kokoda and the Kokoda Trail, still had most of the 39th Australian Infantry Battalion on the Port Moresby side of the range. Only Company B and the 300-man Papuan Infantry Battalion were in the Buna–Kokoda area at the time of the landing. Company B, 129 men at full strength, was at Kokoda; the PIB, part of whose strength was on patrol miles to the north, was at Awala, a few miles east of Wairopi.

A grueling overland march from Port Moresby had brought Company B to Kokoda on 12 July. Its heavy supplies and machine guns reached Buna by sea on the 19th; and company headquarters and one platoon, under the company commander, Capt. Samuel V. Templeton, set out from Kokoda the same day to bring them in. After picking up the supplies and machine guns, Templeton had almost returned to Kokoda when the Japanese landed. He turned back at once when he heard the news, and made

at top speed for Awala to reinforce the PIB.[12]

A PIB patrol first sighted the Japanese at 1750, 22 July, a few miles from Awala. The enemy struck at Awala the following afternoon just as the headquarters of Company B and its accompanying platoon reached the area. After a short skirmish, Templeton's force withdrew, taking up a defensive position that night just short of the Wairopi Bridge. The next day, with the enemy closing in, it pulled back over the bridge and demolished it before the Japanese could make the crossing.[13]

The thrust toward Kokoda caught General Morris, who, as G.O.C. New Guinea Force, was in command at Port Moresby, at a painful disadvantage. He had been ordered to get the rest of the 39th Battalion to Kokoda with all speed, as soon as the Japanese landed,[14] but found himself unable immediately to comply with the order. The problem was that four companies of the 39th Battalion (Headquarters Company and three rifle companies) were on the Port Moresby side of the mountains, including a rifle company in the foothills outside Port Moresby,

[11] *Yokoyama Adv Tai* Orders No. A–2, 16 Jul 42; Fld Log, *Sakigawa Tai,* Jul–Aug 42; Rad, Maj Toyonari Toyofuku, *17th Army* Liaison Offr to CG *17th Army,* 23 Jul 42; *Yokoyama Adv Tai* Rpt, 23 Jul 42. Last two in ATIS EP 28. COIC Rpt No. 316, 25 Jul 42, in G–3 Jnl, GHQ SWPA; *17th Army Opns,* I, 21.

[12] NGF OIs, No. 16, 12 Jun 42, No. 18, 25 Jun 42, No. 20, 22 Jul 42; Brig S. H. Porter, Report on Part Played by 30th Australian Infantry Brigade Headquarters in the Owen Stanley Ranges, copy in OCMH files; ALF, Rpt on New Guinea Opns, Buna–Ioribaiwa.
[13] COIC Rpt No. 316, 25 Jul 42; Msg, Gen MacArthur to Gen Marshall, No. C–160, CM–IN 9267, 26 Jul 42; *Yokoyama Adv Tai* Rpt, 27 Jul 42, in ATIS EP 29; ALF, Rpt on New Guinea Opns, Buna–Ioribaiwa; NGF, Notes on Opns in New Guinea, Ser 3.
[14] Msg, Gen Chamberlin to ALF, No. 4393, 22 Jul 42; Msg, ALF to MilComd, Port Moresby, No. G–34393, 22 Jul 42; Transcript, tel conversation, Col E. L. Sheehan, ALF, G–3 Sec, GHQ SWPA, to Brig R. N. L. Hopkins, ALF Hq, 23 Jul 42. All in 385, G–3 Files, GHQ SWPA.

and there was only one small aircraft at Port Moresby capable of landing on the small and extremely rough airfield at Kokoda.

Morris did what he could. The battalion commander, Lt. Col. William T. Owen, was immediately ordered to Kokoda by air in the one plane capable of landing there; Company C, the rifle company in the western foothills of the range, was ordered to march on Kokoda as quickly as possible; and the remaining three companies of the battalion, still at Port Moresby, were put on the alert for early movement to Kokoda by air if enough aircraft of a type capable of landing at Kokoda could be secured in time.[15]

The Fall of Kokoda

Colonel Owen had been instructed to make a stand immediately east of Kokoda, and, if that failed, to take up a position south of it. He arrived at Kokoda on 24 July to find that there was little he could do to stop the onrush of the Japanese. The demolition of the Wairopi Bridge had not held them up long. By the 25th, they had a hasty bridge over the Kumusi and were advancing rapidly on Kokoda. Captain Templeton (whose original force of little more than a platoon had by this time been reinforced by a second platoon of Company B) made a desperate stand that day at Gorari, about eight miles west of Wairopi. The Japanese, attacking with mortars, machine guns, and light field pieces, quickly outflanked him and forced him to withdraw

to Oivi, a point in the steep foothills of the range, only eight miles by trail from Kokoda.

General Morris had meanwhile been making every effort to get men forward. Early on 26 July, the small transport aircraft at his disposal made two flights to Kokoda, bringing in thirty men from Company D. Holding half of them at Kokoda, Colonel Owen sent the other half on to Oivi where Captain Templeton was trying to hold in the face of heavy odds. The resistance at Oivi did not last long. Templeton was killed that afternoon, and his tiny force was outflanked and encircled.

Colonel Owen now had no choice but to evacuate Kokoda, and did so just before midnight. After he sent New Guinea Force notice of the evacuation, Owen's force—the rest of Company B, and the incoming fifteen men of Company D—crossed over the western side of Eora Creek Gorge. It took up previously prepared positions at Deniki, five miles southwest of Kokoda, and was joined next day by those of the Oivi force who had succeeded in extricating themselves during the night from the Japanese encirclement.[16]

The Fight To Retake the Airfield

New Guinea Force received Owen's evacuation message late on the morning of 27 July. By then the arrival from Australia of another plane had given General Morris' headquarters two aircraft suitable for the Kokoda run, and both of them were in the

[15] NGF OI No. 20, 22 Jul 42; ALF, Rpt on New Guinea Opns, Buna–Ioribaiwa; NGF, Notes on Opns in New Guinea, Ser 3. The Australian battalion consisted at this time of four rifle companies and a large Headquarters Company to which were assigned the heavy weapons, communications, transport, supply, and mess personnel of the battalion.

[16] NGF OI No. 20, 22 Jul 42; Adm Inst to NGF OI No. 20, 22 Jul 42; G–2 Daily Summary Enemy Intel No. 126, 26 Jul 42; Special App to COIC Sitrep No. 318, 27 Jul 42. All in G–3 Jnl, GHQ SWPA. AFL, Rpt on New Guinea Opns, Buna–Ioribaiwa; NGF, Rpt on Opns in New Guinea, Ser 3.

air at the time loaded with troops and supplies. They were at once recalled to Port Moresby. Next morning Owen counterattacked and, after some bitter hand-to-hand fighting, drove the Japanese out of Kokoda. Owen was now desperately in need of the very reinforcements that New Guinea Force had recalled the previous day. Unfortunately the message that he had regained Kokoda did not reach Port Moresby until late in the afternoon, too late for action that day. Meanwhile, two more planes had come from Australia. New Guinea Force, now with four transports that could land at Kokoda, planned to fly in a full infantry company with mortar and antiaircraft elements the first thing in the morning. The planes were never sent. At dawn on the 29th, the Japanese counterattacked and, after two hours of fighting during which Colonel Owen was killed, again drove the Australians out of Kokoda.[17]

Australian reinforcements had meanwhile begun arriving in the forward area on foot. Company C reached Deniki on 31 July, followed the next day by Company A. By 7 August, all five companies of the 39th Battalion were at the front, and MAROUBRA Force totaled 480 men. Supplies were being manhandled over the trail by the incoming troops, and by hundreds of native carriers under the supervision of ANGAU. Food and ammunition were also being dropped from the air—a dry lake bed at Myola, a few miles southeast of Kagi, the forward supply base, served as the main dropping ground.[18]

There were patrol clashes on 7 and 8 August, and early on 10 August MAROUBRA Force, which estimated enemy strength at Kokoda as no more than 400 men counterattacked. Three companies were committed to the assault, with the remaining two held in reserve. While one company engaged the Japanese to the south of Kokoda, a second moved astride the Kokoda–Oivi track via the Abuari–Missima–Fila cutoff and engaged them to the east of Kokoda. The third company marched undetected on Kokoda and took possession of the airfield that afternoon without suffering a single casualty.

The success was short-lived. The company astride the Japanese rear had to be ordered back to Deniki to stem a powerful enemy attack on that point, and the company holding the airfield (whose position had in any event become untenable) had to evacuate it on the night of 11–12 August because of a critical shortage of supplies.[19]

Colonel Yokoyama was now ready to attack with his full force. Early on 13 August, he struck the Australian position at Deniki with about 1,500 men. The Australians were forced to yield not only Deniki but also Isurava five miles away. The Japa-

[17] *Yokoyama Adv Tai* Rpt, 29 Jul 42; Msg, Maj Toyofuku to CofS, *17th Army*, No. 216, 31 Jul 42. Both in ATIS EP 28. ALF, Rpt on New Guinea Opns, Buna–Ioribaiwa; NGF, Notes on Opns in New Guinea, Ser 3. Colonel Owen was posthumously awarded the Distinguished Service Cross, the first Australian infantryman to receive the decoration in World War II. The citation is in GO No. 11. GHQ SWPA, 22 Jan 43.

[18] COIC Sitreps No. 320, 28–29 Jul 42, No. 332, 9–10 Aug 42, G–2 SWPA Daily Summaries Enemy Intel No. 129, 29–30 Jul 42, No. 130, 30–31 Jul 42; GHQ SWPA OI No. 15, 6 Aug 42. All in G–3 Jnl, GHQ SWPA. ALF, Rpt on New Guinea Opns, Buna–Ioribaiwa; NGF, Notes on Opns in New Guinea, Ser 3.

[19] ALF Daily Opns Rpts, No. 117, 10 Aug 42, and No. 121, 14 Aug 42; COIC Sitreps No. 332, 10 Aug 42, No. 334, 12 Aug 42, No. 336, 14 Aug 42; G–2 Daily Summaries Enemy Intel No. 135, 3–4 Aug 42, No. 140, 9–10 Aug 42; G–3 Opns Rpts No. 125, 11 Aug 42, No. 129, 15 Aug 42; Memo, Gen Chamberlin for Gen Sutherland, 14 Aug 42. All in G–3 Jnl, GHQ SWPA. NGF, Notes on Opns in New Guinea, Ser 3.

nese, having no intention at the moment of going any farther, began to dig in.[20]

Kokoda and the Buna–Kokoda track were now firmly in Japanese hands, and a base had been established for the advance on Port Moresby through the Gap. According to plan, the move was to be undertaken as soon as General Horii and the main body of the *South Seas Detachment* reached the scene of operations.

The Main Force Arrives

The Joint Agreement of 31 July

General Hyakutake arrived at Rabaul from Davao on 24 July to find that Colonel Yokoyama had been reporting good progress in his thrust on Kokoda. As the news from Yokoyama continued good, Hyakutake, seeing no reason for further delay, recommended to *Imperial General Headquarters* that the overland operation be undertaken at once. Tokyo, which had been well disposed to the project from the first, quickly gave its blessing and, on 28 July, ordered the operation to be mounted as quickly as possible.[21]

Three days later, on the 31st, General Hyakutake concluded a joint Army-Navy agreement with Vice Adm. Nichizo Tsukahara, commander of the *11th Air Fleet*, and Vice Adm. Gunichi Mikawa, commander of the newly established *8th Fleet*.

Mikawa had just taken over control of naval operations in the New Guinea–Bismarcks–Solomons area from the *4th Fleet*. After stating that the seizure of Port Moresby and other key points in eastern New Guinea was necessary in order to secure control of the Coral Sea, the three commanders adopted a basic plan of attack patterned closely on the draft plan which General Hyakutake had prepared on 18 July, thirteen days before.

The plan provided that General Horii, with both the *South Seas Detachment* and the *Yazawa Detachment* under his command, would move on Port Moresby via Kokoda, and that the *Kawaguchi Detachment*, supported by units of the *8th Fleet*, would take Samarai. As soon as Samarai was taken, a "Port Moresby Attack Force," consisting of the *Kawaguchi Detachment* and elements of the *8th Fleet* would be organized there. Then, in a move timed to coincide with diversionary attacks on the Bulolo Valley by the naval troops at Lae and Salamaua, the attack force would embark for Port Moresby, attacking it from the sea at the precise moment that the *South Seas* and *Yazawa Detachments* cleared the mountains and began attacking it from landward.

The agreement provided specifically that all the forces at the disposal of the participating commanders would be available for these operations, which were to begin on X Day, the day that the main body of the *South Seas Detachment* arrived at Buna. X Day was set as 7 August, the date, interestingly enough, of the projected American landing at Guadalcanal.[22]

---

[20] ALF Opns Rpt, No. 122, 15 Aug 42, in G–3 Jnl, GHQ SWPA; *17th Army* Intel Summary No. 4, 17 Aug 42; *Yazawa Butai* Intel Rpt No. 3, 17 Aug 42, in ATIS EP 28; AMF, Interr of Gen Adachi *et al.;* ALF, Rpt on New Guinea Opns, Buna–Ioribaiwa; NGF, Notes on Opns in New Guinea, Ser 3.

[21] *18th Army* Opns, I, 9; USSBS, *Interrogation of Japanese Officials,* II, 525.

[22] Ltr, Gen Willoughby to Gen Ward, 12 Apr 51; *17th Army* Opns I, 9; *Southeast Area* Naval Opns I, 8.

Under the joint agreement of 31 July, the *8th Fleet* had undertaken to have the airfields at Buna and Kokoda in operation when the main force landed. But this project was not to be easily accomplished. On 29 and 31 July the Allied Air Force caught the enemy supply ships, laden with vehicles and construction materials for the field, while they were en route to Buna. The *Kotoku Maru* was lost and the rest were obliged to return to Rabaul with their cargo undelivered. These mishaps, and the discovery that the airfield site at Buna was very soggy and could not possibly be put into readiness by 7 August, caused X Day to be moved forward to 16 August.[23]

The Landings in the Solomons

Pursuant to the Joint Directive of 2 July, the 1st Marine Division, reinforced, went ashore on Guadalcanal, Tulagi, and adjoining islands in the southern Solomons early on 7 August. The Americans quickly dispersed the weak forces the enemy had on the islands, including a few hundred garrison troops and a couple of thousand naval construction troops on Guadalcanal. By the evening of 8 August the marines were in control of Tulagi, Gavutu, and Tanambogo and held the airfield at Lunga Point on Guadalcanal, the main objective of the landings.

The *8th Fleet* had been busy gathering ships for the Port Moresby operation. Though caught off balance by the landings, it struck back vigorously during the early hours of 9 August. Entering the area between Florida Island and Guadalcanal undetected, the Japanese sank four heavy cruisers, including the Australian flagship *Canberra* which with other ships of Task Force 44, Admiral Leary's main force, was in the Solomons supporting the landings. That afternoon the Allied fleet pulled out of the area in accordance with a decision made the previous evening that its ships were vulnerable and would have to be withdrawn. No sooner was the withdrawal completed than the *8th Fleet* and the naval air units at Rabaul began a day-and-night harassment of the Marine landing force. The next step was to send in troops.[24]

Here the Japanese ran into difficulties. The *8th Fleet* did not have enough naval troops at Rabaul and Kavieng to counter the American landings. The *17th Army*, on the other hand, was at a loss to know which of its forces to order to Guadalcanal. The *South Seas Detachment,* its only unit at Rabaul, was committed to the Port Moresby operation, and the rest of its troops were out of reach at Davao and Palau. After much consultation between Tokyo and Rabaul, it was decided to use the *Kawaguchi Detchment,* less one battalion, which would remain committed to the capture of Samarai and the subsequent landing at Port Moresby. Because there was no shipping immediately available at Palau with which to get the detachment to its destination, a further decision was made to have another force precede it. The *Ichiki Detachment,*

---

[23] Rpt, Comdr *Kusen Tai,* 29 Jul 42; Rad, CofS *17th Army* to *Yazawa Butai,* 30 Jul 42. Both in ATIS EP 28. Fld Log *Sakigawa Tai,* Jul–Aug 42, in ATIS EP 27; Ltr, Gen Willoughby to Gen Ward, 12 Apr 51; *17th Army* Opns I, 22; Naval Account, Japanese Invasion Eastern New Guinea, p. 18. Although the *Kotoku Maru* was sunk, 263 of the men aboard, mostly troops of the *15th Independent Engineers,* managed to get safely to Giruwa in motor launches.

[24] *17th Army* Opns I, 25, 26; *Southeast Area Naval Opns* I, 11; Miller, *Guadalcanal: The First Offensive,* pp. 61–67.

which was already at sea and in position to reach the target quickly, was given the assignment.

These decisions had scarcely been made when Rabaul discovered for the first time that the Allies were building an airfield at Milne Bay and had a garrison there. It was a startling discovery. Realizing that their reconnaissances of the area had been faulty, and that they had almost attacked the wrong objective, the Japanese at once abandoned the Samarai operation and chose Rabi, near the head of Milne Bay, as the new target. It was to be taken by the same battalion of the *Kawaguchi Detachment* which had previously been assigned to the capture of Samarai, plus such naval landing units of the *8th Fleet* as would be available at the time of the operation.[25]

The Japanese Build-up at Buna

At Buna, meanwhile, the Japanese build-up was proceeding. It had been interrupted by the Allied landings in the southern Solomons, but not seriously. For example, a convoy carrying the 3,000 men of the *14th* and *15th Naval Construction Units*, their construction equipment, vehicles, and some army supplies had left Rabaul for Buna on 6 August. It was recalled next day by the *8th Fleet* when it was only part of the way to its destination. Held over at Rabaul till the situation in the Solomons clarified itself, the convoy left Rabaul a second time on the night of 12 August and, though heavily attacked from the air on the way, reached Basabua safely the following afternoon. By early morning of the 14th, the ships were unloaded and on their way

home. Next morning as work began on the Buna strip and on a dummy strip immediately to the west of it, the ships, despite more air attacks, arrived back at Rabaul undamaged.[26]

The main body of the *Nankai Shitai* (less a rear echelon which was to come later) left Rabaul on 17 August in three escorted transports. Aboard were *Detachment Headquarters* under General Horii; the *2d* and *3d Battalions* of the *144th Infantry* with attached gun company, signal unit, and ammunition sections; the two remaining companies of the *55th Mountain Artillery;* the rest of the *47th Field AAA Battalion;* a company of the *55th Cavalry* with attached antitank gun section; part of the divisional medical unit, a base hospital, a collecting station, and a divisional decontamination and water-purification unit. A naval liaison detachment, a couple of hundred more men of the *Sasebo 5th Special Naval Landing Force,* 700 more Rabaul natives, 170 horses, and a large tonnage of supplies were also in the convoy.[27]

Without being detected by Allied air units, the transports reached Basabua in the late afternoon of 18 August and were unloaded

---

[25] Ltr, Gen Willoughby to Gen Ward, 12 Apr 51: *17th Army* Opns I, 25–27, 27–29, 35–36.

[26] *Nankai Shitai* Opns Order No. 96, 12 Aug 42, in ATIS CT 21, No. 267; G–2 Daily Summaries Enemy Intel, Allied Air Force Opns Rpts, Allied Air Force Recon Rpts, COIC Sitreps for the period 12 through 15 Aug 42, in G–3 Jnl, GHQ SWPA; *17th Army* Opns, I, 47–48; Naval Account, Japanese Invasion Eastern New Guinea, pp. 18–20.

[27] *Nankai Shitai* Opns Orders No. 96, 12 Aug 42 Annex No. 5, Table of Disposition of *South Seas Detachment* Aboard Ship, 15 Aug 42, in ATIS CT 21, No. 267; No. 98, 18 Aug 42, No. 99, 21 Aug 42, in ATIS EP 33; *Yazawa Shitai* Intel Rpt No. 3, in ATIS CT 24, No. 293; Naval Account, Japanese Invasion Eastern New Guinea, p. 19; *17th Army* Opns, I, 47, 48. The date of the *Shitai's* arrival at the beachead was moved up from 16 to 18 August because of the delays in getting the *14th* and *15th Naval Construction Units* there.

quickly and without incident. Strangely enough, the transports were not attacked during the entire time they were at anchor, nor even while they were on their way back to Rabaul. The Allied Air Forces had been caught napping. The biggest prize of all, the main body of the *Nankai Shitai* and *Detachment Headquarters,* had landed safely.

The *Yazawa Detachment,* the *41st Infantry Regiment* under its commander, Col. Kiyomi Yazawa, was next to go. The regiment, detached in March 1942 from the *5th Division,* had distinguished itself in Malaya. Like the *Nankai Shitai* and the *15th Independent Engineers,* it was a veteran force with a high reputation for aggressiveness. The *Yazawa Force* had reached Rabaul from Davao on 16 August and upon arrival had come under General Horii's command as an integral part of the *South Seas Detachment.*

Rabaul had planned to have the full strength of the regiment, plus the rear echelon of the *Nankai Shitai,* arrive at the beachhead together. At the last moment, however, it was decided to put aboard a large Army bridge-building and road-construction unit, numbering about a thousand men. This change in plan made it necessary to leave the rear echelon troops and one battalion of the *41st Infantry* for a later convoy. As finally loaded on 18 August, the troop list included regimental headquarters and two battalions of the *41st Infantry,* a regimental gun unit, signal, ordnance and motor transport troops, a veterinary hospital, a water supply and purification unit, and the bridge-building and road-construction unit. Also aboard were a hundred more men of the *Sasebo 5th Special Naval Landing Force,* some 200 more Rabaul natives, 200 more horses, several hundred cases of am-

munition, five tons of medical supplies, a quantity of gasoline in drums, and large stores of food and fodder.

The convoy left Rabaul on 19 August and landed at Basabua on 21 August in the midst of a storm. There was no interference from Allied aircraft, the ships unloaded safely, and the two battalions of the *41st Infantry* made their first bivouac that night at Popondetta about fifteen miles southeast of the anchorage. Except for some 1,500 men—the rear echelon of the *Nankai Shitai* and the remaining battalion of the *41st Infantry,* which were due in the next convoy— the full allocation of troops for the overland push against Port Moresby had arrived at the scene of operations.[28]

Horii would have a hard time getting additional troops, for things had not gone well at Guadalcanal. The advance echelon of the *Ichiki Detachment* had reached the island on 19 August. Though the strength of the force was under a thousand men, its commander had attacked at once without waiting for reinforcements. The attacking force was cut to pieces, and General Hyakutake, as a result, again had to change his plans. He returned the battalion of the *Kawaguchi Detachment,* which had been scheduled for the Milne Bay operations, to its parent detachment for use in the Solomons. Hyakutake then earmarked the *Aoba*

[28] *Yazawa Det* Intel Rpts No. 2, 10 Aug 42, No. 3, 17 Aug 42, in ATIS EP 28; *Nankai Shitai* Opns Orders No. 96, 12 Aug, with Annex [*Myoko Maru* and *Yusukawa Maru*] circa 18 Aug 42, Loading List, in ATIS CT 21, No. 267; No. 98, 18 Aug 42, in ATIS EP 33; *17th Army* Intel Summaries No. 6, 19 Aug 42, No. 9, 22 Aug 42, in ATIS EP 28; *Tomita Butai* Opns Orders No. 7, 19 Aug 42, No. 9, 22 Aug 42, in ATIS CT 24, No. 299; *17th Army* Opns, I, 21, 47–48; Naval Account, Japanese Invasion Eastern New Guinea, p. 19; G–2 SWPA Daily Summaries Enemy Intel, Allied Air Forces Opns Rpts; COIC Sitreps, 18 through 22 Aug 42, in G–3 Jnl, GHQ SWPA.

Detachment, previously in Army reserve, as the landing force for the Milne Bay operation, thus leaving the Army without a reserve force upon which to call in case of need.[29]

General Horii Takes Over

By this time General Horii had a substantial force at his disposal. A total of 8,000 Army troops, 3,000 naval construction troops, and some 450 troops of the *Sasebo 5th Special Naval Landing Force* had been landed safely in the Buna–Gona area since the *Yokoyama Advance Force* had hit the beach at Basabua a month before.[30] Even with combat losses which had been light, the desertion of some of the Rabaul natives, and the diversion of a substantial portion of his combat strength for essential supply and communication activities, it was still a formidable force. But whether such a force would be able to cross the Owen Stanley Mountains in the face of determined opposition and still be in condition to launch a successful attack on Port Moresby when it reached the other side, even General Horii, poised as he was for the operation, probably would have found it difficult to answer.

General Willoughby, General MacArthur's G–2, while admitting the possibility that the Japanese might attempt to cross the mountains in force, found it hard to believe, with the terrain what it was, that they would seriously contemplate doing so. His stated belief in late July was that the Japanese undertook seizure of the Buna–Gona–

Kokoda area primarily to secure advanced airfields in the favorable terrain afforded by the grass plains area at Dobodura. They needed the airfields, he submitted, in order to bring Port Moresby and the Cape York Peninsula under attack, and also to support a possible coastwise infiltration to the southeast which would have as its culmination joint Army and Navy operations against both Port Moresby and Milne Bay. He conceded that the Japanese might go as far as the Gap in order to establish a forward outpost there, but held it extremely unlikely that they would go further in view of the fantastically difficult terrain beyond.[31]

On 12 August, with two landings completed, and a third expected momentarily, General Willoughby still held that "an overland advance in strength is discounted in view of logistic difficulties, poor communications, and difficult terrain." On 18 August, the day that the main body of the *Nankai Shitai* landed at Basabua, he again gave it as his belief that the enemy's purpose seemed to be the development of an air base for fighters and medium bombers at Dobodura and that, while more pressure could be expected in the Kokoda–Gap area, "an overland movement in strength is discounted in view of the terrain."[32]

On 21 August, almost a week after the activity began, Allied air reconnaissance discovered for the first time that the Japanese were lengthening the small low-lying emergency landing strip at Buna which Colonel Robinson had reported as unsuit-

---

[29] *17th Army Opns,* I, 27, 36.

[30] Naval Account, Japanese Invasion Eastern New Guinea, p. 20. These are the official figures of the *8th Fleet,* which transported the troops, and are believed to be accurate.

[31] G–2 SWPA Daily Summaries Enemy Intel, No. 126, 26–27 Jul 42, No. 127, 27–28 Jul 42, No. 129, 29–30 Jul 42, in G–3 Jnl, GHQ SWPA.

[32] G–2 Daily Summaries Enemy Intel No. 142, 11–12 Aug 42, No. 148, 17–18 Aug 42.

able for military use.[33] The discovery that the Japanese were building airfields in the Buna area (if only at Buna rather than as they might have done at Dobodura) led General Willoughby to the conclusion that here at last was the explanation for the Japanese seizure of the beachhead. The fact that they had done so, he thought, had nothing to do with a possible thrust through the mountains, for an overland operation against Port Moresby was to be "discounted in view of the logistical difficulties of maintaining any force in strength" on the Kokoda Trail.[34]

The same day that General Willoughby issued this estimate, General Horii, who had previously been at Giruwa, left the beachhead for Kokoda to take personal charge of the advance through the Gap.[35] The overland operation against Port Moresby, which General Willoughby had been so thoroughly convinced the Japanese would not undertake, was about to begin.

[33] COIC Sitrep No. 343, 21 Aug 42, with Attchd Photo Intel Ser No. 178, Buna Runway, No. 345, 23 Aug 42; G–2 Daily Summary Enemy Intel No. 152, 21–22 Aug 42; Allied Air Forces Recon Rpt, 22 Aug 42.

[34] G–2 Daily Summary Enemy Intel No. 152, 21–22 Aug 42.

[35] *Nankai Shitai* Opns Orders No. A–99, 20 Aug 42, No. 100, 21 Aug 42, in ATIS EP 33.

CHAPTER VI

The Japanese Offensive Collapses

Ten days after the first Japanese landing at Basabua Admiral King wrote to General Marshall that, while he was willing to assume that General MacArthur was "taking all measures in his power to deny the threat of Japanese penetration toward Port Moresby," he doubted that the measures taken (which he described as "airpower supported by minor ground forces north of the Owen Stanley Mountains") would be successful. Since, in his opinion, the holding of Port Moresby and the Buna-Gona area was essential to the ultimate success of operations in both the South and Southwest Pacific Areas, he asked that General Marshall obtain from General MacArthur by dispatch the latter's "views as to the present situation in New Guinea, and his plan to deny further advance to the Japanese, pending execution of Task Two." [1] General Marshall replied the next day. He agreed, he said, with the assumption that General MacArthur was taking all measures in his power to deny the Japanese threat, but he felt it was "a little early to assume that such measures [would] be unsuccessful." Admiral King was assured, however, that General MacArthur was being asked for his plan to counteract the Japanese offensive.

Such a message had, in fact, gone out the day before. [2]

The SWPA: Early August

General MacArthur's Accounting

General MacArthur had a reassuring story to tell. He had just ordered the 7th Australian Infantry Division to New Guinea—the 18th Brigade to Milne Bay, and the 21st and 25th Brigades to Port Moresby. His plan of operations to prevent further enemy encroachment in New Guinea had been greatly hampered, he noted, by a critical shortage of transportation, especially sea transport, and by a dearth of naval convoy ships to protect his supply routes. The work of defending the area had nevertheless gone on despite these difficulties. Before the defenses in New Guinea could be augmented, it had been necessary, as a first step, to move engineers and protective garrisons into the Townsville–Cloncurry area in order to complete a series of airfields there and to develop Port Moresby as an advance jump-off point for the air force. As a second step, the garrison

---

[1] Memo, Admiral King for Gen Marshall, 31 Jul 42, sub: Japanese Operations, Northeast Coast of New Guinea, in 381, OPD PTO, Sec 2.

[2] Memo, Gen Marshall for Admiral King, 1 Aug 42, sub: Japanese Operations, Northeast Coast of New Guinea, in 381, OPD PTO, Sec 2; Msg, Gen Marshall to Gen MacArthur, CM–OUT 9289, 31 Jul 42.

at Port Moresby was doubled to two brigades; engineers and antiaircraft units were sent forward to develop and protect the dispersal facilities in the area; and a beginning was made in developing and securing airfields in the Cape York Peninsula. As a succeeding step, airfields were built at Milne Bay and Merauke to cover Port Moresby from east and west, and troops were ordered forward to secure the crest of the range at Wau and Kokoda.

The experienced 7th Australian Infantry Division would begin moving to the front within the next few days—one brigade to Milne Bay, the other two to Port Moresby. Seven transpacific ships, which would in due course be returned to their regular runs, were being requisitioned to get the division and its equipment forward.

General MacArthur went on to say that the final solution to the problem of defending New Guinea would, of course, come with the completion of Task One and the inception of Tasks Two and Three. After sketching a plan of maneuver for the latter two tasks, he told General Marshall that, while further preparations were necessary for Task Three, immediately after Task One was successfully completed Task Two could begin if the aircraft carriers and the Marine division with its amphibious equipment were made available for the operation.[3]

It was an excellent accounting. Starting in late March with only a few airfields in the Townsville–Cloncurry area and two poor fields at Port Moresby, General MacArthur by early August also had effective bases in the Cape York Peninsula, at Merauke, and at Milne Bay—a remarkable accomplish-

ment in view of the appalling terrain, the shortage of engineer troops, and the difficulties of supply.

General Rowell Takes Over in New Guinea

On 6 August all Australian and American forces serving in Australian New Guinea (Papua and North East New Guinea) were put under New Guinea Force. On 9 August Maj. Gen. Sydney F. Rowell, General Officer Commanding, 1st Australian Corps, took command of all forces in New Guinea. Nine days later, General Rowell became G. O. C. New Guinea Force.[4]

The orders of 6 August gave New Guinea Force a greatly expanded mission. It was to prevent further penetration of Australian New Guinea, hold the crest of the Owen Stanley Range, and retake Kokoda, the Buna-Gona area, and ultimately Lae and Salamaua. It was to carry out active reconnaissance of its area and the approaches thereto, maintain and augment KANGA Force, and establish a special force at Milne Bay. After infiltrating the northeast coast of Papua from East Cape to Tufi, the Milne Bay troops would join with the overland forces on the Kokoda trail in the capture of the Buna–Gona area.[5]

As General Rowell took command in New Guinea, the Japanese on the trail were at Isurava south of Kokoda. Radio intercepts

---

[3] Msg, Gen MacArthur to Gen Marshall, No. Q–147, CM–IN 1607, 2 Aug 42.

[4] GHQ SWPA OI No. 15, 6 Aug 42; LHQ OI No. 30, 9 Aug 42; NGF OI No. 24, 18 Aug 42. General Morris, who in addition to being G. O. C. New Guinea Force had also been Administrator of New Guinea and head of the Australia–New Guinea Administrative Unit, ANGAU, continued in the latter two capacities, thereby making it possible for General Rowell to concentrate exclusively on combat operations.

[5] GHQ SWPA OI No. 15, 6 Aug 42.

and documents captured by KANGA Force revealed that the Japanese intended to land at Samarai shortly.[6] The situation was in crisis, but the Allied defensive position was stronger than it appeared to be—much stronger, in fact, than had been thought possible only a few short weeks before.

The Defense Falls Into Place

The North Queensland Bases

By the third week in August three fields had been completed in the Cape York Peninsula, one for fighters and two for heavy bombers. Three additional fields for heavy bombers were due to be completed by the end of September. The movement of aviation units, garrison troops, and supplies to the bases in northern Queensland was proceeding but was not expected to be complete until sometime in October because of the emergency troop movements to Port Moresby and Milne Bay, and the consequent shortage of shipping.[7]

To alleviate a critical shortage of U.S. engineer troops,[8] and to speed construction

where it was most needed, arrangements were made in August to turn over the task of airfield construction and maintenance in northern Queensland and elsewhere on the mainland either to the RAAF or to the Allied Works Council, a civilian construction agency of the Australian Government staffed for the most part by men who were over age or otherwise exempt from military duty. American engineer troops released in this way were at once transferred to New Guinea. The change-over was a gradual one, but by the end of the year almost all U.S. engineer troops in the Southwest Pacific Area were in New Guinea.[9]

Port Moresby

By 19 August, Brig. A. W. Potts's 21st Australian Infantry Brigade, the leading brigade of the two 7th Division brigades ordered to Port Moresby, had already arrived there. It did not tarry but began moving at once to Isurava, where MAROUBRA Force—by this time a battalion and two companies of the 30th Brigade—was making a stand under the brigade commander, Brig. Selwyn H. Porter. The 25th Brigade, which was to follow the 21st, was delayed by the shipping shortage and was not expected to arrive until early September.

Even so, the Port Moresby garrison, with its three infantry brigades and its Australian and American air, antiaircraft, engineer, and service units, already numbered 22,000 men. When the 25th Brigade, 7th Division headquarters, and other divisional troops arrived, it would total 28,000. The seven-air-

[6] G–2 Daily Summary Enemy Intel, No. 135, 3–4 Aug 42, in G–3 Jnl, GHQ SWPA; ALF, Rpt on New Guinea Opns, Buna–Ioribaiwa.

[7] Msg, Gen MacArthur to Gen Marshall, No. C–301, CM–IN 7017, 19 Aug 42.

[8] General Casey had under his command on 1 May 1942 a total of 6,240 U.S. Engineer construction troops comprising the following units: the 43d and 46th General Service Engineer Battalions, the 808th Engineer Aviation Battalion, the 91st and 96th Separate Engineer Battalions, and the 576th and 585th Engineer Dump Truck Companies. The first three were white units; the remaining four, Negro. Except for the addition of the 69th Topographical Company, and the expansion of the 91st and 96th Battalions to regiments, an increase since May of some 1,200 men, his command was substantially the same at the end of the year. OCE SWPA Annual Rpt, 1942; OCE SWPA, Location and Strength of U.S. Engineer Units, 31 Dec 42. Both in AFPAC Engr File.

[9] Gen Casey, Memo for Record, 11 Aug 42, sub: Conference with General Kenney, Air Vice Marshal William D. Bostock, and Lt Col R. E. Beebe; OCE SWPA, Draft Engr Rpt, 31 Dec 42. Both in AFPAC Engr Files. OCE, AFPAC, *Engineers in Theater Operations* (Washington, 1947), p. 38.

PORT MORESBY *as it looked when the headquarters of the U.S. Advanced Base in New Guinea was established there.*

field program projected for Port Moresby was nearing completion. Four fields were finished and in use—two for fighters, one for medium bombers, and one for heavy bombers. The three remaining fields—two for heavy bombers and one for medium bombers—were expected to be ready by early September.[10]

Plans to make Port Moresby a large supply and communications area were well advanced. On 11 August the U. S. Advanced Base in New Guinea was established by USASOS with headquarters at Port Moresby. Its functions were to aid in the operation of the port and other ports in New Guinea,

to control the activities of U. S. service troops in the area, and, in general, to provide for the supply of all American troops in the battle zone.[11]

The port itself, shallow and suitable only for light traffic, was to be improved. Existing facilities permitted only one ship to be unloaded at a time, and that very slowly, with the frequent result that as many as two or three others had to wait in the roads to unload, exposed all the while to enemy attack. Since the existing harbor site did not lend itself to expansion, General Casey planned to develop Tatana Island (a small island in Fairfax Harbor to the northwest of the existing harbor) into an entirely new

[10] Msg, Gen MacArthur to Gen Marshall, No. C–301, CM–IN 7017, 19 Aug 42.

[11] USASOS SWPA, GO No. 7, 11 Aug 42.

port. The new development, which would permit several ocean-going ships to be unloaded at one time, was to be connected with the mainland by an earth-filled causeway a half-mile long, over which would run a two-lane highway with a freeboard of two feet over high tide. The project was to be undertaken as soon as engineers and engineering equipment became available.[12]

Measures were being taken to improve the air supply situation both in the Owen Stanleys and in the Bulolo Valley. After a careful study of the problem, General Kenney assigned six A–24's, a B–17, and two transports—all the aircraft that could be spared—to the task of dropping supplies to the Australian troops in both areas. It was hoped that the use of these planes if only for ten days, the period of their assignment, would make possible a substantial improvement in the supply situation at both Kagi and Wau.[13]

Milne Bay

By 21 August the 18th Australian Infantry Brigade (the 2/9, 2/10, and 2/12 Australian Infantry Battalions) under Brig. George F. Wootten completed its movement to Milne Bay. There it joined the 7th Australian Infantry Brigade, Citizen Military Forces (the 9, 25, and 61 Australian Infantry Battalions), under Brig. John Field, which had reached Milne Bay in July. The following day, 22 August, Maj.

Gen. Cyril A. Clowes, an experienced officer who had commanded the ANZAC Corps artillery in Greece, took command of Milne Force. His instructions were to protect the airfields and deny Milne Bay to the enemy.

After the company of the 46th U. S. Engineers had arrived in late June and the 7th Brigade, a 25-pounder battery, and some light and heavy Australian antiaircraft in early July, the second of two RAAF fighter squadrons equipped with P–40's and part of a RAAF reconnaissance squadron using Hudsons reached Milne Bay by early August. Two companies of the 43d U. S. Engineers had also arrived by this time as well as the 709th U. S. Airborne Antiaircraft Battery which was equipped with .50-caliber machine guns. The American engineer troops had a few .50-caliber machine guns and some 37-mm. antitank guns in addition to their rifles and light machine guns.[14]

Milne Force, when General Clowes took it over on 22 August, was a good-sized command. Australian troop strength was 7,429 men, of whom 6,394 were combat troops and 1,035 were service troops. American troop strength, mainly engineers and antiaircraft personnel, numbered 1,365 men;

---

[12] Memo, Col Beebe, Air Dir of Opns, Allied Air Forces, for CG, 18 Aug 42, in 385–9, G–3 Files, GHQ SWPA; OCE SWPA, Draft Engr Rpt, 31 Dec 42; OCE SWPA, New Guinea Ports, 1942. Both in AFPAC Engr File.

[13] Ltr, Gen MacArthur to Gen Blamey, 24 Aug 42, in G–3 Jnl, GHQ SWPA; Ltr, Gen Kenney to Gen Ward, 26 Feb 51.

---

[14] Memo, Gen MacArthur for Comdr ALF *et al.*, 2 Jul 42, sub: Reinforcement Fall River; Rad, Movements, Townsville, to GHQ SWPA, No. 2797, 7 Jul 42; Ltr, Gen MacArthur to Comdr ALF, 7 Aug 42. All in 384, FALL RIVER File, G–3 Files, GHQ SWPA. Memo, Gen MacArthur for CG USASOS, 28 Jul 42, sub: Movement of 2d Battalion, 43d Engineers, less one company, in 307.5, Rec Sec Files, GHQ SWPA; Unit Hist, 709 AAA MG Bty, copy in DRB HRS, AGO. The 25-pounder was the standard artillery piece of the Australian and British Army at this time. The caliber was about 3½ inches; the barrel was about 7¾ feet long; and the weight of the shell, as the name of piece suggested, was roughly 25 pounds.

the strength of the RAAF was 664 men.[15] Clowes's total strength was thus 9,458 men.

To guard against Japanese infiltration from the Buna–Gona area patrols were operating between East Cape (the eastern tip of New Guinea) and Goodenough Bay. The overland trails leading into Milne Bay were being patrolled regularly, as was the Mullins Harbor area to the southwest of Milne Bay. General Clowes had neither landing craft, coastal guns, nor searchlights, but the best defense that time would allow had been provided.[16]

The Battle of Milne Bay

The Scene of Operations

Milne Bay, about twenty miles long and five to ten miles wide, lies at the extreme southeast tip of New Guinea. (*Map 5*) The fact that it is often closed in from the air probably accounted for the long time that it took the Japanese to discover the presence of the Allies in the area. On either arm of the bay, mountains 4,000 feet high rise abruptly from the shore. Between the mountains and the sea are narrow coastal corridors consisting for the most part of deep swamp, and dense, almost impenetrable, jungle. The rainfall in the bay area averages 200 inches a year, and during wet weather the corridors are virtually impassable.

At the head of the bay is a large plain into which the coastal corridors merge. This plain, the site in prewar days of an immense coconut plantation operated by Lever Brothers, was the only place in the entire area which was not completely bogged down in mud. Because it already had a small, if inadequate, road net, all the base installations and airfields were concentrated there.

At the time General Clowes took command, one airfield—No. 1 Strip, in the center of the plantation area—had been completed and was being used by the P–40's and Hudsons. The 46th Engineer company was working on No. 2 Strip, which was about four miles inland at the western end of the plantation. The two companies of the 43d Engineers were working on No. 3 Strip, which was just off the north shore.

Although a great deal of hard work, under the most adverse conditions, had gone into the base, much still remained to be done. The roads, for the most part, a corduroy of coconut logs covered with decomposed coral, were in very poor condition. The dock, at Gili Gili, at the very head of the bay, consisted of two barges placed side by side with a ramp leading to the small and inadequate jetty that had been there when the military first arrived. Number 1 Strip, the only runway in operation, and very hastily constructed, consisted of an open-mesh steel mat, laid over a low-lying, poorly drained base. Mud seeped through the mat and caused aircraft using the runway to skid and sometimes crack up. Since there was no time to rebuild the field, all that could be done to remedy the situation was to have bulldozers scrape the mat daily and deposit the mud in piles on either side of the strip. The runway was particularly treacherous during wet weather. Though it

---

[15] Msgs, Gen MacArthur to Gen Marshall, No. C–301, CM–IN 7017, 19 Aug 42, No. C–382, CM–IN 11398, 30 Aug 42; Memo, Gen Chamberlin for Gen Sutherland, 23 Oct 42, sub: Allied Strength at Milne Bay, 25 Aug 42–Sep 42, in G–3 Jnl, GHQ SWPA; Comdr Milne Force, Rpt on Opns, 25 Aug 42–7 Sep 42, copy in OCMH files.

[16] Memo, Gen Sutherland for Gen Blamey, 2 Aug 42, in 385, FALL RIVER File, G–3 Files, GHQ SWPA; ALF Daily Opns Rpt No. 115, 8 Aug 42, in G–3 Jnl, GHQ SWPA.

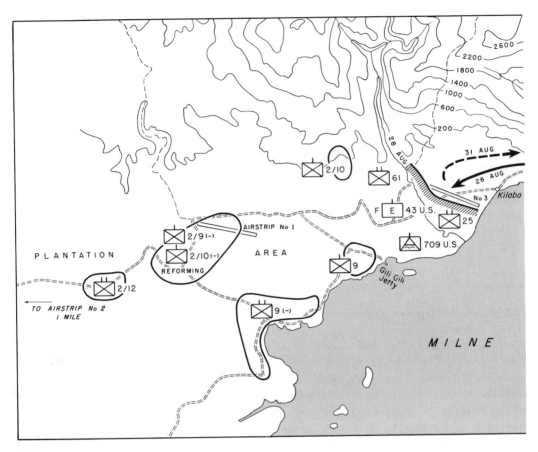

MAP 5

had originally been built as a bomber strip, the P–40's often required its entire length for their take-offs when it had rained for any length of time. When the rainfall was exceptionally heavy they were often unable to take off at all.[17]

[17] Staff Mtg, CGS LHQ, 28 Aug 42, in 337, Conf File, Rec Sec Files, GHQ SWPA; G–3 [GHQ SWPA] Outline of Milne Bay Opns, in G–3 Jnl, GHQ SWPA; Comdr Milne Force, Rpt on Opns, 25 Aug–7 Sep 42; Ltr, Maj Gen Hugh J. Casey to author, 21 Jul 50, in OCMH files. General Casey's explanation of the hasty construction of No. 1 Strip is that the field had to be constructed that way "in order to secure an operable airdrome in the limited time available."

This then was the place that the Japanese had chosen, at the last minute, to capture instead of Samarai. They had made the decision only in mid-August, when they first discovered the Allies were actually there. A few days later they issued the orders to attack.

The Landing

Toward the latter part of August the Japanese decided to launch the Milne Bay operation immediately. The *Aoba Detachment,* the Army force earmarked to land at

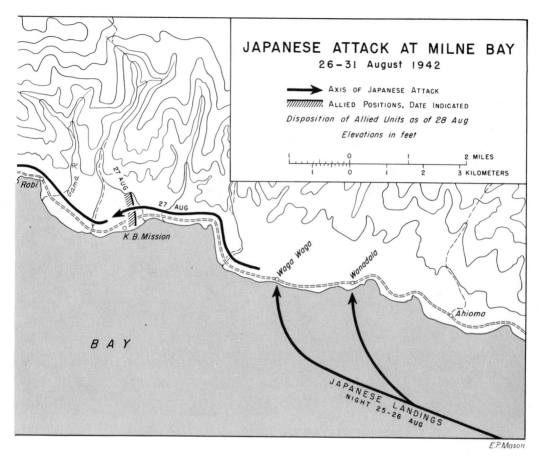

JAPANESE ATTACK AT MILNE BAY
26–31 August 1942

→ AXIS OF JAPANESE ATTACK

ALLIED POSITIONS, DATE INDICATED

Disposition of Allied Units as of 28 Aug

Elevations in feet

0   1   2 MILES

0   1   2   3 KILOMETERS

Rabi

Gama R.

27 AUG

27 AUG

K.B. Mission

Waga Waga

Wanadala

Ahioma

B A Y

JAPANESE LANDINGS
NIGHT 25-26 AUG

E.P. Mason

Milne Bay, was still at Davao. Nevertheless the *8th Fleet,* with naval troops available for action at Kavieng and Buna, decided to proceed with the operation without waiting for the detachment to come in. Judging that Milne Bay was held by two or three infantry companies and twenty or thirty aircraft, Admiral Mikawa on 20 August ordered some 1,500 men to Milne Bay. A total of 1,171 men (612 *Kure 5th Special Naval Landing Force* (SNLF) troops, 362 *16th Naval Pioneer Unit* troops, and 197 men of the *Sasebo 5th SNLF*) were ordered to Milne Bay from Kavieng; the rest, 353

Sasebo 5th SNLF troops, were to come from Buna. Commander Shojiro Hayashi, of the *Kure 5th SNLF,* was in command of the landing forces from Kavieng. His orders were to land at Rabi, a point about three miles from the Gili Gili wharf area at the head of the bay. The troops from Buna were to land at Taupota on the north coast and march on Gili Gili overland.

The first echelon from Kavieng, bearing mostly *Kure 5th* troops, left Rabaul for Rabi in two transports in the early morning of 24 August. The troops of the *Sasebo 5th SNLF* at Buna left for Milne Bay at approxi-

MILNE BAY AREA. *(Photograph taken 1946.)*

mately the same time in seven large motor-driven landing barges.[18]

The seven landing craft were the first to be detected by the Allies. The Coast Watcher at Porlock Harbor sighted them the same afternoon, and early the next morning a reconnaissance aircraft reported that they were nearing Goodenough Island.

[18] Diary, member *Kure 5th SNLF,* in ATIS CT 1, No. 41; Diary, member *Kure 3d SNLF,* in ATIS CT 3, No. 57; Diary, member *Kure 5th SNLF,* in ATIS CT 4, No. 76; *Sasebo 5th SNLF* Opns Orders, tr quoted in G–2 Daily Summary Enemy Intel No. 164, 2–3 Sep 42, in G–3 Jnl, GHQ SWPA; AMF, Interr Gen Adachi *et al.; 17th Army* Opns I, 50–51; *Southeast Area* Naval Opns I, 15; Naval Account Japanese Invasion Eastern New Guinea, pp. 25–28.

Twelve P–40's from Milne Bay (which had been unable to attack previously because of enemy air raids and bad weather) took off for Goodenough Island at noon and shortly thereafter discovered the landing craft beached on the southwestern shore of the island, where the Japanese had put in to stretch their legs and prepare a meal. The P–40's gave the drawn-up barges and ration-littered beach a thorough strafing. When the attack was over, all of the landing craft had been destroyed, and the *Sasebo* unit, its stores, ammunition, and communications equipment gone, was left stranded on Goodenough Island with no way of reaching its objective, or even of returning to Buna.[19]

The convoy bearing the *Kure 5th* troops fared better in its approach to the target. Heavily escorted by cruisers and destroyers, the transports were first sighted off Kiriwina Island, 140 miles northeast of Milne Bay, in the early morning of 25 August, making directly for Milne Bay. General MacArthur's headquarters immediately ordered the Air Force to attack the convoy and destroy it. All available B–25's and B–26's at Townsville and nine B–17's at Mareeba in the Cape York Peninsula took off at once for the attack, which was to be made that afternoon in concert with the RAAF P–40's and Hudsons from Milne Bay.

Fortunately for the Japanese, the weather (except for a short break at noon which the RAAF had exploited to the full in the attack on Goodenough Island) was very bad all day, both at Moresby and Milne Bay. For hours on end planes were unable to take off from either place. Attempts by the B–17's from the Cape York Peninsula and the P–40's and Hudsons from Milne Bay to hit the convoy proved fruitless because of violent rain squalls and a heavy overcast. By late afternoon visibility was down to zero, and despite occasional breaks thereafter the Air Force found it impossible to attack successfully that day.[20]

The Japanese landing began about 2200 hours, 25 August, on the north shore of the bay near Waga Waga and Wanadala—five to seven miles east of Rabi, their prescribed landing point. The landing force set up headquarters at Waga Waga and established a series of supply dumps there and in the Wanadala area. The shore east of K. B. Mission, which the Japanese continued to think for some time was the Rabi area, became their main bivouac site and forward jump-off point. Here, about one mile east of the mission, at 0145 hours on 26 August, elements of Milne Force met the Japanese column in an indecisive engagement when a screening platoon from Company B, 61 Battalion, at K. B. Mission started a fire fight with the Japanese that lasted until nearly dawn. Although the enemy used light tanks in support of his probe, he finally withdrew leaving the Australian detachment in place.[21]

The Advance

The Japanese could scarcely have chosen a worse landing place. Their objectives, the airfields and the wharf, were at the head of Milne Bay, and they had landed several miles from the plantation area on a jungle-covered coastal shelf, flanked on the right by mountains and on the left by the sea. Because the mountains in the landing area were steep and very close to shore, there was virtually no room for maneuver, and the heavy jungle which covered the bay shore made it impossible to find a dry bivouac for the troops anywhere in the area.

It had rained steadily during the preceding few weeks, and the heavy tropical downpour continued. The mountain streams had

[19] Diary, member *Sasebo 5th SNLF,* in ATIS CT 4, No. 84; Allied Air Forces Opns Rpt, 25 Aug 42; GHQ Sitrep No. 347, 25 Aug 42; Interr Gen Adachi *et al.;* Comdr Milne Force, Rpt on Opns, 25 Aug–7 Sep 42; G–3 Outline Milne Bay Opns, 25 Aug 42; G–3 Opns Rpt No. 140, 26 Aug 42; in G–3 Jnl, GHQ SWPA; Naval Account Japanese Invasion Eastern New Guinea, p. 27.
[20] G–3 Outline Milne Bay Opns; G–3 Opns Rpt No. 139, 25 Aug 42, No. 140, 26 Aug 42; Allied Air Forces Opns Rpt, 25 Aug 42.

[21] AMF, Interr Gen Adachi *et al.;* Naval Account Japanese Invasion Eastern New Guinea, pp. 25–28; Comdr Milne Force, Rpt on Opns, 25 Aug–7 Sep 42.

become roaring torrents, and the spongy soil of the corridor a quagmire. The single coastal track that skirted the corridor had in places completely washed away, and the level of the many fords that cut across it had risen to almost three feet. Except for a few abandoned plantations and mission stations, the corridor was a sodden welter of jungle and swamp, an utter nightmare for any force operating in it.[22]

Although they had seriously misjudged Allied strength, and had landed on a muddy coastal shelf thousands of yards from the head of the bay, the Japanese nevertheless enjoyed some significant tactical advantages. Their left flank was secure because they had control of the sea, and their right flank could not easily be turned because of the mountains a few hundred yards away. It was true that they could count on little air power, since Lae and Salamaua, the nearest operational air bases, were more than 300 miles away; but unlike Milne Force, which could barely scrape up a few trawlers, they had plenty of landing craft and could therefore land troops and supplies freely under cover of darkness or of the weather, despite their deficiency in the air.

General Clowes, on the other hand, was a man fighting blind. Because of the dense jungle on the north shore of the bay and frequent heavy overcasts, neither his ground patrols nor his aerial reconnaissance could tell him what the Japanese were doing or what their numbers were. Worse still, he was face to face with the possibility that the Japanese, in addition to landing on the north shore, might land troops on the south shore, or even at the head of the bay. Having no idea as yet of Japanese intentions,

Clowes held the bulk of his force in the plantation area, to be committed to the north shore when it became apparent from the circumstances that the Japanese had no intention of landing troops elsewhere in the bay area.

At the time of the Japanese landings during the night of 25–26 August, the main body of Milne Force was deployed in the plantation area in the vicinity of the airfields and two companies of the 61 Battalion were on the north shore in the path of the Japanese thrust. One of these companies was at Ahioma, just east of Wanadala; the other was at K. B. Mission. There was also a platoon of the 61 Battalion on the northeast coast guarding against an overland attack on Milne Bay from the Taupota side of the mountains, as well as a reinforced company of the 25 Battalion farther to the northwest on Goodenough Bay.

The company at Ahioma did not fare as well as the one at K. B. Mission. The troops at Ahioma had been under orders to return to Gili Gili by water, and two of the three platoons were already on their way in two ketches when the Japanese landings began. Shortly after leaving Ahioma the ketches plowed into a landing wave off Wanadala. In the melee one of the Australian craft was sunk. Some of the militia troops were lost; others struggled ashore and infiltrated back to their own lines. The platoon in the other ketch returned to Ahioma and, with the platoon that had remained there, marched overland to Taupota and thence back over the mountains to Gili Gili where they rejoined their battalion several days later.[23]

[22] Staff Mtg CGS LHQ, 28 Aug 42; OCE SWPA, Draft Engr Rpt, 31 Dec 42; Comdr Milne Force, Rpt on Opns, 25 Aug–7 Sep 42.

[23] Memo, Brig John Field, CO 7th Aust Inf Bde, for Hq, Milne Force, 17 Sep 42, sub: Lessons from Recent Fighting, copy in OCMH files; G–3 Outline Milne Bay Opns; Comdr Milne Force, Rpt on Opns, 25 Aug–7 Sep 42; Naval Account Japanese Invasion Eastern New Guinea, p. 26.

By 0745 that morning, 26 August, the weather had abated sufficiently for the P–40's from No. 1 Strip and the B–17's staging from Port Moresby to go into action. In an extremely successful morning's business, the P–40's managed to destroy most of the food and ammunition that the Japanese had brought with them. The B–17's, almost as successful, inflicted heavy damage on a large Japanese transport unloading offshore.[24]

Toward evening a second Japanese convoy (Commander Hayashi's second echelon) was sighted off Normanby Island in the D'Entrecasteaux Group, making at high speed for Milne Bay. Before it could be dealt with, a heavy fog descended over the area, blotting out the convoy's further movements. The troops aboard landed safely that night, completing the 1,170-man movement from Kavieng.[25]

K. B. Mission had meanwhile been reinforced by a second company of the 61 Battalion. The Japanese, who had reconnoitered the mission during the day, struck again that night in much greater strength than before. The Australian militia was forced out of the mission and all the way back to the line of the Gama River, just east of Rabi. Fortunately for the Australians, the Japanese again chose to break off the engagement at dawn.

The following morning, General Clowes sent the 2/10 Battalion of the 18th Brigade to K. B. Mission. The battalion, intended to be a reconnaissance force, was lightly armed. Its orders were to keep in contact with the Japanese, draw them out, and in general find out what they were up to. Without such essential knowledge, General Clowes was confronted with a cruel dilemma. If he moved his troops onto the north shore, the enemy might counter by landing fresh troops on the south shore or at the head of the bay itself. As he himself was to explain:

The presence of Jap naval elements in the vicinity throughout the operation and the freedom of activity enjoyed by the enemy by sea constituted a continuous menace in regard to possible further landings. These factors necessarily had a marked influence on plans and dispositions made to deal with the enemy. On several occasions, such plans were definitely slowed down or suffered variation through the delay involved in assuring that the south shore was clear, and, further, that reports of the presence of enemy ships at Mullins Harbor were not founded on fact.[26]

The 2/10 Battalion reached the mission unopposed in the late afternoon of 27 August. Under orders to move on again in the morning, the battalion had barely settled itself for the night when the Japanese struck at the mission again, this time with two tanks and all their available combat troops. Despite unceasing tropical rain, the ground in the well-drained and relatively open plantation area was firm enough for tank action. The two tanks, equipped with brilliant headlights that made targets of the Australians and left the attackers in darkness, inflicted heavy casualties on the 2/10 Battalion. The lightly armed Australians,

[24] GHQ SWPA Sitrep No. 347, 26 Aug 42; Msg, Gen MacArthur to Gen Marshall, No. C–361, CM–IN 10432, 27 Aug 42; Comdr Milne Force, Rpt on Opns, 25 Aug–7 Sep 42; Naval Account Japanese Invasion Eastern New Guinea, p. 26.
[25] G–3 Opns Rpt, No. 140, 26 Aug 42; G–3 Outline Milne Bay Opns; Msg, Gen MacArthur to Gen Marshall, No. C–361, CM–IN 10432, 27 Aug 42.

[26] Comdr Milne Force, Rpt on Opns 25 Aug–7 Sep 42; Naval Account Japanese Invasion Eastern New Guinea, p. 26; Interv with Lt Col Peter S. Teesdale-Smith, AMF, 22 Aug 49, copy in OCMH files. At the time the battle was fought, Colonel Teesdale-Smith, then a captain, was intelligence officer of the 2/10 Battalion.

whose only antitank protection was "sticky-type" hand grenades, which would not stick, were unable to knock out the tanks and also failed to shoot out their headlights. After about two hours of fighting the Japanese managed to split the battalion in two. Battalion headquarters and two companies were forced off the track and into the jungle, and the remainder of the battalion was pushed back to the Gama River. A portion of the battalion reached the plantation area that night, but the main body took to the hills in order to get around the enemy's flank and did not get back to the head of the bay until three days later.[27]

With the 2/10 Battalion out of the way, the Japanese continued on to No. 3 strip. There a heavy fire fight at once developed, a fight in which American antiaircraft and engineer troops played a significant part.

The Fighting at No. 3 Strip

The east-west airstrip, just west of Kilabo and only a few miles from Rabi, was an ideal defensive position. The runway, a hundred yards wide and 2,000 yards long, was cleared but only partially graded, and there was a sea of mud at its eastern edge which made it impossible for tanks to get through. It afforded the defenders a broad, cleared field of fire, and, lying obliquely across the mouth of the corridor with its southern end less than five hundred feet from the water, was directly in the path of the Japanese advance.

Brigadier Field, in charge of the defense, ranged his troops along the southern edge of the strip, giving the Japanese no alterna-

tive but to attack frontally. The main burden of holding the strip fell upon the brigade's 25th and 61st Battalions, but the 709th U. S. Airborne Antiaircraft Battery and Companies D and F of the 43d U. S. Engineers held key positions in its defense. The antiaircraft battery with its .50-caliber machine guns was given the task of supporting the Australians at the eastern end of the strip, and the .50-caliber and 37-mm. gun crews of Companies D and F, 43d U. S. Engineers, flanked on either side by Australian riflemen and mortarmen, were stationed at the center of the line at the crucial point where the track from Rabi crossed the runway.

The Japanese reached the area immediately in front of the strip just before dawn. They attacked aggressively but were repulsed and forced to withdraw. No tanks were used in the attack, although two of them (apparently the same two that the Japanese had used with such success at K. B. Mission were brought up, only to be abandoned when they bogged down hopelessly.[28]

The attackers were now within a few miles of No. 1 Strip, and General Clowes, fearful lest they infiltrate it during the night, ordered the P-40's to Port Moresby. Fortunately the Japanese were quiet that night, and the following morning the fighters returned to Milne Bay to stay.[29]

[27] Memo, Brig Field for Hq Milne Force, 17 Sep 42, sub: Lessons from the Recent Fighting; Comdr Milne Force, Rpt on Opns, 25 Aug-7 Sep 42; Interv with Col Teesdale-Smith, 22 Aug 49.

[28] Ltr, Capt Joseph E. Wood, Adj 2d Bn, 43d Engr Regt (GS), to Chief Engr, U.S. Army, SWPA, 18 Sep 42, sub: Rpt of Participation in the Milne Bay Battle by U.S. Engr Troops in this Area; Memo, Gen Casey for Gen Sutherland, 25 Oct 42; Ltr, Maj Ludlow C. Adams, CO 2d Bn, 43d Engrs (GS), to CG USASOS SWPA, 2 Nov 42, sub: Participation of U.S. Engr Troops in the Battle of Milne Bay, 25 Aug-20 Sep 43. All in AFPAC Engr File. Unit Hist 709th AAA MG Bty.
[29] Comdr Milne Force, Rpt on Opns, 25 Aug-7 Sep 42.

AUSTRALIAN RIFLEMEN PASSING ABANDONED JAPANESE TANKS
bogged down near No. 3 Strip.

On 26 August, the day of the landing, and again on the afternoon of the 28th, General MacArthur had ordered General Blamey to see to it that the north shore of Milne Bay was cleared of the enemy at once.[30] Because of defective communications New Guinea Force did not receive the orders of the 26th until late on the 27th, and General Clowes, apparently, not until early the next morning.[31] Early on the 28th Clowes ordered the 7th Brigade to be prepared to move forward at dawn the following day. Strong patrols of the brigade moved out early on the 29th but met stiff enemy opposition, and little progress was registered. Clowes thereupon ordered in the 18th Brigade with instructions to move at once on K. B. Mission. He canceled the orders at 1633 upon learning that another Japanese convoy was on its way to Milne Bay.

[30] G–3 Outline Milne Bay Opns; Ltr, Gen Sutherland to Gen Blamey, 28 Aug. 42, in G–3 Jnl, GHQ SWPA. General MacArthur, in conference with General Blamey on the 26th, gave it as his "professional opinion" that the Japanese would reinforce the landing on the north shore within seventy-two hours.

[31] Ltr, Maj Gen George A. Vasey, DSGS ALF, to Gen Sutherland, 28 Aug 42, in G–3 Jnl, GHQ SWPA; Comdr Milne Force, Rpt on Opns, 25 Aug–7 Sep 42.

His reason for the cancellation—as he was to explain later—was the renewed possibility "of an enemy attempt to land on the west and south shores of Milne Bay." [32]

The convoy, escorted by a cruiser and nine destroyers, unloaded safely under cover of a heavy mist. It brought to the sore-beset Japanese on the north shore nearly 770 reinforcements—568 troops of the *Kure 3d SNLF* and 200 of the *Yokosuka 5th SNLF*—under Commander Minoru Yano, who, being apparently senior to Hayashi, at once took over command of operations. [33]

The daylight hours of the following day, 30 August, were quiet. Milne Force sent patrols to feel out the enemy in preparation for the long-delayed general advance, and the Japanese, hidden in the jungle, consolidated for another attack on No. 3 strip. The climax came that night when the Japanese made an all-out effort to take the strip. Brigadier Field was again ready for them. The only change in his dispositions was to place the .50-caliber machine guns of the 709th Antiaircraft Battery at both ends of the line instead of as before on its eastern end. The .50-caliber machine guns and 37-mm. antitank gun crews of Companies D and F of the 43d Engineers were as before in the center of the line, flanked on either side by the riflemen and mortarmen of the 25th and 61st Battalions. The 25 pounders, about half a mile to the rear, lent their support, as did the P–40's from No. 1 Strip.

When the Japanese made their move against the airstrip, such intense fire hit them that not one man was able to cross the strip alive. The heaviest attack came before dawn. Like the others, it was repulsed with heavy loss to the enemy, who withdrew at first light, leaving 160 dead behind. [34]

The Withdrawal

The Japanese were now in full retreat, and Brigadier Wootten's 18th Brigade, the 2/12 Battalion leading, began the long-delayed task of clearing them from the north shore. Very heavy fighting developed at once along the Gama River and later near K. B. Mission. Between 1 and 5 September the Australians lost 45 killed and 147 wounded. Japanese losses were much heavier. At the Gama River alone, the enemy lost at least 100 killed, and his casualties mounted steadily as the Australians advanced. Hungry, riddled with tropical fevers, suffering from trench foot and jungle rot, and with many wounded in their midst, the Japanese realized the end was near; and Commander Yano, himself wounded, so advised the *8th Fleet*. [35]

[32] Comdr Milne Force, Rpt on Opns, 25 Aug–7 Sep 42. The 18th Brigade was, of course, less the 2/10 Battalion, which at this time was trying to find its way back to the head of the bay.

[33] Diary, owner unknown, in ATIS CT 1, No. 41, 63; Diaries, members *Kure 3d* and *Yokosuka 5th SNLF* in ATIS CT 4, Nos. 63, 65, 67; USSBS, *The Campaigns of the Pacific War*, p. 111; Naval Account Japanese Invasion Eastern New Guinea, pp. 25, 28; *17th Army Opns*, I, 51.

[34] Ltr, Capt Wood to Chief Engr, SWPA, 18 Sep 42, sub: Report of Participation in the Milne Bay Battle by U.S. Engr Troops in this Area; Memo, Gen Casey for Gen Sutherland, 25 Oct 42; Memo, Maj Adams for CG USASOS, 2 Nov 42, sub: Participation of U.S. Engr Troops in the Battle of Milne Bay; OCE SWPA, Draft Engr Rpt, 31 Dec 42; Unit Hist 709th AAA MG Bty; Comdr Milne Force, Rpt on Opns, 25 Aug–7 Sep 42; Naval Account Japanese Invasion Eastern New Guinea, pp. 26, 27; *Southeast Area* Naval Opns I, 21.

[35] Ltr, John Balfour, Office of the Official Australian War Historian, Canberra, to author, 8 Dec 50, in OCMH files; Comdr Milne Force, Rpt on Opns, 25 Aug–7 Sep 42; *Southeast Area* Naval Opns I, 21; Naval Account Japanese Invasion Eastern New Guinea, p. 27.

The commander in chief of the *8th Fleet,* Admiral Mikawa, considered the possibility of reinforcing the landing parties at Milne Bay with the 1,000-man advance echelon of the *Aoba Detachment,* which had finally reached Rabaul on 31 August. It was a sufficient force, he thought, to retrieve the situation if the troops ashore could hold out till it arrived. In an interchange of messages with Yano, Admiral Mikawa offered to land 200 more *Yokosuka 5th* troops immediately, and the *Aoba Detachment* by 12 September, if there was any possibility that the troops at Milne Bay could hold out till the *Aoba Force* arrived. When Yano told him that the troops ashore were physically incapable of making a further stand, Mikawa concluded the situation was hopeless and ordered Milne Bay evacuated.

The wounded were put on board ship on the night of 4 September. The rest of the landing force, except for scattered elements that had to be left behind, took ship the following night from the anchorage at Waga Waga one jump ahead of the 18th Brigade, whose forward elements were actually within earshot when the Japanese pulled out. Some 1,300 of the 1,900 troops landed were evacuated to Rabaul, nearly all of them suffering from trench foot, jungle rot, tropical ulcers, and other tropical diseases. Virtually none of the evacuees, not even those who landed as late as 29 August, were in condition to fight.[36]

The 2/9 Battalion, which was now leading the advance, met with only light and scattered resistance on the morning of 6 September. By the following morning it was clear that organized resistance had ceased. Small bands of stragglers were all that remained of the Japanese landing forces, and these were disposed of in the next few weeks by Australian patrols, which took only a handful of prisoners.

The Japanese lost some 600 killed in the operation, as against 321 Australian ground casualties—123 killed and 198 wounded.[37] American losses in defense of No. 3 Strip were very low—one man killed and two wounded.[38]

The timely return from the Solomons in early September of Task Force 44 made it possible thenceforward for the Allied Naval Forces to cover the sea approaches to Milne Bay;[39] and the dispatch, at approximately the same time, of two 155-mm. guns with attached searchlight units helped further to secure the area.[40]

The base was meanwhile being steadily improved. More and better roads were built. A new wharf was constructed to replace the old inadequate jetty. Number 1 Strip was

---

[36] Intercept, rad *COMCRUDIV 18* to *Comdr Japanese Troops, Milne Bay,* 3 Sep 42; Intercept, rad, *CINC 8th Fleet* to *Comdr Japanese Troops, Milne Bay,* 5 Sep 42; G–3 Opns Rpt No. 149, 4 Sep 42; GHQ Sitrep No. 356, 4 Sep 42. All in G–3 Jnl GHQ SWPA. Comdr Milne Force, Rpt on Opns, 25 Aug 42–7 Sep 42; AMF, Interr Gen Adachi *et al.; Southeast Area* Naval Opns I, 21–22; Naval Account Japanese Invasion Eastern New Guinea, p. 28.

[37] Ltr, Balfour to author, 8 Dec 50; Comdr Milne Force, Rpt on Opns, 25 Aug–7 Sep 42, AMF; Interr Gen Adachi *et al.; Southeast Area* Naval Opns I, 22; Naval Account Japanese Invasion Eastern New Guinea, p. 28.
[38] Ltr, Capt Wood to Chief Engr SWPA, 18 Sep 42, sub: Report of Participation in the Milne Bay Battle by U.S. Engineer Troops in this area; Memo, Maj Adams for CG USASOS, 2 Nov 42, sub: Participation of U.S. Engr Troops in the Battle of Milne Bay; Unit Hist 709th AAA MG Bty.
[39] Msg, Gen MacArthur to Gen Marshall, No. C–267, CM–IN 574, 28 Aug 42; Rad, COMSOPAC to CTF 61 *et al.,* 30 Aug 42, in SOPAC War Diary; Memo, Gen Sutherland for Admiral Leary, 4 Sep 42, sub: Employment of Naval Forces Southwest Pacific Area, in G–3 Jnl, GHQ SWPA.
[40] Memo, Gen Chamberlin for Gen Vasey, 10 Sep 42, sub: 155-mm. GPF Guns for Milne Bay, in 385, G–3, GHQ SWPA Files, in ORB RAC, AGO.

WHARF AT GILI GILI *built to replace old jetty.*

rebuilt, and No. 3 Strip was completed.[41] Bombing of Rabaul and of Japanese airfields in the northern Solomons without the need of crossing the Owen Stanleys became possible for the first time. Equally important the stage was set for a successful investiture of the north coast of Papua from East Cape to Buna.

The Allied victory at Milne Bay had snapped the southern prong of the pincers the Japanese had hoped to apply to Port Moresby. An essential part of the plan of 31 July had failed. The rest of the plan, the overland attack on Port Moresby by the *South Seas Detachment*, was now to be put to the test.

The Road to Ioribaiwa

General Horii Pushes the Australians Back

While the battle of Milne Bay was being fought, the Japanese on the Kokoda Trail were winning some of their most spectacular victories of the campaign. General Horii, who had left for the front on 22 August,

[41] OCE SWPA, Draft Engr Rpt, 31 Dec 42; Ltr, Gen Casey to author, 21 Jul 50. Number 2 Strip was never completed, for it was decided immediately after the battle to discontinue work on it and to concentrate instead on the other two fields.

had issued orders on the 24th for a general offensive. The attack began at dawn on 26 August and developed such power after a week of unremitting pressure that the Australians found themselves unable to stand firm with the forces at hand. They had no choice but to give ground. Not only were they heavily outnumbered, but their supply difficulties were greater than those of the Japanese who were supplied from nearby Kokoda and whose way, once their supply parties had reached the crest of the range, lay down, not up.

The enemy advance continued despite the mountain trail, the bitter resistance of the Australians, and the sustained bombing and strafing of Japanese supply lines by the Allied Air Force. By 7 September, the date organized resistance ceased at Milne Bay, the troops of the *South Seas Detachment* had made tremendous gains. They had driven the Australians from Isurava, Alola, Eora Creek, and Templeton's Crossing. They had gained possession of the Gap, had taken Myola, Kagi, and Efogi on the southern slopes of the range, and stood poised to take Menari, Nauro, and Ioribaiwa, the last villages between them and Port Moresby.[42] (*See Map II.*)

The Opposing Forces

General Horii had opened the attack with the *144th Infantry*, reinforced by elements of the *55th Mountain Artillery*, miscellaneous mortar and machine gun units, and the main body of the *15th Independent Engineers*. The artillery troops had left their

---

[42] *Nankai Shitai* Opns Order No. A–102, 24 Aug 42, in ATIS EP No. 33; ALF, Rpt on New Guinea Opns, Buna–Ioribaiwa; G–2 Daily Summaries Enemy Intel No. 166, 4–5 Sep 42, No. 167, 5–6 Sep 42, No. 168, 6–7 Sep. 42.

guns behind pending a study of how they were to be brought forward, and the engineers were advancing with the infantry troops, improving the track as they went. One of the two battalions of the *41st Infantry*, which had come in from Rabaul a few days before, joined in the attack on 28 August. The remaining battalion was held in reserve in the Kokoda area, where it helped out with supply. On the night of 2–3 September, approximately 1,500 Japanese reinforcements from Rabaul were landed safely at Basabua from a large convoy which managed to elude detection by the Allied Air Force. The reinforcements included the remaining battalion of the *41st Infantry* and the rear echelon of the *Nankai Shitai*—the *67th Line of Communications Hospital,* more service troops, and an "emergency" transport unit including vehicles and 300 pack horses. The incoming battalion was immediately ordered to the front and reached the scene of operations a few days later.

In contrast to General Horii's five reinforced battalions, the Australians, until Efogi was reached, never had more than three battalions in the forward area to oppose the Japanese advance. One of them was the depleted 39 Battalion, which had been in action for more than a month and should have been relieved long before. The Japanese, using continuous flanking operations, had no trouble driving the Australians back. Two regimental combat teams, one under command of Col. Masao Kusunose, commander of the *144th Infantry*, and the other under Colonel Yazawa, commander of the *41st Infantry*, alternated in pressing home the attack. They were thus able to outflank the Australians almost at will and, by bringing pressure to bear from different directions, to push them from one ridge after another.[43]

When the Japanese opened their offensive in late August, the only combat troops facing them were the 39 Battalion, 30th Brigade headquarters, and the 53 Battalion. Two battalions of the 21st Brigade, the 2/14 and 2/16 Battalions (which were to be followed by the third battalion, the 2/27), were on the way to the forward area but had not yet arrived. They began arriving company by company the following day, each company being thrown into battle as soon as it came up.

The fighting was desperate and the Australians, weighed down with heavy packs and cumbersome .303 rifles, outnumbered and repeatedly outflanked, suffered heavy casualties. The 2/14 Battalion relieved the 39 Battalion on 29 August, and the latter unit moved to the rear to reorganize, as did the 53 Battalion which had been badly cut up in the battle. From 1 September to 5 September the 2/14 and 2/16 Battalions, bearing the full brunt of the enemy attack, were under such heavy pressure that they were forced to withdraw through the Gap and take up positions on the other side of the range.[44]

The Australians found it impossible to make a stand, not only because they were outnumbered but also because they were running short of food and ammunition.

Their supplies had come either via native carriers or by airdrops, and neither carriers nor planes had been able to get enough supplies to them for more than hand-to-mouth operations. The forward supply system on the trail, which at best had operated only by fits and starts, collapsed completely when the Myola dropping grounds were lost, and the natives, demoralized by the Japanese advance, began to desert in large numbers.[45] Suffering from exhaustion, fever, and dysentery, the Australians had to pull back to a defensive position closer to their source of supply, from which, after being properly reinforced, they could hope to launch an effective counterattack.

The retreat was bitterly contested but, despite the enemy's superior strength, orderly. The enemy's losses were heavy, but the cost to the Australians, continuously in danger of being surrounded and overwhelmed if they held a position too long, were heavier still. When the 2/14 and 2/16 Battalions fell back on Efogi Spur on 6 September (where they joined the 2/27 Battalion which was already in position there), the 2/14 Battalion was at half-strength and the 2/16 Battalion only a company stronger.[46]

General MacArthur Plans a Turning Movement

All this time General Headquarters had been under the impression that Japanese

---

[43] ALF, Rpt on New Guinea Opns, Buna–Iori-baiwa; *Nankai Shitai* Opns Orders No. A–102, 24 Aug 42, n. n., 29 Aug 42, n. n., 30 Aug 42, No. A–112, 4 Sep 42, in ATIS EP No. 33; *17th Army Intel Summaries* No. 9, 22 Aug 42, No. 11, 26 Aug 42, No. 14, 29 Aug 42, No. 15, 30 Aug 42, No. 16, 31 Aug 42, No. 19, 3 Sep 42, in ATIS EP No. 28.

[44] ALF Daily Opns Rpt No. 138, 31 Aug 42; G–3 Opns Rpt, No. 147, 2 Sep 42; G–2 Daily Summaries Enemy Intel No. 165, 3–4 Sep 42, No. 166, 4–5 Sep 42; ALF, Rpt on New Guinea Opns, Buna–Ioribaiwa.

[45] ALF Daily Opns Rpt No. 141, 3 Sep 42; G–3 Opns Rpt No. 148, 3 Sep 42; G–2 Daily Summaries Enemy Intel No. 164, 2–3 Sep 42, No. 166, 4–5 Sep 42, No. 167, 5–6 Sep 42. White, *Green Armor*, pp. 189–208. White was with the troops at this time, and his account of the retreat is a vivid and compelling one.

[46] G–3 Opns Rpt No. 152, 7 Sep 42; Ltr, Gen Vasey, DCGS ALF, to Gen Chamberlin, 8 Sep 42, in G–3 Jnl, GHQ SWPA.

strength on the trail was slight, and that
the enemy had no real intention of advancing on Port Moresby.[47] It therefore did not
immediately understand the reason for the
swift Japanese advance. General Mac-
Arthur indeed found himself puzzled by the
situation. Being certain, he said, that the
Australians on the trail outnumbered the
Japanese, he had General Chamberlin ask
Allied Land Forces on 7 September for an
explanation of the repeated Australian withdrawals.[48]

The explanation came the next day from
General Rowell himself, and was communicated immediately to General Chamberlin.
General Rowell pointed out that, contrary to
the prevailing opinion at General Headquarters, his forces had been heavily outnumbered during the previous week's fighting. He added that the Japanese appeared
to have on the trail the maximum number
of troops that they could supply there.
While he was certain that he could regain
the initiative with the help of the 25th
Brigade, which was then disembarking at
Port Moresby, he felt that he would need
more troops later on in the operation. Because none of the CMF brigades at Port
Moresby seemed to have enough training
for the task, he asked that one of the two
6th Australian Infantry Division brigades
that had recently come in from Ceylon be
transferred to Port Moresby at once for
action on the trail.[49]

On 9 September the 16th Australian Infantry Brigade of the 6th Division was

GENERAL HARDING

ordered to Port Moresby, and the 25th
Brigade was rushed to the front.[50] Since there
now appeared to be sufficient Australian
troops to contain the Japanese advance,
General MacArthur began to plan a flanking movement by an American regimental
combat team which would cut in on the
enemy's rear and hasten his withdrawal
from the Kokoda–Gap area.

Choice of the unit was left to Maj. Gen.
Robert L. Eichelberger (then newly arrived
in Australia and soon to be promoted to
lieutenant general), to whom as Commanding General, I Corps, U. S. Army, the 32d
and 41st Divisions had been assigned on 5
September. General Eichelberger had already decided that the 32d Division would
precede the 41st to New Guinea. He made

[47] G–2 Daily Summaries Enemy Intel, No. 165,
3–4 Sep 42, No. 168, 6–7 Sep 42.

[48] Untitled Jnl Entry [Gen Chamberlin, Memo
for the Record, 1800, 7 Sep 42], 8 Sep 42, in G–3
Jnl, GHQ SWPA.

[49] Ltr, Gen Vasey to Gen Chamberlin, 8 Sep 42.
The incoming 6th Division units were the 16th and
17th Brigades. The 19th Brigade, it will be recalled,
was at Darwin where it had been since March.

[50] LHQ OI No. 33, 9 Sep 42; ALF, Rpt on New
Guinea Opns, Buna–Ioribaiwa.

this decision because the training camp of the 32d Division at Camp Cable near Brisbane was inferior to that of the 41st Division at Rockhampton. The general believed the 32d should go first because it would in any event have to be moved to another camp. After consulting with General Harding, commanding general of the 32d Division, and learning from him that the 126th Infantry under Col. Lawrence A. Quinn was the best-trained and best-led of his three regiments, General Eichelberger chose the 126th for the task.

The regiment was at once alerted for transfer to New Guinea. The men prepared for immediate movement, and, on General Eichelberger's orders, a Brisbane cleaning establishment began dyeing the men's fatigues a mottled green for action in the jungle.[51]

General MacArthur's plan of maneuver was ready on 11 September, and he communicated it at once to General Blamey, Commander Allied Land Forces, to whom I Corps had been assigned for operational control.[52] He was satisfied, General MacArthur wrote, that the dispatch of the 25th and 16th Brigades to Port Moresby would probably be sufficient to arrest any further forward movement of the Japanese toward Port Moresby, and ultimately to drive them back across the Owen Stanley Range. Since the Japanese were known to be extremely tenacious in holding ground once they had gained it, he believed that to force the Japanese back by direct attack along the Port

Moresby–Kokoda track alone would be a very slow business. To hasten a Japanese withdrawal, he had therefore ordered "a wide turning movement" by the 126th U. S. Infantry to cut in behind the Japanese at Wairopi. This, General MacArthur thought, could best be accomplished by an overland advance from Port Moresby, via Rouana Falls and the Mimani, Irua, Mugoni, and Kumusi Rivers, a route his staff had particularly recommended be used.[53]

The following day, Brig. Gen. Hanford MacNider, of the G–4 Section GHQ SWPA, who had been chosen by General MacArthur to make advance arrangements for the regiment's reception and march over the mountains, left for Port Moresby by air. General MacNider was accompanied by Lt. Col. Joseph S. Bradley, the 32d Division G–4 (who returned to Australia several days later), and members of Colonel Quinn's staff including Maj. Bernd G. Baetcke, his executive officer, Capt. William F. Boice, his intelligence officer, and Capt. Alfred Medendorp, the assistant S–4. Suitable arrangements were made by these officers for the reception of the troops, and two days later, 15 September, the first element of the 126th Infantry left Brisbane for Port Moresby by air, the men's fatigues still wet with dye.

The movement consisted of Company E, a medical officer, Capt. John T. Boet, four aid men, and an attached platoon of Company A, 114th Engineer Battalion. The detachment, 172 men in all, was under command of Capt. Melvin Schultz, commanding officer of Company E. These former National Guard troops, most of them from Big Rapids, Michigan, arrived at Port Moresby

[51] GHQ SWPA GO No. 30, 5 Sep 42; Interv with Maj Gen Edwin F. Harding, 9 Dec 47; Interv with Lt Gen Robert L. Eichelberger, 20 Nov 48. Both intervs in OCMH files. F. Tillman Durdin, "The Grim Hide and Seek of Jungle War," in *The New York Times Magazine,* 7 Mar 43.

[52] GHQ SWPA, GO No. 30, 5 Sep 42.

[53] Ltr, Gen MacArthur to Comdr ALF, 11 Sep 42, sub: Shipment, 126th Inf, 32d U.S. Div, to Port Moresby, in G–3 Jnl, GHQ SWPA.

32D DIVISION TROOPS *gathered to hear an address by General Harding, above; below, preparing to board a transport plane for New Guinea.*

from Amberley Field near Brisbane on the afternoon of 15 September, the first American infantry unit to set foot in New Guinea.[54]

General Harding had come down to Amberley Field to see the company off and, before it left, had given the men a little talk, in which he referred to them as "The Spearhead of the Spearhead of the Spearhead." Pleased with the general's happy phrase, Company E called itself thereafter, "The Three Spearheads." [55]

General MacNider's group had no sooner arrived at Port Moresby than it discovered that the route proposed by General MacArthur's staff for the advance to Wairopi was an impracticable one. Not only did it intersect the Australian rear and extend into an area where troops using it could be cut off by the Japanese, but it was so rough and mountainous that the only way to supply troops using it would be from the air. Consideration was then given to an alternative route—the eighty-five mile trail, Port Moresby–Kapa Kapa–Kalikodobu–Arapara–Laruni–Jaure. From Jaure lesser trails led to Wairopi and Buna. Little was known about the route for it had not been used in years. The coastal natives avoided it because they believed it to be haunted,

especially at the divide; and no white man had passed that way since 1917, a quarter of a century before. Although the route had the advantage that troops operating over it could be supported logistically by land and sea for about a third of the distance, it had also a very serious disadvantage—a 9,100-foot mountain crossing, which the Australians feared was impracticable for marching troops. General Rowell strongly opposed using it and favored an alternative route running from Abau to Jaure where the crossings were under 5,000 feet.

After thinking the matter over, General MacNider and his group decided to send a pathfinder patrol, under Captain Boice, to reconnoiter the Kapa Kapa–Jaure trail; and General Casey, who was at Port Moresby at the time, ordered his deputy, Col. Lief J. Sverdrup, to reconnoiter the Abau route.[56]

On 17 September, the same day that Colonel Sverdrup and a small party left for Abau to reconnoiter the route Abau–Debana–Namudi–Jaure (the Abau track), Captain Boice, accompanied by 1st Lt. Bernard Howes and six enlisted men of Company E, an officer of ANGAU, and forty native carriers, left Port Moresby for Kapa Kapa by lugger to begin the reconnaissance of the track leading from that point to Jaure. The rest of Company E and its attached medical personnel and engineer platoon were moved out to help a company of the 91st U. S. Engineers construct a motor road from Tupeselei (a few miles southeast of Port Moresby) to Kapa Kapa, and thence

<hr>

[54] Ltr, Col Lawrence A. Quinn, CO 126th Inf, to CofS 1st Australian Corps (Brig Hopkins), 3 Oct 42, in 126th Inf Patrol Rpts Jnl, Buna–Papuan Campaign; Interv with Col Bernd G. Baetcke, 17 Nov 50, in OCMH files; 32d Div AAR, Papuan Campaign; 126th Inf CT AAR, Papuan Campaign. All AAR's and other combat records of the 32d Division and its organic and attached units are in DRB HRS, AGO. E. J. Kahn, Jr., "The Terrible Days of Company E," *The Saturday Evening Post,* January 8, 1944, pp. 9–10.

[55] Kahn, "The Terrible Days of Company E," *The Saturday Evening Post,* January 8, 1944, pp. 9–10. The allusion was, of course, to the fact that company E was the spearhead of the 126th Infantry, and the 126th Infantry in its turn was to be the spearhead of the division and corps.

[56] Special Abau Reconnaissance Party, MAPLE, Orders No. 1, 16 Sep 42, in AFPAC Engr File; Memo, Brig Gen Hanford MacNider for Gen Whitlock, 17 Sep 42, copy in OCMH files; Interv with Col Baetcke, 17 Nov 50; Maj Alfred Medendorp, The March and Operations of the Antitank and Cannon Company (32d Inf Div) in the Attack on Wairopi, 4 Oct–28 Nov 42, Infantry School Monograph, copy in TIS Files.

to a rubber plantation at Cobaregari near Kalikodobu where an advanced base was to be established. The opening of the road Tupeselei-Kapa Kapa-Kalikodobu, as General McNider explained, would allow the advance base near Kalikodobu, nicknamed "Kalamazoo," to be supplied both by road and by water and would remove entirely the need for air supply until the mountains were reached.[57]

The main body of the regiment was now ready to move. The combat team, less artillery—180 officers and 3,610 enlisted men—took ship for New Guinea on 18 September. Colonel Quinn, who had been at Brett's Wharf, Brisbane, to see his men off, arrived at Port Moresby by air on the 20th, accompanied by two of his staff officers, Maj. Simon Warmenhoven, the regimental surgeon, and Capt. Oliver O. Dixon, the regimental S-3, and reported at once to General Rowell.

The regiment reached Port Moresby in convoy on 28 September to find that the 128th Regimental Combat Team, also less its artillery, was already there, having completed its move to Port Moresby by air five days before. The two American regiments, each with attached division engineer, medical, and signal troops were parceled out on arrival to different Australian commands.[58] The 128th Infantry, commanded by Col. J. Tracy Hale, Jr., was assigned to the Port Moresby garrison force, and, as such, came

under the operational control of Headquarters, 6th Australian Infantry Division, which was then in charge of Port Moresby's ground defense. It relieved the 808th Engineer Aviation Battalion (which had been pulled from its normal airfield construction duties and given a combat role) and took up a defensive position along the Goldie River, north of Port Moresby. The 126th Infantry and attached troops were assigned directly to New Guinea Force for use in the advance on Wairopi. They went into bivouac at Bootless Inlet and were for the time being kept in garrison reserve.[59]

The reason for the swift and dramatic movement to New Guinea by air of the 128th Infantry (the greatest that the Air Force had undertaken up to that time) soon became obvious. It lay in the continued advance along the Kokoda Trail of General Horii's troops. Not only did Horii still have the initiative, but he seemed to be threatening Port Moresby as it had never been threatened before.

The Japanese Take Ioribaiwa

When General Horii attacked Efogi spur on 8 September, he had five reinforced battalions of infantry in action. The 21st Brigade, on the other hand, was down to nine companies, and only four of them (the four companies of the 2/27 Battalion) had fresh troops. Exploiting their numerical superiority, the Japanese first struck the 2/27 Battalion, cutting it off from the balance of

[57] Memo, Gen MacNider for Gen Whitlock, 17 Sep 42; Rad, Gen MacNider for Gen Whitlock, 5th AF, No. S-136, 17 Sep 42; Rad, Col Matthews, U. S. Adv Base, New Guinea, to CG USASOS, 18 Sep 42. Both rads in 384, G-3 Files, GHQ SWPA. Ltr, Col L. J. Sverdrup to Gen Casey, 19 Sep 42, sub: Rpt No. 1, in AFPAC Engr File; 126th Inf CT AAR, Papuan Campaign; AGS SWPA Terrain Study No. 28, Main Routes Across New Guinea, 18 Oct 42, pp. 49-54, 56-58.

[58] Ltr, Col Quinn to Brig Hopkins, 3 Oct 42; 107th Med Bn AAR, Papuan Campaign.

[59] Ltr, CINC SWPA to Comdr ALF et al., 17 Sep 42, sub: Troop Movement Dir No. 1; LHQ OI No. 35, 17 Sep 42; NGF OI No. 30, 19 Sep 42; Msg, Gen Casey to Gen MacArthur, No. 737, 18 Sep 42; Msg, Gen MacArthur to Gen Casey, No. C-561, 19 Sep 42. All in G-3 Jnl, GHQ SWPA. 126th Inf CT AAR, Papuan Campaign; 128th Inf AAR, Papuan Campaign.

MAROUBRA Force, then pushed the unit completely out of the fight by forcing it off the trail. Another Japanese column struck elements of the 2/14 and 2/16 Battalions echeloned along the trail in rear of the 2/27 positions, established a trail block, and isolated 21st Brigade headquarters and a company from the 2/14 Battalion. With control lost, the command group and the Australian infantrymen fought their way through the block and with the rest of the 2/14 Battalion withdrew through the 2/16 Battalion to Nauro by nightfall on 9 September. General Horii had meanwhile called in his reserve, the *3d Battalion, 41st Infantry.* After its arrival in the front lines about 12 September, the Japanese had two full infantry regiments on the trail, depleted in strength but with engineer and other attached troops, a force of at least 5,000 men.[60]

The 2/14 and 2/16 Battalions, now with a combined strength of 320 men and fighting as a composite battalion, yielded Nauro and fell back to an east-west ridge north of Ioribaiwa during 10–11 September. Already established on the ridge were the 2/1 Pioneer Battalion and the 3 Battalion, 14th Brigade (which had come up from Port Moresby ahead of the 25th Brigade). The 2/31 and 2/33 Battalions, the leading elements of the 25th Brigade, under Brig. Kenneth W. Eather, reached Ioribaiwa on 14 September and attempted to drive past

both flanks of the Japanese position. When these flanking movements were met by a strong counterthrust that pierced the Australian line, a further withdrawal was ordered to the Imita Range, a strong defensive position, a full day's march from Ioribaiwa, and separated from it by the deep valley of Ua-Ule Creek.

The Japanese reached Ioribaiwa on 16 September and took up a position there. The Allied situation was not as difficult as it seemed. The Australians, then only one pack stage away from Uberi, their main rearward supply base, were finally in position to counterattack.[61]

The Japanese supply situation had by this time become impossible. That this was the case was in large part due to General Kenney, who had taken command of the Allied Air Forces on 4 August. The Fifth Air Force, the American element of the Allied Air Forces, which Kenney in the interests of greater operational efficiency had established as a separate command in early September,[62] had completed disrupted Japanese

---

[60] G–2 Daily Summaries Enemy Intel No. 170, 8–9 Sep 42, No. 171, 9–10 Sep 42, No. 172, 10–11 Sep 42: Lanops Bul No. 30, 9 Sep 42, in G–3 Jnl, GHQ SWPA; ALF, Rpt on New Guinea Opns, Buna–Ioribaiwa; *Nankai Shitai* Opns Order No. A–115, 11 Sep 42, in ATIS EP No. 33; Diary, Actg Comdr *No. 2 MG Co, 2d Bn, 144th Inf,* in ATIS CT 29, No. 358. The figure, 5,000, is of course an approximation, but it appears reasonably clear from captured enemy records that General Horii's front-line force, even allowing for heavy losses, and the diversion of part of its strength to supply duties, was at least 5,000 strong at the time.

[61] G–2 Daily Summary Enemy Intel No. 174, 12–13 Sep 42; ALF Daily Opns Rpt No. 156, 17 Sep 42; ALF Rpt on New Guinea Opns, Buna–Ioribaiwa; NGF, Rpt on Opns in New Guinea Opns, Ser 3.

[62] Msg, Gen Kenney to Gen Marshall, No. A–201, CM–IN 1752, 4 Aug 42; Fifth Air Force GO No. 1, 3 Sep 42. When he established the Fifth Air Force, General Kenney drew a clear line of demarcation between its responsibilities and those of the RAAF. Thus, while the Fifth Air Force became responsible for operations in the Northeast Area, the RAAF took over the responsibility for defense of the Australian continent and particularly of the Darwin area. In practice, the Fifth Air Force always had the support of Australian squadrons in its operations to the northeast of Australia, and the RAAF in turn was repeatedly reinforced by Fifth Air Force units, especially at Darwin, which was still under regular Japanese air attack. From Darwin, in turn, attacks were being mounted on strategic points in the Netherlands Indies. AAF, Air Actn in Papua, 21 Jul 42–23 Jan 43, pp. 51–52, copy in USAF Hist Off.

BRIDGE AT WAIROPI. *Note bombed-out portion of bridge and bomb craters in area. (Photograph taken on 1 October 1942.)*

supply. The advance echelon of the air force at Port Moresby, under General Kenney's deputy commander, Brig. Gen. Ennis P. Whitehead, was doing a magnificent job of pulverizing Japanese lines of communication. After considerable experimentation it had been found that the A–20 bomber, modified to carry eight forward machine guns and using a parachute fragmentation bomb invented by General Kenney himself, was particularly effective in low-level attacks on Japanese supply trains, dumps, and landing barges. The runway at Buna and the suspension bridge at Wairopi were under almost continuous attack. As fast as the Japanese naval construction troops at Buna filled in the runway, the Fifth Air Force would see to it that it was pitted again; and efforts of the *15th Independent Engineers* to keep the Wairopi Bridge in use were being continually set at naught by Fifth Air Force and attached RAAF units that would roar in at low levels to demolish it. Because of the relentless air attack, Japanese supply trains were virtually forced off the trails.[63] Food, as a result, though still available to the Japanese in the rear areas, was not getting through to the front lines. Whole battalions of the *South Seas Detachment* were foraging everywhere along the trail for food. Native gardens along the line of march were being stripped of sugar cane, taro, yams, pumpkins, melons, and everything else that was edible, but there was not enough food in that poor upland area to feed such a host for long. By September the front-line ration was down to less than a cupful of rice per day. By 17 September, the day after the Japanese seizure of Ioribaiwa, with the beach at Port Moresby almost visible from the height on which the Japanese found themselves, there was not a grain of rice left on the ridge for issue to the troops.[64]

General Horii's Orders Are Changed

When he first opened his offensive on 26 August, General Horii's objective had been Port Moresby. The deterioration of the situation at Milne Bay, and the difficulty of getting troops ashore at Guadalcanal in the face of Allied naval and air forces operating in the Solomons area, caused General Hyakutake on 29 August to instruct General Horii to halt the *South Seas Detachment* as soon as it had reached the southern foothills of the Owen Stanley Range. The advance was not to be resumed, he was told, until such time as Milne Bay had been taken and the Guadalcanal operation was progressing satisfactorily. *Imperial General Headquarters* concurred in these orders and two days later directed that General Horii go on the defensive as soon as he had crossed the Owen Stanley Range.[65]

Upon receipt of these instructions, General Horii had pressed through the Gap, looking for a defensible position on the other side of the range which he could hold until he was ordered to resume the advance on Port Moresby. Horii's first choice had been Nauro, but after sending out a reconnaissance party forward of Nauro he chose Ioribaiwa as the place to make his stand. The day after its seizure the troops holding it were told that they were to wait there until the middle of the following month, when it was expected that the final push against Port Moresby would be undertaken.[66]

[63] Photo Intel Rpts Buna Runway, Ser 242, 4 Sep 42, Ser 245, 10 Sep 42, Ser 247, 13 Sep 42, in AFPAC Engr File; Allied Air Forces Opns Rpt, 11 Sep 42, 17 Sep 42; G–3 Opns Rpt No. 159, 14 Sep 42; GHQ Sitreps No. 365, 11 Sep 42, No. 370, 17 Sep 42, in G–3 Jnl, GHQ SWPA; GHQ SWPA GO No. 34, 15 Sep 42; *17th Army* Intel Rpt No. 36, 23 Sep 42; USSBS, *The Fifth Air Force in the War Against Japan* (Washington, 1947), p. 27.

[64] *Nankai Shitai* Directions Regarding Economy in the Use of Ammunition and Provisions, 1 Sep 42; *Nankai Shitai* Bul Instns, 6 Sep 42; *Nankai Shitai* Instns Concerning Provisions and Forage, 10 Sep 42; *Nankai Shitai* Bul No. 3, 13 Sep 42. All in ATIS EP No. 33. *17th Army* Intel Rpt, No. 33, 18 Sep 42, in ATIS EP 28; Diary, Actg Comdr No. 2 MG Co, 2d Bn, 144th Inf, in ATIS CT 29.

[65] Ltr, Gen Willoughby to Gen Ward, 12 Apr 51; Hist Rec, *Army Section Imperial General Headquarters*, p. 62; *17th Army* Opns, I, 49, 54, 55; *Southeast Area* Naval Opns I, 19.

[66] *Nankai Shitai* Opns Order No. A–116, 12 Sep 42; Memo, Bde Med Dept to Med Offs *41st Inf*, 12 Sep 42, sub: Matters Relating to Health During the Period of Waiting; *Nankai Shitai* Bul No. 3, 13 Sep 42. All in ATIS EP No. 33. Diary, Actg Comdr No. 2 MG Co, 2d Bn, 144th Inf.

On 20 September General Horii called together his commanders at a hill near his headquarters at Nauro and told them how things stood. He praised them for the way in which they and their men had succeeded in crossing "the so-called impregnable Stanley Range," and explained that the reason for the halt was to regain their fighting strength, so as to be able, at the proper time, "to strike a crushing blow at the enemy's positions at Port Moresby." [67] How this was to be done with the existing state of supply was not explained.

Shortly after General Horii had ordered his subordinate commanders to hold Ioribaiwa he received, as a result of further Japanese reverses at Guadalcanal, instructions which in effect ordered his withdrawal from Ioribaiwa. The *Kawaguchi Detachment,* which had finally reached Guadalcanal in late August, was virtually wiped out on the night of 13–14 September, in the Battle of Edson's or Bloody Ridge. The Japanese were thus left without an effective striking force on the island.[68] Because of this new reverse, and the complete failure of the Milne Bay operation, *Imperial General Headquarters* felt impelled once again to revise its operational plan for Port Moresby. On 18 September new orders were issued which emphasized that everything was to be subordinated to the retaking of Guadalcanal. Existing positions in New Guinea were to be held as long as possible, but the *South Seas Detachment* was to be absolved

of the responsibility of maintaining itself indefinitely in the southern foothills of the Owen Stanley Range. Instead, it was to begin preparations at once for the defense of the Buna–Gona beachhead, which it was to hold as its primary defensive position until again ordered to advance.

By concentrating on the Guadalcanal operation and ordering the *South Seas Detachment* back from the southern foothills of the range to the more easily defended beachhead, *Imperial General Headquarters* could still hope to retrieve the situation in both the Solomons and New Guinea. It was now planned that, as soon as Guadalcanal was retaken, the forces committed to that operation would be diverted to New Guinea. A part would seize Milne Bay and then, in accordance with the original plan, would move on Port Moresby by sea. The rest would be used to reinforce the *South Seas Detachment,* which, at the proper time, would sally forth from the beachhead, recross the mountains, and, in spite of all previous reverses, complete the Port Moresby operation in concert with the forces coming in from Milne Bay.[69]

Complying with his new instructions, General Horii began at once to prepare for an orderly withdrawal that would commit a minimum number of troops while allowing the forces to the rear the maximum possible time to reinforce the beachhead. He left the *1st* and *3d Battalions* of the *144th Infantry* at Ioribaiwa and two companies of the *1st Battalion, 41st Infantry,* immediately to the rear at Nauro. The remaining battalion of the *144th Infantry*

[67] An Address of Instruction by General Horii at a hill west of Wamai (Nauro), 20 Sep 42, quoted verbatim in Diary, Actg Comdr *No. 2 MG Co, 2d Bn,* 144th Inf.

[68] *17th Army Opns,* I, 39, 43, 54, 55, 59, 60; Miller, *Guadalcanal: The First Offensive,* pp. 116–119, 126.

[69] Hist Rec, *Army Section Imperial General Headquarters,* pp. 62, 63; *17th Army Opns,* I, 54, 55, 59 60; *Southeast Area* Naval Opns I, pp. 24, 25.

and supporting troops General Horii ordered to Isurava. The main body of the *41st Infantry*, less the two companies at Nauro and a company at Kokoda, was ordered to the Sanananda–Giruwa coastal area.[70] General Horii's instructions to the main body of the *144th Infantry* were that it was to hold Ioribaiwa as long as possible and then retire northward to be relieved at the proper time by the troops in the Kokoda–Isurava area. As the latter fell back, they would be relieved in turn by troops from the beachhead.

On 24 September, the day the *2d Battalion, 144th Infantry*, was pulled out of the line and sent to Isurava, the *3d Battalion, 41st Infantry*, reached Giruwa. It was followed in a few days by the main body of the *41st Infantry*, under Colonel Yazawa. The naval garrison and the airfield at Buna were under the command of Navy Capt. Yoshitatsu Yasuda, who had come in from Rabaul on 17 September with 280 *Yokosuka 5th SNLF* troops. Colonel Yazawa took over command in the Giruwa coastal area, where were to be found the main Japanese supply dumps and the most important medical installation, the *67th Line of Communications Hospital*. Work on beachhead defenses was well under way by 23 September. There were several thousand service troops in the rear area to do the job, and as each new increment of troops reached the coastal area it joined with the others in building bunkers, emplacing guns, clearing fields of fire, and otherwise preparing the beachhead for defense.[71]

The Australians Take the Offensive

Allied Land Forces lost no time in taking the offensive. On 23 September General Blamey, Commander ALF, arrived at Port Moresby and took over command of New Guinea Force. Lt. Gen. Edmund F. Herring, succeeding General Rowell, became Commander, Advance New Guinea Force.[72] On 26 September, after aggressive patrol action to fix the enemy's position, and a short preparation which included an artillery bombardment by two 25 pounders brought up from Uberi, the 25th Brigade began an all-out attack on Ioribaiwa, taking it with relative ease two days later.

The Japanese had put up only token resistance. Instead of making a stand, they had abandoned their elaborate positions on Ioribaiwa Ridge almost on contact, and had retreated so swiftly up the trail that the Australians, who took up the pursuit, were unable to keep up with them.[73] Like the attempt to take Milne Bay, the Japanese overland offensive had collapsed.

---

[70] *17th Army* Intel Rpts No. 36, 23 Sep 42, No. 38, 24 Sep 42, No. 39, 26 Sep 42, in ATIS EP 28; Diary, Actg Comdr *No. 2 MG Co, 2d Bn, 144th Inf; Yazawa Det* Bivouac Order, 1 Oct 42, Eastern Giruwa, in Fld Staff Diary, Medical Capt Fukunobu Okabu, in ATIS EP 24.

[71] Log, *Yokosuka 5th SNLF*, 28 May–29 Sep 42, in ATIS CT 26, No. 309; Diary, member *Yokosuka 5th SNLF*, in ATIS CT 22, No. 269; *17th Army* Intel Rpts, No. 36, 23 Sep 42, No. 39, 25–26 Sep 42, No. 40, 27–30 Sep 42, in ATIS EP 38; *Yazawa Det* Bivouac Order, 1 Oct 42, in ATIS EP 24; Diary, Actg Comdr *No. 2 MG Co, 2d Bn, 144th Inf.*

[72] Comdr ALF, Rpt on Opns, 23 Sep 42–22 Jan 43, in G–3 Jnl, GHQ SWPA; Rpt of CG Buna Forces on the Buna Campaign, 1 Dec 42–25 Jan 43, p. 45, in DRB HRS, AGO. Upon General Blamey's return to Australia, command of New Guinea Force would revert to General Herring.

[73] ALF Opns Rpts No. 164, 25 Sep 42, No. 165, 26 Sep 42; G–2 Daily Summary Enemy Intel, No. 187, 25–26 Sep 42; G–3 Opns Rpt, No. 190, 28–29 Sep 42; ALF, Rpt on New Guinea Opns, 23 Sep 42–22 Jan 43.

CHAPTER VII

The Advance on the Beachhead

The Japanese had again done the unexpected. Instead of holding Ioribaiwa tenaciously as General MacArthur had assumed they would, they had thinned out their lines and withdrawn after the opening encounter. Their withdrawal, if unexpected, nevertheless enabled GHQ for the first time in the campaign to issue a comprehensive plan on 1 October looking to the envelopment and destruction of the enemy at the Buna–Gona beachhead. This plan and the more detailed instructions of 11 October

provided for the recapture of Goodenough Island and stipulated that the troops available to the Commander, New Guinea Force, would move on the beachhead along three axes of advance: along the Kokoda Trail; via the Kapa Kapa–Jaure track or the Abau–Namudi–Jaure route; and up the coast northwestward from Milne Bay. (*Map 6*) The advance would be in two stages. The troops moving overland would, before any further advance, secure the line of the Kumusi River from the Owalama

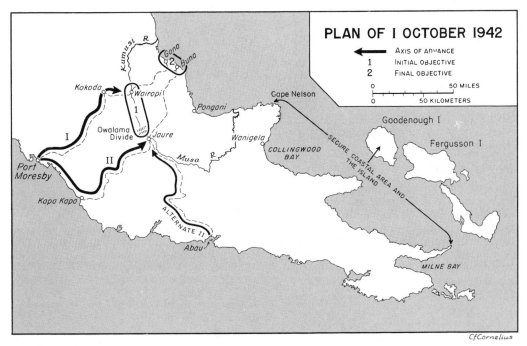

CfCornelius

MAP 6

Divide (north of Jaure) to the crossing of the Buna–Kokoda track at Wairopi. Those moving up from Milne Bay would first secure Goodenough Island and the coastal area to the northward as far as Cape Nelson. When these areas were secured, a concerted advance by all land forces upon the Buna–Gona area would be ordered.[1]

The Approach to the Target

General MacArthur
Explains the Plan

Because General MacArthur always had to consider the possibility that the Japanese might succeed in retaking Guadalcanal, and that they would then throw all their available forces into New Guinea, the plan had been so drawn that his troops could be extricated should they be met by overwhelming force or should their supply lines by sea or across the mountains fail. Emphasizing that the situation in the Solomons had "a direct and vital bearing upon our operations," General MacArthur explained the basic reason for the provision in the Operation Order of 1 October which required that the line of the Kumusi River be secured in preparation for "an offensive against the north coast of New Guinea to be executed upon order from General Headquarters."

. . . the successful employment, [he wrote] of any considerable number of troops on the north shore of New Guinea is entirely dependent upon lines of communication. The enemy has complete control of the sea lanes, and we are not now, nor have any reasonable expectation of being in position to contest that control. In consequence, although we shall employ shipping to the maximum extent possible

in the supply of our troops, our fundamental plans are limited by the fact that the enemy can cut that line at will, even with so small a force as a few torpedo boats. . . .

The general continued:

. . . It must be contemplated that any organization engaged on the north shore of New Guinea must be ready and able to withdraw successfully across the mountains with only such supplies as can be made available by air and by native carriers. A local success attained at a time when the enemy is devoting his attention to the Solomons, must not blind us to the fact that basic conditions which have heretofore limited our action in New Guinea are unchanged, and that in the absence of secure lines of communication on the north coast of New Guinea we still are unable to maintain large forces there. In consequence, our advance must be so planned that if supply lines fail, or if we are met by overwhelming forces, we can withdraw to our previously occupied defensive positions.

It was with an eye to such an eventuality that Colonel Sverdrup (who had meanwhile reported adversely on the Abau–Jaure track) had again been sent to New Guinea with instructions to discover and develop landing strips and dropping grounds in the area beyond the mountains north of Abau.[2]

General MacArthur's purpose was clear. The risks of the advance would be counterbalanced by a secure line of retreat. If the

---

[1] GHQ SWPA OI No. 19, 1 Oct. 42; Plan of Commander, ALF in New Guinea, 11 Oct. 42, copy in OCMH.

[2] Ltr, Gen MacArthur to Gen Blamey, 20 Oct 42, in 384, G–3 Files, GHQ SWPA. Sverdrup, who had just returned to Australia, had found the track extremely difficult for marching and out of the question for use by either jeeps or pack animals. On 14 October GHQ, which had expected to send the 127th Infantry over it, canceled all plans for its use as an axis of advance to the battlefield. Msg, Gen MacArthur to Gen Blamey, No. C–667, 27 Sep 42; GHQ SWPA Troop Dir No. 5, 30 Sep 42; GHQ SWPA OI No. 20, 14 Oct 42; Msg, Gen MacArthur to Gen Blamey, No. C–8533, 14 Oct 42. All in G–3 Jnl, GHQ SWPA. Memo, Gen Casey for Gen Sutherland, 3 Oct 42, sub: Summary of Findings and Recommendations pertaining to Abau Project, in 384, G–3 Files, GHQ SWPA.

maneuver for whatever reason turned out badly, it would at least be possible to extricate the forces and use them to fight again under more favorable circumstances.

Logistic Preparations

As preparations for the offensive gathered momentum, a much-needed consolidation of Australian and U. S. supply services in New Guinea was effected. On 5 October General Headquarters established the Combined Operational Service Command (COSC). The new command was to operate under New Guinea Force and to control all Allied line of communications activities in Australian New Guinea. Brig. Gen. Dwight F. Johns, U. S. A., Deputy Commander, United States Army Services of Supply, was designated its commander, and Brig. V. C. Secombe, Australian Staff Corps, became his deputy. All Australian and U. S. supply elements in the forward area were placed under General Johns's command. In addition to carrying out routine service of supply functions, the new command took over control of a pool of small boats or luggers which were being assembled at Milne Bay for use in operations against Buna.[3]

Dock and port improvements at Milne Bay and Port Moresby were by this time well advanced. The acute shortage of engineer troops in the combat zone was being remedied by the transfer to New Guinea from Australia of all available engineer troops, a process that in the case of the U.S. engineers had begun in earnest in August. At Milne Bay, a permanent T-shape wharf to replace the previous makeshift

was finished in early October. At Port Moresby the half-mile causeway to Tatana Island was completed by the end of the month. The benefit to Allied logistics was very great. Several large ships could be unloaded simultaneously, where previously it had been possible to unload only one. A small tropical anchorage, capable initially of unloading and storing only 500 tons of cargo a day, had been transformed into a busy port which already had several times that capacity, and which ultimately would have a capacity nine times that figure. It was a noteworthy achievement, and one of which General Casey could well be proud.[4]

The airfield construction program was almost complete. With few exceptions, the airfields at both Port Moresby and Milne Bay were either finished or due to be completed shortly, and a 120-day supply level was being built up at both points.[5] A tremendous amount of construction still remained to be done in the forward area, but it could be completed concurrently with the offensive.

The Recapture of Kokoda

To marshal the troops and bring them in concerted fashion before their objective over the mountains and along the coast of a vast,

---

[3] Ltr, CINCSWPA to Comdr ALF, 5 Oct 42, sub: Establishment of an Operational Service Comd in New Guinea, in G–3 Jnl, GHQ SWPA; ALF, Rpt on New Guinea Opns, 23 Sep 42–22 Jan 43.

[4] Msg, Gen Casey to Gen MacArthur, No. 540, 14 Sep 42; Msg, Gen Casey to Gen Sutherland, No. 739, 18 Sep 42; Msg, Col Matthews, US Adv Base New Guinea, to CG USASOS, No. SR 39, 6 Oct 42. All in 826, G–3 Files, GHQ SWPA. Msg, Brig Gen Dwight F. Johns, CG COSC, to Gen MacArthur, No. RA 866, 30 Oct 42, in 385, G–3 Files, GHQ SWPA; Msg, MacArthur to Marshall, No. C–731, CM–IN 07247, 17 Oct 42.

[5] Msg, Col Matthews, Adv Base New Guinea, to CG USASOS, No. 712, 18 Sep 42; Msg, Gen MacArthur to Gen Blamey, No. C–667, 27 Sep 42; in G–3 Jnl, GHQ SWPA; Msg, ALF to G–3, GHQ SWPA, No. 044, 2742, in 385, G–3 Files, GHQ SWPA.

undeveloped, jungle-covered island like New Guinea was to be no easy task. The first drive, that along the Kokoda Trail, was already under way, with the Australians under Maj. Gen. Arthur S. Allen, General Officer Commanding, 7th Australian Infantry Division, in pursuit of the retreating Japanese. After abandoning Ioribaiwa, the latter had withdrawn through the Gap, and by 8 October were at Templeton's Crossing. (*Map III*) Entrenching themselves on high ground on either side of the entrance to Eora Creek Gorge, the Japanese, now principally troops of the *2d Battalion, 144th Infantry*, held for a week and then withdrew to Eora Creek. On orders of General Horii, who was then at Kokoda, the main body of the *144th Infantry* rejoined the *2d Battalion* on 17 October at Eora Creek where a further stand was made.[6]

The Japanese had suffered heavy losses at the hands of the Australians and were being relentlessly bombed and strafed from the air by the Fifth Air Force. Their troops were suffering from beriberi, dysentery, lack of food, and some had already begun to practice cannibalism.[7] Yet they held to their positions tenaciously and could be dislodged only by frontal attack and the same flanking tactics that the Japanese themselves had used so effectively in the advance to Ioribaiwa.

The troops of the 25th Brigade, forced to scale the heights where the enemy troops were entrenched, pushed them out of one strongpoint after the other. The 16th Brigade, under Brig. John E. Lloyd, relieved the 25th Brigade on 20 October. Aided by the 25th Brigade's 2/31 Battalion, the fresh troops of the new brigade soon cleared the Japanese out of the Eora Creek area and, shortly thereafter, forced them out of Alola. The *144th Infantry* next fell back on Oivi where it was relieved on 29 October by a fresh force from the beachhead under command of Colonel Yazawa. The new force, a composite battalion of *41st Infantry* troops strongly reinforced with artillery and engineer elements, was ordered to dig itself in on the heights at Oivi and to hold its positions as long as possible in order to cover the movement of the *144th Infantry* across the Kumusi River. The *41st Infantry* troops, who had brought all the food and ammunition with them that they and hundreds of impressed Rabaul natives could carry, quickly dug themselves in on the heights and prepared for a major stand.

After a short rest the 25th Brigade had again gone into action, and it occupied Kokoda on 2 November. The Australian flag was raised there on that day by Maj. Gen. George A. Vasey, who had taken over command of the 7th Division from General Allen a few days before. With Kokoda airfield in Australian hands, and the 25th and 16th Brigades converging on Oivi, the pursuit was virtually over.[8] The troops along the first axis of advance had almost reached their objective.

---

[6] *Nankai Shitai* Opns Order "KO" No. 127, 14 Oct 42; "KO" No. 128, 15 Oct 42, in ATIS EP 39; Diary, Actg Comdr *No. 2 MG Co. 2d Bn, 144th Inf;* Comdr ALF, Rpt on New Guinea Opns, 23 Sep 42–22 Jan 43.

[7] Diary, Actg Comdr, *No. 2 MG Co. 2d Bn, 144th Inf.* This Japanese officer, then at Eora Creek, noted in his diary on 17 October, that his troops had been reduced to eating roots and grass, and, two days later, wrote that "because of the food shortage, some companies have been eating human flesh [Australian soldiers]."

[8] *Tomita Det* Bivouac Order No. 1, Giruwa, 25 Oct 42, in ATIS EP 24; *Nankai Shitai* Opns Orders "KO" No. 131, 26 Oct 42, "HEI" No. 11, 27 Oct 42, "KO" No. 132, 30 Oct 42, "KO" No. 133, 31 Oct 42, in ATIS EP 39; ALF, Rpt on New Guinea Opns, 23 Sep 42–22 Jan 43; Buggy, *Pacific Victory,* p. 190.

Securing the Coast

The problem still remained how to secure the coast from Milne Bay to Cape Nelson. Since there were then no landing craft in the theater, General MacArthur had issued orders in August that as many shallow-draft boats as possible be assembled at Milne Bay to serve the purpose.[9]

Planning for the move had scarcely begun when the possibility arose that Marine Corps troops would be made available for the task. The initiative had come from Admiral King, who ordered Admiral Nimitz on 8 September to release a regiment of trained amphibious troops to the Southwest Pacific Area. The 8th Marine Regiment was chosen for the task. Notified four days later by General Marshall that the regiment would be turned over to him by Admiral Ghormley on or about 1 October, General MacArthur began at once to plan for the use of the Marine unit in the coastal infiltration.[10]

General MacArthur did not get the Marine regiment. Admirals Nimitz and Ghormley had grave objections to releasing it and told Admiral King that this highly trained amphibious unit should not be used to do a job that General MacArthur's available troops in shallow-draft barges could probably do as well. Admiral King apparently considered the point well taken. The offer of amphibious troops was withdrawn, and General MacArthur was left with the task of securing the northeast coast of Papua as best he could from his own resources.[11]

By this time, it had become clear that to send the troops up the coast by boat would be both slow and dangerous. For one thing there were not nearly enough shallow-draft boats in sight to do the job properly; for another the route between Milne Bay and Cape Nelson and beyond Cape Nelson was strewn with uncharted reefs. Finally, as General Blamey observed to General MacArthur, to use the boats for the forward movement would not only delay the operation but might also result in the troops' meeting the same fate that befell the Japanese on Goodenough Island.

There was fortunately a better way. In July the local Australian authorities had cleared off and barricaded an airstrip at Wanigela Mission on Collingwood Bay, a point within easy marching distance of Cape Nelson. It became possible therefore to get the troops forward by air, and to use the boats to supply them from Milne Bay as soon as a clear channel could be charted through the reefs. The air force, which by this time had the space, undertook to fly the troops in, and a party of coastwatchers in the small motorship HMAS *Paluma* began charting the required clear-water channel to Cape Nelson.[12]

[9] Msgs, Gen MacArthur to Gen Marshall, No. Q–147, CM–IN 1607, 2 Aug 42, No. C–301, CM–IN 7017, 19 Aug 42; GHQ SWPA OI No. 15, 16 Aug 42.
[10] Msg, CINCPAC to COMSOPAC, No. 081736, 8 Sep 42, in Pac Strat File, Exec OPD File; Msg, Marshall to MacArthur, No. 1719, CM–OUT 4272, 12 Sep 42; Ltr, Gen Blamey to Gen MacArthur, 25 Sep 42; Msg, Gen MacArthur to Gen Blamey, No. C–667, 27 Sep 42. Both in G–3 Jnl, GHQ SWPA.
[11] Msg, Marshall to MacArthur, No. 2030, CM–OUT 7382, 22 Sep 42; Msg, MacArthur to Marshall, No. C–554, CM–IN 9987, 23 Sep 42; Msgs, COMSOPACFOR to COMINCH, 0800, 27 Sep 42, 0256, 29 Sep 42, Pac Strat File, OPD Files.
[12] Memo, Cols Sheehan and Larr, G–3 Sec SWPA, for Gen Chamberlin, 30 Jul 42, sub: Immediate Action Required in the Buna-Milne Bay Area; Memo, Gen Sutherland to Gen Blamey, 11 Aug 42, sub: Wanigela Mission; Ltr, Gen Blamey to Gen MacArthur, 25 Sep 42; Msg, Gen Blamey to Gen MacArthur, No. 1314, 1 Oct 42. All in G–3 Jnl, GHQ SWPA. AAF, Air Force Statistical Digest World War II, Tab 93, p. 170, copy in OCMH files; Feldt, *The Coast Watchers*, pp. 186–91.

The 2/10 Battalion of the 18th Brigade and attached U. S. engineer and antiaircraft troops were flown into Wanigela from Milne Bay on 5 and 6 October by the 21st and 22d Transport Squadrons of the Fifth Air Force. The troops immediately began securing the area and preparing it for the reception of more troops. By that time the *Paluma* had completed the charting of the channel to Cape Nelson, and the boats, laden with supplies, began moving forward to Wanigela from Milne Bay.[13]

General Blamey had planned to follow the 2/10 Battalion with the rest of the 18th Brigade as soon as the 17th Brigade (which was to replace it at Milne Bay) arrived there and the supply of the Wanigela area by sea was assured. To wait for the arrival of the 17th Brigade would have meant a considerable delay inasmuch as it was not due at Milne Bay until late October. General Blamey decided therefore to use the 128th Infantry (then still at Port Moresby) to reinforce the Wanigela garrison. By doing so, Blamey believed he would not only save time but would also help out the air force, which was reluctant to use the airfields at Milne Bay for troop movements because they were inferior to those at Port Moresby.[14]

On 13 October the 2/6 Independent Company and the 2d and 3d Battalions of the 128th Infantry were ordered to Wanigela by air, the 3d Battalion, under Lt. Col. Kelsie E. Miller, leading. The air move-

ments began next morning with the initial flights originating at Laloki airfield near Port Moresby. By 18 October, most of the regiment was at Wanigela. The Band, the Antitank Company, the Service Company, and two companies of the 1st Battalion had to be left temporarily at Port Moresby when the field at Wanigela became unusable because of heavy rains.[15]

Preliminary reconnaissance had indicated that there were excellent trails in the Wanigela–Cape Nelson area. It was therefore planned that the troops would march from Wanigela to Pongani, a point on the western shore of Dyke Ackland Bay, about thirty miles from Buna, which was known to be free of Japanese. The men of the Australian Independent Company, who were specially trained in jungle operations, were to go first, and the 3d, 2d, and 1st Battalions, 128th Infantry, were to follow in that order. The trail, which lay diagonally across the neck of the Cape Nelson Peninsula, was cut by the Musa River at Totore, a day's march from Wanigela, and reputedly the only good river crossing in the area.

It was soon discovered that the reconnaissance reports had been mistaken about the condition of the trails in the Wanigela-Pongani area. The river was rising rapidly and most of the trails in the area had been obliterated. Traveling with little but their rifles, the Australian commandos who left on the 14th as planned, managed to reach Pongani, but the heavily loaded 3d Battal-

[13] Memo, Gen Chamberlin for Gen Sutherland, 6 Oct 42; Ltr, Gen Blamey to Gen MacArthur, 7 Oct 42; Msg, Col Matthews to CG USASOS, No. SR 65, 7 Oct 42. All in G-3 Jnl, GHQ SWPA. AAF, Air Action in the Papuan Campaign, pp. 69–70; Feldt, *The Coast Watchers,* p. 190.

[14] Ltr, Gen Blamey to Gen MacArthur, 7 Oct 42; NGF OI No. 35, 8 Oct 42; Msg, Gen Blamey to Gen MacArthur, No. Z–29, 10 Oct 42. All in G-3 Jnl, GHQ, SWPA.

[15] Plan of Comdr Allied Land Forces in New Guinea As Arranged in Conf, 11 Oct 42; Ltr, Gen Harding to Gen Sutherland, 12 Oct 42; NGF OI No. 38, 13 Oct 42; Col J. Tracy Hale, Jr., Answers to Questions by Hist Sec, GHQ SWPA, As to Certain Phases of the Papuan Campaign. All in G-3 Jnl, GHQ SWPA. Ltr Col Miller to Gen Ward, 26 Mar 51; 128th Inf Hist of Papuan Campaign; 32d Div AAR, Papuan Campaign.

ion, only a day behind the Australians, was unable to get through. After floundering in knee-deep swamps, the men reached Totore on the afternoon of 16 October, and went into camp near by at Guri Guri, called by Colonel Miller "the most filthy, swampy, mosquito infested area" that he had ever seen in New Guinea.

A crossing by log raft was attempted at a nearby native village. Reconnaissance on the far side showed that a crossing there would put the battalion on the wrong route, and the project was abandoned in favor of a crossing farther upstream. On 18 October, 1,500 feet of cable was dropped from the air at Guri Guri. No tools, tie wire, clamps, or bolts were dropped with the cable. Company M, under Capt. Frank N. Williams, and a platoon of Company C, 114th Engineer Battalion, carried the cable, strung out by hand, to the upstream site and started establishing the crossing there.

Though still without tools, clamps, or tie wire, Captain Williams soon had a makeshift crossing over the Musa. It too was abandoned when ANGAU passed on the information that the trail leading out of the site was under seven feet of water, and impassable to anything except small boats and native canoes.

On 23 October Company M and the engineer platoon rejoined the 3d Battalion, which had been ordered from Guri Guri to Gobe, west of Porlock Harbor. The battalion was to be shuttled from Gobe to Pongani in such of the boats coming in with supplies from Milne Bay as could negotiate the treacherous waters around Cape Nelson. The 2d Battalion, which had been just behind the 3d on the Wanigela-Totore track, was ordered back to Wanigela, to be moved to Pongani by sea as soon as shipping was available. The elements of the 1st Battal-

ion present at Wanigela were to follow immediately, and the rest of the battalion was to be transferred to Pongani in the same fashion as soon as it reached Wanigela.[16]

The 3d Battalion marched overland from Totore to Gobe in two echelons, taking approximately four days for the move. Some of the men picked up malaria in the mosquito-infested swamps along the Musa, and the weakening effects of the march were apparent in the subsequent operations of the battalion.[17]

The coastal shuttle had meanwhile gone into operation, despite the fact that little was known at that time about the waters past Wanigela. The available information was that boats of up to twelve-foot draft could safely negotiate the coastal waters between Milne Bay and Wanigela, but that only small luggers or trawlers would be able to get around Cape Nelson because of submerged reefs in that area, some of them only a few feet from the surface. The plan for the shuttle was worked out accordingly. Large fishing boats of between 100 and 120 tons, loaded so as to draw not more than twelve feet of water, would bring the supplies forward from Milne Bay to Wanigela, and a flotilla of eight luggers with an aver-

---

[16] Ltr, Gen Blamey to Gen MacArthur, 18 Oct 42, in G–3 Jnl, GHQ SWPA; Ltrs, Gen Harding to Gen MacNider, Wanigela, 19 Oct 42 and 21 Oct 42; Ltr, Gen Harding to Gen Sutherland, 20 Oct 42; Memos, Gen MacNider for Gen Harding, 21 Oct 42 and 22 Oct 42, copies in OCMH files; Interv with Gen Chamberlin, 14 Jan 50; Ltr, Col Miller to Gen Ward, 27 Mar 51; Ltr, Col Miller to author, 7 Jan 52; 114th Engr Bn, Engr Opns in the Papuan Campaign; 128th Inf Hist of Papuan Campaign.

[17] Ltr, Col Alexander J. MacNab to Gen Ward, 7 Mar 51; Ltr, Col Miller to author, 7 Jan 52; Col Hale, Answers to Questions by Hist Sec, GHQ SWPA, as to Certain Phases of the Papuan Campaign; 128th Inf Hist of Papuan Campaign; 32d Div AAR, Papuan Campaign.

age displacement of about 20 tons, would carry them around Cape Nelson to Pongani. The larger boats were to be under control of the Combined Operational Service Command, while the luggers would come under command of Lt. Col. Laurence A. Mc-Kenny, Quartermaster of the 32d Division.[18]

The first two luggers reached Wanigela on 17 October and were at once sent forward to Pongani with men and supplies. Early the following morning, a Fifth Air Force B–25 mistook them for the enemy and bombed the boats off Pongani. Two men were killed: Lt. A. B. Fahnestock, in charge of small boat operations for the COSC, and Byron Darnton, a veteran correspondent of *The New York Times* who had served with the 32d Division during World War I, and had looked forward to reporting its operations in World War II. Several others were wounded, and one of the boats suffered such severe damage that it had to be withdrawn from the run.[19]

Despite this initial error, and the fact that the luggers did not operate during daylight to avoid being attacked by Japanese aircraft, the Wanigela–Pongani shuttle continued in successful operation through the rest of October. The few quartermaster troops under Colonel McKenny's command had a difficult time of it. There were no piers or jetties in the area and no lighters. To unload the luggers they had to pile the cargo on native outrigger canoes, rowboats, or canvas-sided engineer boats. Then, aided wherever possible by natives and tactical forces from the shore, they would take to the water and, stark naked, push the tiny craft through the breakers, unload, and go back again, making dozens of trips through the night without rest in order to be on their way again before daylight.[20]

These small seaborne supply and troop movements had their effect. By 2 November, the day the Australians retook Kokoda, the 128th Infantry, less only the elements still at Port Moresby, was at Pongani and Mendaropu and rapidly growing supply dumps had been established at both points.[21]

The discovery by the *Paluma* in early November that the larger vessels operated by the COSC could safely round Cape Nelson further increased the usefulness of the luggers. The bigger boats from Milne Bay began discharging their cargo at Porlock

---

[18] Msgs, Col Matthews to CG USASOS, No. SR 35, 6 Oct 42, No. SR 65, 7 Oct 42; Msg, Gen MacArthur to Gen Blamey, No. C–892, 18 Oct 42. All in 384, G–3 Files, GHQ SWPA. Msg, ALF to Milcomd, Moresby, No. QM 57797, 24 Oct 42, in 385, G–3 Files, GHQ SWPA; 32d QM Bn, Rpt on Activities, Papuan Campaign; 107th QM Det, Hist Papuan Campaign; Interv with Gen Harding, 29 Jun 49.

[19] Ltr, Lt Col Laurence A. McKenny, QMC, to Gen MacNider, n. d., sub: Report of attack by unidentified bomber at Pongani, New Guinea, 18 Oct 42, copy in OCMH files; Allied Air Force Opns Rpt, 2400, 18 Oct 42. In a letter to General Sutherland, General Harding had this to say of the blunder, "Everyone hereabouts is distressed over the death of Darnton and Fahnestock. I knew Darnton quite well . . . and considered him one damn good correspondent and swell guy. He was hot to be on the spot for the first contact of American Army ground troops with the Japs. I told him that this would probably be it and gave him permission to go." Ltr, Gen Harding to Gen Sutherland, 20 Oct 42, copy in OCMH files.

[20] 32d QM Bn, Rpt on Activities, Papuan Campaign; 107th QM Det, Hist Papuan Campaign; 32d Div AAR, Papuan Campaign; E. J. Kahn, Jr., *G. I. Jungle* (New York, 1943), p. 88.

[21] Msg, Gen Blamey to Gen MacArthur, No. Z–108, 2 Nov 42, in G–3 Jnl, GHQ SWPA; Msg, Col Matthews to CINCSWPA, No. P–48, 5 Nov 42, in 384, No. 2, New Guinea File, G–3 Files, GHQ SWPA.

COASTAL SHUTTLE OPERATIONS

Harbor, and the luggers, in turn, began shuttling between Porlock and Pongani.[22]

The Recapture of Goodenough Island

GHQ had ordered that, in addition to securing the coast between Milne Bay and Cape Nelson, the Commander, New Guinea Force, was to recapture Goodenough Island, a flanking position which in enemy hands could imperil the advance along the northeast coast of Papua. The task of taking the island went to the 2/12 Battalion of the 18th Brigade, then still at Milne Bay. The troops, in two destroyers, were landed on both sides of the island's southern tip on the night of 22–23 October and drove inland.[23]

There were some 290 Japanese on the island, sixty of the 353 troops of the Sasebo 5th SNLF who had been stranded there on 26 August having been evacuated to Buna by submarine before the Australians landed.[24] The submarine had brought in food and ammunition, and the remaining Japanese, well dug in, resisted tenaciously during the daylight hours of the 23d, but only to gain time. That night, the submarine came in again. Shuttling back and

forth through the night, it deposited 250 Japanese troops on nearby Fergusson Island, where they were picked up by a cruiser and taken to Rabaul. The few stragglers left behind on Goodenough were quickly mopped up by the Australians who at once took appropriate measures for the island's security.[25]

The March to Jaure

On the Kapa Kapa trail, meanwhile, Captain Boice and a small party were advancing toward Jaure and Major Baetcke, in command at "Kalamazoo," was building a forward supply base at Arapara, about thirty miles away by trail. Though the road was still unfinished, it was possible by this time for jeeps to travel over it as far as Nepeana, a distance of about fourteen miles. Over the remaining sixteen miles the track was so steep and so rough that native carriers had to be used to do the job. Supervised by ANGAU officers the natives were hard at work moving the supplies forward on their backs.[26]

The results of Captain Boice's reconnaissance were soon in. After being delayed at Laruni, about fifty miles out, because he had run out of rations and an airdrop that he had asked for had not materialized in time, Boice had finally reached Jaure on 4 October. Next day he reported by radio that the trail although taxing was practicable for marching. General Harding, who had moved the divisional CP to Kalamazoo,

[22] Msg, Gen MacArthur to CG USASOS, No. C–1065, 3 Nov 42, in 384, G–3 Files, GHQ SWPA; Memo, NOIC Port Moresby for NGF, 4 Nov 42, sub: Milne Bay to Buna Sea Route, in G–3 Jnl, GHQ SWPA; Interv with Gen Harding, 9 Dec 47.

[23] NGF OI No. 19, 1 Oct 42, and No. 39, 17 Oct 42; ALF, Rpt on New Guinea Opns, Goodenough Island and Milne Bay.

[24] AMF, Interr Gen Adachi et al.; Naval Account, Japanese Invasion Eastern New Guinea. An enemy diary captured at Buna recounts that since the Japanese troops stranded on Goodenough Island "were without provisions and communications facilities, three messengers were sent [to Buna] for help. Before departure, these three men burned their skin to look like natives. They accomplished their mission after covering more than 100 nautical miles in a canoe." Diary, member 15th Naval Pioneer Unit, in ATIS CT 14, No. 176.

[25] AMF, Interr Gen Adachi et al.; Naval Account, Japanese Invasion Eastern New Guinea, p. 27; ALF, Rpt on New Guinea Opns, Goodenough Island and Milne Bay.

[26] Memo, Col Quinn for Brig Hopkins, 3 Oct 42, sub: Report of Reconnaissance, Cobaregari–Jaure track, in 126th Inf CT Patrol Rpts Jnl; Interv with Col Baetcke, 1 Nov 50.

KAPA KAPA TRAIL, SEPTEMBER 1942

at once secured permission from New Guinea Force to send forward an advance echelon of the 126th Infantry. Except for Company E, at Nepeana, the regiment was then encamped at Bootless Inlet near Port Moresby. The advance unit was to be composed of the 2d Battalion, 126th Infantry, supported by troops of the regimental Antitank and Cannon Companies operating as riflemen, who were to go first.

The Antitank and Cannon Companies and a small medical detachment, all under the command of Captain Medendorp, left Kalikodobu for Nepeana en route to Jaure on 6 October. At Nepeana, Medendorp was to use forty-five men from Company E—a five-man communications detachment un-

der 1st Lt. James G. Downer and a forty-man rifle platoon under 1st Lt. Harold B. Chandler, Jr.—as his advance guard. The force as it left Kalikodobu numbered 250, with 100 natives attached. Medendorp's orders were to establish dropping grounds at Laruni and Jaure and to build up stocks of food and supplies there for the use of the main force when it began moving. By arrangement with the air force, the Band, Service, and Casual Companies were to load the planes and do the actual dropping.

Because the troops were fresh to the jungle, too heavily burdened, and not in top condition, the first day's march to Nepeana (where Company E was encamped) did not go well. Hearing that the troops had fared badly, General Harding, who reached Nepeana by jeep early the next morning to see the men off, gave orders that their packs be lightened and their ammunition cut down. In addition, he ordered the forty-five men detailed as advance guard to push ahead for Jaure "without regard to the progress of the other two companies. . . ." Lieutenants Downer and Chandler—Downer going first—were to come under command of Captain Boice upon their arrival at Jaure, where they were ultimately to be reunited with their company.[27]

The second day's march, through comparatively easy country, went off without difficulty. The next day when the foothills of the range were reached told a different story, especially for the troops of the Antitank and Cannon Companies. These men were in much poorer condition than the men of the advance guard, who had been longer in the area and had had a chance to toughen up while helping the engineers build the road to Nepeana.

As Medendorp recalls the situation:

The troops had no trail discipline. The hills were steeper. Footing was insecure. Leeches and insects began to be a nuisance. The trail was strewn with cast-off articles. Leather toilet sets, soap, socks, and extra underwear told a tale of exhaustion and misery. Upon reaching streams, the men would rush to them and drink, regardless of the fact that upstream some soldier might be washing his feet. The trail was filled with struggling individuals, many lying on one side panting for breath. The medical officer bringing up the rear,

reached the bivouac that night with a platoon of limping and dazed men. There were no stragglers however, for it was feared all through the march that stragglers might be killed by a Jap patrol.[28]

On the fourth day the troops reached Arapara, halfway to Laruni, and the last point which could be supplied from Kalamazoo.[29] The next day most of the native carriers deserted, and the weary troops were left to carry their rations and heavy supplies themselves.

After a hard uphill climb the Medendorp force reached Laruni, which was on a mountain top, on 13 October. The advance guard, traveling light and moving fast, was a day ahead. On 14 October, just as the Medendorp force began establishing a dropping ground at Laruni, the 2d Battalion, 126th Infantry, under the battalion commander, Lt. Col. Henry A. Geerds, began leaving Kalikodobu for Jaure. Attached was the 19th Portable Hospital and a platoon of the 114th Engineer Battalion. The force was almost 900 strong and had several hundred native carriers accompanying it. The companies were following each other at a day's interval, with Company E,

---

[27] Memo, Col Quinn for Brig Hopkins, 3 Oct 42, sub: Report of Reconnaissance, Cobaregari–Jaure track; Memo, Col Quinn for Gen Harding, 15 Oct 42. Both in 126th Inf CT Patrol Rpts Jnl. Ltr, Gen Harding to Gen Sutherland, 12 Oct 42; Maj Medendorp, The March and Operations of the Antitank and Cannon Companies, 126th Infantry, 4 Oct–28 Nov 42.

[28] Maj Medendorp, The March and Operations of the Antitank and Cannon Companies, 126th Infantry, 4 Oct–28 Nov 42.

[29] Just as the troops were settling themselves for the night, thirty-five men of the 21st Brigade, whom the Japanese had cut off on the Kokoda Trail almost a month before, staggered into camp. The Australians, starving, exhausted, and nursing old untreated wounds, were in a pitiful state. After they had been given food, and Capt. Lester Segal, the medical officer, had taken care of their wounds, they were directed to Kalamazoo, where, Colonel Baetcke recalls, twenty of the thirty-five had to be hospitalized immediately upon arrival. Ltr, Capt Medendorp to Col Quinn (by hand via Maj Baetcke), 9 Oct 42, sub: Daily Report, in 2d Bn, 126th Inf, Trail Opns Jnl; Interv with Col Baetcke, 17 Nov 50.

under Captain Schultz, leading, and Company F, under Lt. Erwin Nummer, immediately behind.

After leaving a forty-two-man detachment at Laruni to take care of the dropping ground, Medendorp pushed on to Jaure and reached it on 20 October, four days after Downer and Chandler got there. The next day, on orders of New Guinea Force, he sent a fifty-man detachment of the Cannon Company northeastward into the Kumusi River Valley. These men were to be joined immediately by the rest of the troops of the Antitank and Cannon Companies, in order to prevent a possible Japanese attack on Jaure from the Wairopi area.

The march was much more difficult for the 2d Battalion than for the troops with Boice and Medendorp because, while it had rained spasmodically during the first two weeks of October, the heaviest rains fell just as the battalion began leaving Kalikadobu. Beginning 15 October a steady downpour gave the men no respite through five days and five nights. Even after the elements abated a little, heavy rains during the afternoon and at night left the troops drenched and miserable.

The Owen Stanley divide at Mount Suwemalla (or, as the troops called it, "Ghost Mountain"), was a dank, eerie place a few days out of Laruni. It rose 2,000 feet higher than the Gap, and the terrain was, without qualification, rougher and more precipitous than that over which the Australians and Japanese were struggling further to the northwest. Captain Schultz reported that the trail was so narrow that "even a jack rabbit couldn't leave it." The troops had to march in single file, and there was usually no place on either side of the trail for a bivouac. In the jungle the men stumbled

over vines and roots with every step as they made their way through the muck and slime. The ever-present mud was sometimes so deep that the men sank into it up to their knees and had to have help in extricating themselves. The swollen mountain streams through which the men had to wade had currents of up to twenty miles per hour—sufficient to knock a man down during some of the crossings.

To follow the stream beds gave no relief. Not only were they cluttered with immense boulders but the streams became roaring torrents at a moment's notice, and the men had no choice but to take to the trail again.

Immense ridges, or "razorbacks," followed each other in succession like the teeth of a saw. As a rule, the only way the troops could get up these ridges, which were steeper than along the Kokoda Trail, was either on hands and knees, or by cutting steps into them with ax and machete. To rest, the men simply leaned forward, holding on to vines and roots in order to keep themselves from slipping down the mountainside.

Plunging down the face of one such ridge, the troops would find themselves faced with the towering slope of another only a stone's throw away. Four or five ridges—only a few miles as the crow flies—meant a day's march. The same troops that, in one instance, stumbled, slipped, or fell more than 2,000 feet in forty minutes on a downward slope took almost eight hours, most of it on hands and knees, to cover the last 2,000 feet of the 9,000-foot divide.

Profiting from the experience of Boice and Medendorp, the battalion had stripped for the march. Gas masks, helmets, mess kits, and heavy weapons had been left behind, and the ammunition load had been cut down. But so rough was the trail and so arduous the march that even the lightened packs proved too heavy. Piece by piece, the men discarded toilet articles, raincoats, shelter-halves, mosquito nets, and even blankets. As a result the troops, who were constantly at the mercy of chiggers, mites, mosquitoes, and leeches, spent their nights being cold as well as wet.[30]

The men had been poorly fed. They were, for the most part, on the Australian ration— hardtack, bully beef, and tea, supplemented by a little rice. Because the unceasing wet had made it virtually impossible for them either to heat the ration or to boil water for tea, most ate the food cold and threw away the tea. The bully beef (corned, preserved beef of Australian manufacture) came in large, four- or five-pound tins. It was not only unappetizing, it often had a revolting fish-oil taste that caused some of the troops to retch when they tried eating it. Many of the tins had become contaminated: some had been contused or sprung when they were dropped from the air; others had been left out in the open without cover and had rusted. This contamination, together with the impossibility of sterilizing the few eating utensils the troops had with them, and the tendency of the oversize cans of beef to spoil before they were completely consumed, had its effect. Acute diarrhea and dysentery gripped most of the battalion, and many of

the men had to cut holes in the seats of their trousers, so completely had they lost control of their bowel movements.[31]

The medical officers marching at the rear of the column did what they could for those who because of exhaustion, dysentery, and other ailments could not keep up. It was a great deal, and in the opinion of one who made the march, many members of the battalion owed their lives to these doctors who picked them up and cared for them when they were so sick and weak that "they were ready to call it 'quits' and die."[32]

The 1st Sergeant of Company E, Paul R. Lutjens, recalls the march in these words:

It was one green hell to Jaure. We went up and down continuously; the company would be stretched over two or three miles. We'd start at six every morning by cooking rice or trying to. Two guys would work together. If they could start a fire which was hard because the wood was wet even when you cut deep into the center of the log, they'd mix a little bully beef into a canteen cup with rice, to get the starchy taste out of it. Sometimes we'd take turns blowing on sparks trying to start a fire, and keep it up for two hours without success. I could hardly describe the country. It would take five or six hours to go a mile, edging along cliff walls, hanging on to vines, up and down, up and down. The men got weaker; guys began to lag back. . . . An officer stayed at the end of the line to keep driving the stragglers. There wasn't any way of evacuating to the rear. Men with sprained ankles hobbled along as well as they could, driven on by fear of being left behind. . . ."[33]

---

[30] Msg, Capt Melvin Schultz to Col Quinn, 0200, 25 Oct 42, in 2d Bn, 126th Inf, Trail Opns Jnl; Interv, Col Harry Knight, CAV, with Lt Col Henry A. Geerds, n. d. [Circa 15 Nov 42], abstract in OCMH files, original in Mr. Hanson W. Baldwin's personal possession; Robert H. Odell, Buna, 12 Dec 42, abstract in OCMH files; Interv with Maj Robert H. Odell, 14 Dec 50; Kahn, "The Terrible Days of Company E," The Saturday Evening Post, 8 Jan 44, pp. 43–44; Hanson W. Baldwin, "Doughboy's March a High Point in the War," The New York Times, 7 May 44.

[31] Odell, Buna, 12 Dec 42; Interv with Maj Odell, 14 Dec 50; Ltr, Maj Gen C. A. Martin to Gen Ward, 6 Mar 51; Durdin, "The Grim Hide and Seek of Jungle War," The New York Times Magazine, 7 Mar 43; Kahn, "The Terrible Days of Company E," pp. 43–44.

[32] Ltr, Col Herbert M. Smith to General Ward, 9 Mar 51.

[33] Kahn, "The Terrible Days of Company E," p. 43.

As the march continued, the suffering of the men increased, and Sergeant Lutjens wrote in his diary: ". . . Our strength is about gone. Most of us have dysentery. Boys are falling out and dropping back with fever. Continual downpour of rain. It's hard to cook our rice and tea. Bully beef makes us sick. We seem to climb straight up for hours, then down again. God, will it never end?" [34]

After plunging through gorges, wading neck-deep streams, scaling cliffs, and slogging over muddy trails, the men of Schultz's company reached Jaure on 25 October exhausted, their clothing in tatters and their shoes moldy and worn out. The march had been too much for Colonel Geerds. He suffered a heart attack on the trail and had to be evacuated to Port Moresby. Ordered forward from Kalikadobu, Maj. Herbert M. Smith, previously supply liaison officer for the regiment, took over as battalion commander. [35]

By 28 October, the other companies had reached Jaure and the main body of the battalion began leaving Jaure for Natunga and Bofu, points in the steep foothills of the range northeast of Jaure leading to the Buna area. Companies E and F, the first to arrive, had gone on ahead to prepare dropping grounds at Natunga and Bofu. Already in place to the west, where they were guarding the battalion's flank and rear, were the Antitank and Cannon Companies under Captain Medendorp. The Medendorp force, now known as the W or Wairopi Patrol, had elements operating on

the east bank of the Kumusi in the shadow of Mount Lamington. With a base camp and dropping ground at Kovio and, two days away, an advance post at Barumbila, ten miles south of Wairopi, it was actively patrolling the area forward of Barumbila. [36]

Completing the Deployment

The Discovery of the Airfields

The 2d Battalion, 126th Infantry, with attached regimental and divisional troops, was the only American force to march over the Owen Stanleys since a better way had been found to get the troops forward. Acting on his own volition, Cecil Abel, a missionary and long-time resident of the Abau district, came to Port Moresby with the information that there was an excellent airfield site near Fasari, in the upper valley of the Musa River. General MacNider and Colonel Bradley, recognizing the importance of the information, rushed Abel to Kalamazoo to see General Harding. Having realized the difficulty of getting any sizable body of troops across the Owen Stanleys by marching, Harding welcomed the news. He saw in the field of which Abel spoke a way of getting his remaining troops across the mountains swiftly, and without dulling their physical edge. He was con-

---

[34] *Ibid.*

[35] Odell, Buna, 12 Dec 42; Interv with Maj Odell, 14 Dec 50; Hist Adv Det and 2d Bn, 126th Inf, Papuan Campaign; Kahn, "The Terrible Days of Company E," pp. 43–44.

[36] Msgs, 14–29 Oct 42, in 126th Inf CT Trail Opns Jnl; Ltr, Col Quinn to Gen Harding, 5 Nov 42, sub: Plan of Withdrawal from Wairopi–Bofu area, in 126th Inf CT, S–2, S–3 Jnl; 32d Div Sitreps, Nos. 5–10, 22–27 Oct 42, No. 36, 8 Nov 42; 114th Engr Bn (C) Hist Papuan Campaign; Hist Adv Det and 2d Bn, 126th Inf, Papuan Campaign; 126th Inf Hist Papuan Campaign; Maj Medendorp, The March and Operations of the Antitank and Cannon Companies, 126th Inf, 4 Oct 42–28 Nov 42.

vinced of the feasibility of the idea when Abel assured him that a trail on high ground, suitable for marching, led from the site of the airfield to Pongani, forty-five miles away. Returning to Port Moresby the next day, Harding enlisted the aid of General Whitehead, who was also much taken with the idea. Abel returned at once to Fasari and, with the aid of native labor and hand tools dropped from the air by the Fifth Air Force, soon had a field there suitable for the use of transports. Thus, when Colonel Sverdrup reached the upper Musa on 19 October, after toiling laboriously over the mountainous Abau track, he found C–47's already using the field, the first plane having landed there that day.[37]

Within days of the completion of the strip, which was fittingly given the name Abel's Field, three other promising sites were found in the same general area. The first, suitable only for emergency landings, was at Embessa, a few miles north of Abel's Field; the second, a much better site, was at Kinjaki Barige, about twenty-five miles farther and northwest from Embessa; the third, also an excellent site, was at Pongani itself.[38] As had been the case at Abel's Field, little more was required to convert these sites into acceptable landing fields than cutting over and burning tall grass and small trees. By early November Colonel Sverdrup had finished the job, using native labor at Embessa and Kinjaki Barige, and members

of Company C, 114th Engineer Battalion, at Pongani.[39]

General Blamey's Proposal

The question as to whether the Kapa Kapa–Jaure track would be used for further troop movements was not easily dismissed. On 19 October, the day that he received word that Abel's field was ready for use, General Harding asked permission from New Guinea Force to fly in the 1st and 3d Battalions, 126th Infantry, to the field. From there the two units would march to Pongani. General Herring had been in favor of the plan, but General Blamey had turned it down on the ground that, except for Abel's word, there was no proof that a practicable trail to Pongani existed. On 30 October Harding proposed that the 1st and 3d Battalions be flown across the mountains to Pongani and Kinjaki Barige. This time, Blamey approved the plan, and at once asked General MacArthur's concurrence for the transfer by air to Pongani of the two battalions, and for the immediate landing of supplies for their support at Abel's field and Kinjaki Barige.[40]

---

[37] Ltrs, Gen Harding to Gen Sutherland, 12 Oct 42 and 14 Oct 42, copies in OCMH files; Interv with Gen Harding, 29 Jun 49; Ltr, Gen Harding to author, 24 Jul 51.

[38] Msg, Gen MacArthur to Gen Blamey, No. C–818, 11 Oct 42, in G–3 Jnl, GHQ SWPA; Ltr, Gen Harding to Gen Sutherland, 12 Oct 42.

[39] Msgs, Col Sverdrup to Gen Casey, No. 930, 19 Oct 42, n.n., 26 Oct 42, n.n., 27 Oct 42, No. 1686, 29 Oct 42, No. RQ–902, 30 Oct 42. All in 384, G–3 Files, GHQ SWPA. 114th Engr Bn (C) Hist Papuan Campaign; 32d Div AAR, Papuan Campaign. For the native labor required to build these airfields the United States paid the following: 1,500 lbs. of trading tobacco, 50 bolts of cloth, 1,000 Boy Scout knives, 50 cases of canned meat, 200 lbs. of salt, 1,000 tin-plate bowls, 1,000 spoons, and 1,000 packages of garden seed. Ltr, Gen Casey to Agent, Finance Officer, Base Sec 3, Brisbane, 1 Oct 42, with indorsements, in 384, G–3 Files, GHQ SWPA.

[40] Ltr, Gen Harding to Gen MacArthur, 30 Oct 42; Ltr, Gen Harding to Gen Sutherland, 31 Oct 42. Copies in OCMH files. Msg, Gen Blamey to Gen MacArthur, No. Z–105, 31 Oct 42, in G–3 Jnl, GQH SWPA; Ltr, Gen Harding to author, 24 Jul 51.

Because of events in the Solomons, General MacArthur did not immediately give his concurrence. The situation in the South Pacific (where Vice Adm. William F. Halsey had succeeded Admiral Ghormley as Commander, South Pacific Area, on 18 October) had become critical. After successfully landing troops on Guadalcanal, the Japanese on 23 October had launched a fierce attack on the airfield. The land attack was co-ordinated with a move southward from Rabaul of heavy Japanese naval forces, including carriers. On 26–27 October the attacks, both by land and by sea, were repulsed with heavy losses to the enemy. The situation, however, continued grave, for the American fleet, after losing one of its two carriers and suffering heavy damage to the other, had been forced to withdraw, leaving the Japanese free to continue with the reinforcement of their expeditionary force on Guadalcanal.[41]

General MacArthur had already prepared a plan for withdrawal from the north coast and, if necessary, from New Guinea, should the Japanese take Guadalcanal and then turn their full strength on New Guinea.[42] He therefore answered General Blamey that as long as the situation in the Solomons remained indecisive, and the enemy had afloat large bodies of troops which could be easily turned against New Guinea, it was unsafe to concentrate as large a force as two regiments, less one battalion, in the Pongani area—at least before the line of the Kumusi River was secured. General Mac-

Arthur added that the original plan to combine the advance along the Kokoda Trail with an envelopment from Jaure was still the safest line of action, since it could be followed by a movement on Buna in conjunction with envelopments from both Jaure and Pongani.[43]

General Blamey assured General MacArthur that he had never intended to concentrate the remaining units of the 126th Infantry at Pongani. His intention had been rather to consolidate the regiment (less the 250 men in the Kumusi Valley) at Bofu. The troops would be flown to the Pongani area only because the airfields were there, and there was nowhere else to land them. Immediately upon disembarking, they would leave the coastal area and march inland to Bofu and join the 2d Battalion. The march from Pongani to Bofu would be by a route south of, and protected by, Hydrographer's Range. For additional protection, the 2/6 Independent Company, at Pongani, would be assigned to patrol the trails north of the range. The 250-man force in the Kumusi Valley would remain there to harass enemy communications and would come under 7th Division command when the Australians crossed the Kumusi River.

Having clarified his proposal, General Blamey asked General MacArthur to give further consideration to the request that the remaining units of the 126th Infantry be flown to the north shore. Lines of withdrawal Blamey added, were available both from Pongani and Bofu and, while not easy to use, were believed to be no more difficult than those over the Kokoda Trail.[44]

[41] Miller, *Guadalcanal: The First Offensive*, pp. 138–39, 156–59, 166–69; USSBS, *The Campaigns of the Pacific War*, pp. 119–23.

[42] PETERSBURG Plan, Redistribution of Allied Forces, Southwest Pacific Area, in the event of Japanese Success in the Solomon Islands, 31 Oct 42, abstract in OCMH files.

[43] Msg, Gen MacArthur to Gen Blamey, No. C–1045, 1 Nov 42, in G–3 Jnl, GHQ SWPA.

[44] Msg, Gen Blamey to Gen MacArthur, No. Z–108, 2 Nov 42, in G–3 Jnl, GHQ SWPA.

CROSSING A BRANCH OF ERORO CREEK, *elements of the 32d Division make their way to Embogo, 5 November 1942.*

The Final Decision

After reconsidering the matter, General MacArthur told General Blamey that he was very much in favor of an early attack and would be in complete accord with such a proposal if sufficient supplies could be provided by air in time to assure its success. This meant, he stipulated, that at least ten days' rations and appropriate amounts of ammunition and medical supplies would have to be in place behind each of the three columns before an advance was ordered. What was more, the air supply movements

to Kokoda, Bofu, and Pongani would have to be completed before the movement of the 126th Infantry from Port Moresby began. Since these movements would place a tremendous strain upon the air force, Blamey was told to make sure that the attack was logistically feasible before the troops were ordered forward.[45]

That same day, 2 November, General MacArthur picked 15 November as the tentative date of attack. The following day,

[45] Msg, Gen MacArthur to Gen Blamey, No. C–1060, 2 Nov 42, in G–3 Jnl, GHQ SWPA.

CHOW LINE ALONG THE MUDDY TRAIL. *128th Infantrymen en route to Oro Bay from Pongani.*

New Guinea Force ordered the 32d Division to patrol up to, but to make no move beyond, the Oro Bay–Bofu–Wairopi line until so ordered. On 6 November an advance echelon of General Headquarters opened at Port Moresby, and General MacArthur arrived there the same day to direct the operations.[46]

Drawing the Noose Tight

Oivi and Gorari

Progress on the main axis of advance accelerated when Kokoda was recaptured. The airfield was quickly reconditioned and lengthened to accommodate C–47's, and the Fifth Air Force at once began using it to fly in food, guns, and ammunition in support of the Australian advance. Vehicles, bridging equipment, and other paraphernalia followed. The supply nightmare that had beset the Australians in the Owen

---

[46] Msq, NGF to 32d Div, Ser 430, 3 Nov 42, in 32d Div G–2, G–3 Jnl; Msg, Gen MacArthur to CG ALF, New Guinea, No. C–1102, 6 Nov 42, in G–3 Jnl, GHQ SWPA. Msg, Gen MacArthur to Gen Marshall, No. C–940, CM–IN 3061, 7 Nov 42.

Stanleys was over. What 2,000 natives and dropping from the air could not do in days, it was now possible to accomplish by plane in minutes. With Kokoda airfield as their rearward base, the Australians could advance on the beachhead with confidence.[47]

Colonel Yazawa's troops, having come in from the beachhead, were well dug in when the 16th Brigade, advancing over the Abuari–Missima–Fila cutoff, attacked toward Oivi on 4 November. The Japanese had artillery emplaced on the heights and, as both Colonel Yazawa and General Horii hoped, enough food and ammunition for at least a week's stand, followed by an orderly withdrawal. The *3d Battalion, 144th Infantry,* with attached engineer troops was at Gorari, a few miles to the east, where it had been sent the day before by General Horii to prevent an Australian break-through on Colonel Yazawa's left rear. The rest of the *144th Infantry* and attached divisional and regimental units were in bivouac at Ilimo. They were resting and recovering their strength preparatory to crossing the Kumusi River. Since Colonel Kusunose had been evacuated to Rabaul in late October because of sickness and wounds, Colonel Tsukamoto, commander of the *1st Battalion, 144th Infantry,* who had led the initial attack on Kokoda, was temporarily in command of the regiment.[48]

The 16th Brigade met stiff resistance when it attacked toward Oivi. Reinforced by the 3d Australian Infantry Battalion, a militia unit, the brigade began flanking on right and left. By 8 November elements of the 2/1 Battalion, moving around the Japanese south (left) flank, were in contact with the enemy southeast of Gorari. On 9 November the 25th Brigade joined the 2/1 Battalion, and the Australians pounced on the Japanese at Gorari.

With the Australians in front and rear, Colonel Yazawa realized it was time to pull out. That night he evacuated Oivi unobserved with what was left of his force—900 men. With him were General Horii and several members of the *Shitai* staff, who had apparently been inspecting Yazawa's position when the Australians cut between it and Gorari. Abandoning guns and ammunition, and indeed everything that would impede their flight, the Japanese took the only remaining route of escape left to them—the rugged jungle country northeast of Oivi. Since the mouth of the Kumusi was only about twenty miles north of Gona, Yazawa planned to follow the river bank to the sea and then move to Gona by way of the coast.

After circling through the jungle, the troops of the *Yazawa Force* came out on the left bank of the Kumusi, well north of the Australians. Shaking off all attempts of the latter to overtake them, they struck off toward the river's mouth—their ultimate destination, Gona.

Gorari was completely overrun by 12 November. More than 500 Japanese were killed there; guns, small arms, and ammunition were captured; and some 200 Rabaul natives were liberated. The Japanese suffered heavily at Gorari, but the much larger body of Japanese at Ilimo, as well as a remnant of the Gorari force, got away. Japanese sick and wounded began crossing

---

[47] NGF OI No. 40, 31 Oct 42, and No. 42, 14 Nov. 42; Msg, Gen Sutherland to Gen MacArthur, No. P–48, 6 Nov 42, in G–3 Jnl, GHQ SWPA; ALF, Rpt on New Guinea Opns, 23 Sep 42–22 Jan 43; AAF, Air Actn in the Papuan Campaign, p. 72.

[48] 67th LofC Hospital Orders, 31 Oct 42, in ATIS EP 24; Nankai Shitai Opns Orders: "KO" No. 133, 31 Oct 42, "KO" No. A–135, 3 Nov 42, "KO" No. 136, 3 Nov 42, in ATIS EP No. 39; No. A–136, 3 Nov 42, in ATIS CT 4, No. 103.

the Kumusi on 10 November, and the main body crossed on the night of 12–13 November, covered by a small rear guard which dug itself in at Ilimo. With the sick and wounded, some 1,200 men crossed the river, mostly on rafts. The incoming troops reached Giruwa several days later, hungry and mostly weaponless, having lost most of their equipment, stores, and ammunition either before or during the crossing.[49]

The Japanese had taken heavy losses at Oivi and Gorari, and their forces had been scattered. Colonel Yazawa had held at Oivi almost as long as he had intended, but the orderly withdrawal that General Horii had planned for had become a rout.

On 13 November the 25th Brigade wiped out the enemy rear guard which had been covering the crossing. A temporary bridge was completed at Wairopi that night. The next morning, while the air force dropped bridging equipment for a more permanent structure, the leading element of the brigade began crossing the river.[50]

The Americans Reach the Front

By this time the movement of the American forces into the concentration areas was almost complete. The 2d Battalion, 126th Infantry, which had started leaving Jaure on 28 October, closed into the Natunga area on 2 November, after a comparatively easy march from Jaure. After spending more than a week in the area drawing rations, helmets, boots, and other equipment at the Natunga dropping ground, the battalion pushed on to Gora and Bofu, reaching the latter point on 12 November.

Captain Boice had been unable to find even one good dropping ground between Jaure and Natunga. As a result, most of the rations dropped from the air between those two points had been lost, and the troops (who were reduced to eating bananas and papayas or whatever else they could find) had gone hungry. Colonel Quinn had made it his business to fly with the air-dropping planes in the hope of working out dropping techniques which would get food to his troops. He was killed on 5 November while in a plane dropping supplies to the troops at Natunga. A cargo parachute that caught in the plane's tail assembly sent the plane out of control, and everyone aboard died in the crash.

Colonel Quinn's loss was a blow to the division. General Harding, in a letter to General Eichelberger, described Quinn as "my best regimental commander, and that by a wide margin." Harding chose Lt. Col. Clarence M. Tomlinson, commanding officer of the 3d Battalion, to command the regiment, and Tomlinson was promoted to colonel in short order. Maj. George Bond took command of the 3d Battalion.[51]

The air movement from Port Moresby of regimental headquarters and of the 1st and 3d Battalions began on 8 November, the 1st Battalion going first. Because heavy

[49] ALF, Daily Opns Rpts No. 204, 4 Nov 42, No. 215, 15 Nov 42; G–3 Opns Rpt No. 225, 17–18 Nov 42, in G–3 Jnl, GHQ SWPA. *Nankai Shitai* Opns Orders "KO" No. 140, Ilimo, 9 Nov 42, in ATIS EP No. 39; *Tomita Butai* Orders, n.n., 15 Nov 42, in ATIS EP No. 29; Msg, Col Tomita to CofS, *Army Hq*, Rabaul, 28 Nov 42, in ATIS CT 26, No. 314; *17th Army* Opns I, 129; *18th Army* Opns I, 15.

[50] ALF, Opns Rpts, No. 215, 15 Nov 42, No. 216, 16 Nov 42, No. 217, 17 Nov 42, in G–3 Jnl, GHQ SWPA; ALF, Rpt on New Guinea Opns, 23 Sep 42–22 Jan 43.

[51] Ltr, Gen Harding to Gen Eichelberger, 5 Nov 42, copy in OCMH files. Ltr, Maj Gen Albert W. Waldron to Gen Ward, 28 Mar 51; 126th Inf CT AAR, Papuan Campaign; 32d Div AAR, Papuan Campaign.

TAKING A BREAK. *Troops from the 3d Battalion and regimental headquarters of the 126th Infantry rest along a trail between Boreo and Dobodura.*

rains had made the airfield at Pongani temporarily unsafe for the landing of troops, 590 men of the 1st Battalion—Battalion Headquarters, Company A, Company B, two platoons of Company C, and a squad of Company D—under the battalion commander, Lt. Col. Edmund J. Carrier, were flown instead to Abel's Field. Upon arrival there, they began marching to Pongani.[52]

Work on a new all-weather airfield had been proceeding at Pongani. The field, on a well-drained site and covered with gravel

from a nearby pit, was finished on 9 November, the day after the movement to Abel's Field began. The air force, previously under the impression that only Abel's Field was open, tested the new field, found it acceptable, and at once began flying in the rest of the 126th Infantry to Pongani.[53]

Within hours of Colonel Carrier's arrival at Abel's Field, the rest of the 1st Battalion, 218 men—Company D, less one squad, and Company C, less two platoons—under Maj.

---

[52] 1st Bn, 126th Inf Jnl, Sers 293, 294, 8 Nov 42, Sers 297, 298, 299, 9 Nov 42, Sers 330, 331, 19 Nov 42.

[53] Msgs, Gen MacNider to Gen Harding, No. 476, 5 Nov 42, No. 535, 8 Nov 42, No. 575, 9 Nov 42, in 32d Div G–2, G–3 Jnl; Ltr, Gen Harding to Gen MacNider, 8 Nov 42, copy in OCMH files.

TAKING A BREAK. *Lt. Col. Alexander J. MacNab (right), Executive Officer of the 128th Infantry, pauses with two of his men for a cigarette on the trail.*

Richard D. Boerem, executive officer of the battalion, had landed at Pongani and at once began marching to Natunga. Colonel Tomlinson and regimental headquarters reached Pongani by air on 11 November, as did the 3d Battalion, all elements moving out to Natunga immediately on arrival. By 14 November Major Boerem's detachment was approaching Natunga, and regimental headquarters and the 3d Battalion were moving forward rapidly behind it. Almost all of Major Smith's 2d Battalion was at Bofu, and the remaining troops of the 1st Battalion, under Colonel Carrier, after having struggled through swampy terrain

since 9 November, were approaching Pongani.[54]

On the coastal flank, General MacNider's command, the 128th Infantry and the 2/6 Independent Company, known by this time as Warren Task Force, was consolidating in the Oro Bay–Embogo–Embi area. Its

---

[54] Msg, Gen MacNider to Gen Harding, No. 575, 9 Nov 42; Msg, Gen Harding to Gen MacNider, No. 576, 10 Nov 42; Msg, Gen Harding to Lt. Col. Clarence M. Tomlinson, Ser. 654, 15 Nov 42, in 32d Div G–2, G–3 Jnl; 126th Inf S–2, S–3 Jnl, Papuan Campaign; Jnl, Maj Boerem's Det, Part 1st Bn, 126th Inf, 10, 13, 14 Nov 42; 126th Inf CT AAR, Papuan Campaign; 32d Div AAR, Papuan Campaign.

patrols were operating inland as far as Borio and up the coast as far as Cape Sudest. The last two companies of the 1st Battalion, 128th Infantry, had been flown to Wanigela from Port Moresby on 8 November and brought forward immediately by boat. Except for Company A, which had been left at Pongani to guard the supply dumps there, the battalion was now at Embogo under Lt. Col. Robert C. McCoy. The 2d Battalion, under Lt. Col. Herbert A. Smith, was at Eroro Mission, and the 3d Battalion, under Colonel Miller, was near Embi. The Australian Independent Company, under Maj. Harry G. Harcourt, was at Pongani preparing to move forward after its extensive patrols of the trails north of Hydrographer's Range and of the Natunga–Pongani track. There was a forward dump at Embogo, and Colonel McKenny was planning an even more advanced dump at Hariko. General MacNider, in turn, planned to move his headquarters to Hariko as soon as there were boats available for the movement.[55]

Artillery was to be Australian. A two-gun section of 3.7-inch mountain artillery was at Embogu, and four 25-pounders had reached Oro Bay. The crews were under 32d Division command. Reinforcements, consisting of the 127th Regimental Combat Team, less artillery, had at last begun loading at Brisbane for Port Moresby on 14 November.[56]

The Americans were now finally in position for the forthcoming attack and the Australians soon would be. Up to this time the campaign had cost the latter 2,127 casualties,[57] but the enemy was back at the beachhead on which he had landed in July. His back was to the sea, and the noose around him was being drawn tight.

[55] Ltr, Gen Harding to Gen MacNider, 28 Oct 42, copy in OCMH files; Ltr, Lt Col Chester C. Beaver, 128th Inf, to Gen Harding, 6 Nov 42; Ltr, NGF to 32d Div, 9 Nov 42. Last two in 32d Div G–2, G–3 Jnl; 32d Div Sitreps, No. 45, 13 Nov 42, No. 47, 16 Nov 42, 128th Inf AAR, Papuan Campaign; 32d Div AAR, Papuan Campaign.

[56] Msg, NGF to 32d Div, No. 609, 11 Nov 42, in 32d Div G–2, G–3 Jnl; Msg, Gen MacNider to Gen Harding, 15 Nov 42, in OCMH files. Ltr, Gen Waldron to Gen Ward, 5 Mar 51; 32d Div Hist of Arty, Papuan Campaign. The 3.7-inch pack howitzer was a standard British piece, much used by the Australians. It was about 94-mm.; the projectile weighed 19½ pounds; and the maximum range was 6,000 yards.

[57] Australian casualty figures for the period 22 July 1942 to 16 November 1942, for ground troops only, are as follows: 709 killed in action; 132 died of wounds and other causes; 1,286 wounded in action. Ltr, Balfour to author, 15 Feb 50; Sig, Australian Army Headquarters, Melbourne to Australian Military Mission, Washington, No. MW–179, 22 June 50, copy in OCMH files.

CHAPTER VIII

The Allies Close In

Just as the Allies prepared to close on Buna the turning point came in the struggle for the southern Solomons. In the naval battle of Guadalcanal (12–15 November), Admiral Halsey's forces virtually wiped out an eleven-ship enemy convoy, carrying almost all the reserves the Japanese had available for action in the South and Southwest Pacific. After this catastrophic setback, the Japanese gave up trying to reinforce their troops on Guadalcanal, contenting themselves with desperate attempts to keep them supplied so as to prolong resistance as long as possible. With the island sealed off, Marine Corps troops, reinforced by Army troops (who were arriving on the scene in increasing numbers to replace the marines), could proceed uninterruptedly with the task of destroying the large Japanese garrison left on the island.[1] The battle for Guadalcanal had entered an advanced phase just as that for Buna began.

Mounting the Attack

The Scene of Operations

The scene of operations was the Buna–Gona coastal plain, commonly referred to as the Buna area. (*Map IV*) Lying between the sea and the foothills of the Owen Stanley Range, the region is quite flat. In the Buna strips area the elevation is about three feet. At Soputa, some six and one-half miles inland, it is only a few feet higher. The terrain consisted mainly of jungle and swamp. The jungles, mostly inland, were a tangle of trees, vines, and creepers, and dense, almost impenetrable undergrowth. The swamps, filled with a frenzied growth of mangrove, nipa, and sago trees, were often shoulder-deep, and sometimes over a man's head.

Scattered through the region were groves of coconut palms, areas of bush and scrub, and patches of kunai grass. The coconut palms, some of them 125 feet high, were to be found principally along the coast at such points as Cape Endaiadere, Buna Mission, Giruwa, Cape Killerton, and Gona, but there were also a few groves inland, surrounded in the main by swamp. Generally the bush and scrub were heavily overgrown, and the undergrowth was almost as impenetrable as that in the jungle. The kunai grass, shoulder-high, and with knife-sharp edges, grew in thick clumps, varying in size from small patches that covered a few square feet to the Dobodura grass plains that extended over an area several miles square.

The rainy season had begun and the Girua River, which divided the area in two,

---

[1] Hist Rec *Army Section, Imperial General Headquarters,* pp. 65, 67; *Southeast Area* Naval Opns, I, 45–50; *17th Army* Opns, I, 114–115; USSBS, *The Campaigns of the Pacific War,* pp. 125–139; Miller, *Guadalcanal: The First Offensive,* pp. 177–89, 230–31.

was in flood. After losing itself in a broad swampy delta stretching from Sanananda Point to Buna Village, the Girua emptied into the sea through several channels. One of these, Entrance Creek, opened into the lagoon between Buna Village and Buna Mission. Between Entrance Creek and Simemi Creek to the east was an immense swamp. This swamp, formed when the overflow from the river had backed up into the low-lying ground just south of Buna Mission, reached as far inland as Simemi and Ango. It was believed to be impassable, and its effect was to cut the area east of the river in two, making the transfer of troops from one part to the other a slow and difficult process.[2]

Because of the swamp, there were only three good routes of approach to the Japanese positions east of the river. The first led from Soputa and Ango Corner along the western edge of the swamp to a track junction three quarters of a mile south of Buna Mission which was to become known to the troops as the Triangle. From this junction, one trail led to Buna Village and the other to Buna Mission. A second route of approach was from Dobodura and Simemi along the eastern end of the swamp and along the northern edge of the Old Strip to Buna Mission. A third approach lay along the coastal track from Cape Sudest to Cape Endaiadere, where the trail back-tracked diagonally through Duropa Plantation to the New Strip, and ran thence to Buna Mission.

The situation was the same on the western side of the river. There were only two good approaches to the Japanese beachhead positions in that area, and both of them lay through swamp. One was the trail that ran to Gona via Amboga Crossing and Jumbora; the other was the main trail to Sanananda via Popondetta and Soputa. In addition, several branch trails forked from the Soputa–Sanananda track to Cape Killerton, where they joined the coastal trail to Sanananda, Sanananda Point, and Giruwa.

In the hot and muggy climate of the Buna–Gona area the humidity averages 85 percent, and the daily temperature, 96° F. The area was literally a pesthole. Malaria, dengue fever, scrub typhus, bacillary and amoebic dysentery were endemic there, as were the lesser ills—jungle rot, dhobie itch, athlete's foot, and ringworm.[3] Unless the campaign came to a quick end, disease would inevitably take heavy toll of the troops.

The Plan of Attack

New Guinea Force published the over-all plan of attack on 14 November. The orders provided that the 7th Australian Division and the 32d U. S. Division would destroy the enemy in the area bounded by the Kumusi River, Cape Sudest, and Holnicote Bay. The boundary between the two divisions was to be a line running from the mouth of the Girua River to Hihonda, thence southwesterly along a stream halfway between Inonda and Popondetta. The 7th Division was to operate on the left of the boundary, the 32d Division on the right. The 21st Brigade, now to serve its second

[2] Actually there was no mission at Buna, and what was known as Buna Mission was really Buna Government Station. Likewise, what the Board of Geographic Names officially calls the Senimi River was known as Simemi Creek. Since nearly all records of the campaign refer to "Buna Mission" and "Simemi Creek," these names will be used throughout this volume.

[3] Rpt, CG Buna Forces on the Buna Campaign, pp. 2–8, with app. Map B, Buna Campaign Area; WD, Survey of Northeast New Guinea and Papua.

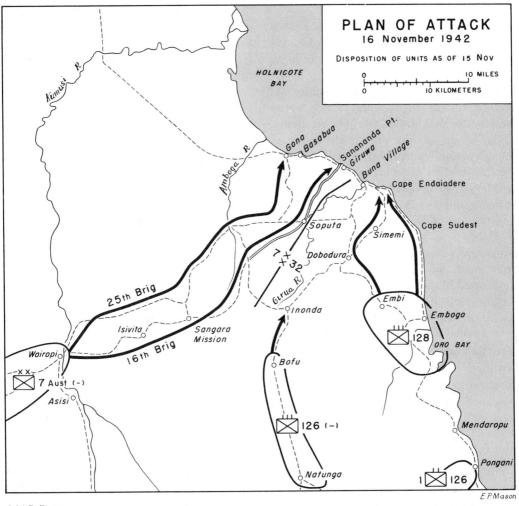

PLAN OF ATTACK
16 November 1942

DISPOSITION OF UNITS AS OF 15 NOV

MAP 7

tour of duty in the campaign, was to be flown in from Port Moresby and go into 7th Division reserve near Wairopi. (*Map 7*)

The troops were to begin moving forward on 16 November, the 32d Division against Buna, and the 7th Division against Gona and Sanananda. Units on either side of the interdivisional boundary were to take particular care not to uncover their inward flank. Each division was to be prepared to

strike across the boundary against the enemy's flank or rear should the opportunity offer. The 32d Division, in addition to carrying on its combat role, was to establish a landing strip at Dobodura, secure and hold the crossing of the Girua River near Soputa, and provide for the security of the right flank from enemy sea-borne attack.[4]

---

[4] NGF OI No. 42, 14 Nov 42.

The LILLIPUT Plan

Hopeful of an early victory, New Guinea Force issued a plan for defense of the Buna area the next day. Under LILLIPUT (as the plan was called) the 32d Division would become responsible for Buna's defense as soon as the area was cleared of the enemy. To assist the division in the discharge of that responsibility, Australian artillery, anti-aircraft, and air-warning units were to be sent forward to Buna at the earliest possible moment and come under its command. The first echelon of LILLIPUT, including several K. P. M. ships, had already been called forward and was due to arrive at Milne Bay from Australia on 18 November.[5]

General Blamey had asked General Mac-Arthur for a few destroyers to protect the LILLIPUT ships as they passed through the area beyond Cape Nelson and while they were unloading at Buna, but Vice Admiral Arthur S. Carpender, who had succeeded Admiral Leary as Commander of the Allied Naval Forces in September, had voiced strong objections to sending destroyers into the "treacherous" waters off Buna. In a letter to General MacArthur, he made his position clear. The entire area between Cape Nelson and Buna, he wrote, was so filled with reefs that there was virtually no "sea room" in which destroyers could maneuver. The Japanese, using the northern approach route from Gasmata, a small island off the south coast of New Britain, did not have this difficulty, for there were deep-water areas suitable for the maneuvering

of cruisers and destroyers all the way between it and Buna. To put a "minor surface force" in the Buna area would serve no useful purpose in the face of the much heavier forces the enemy could easily send in from Rabaul. General Blamey could have one or two shallow-draft antisubmarine vessels for the escort of the LILLIPUT ships, but no destroyers; the latter were not to be used for escort duty north of Milne Bay.[6]

Since Admiral Carpender had objections also to sending submarines into the Buna area,[7] it became clear that the only help the Allied forces closing in on Buna could expect from the fleet was a few small patrol boats. The air force, in addition to bearing its close support and supply responsibilities, would have to carry almost the entire burden of protecting Allied supply movements northward of Milne Bay, and of beating back enemy attempts to reinforce the beachhead.

The Forces Move Up

On 15 November General Harding issued the divisional plan of attack. In Field Order Number One of that date, he ordered one battalion of the 128th Infantry to march along the coast via Embogo and Cape Sudest to take Cape Endaiadere. A second battalion was to move on the Buna airfield via Simemi. The remaining battalion, which would be in division reserve, was to proceed to the Dobodura grass plains area and pre-

[5] NGF OI No. 43, 15 Nov 42. Msg, Gen Chamberlin to Gen Sutherland, No. C–1237, 14 Nov 42; Msg, P–146, Gen Sutherland to Gen Chamberlin, 14 Nov 42. Both in 384, G–3 Files, GHQ SWPA.

[6] Ltr, Gen Blamey to Gen MacArthur, 7 Nov 42; Ltr, Vice Admiral Arthur S. Carpender, Comdr ANF, to Gen MacArthur, A16–3, Ser 00521, 10 Nov 42, sub: Opns for Capture of Buna. Both in G–3 Jnl, GHQ SWPA.
[7] R&R, Gen Chamberlin to Gen Sutherland, 10 Nov 42, in 385, G–3 Files, GHQ SWPA.

SIMEMI VILLAGE, *along the route of Company M, 128th Infantry, on its way to an advanced position.*

pare a landing strip for transports. Each battalion was to have an engineer platoon and a body of native carriers attached. H Hour for Warren Force was set at 0600, 16 November. The 126th Infantry (less the elements of the 1st Battalion arriving at Pongani) would close on Inonda. It would move from Inonda on Buna by a route to be specified later.[8]

While Colonel Tomlinson's force would have to be supplied by airdropping until

the field at Dobodura was in operation, Warren Task Force was, as far as possible, to be supplied by sea. There was to be a deepwater harbor at Oro Bay, Col. John J. Carew, the Divisional Engineer, having investigated the harbor area and reported favorably on the project.[9] Its completion, and the completion ultimately of an access road from it to Dobodura, would make it

---

[8] 32d Div FO No. 1, 15 Nov 42, copy in DRB HRS, AGO.

[9] Ltr, Col John J. Carew, CO 114th Engr Bn, to Gen Harding, 14 Nov 42, sub: Preliminary Reconnaissance Rpt, Oro Bay Area, Ser 647, in 32d Div G-2, G-3 Jnl; Memo, Gen MacNider for Gen Harding, 15 Nov 42, in OCMH files.

LT. COL. HERBERT A. SMITH *leading troops across a river on the way to Embogo.*

possible for large ships to anchor there and would also make possible the development of Dobodura into a major air base, not only for fighters and transports, but also for all types of bombers.

General MacNider's troops were given an extra ration of rice before they left their lines of departure on 16 November. Colonel Tomlinson's headquarters, the 3d Battalion, 126th Infantry, and Major Boerem's detachment (which according to plan was to be reunited with the rest of the 1st Battalion at Dobodura as soon as possible) pushed off from Natunga to Bofu. The 2d

Battalion, already at Bofu, began moving on Inonda.[10]

Early on 16 November, just as the Americans marched out to the attack, the Australians completed the crossing of the Kumusi River. Leaving an engineer detachment to clear an airstrip on the east bank of the river, the 25th Brigade began marching on Gona, and the 16th Brigade, on

---

[10] Gen Harding's Diary, 15 Nov 42; Msg, Col Tomlinson to Gen Harding, Ser 715, Ser 754, 16 Nov 42, in 32d Div G-2, G-3 Jnl; 32d Div Sitrep No. 47, 16 Nov 42; 32d Div Rpt of Actn, Papuan Campaign.

GENERAL MacNIDER *(center, facing forward) mapping plans to take Buna.*

Sanananda. Advance Headquarters, 7th Division, crossed the river on the 16th just behind the 16th Brigade, and Captain Medendorp, whose Wairopi Patrol had had a light brush with the enemy at Asisi a few miles south of Wairopi a week before, reported to General Vasey the same day.[11]

The attack was on, but the condition of many of the attacking troops left a great deal to be desired. The 16th and 25th Bri-

gades, which had chased the enemy nearly all the way across the Owen Stanleys, had been in continuous action under the most arduous conditions for almost two months. They had lost many men, and those that remained were very tired. The 21st Brigade, General Vasey's reserve, though rested and regrouped, was far below strength.[12] Only the untried Americans, numbering at the

---

[11] ALF Opns Rpt No. 215, 15 Nov 42; No. 216, 16 Nov 42; No. 217, 17 Nov 42; No. 218, 18 Nov 42. All in G–3 Jnl, GHQ SWPA; Comdr ALF, Rpt on New Guinea Opns, 23 Sep 42–22 Jan 43.

[12] Ltr, Gen Blamey to Gen MacArthur, 27 Oct 42, in G–3 Jnl, GHQ SWPA; Comdr ALF Rpt on New Guinea Opns, 23 Sep 42–22 Jan 43; NGF, Notes on Opns in New Guinea, Ser 3.

time just under 7,000 men,[13] could be considered fresh troops, and many of them because of sickness and exhausting marches were far from their physical peak.

The 32d Division
on the Eve of Combat

Training and Equipment

Troops in the opening engagements of every war are often found to be ill prepared to wage the kind of war they actually have to fight. This was the case with the 32d Division when its leading elements marched out to meet the enemy in mid-November 1942. Not only were the troops inadequately trained, equipped, and supported for the task in hand, but many of the difficulties they were to meet at Buna had been neither foreseen nor provided for.

The division, whose insignia is a Red Arrow with a crosspiece on the shaft, was a former Michigan and Wisconsin National Guard unit. It had a record of outstanding service in World War I, having fought with great distinction on the Aisne–Marne, the Oise–Aisne, and in the Meuse–Argonne drive. The division was inducted into the federal service on 15 October 1940 as a square division. The following April some 8,000 Michigan and Wisconsin selectees were added to its strength. After participating in the Louisiana maneuvers, the division was triangularized into the 126th, 127th, and 128th Infantry Regiments. The 120th, 121st, 126th, and 129th Field Artil-

lery Battalions were assigned as divisional artillery. The 121st Field Artillery Battalion was equipped with 155-mm. howitzers. The other battalions, which had trained with World War I 75's, received 105's just before embarkation.[14]

The 32d Division had expected to fight in the European theater and, in late December 1941, had actually been earmarked for operations there. General Harding joined it in Louisiana in early February 1942. In late February the division was sent to Fort Devens, Massachusetts, and instructed to prepare for immediate movement to Northern Ireland. Ordered at the last moment to the Pacific, the division took on more than 3,000 replacements at San Francisco and reached Adelaide, Australia, on 14 May. Training had scarcely got under way when the division was again ordered to move— this time to Brisbane. The move was completed in mid-August, and training had just got into its stride again at Camp Cable, the division's camp near Brisbane, when the first troops started moving to New Guinea.

These moves served the division ill. Not only was it difficult to harden the men because they were so much in transit, but the weeks spent in moving, in making each successive camp livable, and in providing it with bayonet courses, rifle range, infiltration courses, and similar installations before infantry training could begin cut heavily into the division's training time. This was a serious matter since the division had arrived in Australia only partially trained, and many

---

[13] As of 14 November, the 126th and 128th Combat Teams, and the forward echelon of division headquarters totaled 6,951 men, with more engineer and medical troops still to come. Ltr, CG 32d Div to GOC NGF, 14 Nov 42, sub: Strength Rpt, in OCMH files; Ltr, Gen Harding to author, 26 Feb 50.

[14] *Order of Battle of the United States Land Forces in the World War, American Expeditionary Forces,* (Washington, 1931), pp. 176–91; Annual Rpt, National Guard Bureau, 1941, Table VII, p. 29; AGF, Fact Sheet on 32d Inf Div, 1 Mar 47, in DRB HRS, AGO; Ltr, Gen Harding to author, 26 Feb 50.

of its officers, new to the division, had not yet had time to know their men.

There was another difficulty. Like the 41st Division, the 32d was part of the garrison of Australia. The main emphasis in its training had been on the defense of Australia, a type of training from which the troops had little new to learn for it repeated the training that they had received at home. What they really needed—training in jungle combat—they got very little of.[15]

General Richardson, Commanding General, VII Corps, then on a mission in the Pacific for General Marshall, inspected the troops in early July and reported that as far as their training was concerned they were "still in the elementary stages" and would not be ready for combat "by some few months." General Eichelberger reached Australia in early September and found the division still not ready for combat. He rated its state of training as "barely satisfactory" and told General MacArthur it needed further hardening as well as a vast amount of training, especially in jungle warfare.[16]

As quickly as he could, Eichelberger instituted a stepped-up training and hardening program, but the 126th and 128th Infantry Regiments had already moved out to New Guinea before the new program could

go into effect. Thus when the two regiments entered combat they were not in top physical condition, had received very little training in scouting, night patrolling, or jungle warfare, and had been fired over in their training either very briefly or not at all.[17]

Looking back at it all, General Harding had this to say of the training of the division before it entered combat:

I have no quarrel with the general thesis that the 32d was by no means adequately trained for combat—particularly jungle combat. A Third Army (Krueger) training inspection team gave it a thoroughgoing inspection about a month before I joined it and found it deficient on many counts. I got a copy of this report from Krueger and it was plenty bad. . . .

On the other hand I found the division well disciplined, well behaved, and well grounded in certain elements of training. . . . My estimate of training when I took over is that it was about on a par with other National Guard divisions at that time.

Unfortunately we had no opportunity to work through a systematic program for correcting deficiencies. From February when I took over until November when we went into battle we were always getting ready to move, on the move, or getting settled after a move. No sooner would we get a systematic training program started than orders for a move came along to interrupt it. As you know, you just can't formulate and get set up for a realistic training program in a couple of days. As a matter of fact, realistic training for modern war requires an enormously elaborate installation of training aids, courses, etc. without which really good training can't be complete. Such installations were out of the question

---

[15] Durdin, "The Grim Hide and Seek of Jungle War," *The New York Times Magazine*, 7 Mar 43; Interv with Gen Harding, 9 Dec 47; Interv with Gen Eichelberger, 3 Feb 50; Ltrs, Gen Harding to author, 26 Feb 50; 24 Jul 51; Ltr, Gen Waldron to Gen Ward, 5 Mar 51; Gen Eichelberger, *Our Jungle Road to Tokyo*, (New York, 1950), pp. 7, 11. Mr. Durdin was on the ground throughout the campaign, having taken over as *New York Times* correspondent upon Byron Darnton's death.

[16] Memo, Gen Richardson for Gen Marshall, 9 Jul 42, Report No. 5, in SWPA–MacArthur File, OPD Exec File: Interv with Gen Eichelberger, 6 Feb 50; Gen Eichelberger, *Our Jungle Road to Tokyo*, pp. 11, 12.

[17] Ltr, Gen Eichelberger to Gen Sutherland, 24 Dec 42, copy in OCMH files; Interv with Gen Eichelberger, 6 Feb 50; Ltr, Col Harry Knight, Cav, to CG AGF, 4 Jan 43, sub: Report of Col Harry Knight in the Southwest Pacific, with incl. U.S. Troops in the Battle of Buna; Ltr, Col Herbert B. Laux, Inf, to CG AGF, 20 Feb 43, with incl. Both ltrs in 381, OPD SWPA File, Sec 4. Ltrs, Gen Harding to author, 26 Feb 50 and 26 Jul 51.

for us, although we managed to set up a few simplified modifications of the real thing which would have served fairly well, had we ever had time to run more than a fraction of the command through them.[18]

Although the troops had much of the standard equipment of the day, not all of it was to prove suitable for the area in which they were to fight. Much of their radio equipment, for instance, had already failed to function, and they did not have the carbine which would have been an ideal weapon in the tangled, overgrown beachhead area. Although the carbine was available elsewhere, it was to be months before the first carbines reached the Southwest Pacific Area and were distributed among the troops.[19]

The troops had none of the specialized clothing and equipment which later became routine for jungle operations. Their clothing—dyed to aid concealment in the jungle—was already causing them great discomfort. Not only did the dye run, but its residuum stopped up the cloth and made it nonporous. The garments, as a result, became unbearable in the extreme tropical heat and caused hideous jungle ulcers to appear on the bodies of nearly all the troops wearing them.[20]

Though they were about to enter a jungle area overgrown with vines and creepers and teeming with noxious insects, the men were critically short of machetes, and had no in-

sect repellants. Nor had anyone thought to issue them small waterproof boxes or pouches for the protection of their personal effects and medical supplies from the extreme heat and wet. Cigarettes and matches became sodden and unusable, and quinine pills, vitamin pills, and salt tablets,—then usually issued in bulk a few days' supply at a time—began to disintegrate almost as soon as the men put them in their pockets or packs, and the same thing sometimes happened to the water chlorination tablets.[21]

Various expedients had been adopted to lighten the weight each man would have to carry in the jungle. The marching troops were equipped as far as possible with Thompson submachine guns, and the heavier weapons, including most of the 81-mm. mortars, were put aside to be sent forward later by boat. Medical and communications equipment were stripped to the bare essentials, and field ranges and accompanying heavy mess equipment were left behind at Port Moresby.[22]

The medical units were using gas stoves, kerosene burners, and even canned heat to sterilize their instruments and provide the casualties with hot food and drink, but the front-line troops had none of these things. Without their normal mess equipment, they no choice but to use tin containers of all kinds to heat up their rations, prepare their coffee (when they had coffee), and wash their mess gear. Since it rained almost continually and there was very little dry fuel available, it was usually impossible to heat

[18] Ltr, Gen Harding to author, 26 Feb 50.

[19] Ltr, Gen Eichelberger to Gen Sutherland, 8 Dec 42; Rpt, CG Buna Forces on the Buna Campaign, p. 84; Ltr, Maj David B. Parker, CE, to CG USASOS, 2 Dec 42, sub: Notes on Operations near Buna, New Guinea, 14–23 Nov 42, in AFPAC Engr File; Durdin, "The Grim Hide and Seek of Jungle Warfare," 7 Mar 43.

[20] Ltr, Col John E. Grose to Gen Ward, 26 Feb 51, with incl; Durdin, "The Grim Hide and Seek of Jungle War," 7 Mar 43; Eichelberger, Our Jungle Road to Tokyo, p. 39.

[21] Ltr, Col Carl Hanna, MC, Surgeon 32d Div, to Chief Surgeon USASOS SWPA, 10 Dec 42, in Surgeon General's Hist File; Ltr, Col Hanna to author, 25 Nov 50; Maj Parker's Buna Rpt; Interv with Maj Odell, 14 Dec 50.

[22] Col Knight's Buna Rpt; Ltr, Col Hanna to author, 14 Oct 50; Ltr, Gen Harding to author, 26 50.

water sufficiently to sterilize the tins and mess gear from which the troops ate—an open invitation to the same type of diarrhea and dysentery that had already overtaken 'the 2d Battalion, 126th Infantry, in its march over the mountains.[23]

Artillery and Engineer Support

As the troops marched out for the attack, there was a widespread belief at higher headquarters that the mortars, direct air support, and the few Australian pieces already available in the area would be enough to clear the way for the infantry.[24] Even this represented better support than that advocated by General Kenney, who, in a letter to Lt. Gen. H. H. Arnold on 24 October, told the latter that neither tanks nor heavy artillery had any place in jungle warfare. "The artillery in this theater," he added, "flies." [25]

Neither General Harding nor his artillery commander, Brig. Gen. Albert W. Waldron, believed that the infantry could get along very well without the artillery. Strongly supported by Harding, Waldron kept asking that the divisional artillery be brought forward. General MacArthur's headquarters did not have the means either to bring all the artillery forward or to keep it supplied when it got there. Not being at all sure that artillery could be used effectively or even be manhandled in the swampy terrain of the beachhead, GHQ was cool to the proposal.

In the end, by dint of great persistence, and with the held of the Australian artillery commander, Brig. L. E. S. Barker, who thought as he did on the subject, Waldron got a few pieces of artillery—not his own, and not as much as he would have liked, but better than no artillery at all.[26]

If the division's artillery support—two 3.7-inch howitzers and the promise of a four-gun section of 25-pounders which had yet to arrive at the front—was scanty, its engineer support was even scantier. Almost half of General Horii's original force had either been combat engineers or Army and Navy construction troops. Yet, General Harding, with the rainy season at hand, and every possibility that roads, bridges, and airfields would have to be built in the combat zone, had only a few platoons of the 114th Engineer Battalion attached to his two combat teams. And these engineer troops reached the front almost empty-handed. They had no axes, shovels, or picks, no assault boats, very little rope, and not a single piece of block and tackle. The theory was that all these things would come up by boat with the heavy equipment. In practice, however, the failure to have their tools accompany them meant that the engineer troops could do only the simplest pioneer work at a time when their very highest skills were needed.[27]

The Condition of the Troops

Medical supplies at the front were critically short as the troops marched out for the attack. Bismuth preparations for the treatment of gastrointestinal disturbances were almost unprocurable, and there was not

[23] Ltr, Col Hanna to author, 14 Oct 50; Interv with Maj Odell, 14 Dec 50; Hist Medical Activities 32d Div, Papuan Campaign, in Surgeon General's Hist File.

[24] Ltr, Col H. F. Handy, FA, to CG AGF, 13 Feb 43, sub: Rpt of Military Observer in the Southwest Pacific Theater of Operations, in 381, OPD SWPA File, Sec 2; Interv with Gen Harding, 9 Dec 47; Ltr, Gen Harding to author, 24 Jul 51.

[25] Quoted in AAF, Air Action in the Papuan Campaign, p. 72.

[26] Ltr, Gen Waldron to Gen Ward, 5 Mar 51; Ltr, Gen Harding to author, 25 Jul 51.

[27] Col Knight's Buna Rpt; Maj Parker's Buna Rpt.

107TH MEDICAL BATTALION CORPSMEN AT WARD'S DROME *near Port Moresby awaiting a flight to Pongani.*

enough quinine sulphate, the malaria suppressive in use at the time, for regular distribution to the troops. There was no atabrine, and none was to be received throughout the campaign.[28]

General Harding had arranged to have his medical supplies go forward by boat, only to find at the last minute that the boats were busy carrying other things. He did what he could in the emergency. Getting in

touch immediately with General Whitehead, Harding explained to him that the medical supply situation was "snafu" and asked him to fly in the most urgently needed items "to take care of things until we can get the boat supply inaugurated."[29]

Most of the troops had gone hungry; some had nearly starved during the approach march, and food was still in short supply. Rations had accumulated in the rearward dumps between Wanigela and the front, but there was only a few days' supply at the front itself. It was assumed that this

[28] Ltr, Gen Harding to Brig Gen Ennis P. Whitehead, 14 Nov 42, copy in OCMH files; Ltr, Maj Herbert C. Wallace, M. C., Actg Surgeon 32d Div, to TAG, 28 Feb 43, sub: Monthly Sanitary Report, in Surgeon General's Hist File; Ltr, Col MacNab to author, 14 Nov 49; Ltr, Col Herbert M. Smith to author, 16 Mar 50.

[29] Ltr, Gen Harding to Gen Whitehead, 14 Nov 42.

deficiency and other supply shortages would be made good as the attack progressed.[30]

Except for the latest arrivals (the 1st and 3d Battalions, 126th Infantry) the troops presented anything but a soldierly appearance. Their uniforms were stained and tattered, few had underwear or socks, and their shoes in most cases were either worn out or in the process of disintegration. Most were bearded and unkempt, virtually all were hungry, and some were already showing unmistakable signs of sickness and exhaustion.[31] The 2d Battalion, 126th Infantry, and the troops who had marched with it across the mountains had been severely affected by the ordeal. The 128th Infantry, whose name for Pongani was "Fever Ridge," was not in much better condition. As the commander of the 2d Battalion recalls the matter, the trouble was that the men had been on short rations since mid-October; that they had made some extremely exhausting marches through the jungle "on a diet of one-third of a C-ration and a couple of spoonfuls of rice a day"; and that many of them already had "fever, dysentery, and jungle rot." [32] General Eichelberger put the whole matter in a sentence when he wrote that, even before the 32d Division had its baptism of fire, the troops were covered with jungle ulcers and "riddled with malaria, dengue fever, [and] tropical dysentery." [33] Sickness and exhaustion had already claimed many vic-

tims; they would claim many more as the fighting progressed.

The Division's Estimate of Enemy Strength

For all their hunger, their exhaustion, and their sickness, the troops were cocky and overconfident about the task that lay ahead. They had been told and they believed that Buna was a "push over," and neither they nor their commanders saw any reason why it should not be theirs in a few days. No one—either at Port Moresby or at the front—believed that there would be any difficulty in taking Buna. Natives (who as was soon to become evident had no conception of numbers) had spied out the land and come back with reports that there were very few Japanese in the area. The air corps, similarly, had been reporting for more than a month that there were no Japanese to be seen at the beachhead and that there was no evidence that it was fortified or that the enemy had serious intentions of defending it.[34]

As these reports of enemy weakness poured in, the 32d Division began to think in terms of a quick and easy conquest of Buna. "I think it is quite possible," wrote General Harding on 14 October, "that the Japanese may have pulled out some of their Buna forces. . . ." "We might find [Buna] easy pickings," he added, "with only a shell of sacrifice troops left behind to defend it." By 20 October General Harding felt that there was "a fair chance that we will have

[30] Msg, Gen MacNider to Gen Harding, Ser 769, 17 Nov 42; Msg, Col John Mott, CofS 32d Div, to Gen MacNider, Ser 777, 17 Nov 42. Both in 32d Div G-2, G-3 Jnl. Ltr, Col Herbert A. Smith to author, 20 Jan 50; Ltr, Lt Col Herbert M. Smith to author, 16 Mar 50.

[31] Ltr, Col Herbert A. Smith to author, 20 Jan 50; Interv with Col Baetcke, 17 Nov 50; Interv with Maj Odell, 14 Dec 50; Kahn, *G. I. Jungle*, pp. 108, 121, 122.

[32] Ltr, Col Herbert A. Smith to author, 20 Jan 50.

[33] Eichelberger, *Our Jungle Road to Tokyo*, p. 23.

[34] 32d Div G-2 Intel Summaries No. 6, 13 Oct 42, No. 7, 21 Oct 42, No. 8, 29 Oct 42, No. 9, 5 Nov 42, in DRB HRS, AGO; Col Handy's Buna Rpt; Col Knight's Buna Rpt; Ltr, Col MacNab to author, 15 Nov 49; Ltr, Col Herbert A. Smith to author, 20 Jan 50; Ltr, Lt Col Herbert M. Smith to author, 5 Jun 50.

Buna by the first of November." At the end of the month, he wrote that all information to date was to the effect that Japanese forces in the Buna–Gona area were relatively light and asked how GHQ would look upon November 5 as a suitable date for D Day. "Things look pretty favorable right now," he said, "for a quick conquest of Buna." [35]

A Ground Forces observer, Col. H. F. Handy, noted that, as November opened, many in the 32d Division felt "that Buna could be had by walking in and taking over." [36] Another Ground Forces observer, Col. Harry Knight, noted that "the lid really blew off, when the order was received on 3 November that American troops were not to move forward from Mendaropu and Bofu until further instructed. The reason for the order was, of course, to gain time in which to stockpile supplies for the impending advance, but the division, restive and eager to be "up and at 'em" did not see it that way.

. . . Opinions were freely expressed by officers of all ranks . . . [Colonel Knight recalls] that the only reason for the order was a political one. GHQ was afraid to turn the Americans loose and let them capture Buna because it would be a blow to the prestige of the Australians who had fought the long hard battle all through the Owen Stanley Mountains, and who therefore should be the ones to capture Buna. The belief was prevalent that the Japanese had no intention of holding Buna; that he had no troops there; that he was delaying the Australians with a small force so as to evacuate as many as possible; that he no longer wanted the airfield there; . . . that no Zeros had been seen in that area for a month; and that the Air Corps had prevented any reinforcements from coming in . . . and could prevent any future landing . . . .[37]

On 6 November Maj. W. D. Hawkins, General Harding's G–2, noted that both ground and air reconnaissance reports indicated that Buna, Simemi, and Sanananda each held perhaps 200–300 Japanese with only "a small number" of enemy troops at Gona. He went on to guess that the enemy was already reconciled to the loss of Buna and probably intended to evacuate it entirely. Major Hawkins thought the Japanese would be most likely to try evacuating their forces by way of the Mambare River so as to be able to take them off at the river's mouth. They would do this, he suggested, in order to avoid a "Dunkirk" at Buna, since Buna was an open beach from which embarkation by boats and barges would lay the evacuees open to heavy air attack.[38]

These optimistic views on the possibilities of an early Japanese withdrawal did not agree with General Willoughby's estimates of the situation. Willoughby estimated enemy strength on 10 November as two depleted regiments, a battalion of mountain artillery, and "normal" reinforcing and service elements—about 4,000 men in all. He thought that an enemy withdrawal from Buna was improbable, at least until the issue was decided at Guadalcanal. It was known, he said, that General Horii's orders were definitely to hold Buna until operations in the Solomons were successfully completed. These orders, the Japanese hope of success in the Solomons, and what was known of the character and mentality of the Japanese commanders involved made it highly unlikely, General Willoughby thought, that there would be "a withdrawal at this time."

By 14 November General Willoughby began to have doubts that the enemy had two regiments at Buna. He thought that the

[35] Ltrs, Gen Harding to Gen Sutherland, 14 Oct 42, 20 Oct 42, 31 Oct 42, copies in OCMH files.
[36] Col Handy's Buna Rpt.
[37] Col Knight's Buna Rpt.
[38] 32d Div G–2 Daily Summary, No. 9, 6 Nov 42.

mauling taken by the Japanese at Oivi and Gorari had left them with about "one depleted regiment and auxiliary units" and that these, pending the outcome of the Solomons operation, were capable only of fighting a delaying action. It was therefore likely, General Willoughby suggested, that there would be close perimeter defense of the airfield and beachhead at Buna, followed by a general withdrawal, if the Japanese effort in the Solomons failed. That the enemy would attempt further reinforcement of the Buna area he thought improbable "in view of the conditions in the Solomons, and the logistic difficulties and risks which are involved." [39]

General Vasey's estimate of the enemy's strength based on prisoner of war interrogations was, as of 14 November, 1,500 to 2,000 men [40]—roughly the same figure that General Willoughby seems to have had in mind in his revised estimate of the same day. General Harding, who had Vasey's estimate, but had probably had no chance as yet to see Willoughby's, was more optimistic than either. Relying principally on information supplied by the natives, his G-2 had estimated that the "Buna area was garrisoned by not more than a battalion with purely defensive intentions." [41] Harding accepted this estimate, and the intelligence annex in his first field order of the campaign read as follows:

The original enemy force based at Buna is estimated as one combat team with two extra infantry battalions attached. This force has been withdrawing steadily along the Kokoda Trail for the past six weeks. Heavy losses and evacuation of the sick have reduced them to

an estimated three battalions, two of which made a stand in the Kokoda-Wairopi area, with the third occupying Buna and guarding the line of communications. Casualties in the two battalions in the Wairopi area have reduced them to approximately 350 men, who, it is believed, are retiring northward along the Kumusi River Valley. . . .[42]

By the time the story got to the men it was to the effect that there were not over two squads of Japanese in Buna Village and that other enemy positions were probably as weakly held. Told by their officers that the operation would be an easy one, and that only a small and pitiful remnant of the enemy force which had fought in the Owen Stanleys remained to be dealt with, the troops were sure that they could take Buna in a couple of days, and that about all that remained to be done there was to mop up.[43]

This was a sad miscalculation. The Japanese were present in much greater strength than the 32d Division supposed, and superbly prepared defensive positions stood in its way, as well as in the way of the 7th Division which was to attack farther to the west.

The Enemy Position

The Japanese Line

The Japanese had established a series of strong defensive positions along an eleven-mile front extending from Gona on their

---

[39] GHQ SWPA OI No. 23, 10 Nov 42; G-2 Daily Summaries Enemy Intel No. 235, 12-13 Nov 42, No. 237, 14-15 Nov 42.

[40] Msg, 7th Aust Div to Adv NGF, Ser 733, 14 Nov 42, in 32d Div G-2, G-3 Jnl.

[41] 32d Div Intel Rpt, Papuan Campaign.

[42] 32d Div, FO No. 1, 15 Nov 42.

[43] Memo, Col Russel Reeder, WDGS, for Col William L. Ritchie, Chief, Southwest Pacific Gp OPD, 22 Feb 43, in 381 OPD SWPA, Sec 1; Col Knight's Buna Rpt; Col Handy's Buna Rpt; Col Hale, Answers to Questions by Hist Sec, GHQ SWPA, as to Certain Phases of the Papuan Campaign; Ltr, Lt Col Herbert M. Smith to author, 5 Jun 50; Eichelberger, Our Jungle Road to Tokyo, pp. 19, 20.

extreme right to Cape Endaiadere on their extreme left. The enemy line enclosed a relatively narrow strip along the foreshore. It varied from a few hundred yards to a few miles in depth and covered an area of about sixteen square miles. (*Map V*)

The Japanese defense was built around three main positions. One was at Gona, another was along the Sanananda track, and the third was in the Buna area from Girua River to Cape Endaiadere. Each was an independent position, but their inward flanks were well guarded, and lateral communications between them, except where the coastal track had flooded, were good. Gona, a sandy trail junction covering the Army anchorage at Basabua, was well fortified, though its proximity to the sea made impossible defense in any depth. There were strong and well-designed defenses along the Sanananda track and at the junction of the several branch trails leading from it to Cape Killerton. On the other side of the Girua River equally formidable defenses covered the Buna Village, Buna Mission, and Buna Strip areas.

The main Japanese base was at Giruwa. The largest supply dumps and the *67th Line of Communications Hospital* were located there. On this front the main Japanese defensive position was about three and one-half miles south of Sanananda Point, where a track to Cape Killerton joined the main track from Soputa to Sanananda Point. A lightly wooded area just forward of the track junction, and the sandy and relatively dry junction itself, bristled with bunkers, blockhouses, trenches, and other defensive positions. Beginning a couple of miles to the south, several forward outposts commanded the trail. About half a mile to the rear of the junction, where another trail

branched from the main track to Cape Killerton, there was a second heavily fortified position, and beyond it, a third. These positions were on dry ground—usually the only dry ground in the area. They were flanked by sago swamp, ankle to waist deep, and could be taken only by storm with maximum disadvantage to the attackers.[44]

East of the Girua River, the Japanese line was even stronger because it presented a continuous front and could not be easily flanked. The line began at the mouth of the Girua River. Continuing southeastward, it cut through a coconut grove and then turned southward to the trail junction where the Soputa–Buna track forks to Buna Village on the one hand and to Buna Mission on the other. Sweeping north, the line enclosed the Triangle, as the fork was called, and then turned eastward from that narrow salient to the grassy area known as the Government Gardens. From the Gardens, it led south and then east through the main swamp to the grassy area at the lower or southern edge of the Old Strip. It looped around the strip and, continuing southward, enclosed the bridge between the strips. Then making a right-angled turn to the New Strip and following the southern edge of the strip to within a few hundred yards of the sea, it cut sharply northeast, emerging on the sea at a point about 750 yards below Cape Endaiadere.[45]

Because the three-foot water table in the

---

[44] [Japanese] Estimate of the Situation, 16–17 Nov 42, in ATIS EP 29; ALF, Rpt on New Guinea Opns, 23 Sep 42–22 Jan 43; Rpt, CG Buna Forces, pp. 9, 39; 163d Inf CT, The Battle of Sanananda, in DRB HRS, AGO; Buggy, *Pacific Victory*, pp. 196–97.

[45] Rpt, CG Buna Forces, p. 10; Buna Target Plan [Map] No. 24, in DRB HRS, AGO.

area ruled out the possibility of deep trenches and dugouts, the region was studded instead with hundreds of coconut log bunkers, most of them mutually supporting and organized in depth. In general, they were of two types: heavily reinforced bunkers located in more or less open terrain, and smaller, less heavily reinforced bunkers built where the terrain was overgrown with trees and vegetation that offered the defenders a measure of protection against air bombardment or artillery fire.

There were a few variations. Now and then where the terrain particularly favored them, the Japanese had large, squat, earth-covered blockhouses, each capable of holding twenty or thirty men. In addition, they had a few concrete and steel pillboxes behind the New Strip.

Except for these variations, which were on the whole rare, the standard Japanese bunker in the area was of heavy coconut log and followed a common pattern. The base was a shallow trench, perhaps two feet deep. It was six to eight feet long and a few feet wide for the smaller bunkers, and up to thirty feet long and ten feet wide for the larger ones. Heavy coconut logs, about a foot thick, were used for both columns and crossbeams. The logs were cut to give the bunkers an interior height of from four to five feet, depending on the foliage and terrain. The crossbeams forming the ceiling were laid laterally to the trench. They usually overlapped the uprights and were covered by several courses of logs, and often by plates of sheet steel up to a quarter of an inch thick. The walls were revetted with steel rails, I-beams, sheet iron, log pilings, and forty-gallon steel oil drums filled with sand.

As soon as the framework was up, the entire structure was covered with earth,

rocks, and short chunks of log. Coconuts and strips of grass matting were incorporated into the earth fill to assist in cushioning the pressures set up by high explosive, and the whole structure was planted with fast-growing vegetation. The result could scarcely have been improved upon. The bunkers, which were usually only about seven or eight feet above ground, merged perfectly with their surroundings and afforded excellent concealment.

As a further aid to concealment, firing slits were usually so small as to be nearly invisible from the front. In some cases (as when the bunkers were intended merely as protection from artillery and air bombardment) there were no slits at all. Entrance to the bunkers was from the rear, and sometimes there was more than one entrance. The entrances were placed so that they could be covered by fire from adjacent bunkers, and they were usually angled to protect the occupants from hand grenades. The bunkers either opened directly onto fire trenches or were connected with them by shallow crawl tunnels. This arrangement permitted the Japanese to move quickly from fire trench to bunker and back again without fear of detection by troops only a few yards away.

These formidable field fortifications were cleverly disposed throughout the Buna position. Bunker and trench systems, within the Triangle, in the Government Gardens, along Entrance Creek, and in the Coconut Grove on the other side of the creek, protected the inland approaches to Buna Village and to Buna Mission, and the approaches, in turn, were honeycombed with enemy emplacements. The main swamp protected the southern edge of the Old Strip, and bunkers, fire trenches, and barbed wire covered its northern edge. The

COCONUT LOG BUNKER WITH FIRE TRENCH ENTRANCE *in the Buna Village area.*

bridge between the strips had bunkers and gun emplacements both at front and rear, and the bridge area could be swept by fire from both strips. There were bunkers, fire trenches, and breastworks behind the New Strip and in the Duropa Plantation, and fire in defense of the strip could also be laid down from the bridge area, from the Old Strip, and from the Y-shaped dispersal bays at its eastern end. The airstrips afforded the Japanese cleared fields of fire and made it possible for them to lay down bands of fire on troops who sought to flank the New Strip by crossing the bridge between the strips, or who tried advancing along its northern edge.[46]

The Japanese line at Buna was, in its way,

---

[46] Tel Msg, 18th Bde to 32d Div, Ser 3609, 18 Dec 42; Msg, NGF to 32d Div, Ser 3740, 19 Dec 42; Memo, Maj W. D. Hawkins, 32d Div G-2, Ser 3814, 21 Dec 42, sub: Constructional Details of Enemy Emplacements. All in 32d Div G-3 Jnl. 127th Inf Jnl, Ser 32, 21 Dec 42; Memo, Lt Col A.F.A. Irwin, RAE, 6th Aust Div, to Brig George F. Wootten, 18th Bde, 4 Jan 43, sub: Japanese Strong Points—Expedients in Assisting Attack, copy in OCMH files; Rpt. CG Buna Forces, pp. 96–98; 163d Inf TC, The Battle of Sanananda, with incis.

INTERIOR OF COCONUT LOG BUNKER *reinforced with sand-filled oil drums near, Duropa Plantation.*

a masterpiece. It forced the 32d Division to attack the enemy where he was strongest—in the Triangle, along the trail leading to the bridge between the strips; along the northern edge of the strip; and frontally in the Duropa Plantation. By canalizing the Allied attack into these narrow, well-defended fronts, the Japanese who had short, interior lines of communication, and could shift troops from front to front by truck and landing craft, were in a position to exploit their available strength to the maximum, no matter what its numerical inferiority to that of the Allies.

The Garrison

Shortly after contact was lost with General Horii, Colonel Yokoyama, commanding officer of the *15th Independent Engineers*, took charge of all Japanese forces west of the river. Captain Yasuda, as the senior naval officer present, took command of those east of it.[47]

---

[47] *Yokoyama Det* Orders, 18 Nov 42, in ATIS EP 29; *17th Army* Opns I, 130; *18th Army* Opns I, 22.

On 16 November, the day the Allies marched out for the attack, the Japanese garrison in the beachhead area was a jumble of broken Army and Navy units. Though riddled by battle casualties and disease, it still numbered approximately five and a half thousand effectives.[48] Army units included the remnants of the *144th Infantry,* of the *15th Independent Engineers,* the *3d Battalion, 41st Infantry,* the divisional cavalry detachment, and the *47th Field Antiaircraft Artillery Battalion.* In addition, a few field artillery batteries had been left to guard the beachhead along with a number of rear echelon units that had never been in combat. There were about 500 *Yokosuka 5th* and *Sasebo 5th* special naval landing troops in the area, and perhaps twice that number of naval laborers from the *14th* and *15th Naval Pioneer Units.*[49]

---

[48] Rad, *67th LofC Hospital,* Giruwa, to CofS *17th Army,* 15 Nov 42, in ATIS EP 29; AMF Interr Gen Adachi *et al.;* *17th Army* Opns I, 129–30. No precise figure can be given for Japanese strength at the beachhead in mid-November, but it is possible to support the figure given above. When questioned at Rabaul in 1945, General Adachi (who should have known as he took charge of New Guinea operations two weeks later) gave the total Japanese strength on 15 November as 9,000. His figure, however, included approximately 900 troops who were then with Colonel Yazawa on the other side of the Kumusi, and another 900 who did not reach the beachhead from Rabaul until two days later. As it is known that some 1,800 men were hospitalized at the time in the *67th Line of Communications Hospital,* it can be estimated that there were at least 5,500 effectives at the beachhead in mid-November, including of course, Army and Navy laborers.
[49] *Nankai Shitai* Opns Orders TEI No. 35, 6 Oct 42, in ATIS EP 29; *67th LofC Hospital* Fld Staff Diary, 1–31 Oct 42, in ATIS EP 24; *18th Army* Opns I, 20–21; Rpt, CG Buna Forces, pp. 42–44. The Japanese had been evacuating their sick and wounded to Rabaul whenever the opportunity offered, and appear to have returned a number of their naval construction troops as well, presumably for more pressing construction work elsewhere.

The Condition of the Enemy Troops

The Japanese were in a bad way. In the long retreat from Ioribaiwa (and especially at Oivi and Gorari) and in the crossing of the Kumusi, they had lost irreplaceable weapons and supplies. Their most critical shortages were in small arms, food, and medical supplies—items that Lt. Col. Yoshinobu Tomita, the detachment supply officer, had for some time been doling out with a careful hand.

All the weapons that could be scraped together were either in the front lines or stacked where they would be readily available when the front-line troops needed them. Except for troops immediately in reserve, most of the men to the rear had no weapons. Worried by the situation, Colonel Yokoyama issued orders for all troops without arms to tie bayonets to poles. If they had no bayonets, they were to carry wooden spears. These "weapons" were to be carried at all times; even the patients in the hospital were to have them at their bedsides.[50]

The troops had been on short rations for a long time, and the ration was progressively decreased. To eke it out, the few horses that were left were being gradually butchered for food.

There was a great deal of sickness. Nearly all the troops being admitted to the hospital for wounds and disease were found to be suffering as well from exhaustion and general debility. There had been serious outbreaks of malaria in the ranks, and a large proportion of the men had dysentery of an aggravated kind.

Things were at their worst at the base hospital at Giruwa. There was very little medicine, and not enough food to promote

---

[50] *Yokoyama Det* Bul, 2 Dec 42, in ATIS EP 24.

the recovery of the patients. Water had seeped into the wards, and the seepage, the extreme humidity, and heavy rains had caused clothes, bedding, and medical equipment to mold, rot, or rust away. As November opened, the medical staff had reported that food and medicine were so short as "to militate absolutely against the recovery of the patients," and the situation, instead of improving, had become progressively worse.[51] Toward the end of the month, a Japanese soldier was to write in his diary: "The patients in the hospital have become living statues. There is nothing to eat. Without food they have become horribly emaciated. Their appearance does not bear thinking upon."[52]

Despite these difficulties, the position of the Japanese was by no means hopeless. They had good stocks of ammunition, a strong defensive position, and enough men and weapons to hold it for a long time. What was more, they had every reason to expect that Rabaul would quickly reinforce and resupply them. Their orders were to hold, and, with a little help from Rabaul, they were prepared to do so indefinitely.

Enemy Dispositions

Colonel Yokoyama sent some 800 troops to Gona—a key position since it covered the all-important anchorage at Basabua. This force included an Army road-building unit

of about 600 men, the troops of a divisional water-purification and decontamination unit, and some walking wounded. The commander of the road-building unit, Maj. Tsume Yamamoto, was put in charge of the defense.[53]

Colonel Yokoyama himself took over the defense of the vital Sanananda–Giruwa area. He ordered some 1,800 men—headquarters and one company of the *3d Battalion, 41st Infantry*, the main body of the *1st Battalion, 144th Infantry*, a portion of the *15th Independent Engineers*, a 700-man contingent of Formosan naval laborers, and some walking wounded—to front-line positions at the main junction of the Sanananda and Cape Killerton trails. The salient, known to the Japanese as South Giruwa, was divided into northern, central, and southwestern sectors, and put under command of Colonel Tsukamoto. In reserve at the second trail junction a half-mile to the north, Colonel Yokoyama stationed a second company of the *3d Battalion, 41st Infantry*, a mountain gun battery, about 300 men of the *15th Independent Engineers*, and a portion of the antiaircraft battalion. Colonel Yokoyama moved his headquarters to Sanananda at the head of the trail and there stationed a second mountain artillery battery, the cavalry troop, the rest of the *41st Infantry*, and most of the naval construction troops in the Giruwa area.

At Buna, Captain Yasuda had under his command the naval landing troops, an element of the *15th Independent Engineers*, a section of the antiaircraft battalion, about 450 naval laborers, and a few hundred Army service troops. He had some 75-mm. naval guns, a number of 13-mm. guns, several 37-mm. pompoms, and half a dozen

[51] *67th LofC Hospital* Rpt of Service, 31 Oct 42, in ATIS EP 24; Rad, CO *67th LofC Hospital* to CofS *17th Army*, 15 Nov 42; *Yokoyama Det* Bul, Giruwa, 22 Nov 42; Rad, Lt Col Yoshinobu Tomita to CofS *17th Army*, 23 Nov 42. All in ATIS EP 29. Interr, Lt Zengoro Sawatari, Med Off, *144th Inf*, in 32d Div Interrogation and Translation File; *18th Army* Opns I, 25.
[52] Captured Japanese Diary, owner unknown, entry 27 Nov 42, Ser 3624, 18 Dec 42, in 32d Div G–3 Jnl.

[53] *18th Army* Opns I, 21, 24.

3-inch antiaircraft guns. The engineers, the antiaircraft troops, and the service troops were assigned to the defense of the plantation, the New Strip, and the bridge between the strips. The *Yokosuka 5th* and *Sasebo 5th* troops, as well as the naval laborers, were deployed in Buna Village, Buna Mission, the Coconut Grove, and the Triangle.[54]

Reinforcements were quickly forthcoming. Tokyo had realized for some time that, despite the emphasis on retaking Guadalcanal, troops would also have to be sent to the Buna–Gona area if the beachhead was to be held. The troops immediately available for the purpose were several hundred *144th Infantry* replacements who had just reached Rabaul from Japan and the *3d Battalion, 229th Infantry*, a *38th Division* unit whose two sister battalions were on Guadalcanal. The *229th Infantry* had had combat experience in China, Hong Kong, and Java and was rated an excellent combat unit.

The battalion under its commander, Maj. Hiaichi Kemmotsu, together with 300 *144th Infantry* replacements and the new commander of the *144th Infantry*, Col. Hiroshi Yamamoto, was ordered to Basabua on 16 November and arrived there by destroyer the following evening. There were about 1,000 men in the convoy, and their arrival brought effective enemy strength at the beachhead to some 6,500 men, not including troops that might be released from the hospital later on and sent to the front.

The incoming troops were transferred to Giruwa by barge and then sent on to the Cape Endaiadere–Durope Plantation–Buna Strips area. Colonel Yokoyama took command of that area, and Captain Yasuda of the area west of it as far as the Girua River.

The picture at Buna had changed. The Japanese there now had more than 2,500 troops to man the defenses on that side of the river—almost half of them newly equipped and fresh from Rabaul.[55]

The Situation at Rabaul

On 16 November, the day that Colonel Yamamoto was ordered to Buna, a new area command was established to control operations in New Guinea and the Solomons. The new command, the *8th Area Army*, under Lt. Gen. Hitoshi Imamura, was to have under it two armies—the *17th Army* under General Hyakutake, which was to operate exclusively in the Solomons, and the *18th Army*, under Lt. Gen. Hatazo Adachi, which was to operate in New Guinea. General Adachi arrived at Rabaul on 25 November and assumed command of the *18th Army* the same day. His first task was to retrieve the situation in Papua—a very difficult assignment as he was soon to discover.[56]

---

[54] *Yokoyama Det* Orders, 16 Nov 42, in ATIS EP 29; Japanese Strength and Dispositions on the Soputa–Sanananda Track, 20 Nov 42, translation of an enemy map captured at Gona by New Guinea Force, 8 Dec 42, in OCMH files; *18th Army* Opns I, 20–21; US Buna Forces G–2 Periodic Rpt, 14 Dec 42–4 Jun 43, in DRB HRS, AGO; Rpt, CG Buna Forces, pp. 43, 77.

[55] [Japanese] Estimate of the Situation, 16 Nov 42, 17 Nov 42; *Tomita Det Bivouac* Orders, Giruwa, 17, 18 Nov 42. All in ATIS EP 29. *17th Army* Opns I, 129–30; *18th Army* Opns I, 16, 21.

[56] 1st Demob Bur, GHQ FEC, Japanese Studies in World War II, No. 37, *8th Area Army* Opns, p. 1; *17th Army* Opns I, 131; *18th Army* Opns I, 22–23.

CHAPTER IX

The Opening Blows in General Vasey's Area

On 16 November the 32d Division under General Harding and the 7th Division under General Vasey moved out against the enemy positions at the Buna–Gona beachhead. The Americans were on the right, and the Australians on the left. (*See Map V.*) Between them ran the Girua River, the divisional boundary. East of the river, the 126th Infantry troops under Colonel Tomlinson pushed off from Bofu and marched on Buna Village and Buna Mission by way of Inonda, Horanda, and Dobodura. Warren Force, the 128th Infantry and supporting elements, under General MacNider, sent out two columns from its positions along the coast: one along the coastal track leading to Cape Endaiadere; the other against the bridge between the strips. On the other side of the river, the 25th Brigade under Brigadier Eather left the Wairopi crossing early on the 16th and moved on Gona by way of Awala, Amboga Crossing, and Jumbora. Crossing the Kumusi close on the heels of the 25th Brigade, the 16th Brigade under Brigadier Lloyd began moving on Sanananda the same day via Isivita, Sangara, Popondetta, and Soputa. Believing like the Americans on the other side of the river that only a small number of the enemy remained, the Australians advanced confidently, sure of a quick and easy victory.

The Attacks on Gona

The 25th Brigade Bogs Down [1]

Gona was forty miles from Wairopi, and the trail, a poor one frequently lost in mud, lay through bush, jungle, kunai flat, and swamp. The 25th Brigade moved out toward Gona on 16 November, the 2/33 Battalion leading and the 2/25 Battalion bringing up the rear. There was no enemy contact on either the 16th or the 17th but the heat was intense and men began dropping out with malaria and collapsing with heat prostration. The 2/33 Battalion, Lt. Col. A. W. Buttrose commanding, reached Jumbora on the afternoon of 18 November and started to prepare a dropping ground. One of its companies moved forward to Gona to find out if the place was defended.

The company quickly discovered that there were Japanese at Gona. Major Yamamoto's original allotment of 800 men had been reinforced by an additional hundred

[1] Except for the passages on the Japanese side, which are to be found in *18th Army* Opns I, 24, the following subsection is based mainly on the official Australian manuscript history, Dudley McCarthy, The Southwest Pacific Area: The First Year, Ch. 16, Gona. Other pertinent sources are the ALF Daily Opns Rpts for the days in question, and NGF Notes on Opns in New Guinea, Ser 3.

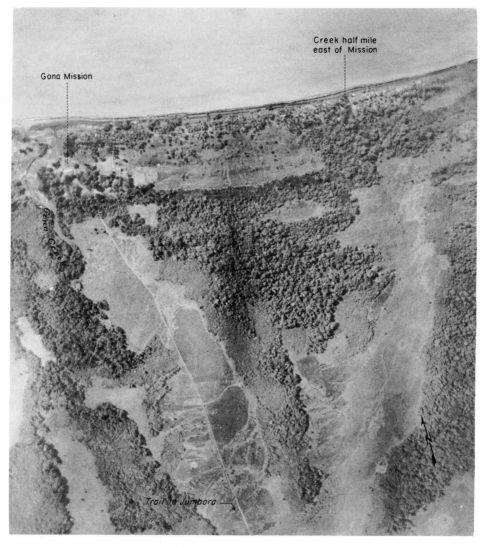

GONA MISSION AREA

men—eighty from the *41st Infantry,* and the rest walking wounded from the hospital. The Japanese defense was centered on Gona Mission at the head of the trail. The mission and the surrounding native village area were honeycombed with bunkers, trenches, and firing pits, and every approach was covered. On the west lay the broad mouth of Gona Creek, an expanse of water just wide enough to make an attack from the other side of the creek unlikely. Immediately to the south, and along the east bank of the creek, was an overgrown timbered area which bristled with defense works. To the east a labyrinth of hidden firing pits with overhead cover extended along the shore for a distance of about three quarters of a mile. With such defenses at their disposal, a resolute garrison could hope to hold for a long time.

The company of the 2/33d which had gone on ahead to investigate ran into the most southerly of the Japanese defenses late on 18 November. The position, a strong, well-prepared one with cleared fields of fire, was about 1,000 yards south of the mission. Next morning when the 2/31 Battalion, which was now in the lead, came up, it found the sixty men of the company in an intense fire fight with an enemy who was well hidden and well dug in, and whose fire commanded every approach. The 2/31st, under its commander, Lt. Col. James Miller, attacked vigorously but could not penetrate the enemy's protective fires. By nightfall, when it was ordered to disengage, the battalion had lost thirty-six killed and wounded.

By this time the brigade had outrun its supply. Ammunition had run low, and the troops, hungry, and racked with fevers, were without food. The supply situation righted itself on 21 November when supply planes came over Jumbora and dropped what was needed. Brigadier Eather at once assigned a company of the 2/33 Battalion to guard the supply dump. When a forty-five man detachment of the 2/16 Battalion which had previously been operating in the Owen Stanleys was made available to him that day, he ordered it to take up a position on the west bank of Gona Creek in order to cover his left flank. The 25th Brigade was finally ready to attack.

Eather's command now numbered less than 1,000 men. Thus far he had no idea of how strong an enemy force was facing him. He did not yet realize that the Japanese de-

fending Gona from carefully prepared positions had roughly the same number of troops that he had.

The attack began early on 22 November. The 2/33 Battalion attacked frontally along the track; the 2/25 Battalion, in reserve, moved out on the left of the track to be in position to attack from the southwest if called upon; the 2/31 Battalion, which was to launch the main attack, pushed forward on the right toward the beach, turned left, and attacked from the east.

Moving through swamp, the troops got as close as they could to the Japanese positions and then went in on the run with bayonets fixed. They did not go far. The leading troops had scarcely reached the Japanese front-line positions when the entire attacking wave was met by such intense enfilading fire from right and left that the troops had to pull back into the swamp. This abortive attack cost the 2/31 Battalion sixty-five killed and wounded.

The next day Brigadier Eather tried again. He switched the 2/25 Battalion from the left flank to the right and ordered it to launch a new attack from the east that afternoon. The 2/25th, Lt. Col. Richard H. Marson commanding, passed through the 2/31st and attacked westward, supported by fire from its sister battalion. The result was the same. No sooner had the troops approached the enemy position than enfilading fire drove them back into the swamp, like the 2/31 Battalion before them. The 2/25th lost sixty-four men in the day's fighting, only one less than the 2/31st in the attack of the day before.

The situation had turned serious. In only three days of fighting, the brigade had lost 204 killed and wounded. There was little to show for these losses. Although the Japanese had pulled back along the track, they were still holding the village and the mission and had apparently given as good as they got.

Realizing only too well now that he faced a strong, well-entrenched enemy, Brigadier Eather called for an air strike to soften up the Japanese position. When it was over, he planned to attack again with the 3d Infantry Battalion which had meanwhile come under his command.

The air force flew over Gona on 24 November and gave the place a thorough bombing and strafing. On the next day the 3d Battalion, now less than 200 strong, attacked Gona from the southwest. For the first time the attack was well prepared. Not only did the 2/25 and 2/31 Battalions fire in its support, but four 25-pounders which had reached Soputa on 23 November fired 250 rounds of preparatory fire before the troops jumped off. Under the command of Lt. Col. Allan G. Cameron, the battalion got about fifty yards inside the Japanese position but, as in the case of the other attacks, was met by such intense fire that it too had to withdraw. The attack, though a failure like the rest, had one redeeming feature: unlike the inadequately prepared attacks which had preceded it, casualties were relatively light.

The 21st Brigade Opens Its Attack

By now the 25th Brigade was no longer in condition to attack. The total strength of its three battalions amounted to less than 750 men—two were under 300 men, and one, the 2/31st, was under 200. The troops were exhausted, and the number of sick from malaria and other causes was increasing daily. What was left of the brigade could still be used to contain the enemy but could

scarcely be expected to do more. The task of clearing Gona fell therefore to General Vasey's reserve unit, the 21st Brigade, Brig. Ivan N. Dougherty commanding. It was only about 1,100 strong, but the men, after a long rest at Port Moresby, were fit and ready to go.

Advance elements of the new brigade began moving into the line on 28 November. By 30 November the brigade had completely taken over. Pending the receipt of orders returning it to Port Moresby, the 25th Brigade took up a position along the track just south of Gona and lent such support as it could to the 21st Brigade, whose opening attacks on the place were, to Brigadier Dougherty's chagrin, proving no more successful than its own.[2]

The capture of Gona, which the Australians had thought initially to be undefended, had turned out to be an extremely difficult task. After almost two weeks of attack, it was still in enemy hands. The Japanese had suffered heavy losses and had been forced to contract their lines until they held little more than a small area immediately around the mission, but they were still resisting with the utmost tenacity, and their perimeter had yet to be breached. The almost fanatical resistance of Major Yamamoto's troops served its purpose. Australian troops that might otherwise have been available for use elsewhere in the beachhead area were at the end of the month still trying to take Gona.

---

[2] ALF Daily Opns Rpt No. 230, 30 Nov 42; Allied Air Forces Opns Rpt, 29–30 Nov 42; G–3 Opns Rpts, No. 237, 29–30 Nov 42, No. 238, 30 Nov–1 Dec 42; Msg, 7th Div to 32d Div, Ser 29, 1 Dec 42, in G–2 Jnl; 32d Div; NGF Notes on Opns in New Guinea, Ser 3; ALF Rpt on New Guinea Opns, 23 Sep 42–22 Jan 43; McCarthy, op. cit., Ch. 16.

The 16th Brigade Moves on Sanananda

*The Australians Reach
the Track Junction*

The leading battalion of the 16th Brigade, the 2/2d, Lt. Col. C. R. V. Edgar commanding, was across the Kumusi by the early morning of 16 November. Edgar struck out at once for Popondetta. Behind him in order were Brigadier Lloyd and his headquarters, the 2/3 Battalion, and the 2/1 Battalion.

The men plodded along without rations, tired and hungry. They were gnawing green papayas and sweet potatoes, whatever they could find. Some were so hungry they chewed grass.

A torrential rain struck the next day, turning the track into a sea of mud. Even minor creeks were almost impossible to ford. The troops still had no food, and that day fifty-seven men of the 2/2d collapsed on the trail from exhaustion, heat prostration, and hunger.

There was no food on the 18th—only a rumor that the planes would drop some at Popondetta. The 2/2d reached Popondetta that evening, but there was no food there either. Rations would be waiting for them, the troops were told, at Soputa, a day's march away.

Leaving some troops at Popondetta to prepare an airstrip, the brigade pushed off for Soputa on 19 November, the 2/3 Battalion leading. Rations had been dropped during the morning at Popondetta and caught up with the troops by noon, at which time the men had their first meal in three days. The battalion approached Soputa toward evening and ran into resistance just outside the village. Maj. Ian Hutchinson, the battalion commander, at once deployed

his troops for attack. Darkness fell before the battalion could clear out the enemy, and the weary troops dug in.

Next morning the Japanese were gone. Brigadier Lloyd sent a covering force to the Girua River crossing, about half a mile east of Soputa, and the 2/3 Battalion marched out along the track in pursuit of the Japanese. Finding no enemy after a half-hour march, the troops were busily eating breakfast by the side of the track, when the 2/1 Battalion, taking the lead, pushed past them. After about fifteen minutes of marching through brush and scrub, the 2/1 began debouching onto a broad kunai flat and there was met by heavy enemy fire, including artillery fire.[3]

The 2/1st had to run into Colonel Tsukamoto's most southerly outpost. This outpost was manned by a covering detachment whose mission was to delay an advancing force, thus giving Tsukamoto time to complete preparations for the defense of his main position at the junction of the Cape Killerton and Soputa–Sanananda tracks.

Lt. Col. Paul A. Cullen, the battalion commander, ordered an immediate attack. One company of the 2/1 started moving frontally up the track. A second company started flanking on the right. A third composite company moved out wide on the left. The troops in the center and on the right made some gains at first, but by noon they were meeting strong resistance that balked further progress that day. The company on the left under command of a particularly aggressive young officer, Capt. B. W. T. Catterns, did better. This force, ten officers and eighty-one enlisted men (all that was left of two companies), made a wide detour

---

[3] ALF Daily Opns Rpt No. 220, 20 Nov 42; McCarthy, *op. cit.*, Ch. 17; Maj. J. W. Dunlop, 2/2 Bn, The Sanananda Track, abstract in OCMH files.

around the Japanese right flank, taking particular care to keep clear of the kunai flat which the enemy was defending. By evening Catterns was about two miles behind the Japanese and in position to come in on their right rear.

Creeping stealthily forward, the Australians surprised a number of Japanese at their evening meal, killed about eighty of them, and established a strong, all-around perimeter just east of the track. The Japanese attacked Catterns all day on 21 November, hitting him repeatedly from three sides. Though they were running short of ammunition, Catterns' troops in a stirring defense not only beat off the enemy but inflicted heavy casualties upon him.

The Australians on the right were quick to profit from the enemy's absorption in Catterns' attack. Two companies of Colonel Edgar's 2/2 Battalion, under Capts. Athelstan K. Bosgard and Jack M. Blamey, pushed around the enemy's left flank and kept going. By evening they had gained 3,000 yards and had taken an enemy rice dump in an abandoned banana plantation, about 600 yards east of the track. As the Australians moved into the dump area, the Japanese rallied, mounted a strong attack, and brought the drive on the right to a complete halt.

Catterns had meanwhile won his battle. Unable to dislodge him, the Japanese covering force fell back that night to the track junction, abandoning still another prepared defensive position on the kunai flat which it was now no longer in a position even to try to hold.

Catterns lost sixty-seven of his ninety men in the engagement, but his attack was a brilliant success. Not only had it turned the enemy's flank, but it had made possible the deep penetration on the right. Left with no

choice but to withdraw, the Japanese had pulled all the way back to their main defenses in the track junction.

When the attack was over and Catterns' company had been relieved by a company of the 2/3 Battalion, the Australians had a new east-west front line which was pivoted on the track and lay within easy attacking distance of the enemy positions immediately south of the track junction. The Australian left was just south of the perimeter Catterns had held on the 21st, a slight withdrawal having been ordered there for tactical reasons. In the center the Australians were astride the track several hundred yards to the south of the main Japanese defenses covering the track junction. On the right, to the southeast of the junction, they held the banana plantation and the rice dump, their forward foxholes in the relatively open plantation area being only thirty or forty yards away from those of the enemy.

By this time the strength of the brigade after not quite two months of action had gone down from almost 1,900 officers and men to a force of barely 1,000. Most of the companies in the line were at half strength or less. Catterns' company, for instance, had only twenty-three officers and men, and the company of the 2/3 Battalion that relieved his unit had less than fifty men. The two companies on the right under Captains Bosgard and Blamey did not exceed forty men each, and the other companies were similarly depleted.

Despite their dashing showing on 21 November, the troops of the brigade were in poor physical condition. They were feverish, hungry, and exhausted, and an ever increasing number were being hospitalized for malaria and other diseases. The brigade was still a fighting force. It could still hold, but its men, for the present at least, were too worn out to do more. Until they had a little rest another force would have to take over the attack. That force, by decision of General MacArthur, was to be Colonel Tomlinson's 126th U. S. Infantry, the regiment to which General Harding had given the task of taking Buna Village and Buna Mission.[4]

General Vasey Is Given the 126th Infantry

Because he could make no radio contact with the 7th Division, and had no assurance that the Australians would get to Soputa in time to close his inward flank, General Harding ordered Colonel Tomlinson on the morning of 18 November to march on Buna via Popondetta and Soputa. Tomlinson, who was then at Inonda, was told that, if the Australians were at Popondetta by the time his leading elements got there, he was to order his troops back to Inonda and, as previously planned, move them on Buna via Horanda and Dobodura.

Early on 19 November Colonel Tomlinson sent Major Bond and Companies I and K, 126th Infantry, across the Girua River to find out if the Australians had as yet reached Popondetta. Bond made contact with an Australian unit just outside of Popondetta at 1130 that day. When he learned that the main Australian force had already passed Popondetta and was on its way to Soputa, Bond ordered his two companies back to Inonda. The regiment, which had been down to its last C ration on 18 November, had rations and ammunition dropped to it at Inonda on the 19th and began marching on Buna, via Horanda,

and Dobodura, the 2d Battalion as before leading.[5]

At Port Moresby meanwhile, higher headquarters, with General MacArthur's approval, had decided to give the 126th Infantry to General Vasey for action on the Sanananda track, rather than let it proceed as originally planned to Buna. The point was made that there seemed to be more Japanese in General Vasey's area than in General Harding's, and that the main effort would therefore have to be made west of the Girua River. If need be, higher headquarters decided, this was to be accomplished at the expense of the offensive effort on the eastern side of the river.

After this decision, General Vasey was told that he could have the 126th Infantry if he thought he needed it to take Sanananda. Knowing only too well how tired and depleted the 16th Brigade was, General Vasey accepted the offer with alacrity, and General Herring at once ordered Colonel Tomlinson to Popondetta with instructions to report to General Vasey.[6]

The diversion of the 126th Infantry to General Vasey's command greatly disturbed General Harding, who could see little justification for the diversion of half his troop strength to General Vasey just as he was about to use it to take Buna. In a message "For General Herring's eyes only," he urged that the decision to take the 126th Infantry away from him be reconsidered as likely to lead to confusion, resentment, and misunderstanding. The message went out at 0100, 20 November, and General Herring,

---

[4] Msg, NGF to 126th Inf (repeated to 32d Div) 1840, 19 Nov 42, in 32d Div G-2, G-3 Jnl; Maj Dunlop, The Sanananda Track; McCarthy, op. cit. Ch. 17.

[5] 126th Inf Jnl, Ser 17, 18 Nov 42, Ser 6, 9, 10, 19 Nov 42.

[6] Msg, NGF to 32d Div, No. 933, 19 Nov 42; Msg, NGF to 126th Inf, No. 941, 19 Nov 42; Msg, NGF to 7th Aust Div, No. 966, 19 Nov 42; Msg, Gen Herring to Gen Harding, No. 1068, 20 Nov 42. All in 32d Div G-2, G-3 Jnl.

in a stiff note, replied at 1420 that the decision would have to stand, and that he was counting on Harding to make no further difficulties in the matter.[7] General Harding had no further recourse. He would have to make out as best he could at Buna without Colonel Tomlinson's troops.

The Regiment Arrives at Soputa

On 19 November Colonel Tomlinson was ordered by New Guinea Force to report to the 7th Division. Surprised by the order, Tomlinson immediately tried checking with General Harding by radio to make sure that there was no mistake. Unable to make radio contact with Harding, he got in touch with the rear echelon of the regiment at Port Moresby. Learning from the regimental base that he had indeed been released from the 32d Division, he began moving on Popondetta early on the 20th. Accompanied by a small detail, including Captain Boice, his S–2, and Captain Dixon, his S–3, he reported to General Vasey at Popondetta that afternoon. Vasey at once sent him to Soputa where he was to come under the command of Brigadier Lloyd.

The regiment had already begun moving. Major Bond and the men of Companies I and K, who had been on their way back to Inonda when the orders came for the regiment to cross the Girua and come under Australian command, led the march to

Soputa. Major Baetcke, whom Colonel Tomlinson had left in command at Inonda, departed for Soputa with the rest of the regiment the same afternoon. Only an air-dropping detail and a couple of hundred natives were left at Inonda. Their instructions were to bring forward all the supplies accumulated there as quickly as possible.

Although it had rained during the preceding few days and the march was through heavy mud, the troops made good time. By the evening of 21 November, the whole force—regimental headquarters, Major Boerem's two companies and platoon of the 1st Battalion, Major Smith's 2d Battalion, the 17th Portable Hospital, the Service Company, and a platoon of Company A, 114th Engineer Battalion—had reached Soputa. The men arrived wet and hungry. They were at once attached to the 16th Brigade and assigned a bivouac near Soputa.

General Vasey in the meantime had set 22 November as the day that the Americans were to be committed to action. With the successful advance of the 16th Brigade on 21 November, the plan now was that the brigade would hold and make no further attempt to advance until the Americans had taken the track junction.[8]

The situation was to the liking of the depleted and exhausted 16th Brigade. As the Australian historian Dudley McCarthy puts it, ". . . the Australians were content to sit back for a while and watch the Americans. There was a very real interest in their observation and a certain sardonic but concealed amusement. The Americans had told some of them that they 'could go home now' as

[7] Msg, Gen Harding to Gen Herring, 0100, 20 Nov 42; Msg, Gen Herring to Gen Harding, No. 1068, 20 Nov 42. Both in 32d Div G–2, G–3 Jnl; Interv with Gen Harding, 27 Jun 49. Although General Harding's message is mentioned by number in General Herring's message, no copy of it is to be found in the records of the 32d Division. Its gist as given above is from General Harding's personal recollection on the matter.

[8] 126th Inf Jnl, Sers 5, 14, 19 Nov 42, Sers 4, 6, 20 Nov 42; 126th Inf CT AAR, Papuan Campaign; Ltr, Col Tomlinson to Gen Ward, 7 Mar 51; McCarthy, op. cit., Ch. 17.

they (the Americans) 'were here to clean things up.' " [9]

The Americans Take Over

The Troops Move Out for the Attack

On the evening of 21 November Colonel Tomlinson, who, with Captains Boice and Dixon, had already reconnoitered the front in the company of both General Vasey and Brigadier Lloyd, met with his battalion commanders to plan the next morning's attack. Little was known about the terrain ahead. The map being used at the time by the 16th Brigade was the provisional 1-inch-to-1-mile Buna Sheet. In addition to being inaccurate, it was blank as far as terrain features in the track junction were concerned. All that it showed was the junction, the Cape Killerton track, and the Soputa–Sanananda track. The rest was left to the troops to fill in.

As he started planning for the attack, Colonel Tomlinson knew only that heavy bush, jungle, and swamp lay on either side of the junction, and that the junction itself was covered by well-prepared enemy defenses, location and depth unknown. The Japanese position, he noted, was an inverted V. To flank it, he would have to attack it in a larger V. His plan was therefore to use Major Bond's 3d Battalion to probe the enemy position and move behind it in a double envelopment from right and left. When that maneuver was completed, he would send in Major Smith's 2d Battalion and, as he phrased it, "squeeze the Japanese right out."

Tomlinson quickly worked out the details of the attack. While Major Boerem's detachment tried attacking frontally along the track, Major Bond's battalion would move up into the 16th Brigade's area and, from a central assembly point about four miles north of Soputa, would march out on right and left to begin the envelopments. The 2d Battalion, in need of rest after its march over the Owen Stanleys, was to remain in the Soputa area in reserve, to be called upon when needed. [10]

The 2d Battalion had no sooner settled itself in its bivouac than New Guinea Force ordered it back across the Girua River to rejoin the 32d Division. General Herring gave the order in response to a request from General Harding for the reinforcement of the 2d Battalion, 128th Infantry, which had run into difficulties on General Harding's left flank. Major Smith's battalion left Soputa for the river crossing, half a mile away, early on 22 November. It got there only to discover that the river, which was unbridged, was in flood and could not be forded. A cable was thrown over the river, and the troops crossed in hastily put together rafts, which were guided to the other side by the cable. The battalion finished crossing the river late that evening and fought thereafter on the eastern side of the river. [11]

Major Smith's battalion and the bulk of Colonel Carrier's battalion—some 1,500 men—were now both east of the Girua

---

[9] McCarthy, op. cit., Ch. 17.

[10] 126th Inf Jnl, Ser 23, 21 Nov 42; Interv with Col Baetcke, 17 Nov 50; Ltr, Col Clarence M. Tomlinson to author, 28 Nov 50; McCarthy, op. cit., Ch. 17.

[11] Msg, Gen Harding to NGF, Ser 1099, 21 Nov 42; Msg, NGF to 32d Div, No. G–01559, 22 Nov 42; Msg, Maj Smith to 32d Div, Ser 1254, 23 Nov 42. All in 32d Div G–2, G–3 Jnl; 126th Inf Jnl, Sers 8, 49, 22 Nov 42; Interv with Maj Odell, 14 Dec 50.

River.[12] Colonel Tomlinson was left with the comand only of the 126th Infantry troops west of it—Headquarters and Headquarters Company, Major Boerem's detachment, Major Bond's 3d Battalion, the regimental Cannon and Antitank Companies, a detachment of the Service Company, and attached medical and engineer troops—a total of 1,400 men.[13] The Cannon and Antitank Companies were still at Wairopi and would not arrive at Soputa for some time. The envelopments would have to be made with the troops at hand—Major Boerem's detachment and Major Bond's battalion.

Though he was now without his reserve battalion, Colonel Tomlinson proceeded as planned with the envelopments. Major Boerem's detachment would engage the enemy frontally along the track, and the 3d Battalion—Companies I and K on the left and Company L on the right—would make the envelopments, supported by elements of Company M.

Companies I, K, and L, strengthened in each case by machine gun and mortar elements from Company M, left the regimental bivouac area near Soputa at 0640, 22 November, their faces daubed with green for action in the swamp and jungle terrain facing them. The troops had been issued two

days' rations, hand grenades, and as much .30-caliber and .45-caliber ammunition as they could carry. Twenty rounds had been issued for each mortar, and arrangements had been made to have additional rations, equipment, and ammunition brought forward as needed by native carriers and by Company M.

The 3d Battalion moved up to its designated assembly area, and there, about four miles north of Soputa and about 1,000 yards south of the track junction, Major Bond established his CP. Continuing up the track, Major Boerem's detachment passed through a company of the 2/3 Battalion under Capt. N. H. L. Lysaght, the most advanced unit on the trail, and began moving into position immediately to Lysaght's front. Companies I and K, Capt. John D. Shirley and Lt. Wilbur C. Lytle commanding, accompanied by Capt. Meredith M. Huggins, battalion S–3, moved out on the left at 0940; Company L, under Capt. Bevin D. Lee, pushed off on the right an hour and a half later. Company M, under Capt. Russell P. Wildey, less such of its machine gun and mortar elements as were with the companies in attack, went into bivouac 200 yards to the rear of Major Bond's CP. (*Map 8*)

By 1100 Companies I and K had passed through the Australian troops on the left— two companies of the 2/2 Battalion under command of Capt. Donald N. Fairbrother. At 1445 Company L had reached the right-flank position in the banana plantation held by the remaining two companies of the 2/2d under Captains Bosgard and Blamey. By this time Major Boerem's detachment had passed through Captain Lysaght's company and was dug in immediately to its front. The rest of the 2/3 Battalion was in position behind Lysaght to give the center

---

[12] It will be recalled that Colonel Carrier and most of the 1st Battalion, 126th Infantry, 589 officers and men, had been flown from Port Moresby to Abel's Field, when the landing field at Pongani had closed temporarily because of heavy rains, and that the next day the rest of the troops 218 men, under Major Boerem, had been flown to Pongani upon the opening there of a new all-weather field. The two detachments became separated. The bulk of the battalion, under Colonel Carrier, fought thereafter east of the river. Major Boerem's detachment (which with late comers and attached troops was to reach a strength of about 250 men) fought west of it.

[13] Ltr, Gen Eichelberger to Gen MacArthur, 14 Jan 43, copy in OCMH files.

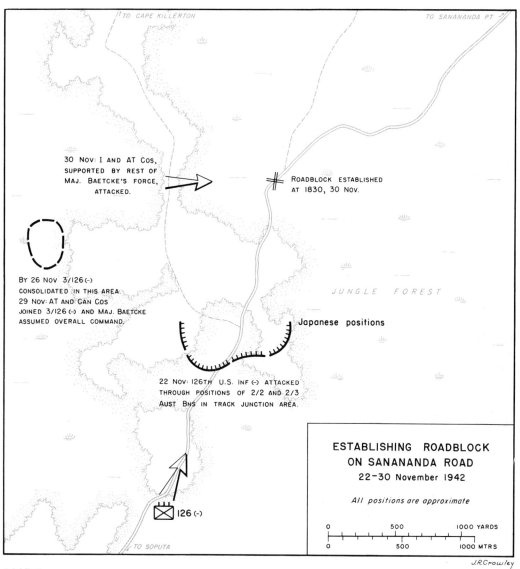

TO CAPE KILLERTON

TO SANANANDA PT

30 NOV: I AND AT COS, SUPPORTED BY REST OF MAJ. BAETCKE'S FORCE, ATTACKED.

ROADBLOCK ESTABLISHED AT 1830, 30 NOV.

BY 26 NOV 3/126 (-) CONSOLIDATED IN THIS AREA. 29 NOV: AT AND CAN COS JOINED 3/126 (-) AND MAJ. BAETCKE ASSUMED OVERALL COMMAND.

JUNGLE FOREST

Japanese positions

22 NOV: 126TH U.S. INF (-) ATTACKED THROUGH POSITIONS OF 2/2 AND 2/3 AUST BNS IN TRACK JUNCTION AREA.

126 (-)

ESTABLISHING ROADBLOCK ON SANANANDA ROAD
22-30 November 1942

All positions are approximate

| 0 | 500 | 1000 YARDS |
| 0 | 500 | 1000 MTRS |

TO SOPUTA

J.R.Crowley

MAP 8

depth and serve as a backstop should the Japanese try to break out from the track junction. Colonel Tomlinson's attack was almost ready to go.[14]

[14] 126th Inf Jnl, Ser 23, 21 Nov 42, Sers 12, 14, 18, 24, 22 Nov 42; Jnl, Maj Boerem's Det; 126th Inf CT AAR, Papuan Campaign; McCarthy, *op. cit.*, Ch. 17.

The Envelopments Begin

At 1100 Company K under Lieutenant Lytle moved out into the no man's land on the Australian left. Company I under Captain Shirley followed immediately, swinging wide around Lytle's left. Colonel

Tsukamoto had patrols in the area, and Company K ran into the first of them at 1110, only ten minutes out. The patrol was a small one, and Lytle had no trouble dispersing it. Company I, which was covering Company K from the left, ran into a much larger force at 1215. Shirley started flanking on right and left, and the Japanese after a heavy exchange of fire withdrew. At 1300 Company K again received fire, probably from the same force which had tried to ambush Company I. Lieutenant Lytle started flanking, and the enemy again withdrew.

The two companies suffered light casualties in these encounters—four killed and four wounded. The terrain was heavy bush and swamp, hard to get through, and with no prominent terrain features from which to take a bearing. Having had very little training in patrolling, the troops got their directions skewed during the frequent harassing encounters with the enemy. By the end of the day they found themselves only about 350 yards north of the Australians and not, as they had planned, several times that distance from them.

Captain Lee's Company L, with a platoon of Company M attached, left the banana plantation, which was on the west bank of a small, easily forded stream, at about 1500 and attacked in a northwesterly direction. After gaining perhaps 200 yards, the company was stopped in its tracks by heavy crossfire. It lost three killed and several wounded and made no further advance that day.

The company had just dug itself in for the night when Colonel Tsukamoto attacked with several hundred fresh *144th Infantry* replacements who had reached Basabua the night before and had been immediately assigned to his command. Company L, helped by the two Australian companies, threw back the attack and inflicted heavy losses to the enemy. Company L alone claimed to have killed forty Japanese that night, with a further loss to itself of two killed and one wounded.[15]

Colonel Tomlinson had planned to continue the attack during the afternoon of 23 November. But with Companies I and K completely out of position on the left, and Company L on the right stopped almost as soon as it moved out of the plantation area, he had to postpone the attack until his flanking companies were more advantageously situated to launch it.

The delay would be an advantage for the front by this time was rapidly becoming organized. The airstrip at Popondetta opened for traffic on 23 November, and a section of four 25-pounders of the 2/1 Australian Field Regiment, Maj. A. G. Hanson commanding, was flown in and went into action the same day from a point north of Soputa. Additional 81-mm. mortars were rushed to Company L, and the available native carriers and troops of Company D began bringing out the wounded and carrying rations to the troops on both flanks.[16]

Companies I and K, trying to get into position for the attack after their slow advance of the day before, got off to an early start on 23 November. Except for some heavy firing at daybreak, which caused

---

[15] 126th Inf Jnl, Sers 4, 5, 23 Nov 42; *Tomita Butai* Orders, 22 Nov 42; *Yokoyama Det* Orders, 22 Nov 42. Last two in ATIS EP 29; *17th Army Opns I*, 131; *18th Army Opns I*, 20, 21. About 500 replacements had come in from Rabaul on 21 November. The larger portion were at once assigned to Colonel Tsukamoto for front-line action, and the rest were left in reserve to the rear of the track junction.

[16] 126th Inf Jnl, Ser 5, 23 Nov 42; G-3 Opns Rpt, No. 231, 23–24 Nov 42, in G-3 Jnl, GHQ SWPA; NGF, Notes on Opns in New Guinea, Ser 3; McCarthy, *op. cit.*, Ch. 17.

them no casualties, the two companies met no interference from the enemy all day. Progress was steady, and by 1410 Captain Shirley was able to report an uninterrupted advance.

Though they themselves were not too sure of their location, Companies I and K had by the following evening reached a clearing in the swamp to the left of the track, about 1,200 yards north of their line of departure and about 1,000 west of the Killerton trail. The two companies, now together and in position to attack, settled themselves in the clearing for the night, preparatory to attacking eastward in the morning. After three sleepless nights the weary men were not as alert as they should have been. Japanese patrols approached to within a short distance of their perimeter and suddenly subjected them to heavy crossfire. Taken completely by surprise, the troops pulled back into the swamp in disorder.

Learning of the new setback, Colonel Tomlinson, who had counted on finally attacking on 25 November, at once ordered Major Bond forward to take command of the two scattered companies and to attack on the 26th.

On the right Company L had been making virtually no progress. By the evening of 24 November, it was just where it had been on the evening of the 22d—on the outskirts of the rice dump, about 200 yards from its line of departure.

The next day, 25 November, the 25-pounders and the mortars gave the Japanese positions a thorough going over. In the process, however, an 81-mm. mortar shell fell short and landed in the command post that Captain Lee was sharing with Captain Blamey. Blamey and one other Australian were killed, and Captain Lee and five others—Australians and Americans—were

wounded. Captain Bosgard took over command of the Australians in the area, and Maj. Bert Zeeff of the Americans. Major Zeeff, executive officer of the 3d Battalion, went forward that night from battalion headquarters. Zeeff reached the plantation area with a few men from Battalion Headquarters Company at about 0100 on the 26th. He slept in the same CP in which Captain Blamey had been killed. At daybreak, after a heavy mortaring of the plantation area by the Japanese, Zeeff inspected the Allied position. He found the Australians in the center of the line, with the Americans in a semicircular position on left and right. The Australians were behind a heavy log breastwork, which, as Zeeff recalls, was "grooved and creased" with enemy fire. The attack obviously was making no progress, and it was clear to Zeeff that he would have to use some other axis of approach if he was to reach the track.

Instead of trying to crash through the strong enemy positions forward of the plantation area, Zeeff tried a new tactic. Leaving part of Company L and twenty men from 3d Battalion headquarters in place in the plantation area, he recrossed the stream with the rest of his force, about 100 men, sideslipped along the stream for about 600 yards, and prepared to hit the enemy through the gap between Boerem's positions on the track and the allied right flank.[17]

---

[17] Jnls, Cos I, K, and L, 126th Inf, 23 Nov 42, 24 Nov 42, 25 Nov 42; 126th Inf Jnl, Sers 12, 14, 16, 19, 23 Nov 42, Sers 4, 16, 28, 24 Nov 42, Sers 9, 19, 25 Nov 42; Ltrs, Lt Col Bert Zeeff to author, 5 Oct 50, 25 Oct 50, 11 Sep 51. Capt. Jack M. Blamey, a nephew of General Blamey, who had distinguished himself by his bravery during this period as well as during the fighting in the Owen Stanleys, was posthumously awarded the Distinguished Service Cross. The citation is in GHQ SWPA GO No. 54, 3 Dec 42.

NATIVES WITH SUPPLIES AND AMMUNITION *for the front lines taking a brief rest along a corduroy road.*

The long-delayed attack was now finally ready. The 25-pounders and the mortars opened up about 1300, 26 November, shortly after Companies I and K, under Major Bond, pushed off to the eastward toward the Killerton trail. At 1320 the artillery and mortar fire ceased. Companies C and D, Major Boerem's two companies, attacked straight north along the track, and Company L, with attached elements of Company M and battalion headquarters, under Major Zeeff, crossed the stream and pushed northwestward.

Major Bond's eastward thrust hit stiff resistance. After several hours of indecisive fighting and the loss of five killed and twenty-three wounded, Bond's two companies consolidated about 700 yards west of the Killerton trail. Major Boerem's companies ran into such heavy machine gun and mortar fire that they were stopped after an advance of less than a hundred yards. Colonel Tomlinson, Captain Boice, Captain Dixon, and other members of the regimental staff who were observing Boerem's attack were pinned to the ground and managed to extricate themselves only after the enemy fire lifted. Zeeff did somewhat better. He pushed ahead for about 350 yards before running into heavy fire from several hidden machine guns that killed and wounded several of his men. The advance, which had begun so promisingly, was brought to a complete halt. The troops began aggressive patrolling to pinpoint the enemy positions, but so skillfully were they

"FUZZY WUZZY" NATIVES *carrving a wounded soldier to a first aid station in the rear area.*

hidden that Zeeff's patrols could not at once locate them. Dusk came, and the troops dug in for the night in foxholes which immediately filled with water.[18]

---

[18] 126th Inf Jnl, Sers 1, 7, 20, 27, 33, 39, 48, 52, 54, 56, 59, 26 Nov 42; Jnls, Cos I, K, and L, 26 Nov 42; Jnl, Maj Boerem's Det, 26 Nov 42; Ltrs, Col Zeeff to author, 5 Oct 50, 25 Oct 50. Maj. Simon Warmenhoven, the regimental surgeon, while on his way that day to Major Boerem's CP with other members of the regimental staff, saw a mortar shell land on a platoon of the 2/3 Battalion, which was in position immediately to Boerem's rear, killing five and wounding eight. Though the position was under heavy fire, Warmenhoven at once went to the aid of the wounded Australians and stayed with them until all had received medical attention and been evacuated. Warmenhoven was later awarded the Distinguished Service Cross. The citation is in Hq USAFFE GO No. 34, 21 Jun 43.

The Establishment of the Roadblock

Early on 27 November Major Bond reported that, although everything on his front was at a stalemate, he was holding and preparing to attack. The next morning, while Colonel Tomlinson was adding up his battle casualties (which by that time were more than 100 killed, wounded, and missing), the Cannon and Antitank Companies under Captain Medendorp finally reached Soputa from Wairopi. The men, exhausted and very hungry, were given food and allowed to rest, their first respite in some time.

Colonel Tsukamoto meanwhile continued attacking savagely on his left, on the assumption apparently that the Allied troops on that flank presented the greatest threat to his position in the track junction. The Japanese attacked all day on 27 November. Their pressure was directed principally at Zeeff, whose forward perimeter was now between 300 and 400 yards from the track, but intermittent glancing blows were sent also against the Australian and American positions in the banana plantation. The heaviest attack of the day came toward evening. It was beaten off with the help of Major Hanson's 25-pounders and the excellent observation of one of Hanson's forward observers, Lt. A. N. T. Daniels, who was with Zeeff. Daniels switched the artillery fire from Zeeff's front to Bosgard's and back again to such good effect that the Japanese attack soon dwindled to nuisance fire only. In repelling the Japanese, Zeeff's troops suffered considerable casualties, and the Australians in the plantation area, now down to about fifty men, lost Captain Bosgard, whose death came only two days after Captain Blamey's.

Zeeff had meanwhile been joined by seventy men from Major Boerem's detachment—thirty-seven men from Company C and thirty-three from Company D. Still facing the task of cleaning out the Japanese immediately to their front, the group spent the day of the 28th in patrolling and locating the hidden enemy positions. One of Zeeff's platoon leaders, 1st Lt. Henry M. Crouch, Jr., accompanied by Lieutenant Daniels, stalked and ambushed a party of eight Japanese. In a particularly daring foray, Sgt. Robert R. McGee of Company L led the patrol that located the main enemy position standing in the way of the advance and helped to wipe it out. The next day, rations, ammunition, and hand grenades were brought forward and distributed to the troops. Zeeff was ready to push for-

ward again. His orders were to move northwest to make contact with the troops on the left flank, who, he was told, would try to hit the Soputa–Sanananda track the next day.[19]

General Vasey had hoped to open up a new front for his Australians by having them cut over from the Killerton trail to the Soputa–Sanananda track at a point well to the north of the area in which the Americans were operating. On 28 November, on the very eve of the American attack, he learned that the plan was impracticable. Strong Australian patrols sent out on 24 and 26 November reported that the intervening swamp barred access from one track to the other that far north. The farthest north the crossing could be made, General Vasey was told, was where the Americans were about to make it. The Americans, in short, had stumbled upon exactly the right spot to make the envelopment, and the envelopment was ready to go.

The main effort was to be on the left. On 29 November Colonel Tomlinson ordered Major Baetcke, his executive officer, to proceed to Major Bond's position on the left flank and take command of the troops there. These troops now included Companies I and K, elements of Company M and 3d Battalion headquarters, and the Cannon and Antitank Companies. The last two units had moved up from Soputa and taken up a position on Bond's rear. Baetcke's instructions were to attack eastward on 30 November and, in concert with a further frontal attack by Major Boerem, and an

---

[19] 126th Inf Jnl, Sers 19, 24, 27 Nov 42, Sers 2, 13, 28 Nov 42; Jnl, Co L, 126th Inf, 27–30 Nov 42; Ltrs, Col Zeeff to author, 5 Oct 50, 25 Oct 50; Interv with Col Baetcke, 18 Nov 50. Sergeant McGee was later awarded the Distinguished Service Cross. The citation is in Hq USAFFE GO No. 32, 15 Jun 43.

attack on the right by Major Zeeff, to establish a roadblock to the rear of the main enemy position in the track junction.

Baetcke reached Bond's position late on the morning of 29 November. He was accompanied by 1st Lt. Peter L. Dal Ponte, commanding officer of the Service Company, whom he had chosen to be his assistant. As nearly as could be made out, Bond's position to the west of both the Cape Killerton trail and the Soputa–Sanananda track lay about 700 yards from the one and 1,600 yards from the other. Baetcke quickly worked out a plan of attack. The line of departure was to be about 200 yards northeast of Bond's main position and about 500 west of the Killerton trail. At the prescribed time the troops would attack straight east and move astride the Soputa–Sanananda track 1,400 yards away.

The units in assault would be under command of Major Bond, who was to be accompanied by Lieutenant Daniels. The attacking force of 265 men was to include Company I under Captain Shirley, the Antitank Company under its commanding officer, Capt. Roger Keast, a light machine gun section of Company M, and a communications detachment from 3d Battalion headquarters. Company K and the Cannon Company, both under command of Captain Medendorp, were to be in support. Led by Lieutenant Lytle, Company K would take up a position behind the line of departure and execute a holding attack by fire. The Cannon Company, under its commander, 1st Lt. John L. Fenton, would remain in reserve to the rear of Company K and would come to its aid should it come under enemy attack.

Early on the morning of 30 November the 126th Infantry attacked the Japanese on the right, in the center, and on the left. The attack on the right by Company L met no opposition for about 150 yards but was then brought to a complete halt by a strong Japanese force that Colonel Tsukamoto had deployed there for just that purpose. Companies C and D in the center did not do as well and gained only a few yards. The real success of the day was registered on the left.

Major Bond's force left the line of departure at 0900, after a ten-minute artillery and mortar preparation. It moved in column of companies, Company I leading. The supporting fire of Company K proved very effective and drew strong, retaliatory fire from the enemy. At first the troops had no trouble dealing with the enemy to the front. About four hundred yards beyond the line of departure, as they started moving through a large kunai patch, they were met from virtually all sides by hostile rifle, mortar, and machine gun fire. Major Bond was wounded about 0930 and had to be evacuated. The attack lost its momentum and for a time bogged down completely. Learning of the difficulty, Major Baetcke came up from the rear, rallied the troops, and, leading the way, cleared the enemy out of the kunai flat. Captain Shirley took command and the attack continued.

After eliminating the resistance on the kunai flat, the troops fought several minor skirmishes with small parties of the enemy who seemed to be patrolling the area. About a thousand yards out, they ran into jungle and swamp terrain more difficult than anything they had previously encountered. The undergrowth in the jungle was almost impenetrable, but the real difficulty came when the men reached a 300-yard stretch of knee-deep swamp. The Japanese, who had cut fire lanes commanding the swamp, temporarily stopped Captain Shirley's troops with knee-mortar and machine gun fire just as they were trying to clear it. Shirley's men finally succeeded in crossing the swamp and dispersing the enemy. A little way out of the swamp the troops came upon a well-traveled trail leading generally eastward and followed it. At 1700 Company I's scouts reported an enemy bivouac area directly ahead. [20] What followed is best told by one who was present.

At this point Captain Shirley ordered his Company I, deployed with two platoons abreast and supporting platoon following in center rear, to insert bayonets and assault the . . . enemy position (endeavoring to get his objective prior to darkness). The attack was well executed and successful. Captain Shirley, after driving the enemy from this position, organized perimeter defense by emplacing his rifle platoons of Company I west of the road; 1 LMG Squad, Company M, near the road on the northern portion of the perimeter; and 1 LMG Squad, Company M, on the southern portion of the perimeter. AT Company had been [deployed] east of the road. The perimeter was in and established by about . . . 1830. . . . About two hours later we were getting heavy mortar fire in the perimeter and later attacks from the northeast on the AT Company's sector, and subsequently from the northwest on Company I's sector. Both were repulsed with few casualties.[21]

In storming the bivouac area, the Shirley force had killed a score of Japanese; it had captured two disabled Ford trucks, a variety of auto repair tools, a little food, and some medical supplies; most important of all, it had gained its objective. The captured bivouac area, a comparatively open, oval-shaped space about 250 yards long and 150 yards wide, lay astride the track 1,500 yards to the north of the track junction and approximately 300 south of the Japanese second line of defense higher up on the track. The long-sought roadblock, to the rear of the Japanese positions in the track junction, had finally been established.[22]

Zeeff's Recall

Now that the Shirley force had cut through the Japanese line and established itself on the track, it remained to be seen whether the Zeeff force, now only a few hundred yards south of it, could link up with Shirley. Held up on 30 November while Shirley was moving steadily to his goal, Major Zeeff experienced no difficulty moving forward the next day. His men advanced northwest in order to join Shirley in the roadblock. The Japanese, apparently diverted from the threat on their left by the new threat on their rear, had relaxed their pressure, and Zeeff's force moved steadily ahead.

Early that afternoon Zeeff's troops crossed the track and, moving to a point about 250 yards west of it, surprised and wiped out a party of thirty-five to forty Japanese. Zeeff reported the skirmish to Colonel Tom-

[20] 126th Inf Jnl, Sers 16, 21, 29 Nov 42, Sers 6, 8, 9, 12, 13, 30, 31, 35, 37, 38, 30 Nov 42; Jnls, Cos I, K, and L, 126th Inf, 29 and 30 Nov 42; Col Baetcke, Notes on the American Force on the Sanananda Trail, 25 May 43; Memo, Maj Peter L. Dal Ponte for author, 12 Jul 50; McCarthy, *op. cit.*, Ch. 17. For his action in rallying and leading the troops on the kunai flat, Major Baetcke was later awarded the Distinguished Service Cross. The citation is in Hq, USAFFE GO No. 32, 15 Jun 43.

[21] Memo, Maj Dal Ponte for author, 12 Jul 50.

[22] 126th Inf Jnl, Sers 62, 69, 73, 74, 75, 76, 30 Nov 42; Jnls, Cos I and K, 126th Inf, 30 Nov 42; Col Baetcke, Notes on the American Force on the Sanananda Trail, 25 May 43; Ltr, Col Baetcke to ACofS, G–3, SWPA, 9 Jul 43, Statement on the Soputa—Sanananda (Huggins) Roadblock, in G–3 Jnl, GHQ SWPA; Memo, Maj Dal Ponte for author, 12 Jul 50; Interv with Col Baetcke, 17 Nov 50.

linson at 1515 and, told him that he thought his troops had crossed the track. To prevent enemy interception of the message Zeeff spoke in Dutch, a language familiar to many of the Michigan troops present, and a Dutch-speaking sergeant at headquarters interpreted for Colonel Tomlinson.

Zeeff dug in at 1625 on Tomlinson's orders. Within the hour the Japanese struck from right and front. After a brisk fire fight in which Zeeff lost two killed and three wounded, the enemy withdrew. At 2100 Colonel Tomlinson ordered Zeeff to move back to the east side of the road as soon as he could and to push northward from there to make the desired juncture with the troops in the roadblock. At that point the wire went dead, and Zeeff was on his own.

The troops fashioned stretchers for the wounded from saplings, telephone wire, and denim jackets, and the next morning began moving from their night perimeter on a northeasterly course to recross the track as ordered. Their withdrawal was no easy task. The enemy kept up a steady fire, and it was here that Pvt. Hymie Y. Epstein, one of Zeeff's last medical aid men, was killed. Epstein had distinguished himself on 22 November by crawling to the aid of a wounded man in an area swept by enemy fire. He had done the same thing on 1 December. This is the scene on the afternoon of the 1st, as Zeeff recalled it:

I was prone with a filled musette bag in front of my face; Epstein was in a similar position about 4 or 5 feet to my left. Pvt. Sullivan was shot through the neck and was lying about 10 feet from me to my right front. Epstein said, "I have to take care of him." I said, "I'm not ordering you to go, the fire is too heavy." [Despite this], he crawled on his stomach, treated and bandaged Sullivan, then crawled back. A few minutes later, Sgt. Bur-

nett . . . was shot in the head, lying a few feet from Sullivan. Epstein did the same for Burnett, and managed to crawl back without being hit.

Epstein's luck did not hold. To quote Zeeff again: "The next morning just before daybreak, Pvt. Mike Russin on our left flank was hit by a sniper. Epstein went to him, . . . but did not return as he was shot and killed there. We buried him before moving out . . . ." [23]

Toward evening, while the troops were digging in for the night at a new perimeter a few yards east of the track and about 500 south of the roadblock, Sergeant McGee, whom Zeeff had sent out to reconnoiter the area immediately to the northward, came back with discouraging news. Strong and well-manned enemy positions, beyond the power of the Zeeff force to breach, lay a couple of hundred yards ahead. Zeeff had scarcely had time to digest the news when the Japanese were upon him again. After a wild spate of firing, the attack was finally beaten off at a cost to Zeeff of five killed and six seriously wounded.

By this time Colonel Tomlinson was satisfied that Zeeff could neither maintain himself where he was nor break through to the roadblock. His perimeter was directly in the line of Allied fire, and there was no alternative but to get him out of there as quickly as possible before he was hit by friendly fire or cut to pieces by the enemy. The wire had been repaired, and at 2000 that night Tomlinson ordered Zeeff to leave the area immediately, warning him that it was to be mortared the next day. Zeeff was to bring

---

[23] Ltr, Col Zeeff to author, 11 Sep 51. Private Epstein was posthumously awarded the Silver Star. The citation is in Hq, 32d Div GO No. 28, 6 Apr 43.

MAKING LITTERS FOR THE WOUNDED

back his sick and wounded but was not to bother burying the dead.

The job of making litters for the six newly wounded began at once and went on through the night. Saplings were cut and stretchers made. By 0330 the stretchers were loaded and the march began. Walking in single column, and guiding themselves in the dark with telephone wire, the troops moved south for about 900 yards and then turned east toward the familiar little stream that flowed past the banana plantation.

The terrain was swampy, and the march slow. The men were spent and hungry, and eight soldiers had to be assigned to each stretcher. Four would carry it for fifty yards, and then the other four would take over.

Two of the stretchers broke down en route, and the troops struggled forward with the two wounded men as best they could. Shortly after daybreak the procession reached the stream, where Captain Dixon was waiting with stretchers and stretcher bearers. The wounded were attended to immediately, and the rest of the troops, most of whom had been eleven days in combat, returned to regimental headquarters and were allowed to rest.

Zeeff had not accomplished his mission, but he and his troops had done something that in retrospect was electrifying. They had threaded their way through the main Japanese position on the track, manned by some 2,000 enemy troops, and had come out in good order, bringing their wounded with them.[24]

The Ensuing Tasks

General Vasey had by now lost all hope of an early decision on the Soputa–Sanananda track. He simply did not have enough troops to secure such a decision. The 16th Brigade had less than 900 effectives left and was wasting away so rapidly from malaria and other sicknesses that there was no longer any question of assigning it any further offensive mission, especially if the mission was of a sustained nature as any offensive thrust

on the track was likely to be. All that the brigade was now in condition to do was hold. If not relieved in the near future, it would soon be unable to do even that.[25]

The weight of the attack would therefore have to continue on the Americans. But they too were beginning to sicken with malaria, and their effective strength was between 1,100 and 1,200 men, not the 1,400 it had been on 22 November when they had first been committed to action. This was scarcely a force sufficient to reduce a position as strong as that held by Colonel Tsukamoto, especially since the later actually had more men manning his powerful defense line than the Allies had available to attack it.

---

[24] Jnl, Co L, 126th Inf, 1–3 Dec 42; 126th Inf Jnl, Sers 18, 19, 27, 31, 1 Dec 42, Sers 5, 23, 2 Dec 42, Sers 1, 4, 3 Dec 42; Ltrs, Col Zeeff to author, 25 Oct 50, 11 Sep 51; Ltr, Col Tomlinson to author, 28 Nov 50.

---

[25] McCarthy, *op. cit.*, Ch. 17.

CHAPTER X

The First Two Weeks at Buna

On 16 November the troops east of the Girua River started for the positions from which they were to attack the enemy in the Cape Endaiadere–New Strip area. (*See Map V.*) The 128th Infantry moved out to the attack in early morning. Colonel McCoy's 1st Battalion (less Company A which was still at Pongani) advanced up the coast from Embogo, crossed the Samboga River, and by nightfall was in position at Boreo, a creek mouth about a mile north of Hariko where General MacNider now had his headquarters. Colonel Miller's 3d Battalion, with Colonel Smith's 2d Battalion marching immediately behind it, moved up from Warisota Plantation—three miles west of Embogo—and Embi, scattered a small Japanese patrol at Dobodura that afternoon, and started for Simemi, its jump-off point for the attack on the bridge between the strips. The troops still at Pongani—Company A, 128th Infantry, Company A, 114th Engineer Battalion, Colonel Carrier's 1st Battalion, 126th Infantry, and Major Harcourt's 2/6 Australian Independent Company—were to leave for the front the next day, in the same luggers which were bringing forward the supplies. Artillery was already in place. Using a Japanese barge captured at Milne Bay, General Waldron, the division artillery officer, had come in during the night with the two Australian 3.7-inch mountain howitzers allotted to the operation, their crews, and 200 rounds of ammunition. Waldron had left before daybreak for Oro Bay to pick up the 25-pounders that were waiting there. His executive officer, Lt. Col. Melvin McCreary, who had been put ashore at Hariko with the two mountain guns, had them assembled and ready to fire from an advanced position at Boreo that evening.[1]

General Harding Readjusts His Plans

The Disruption of the Supply Line

It was clear as the advance got under way that the 32d Division's weakest point was its supply line. Until an airfield was completed at Dobodura the division's supply, except for emergency dropping from the air, would be entirely dependent upon the six remaining luggers or trawlers with which Colonel McKenny was carrying supplies up the coast from Porlock Harbor, as well as upon the Japanese barge General Waldron was using to bring in the 25-pounders from Oro Bay. The boats had thus far not been interfered with by the enemy, but Japanese naval aviation at Lae had marked the Allied coastal movements well, and struck the very day the advance began.

---

[1] 128th Inf Jnl, Ser 70, 17 Nov 42; 3d Bn, 128th Inf, Jnl, 17 Nov 42; 32d Div Hist of Arty, Papuan Campaign; Ltr, Gen Waldron to Gen Ward, 5 Mar 51.

In the late afternoon of 16 November three of Colonel McKenny's luggers—the *Alacrity*, the *Bonwin*, and the *Minnemura*—joined by the Japanese landing barge, which had just come in from Oro Bay, left Embogo for Hariko. The *Alacrity* was carrying ammunition, and the equipment and personnel of the 22d Portable Hospital. The *Bonwin* was loaded with rations and ammunition, and the *Minnemura*, largest of the three luggers, held ammunition, rations, radio supplies, 81-mm. mortars, .50-caliber machine guns, and other heavy equipment not easily carried by the troops. The Japanese barge, also heavily laden, carried two 25-pounders, their crews, and all the 25-pounder ammunition for which space could be found. General Waldron and Col. H. F. Handy, an Army Ground Forces observer, were on the barge. General Harding, who was on his way to the front, was on the *Minnemura*, as was another AGF observer, Col. Herbert B. Laux.

The luggers and barge, protected only by machine guns mounted on their decks, were proceeding without air cover. Though it was still light, Allied fighter aircraft patrolling the coast had left for Port Moresby some time before in order to get back to their bases before dark. While the boats were rounding Cape Sudest, and a small lighter from the shore was off-loading ammunition from the *Alacrity*, which had stopped momentarily for that purpose, the flotilla was attacked by eighteen Japanese Zero-type fighters that appeared without warning from the northwest. The enemy planes gave the ships a thorough strafing. The troops aboard replied with machine guns and rifles but their fire was entirely without effect. In a few moments the barge and all three luggers were ablaze. The ammunition began to explode and all aboard had to take

to the water. General Harding, General Waldron, and Colonel Handy swam ashore. Colonel Laux, who was no swimmer, got there safely in a dinghy which had been riding behind the *Minnemura*.

The luggers, the Japanese barge, and virtually all of the cargo they were carrying were a total loss. The lighter that had been loading ammunition from the *Alacrity* reached shore under fire. At great personal risk 1st Lt. John E. Harbert, a divisional ordnance officer, went aboard and took off the ammunition. Casualties were heavy. Colonel McKenny and twenty-three others were killed, and there were many wounded. The loss of life would have been even greater but for a number of daring rescues from the shore. Braving the enemy fire, the exploding ammunition, and the flaming debris, rescue parties under Colonel Carew, commanding officer of the 114th Engineer Battalion, and 1st Lt. Herbert G. Peabody, of Division Headquarters Company, saved the lives of many who might otherwise have drowned or burned to death.[2]

The next morning, in attacks which took place before the air force could intervene, four Zeros hit two of the remaining three luggers, one at Embogo, and the other at Mendaropu. The first lugger, the *Two Freddies*, was badly smashed up and had to limp back to Milne Bay for repairs; the

---

[2] Maj Parker's Buna Rpt; Col Handy's Buna Rpt: Gen Harding's Diary, 16 Nov 42. Colonel Carew and Lieutenants Harbert and Peabody were later awarded the Distinguished Service Cross, as were the following enlisted men who participated in the rescues: S. Sgt. John R. MacGowan, Sgt. Howard J. Weiss, Cpl. Gordon C. Snyder, Pfc. Donald R. Price, Pvt. Maro P. Johnson, Pvt. Homer McAllister, and Pvt. Cloyd G. Myers. Price, Johnson and McAllister were from the 107th QM Battalion; the others were from Headquarters Company and Companies I and H, 128th Infantry. The citations are in GHQ SWPA GO No. 64, 28 Dec 42, and GO No. 1, 1 Jan 43.

AUSTRALIAN 3.7-INCH PACK HOWITZER *is dismantled before being loaded on a Japanese motor-driven barge which was captured at Milne Bay.*

second lugger, the *Willyama* suffered even greater damage and had to be beached, a total loss. Only one small lugger, the *Kelton*, was left to supply the troops east of the river.

The loss of the boats was a catastrophe of the first magnitude. There were no replacement vessels immediately in sight, and artillery pieces, mortars, machine guns, and other essential matériel, which could not be replaced for days, had been lost on the very eve of the attack. The whole supply plan for the operation had been disrupted. Since the stores of rations and ammunition ac-

tually at the front where the troops could use them were in dangerously short supply, and the one small remaining lugger could not possibly handle more than a small fraction of the division's immediate requirements, Maj. Ralph T. Birkness, Colonel McKenny's successor, then at Port Moresby, at once arranged with the air force to have the most critically needed items dropped from the air.[3]

[3] Msg, Gen MacNider to Gen Harding, Ser 769, 17 Nov 42; Msg, Col John W. Mott, CofS 32d Div, to Gen MacNider, Ser 787, 17 Nov 42; Msg, Gen Harding to Maj Ralph T. Birkness, Moresby, Ser 844, 18 Nov 42. All in 32d Div, G–2, G–3 Jnl.

GENERAL WALDRON (*center, facing forward*) *discusses plans for the impending battle 15 November 1942.*

The dislocation caused by the loss of boats and cargo on 16 and 17 November forced General Harding to make some last-minute changes in plan. General MacNider was ordered to hold up his advance until the *Kelton* could come in and make up at least part of his supply deficiencies, and the troops at Pongani who were to have been moved to Embogo by boat were ordered instead to proceed to the front on foot. Except for the engineer company which was sent to Dobodura, the troops were ordered to Boreo where they were to join with Colonel Mc-Coy's battalion in the attack toward Cape Endaiadere.[4]

Colonel Smith Is Ordered to the Left

On 18 November, with the 1st and 3d Battalions, 128th Infantry, in position at Boreo and Simemi respectively, General Harding set H Hour as 0700 the following

[4] Msg, Col Mott to Maj Harry G. Harcourt, 2/6 Aust Ind Co, Ser 791, 17 Nov 42; Msg, Gen Harding to Col Mott, Ser 848, 18 Nov 42. Both in 32d Div G-2, G-3 Jnl; Gen Harding's Diary, 17 Nov 42.

128TH INFANTRYMEN. *Above, .30-cal. Browning machine gun position in 1st Battalion area, Embogo River; below, four men from the 2d Battalion cook breakfast near the beach at Embogo.*

128TH INFANTRYMEN. *Above, 3d Battalion troops cross a stream near Boreo; below (left to right), Capt. Jack Martin, Capt. Emil Khail, Colonel Miller, and Colonel MacNab discuss attack plans at Warisota Village.*

morning, 19 November. Three companies of the 2d Battalion, 128th Infantry, which were to be in division reserve, were ordered from Dobodura to Ango in order to cover the junction of the Soputa–Buna and Ango–Dobodura tracks until such time as the 126th Infantry could come in and take over the left-flank attack on Buna Village and Buna Mission. The remaining company, joined by the engineer company when it came in from Pongani, was to remain at Dobodura to help prepare an airfield there.

The diversion next day to General Vasey's command of the 126th Infantry, even as it was marching from Inonda toward Buna to attack on Harding's left, upset these plans. Robbed at the last minute of his left-flank force, General Harding had to commit his reserve, the 2d Battalion, 128th Infantry. In ordering Colonel Smith to take Buna, General Harding was well aware that he was sending a battalion to do a job to which a full regiment had previously been assigned. He had no other force available, however, and sent Smith forward anyway, hoping apparently that he might, with luck, do the job. The company at Dobodura was immediately ordered to Ango, and the battalion moved out on the 20th with orders to attack Buna Mission.[5]

The Battle Opens

The Attacks on the Right

Torrential rains that lasted all day began early on 19 November, the day of the at-

tack. The troops were drenched to the skin, and all aircraft were grounded. At 0700, after the two mountain guns fired a few unobserved rounds, the 1st Battalion, 128th Infantry, under Colonel McCoy, moved forward from Boreo, and the 3d Battalion, 128th Infantry, under Colonel Miller, marched out from Simemi. Because of the supply dislocation, the men had only one day's rations with them, and only as much ammunition as was immediately available—little more than a day's supply.

Colonel McCoy's troops, in column of companies, with Company C leading, crossed the creek mouth near Boreo, and began moving along a narrow, muddy path in the jungle about twenty yards inland. Their objective was Cape Endaiadere, two miles away.

Colonel Yamamoto was ready. He had had two full days to get his fresh, well-armed *144th* and *229th Infantry* troops into position. His main line of resistance, between 750 and 800 yards south of Cape Endaiadere, ran from the sea through the Duropa Plantation to the eastern end of the New Strip and past it to the bridge between the strips. (*Map 9*) At the immediate approaches to this well-built and strongly held defense system he had an outpost line of emplacements. Although not continuous like the main line, it was very strong because of its cleared fields of fire. It was covered by troops who manned concealed and cleverly disposed machine gun nests along the track at the lower (southern) end of the Duropa Plantation, and in the plantation itself.

The 1st Battalion made its first enemy contact halfway between Boreo and the plantation. It was met by heavy machine gun and rifle fire from hidden enemy ma-

[5] Msgs, Gen Harding to Col Mott, Ser 848, 18 Nov 42, Ser 964, 19 Nov 42; Msgs, Gen Harding to NGF, Sers 967, 968, 20 Nov 42. All in 32d Div G–2, G–3 Jnl. 32d Div Sitreps No. 52, 18 Nov 42, No. 53, 19 Nov 42, No. 54, 20 Nov 42; Gen Harding's Diary, 18, 19 Nov 42.

chine gun positions west of the track. The troops deployed and attacked, but the heavy overhead jungle growth made it difficult for them to use their mortars effectively and their grenades were of little use because they did not know where the enemy was or where the fire was coming from. The Japanese weapons gave off no flash, and the reverberation of their fire in the jungle made it impossible to ascertain their whereabouts by sound. To complicate matters, the Japanese made it a practice to rotate their weapons among several hidden positions, causing the inexperienced Americans, until they saw through the trick, to imagine themselves covered by automatic weapons from all sides.[6]

Maj. David B. Parker, an engineer observer who was present wrote:

The first opposition from the enemy here was a surprise and shock to our green troops. The enemy positions were amazingly well camouflaged, and seemed to have excellent fields of fire even in the close quarters of the jungle. . . . Snipers were everywhere, . . . and they were so well camouflaged that it was nearly impossible to discern them. The enemy habitually allowed our troops to advance to very close range—sometimes four or five feet from a machine gun post—before opening fire; often they allowed troops to by-pass them completely, opening fire then on our rear elements, and on our front elements from the rear.

Major Parker was particularly impressed by "the deadly accuracy and strength of the enemy machine gun and rifle fire from their camouflaged positions." He added:

. . . Our troops were pinned down everywhere by extremely effective fire. It was dangerous to show even a finger from behind one's cover, as it would immediately draw a burst of fire. It was impossible to see where the enemy fire was coming from; consequently our own rifle and machine gun [fire] was ineffective during the early stages. . . . Grenades and mortars . . . were difficult to use because, first, it was difficult to pick out a nest position to advance upon with grenades, second, the thick jungle growth, and high grass, made throwing and firing difficult, and, third, because it was nearly impossible to observe our fire.[7]

Yielding a dozen or so yards at a time when strongly pressed, the Japanese covering troops gradually fell back. Out of rations, and with the greater part of its ammunition used up, the 1st Battalion ended the day a badly shaken outfit. The troops had entered the battle joking and laughing, and sure of an easy victory. Now they were dazed and taken aback by the mauling they had received at the hands of the Japanese. Nor did it escape them that the bodies of the few Japanese left on the field were those of fresh, well-fed, well-armed troops—not, as they had been led to expect, the tired, emaciated, and disease-ridden survivors of the fighting in the Owen Stanleys. It was to be some time before they and their fellows recovered from the shock of finding that the battle was to be no pushover and that,

---

[6] Maj Parker's Buna Rpt; Capt E. Khail, S-2, 128th Inf, to Col Hale, CO, 128th Inf, 28 Nov 42, sub: Japanese Tactics, in 32d Div G-2, G-3 Jnl; Ltr, Col MacNab to author, 19 Nov 51. It should be noted here that the map then in use on the front, the Buna Target Plan No. 24, was later found to be inaccurate. Its inaccuracy led to errors in the daily situation reports of the forces engaged.

[7] Maj Parker's Buna Rpt. During this attack, T/5 Edwin C. De Rosier, a medical aid man from the 107th Medical Detachment, moved out into the open in the face of intense enemy fire and repeatedly went to the aid of the wounded, saving the lives of several. Killed in action two weeks later, De Rosier was posthumously awarded the Distinguished Service Cross. The citation is in GHQ SWPA GO No. 14, 30 Jan 43.

instead of a short and easy mop-up, a long cruel fight lay ahead of them.[8]

Colonel Miller's troops had an even ruder awakening. As the 3d Battalion approached the trail junction between the Old and New Strips, the Simemi trail degenerated into a narrow causeway with swamp on either side. Attempts to get the troops through an open area about 300 yards south of the junction were met by such intense fire from the western end of the New Strip, from behind the bridge between the strips, and from machine guns forward of the junction itself that no further advance was possible that day.

Nor could Miller do much to blast out the enemy with fire. He had no 81-mm. mortars; a large percentage of his grenades failed to go off; his .30-caliber ammunition ran dangerously low, and he had to call for a fresh supply to be dropped to him from the air.[9] A member of the regimental staff recalled the situation in the following words:

Miller had to attack through swamps which were sometimes waist and chest deep, and through which it was impossible to carry any but light weapons. Here too, grenades (Mills bombs obtained from the Australians) became ineffective when wet. One of Miller's patrols threw seven grenades into a group of ten or twelve Japs whom they stalked only to have all the grenades fail to explode and to suffer about 30 percent casualties from return grenade fire.[10]

At the end of the day, Miller's troops were still at the edge of the clearing south of the junction. The battalion had suffered heavy casualties, and made no further gain. As Colonel Miller himself put the matter late that afternoon, it had been "stopped cold." [11]

Pinned down on a narrow front, out of rations, and with nearly all the ammunition expended, Miller's troops made no progress whatever the next day. They were fortunate that Colonel Yamamoto did not counterattack.

McCoy, better supplied with ammunition, resumed his attack on the 20th. After a sketchy preparation which included some unobserved fire from the mountain guns and a brief bombardment of the Cape Endaiadere area by a few B–25's and A–20's, the battalion attacked from a point about 1,800 yards south of the cape. Company C was on the right, along the coast; Company B was on the left, a short distance inland. The enemy was as well hidden and as well prepared as before, but the Americans had a better idea by this time what they were about. Led by 1st Lt. John W. Crow, who was reported missing in action that afternoon, Company C succeeded in infiltrating and knocking out several enemy machine gun nests. The line moved forward several hundred yards—as far as it was to go that day.[12]

[8] Msgs, Gen MacNider to Gen Harding, Nos. 946, 976, 977, 19 Nov 42, in 32d Div G–2, G–3 Jnl; 1st Bn, 128th Inf, Jnl, Sers 10, 12, 19 Nov 42; Memo, Col Reeder, WDGS, for Col Ritchie, Chief, Southwest Pacific Gp, OPD, WDGS, 22 Feb 43, sub: Observer Interrogation of Officers at Buna and Sanananda; Col Hale, Answers to Questions by the Hist Sec SWPA As to Certain Phases of the Papuan Campaign. An Australian journalist who was present describes the scene thus: ". . . [The Americans] went into action laughing. . . . There was bad psychology somewhere." George H. Johnson, *Pacific Partner* (New York, 1944), p. 203.
[9] 3d Bn, 128th Inf, Jnl, Sers 1250, 1333, 1650, 19 Nov 42; Msg, Gen Harding to Maj Birkness, No. 936, 19 Nov 42, in 32d Div G–2, G–3 Jnl.

[10] Ltr, Col MacNab to author, 15 Nov 49.
[11] 3d Bn, 128th Inf, Jnl, 1715, 19 Nov 42.
[12] 1st Bn, 128th Inf, Jnl, Sers 1, 7, 11, 20 Nov 42 Ltr, Col MacNab to author, 15 Nov 49. Lieutenan Crow, last seen charging an enemy machine gur post, submachine gun in hand, was posthumousl awarded the Distinguished Service Cross. The cita tion is in GHQ SWPA GO No. 14, 30 Jan 43.

Rations and ammunition had been dropped at Hariko and Simemi that morning and by late afternoon had been distributed to both McCoy and Miller. In the evening, Colonel Carrier's battalion and Major Harcourt's Independent Company reached the 1st Battalion's front and went into bivouac immediately to McCoy's rear. The incoming troops, who arrived at the front exhausted after a twenty-five mile march from Pongani with full pack, were to join McCoy's battalion in a further attack on Cape Endaiadere in the morning.[13]

The attack of 21 November was to be in greater strength, better supported, and better supplied than the efforts of 19 and 20 November. The plan of attack called for McCoy's and Carrier's battalions (the 128th Infantry troops on the right, and those of the 126th Infantry on the left) to move north on Cape Endaiadere on a 300-yard front. While the attack was proceeding along the coast, the 2/6 Independent Company would infiltrate the eastern end of the New Strip, and the 3d Battalion, 128th Infantry, from its position astride the Dobodura–Simemi track, would attempt to seize the bridge between the strips. The attack would be preceded by a heavy air bombardment, following which the troops would attack. The time of the attack would be communicated to the battalion commanders as soon as it was definitely learned from the air force when the bombers would come over.

The air attack, executed by A–20's and B–25's, took place at the appointed time, and a few enemy machine gun nests were knocked out from the air. However, no ground attack followed the bombardment. Because of faulty co-ordination—apparently an oversight on the part of regimental headquarters—neither Colonel McCoy nor Colonel Miller received prior notice of the bombardment or, for that matter, orders telling them when to attack. Worse still, one of the planes, instead of dropping its bombs on the Japanese, dropped them on some of Colonel Miller's forward troops, killing four and wounded two others. Orders from regiment calling for an attack at 0800 were finally received by Colonel Miller at 0840, and by Colonel McCoy at 0850—forty and fifty minutes, respectively, after the air bombardment had ceased.

General Harding arranged to have the air force attack again at 1245. The air attack was to be followed by an artillery and mortar barrage, and the troops would jump off at 1300.

This time, no planes showed up for the attack. Fearing that it would not be able to complete the attack within the appointed time the air force had held its planes back rather than run the risk of again hitting friendly troops.[14]

Determined that there would be an attack that day, General Harding got the air force to try again. The air bombardment, as before by A–20's and B–25's, began at 1557 and was over by 1603. It was not a success. Most of the planes were unable to find the target area, and a flight of A–20's that did overshot the beachhead and dropped its bombs into the sea. One B–25 unloaded its bomb load squarely in the midst of Colonel McCoy's two lead com-

---

[13] 1st Bn, 126th Inf, Jnl, Sers 331, 332, 20 Nov 42; 1st Bn, 128th Inf, Jnl, Sers 19, 20, 20 Nov 42.

[14] 1st Bn, 128th Inf, Jnl, Sers 9, 10, 11, 13, 21 Nov 42; 3d Bn, 128th Inf, Jnl, Sers 1, 2, 3, 7, 21 Nov 42; Maj Parker's Buna Rpt; Col Knight's Buna Rpt.

panies—Companies B and C—killing six, wounding twelve, and almost burying seventy others.

This accident had a most disheartening effect on the 1st Battalion. Some of the men withdrew from the line of departure, and their commanders had to order them to return. The attack finally got under way at 1630, after a short unobserved artillery preparation by the mountain guns and a brief barrage by the mortars. As soon as the advance began, it was discovered that the preparation had done the well dug in enemy little or no harm. Once again the troops had to attack an enemy who was virtually untouched by Allied fire.

The attackers had few heavy weapons. Most of their 81-mm. mortars and heavy machine guns either had been lost or had not arrived. All the mortar shells reaching the front—including the light 81-mm. mortar shell, the only shell available at the time for the mortars—were fused superquick so that the shells went off on contact and had little effect against the Japanese bunkers. Forward observers were handicapped by the heavy jungle growth, Japanese camouflage discipline, and communications failures. The SCR 536, the small handset radio with which the mortar platoons were equipped, refused to work in the jungle.

The troops along the coastal track fought desperately with rifles, Thompson submachine guns, light machine guns, and hand grenades. They knocked out a few machine gun nests during the day, as did the Australian Independent Company which was operating near the eastern end of the strip. Otherwise there was little progress. Casualties were heavy. In three days of combat, Company C lost sixty-three men, including all four of its officers. Two ser-

geants, killed within a few hours of each other, commanded it on the 21st.[15]

Colonel Miller's battalion failed even to reach the bridge between the strips. A twenty-round barrage by the 60-mm. mortars, fired without observation and with the aid only of a photomap, had followed the air bombardment. The troops had jumped off at 1628 and at first had made good progress. They moved through the clearing where they had been held up on the 19th and 20th, swept past the junction, and several of the lead platoons actually advanced to within a short distance of the bridge. At its approaches a withering crossfire completely pinned them down. The battalion lost forty-two killed, wounded, and missing in the attack and, try as it would, could not advance. At 1750, Colonel Miller ordered the troops to pull back to a less-exposed position south of the track junction.

It was clear by this time that the 3d Battalion was not going to take the bridge. At 2015 that night Colonel Miller was ordered to leave one company suitably provided with ammunition and supplies to hold the existing position. The rest of the battalion was to march to the coast, where it was to operate thenceforward on the right flank, against Cape Endaiadere. The march was to be accomplished as swiftly as possible and in such a way that the Japanese would be unaware of the transfer. Company I, under 1st Lt. Carl K. Fryday, was chosen to stay

---

[15] 1st Bn, 126th Inf, Jnl, Sers 339 through 350, 21 Nov 42; 1st Bn, 128th Inf, Jnl, Sers 21 through 25, 21 Nov 42; 3d Bn, 128th Inf, Jnl, Sers 8, 11, 21 Nov 42; Allied Air Forces Opns Rpt, 21 Nov 42; Ltr, Col MacNab to author, 15 Nov 49. The two sergeants, 1st Sgt. Reuben J. Steger, and S.Sgt. Carl Cherney, both from Marshfield, Wisconsin, were posthumously awarded the Distinguished Service Cross. Steger's citation is in GHQ SWPA GO No. 1, 1 Jan 43; Cherney's is in GO No. 14, 30 Jan 43.

behind, and the rest of the battalion was moved back to Simemi early the following morning. By 1800 that evening the troops were bivouacked to the rear of the position held by Colonel McCoy's battalion.[16]

The supply picture had brightened slightly. The airstrip at Dobodura opened for limited traffic on 21 November, and five additional luggers arrived on the scene from Milne Bay the same day. One of them broke up on a reef immediately upon arrival, but the remaining four brought in their cargo safely. With the *Kelton,* Major Birkness now had five luggers for the coastwise operation. There was still a chance that the division's supply, disrupted though it was, could be put on an even keel.

The artillery picture had also improved. On 21 November General Waldron brought in the two remaining 25-pounders, their Australian crews, and 200 rounds of ammunition. Japanese Zeros came over just as the guns were ready to be emplaced and knocked the sights off one of them, putting it out of action for several days. This left only three guns—the two mountain guns and a 25-pounder—immediately available for the attack on the powerful Japanese positions in the Duropa Plantation.[17]

It had not taken General Harding long to realize that he was up against a strong enemy bunker line, and that the only way to reduce it in a hurry was with tanks. Judging

correctly that the Duropa Plantation was suitable for tank action, he asked Milne Force (which then had some light General Stuart tanks on hand) to send three of them to Oro Bay by barge. General Clowes did his best to comply with the request, but when the first of the tanks were loaded on some captured Japanese barges—the only craft available for the purpose—the barges sank, taking the tanks with them. Advised that there was no way to get the tanks to him, Harding was left with the task of trying to reduce the formidable Japanese positions without armor.

Dissatisfied with the co-ordination between the various units of Warren Force, Harding ordered Lt. Col. Alexander J. MacNab, executive officer of the 128th Infantry, an experienced and aggressive soldier in whom he had great confidence, to report to General MacNider, under whom he was to co-ordinate the coastal drive. MacNab reached the front on 22 November and at once began laying plans for a stepped-up attack.[18]

One of the first things that MacNab did was to place all the available mortars at the front in battery, connecting them by field telephone with a central observation post in a tall coconut tree overlooking the front. It was not a very good observation post—a much better one was to be found later—but it gave the mortars and the artillery infinitely better observation than was obtainable before. Next morning the artillery pieces registered on the enemy positions along the coastal track and in the New Strip

---

[16] 3d Bn, 129th Inf, Jnl, 1635 through 2015, 21 Nov 42, 0915 through 1800, 22 Nov 42; 32d Div Sitrep No. 57, 22 Nov 42; Maj Parker's Buna Rpt.

[17] Tel Msg, 1st Lt Robert B. Wingler to 32d Div, Ser 1030, 20 Nov 42; Tel Msg, Gen Waldron to 32d Div, Ser 1120, 21 Nov 42; Msg, Capt Lincoln B. Grayson, 114th Engr Bn, to 32d Div, Ser 1147, 22 Nov 42; Msg, 32d Div to NGF, Ser 1153, 22 Nov 42. All in 32d Div G-2, G-3 Jnl. Ltr, Gen Harding to Gen Herring, 28 Nov 42, copy in OCHM files; 32d Div Hist of Arty, Papuan Campaign; Col Knight's Buna Rpt.

[18] Rad, Gen Harding to Milne Force (through NGF), Ser 972, 20 Nov 42; Rad, Milne Force to NGF (for Harding), Ser 1295, 20 Nov 42. Both in 32d Div G-2, G-3 Jnl. 1st Bn, 128th Inf, Jnl, 1330, 1830, 22 Nov 42, 0900, 23 Nov 42; Interv with Gen Harding, 9 Dec 47.

area. The fire was to such good effect that, when Colonel McCoy's and Colonel Carrier's lead companies attacked that day, they were able to push the Japanese back against their main line of resistance. The 2/6 Independent Company, operating off the eastern end of the strip, also made a little progress that day. Ordered to hold tight, Lieutenant Fryday's unit, Company I, 128th Infantry, still in position off the southwest end of the New Strip, remained where it was.[19]

General MacNider had come up during the afternoon from his headquarters at Hariko to observe the fighting. He was wounded at 1830 by an enemy rifle grenade while inspecting the front lines and was immediately evacuated. On General Harding's instructions, Colonel Hale succeeded him as commander of Warren Force.[20]

The next two days, 24 and 25 November, were quiet. Colonel Miller's troops relieved Colonel McCoy's in the front lines, but no advance was attempted either day. The lull was being used to prepare for a co-ordinated attack on Cape Endaiadere and both ends of the New Strip, on the 26th, Thanksgiving Day.

This was to be a strong effort. Eight artillery pieces—six 25-pounders and the two 3.7-inch howitzers—would be in support, four more 25-pounders having been brought in by air on the 25th and emplaced near Ango. A dozen 81-mm. mortars and several more heavy machine guns would be available, as well as thirty-five planes—the largest concentration of aircraft for an attack to date.

The action would open with a thorough bombing and strafing of enemy positions in the Cape Endaiadere–New Strip area. When the air attack was over, the mountain guns would fire on Cape Endaiadere and the 25-pounders would let loose on the bridge between the strips and on the western end of the New Strip. The troops would start from a line of departure about 900 yards south of the cape. Colonel Miller's 3d Battalion, 128th Infantry (less Company I), would thrust directly north along the coastal track and Cape Endaiadere. Colonel Carrier's battalion would move out on Miller's left. Colonel McCoy's troops were to follow Colonel Carrier's at an interval of 1,000 yards, prepared to push through them if necessary. The 2/6 Independent Company would continue attacking on the eastern end of the New Strip, and Company I, 128th Infantry, from its position below the track junction, would attempt to establish itself on the western end of the strip.[21]

High hopes were held for the success of the attack. General Harding left his headquarters at Embogo the night before to observe it personally. Having no motor boat for command use, he caught a ride on the lugger *Helen Dawn*, which was carrying ammunition to the forward dump at Hariko. About seven miles out the lugger ran onto a sand bar, and General Harding had to complete the remaining three miles of his journey in a row boat, with which, fortunately, the *Helen Dawn* had come

[19] 1st Bn, 126th Inf, Jnl, Sers 363, 366, 23 Nov 42; 1st Bn, 128th Inf, Jnl, Sers 19, 20, 23 Nov 42; Ltr, Col MacNab to author, 15 Nov 49.
[20] Msg, 32d Div to NGF, Ser 1280, 23 Nov 42, in 32d Div G-2, G-3 Jnl; 1st Bn, 128th Inf, Jnl, Ser 20, 23 Nov 42; Interv with Gen Harding, 9 Dec 47.
[21] 1st Bn, 126th Inf, Jnl, Ser 384, 25 Nov 42; 1st Bn, 128th Inf, Jnl, 1500, 25 Nov 42; 3d Bn, 128th Inf, Jnl, 0730, 25 Nov 42; 128th Inf, Jnl, 1210, 25 Nov 42; Allied Air Forces Opns Rpt, 26 Nov 42; 32d Div Hist of Arty, Papuan Campaign.

equipped. Harding arrived at Colonel Hale's command post at Hariko at 0445. After visiting Colonel McCoy and Colonel Carrier in their command posts, he moved on to Colonel Miller's CP.[22]

The attack went off as scheduled. It opened with strafing by Beaufighters and P–40's, and bombing by A–20's and B–25's. At 0930, after a short preparation by artillery, mortars, and heavy machine guns, Colonel Miller's battalion moved forward on the right. Fifteen minutes later Colonel Carrier's troops jumped off on the left.

Allied preparatory fire had hit the target area but had done the enemy troops little harm. Retiring into their bunkers, the Japanese waited until it was over, and then emerged unscathed to meet the American infantry attack from hidden firing positions that commanded every approach.

Colonel Miller's troops, coming up against the strongest section of the Japanese line, were stopped almost at once. They suffered fifty casualties by noon and could not move forward. Company K, which had sustained the bulk of the casualties, was pinned down completely, and Company L, out of contact with Carrier's battalion, was immobilized. Japanese fighter planes from Lae (which destroyed the *Helen Dawn* when they found it still caught on the sand bar succeeded in bombing and strafing Miller's battalion despite Allied attempts at interception.

Carrier's attack was also a disappointment, and narrowly missed being a fiasco. Moving through waist-deep swamp, Car-

rier's lead troops, though following a compass course, seem to have misjudged both their direction and their distances. Turning apparently too sharply to the west, and then cutting too soon to the east, they managed to get themselves completely turned around. At 1400 Carrier reported that his troops were nearing the sea, and at 1503 he found to his embarrassment that they were coming out on the coast on Miller's rear. Realizing his error, Carrier resumed the attack, this time striking toward the Duropa Plantation. He made some minor gains against strong enemy opposition, and by morning the two battalions presented a continuous front to the enemy.

Nor did the Australian Independent Company and Company I, 128th Infantry, to the east and west respectively of the New Strip, make any gains that day. Both were stopped in their tracks almost as soon as they tried to move forward. The attack on which so much hope had been placed had been a complete failure.[23]

The next day, Allied aircraft in the course of bombing Japanese positions along the New Strip dropped a string of demolition bombs on Lieutenant Fryday's position

---

[22] 1st Bn, 128th Inf, Jnl, Ser 5, 26 Nov 42; 3d Bn, 128th Inf, Jnl, Sers 5, 11, 26 Nov 42; Gen Harding's Diary, 26 Nov 42; Ltr, Col Miller to Gen Ward, 27 Mar 51; Ltr, Gen Harding to author, 24 Jul 51.

[23] 1st Bn, 126th Inf, Jnl, Sers 392, 393, 396, 26 Nov 42; 3d Bn, 128th Inf, Jnl, Sers 1 through 12, 15, 17, 26 Nov 42; Msgs, 32d Div to NGF, Sers 1476, 1477, 26 Nov 42; Allied Air Forces Opns Rpt, 26 Nov 42; Gen Harding's Diary, 26 Nov 42; Ltr, Col Miller to Gen Ward, 27 Mar 51. During the heavy fighting on Colonel Carrier's front that afternoon, Pvt. Howard M. Eastwood of Company C, 126th Infantry, single-handedly attacked a ten-man party of the enemy whom he had discovered to his front on a scouting mission. Standing upright in the tall grass, he engaged the Japanese with fire from his submachine gun, killing several and dispersing the others. Killed by an enemy sniper in the area, Eastwood was posthumously awarded the Distinguished Service Cross. The citation is in GHQ SWPA GO No. 9, 19 Jan 43.

southwest of the strip. Three men were seriously wounded, and Fryday temporarily pulled his company back into the jungle, south of the position from which the first attack of the 3d Battalion, 128th Infantry, had been launched on 19 November.[24]

The Attack on the Left

Things had gone no better on General Harding's left flank. Colonel Smith's 2d Battalion, 128th Infantry, had begun moving from Ango toward Buna during the morning of 21 November. The battalion's orders were to advance on Buna Mission by way of the Triangle, the jungle-covered track junction from which the Dobodura–Buna track forked to Buna Village and Buna Mission. Captain Yasuda, whose *Yokosuka 5th, Sasebo 5th,* and supporting naval pioneer troops totaled more than double the strength of Smith's battalion, was ready. He had a series of concealed machine gun positions south of the Triangle covering the track, and an elaborate system of bunkers in the Triangle itself. There was heavy swamp on either side of the Triangle, and the bunkers had the effect of turning it into a position of almost impregnable strength. Strong bunker positions in the Coconut Grove north of the Triangle, and in the Government Gardens northeast of it, lay astride the trails leading to the village and the mission, both of which were also honeycombed with bunkers.

Yasuda's defensive position was excellent. His short, secure, interior lines of communication enabled him to concentrate almost his full strength at any threatened point and, when the threat passed, or he chose to withdraw, to use the same troops to beat off another attack elsewhere.

The 2d Battalion, 128th Infantry, moving forward toward the Triangle along the Dobodura–Buna track, knew nothing of the Japanese defenses in the area and very little about the terrain. At 1330 Sgt. Irving W. Hall of Company F, leading the point, caught a swift glimpse of an enemy machine gun about fifty yards away. Coolly turning his back on the gun so as to give the impression that he had not seen it, Hall motioned his men off the track. Before the Japanese knew what he was up to he turned around and fired a burst at them from his submachine gun. In the heavy fire fight that ensued, the point suffered one casualty.[25]

Stopped on the trail by apparently strong enemy positions, Colonel Smith at once began flanking operations. Company G was ordered to move out on the right and Company F on the left. Company H was given orders to engage the enemy frontally, and Company E went into reserve.[26]

At 2130, Colonel Smith reported to General Harding that he had run into opposition at the junction and that, while he was moving forward slowly on either side of that position in an attempt to flank it, he was being delayed by heavy swamp which was causing him more trouble than the enemy. General Harding immediately asked New Guinea Force to reinforce Smith with a battalion of the 126th Infantry from the other side of the Girua. Harding pointed out

[24] Msg, Col Hale to Gen Harding, Ser 1550, 27 Nov 42; in 32d Div G–2, G–3 Jnl; 128th Inf Jnl, 0910, 1035, 27 Nov 42.

[25] 2d Bn, 128th Inf, Jnl, 1000, 1330, 21 Nov 42. Hall was later awarded the Silver Star. The citation is in HQ US Forces, Buna Area, GO No. 14, 20 Jan 43.
[26] 2d Bn, 128th Inf, Jnl, 1330, 21 Nov 42.

126TH INFANTRYMEN PASSING THROUGH HARIKO *on their way to the front lines.*

that it could march directly to Buna via the Soputa–Buna track.[27]

General Herring quickly acceded to General Harding's request and ordered the 2d Battalion, 126th Infantry, across the river. Maj. Herbert M. Smith, commanding officer of that battalion, reached Colonel Smith's command post at 0930, 23 November. The two 2d Battalions thereupon took the name of Urbana Force, and Colonel Smith, as senior officer present, took command. To avoid confusion in radio messages, General Harding designated Colonel Smith as White Smith, and Major Smith as Red Smith.[28]

The terrain Urbana Force had run into, especially on the right, was (as Colonel Smith had already intimated to General Harding) appalling. The main track was

---

[27] Msg, Lt Col Herbert A. Smith to Gen Harding, Ser 1100, 1101, 21 Nov 42; Msg, Gen Harding to NGF, No. 1099 [*sic*], 21 Nov 42. Both in 32d Div G–2, G–3 Jnl. The fact that the serial of General Harding's message to New Guinea Force is lower than the serials on the messages from Colonel Smith to General Harding was apparently due to an error in filing, since the messages from Smith were received at 32d Division headquarters at 2130, and Harding's message to New Guinea Force did not go out until 2205—thirty-five minutes later.

[28] Msg, Maj Smith to 32d Div, Ser 1254, 23 Nov 42; Msg, Gen Harding to Maj Smith, Ser 1257, 23 Nov 42. Both in 32d Div G–2, G–3 Jnl. 2d Bn, 128th Inf, Jnl, 0930, 23 Nov 42.

deep in mud, and Company G, 128th Infantry, attempting to advance on the right, hit stretches of swamp in which the troops sometimes found themselves up to their necks in water. Company F, 128th Infantry, met better terrain on the left but discovered that Entrance Creek, which paralleled the left-hand fork of the Triangle, not only was tidal and unfordable but seemed to be covered by enemy machine guns at every likely crossing.[29]

Company G's experience in the swamp had been particularly wearing. The men had moved out into the swamp to the right of the Triangle in the late afternoon of 21 November. As they made their way eastward, darkness fell. The acting company commander, 1st Lt. Theodore Florey, decided to go on, but the swamp kept getting deeper. Since there seemed to be little chance of reaching dry ground before morning, Florey finally called a halt at 2100. The company spent a miserable night. A few of the men were able to find perches on the roots of trees, but the rest waited in the mire for morning. Wet to the skin and in need of sleep, the men started moving again at daybreak. After a slow and difficult march, they hit dry land at about noon. Taking their bearings, the troops discovered that they were on one of two kunai flats running southeast of the Triangle, and that only about 200 yards of sago swamp lay between them and the flat adjacent to their objective.

Though he now had a company in position to strike, Colonel Smith had grave doubts whether an attack from that quarter would be practicable. Reports from Company G, from the Ammunition and Pioneer Platoon, which was carrying rations forward to it, as well as from wire-laying parties of Headquarters Company, which were having a difficult time laying wire on the right, convinced him that it would be virtually out of the question to try to supply Company G in the terrain in which it found itself. Since the reports from Company F were much more favorable and indicated that the swamp on the left of the Triangle was never more than waist-deep, he decided to pull Company G back from its untenable position on the right and concentrate his entire force on the left where the going, though far from good, was obviously much better.[30]

On 23 November Colonel Smith sent a message to division headquarters informing it of his plan. The supply route to Company G, he wrote, was "neck-deep in mud and water," and he asked permission for the company's withdrawal.[31] After waiting until about 1400 for a reply and receiving none, Smith ordered the company to pull out of the swamp and report to him for further orders. So ordered, the company severed its wire connection with battalion headquarters and started for the rear. Division headquarters had received Smith's message about 1400 and, because of an error on the part of the decoding clerk, understood it to say that the supply route to Company G was "knee-deep in mud and water," and not, as Colonel Smith sent it, "neck-deep." The headquarters replied at 1425 that Smith was under no circumstances to with-

---

[29] Msgs, Col Smith to Gen Harding, Sers 1100, 1101, 21 Nov 42; Tel Msg, Capt Grayson to Gen Harding, Ser 1166, 22 Nov 42; Msg, Col Smith to Gen Harding, Ser 1189, 22 Nov 42. All in 32d Div G–2, G–3 Jnl.

[30] Ltr, Col Herbert A. Smith to author, 20 Jan 50.
[31] Msg, Col Smith to 32d Div, Ser 1246, 23 Nov 42, corrected in Ser 1277 of the same date, in 32d Div G–2, G–3 Jnl.

draw, but was instead to proceed with the attack.[32]

Colonel Smith sent a messenger to intercept Company G and return it to its former position. Having only limited knowledge of the enemy positions he was supposed to attack, he asked division for a delay of a day or two in which to learn more about the enemy and the terrain, and perhaps find a better route of supply to Company G. Division would not give him the time. At 2045 it informed him that there would be an air strike on the Triangle at 0800 the next morning, 24 December, following which he and Major Smith were to attack.[33]

At 2330 the two Smiths held a staff meeting at Colonel Smith's command post, 1,200 yards south of the nearest Japanese positions below the Triangle. There they worked out a plan which envisaged simultaneous thrusts at the Triangle from left, front, and right. The three-way attack would be preceded by air bombardment and strafing scheduled for 0800, and the troops were to jump off as soon as the air attack was over. Four 25-pounders which had just reached Dobodura that day would fire from Ango in support of the attack as soon as they got the range.[34]

The attack opened at 0800 the next morning with an attempt by the air force to strafe the Triangle. Twelve P–40's made one pass over the objective and missed it altogether. No bombers followed the fighters, and there was no attempt by the P–40's to try to hit the Triangle again, since they apparently thought they had executed their mission.

Because the air attack had been a complete failure, the ground attack was held up to give the air force a chance to try again. It was arranged that this time eight P–39's and four P–40's would attack at 1355. There was to be no bombardment, since no bombers were available.

At the appointed time only the four P–40's showed up. Instead of strafing the Japanese in the Triangle, they strafed Colonel Smith's command post. Fortunately only one man was wounded in the strafing, and he only slightly, but the Japanese positions in the Triangle were left completely untouched.

After the last of the P–40's had finished strafing his command post, Colonel Smith waited a few moments to see if any more planes would follow. No more planes arrived; so he ordered the attack to begin without further support from the air force. Following a short mortar preparation, principally by the 60-mm. mortars (the two battalions then had only two 81-mm. mortars apiece and little ammunition for them), the troops jumped off at 1428. At 1437 the 25-pounders at Ango found the range, and joined in the attack.[35]

On the left, Company E, 126th Infantry, began by swinging wide around Entrance Creek; then it moved north about 400 yards and turned northeast. Just as it had finished covering another 400 yards and was approaching a small bridge over the creek

[32] Msg, Gen Harding to Col Smith, Ser 1247, 23 Nov 42, in 32d Div G–2, G–3 Jnl; Ltr, Col Herbert A. Smith to author, 20 Jan 50.

[33] Msg, 32d Div to Col Smith, Ser 1276, 23 Nov 42; 2d Bn, 128th Inf, Jnl, 2330, 23 Nov 42; Ltr, Col Herbert A. Smith to author, 20 Jan 50.

[34] 2d Bn, 126th Inf, Jnl, 23 Nov 42; 2d Bn, 128th Inf, Jnl, 2330, 23 Nov 42, 1420, 24 Nov 42; Ltr, Col Herbert A. Smith to author, 20 Jan 50.

[35] Msg, Col Smith to Gen Harding, Ser 1339, 24 Nov 42, in 32d Div G–2, G–3 Jnl; 2d Bn, 126th Inf, Jnl, 24 Nov 42; 2d Bn, 128th Inf, Jnl, 0800, 1355, 1400, 24 Nov 42; Allied Air Forces Opns Rpt, 24 Nov 42, in G–3 Jnl, GHQ SWPA; Ltr, Col Herbert A. Smith to author, 20 Jan 50.

northwest of the Triangle, a strong Japanese force struck with accurate machine gun fire. The troops dug in at once in foxholes which immediately filled with water. They went no further that day.

Company F, 126th Infantry, though soon joined by Company H, Colonel Smith's heavy weapons company, did little in its frontal attack on the Triangle. It moved forward about 300 yards, only to find heavy barbed wire entanglements strung across the track. The enemy covering the wire was laying down intense fire. Having neither wire cutters nor the materials with which to make Bangalore torpedoes, the Americans dug in and requested engineers with explosives to clear the way.[36]

Companies E and G, 128th Infantry, on the right, fared worst of all. Using newly found short cuts through the deep swamp, Company E managed to reach the kunai flat in much less time than Company G had taken to reach it after its groping efforts of 21 November. The men of Company E therefore joined up with Company G in plenty of time for the attack.

Leaving its weapons platoon on the flat with Company E, Company G under Lieutenant Florey started moving northwest through the sago swamp to flank the Triangle. A little less than 200 yards out, the leading platoon came upon a small grassy area, just outside the Triangle, where it surprised a group of Japanese working on what appeared to be an antiaircraft position. The Americans opened fire, but there were more Japanese about than they

thought, and the company, after suffering several casualties, was forced back into the swamp. Attempts to maneuver around the grassy strip were unsuccessful because of intense automatic weapons fire which greeted the company at every turn. Darkness found the troops pinned down at the edge of the strip, where the slope of the ground leading into the swamp afforded them a little cover.

While the main body of Company G was held up just outside the right-hand fork of the Triangle, the Japanese from the Government Gardens moved forward to within firing distance of the kunai flat held by Company E and the weapons platoon of Company G. They attacked just as it was turning dark, killing one man and wounding five others and greatly disheartening the troops on the flat, most of whom were under enemy fire for the first time.

The weapons platoon of Company G had had two days to get its weapons in order after its march through the swamp, and Company E had been on the kunai flat five or six hours, long enough for it to do the same. But the Americans apparently lacked oil, and parts of the equipment were wet, and they may have been negligent. Whatever the reason, when they were caught in the open, with the sounds of Japanese yells coming from a short distance away, the men tried to hit back at the unseen enemy as best they could, only to find that their weapons would not function properly. ". . . Mortars fell short because increments [the propelling charges in the mortar ammunition] were wet. Machine guns jammed because web belts were wet and dirty and had shrunk. Tommy guns and BAR's were full of muck and dirt, and even the M1's fired well only for the first clip, and then jammed because clips taken from the belts were wet and full

    [36] 2d Bn, 126th Inf, Jnl, 24 Nov 42, 25 Nov 42; 2d Bn, 128th Inf, Jnl, 1412, 1530, 1552, 1660, 1930, 24 Nov 42; Kahn, "The Terrible Days of Company E," in *The Saturday Evening Post*, January 15, 1944, p. 76.

of muck from the swamp." [37] Low on ammunition, completely out of food, and fearing that they had been ambushed, the troops pulled back hastily into the swamp, leaving some of their crew-served weapons behind them.[38]

Colonel Smith in the meantime had been in communication with Company E by telephone. Learning that the Japanese attack had driven the company off the flat and into the swamp, he ordered the troops to remain where they were until he could come up in the morning and give them further instructions. At that point the phone went dead, and Smith could make no further contact with the two companies.

Company E was at this time strung out in a single file all the way back from the kunai flat, with the weapons platoon of Company G somewhere in the middle of the line. At the far end of the line, nearest to battalion, was the executive officer of Company E, 1st Lt. Orin Rogers, and at the head of it, nearest to the flat and the dead telephone, was the commanding officer of Company E, Capt. A. T. Bakken.

Shortly after darkness fell, an order passed along the line to Lieutenant Rogers to move back to the battalion command post. Rogers assumed at the time that the phone at Captain Bakken's end of the line was working again and that there had been a change in orders. He nevertheless made it a point to ask if the order had come from the captain. The answer came back a few minutes later that it had. Thinking no more of the matter, Rogers started the lead troops back to the command post. At the other end of the line, Captain Bakken had also re-

ceived an order to move to the rear. Knowing that the phone near him was out, he assumed that a messenger from battalion headquarters had delivered such a message to Lieutenant Rogers. Just to make sure, he asked whether the message had come from battalion headquarters. The answer came back (again via the chain method) that it had, and the entire column started moving to the rear, the weapons platoon of Company G with it.[39]

The rest of Company G, under Lieutenant Florey, still pinned down just outside the grassy strip leading to the Triangle, had sent a runner back with orders to the weapons platoon to bring up more mortars. The runner returned with the report that Company E and the weapons platoon were gone. An officer was sent back to the kunai flat to check. When he returned with confirmation of the report, Company G, after waiting for further orders and receiving none, also began to move to the rear.

Company E, 128th Infantry, and the weapons platoon of Company G reached Colonel Smith's command post in the early morning hours of 25 November, and Company G, except for a few stragglers, arrived there by 1007. At 1020 Colonel Smith, who only the night before had informed General Harding that he had instructed the men to remain near the edge of the kunai flat until morning, gave "faulty communica-

[37] Ltr, Col Herbert A. Smith to author, 20 Jan 50.
[38] 2d Bn, 128th Inf, Jnl, 2145, 24 Nov 42, 1230, 25 Nov 42.

[39] Ltr, Col Herbert A. Smith to author, 20 Jan 50. Despite a thorough investigation of the matter, Colonel Smith was never able to find out who originated the message for the troops to return to the rear. As he put it in the letter cited above: "A number of men told of passing the messages back and forth, but no one could say definitely where they originated, and many of the men did not even know who stood next to them, especially where Company E and the Weapons Platoon of Company G were badly intermingled."

tion" as the reason for their return to the rear in apparent contravention of his orders.[40]

Because the men were exhausted and hungry, and also because he did not believe that an attack on the right would succeed, Smith decided against ordering the men back into the swamp. His decision, as he himself phrased it, was "to abandon for the time being any action on the right and concentrate on the left, and to continue patrolling on the right in the hope of finding a more suitable route forward."[41]

Though he now shared Colonel Smith's views about the impracticality of an attack on the right and the need to make the main effort on the left, General Harding had gone one step further in his thinking. A study of the trail which led from the left-hand fork of the Triangle to Buna Village and Buna Mission had convinced him that it would be possible to bypass the Triangle and at the same time take both the village and the mission, if troops could be gotten onto the large grassy area northwest of the Triangle through which, in his own phrase, "the left hand road to Buna" ran. He therefore ordered Smith to contain the Triangle with a portion of his troops and to deploy the rest in the swamp south of the grassy area in question, preparatory to seizing it and moving westward on Buna Village.

Smith began deploying his troops in accordance with this tactical plan early on 26 November. Company F, 128th Infantry, and Company G, 126th Infantry, moved into the area west of the bridge over En-

trance Creek which had been occupied and patrolled by Company E, 126th Infantry, since 24 November.[42]

The troops had scarcely begun moving when General Harding, who had for some time felt that the attack on the Urbana front was not being pressed with sufficient vigor, ordered his chief of staff, Col. John W. Mott, to that front. Mott's instructions were to take strong action when he got there and, if he thought the situation required it, to take command.[43]

Colonel Mott reached Colonel Smith's command post on the afternoon of the 27th. Surveying the situation quickly, he came to the conclusion that he would have to assume command and did so at once. He relieved the captains of Companies E and G, 128th Infantry, of their commands and ordered them to take patrols into the area forward of the kunai flat from which the Japanese had driven Company E and the weapons platoon of Company G two days before. In addition, he ordered Companies E and G under their new commanders to retrieve their abandoned weapons on the kunai flat. They did so by sundown, but Company E returned without one of its mortars and had to be sent back a second time to get it.[44]

[40] 2d Bn, 128th Inf, Jnl, 2145, 24 Nov 42, 0908, 1007, 1020, 25 Nov 42.
[41] Ltr, Col Herbert A. Smith to author, 20 Jan 50.

[42] 2d Bn, 126th Inf, Jnl, 26 Nov 42; 2d Bn, 128th Inf, Jnl, 0832, 26 Nov 42.
[43] Gen Harding's Diary, 26 Nov 42; Ltr, Gen Harding to Gen Herring, 28 Nov 42; Col Mott, Memorandum, 10 Dec 42. Copies of last two in OCMH files.
[44] 2d Bn, 128th Inf, Jnl, 1412, 1545, 1550, 27 Nov 42, 0700, 28 Dec 42; Col Mott's Memo; Ltr, Col Herbert A. Smith to Gen Ward, 20 Mar 51. Capt A. T. Bakken of Company E was reinstated shortly thereafter, and Capt H. Spraetz of Company G, who was sick at the time his company was in the swamp, went to the hospital and did not return. Ltr, Col Herbert A. Smith to author, 20 Jan 50.

Mott at once prepared to attack. He adopted a suggestion made to him by Major Smith, that the attack on the grassy strip leading to the village be mounted initially from two smaller grass strips just south of the larger kunai patch, and made his dispositions accordingly. Major Smith's battalion was ordered to assemble near the Girua River, directly below the two strips that Smith had proposed as the jump-off point for the attack. Company F, 128th Infantry, occupied the area west of the bridge over Entrance Creek. Companies G and H, under Colonel Smith, were ordered to take over the positions south of the Triangle in order to contain the enemy there. Company E, left in reserve, was deployed around task force headquarters.

Mott reported his dispositions to General Harding on the evening of 28 November, and the division commander approved them. Following a suggestion from General Herring that he try night attacks, Harding ordered an attack on Buna Village that night. Pleading that he was not ready to attack, Mott asked for a twenty-four-hour delay. Harding granted his request, and the attack was set for the last night of the month—29–30 November.[45]

The Attacks of 30 November

Integrating the Attacks

On the Warren front, a two-day lull had followed the reverse of 26 November. On the 28th General Harding ordered Colonel Hale to prepare to attack the next day. A report that evening, subsequently found to be false, that the Japanese were making a ground attack on Dobodura caused General Harding to postpone the attack to the early morning of the 30th. (*Map 10*)

Both Urbana Force and Warren Force were now scheduled to attack on the 30th, Urbana Force a few hours before Warren Force. Each was still suffering from the most acute deficiencies of supply, all but one of the luggers that had come in on 21 November having by this time either gone aground or been destroyed by the enemy.[46]

Colonel Mott's Attack

Preparations for the attack on the Urbana front were complete by evening of the 29th. In a large coconut tree that overlooked the front, Colonel Mott had an observation post connected by telephone with the artillery at Ango and the mortars. Both artillery and mortars were registered on the objective—the large grassy area just north of the two clearings below which Urbana Force was preparing the attack. Mott's command post was a hundred yards behind the most forward element of Company E, 126th Infantry. His aid station and part of a collecting company were in place near the Girua River.

The final details of the attack were worked out with Major Smith. The troops would move off toward the main strip as soon after midnight as possible. A thirty-minute mortar and artillery preparation would be laid down on the strip. Immediately afterward the men would proceed to their objective in darkness. Lacking white

[45] 2d Bn, 126th Inf, Jnl, 26 Nov 42, 27 Nov 42, 28 Nov 42; 2d Bn, 128th Inf, Jnl, 0832, 1412, 1458, 1643, 27 Nov 42, 0745, 1231, 1431, 1910, 28 Nov 42; Col Mott's Memo; Gen Harding's Diary, 28 Nov 42; Ltr, Lt Col Herbert M. Smith to author, 16 Mar 50.

[46] Msg, 32d Div to NGF, Ser 1770, 29 Nov 42, in 32d Div G–2, G–3 Jnl; 128th Inf Jnl, 2050, 2150, 27 Nov 42, 2122, 2215, 28 Nov 42; Ltr, Gen Harding to Gen Herring, 28 Nov 42, copy in OCMH files; Gen Harding's Diary, 28 Nov 42.

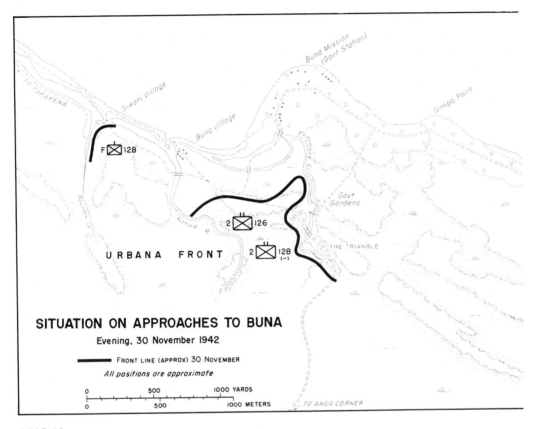

SITUATION ON APPROACHES TO BUNA

Evening, 30 November 1942

━━━━━ FRONT LINE (APPROX) 30 NOVEMBER

All positions are approximate

MAP 10

material for armbands, even underwear, the men would have to keep in close contact with one another. Companies E and F, 126th Infantry, would attack in a northeasterly direction and occupy the main strip, making sure that they first secured that part of it which was nearest to the Coconut Grove, a small coconut plantation immediately north of the bridge over Entrance Creek. Company G, 126th Infantry, would attack along the track and take Buna Village. Company F, 128th Infantry, after being relieved in its present positions by Company E, 128th Infantry, would proceed to Siwori Creek, seize the crossing near its mouth, and outpost the area between the creek and the Girua River. Company H, 128th Infantry, would be immediately behind Companies E and F, 126th Infantry, and would support them with fire. Company E, 128th Infantry, operating immediately to the right of Company E, 126th Infantry, would clear the Japanese out of the Coconut Grove. Company G, 128th Infantry, under Colonel Smith, would operate south of the Triangle and thus cover the track, the artillery at Ango, and the rear of the forces attacking toward Buna Village.[47]

[47] 2d Bn, 126th Inf, Jnl, 29 Nov 42; Col Mott's Memo; Ltrs, Lt Col Herbert M. Smith to author, 16 Mar 50, 5 June 50.

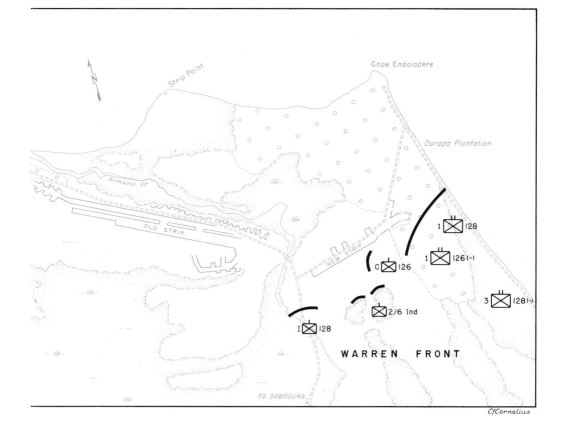

CfCornelius

The jump-off was delayed. Enemy fire from the strip, flares from enemy aircraft that flew over the area during the night, the rising tide in the swamp, and the confusion attendant upon moving so many men through the treacherous swamp terrain in the dark held up the attack for several hours.

Robert H. Odell, then a lieutenant and platoon leader in Company F, 126th Infantry, has this recollection of the matter:

As soon as it was dark, preparations began. When these were completed, we each grasped the shoulder of the man in front, and slowly shuffled forward in the pitch black of the night. Our only guide was the telephone wire leading to the jump-off point, and the troops in the foxholes along the way who had been holding the ground recently captured. There was no trail and consequently several hours were required to travel as many hundreds of yards. We all had bayonets. Rifle fire was forbidden until after the attack was well under way. Japs encountered along the way were to be dealt with silently.

At 0400, Companies E, F, and G, 126th Infantry, finally attacked. It was still dark, and about one hundred yards out, they made their first enemy contact—a line of machine gun posts dead ahead. At that moment, Odell recalls:

All hell broke loose. There was more lead flying through the air . . . than it's possible to estimate. Machine gun tracers lit the entire area, and our own rifle fire made a solid sheet of flame. Everywhere men cursed, shouted, or screamed. Order followed on order. . . . Brave men led and others followed. Cowards crouched in the grass literally frightened out of their skins. . . .[48]

The attack gathered momentum. The two companies—E and F, 126th Infantry—overran the enemy outposts and gained their objective—the eastern end of the main strip. There they found and dispatched an indeterminate number of Japanese, and began to consolidate.[49]

Company G, 126th Infantry, which was to have taken the track to Buna Village as soon as it gained the western end of the strip, accomplished only part of its mission. Led by its commander, 1st Lt. Cladie A. Bailey, it overran strong enemy opposition on its part of the strip but lost its way when it tried moving toward the village. When daylight came, the company found itself in the swamp along the northern edge of the strip.[50] Finding Company G out of reach, Colonel Mott immediately assigned Company E, 126th Infantry, to the task of taking the village. Moving directly on Buna Village by way of the main track, the company attacked at 0600. About 300 yards out of the village, it ran into a well-manned enemy bunker line and found itself unable to advance because of enemy crossfire.

On Major Smith's orders Capt. Harold E. Hantlemann of Company H came up with Lieutenant Nummer, commanding officer of Company F, and some troops from Headquarters Company. Putting Hantle-

mann in charge of the mortars, and Nummer in command of front-line action, Smith made a determined effort to take the village. Preceded by the heaviest concentration of mortar fire yet seen on the Urbana front, the second attack met even fiercer resistance than before. Again the troops could make only slight advances. When the attack was finally called off that afternoon, they had taken considerable casualties but gained very little ground.[51]

Company F, 128th Infantry, which had been given the task of securing the left flank of Urbana Force from enemy attack and cutting the enemy's land communications between Buna and Sanananda, succeeded in its mission. It secured the crossing over Siwori Creek and outposted the trail between it and the bridge over the Girua River. The troops east of Siwori Village had already killed several Japanese from Buna who had tried to cross the bridge, presumably to get to Giruwa or Sanananda.

The other companies of the 2d Battalion, 128th Infantry, had been less successful. Company E, attacking from the southeast end of the strip, failed to take the Coconut Grove, and Company G had very little success in its attacks into the southern tip of the Triangle. Both were subsequently ordered by Colonel Mott to contain these ob-

[48] Odell, Buna.

[49] 2d Bn, 126th Inf, Jnl, 30 Nov 42; 128th Inf Jnl, 1000, 30 Nov 42; Col Mott's Memo; Ltr, Lt Col Herbert M. Smith to author, 16 Mar 50.

[50] For this night's fighting Lieutenant Bailey was later awarded the Distinguished Service Cross. The citation is in GHQ SWPA GO No. 1, 1 Jan 43.

[51] 2d Bn, 126th Inf, Jnl, 30 Nov 42; Col Mott's Memo; Gen Harding's Diary, 30 Nov 42; Ltr, Lt Col Herbert M. Smith to author, 16 Mar 50. Lieutenant Nummer was wounded in the course of the attack but continued in command in spite of his wounds. He was later awarded the Distinguished Service Cross. The same award, though posthumous, went to Sgt. Boyd L. Lincoln, a squad leader of Company E, 126th Infantry, who was killed that afternoon after leading his squad with great distinction all day against the enemy outpost on the outskirts of the village. Nummer's citation is in GHQ SWPA GO No. 3, 6 Jan 43; Lincoln's, in GO No. 1, 1 Jan 43.

jectives and to make no attacks upon them until otherwise ordered.

In the mop-up of the large grassy strip, the troops overran a Japanese headquarters area from which apparently a considerable number of troops had very recently fled. The place consisted of a headquarters building, an infirmary, and several huts containing weapons, ammunition, food, and medicine. The two main buildings had bunkers to the rear with which they connected by tunnels. The buildings were of canvas and frame construction and had wooden floors covered with floor mats. When overrun, the headquarters building was strewn with military documents, codes, and diaries, and contained a large radio set which took eight men to carry. After removing the papers, the radio, the food, and the medical supplies, the buildings were burned to the ground and the connecting bunkers blown up.[52]

Colonel Hale's Attack

The attack on the Warren front, though more heavily supported than that on the Urbana front, was even less successful. By this time General Waldron and his second-in-command, Colonel McCreary, had opened an artillery command post at Dobodura and had established firing data for all

known targets in the area. The Australian artillery consisted of the eight 25-pounders and two 3.7-inch mountain howitzers of the Manning, Hall, and O'Hare Troops. The Manning Troop, four 25-pounders, was north of Ango; the Hall Troop, the remaining 25-pounders, and the O'Hare Troop, the two mountain howitzers, were at Boreo. A flight of Australian Wirraways had just arrived from Port Moresby to aid the artillery in its spotting of enemy targets, and one 105-mm. howitzer of Battery A, the 129th U.S. Field Artillery Battalion (the only U.S. field piece to be used in the campaign) had reached Debodura by air the day before with its crew and 400 rounds of ammunition. The gun, under command of Capt. Elmer D. Kobs, was emplaced at Ango on the 30th, too late however to take part in the attack.[53]

General Harding, more than ever convinced that it would take tanks to clean out the enemy bunker defenses in the Duropa Plantation, had meanwhile continued to plead for armor. He radioed General Johns of the Combined Operational Service Command (COSC) on 27 November and asked him to do his best to get the tanks at Milne Bay to him. He suggested that Johns try to get some of the Japanese landing barges captured on Goodenough Island in the hope that they might prove big enough for the task. New Guinea Force replied for Johns that there were no barges anywhere in the area big enough to carry the tanks, and that they were sending him Bren carriers instead. Thirteen carriers, tracked, lightly armored reconnaissance vehicles mounting

---

[52] Col Mott's Memo; Ltr, Lt Col Herbert M. Smith to author, 5 June 50; Ltr, Col Herbert A. Smith to Gen Ward, 20 Mar 51; Interv with Maj Odell, 14 Dec 50. Odell recalls that the troops had also found a locked safe—the only one in the area. Blowing it open, they found to their amazement that its only contents were numerous small rolls of thin, white paper. Assuming as a matter of course that the rolls were toilet paper, they used them as such, little realizing that what they had found was in fact writing paper, which, in the Japanese style, was rolled so as to permit the writer to cut it to any length that his letter or the business at hand required.

[53] Msg, 1st Lt Herbert G. Peabody, Dobodura, to 32d Div, Ser 1551, 27 Nov 42; Col Handy's Buna Rpt; 32d Div Rpt of Arty, Papuan Campaign. The Wirraways were based at Port Moresby and were thus available to the division for only a few hours a day.

Bren machine guns, arrived with their crews at Porlock Harbor from Milne Bay the same day, 27 November. Advised that at least four of the carriers would reach him in the next couple of days, Harding immediately drew up plans for their use by Warren Force on the 30th.[54]

The plan of attack on the Warren front called for Colonel McCoy's battalion (re-organized into two rifle companies and one heavy weapons company) to move straight up the track in column of companies, with Company A leading. The advance would be on a 350-yard front, and two of the Bren carriers would spearhead the attack. Colonel Carrier's troops with the two remaining Brens leading, and the 2/6 Independent Company on its left, were to strike westward in the area immediately below the New Strip preparatory to a break-through in that area. Besides the Australians and the Bren carriers, four 81-mm. mortars from Company M, 128th Infantry, would support Carrier's force. Colonel Miller's battalion, less Company I, would be in reserve, ready to assist either McCoy or Carrier, as required. Company I would remain in its blocking position astride the Dobodura–Simemi track, a few hundred yards south of the bridge between the strips.

H Hour was to be 0630. Between H minus 15 and H Hour, the 25-pounders would lay down fire on the southwest end of the New Strip. Thereafter they would fire on the woods northeast of the strip to knock out known Japanese mortar and artillery concentrations. The 3.7-inch mountain guns would first fire a preparation on Cape Endaiadere and then switch to local support of Colonel McCoy's advance. The air force, then fighting off an enemy convoy bound for Buna, would bomb and strafe enemy positions whenever it could find the planes to do so.

Because of an acute shortage of shipping at Porlock Harbor, the Bren carriers failed to arrive as scheduled, and the attack was launched without them. The 105-mm. howitzer was not yet ready to fire and took no part in the attack. Nor was there the usual preliminary air bombardment, since the air force was still busy with the enemy convoy.

The 25-pounders, the mountain guns, and the mortars opened up at 0615, and the troops jumped off at the appointed time, 0630. Allied bombers, after successfully chasing the enemy convoy back to Rabaul, joined in the fray at 0900. At 0945 there was a further friendly artillery barrage, and at 1345 and 1448 Allied planes came over again, strafing and bombing.

Despite this support, Warren Force made very little progress that day. Pressed tightly against the Japanese defensive positions and without tanks or enough heavy artillery using projectiles with delayed fuse to demolish the enemy fortifications, the Americans could make little headway. The troops fought desperately, but could not get through the enemy's protective fire.

Company A, 128th Infantry, leading the attack along the coast, advanced less than a hundred yards when it ran into a massive log barricade which Colonel Yamamoto's troops had thrown across the trail. Automatic fire from behind the barricade and from concealed positions on its left soon

[54] Msg, 1st Lt Jay W. Moon, Porlock Harbor, to 32d Div, Ser 1554, 27 Nov 42; Msg, 32d Div to CG COSC, Ser 1582, 27 Nov 42; Msg, 32d Div to Lt Moon, Ser 1633, 28 Nov 42; Msg, Gen Harding to Cmdr J. L. Sinclair, NOIC, Porlock Harbor, Ser 1647, 28 Nov 42; Msg, NGF to 32d Div, Ser 1765, 29 Nov 42. All in 32d Div G-2, G-3 Jnl. 1st Bn, 126th Inf, Jnl, Ser 10, 29 Nov 42; 3d Bn, 128th Inf, Jnl, 1015, 1550, 29 Nov 42; 128th Inf Jnl, 0915, 1145, 29 Nov 42.

brought the company's advance to a complete halt. The artillery at Boreo was unable to reduce the barricade, and sustained fire from 81-mm. mortars and from a 37-mm. gun brought up specifically for the purpose seemed to make no impression upon it. By noon Company A had been definitely stopped, and the men began to dig in, in the intense heat of the day. When Company A was relieved by Company B that night, it was about 900 yards south of the Cape. Its right flank was still in front of the barricade, and its left, which had not kept up, was curved almost all the way back to the line of departure.[55]

Colonel Carrier, on McCoy's left, facing west, had fared a little better. Ordered to infiltrate the eastern end of the New Strip with a view to striking along its northern edge, Company B tried to fight north into the fork but was stopped by enemy fire from a strongpoint dominating the spur and the strip. Company C, with the Independent Company on its left, was to flank the strip by advancing westward along its southern edge. It advanced to about the center of the strip before enemy fire became so heavy that it too had to dig in. Except for the slight progress on Colonel Carrier's front, the attack had again failed.[56]

The situation was serious. Despite repeated attacks on it, the Japanese line stood intact. In the two weeks since the 32d Division had marched out so confidently on the enemy positions at Buna, it had sustained 492 battle casualties but had made not so much as a single penetration of the enemy line.[57] It was obvious that something would have to be done to intensify the attack.

------

[55] Msg, 32d Div to NGF, Ser 1783, 30 Nov 42, in 32d Div G–2, G–3 Jnl; 1st Bn, 128th Inf, Jnl, Sers 1 through 7, 30 Nov 42; 3d Bn, 128th Inf, Jnl, 0810, 30 Nov 42; 128th Inf Jnl, 0725, 0830, 1100, 1233, 30 Nov 42; G–3 Opns Rpt, No. 238, 30 Nov–1 Dec 42; *18th Army* Opns I, p. 22.

[56] 1st Bn, 126th Inf, Jnl, Sers 423, 426, 428, 433, 30 Nov 42; 128th Inf Jnl, 0835, 0945, 1035, 30 Nov 42.

[57] Msg, Gen Harding to NGF, Ser 1681, 28 Nov 42, Ser 1860, 1 Dec 42; Msgs, Capt Joseph M. Stehling to 32d Div, Ser 1713, 28 Nov 42, Ser 1900, 1 Dec 42. All in 32d Div G–2, G–3 Jnl. A breakdown of the casualty figure follows: killed in action, 82; wounded in action, 325; missing in action, 85. The bodies of many of those listed as missing in action were later recovered and went to swell the number killed.

CHAPTER XI

I Corps Reaches the Front

The failure of the 32d Division to take Buna by the end of November had strong repercussions at Port Moresby. The feeling there was that the division had bogged down because of poor leadership,[1] a feeling that was to cost General Harding his command.

The Situation: 30 November

The Condition of the Troops

The men on both the Urbana and Warren fronts were tired and listless. They had not been sufficiently hardened for jungle operations and, with few exceptions, had not been fresh when they reached the combat zone. Thrown into battle in an exhausted state, most of them had had no chance to rest since. The loss of the 126th Infantry to the Australians on 19 November had left General Harding without a reserve. Nor had the return of the far-from-fresh 2d Battalion to his command on 23 November remedied the situation, for the battalion was immediately incorporated into Urbana Force, and the division still had no reserve.

As General Harding explained the matter to General Herring the men, especially during the first five days of combat, had been without rest, and every combat element had, during that time, been "to all intents and purposes continuously engaged." [2]

The troops were half-starved. Most of them had been living on short rations for weeks and their food intake since the fighting began had averaged about a third of a C ration per day—just enough to sustain life.[3] They were shaggy and bearded and their clothes were ragged. Their feet were swollen and in bad shape. Their shoes, which had shrunk in the wet, often had to be cut away so that the troops could even get their feet into them.

The men had very little tentage to protect themselves from the heavy rains. Those who had lost or thrown away their shelter halves during the approach march were still without them and had to sleep in the open. Quinine sulphate, salt tablets, vitamin pills, and chlorination pellets were in short supply, and sicknesses—malaria, "jungle

---

[1] Interv, Louis Morton with Gen Sutherland, Washington, D. C., 12 Nov 46; Intervs with Gen Eichelberger, 20 Nov 48, 6 Feb 50, 12 May 50; Interv with Gen Chamberlin, 14 Jan 50; Kenney, *General Kenney Reports,* pp. 150–151, 154, 156–157.

[2] Ltr, Gen Harding to Gen Herring, 28 Nov 42, copy in OCMH files.

[3] Ltr, Gen Harding to Gen Herring, 28 Nov 42; Ltr, Gen Eichelberger to Gen Sutherland, 3 Dec 42; Ltr, Lt Col Herbert M. Smith to author, 16 Mar 50; Rpt, CG Buna Forces, p. 17.

rot," dengue fever, and dysentery—were beginning to take an increasing toll.[4]

Dysentery was the most widespread affliction. Tainted rations, the long periods that the troops had gone without food, and the lack of sterilizing equipment had all contributed to that result. There were those who were careless with their drinking water, but they were a small minority.[5] The fact was that even those who were extremely careful caught the disease. Thus, Colonel MacNab recalls that although he never drank water that was not chlorinated he "suffered from dysentery as much as any of the troops." [6]

The troops were having trouble with their weapons, partly because of the wet, but mostly because they were not getting gun oil, patches, and other cleaning aids. The M1's had been issued without oil and thong cases. Though gun oil was reaching the front it arrived in large containers that made wide distribution of it impracticable, with the result that some of the troops had to go completely without oil for considerable periods of time. Their weapons therefore— especially the BAR's and machine guns— kept jamming.

There were other serious supply deficiencies. Spare parts and rifle clips were hard to come by, and the troops frequently ran short of ammunition, especially mortar shells. Some had lost their intrenching tools, and so disrupted was supply that they had not been replaced.[7]

Morale was low. Instead of being met, as they had been led to expect, by a few hundred sick and starving Japanese, they found themselves facing apparently large numbers of fresh, well-fed, well-armed troops in seemingly impregnable positions, against whom in almost two weeks of fighting they had failed to score even one noteworthy success.[8]

Most frustrating of all, however, was the realization that they did not have the proper weapons to reduce the bunkers that stood in their way. They were without tanks, grenade launchers, or flame throwers, and mortars, artillery, and air bombardment seemed to have no effect on the enemy's formidable bunker positions. About the only method they could use to reduce the enemy bunkers was to crawl forward as close as the Japanese protective fire would allow and then make a sudden rush in the hope of getting close enough to push hand grenades through the firing slits. This was a course in which, as one who was present was to observe, "Many more failed than succeeded, but for the most part, there was no other way." [9]

[4] Msg, Gen Harding to Maj Birkness, Ser 1911, 2 Dec 42, in 32d Div G–3 Jnl; Interv with Maj Odell, 14 Dec 50; Ltr, Col Herbert A. Smith to author, 20 Jan 50; Lt Col Francis L. De Pasquale, MC Med Hist 32d Div, 1–30 Jan 43. Although there are no sickness figures for this period, the fact that the troops were rapidly sickening at this time was common knowledge, and the final figures compiled at the end of the campaign suggest that a substantial portion of the command was already affected.

[5] Ltr, Col Carl Hanna, MC, to author, 14 Oct 50: Interv with Maj Odell, 14 Dec 50; Ltr, Maj Gen Clarence A. Martin to Gen Ward, 6 Mar 51.

[6] Ltr, Col MacNab to author, 15 Nov 49.

[7] Tel Msg, 1st Lt John E. Harbert, Ord Off, to 32d Div, Ser 1412, 25 Nov 42; Msg, 32d Div to NGF, Ser 1681, Nov 42. Both in 32d Div G–2, G–3 Jnl. Ltr, Gen Eichelberger to Gen Sutherland, 8 Dec 42; Ltr, Lt Col Herbert M. Smith to author, 26 Jun 50; Maj Parker's Buna Rpt.

[8] Memo, Col Reeder, WDGS, for Col Ritchie, Chief, Southwest Pacific Gp, OPD WDGS, 22 Feb 43, sub: Observer Interrogations of Officers at Buna and Sanananda, in OPD 381, PTO Sec 4; Col Hale, Answers to Questions by Hist Sec, GHQ SWPA, As to Certain Phases of the Papuan Campaign; Col Knight's Buna Rpt; Col Handy's Buna Rpt.

[9] Ltr, Col Herbert A. Smith to author, 20 Jan 50.

FIRST AID STATION, SIMEMI, *November 1942.*

Supply

Adequate supply, a basic ingredient of good morale, was simply out of the question at Buna during the latter part of November and the first few days of December, for the Japanese by the end of November had succeeded in cutting the division's supply line by sea. The division had had six luggers in operation on 21 November, but only one was still making the run on the 28th. The rest had either broken up on the reefs or been destroyed by the enemy. Everything now depended on the airlift, which was still too small to fill more than a fraction of the division's needs. By the end of the month, less than sixty tons of freight had been brought in by air—about the equivalent of what one lugger could bring in two trips.[10]

With air space strictly limited, there had been a mad scramble for priorities, and the division, intent on getting enough food and ammunition to the troops to keep the fighting going, found itself competing for space with its supporting elements. In a message to Major Birkness at Port Moresby, Col. Joseph S. Bradley, Division G–4, wrote that

[10] Msg, 32d Div to CG, COSC, Ser 1634, 28 Nov 42, in 32d Div G–2, G–3 Jnl; 32d Div, Rear Echelon Rec of Air Shipments.

FIRST AID STATION, HARIKO, *November 1942.*

the "many priorities by the medics, antiaircraft people, engineers, and others are causing essential chow and ammunition for the
fighting men to be held up." He closed his
message with the plea that Birkness lose no
time in bringing the difficulty "to the attention of the Big Boys." [11]

General Harding described the situation
to General Herring in succinct fashion on 28
November. "Everything," he wrote, "had
been going beautifully until November the
16th, the day they blitzed the four ships, all

of which were loaded with supplies and ammunition." Since then, he added, everything
had been on a "hand-to-mouth, catch-as-
catch-can basis." Nor had the situation improved with the arrival of new luggers on the
21st.

. . . The little ship situation [General
Harding continued] has gone from bad to
worse. One went on the reefs a little while ago,
another got stuck on a sandbar on the 25th,
and was bombed by the Japs the following
day, and three more have been shot up and
bombed while at anchor, one at Mendaropu,
one off Embogu, and one yesterday in Oro
Bay. That finishes the Red Arrow freighters.
There's nothing left except one small craft

[11] Msg, Col Joseph S. Bradley to Maj Birkness,
Ser 1472, 26 Nov 42, in 3d Div G-2, G-3 Jnl.

114TH ENGINEER BATTALION *builds a corduroy road with the help of natives.*

with a kicker that will make about two knots. . . .[12]

Though the division now had to get almost all of its supplies from Dobodura, the process was difficult because no roads existed between the airfield and the front suitable for the use of vehicles. The engineers were building a jeep track between Dobodura and Simemi to speed up the transfer of material to the front lines, but there were not enough engineer troops and engineer tools in the area to do the job quickly. Until the road was completed, native carriers, too few for the task, had to carry the supplies

forward from Dobodura on their backs. Because the carriers would not go into the front lines, it became necessary to use combat troops to complete the deliveries.[13]

The Question of Additional Support

General Harding had little luck in his pleas for additional support. When he asked for tanks he had been promised Bren gun carriers, but even the carriers had not ar-

---

[12] Ltr, Gen Harding to Gen Herring, 28 Nov 42, copy in OCMH files.

[13] Tel Msg, 1st Lt Clifton P. Hannum, S–3, 1st Bn, 126th Inf, to 32d Div, Ser 1501, 26 Nov 42; Rad, Gen Harding to Maj Birkness, Ser 1644, 28 Nov 42; Msg, Gen Harding to NGF, Ser 1908, 2 Dec 42. All in 32d Div G–2, G–3 Jnl. Maj Parker's Buna Rpt; 114th Engr Bn AAR, Papuan Campaign; Eichelberger, *Our Jungle Road to Tokyo,* p. 39.

rived. When he asked for ten more artillery pieces, he was promised four—sometime in December.[14] When he asked for all or part of the 127th Infantry (which had finally reached Port Moresby on Thanksgiving Day), General Herring had disapproved the request with the remark, "I cannot see what it is needed for, as you seem to have ample reserves." [15]

On 29 November Harding moved his headquarters from Embogo to Dobodura. The next day he had an opportunity to renew his plea for additional support. Not only did General Herring visit him, but General Sutherland flew in from Port Moresby.

Herring, who had just opened his headquarters at Popondetta, reached Dobodura by air early in the morning of the 30th, ahead of Sutherland. After the usual amenities, the two generals seated themselves on some empty ammunition boxes and plunged into a discussion devoted principally to Harding's request for the 127th Infantry.

After expressing his dissatisfaction over the diversion to General Vasey of Colonel Tomlinson's 126th Infantry troops, and getting no promise of their return, Harding began to press Herring for at least part of the 127th Infantry. This is the way Harding reported the discussion in his diary,

The chief topic we discussed was the bringing in of part or all of the 127th Infantry. In one of his letters to me, General Herring had stated that he disapproved of previous requests that part or all of the regiment be thrown in, on the ground that we had plenty of reserves. I explained somewhat heatedly, that we had *no* reserves, and I argued to the best of my ability for additional troops, not to relieve those in the line, but to strike in another quarter. General Herring remained unconvinced of the need or desirability of the proposed move despite all my protestations.[16]

Recalling the matter, Harding was to write:

I tried to give Herring the picture by letter, radio, and finally face to face, but he never seemed to get it. He was a gentleman . . . a scholar, and a pretty good guy withal, but his heart, I am sure, was with the Australians. He seemed to take an almost detached view of the trials and tribulations of my all-American contingent. I felt all along that he had very little scope for independent decision.[17]

Harding and Herring were still discussing the problem when Sutherland arrived. Sutherland was also opposed to bringing in the regiment. His argument was that the problem of supplying the troops already in the area was taxing the transport facilities of the air force to the utmost, and that it would be unwise to bring in more troops until a stockpile had been built up at Dobodura. General Harding then pleaded for at least one battalion of the 127th Infantry to strike in a new quarter, but General Sutherland was adamant. The supply level would have to be raised, he said, before such a move could be considered. A further request by Harding that Colonel Tomlinson be returned to him was also refused. General Harding, who did not take kindly to these refusals, considered that he had been given "the brush-off." [18]

---

[14] Msg, NGF to 32d Div, Ser 1768, 29 Nov 42, in 32d Div G–2, G–3 Jnl.

[15] Ltr, Gen Herring to Gen Harding, 28 Nov 42, copy in OCMH files.

[16] Gen Harding's Diary, 30 Nov 42.

[17] Ltr, Gen Harding to author, 24 Jul 51.

[18] Gen Harding's Diary, 30 Nov 42; Interv with Gen Harding, 9 Dec 47.

*General Eichelberger
Is Ordered Forward*

*General Sutherland
Stays for Lunch*

At the close of the discussion General Herring flew back to Popondetta, and General Sutherland, who had more to say, stayed for lunch. During the course of the meal, Harding again pressed him about the 127th Infantry.

. . . I asked [he noted in his diary] if the Australians were going to use it on the other side of the river. His reply was startling. He said that that had been discussed, and that Blamey had spoken disparagingly of the fighting qualities of the American troops, and told MacArthur that he preferred to use his militia brigade in that quarter. He had also dropped one or two remarks to the effect that the Americans weren't showing the fight they should. I told him that anyone who thought that didn't know the facts—that while we hadn't made much progress, it wasn't because we weren't in there fighting, and I reminded him that our casualties would testify to the hard fighting that had been going on.[19]

General Blamey had indeed spoken disparagingly to General MacArthur of the performance of the 32d Division. The conversation had taken place five days before at Government House, General MacArthur's headquarters at Port Moresby. General Kenney, who had been present (and had made a note of General Blamey's remarks), felt that it had been "a bitter pill for General MacArthur to swallow."[20] It must have been, for it was about this time,

as General Kenney recalls further, that General MacArthur "began to be worried about the caliber of his infantry." Stories that American troops were fighting badly and that some had even thrown away their machine guns and fled in panic from the enemy were reaching headquarters,[21] as were observers' reports which were distinctly unfavorable in tone. The observers noted that the troops and their officers seemed to lack aggressiveness, that many of the junior leaders did not seem to know their business, and that "too many" commanders were trying to conduct operations from a command post. At least one of the observers seems to have gone so far as to say that the 32d Division would not fight.[22]

Matters came to a head when Colonel Larr, General Chamberlin's deputy, visited the front on 27 and 28 November and returned to Port Moresby with an extremely adverse report on conditions there.[23] General Sutherland, whose visit was apparently occasioned by Larr's report, mentioned it to Harding during lunch. He told Harding that because of its unfavorable tone General MacArthur had sent for General Eichel-

---

[19] Gen Harding's Diary, 30 Nov 42. The militia brigade was Brigadier Porter's Infantry Brigade, whose 39 Battalion had performed with such distinction in the Owen Stanleys.

[20] Kenney, *General Kenney Reports,* p. 153.

[21] *Ibid.,* pp. 150, 154, 156, 157. The incident which had given rise to these stories occurred on 24 November (see above, p. 186). The units involved were Company E, 128th Infantry, and the Weapons Platoon of Company G, 128th Infantry, then in their first day of combat.

[22] Col Knight's Buna Rpt. Colonel Knight summarizes these unfavorable reports without mentioning specifically who originated them.

[23] Gen Harding's Diary, 30 Nov 42; Interv with Gen Harding, 9 Dec 47; Interv with Gen Eichelberger, 6 Feb 50; Ltr, Gen Harding to author, 24 Jul 51. Larr's report was apparently by word of mouth, since the G–3 files for the period contain no written report on the subject. The author's knowledge of its content comes from the sources cited above. No confirmation could be secured from Colonel Larr on the subject since he was dead at the time that the chapter was written.

berger and would probably order him to the front. Sutherland then asked Harding (whose two field commanders, Colonels Mott and Hale, were ill-regarded by both I Corps and GHQ) whether he intended to make any changes in his top command.[24]

Though Harding knew that Mott had a "notable talent for antagonizing superiors, subordinates, and contemporaries," [25] and was not particularly impressed with Colonel Hale's ability as a regimental commander,[26] he nevertheless replied in the negative. Mott, he pointed out, appeared to be doing an excellent job on the Urbana front and, while he "frankly . . . questioned whether Hale had the qualifications to lead a regiment in battle," he considered that he was "doing fairly well in the only chance he had had to show his stuff." [27]

Harding's reply apparently was enough for General Sutherland. The latter returned to Port Moresby that same afternoon, 30 November, and recommended to General MacArthur that General Harding be relieved at once on the ground that he insisted on keeping in command subordinates whose competence was open to question.[28]

General Eichelberger Is Given His Orders

As Sutherland had told Harding, General MacArthur had already ordered General Eichelberger to Port Moresby.[29] Eichelberger was at Rockhampton training the 41st Division in jungle warfare at the time the summons was received. It was 29 November, a summery and quiet Sunday, the last quiet day General Eichelberger was to enjoy for a long time. There were two messages. The first was an alerting order from General Chamberlin at Brisbane telling Eichelberger to stand by and advising him that if it was decided that he and a small staff were to go to Port Moresby he would be told that night. Late at night the second message came ordering them to go. By that time General Eichelberger, Brig. Gen. Clovis E. Byers, his chief of staff, six staff officers, his aide, and nine enlisted men, mostly clerks, were packed and ready. They took off in two C–47's for Port Moresby early the next morning, 30 November, and, after an uneventful flight over the Coral Sea, landed at Seven Mile Airdrome late in the afternoon. They were met at the airstrip by Colonel Larr, who told

---

[24] Gen Harding's Diary, 30 Nov 42; Interv with Gen Harding, 9 Dec 47.

[25] Ltr, Gen Harding to author, 24 Jul 51. More to the point, he also knew that Mott and Larr were openly antagonistic and had been for some time.

[26] Interv with Gen Harding, 9 Dec 47.

[27] Gen Harding's Diary, 30 Nov 42. General Harding's feeling in the matter was that Hale, as his last regimental commander from the National Guard, in a division in which the bulk of the officers were from the Guard, should be given a chance to show what he could do, especially since Colonel MacNab, who was on the ground, could be trusted to keep him out of trouble. Interv with Gen Harding, 9 Dec 47.

[28] Interv, Louis Morton with Gen Sutherland, 12 Nov 46.

[29] Eichelberger, promoted to lieutenant general on 15 October 1942, had been at Port Moresby in mid-November to observe the 32d Division in action. He had been ordered back to Australia before the fight for the beachhead began in order to prepare a camp for the 25th U.S. Infantry Division, which was then on the alert for movement to Australia from Hawaii. The mission had come to nothing since the division had been diverted at the last moment to Guadalcanal in order to make possible the relief of the 1st Marine Division and its transfer to Australia for rest and rehabilitation. Ltr, CINCSWPA to CG USASOS *et al.*, 22 Nov 42, sub: Reinforcements, in G-3 Jnl, GHQ SWPA; Msgs, Gen Marshall to Gen MacArthur, No. 3874, CM–OUT 6906, 23 Nov 42; No. 4131, CM–OUT 9526, 30 Nov 42; Interv with Gen Eichelberger, 21 Nov 48.

Eichelberger that he would be given four or five days to be briefed on the situation at Buna before he and his staff went over the mountains.

Eichelberger and Byers were given quarters at Government House, General MacArthur's headquarters, a comfortable sprawling place, which in prewar days had been the official residence of the lieutenant governor of Papua. They had scarcely reached their rooms when they were ordered to report to General MacArthur immediately. The two officers preserved a vivid recollection of what followed. They found General MacArthur with Generals Kenney and Sutherland on the long breezy veranda at the front of the house. General Kenney gave them a welcoming smile when they were ushered into MacArthur's presence, but General Sutherland, who had come in earlier in the afternoon with the news that General Harding had no intention of relieving his subordinate commanders, sat at a desk, stern and unsmiling.[30] Aware that General Sutherland had just returned from Dobodura, General Eichelberger, who had been surprised at the abruptness of the summons to report to General MacArthur, was surprised no longer. It was plain to see, he wrote later on, that Sutherland's report had been the cause.[31]

Striding up and down the veranda, grim and intense, General MacArthur without preliminary plunged into the matter at hand. American troops, he told the officers, had dropped their weapons and run from the enemy. He had never been so humiliated in his life, and it was the kind of thing that he would not stand for. Harding, he said, had failed and the blame for what had hap-

pened was his.[32] What was needed at Buna, he told Eichelberger, was aggressive leadership. He knew, he continued, that the troops were not trained for operations in the jungle, that they were sick, and that the climate was wearing them down, but he was convinced that "a real leader could take these same men and capture Buna."[33]

General MacArthur told Eichelberger that he was to relieve Harding and his subordinate commanders, "or," he flung out, "I will relieve them myself and you too." "Time was of the essence," he said, for the Japanese might land reinforcements "any night." Continuing his restless pacing up and down the veranda, he told Eichelberger, "Go out there, Bob, and take Buna or don't come back alive." Then pointing to General Byers, he added, "And that goes for your chief of staff, Clovis, too."

MacArthur went on to tell Eichelberger and Byers that he knew his staff thought they should have four or five days to be briefed on the situation before they went over the mountains. Things, however, were too serious for that, and he would therefore give them not even one day. They were to get ready immediately and leave for Buna in the morning.[34]

General Eichelberger's First Day at Buna

Subsequent briefings and conferences lasted far into the night. In the morning, immediately after breakfast, General Eich-

---

[30] Interv with Gen Eichelberger and Maj Gen Clovis E. Byers, 1 Jun 50.

[31] Eichelberger, *Our Jungle Road to Tokyo*, p. 21.

[32] Interv with Gens Eichelberger and Byers, 1 Jun 50.

[33] Kenney, *General Kenney Reports*, p. 157. The author's interview with Generals Eichelberger and Byers, and interviews with General Eichelberger alone are to the same effect.

[34] Interv with Gens Eichelberger and Byers, 1 Jun 50.

elberger and his party left for Buna.[35] They landed at Dobodura at 0958, and, at 1300, General Eichelberger, as commander of I Corps, assumed command of all U.S. troops in the Buna Area.[36]

Harding, who had been in the midst of a letter to General Sutherland when Eichelberger and the corps staff arrived, noted in his diary that night:

Eichelberger had come fresh from the presence of MacArthur who had given him an earful of instructions concerning what he, Eichelberger, was expected to do. First of all, he was to take command of American troops in the sector. I wasn't sure just where that left me, but I gathered MacArthur was much dissatisfied with way things were going. Among other things, he had told Eichelberger that he was to take Buna or die before it.[37]

After explaining how General MacArthur felt about the situation at Buna, Eichelberger asked Harding what changes he proposed making in his command in order to get things moving. When Harding replied that he intended to relieve no one and that most of his commanders deserved to be decorated not relieved, Eichelberger pushed the matter no further. He decided to spend the day at Dobodura, find out what he could there, and inspect the front the following day. Two of his staff officers, Col. Clarence

A. Martin, his G–3, and Col. Gordon Rogers, his G–2, would observe the attack on the Warren front, while he himself would observe it on the Urbana front.[38]

That night General Eichelberger wrote to General Sutherland that, to judge from what he heard during the day, things did not appear to be as bad as he had been led to expect. Colonel Mott, for instance, was reporting progress, and seemed to be within a hundred yards of Buna Village. Eichelberger referred to a conversation that he had had that day with Brig. R. N. L. Hopkins, General Herring's chief of staff. Hopkins, he said, had stated that General Herring wanted Buna Mission taken and was not particularly interested in the capture of Buna Village. "I told him," General Eichelberger wrote, "that I had directed, prior to seeing him, that Buna Village be captured tonight, and while I was anxious to get in Buna Mission, I did not want to leave the force in Buna Village on our front and rear."

"I shall go forward in the morning," General Eichelberger continued, "to gain a first hand knowledge of the situation." While he was not willing to admit anything, he said, until he had "personally surveyed the situation well forward," he nevertheless felt that he could already recommend the dispatch to the beachhead of "at least one battalion less two companies of the

---

[35] MacArthur was at breakfast. In contrast to his mood of the afternoon before, he was relaxed and affable. He told Eichelberger to take good care of himself for he was "no use to him dead"—a statement that General Kenney in *General Kenney Reports* claims (apparently in error) he made the day before. When breakfast was over, MacArthur drew Eichelberger to one side, promised to decorate him if he took Buna, and told him, in effect, that he was to take the place regardless of casualties. Interv with Gens Eichelberger and Byers, 1 Jun 50.

[36] Rpt, CG, Buna Forces, p. 19.

[37] Gen Harding's Diary, 1 Dec 42.

[38] Interv with Gen Eichelberger 31 May 50; Interv with Gens Eichelberger and Byers, 1 Jun 50; Ltr, Gen Harding to author, 18 Oct 51; Rpt, CG Buna Forces, p. 19; Eichelberger, *Our Jungle Road to Tokyo*, p. 25. General Eichelberger's decision had first been to send Colonel Rogers and Lt. Col. Frank S. Bowen, Jr., the assistant G–3, to the Warren front, but at the last moment he substituted Martin for Bowen. Ltr, Gen Martin to Gen Ward, 6 Mar 51.

127th Infantry, because we may need a fresh impetus to carry into Buna Village." [39]

Buna Operations: 1 and 2 December

The Urbana Front

The night of 30 November–1 December had been an uneasy one on the Urbana front. (*See Map 10.*) The 25-pounders and the mortars had laid down a desultory fire on Buna Village, and a few unarmed Japanese were killed trying to get back to the large grassy strip where the headquarters area had been, in an effort apparently to recover some of the food and weapons left there. There was actually little action during the night, but the exhausted troops, who were expecting a counterattack, got little real rest.

In the morning Urbana force made another attempt to take Buna Village. Detachments from the Headquarters Companies of both 2d Battalions, and a section of machine guns from Company H, 126th Infantry, were sent forward to reinforce Company E, 126th Infantry. This time the plan was to move on Buna Village through the relatively open area just below the bridge over the Girua River, instead of directly up the main track. The attempt was preceded by fire from the 25-pounders at Ango and from all the available 60-mm. and 81-mm. mortars in battery, the latter being, as before, under Captain Hantlemann of Company H. At the start the action went well, and several bunkers were knocked out. Then, just as the troops seems to be on the point of going through, Company E, instead of continuing to press forward, withdrew.

Whether it did so because there was a mixup in signals or because the men were "jumpy," Colonel Mott was unable to ascertain. [40]

Although his front line was now less than 300 yards from Buna Village, Colonel Mott decided to make no further attacks that day. His plan was to attack again in the morning with the aid of the Cannon Company, 128th Infantry, which had meanwhile been promised him by General Harding. [41]

There was intermittent firing during the night, most of it by enemy mortars and machine guns. A few Japanese again tried, unsuccessfully, to reach the large grassy strip. Otherwise, the night was quiet and the troops got a little rest.

By the following morning Colonel Mott had available for the attack on the village Companies E and H, 126th Infantry, the Cannon Company, and a platoon of Company F, 128th Infantry, which he had ordered up from the other side of the Girua River. He had also the eight additional mortars that General Harding, true to his promise, had rushed to him.

At 0950 the artillery opened a heavy concentration of fire on the bunkers holding up the advance. The artillery was followed by Captain Hantlemann's massed 60-mm. and 81-mm. mortars. The artillery fire was accurate, and the mortar barrage intense and

---

[39] Ltr, Gen Eichelberger to Gen Sutherland, 1 Dec 42, copy in OCMH files.

[40] Col Mott's Memo. Pvt. John E. Combs of Company E distinguished himself on this day for a superb job of scouting, during the course of which he maneuvered himself behind an enemy bunker that had been holding up the advance, killed twelve Japanese single-handed, and enabled his platoon to take the position. For this exploit, Combs was later awarded the Distinguished Service Cross. The citation is in the GHQ SWPA, GO No. 1, 1 Jan 43.

[41] 2d Bn, 126th Inf, Jnl, 30 Nov 42, 1 Dec 42; 2d Bn, 128th Inf, Jnl, 2240, 1 Dec 42; Col Mott's Memo.

well placed. As soon as the American infantrymen attempted to move forward, however, they were stopped by heavy bands of fire across every axis of approach. Colonel Mott was again forced to call off the attack in order to give his battered troops at least one day's rest before they attacked again.[42]

Weakened by fever and suffering from hunger and exhaustion, the men by this time were in pitiable condition. Maj. Roger O. Egeberg, a visiting medical officer from Milne Bay, who saw the troops on 1 December, reported to General Eichelberger in General Harding's hearing that they looked like "Christ off the Cross." [43]

As Colonel Mott observed, the men were suffering from the continuous round of fighting, lack of food, and lack of sleep, as well as from "the long marches and short rations on which they had been subsisting even before the fighting started." [44] An entry on 2 December in the journal of the 2d Battalion, 126th Infantry, made just after the Japanese had repulsed Company E's fifth attack on Buna reads, "The troops that we have left are weak and tired and need rest and reinforcement." [45] It was clear that until they got both, it would be impossible to close the last few yards between them and Buna Village.

The Warren Front

General Harding had already concluded that to attack Cape Endaiadere and the New Strip simultaneously was tactically unsound because the attacks from the eastern end of the New Strip were on divergent lines. He decided therefore to shift the main attack to the New Strip. At 1045 on 1 December he ordered Colonel Hale to stop pressing the attack on Cape Endaiadere and to lend all possible support instead to Colonel Carrier in an attack on the New Strip. One of Colonel McCoy's companies was to be left in place along the coastal track to hold the position there, and the other two companies were to support Colonel Carrier in his operations against the strip.[46]

The plan of action, including air and artillery support, called for Company B, 128th Infantry, to remain in position about 900 yards south of Cape Endaiadere and to launch a series of demonstrations intended to deceive the enemy into thinking that the main Allied effort was still against the cape. The real attack would be against the New Strip. Its object was essentially exploratory: to discover a weak spot in the enemy line and to "go all out" if it found a hole.[47]

Company A, 128th Infantry, with Company B, 126th Infantry, and what was left of Company C, 128th Infantry, would launch an east-west attack from the coastal flank toward the dispersal bays off the

---

[42] Msgs, Gen Eichelberger to NGF, Sers 1882 and 1933, 2 Dec 42; Msg, Urbana Force to 32d Div, Ser 1898, 2 Dec 42. All in 32d Div G–2, G–3 Jnl. 2d Bn, 126th Inf, Jnl, 2 Dec 42; 2d Bn, 128th Inf, Jnl, 0030, 0954, 2 Dec. 42. Two men particularly distinguished themselves in the day's attack—Captain Hantlemann, and 1st Lt. James I. Hunt of Battalion Headquarters Company, who at his own request led a platoon in the attack on the village. Each was later awarded the Distinguished Service Cross. The citations are in GHQ SWPA, GO No. 1, 1 Jan 43.

[43] Interv with Gen Harding, 9 Dec 47; Ltr, Gen Harding to author, 24 Jul 51.

[44] Col Mott's Memo.

[45] 2d Bn, 126th Inf, Jnl, 2 Dec 42.

[46] 128th Inf Jnl, Ser 13, 1 Dec 42.

[47] 128th Inf Jnl, Ser 20, 1 Dec 42; Overlay, 32d Div, 1 Dec 42, in 32d Div Overlays, Papuan Campaign; 32d Div Sitrep, No. 77, 2 Dec 42; Ltr, Col MacNab to author, 15 Nov 49; Ltr, Col Hale to Gen Harding, 7 Nov 49, copy in OCMH files.

eastern end of the strip. At the other end of the strip, Company A, 126th Infantry, would join Company I, 128th Infantry, in an attack on the bridge between the strips. The 2/6 Australian Independent Company would patrol the area facing the strip and serve to connect the forces attacking at its other end. The drive from east to west would be under command of Colonel Mc-Coy; that from south to north, under Colonel Carrier.[48]

The air strafing and bombing of Buna Village, the New Strip, and the bridge between the strips took place between 0800 and 0815, and most of the bombs hit the target area. The last flight, however, forgot to drop flares (the prearranged signal that the air bombing was over), and the artillery and mortars as a result took up the bombardment only after an appreciable interval. The troops, who had pulled back temporarily to avoid being hit by friendly fire, jumped off at 0830 but made little progress. Colonel Yamamoto's troops had not been taken in by the feint of Company B, 128th Infantry, toward Cape Endaiadere. When the bombing began, they took shelter in the bunkers. When it was over, they emerged from their shelters and laid down such heavy fire that the advance stalled almost immediately and soon came to a complete halt.

The results of the day's fighting were not encouraging. The heat was intense, and there were as many casualties from heat prostration as from enemy fire. The troops on Colonel McCoy's front knocked out only

a few bunkers before they were completely stopped by the enemy. On Colonel Carrier's front the troops initially registered small gains, only to be stopped in their turn by flanking machine gun fire from positions in the western part of the strongpoint between the strips. The attack on the Warren front had once again been a failure.[49]

General Harding's Relief

I Corps Inspects the Front

For the Corps inspection of 2 December, General Eichelberger, accompanied by his aide, Capt. Daniel K. Edwards, General Harding, General Waldron, and several others, left Dobodura for the Urbana front at 0930. Half an hour later Colonel Martin and Rogers left for the Warren front. Both parties were able to go only a short distance by jeep; the rest of the way, they had to go on foot.

General Eichelberger's party reached its destination first. Just before it arrived at the front, Eichelberger stopped at the Urbana force aid station. There he found a number of unwounded men who had been sent to the rear for a few days to recover from dengue fever or exhaustion. Some had

---

[48] 1st Bn, 126th Inf, Jnl, Ser 450, 459, 1 Dec 42; 1st Bn, 128th Inf, Jnl, Sers 11, 19, 22, 23, 1 Dec 42; 128th Inf Jnl, Sers 11, 18, 19, 22, 23, 1 Dec 42; 32d Div Sitrep, No. 77, 2 Dec 42; Ltr, Col Hale to Gen Harding, 7 Nov 49; Ltr, Col MacNab to author, 15 Nov 49.

[49] Tel Msg, Col Hale to Gen Byers, Ser 1897, 2 Dec 42, in 32d Div G-2, G-3 Jnl; 1st Bn, 126th Inf, Jnl, Sers 454 through 465, 2 Dec 42; 1st Bn, 128th Inf, Jnl, Sers 9, 15, 17, 24, 51, 72, 2 Dec 42; 128th Inf Jnl, Sers 4, 9, 10, 15, 27, 42, 46, 2 Dec 42; 32d Div Sitreps, No. 78, 2 Dec 42; No. 79, 3 Dec 42; Ltr, Col MacNab to author, 15 Nov 49. During the day's operations, S. Sgt. Delmar H. Daniels, of Company B, 126th Infantry, led three volunteers against an enemy strongpoint near the dispersal bays at the eastern end of the strip, which had held up the company for some time, only to be killed as he attempted to clear out the enemy position. Daniels was posthumously awarded the Distinguished Service Cross. The citation is in GHQ SWPA GO No. 14, 30 Jan 43.

cracked up in combat.[50] Eichelberger made it a point to question several of them closely as to why they were not at the front. The most common answer was that they had been sent to the rear for a rest, and the same answer was given by two or three other unwounded individuals closer to the front, who either were dozing at the roots of trees or were on their way to the aid station.[51]

The three generals reached Colonel Mott's command post at 1140. The artillery was still firing, and it was hoped that this time the bunkers which had held up the previous attack would be destroyed. When the news came that the attack had failed, General Eichelberger announced that he was going forward to see for himself how things were. Ordering General Waldron to remain in the CP, he went up front. General Harding, who refused to remain behind, went with him. The Japanese, after repulsing a whole series of attacks, were not firing, and the two generals were able to inspect the front line without drawing enemy fire.[52]

In General Harding's opinion, General Eichelberger had been in an exceedingly censorious mood before. Now he found a great deal to be angry about in his tour of the front. He had been told (and had in good faith reported to New Guinea Force) that there had been a strong Japanese counterattack. On questioning Major Smith he discovered that there had been no counterattack, only a feeble attempt by a few Japanese to get back into the main strip

southeast of the village.[53] He noticed both light and heavy machine guns standing in the open neither dug in nor concealed. Though he was to learn later what the men already knew, that fires made with wet jungle wood raised dense columns of smoke, he was extremely indignant when he discovered that the front-line troops, though ravenously hungry, had not been permitted to cook some captured Japanese rice lest by doing so they draw enemy fire. He seemed to think that lack of aggressiveness kept the troops from firing and he was greatly angered that, when he asked for volunteers to see what lay immediately ahead, the troops he spoke to did not respond.[54]

While General Eichelberger was questioning the troops, he interviewed three machine gunners on the front line. In response to his question, they told him that they knew that there was an enemy machine gun immediately ahead because it had opened fire only a few hours ago on the troops who tried to go that way. General Eichelberger asked if any of them had gone down the trail since that time to see if the machine gun was still there. The men said they had not. The general then offered to decorate the man who would go forward fifty yards to find out. Satisfied that the enemy weapon was still there, neither the gunners nor any of the other troops volunteered for the job. Instead, Captain Edwards, the general's aide, using a different route and crawling on his belly, made his way to the outskirts of Buna

---

[50] Gen Harding's Diary, 2 Dec 42; Col Mott's Memo.

[51] Interv with Gen Eichelberger, 31 May 50; Ltr, Gen Harding to author, 24 Jul 51.

[52] 2d Bn, 128th Inf, Jnl, 1140, 2 Dec 42; Gen Harding's Diary, 2 Dec 42; Col Mott's Memo; Interv with Gen Harding, 9 Dec 47; Interv with Gen Eichelberger, 21 Nov 48.

[53] Msg, Gen Eichelberger to NGF, Ser 1864, 1 Dec 42, in 32d Div G–2, G–3 Jnl; Ltr, Lt Col Herbert M. Smith to author, 16 Mar 50; Ltr, Gen Waldron to Gen Ward, 5 Mar 51. Smith did not know at the time that Colonel Mott had reported this minor brush with the enemy as a counterattack.

[54] Gen Harding's Diary, 2 Dec 42; Col Mott's Memo; Interv with Gen Eichelberger, 21 Nov 48; Ltr, Gen Harding to author, 24 Jul 51.

Village and returned without being fired on, an exploit that only deepened the general's irritation with the troops over their failure to show any disposition to fight.[55]

The upshot was an angry scene in Colonel Mott's command post. General Eichelberger (who told the troops later on that he had not realized at the time "what they were up against") had some "caustic comments" to make on what he had seen at the front.[56] He delivered pointed remarks on the unwounded men at the aid station, the exposed machine guns, the apparent hesitancy to stir up enemy fire, and the failure of frontline troops to volunteer "even for a decoration." [57] At one point, he went so far as to say that he was not even sure that the troops had fought. Colonel Mott flared up at this. He spoke of the hardships his men had been through and argued vehemently in their defense—a point of view with which General Harding made it clear he agreed by demonstratively dashing his cigarette to the ground when Mott finished speaking.[58] This is Mott's recollection of what followed:

His [General Eichelberger's] voice rose and he said, "You're licked," and indicated in various ways that the troops had done a very poor job and included a great many cowards. After having observed General Eichelberger's manner, I refrained from further attempts to state my side of the case and that of the soldiers under me, and shortly thereafter General Eichelberger . . . left my command post.[59]

Nor had the inspection gone much better on the Warren front. Colonels Martin and Rogers reached Colonel Hale's headquarters at Hariko about noon, after catching a lift part of the way to Simemi in a jeep. They left Hariko at 1410 and at 1528 had reached Colonel McCoy's command post. After a short visit there, they went forward with Colonel MacNab to the area off the eastern end of the New Strip. Before they came, the fighting had raged fiercely and every available man had been on the line. When they arrived, however, the action had died down to virtually nothing.

There was no firing, and, as Martin recalls, there were times when the front was "as quiet as the inside of an empty church." Having beaten off a succession of American attacks, the Japanese were resting and taking things easy. They were not firing even on targets in plain view. Nor did the Americans seem anxious to stir up Japanese fire. After the bloody nose that the enemy had given them, they were content to let well enough alone and were using the respite to dig in, bring up supplies, and prepare for the next day's attack. Although Martin admitted "in the light of subsequent knowledge" that the attacks could not possibly have succeeded even had they been "continued throughout the day with the utmost vigor and daring," the total absence of fight-

[55] Gen Harding's Diary, 2 Dec 42; Col Mott's Memo; Interv with Gen Eichelberger, 21 Nov 48; Ltr, Gen Harding to author, 24 Jul 51. Edwards was later awarded the Silver Star. The citation is in Hq I Corps, GO No. 102, 4 Dec 42.
[56] Ltr, Lt Col Herbert M. Smith to author, 16 Mar 50. Smith as commanding officer of the 2d Battalion, 126th Infantry was in the CP at the time and witnessed the scene.
[57] Interv with Gen Eichelberger, 31 May 50.
[58] Gen Harding's Diary, 2 Dec 42; Col Mott's Memo; Ltr, Gen Harding to author, 24 Jul 51; Interv with Gen Eichelberger, 21 Nov 48. That night General Harding wrote in his diary that in the light of his remarks General Eichelberger "showed no appreciation of what the men had been through, or the spirit shown by most of them in carrying on despite heavy casualties, the roughest kind of opposition, and the most trying conditions." Of Colonel Mott's outbursts, he wrote, "I approved of every word he said and of the vehemence with which he stated the case."

[59] Col Mott's Memo.

ing when the inspection team reached the front led the inspectors to wonder whether there had really been any fighting at all that day.[60]

The inspection team was particularly struck by the poor physical condition of the troops. Colonel Rogers (who subsequently put his criticism in writing) described their condition as "deplorable," and took special note of their dirty beards, ragged clothing, and worn-out shoes, and of the fact that they were not getting enough to eat. Colonel Martin noted that the morale of the troops was poor, that the men seemed to have a "sorry for ourselves" attitude, and that they appeared to be interested above all else in being relieved. Rogers was critical of Colonel Hale for remaining too far behind the lines and thought it remarkable that there had been so little action at the front when the inspection team arrived. Martin was struck by the fact that unsanitary conditions had been allowed to develop at the front, and recalls seeing a great deal of unnecessary litter, quantities of unsalvaged equipment, and piles of empty ration tins swarming with flies.[61]

The two colonels were back at Colonel McCoy's CP by 1702, and left on foot for the rear at 1820. They reached Dobodura about 2200, to discover that General Eichelberger had relieved General Harding only a short while before and that General Waldron was in command of the division.[62]

General Eichelberger Comes to a Decision

General Eichelberger was well aware that General MacArthur had spoken in anger on 30 November when he ordered him to relieve Harding. As corps commander, Eichelberger knew, he was under no obligation to take the step if he thought the relief unnecessary. After his visit to the Urbana front, he nevertheless concluded that Harding would have to go.[63] That evening, shortly after his return from the front, he called in General Byers and other immediately available members of the corps staff and told them how things had gone on the left flank. He described the scene in Colonel Mott's command post, informed them that General Harding had appeared to be in sympathy with Mott throughout, and asked them what they would do if they were in his place. The staff members present unanimously told him that he had only one choice: to comply with General MacArthur's instructions and relieve Harding.[64]

Shortly after the staff meeting, General Harding approached General Eichelberger in his tent in order to discuss a new plan to take Buna. He described the plan, which envisaged an air bombardment and an artillery preparation, both co-ordinated on a split-section schedule with the infantry attack. General Waldron was in Eichelberger's tent at the time, and this, as Harding entered it in his diary that night, is what followed:

Eichelberger listened but did not seem to be impressed. He had other matters on his mind, and I soon found out what they were.

---

[60] 128th Inf Jnl, Sers 49, 54, 2 Dec 42; 1st Bn, 128th Inf, Jnl, Sers 69, 70, 2 Dec 42; Ltr, Gen Martin to Gen Ward, 1 Mar 51; Eichelberger, *Our Jungle Road to Tokyo*, p. 25.

[61] Ltr, Gen Martin to Gen Ward, 6 Mar 51; Eichelberger, *Our Jungle Road to Tokyo*, p. 25.

[62] 1st Bn, 128th Inf, Jnl, Sers 71, 73, 2 Dec 42; 128th Inf Jnl, Sers 65, 67, 2 Dec 42; Ltr, Gen Martin to Gen Ward, 6 Mar 51.

[63] Ltrs, Gen Eichelberger to Gen Sutherland, 3 Dec 42, 9 Dec 42, copies in OCMH files.

[64] Interv with Gens Eichelberger and Byers, 1 Jun 50.

He started talking about what he had found out that day that was allegedly wrong. I took issue on one or two points, and finally said, "You were probably sent here to get heads, maybe mine is one of them. If so, it is on the block." He said, "You are right, it was, and I am putting this man—pointing to Waldron—"in command of the division." I said. "I take it I am to return to Moresby." He said, "Yes." I stood up, and stepped outside the tent.[65]

The New Task Force Commanders

As soon as General Harding left the tent, General Eichelberger offered to replace Colonel Hale with Colonel Martin, an offer that Waldron promptly accepted.[66] Some time later, while Waldron was still in Eichelberger's tent, Colonel Martin and Colonel Rogers reported to General Eichelberger. On the way in, Martin had confided to Colonel Rogers that he thought the reason General Eichelberger had sent him to the Warren front in the first place was that he probably wanted him to take command there. Colonel Martin was nevertheless taken aback by what followed. For scarcely had he, as Roger's senior, started to give the report of what he had seen at the Warren front, when as he recalls,

. . . General Eichelberger, turning to General Waldron, stated rather than asked, "Shall we tell him now." Whereupon he turned again

to me and said, "Clarence, my boy, you have always said you would like to command a regiment. I am going to give you one. You will take command of the 128th Infantry and the Warren front. My conclusion . . . confided to Rogers . . . was confirmed. I immediately replied, "Yes, Sir, that is true, but I never imagined it would be under circumstances such as these." Then, I added, "Since I am to take command of the 128th Infantry I would prefer [that] Colonel Rogers made the report." Rogers then continued and made the report orally. We had just returned, it was dark, and there had been no time to write a report.[67]

General Harding's relief was followed the next day by that of Colonels Hale and Mott. Colonel Martin replaced Colonel Hale as commander of Warren Force, and Colonel McCreary took over from Colonel Mott as commander of Urbana Force. McCreary was replaced on 4 December by Col. John E. Grose, General Eichelberger's inspector general, whom Waldron accepted for the post after deciding that he needed McCreary to command the artillery.[68]

I Corps had taken over completely, and the responsibility for taking Buna was now General Eichelberger's.

---

[65] Gen Harding's Diary, 2 Dec 42.
[66] Ltr, Gen Waldron to Gen Ward, 5 Mar 51.

[67] Ltr, Gen Martin to Gen Ward, 6 Mar 51.
[68] 1st Bn, 128th Inf, Jnl, Ser 29, 3 Dec 42; 2d Bn, 126th Inf, Jnl, 3 Dec 42, 4 Dec 42; 128th Inf Jnl, Sers 16, 20, 3 Dec 42; Col Mott's Memo; Ltr, Gen Eichelberger to Gen Sutherland, 3 Dec 42; Ltr, Gen Waldron to Gen Ward, 5 Mar 51.

CHAPTER XII

The Fighting West of the Girua

The 900 men of Colonel Yazawa's *41st Infantry* force, which had extricated itself from Oivi on 10 November and fled northward with General Horii along the west bank of the Kumusi River, reached the river's mouth twelve miles north of Gona toward the end of the month. While trying to cross the turbulent Kumusi on a raft, General Horii and his chief of staff were drowned at Pinga, west of Gona. (*See Map III.*) Otherwise the force was intact. Since Yazawa was in no position to fight his way down the coast, Colonel Yokoyama undertook to bring his force back into the battle area by sea. On 28 November Yokoyama sent all the landing craft he had to the mouth of the Kumusi. The craft picked up as much of Yazawa's force as they had space for, but most of the *1st Battalion, 41st Infantry,* was left behind. The boats were attacked on the way by Allied aircraft and several were sunk, but Yazawa and perhaps 500 of his force reached Giruwa early on 29 November, a welcome reinforcement for the hard-pressed beachhead garrison.[1]

Operations in the Gona Area

Fresh Japanese Troops Reach the Kumusi

Rabaul, meanwhile, was making every effort to reinforce the beachhead. On 22 November a fresh *18th Army* unit, the *21st Independent Mixed Brigade*, principally the *170th Infantry Reinforced*, arrived at Rabaul from Indochina under command of Maj. Gen. Tsuyuo Yamagata. The brigade, a former Indochina garrison unit without previous combat experience, was immediately put on orders for Basabua but, because of the brightness of the moon, was held over at Rabaul for the better part of a week. The first echelon, totaling 800 men and consisting of General Yamagata, his staff, the *1st Battalion, 170th Infantry,* and a portion of the *1st Battalion, 38th Mountain Artillery,* finally left Rabaul on the night of 28–29 November in four destroyers which made for Basabua via the northern route. Apparently thinking that the favorable moon and the speed and maneuverability of the destroyers would see them through, General Adachi (who had reached Rabaul only three days before) failed to provide the movement with air cover. This was a mistake, as he was to discover early the next morning when Allied bombers hit the destroyers in Vitiaz Strait and damaged them

---

[1] Allied Air Forces Opns Rpt, 30 Nov 42; G–3 Opns Rpt, No. 238, 30 Nov 42–1 Dec 42; *Yokoyama Force* Buls, 26 Nov 42, 28 Nov 42, in ATIS EP 29; Msg, Col Tomita to CofS *Army Hq*, Rabaul, 28 Nov 42, in ATIS CT 26; *Yokoyama Force* Orders No. A–12, 30 Nov 42, in ATIS CT 18, No. 229; *17th Army* Opns I, 129, 130; *18th Army* Opns I, 15, 20, 23, 25.

so heavily that they were forced to return to Rabaul.

By then the second echelon of Yamagata's Force, totaling about 800 men, was loaded and ready to go in four other destroyers. It consisted of the *3d Battalion, 170th Infantry,* less one company, and attached troops, including a complete headquarters communications unit. To save time, General Yamagata and his headquarters attached themselves to the *3d Battalion,* and the convoy left Rabaul late on 30 November, taking the southern route through St. George's Channel.

This time it had a strong fighter plane escort, mostly naval Zeros. About forty miles southeast of Gasmata, the ships were attacked by six B–17's, but the bombers were successfully intercepted by seventeen to twenty Zeros. Further attacks closer to Buna, first by four B–17's and then by six B–25's, were also intercepted, and the ships managed to reach the anchorage at Basabua safely before daybreak on 2 December. They did not remain long. Before they could even begin to unload, a heavy concentration of Allied aircraft struck at them and forced them to flee the anchorage. The ships moved north and began landing the troops by barge near the mouth of the Kumusi. Dropping flares because it was still dark, Allied planes dived in to disrupt the landing. They bombed and strafed ships and landing craft, but about 500 of the troops aboard and a large part of their supplies managed to reach shore. There they were joined by the *41st Infantry* troops whom Colonel Yazawa had been forced to leave behind a few days before.[2]

Although General Yamagata was ashore and had a sizable force at his disposal, his troubles had only begun. With the Australians between him and Gona, his problem was no mean one. It was how to get his men south where they would be of use in the defense of the beachhead.

The Fall of Gona [3]

The fighting at Gona had meanwhile entered its final stages, though the Australians were to suffer very heavy losses before they cleared the Japanese out of their burrows in the mission area. The 2/14 and 2/27 Battalions, the first units of the 21st Brigade to reach the Gona area, were committed to action there on the afternoon of 28 November. A patrol of the 2/14 Battalion was sent to investigate a small creek on the beach half a mile east of the mission, from which it was planned that the battalion would attack the next morning. (*See photo, page 148.*) The patrol reported the area clear of the enemy, and the battalion at once began moving into position. When it broke out at dusk on the coast 200 yards east of the creek, it ran into a hornet's nest of opposition. From a network of concealed and well prepared positions the Japanese hit the battalion hard, inflicting thirty-two casualties on the Australians before they could disengage.

The next day, after an air strike on known enemy positions east of the mission, the 2/27 Battalion under its commander, Lt. Col. Geoffrey D. Cooper, moved into position west of the creek. Swinging wide through bush and swamp, the 2/14th, Lt. Col. Hugh B. Challen, commanding, debouched onto

---

[2] Allied Air Forces Opns Rpts, 28 Nov–3 Dec 42; G–2 Daily Summary Enemy Intel, No. 254, 1–2 Dec 42; AMF, Interr Gen Adachi *et al.; 21st IMB* Troop List, in ATIS CT 18, No. 234; *17th Army* Opns I, 131; *18th Army* Opns I, pp. 19–24.

[3] Except where otherwise noted, this subsection is based on the official Australian manuscript history, McCarthy, The Southwest Pacific: The First Year, Ch. 16.

the beach several hundred yards east of the creek. The 2/27th was to attack westward along the beach, and the 2/14th, in addition to clearing out any remaining opposition east of the creek, was to send a detachment eastward to deny the enemy the anchorage at Basabua.

The 2/27th was slow in moving forward. When it finally attacked, it met very heavy opposition from hidden enemy positions and in short order suffered fifty-five casualties. The 2/14 Battalion, moving west to clear out the enemy east of the creek, encountered the same kind of opposition and sustained thirty-eight casualties. The pattern was familiar. Heavy losses had thus far characterized every attack on Gona, and the 21st Brigade's first attack on the place was no exception. Although the brigade had not gone into action until the 28th, it had already lost 138 men and gained little more than a favorable line of departure from which to mount further attacks.

On 30 November, the 2/27th continued its attack westward and again met strong opposition from the hidden enemy. This time it lost forty-five men. The 2/14th, meeting lighter opposition, lost only eleven men and finished clearing the enemy out of his positions east of the creek. The Australians now held most of the beach between Basabua on the right and Gona on the left, but Gona itself was still firmly in Japanese hands.

That evening, Brigadier Dougherty drew up the plan for another attack the next day, 1 December, which would include part of Lt. Col. Albert E. Caro's newly arrived 2/16 Battalion. The plan provided that the 2/27 Battalion, with a company of the 2/16th on its left, would attack straight east in the morning. At a designated point, the 3 Infantry Battalion, coming up from the head-

quarters area to the south, would move in on the left and join with the AIF in the reduction of Gona, which lay immediately to the Australian left front.

About 0200 the next morning the Japanese at Giruwa made a last attempt to reinforce Gona. Loaded with 200 *41st Infantry* troops, who had come in from the mouth of the Kumusi the night before, three barges tried to land about 600 yards east of Gona, but patrols of the 2/27 Battalion drove them off. The barges returned to Giruwa, their mission a failure.[4]

Shortly after the Japanese landing craft had been driven off, the day's attack on Gona began. At 0545 artillery and mortars opened up on the enemy, and at 0600 the troops attacked with bayonets fixed. The attack on the beach started off well, but the 3 Battalion mistook its rendezvous point and did not move far enough north. As a result, it failed to link up, as planned, with the company of the 2/16 Battalion on the 2/27th's left.

Everything went wrong after that. Swinging southwest to cover the front along which the 3 Battalion was to have attacked, the company of the 2/16th on the left and part of a company of the 2/27th on its right, broke into the village that morning, but the Japanese, who were there in strength, promptly drove the Australians out. Casualties were heavy: the company of the 2/16th alone lost fifty-eight killed, wounded, and missing in the abortive attack.

On 3 December, Lt. Col. R. Honner's 39 Battalion, leading Brigadier Porter's 30th Brigade, reached the front, rested and rehabilitated after its grueling experience in the Owen Stanleys' in July and August.

---

[4] *Yokoyama Det* Opns Orders No. A–12, 30 Nov 42, in ATIS CT 18, No. 229.

General Vasey had planned to send the battalion to Sanananda, but the 21st Brigade's losses—430 killed, wounded, and missing, in the five days that it had been in action—left him no choice but to give it to Brigadier Dougherty. Ordering the rest of the 30th Brigade to Sanananda, Vasey assigned the battalion to Dougherty for action in the Gona area.

Next day, the 25th Brigade, which had been relieved by the 21st Brigade on 30 November, was further relieved, along with its attached 3 Infantry Battalion, of its supporting role in the Gona area. The troops, who had long since earned the respite, received their orders to return to Port Moresby on 5 December and at once began moving to the rear. Their part in the campaign was over.

On the 6th, Brigadier Dougherty launched still another attack on Gona. The remaining troops of the 2/16 and 2/27 Battalions, now organized as a composite battalion, jumped off from their positions east of the mission and attacked straight west along the beach. The 39 Battalion, following a now-familiar tactic, moved up from the south and attacked northwest, hoping to reduce the village. The result was the same as before: heavy casualties and only a slight improvement in the Australian position.

Yet for all their losses, the Australians were doing much better than they thought. The Japanese had taken a terrific pounding. They were utterly worn out and there were only a few hundred of them left. The time had come for the knockout blow.

It was delivered on 8 December. At 1245, after a fifteen-minute artillery and mortar preparation, the 39 Battalion attacked Gona from the southeast. It broke into the village without great difficulty and began system-

atically clearing the enemy out. Exactly an hour later, the composite 2/16–2/27 Battalion, which had been supporting the 39 Battalion's attack with fire, moved forward—the troops of the 2/27th along the beach, and those of the 2/16th from a start line a few hundred yards south of it. By evening the militia and the AIF had a pincers on the mission, and only a small corridor 200 yards wide separated them.

Acting on Colonel Yokoyama's orders, Major Yamamoto, still leading the defense, tried to make his way by stealth to Giruwa that night with as much of his force as he could muster—about 100 men. The attempt failed, and the Japanese were cut down in the darkness by the Bren guns of the Australians.

The end came next day. Early on 9 December patrols of the 2/16, 2/27, and 39 Battalions moved into the mission area to mop up. It was a grim business with much hand-to-hand fighting, but the last enemy positions were overrun by 1630 that afternoon. The Australians found a little food and ammunition and took sixteen prisoners, ten of them stretcher cases.

The Japanese at Gona had fought with such single-minded ferocity that they had not even taken time to bury their dead. Instead, they had fired over the corpses and used them to stand on or to prop up their redoubts. Toward the end, the living had been driven to put on gas masks, so great was the stench from the dead.

The stench was indeed so appalling that it had nauseated the Australians. When the fighting was over and the victors were able to examine the Japanese positions, they wondered how human beings could have endured such conditions and gone on living. An Australian journalist who was with the troops describes the scene thus:

. . . Rotting bodies, sometimes weeks old, formed part of the fortifications. The living fired over the bodies of the dead, slept side by side with them. In one trench was a Japanese who had not been able to stand the strain. His rifle was still pointed at his head, his big toe was on the trigger, and the top of his head was blown off. . . . Everywhere, pervading everything, was the stench of putrescent flesh.[5]

The Australians buried 638 Japanese dead at Gona, but they themselves had lost more than 750 killed, wounded, and missing. Nor did capture of the village mean the end of fighting in the Gona area. General Yamagata had moved his force from the mouth of the Kumusi to the east bank of the Amboga River, a small stream whose mouth was about two miles northwest of Gona. His hope apparently was to find a weak spot on the Australian left flank and cut his way through to Gona. Australian patrols began clashing with Yamagata's force on 4 December, the day it crossed the Amboga. The clashes increased in violence, and on 9 December, the day that Gona fell, Brigadier Dougherty ordered the 39 Battalion westward to deal with the enemy.[6]

General Oda Gets Through

General Adachi meanwhile had not relaxed his efforts to reinforce the beachhead. Early on 7 December, a second landing force of about 800 men—the *1st Battalion, 170th Infantry,* the remaining company of the *3d Battalion, 170th Infantry,* the regimental gun company, and a heavy machine gun company—left Rabaul in six destroyers.

Covered by approximately twenty Zero fighter planes—the convoy took the southern route through St. George's Channel. A Fifth Air Force B–24 on armed reconnaissance spotted the ships at 1020 the next morning, just as they were leaving the channel for the open sea. The B–24 attacked immediately and scored a hit on one of the destroyers. It was not fatal, and the six ships moved steadily onward to their destination. Late that afternoon, despite strong fighter interception, they were attacked by nine B–17's which hit them in successive waves. Three of the destroyers were set afire, and seven of the fighters were shot out of the sky without the loss of a single B–17. By 1625 the Japanese had had enough. With dead and wounded aboard, and fires raging on three of the six destroyers, they reversed course and limped home to Rabaul. The air force had successfully turned back the second attempt of the *1st Battalion, 170th Infantry,* to reach the beachhead.[7]

General Yamagata's position had now become very precarious. His troops were being bombed relentlessly from the air, and the Australians were taking increasingly heavy toll of them. Rather than retreat, he ordered his remaining troops to throw up a defensive line in the Napapo–Danawatu area, a few miles northwest of Gona. There they were to hold, awaiting the arrival of reinforcements.[8]

The reinforcements were not long in coming. The *1st Battalion, 170th Infantry,*

[5] ALF Daily Opns Rpt Nos. 235–243, 5–13 Dec 42, in G–3 Jnl, GHQ SWPA; *18th Army* Opns I, 25. Quoted excerpt is from Ian Morrison, *Our Japanese Foe* (New York, 1943), pp. 6, 7.
[6] ALF Daily Opns Rpt Nos. 236–238, 6–8 Dec 42; *18th Army* Opns I, 25; McCarthy, *op. cit.,* Ch. 16.

[7] G–3 Opns Rpt No. 245, 7–8 Dec 42; Allied Air Force Opns Rpt, 8 Dec 42; G–2 Weekly Summary Enemy Naval Intel, 13 Dec 42, in G–3 Jnl, GHQ SWPA; Diary, Maj Nojiri, Staff Off and later CO, *1st Bn, 170th Inf,* in ATIS CT 29, No. 350; *18th Army* Opns I, 25.
[8] Allied Air Force Opns Rpts, 2, 9, and 12 Dec 42; Allied Air Force Rpt, 4 Dec 42, 9 Dec 42; ALF Daily Opns Rpt No. 224, 14 Dec 42; *18th Army* Opns I, 25.

which had been forced to return to Rabaul on 8 December, was ordered forward again on the 12th for the third time. In five destroyers, the force of about 800 men left Rabaul under command of Maj. Gen. Kensaku Oda, new commander of the *South Seas Detachment,* succeeding General Horii. General Oda's orders were to report to General Yamagata, his senior in rank, for further instructions.

Fortunately for Oda and the troops of Yamagata's brigade, the weather turned bad. Protected by poor visibility, the Japanese this time used a northern route which led past Madang and through Vitiaz Strait and got through safely. An attempt was made to bomb the ships on 13 December when they were glimpsed fleetingly off Madang, but it was unsuccessful. The weather continued bad, and the destroyers managed to reach the mouth of the Mambare River about thirty miles north of the mouth of the Kumusi at 0200 on the 14th without being detected by the air force. The ships came prepared for a quick getaway. Their decks were loaded down with waterproofed cases of supplies lashed to drums or buoys, and they had brought along plenty of landing craft. Unloading operations began at once. The troops made for shore in the landing barges, and the supplies were pushed overboard into the sea to be washed ashore by the tide.

The air force reached the scene at 0600. By that time unloading was virtually complete. The destroyers had already pulled out of the area, and efforts to bomb them were unsuccessful. However, some of the supplies and a few of the landing barges were still offshore, and the air force lost no time in bringing them as well as the landing beaches under attack. The Japanese lost some barges, men, and supplies, but their

losses were on the whole small.[9] Thanks to the weather the Japanese could congratulate themselves on an unusually successful run. They were some forty miles north of the beachhead, but they had their launches with them and could hope to reach it by coastwise infiltration.

Though the Japanese had everything ashore and under cover, neither they nor their supplies were beyond Allied reach. Unknown to them, an Australian coast watcher, Lt. Lyndon C. Noakes, AIF, had his camp on a ridge about two miles from the mouth of the Mambare. Discovering the landing almost as soon as it was made, Noakes scouted the Japanese encampment, fixed the position of the tents and supply dumps in relation to a sandy beach easily seen from the air, and then had his radio operator send out a signal giving the exact position of the Japanese camp and dump area. Early the next morning the air force came over and scored hits on the Japanese supply dumps and destroyed several of General Oda's precious launches. As soon as the bombers left, the Japanese tried shifting remaining supplies to what they apparently thought would be a more secure place, but to no avail. They reckoned without Noakes, who at once reported the shift to the air force. Bombers came over again the next morning and blew up more of General Oda's supplies and sank more of his launches, repeating the process every time the Japanese tried moving their supplies to a new place.

Oda was delayed several days at the mouth of the Mambare. Critically short of landing craft, he finally managed to move forward to the Amboga with only a portion

---

[9] Allied Air Force Opns Rpt, 13 Dec 42, 14 Dec 42; G–3 Opns Rpt No. 251, 13–14 Dec 42; Allied Air Forces Intel Summary DOI, No. 260, 15 Dec 42; Diary, Maj Nojiri; *18th Army* Opns I, 25.

of the *1st Battalion, 170th Infantry.* Hugging the coast, and moving only at night, he and the battalion's advance echelon reached the mouth of the Amboga on 18 December and at once reported to General Yamagata,[10] whose headquarters, previously at Napapo, about three miles northwest of Gona, was now at Danawatu about five miles northwest of it.

By this time the 2/14 Battalion, after leaving a portion of its strength to outpost the Basabua anchorage, had moved west to the Amboga River area and joined the 39 Battalion in operations against General Yamagata's force in that area. The fighting had been extremely costly to the Japanese. By mid-month they had lost so many men that when General Oda reported to him on the 18th, Yamagata immediately ordered into the line around Danawatu all the troops that Oda had brought with him. Oda himself he ordered to Giruwa with instructions to take command upon his arrival there. Oda and his staff reached Giruwa safely by launch on 21 December, and the general at once took command in place of Colonel Yokoyama.[11]

As commander at Giruwa Colonel Yokoyama had concerned himself, since the Allies had marched out on the beachhead, chiefly with operations along the Soputa–Sanananda track, and General Oda at once moved his headquarters forward to Sanananda to take personal charge of them.

---

[10] Allied Air Force Opns Rpts, 15, 16, and 17 Dec 42; Feldt, *The Coast Watchers,* pp. 194–96; Maj Nojiri's Diary; *18th Army* Opns I, 27.

[11] ALF Daily Opns Rpt No. 247, 17 Dec 42, No. 248, 18 Dec 42; G–3 Opns Rpt No. 256, 18–19 Dec 42; *Nankai Shitai* Orders No. 3, 22 Dec 42, in ATIS CT 18, No. 232; Interr, Sgt Jinsaburo Hirose, *1st Bn, 170th Inf,* in 32d Div G–2 Enemy Interrogations and Translations File; Maj Nojiri's Diary; *18th Army* Opns I, 27.

The Sanananda Front

The Roadblock Garrison Holds Its Own

Establishment of the roadblock on 30 November by units of the Baetcke force under Captain Shirley had cut off the Japanese forward units at the junction of the Killerton trail and the Soputa–Sanananda track, the only notable gain since operations against the enemy positions in the track junction began. Shirley's men, however, had their difficulties. The garrison (Company I, the Antitank Company, a machine gun section of Company M, and a communications detachment of 3d Battalion headquarters) was itself in a precarious position. Not only was its supply line exposed and vulnerable, but the troops manning the position were subject to continuous attack from almost every direction by enemy forces who outnumbered them several times over. (*Map 11*)

Situated in a comparatively open space in the midst of a swampy jungle, the roadblock was a position not easy to defend. It was only a few feet higher than the surrounding swamp and lacked natural cover except for a few small trees and a profusion of broad-leaved vines. Tall jungle trees, 25 to 100 feet high, standing over dense undergrowth, surrounded it and afforded the enemy every advantage in sniping or mounting surprise attacks.

The men had dug themselves in as soon as the roadblock was secured. The two machine gun squads of Company M took up their position at the northern end and southern ends of the perimeter. Company I moved into position west of the road, and the Antitank Company dug in east of it. Two 60-mm. mortars were emplaced

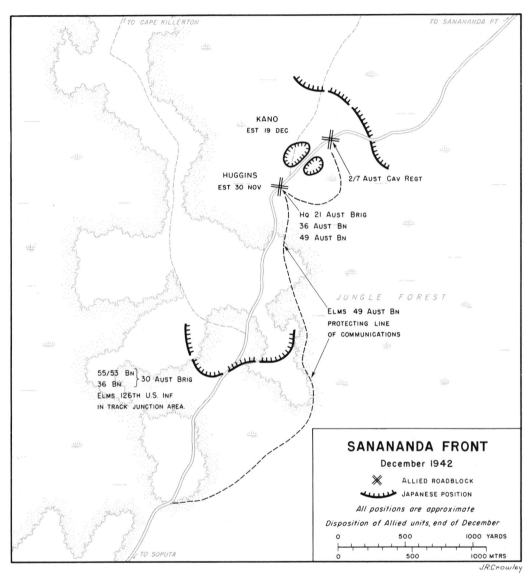

MAP 11

inside Company I's perimeter west of the road.

The night the roadblock was established, the Antitank Company repulsed a heavy attack from the northeast and Company I, one from the northwest. Next morning Captain Keast and a strong patrol including

Lieutenant Daniels, the Australian forward observer who had done such effective work for Major Zeeff on the right, tried a probing attack just off the southwest end of the perimeter. They ran into a well-laid enemy ambush. Keast and Daniels were killed and nine others were wounded. As quickly as they could, the men pulled back into the perimeter, the 1st Sergeant of Company I, Alfred R. Wentzloff, and five men of the company successfully covering their retreat by fire. Beginning in the late afternoon of 1 December and continuing till after midnight, at least five separate counterattacks hit the roadblock troops from the southwest, north, northwest, and northeast. All were thrown back with only small casualties to the garrison.[12]

During this action Major Baetcke, the task force commander, and the rest of his force, Company K and the Cannon Company, were in position in the 3d Battalion area, west of the roadblock. Originally they had planned to move into the roadblock as soon as it was established. They were to make their move, however, only if Major Boerem's frontal attack on 30 November succeeded in piercing the Japanese positions in the track junction, and if Boerem was able, in consequence, to reach the roadblock. Boerem's attack had failed, but the proposal was made on 1 December to send Company K and the Cannon Company into the roadblock anyway. It was argued that Companies I and K and the Cannon and Antitank Companies combined might be able to attack the Japanese rear successfully before the enemy could stabilize his defenses in the area. Major Baetcke finally discarded the plan as too risky. To put it into execution might cause the troops in the roadblock to lose all communication with the rear and could very easily result in the destruction of the entire force. Baetcke's feeling therefore

was that he had to keep Company K and the Cannon Company in position west of the roadblock to supply it and guard its tenuous line of communications.

Supplies came up from the rear on 1 December, and the following morning Major Baetcke sent out the first ammunition and ration party, under command of Captain Huggins, S–3 of the 3d Battalion, 126th Infantry. It had to fight its way into the perimeter but reached it safely about 1100. Shortly afterward, the Japanese launched a heavy counterattack and succeeded in nibbling off fifty yards from the northeast end of the perimeter. Captain Shirley was killed at 1240 and Captain Huggins took over command of the roadblock, which for the following month was to bear his name.[13]

The Japanese attacked the roadblock repeatedly that day and the next but were repulsed. Major Boerem's troops could not cut their way through to the roadblock, and Major Zeeff had to be recalled. Action on the track had crystallized into a fight to maintain the roadblock, a situation that scarcely required the presence of a regimental headquarters. Thus on 3 December, when General Eichelberger requested the transfer to the other side of the river of

---

[12] 126th Inf Jnl, Ser 13, 1 Dec 42; Jnl, Co I, 126th Inf, 1 Dec 42; Memo, Maj Dal Ponte for author, 15 Jul 50. Sergeant Wentzloff was later awarded the Silver Star. The citation is in Hq USAFFE GO No. 32, 15 Jun 43.

[13] Jnl, Maj Boerem's Det, 1 Dec 42; 126th Inf Jnl, Sers 7, 13, 19, 22, 2 Dec 42; Jnl, Co I, 126th Inf, 2 Dec 42; Ltr, Col Baetcke to author, 10 Jan 50; Memo, Maj Dal Ponte for author, 12 Jul 50. On Major Baetcke's orders, Lieutenant Dal Ponte returned to task force headquarters with the ration party that Captain Huggins had led into the roadblock that morning. Colonel Baetcke recalls that Dal Ponte brought back with him some dried onions captured in the roadblock. Considering them a great delicacy, he and Dal Ponte mashed them up with biscuit, and added a little water. They ate the resulting gruel with great relish, counting spoonfuls so that one man would not get more than the other. Interv with Colonel Baetcke, 17 Nov 50.

Colonel Tomlinson and his headquarters, General Herring had no difficulty acceding to the request, even though he had specifically denied a similar request from General Harding a few days before. The transfer was made the next day, 4 December. Tomlinson reached Dobodura by air early that morning, and Captain Boice, his S–2, Captain Dixon, his S–3, and sixty enlisted men of Headquarters Company, under command of 1st Lt. Charles W. Swank, crossed the Girua on foot early the same day. Major Baetcke thereupon assumed command of the remaining American troops west of the Girua, and Major Zeeff became Baetcke's executive officer.[14]

Brigadier Lloyd ordered a new attack for 5 December. The plan of action provided that Major Baetcke from his position west of the roadblock would strike the Japanese right rear north of the junction, while Major Boerem attacked their left-front positions south of it. Baetcke would use the eighty men of Company K, and Boerem, the 220 men of Companies C and L. Company L had been assigned to Boerem upon Zeeff's recall from operations on the right.

At 0715 on the 5th, all the Allied guns and mortars on the front opened up. Fifteen minutes later the troops jumped off for the attack. Leaving the Cannon Company in position under Captain Medendorp, Major Baetcke pushed straight south with his eighty-man force. Advancing through a heavy field of kunai grass which made it impossible to see more than a few feet ahead, Major Baetcke's force covered about 300 yards before it was halted by heavy machine gun and mortar fire. Major Boerem, with his 220 men, did not do as well. Running into very heavy opposition, he gained less than 100 yards before his attack was also stopped. Losses were heavy. Baetcke and Boerem between them lost ninety men that day out of the 300 engaged—two killed, sixty-three wounded, and twenty-five missing.[15] It was clear that Colonel Tsukamoto's troops were firmly entrenched and that rooting them out would be no easy task.

At the roadblock the garrison had been heavily engaged. The Japanese had thrust from several directions on 3 December and had repeated the performance the next day. Captain Huggins was wounded on the 5th, the day that the attack put on by Majors Baetcke and Boerem had failed, but remained in command for lack of someone else to take his place.

The enemy had tried to infiltrate Company K's position west of the roadblock on the 4th and laid a skillful ambush about 300 yards out of the roadblock on the 5th. When Lieutenant Dal Ponte tried to lead a sixty-man ration and ammunition party into the block that morning, the hidden Japanese tried to entrap him. Although Dal Ponte's party consisted mainly of cooks, clerks, and mortarmen, each carrying a forty-pound load, the men gave a good account of themselves. Not only did the ambush fail, but the heavily burdened troops turned the tables on the enemy and at one point almost broke through to the roadblock. After fighting all day and suffering a half-dozen casualties including two killed, the troops were finally forced to withdraw when the Japanese,

---

[14] Msg, Adv NGF to 32d Div, Ser 2086, 3 Dec 42, in 32d Div G–3 Jnl; 126th Inf Jnl, Sers 9, 25, 31, 32, 3 Dec 42, Sers 1, 2, 3, 4 Dec 42; 3d Bn, 126th Inf Jnl, Ser 1, 4 Dec 42.

[15] 3d Bn, 126th Inf, Jnl, Sers 16, 17, 20, 22, 23, 24, 4 Dec 42, Sers 3, 4, 5, 12, 13, 14, 16, 18, 25, 28, 31, 5 Dec 42, Ser 1, 6 Dec 42; Jnl, Maj Boerem's Det, 4, 5, 6 Dec 42; Col Baetcke, Notes on American Force on the Sanananda Trail.

strongly reinforced, seemed about to envelope them.[16]

Another attempt to get rations and ammunition through to the roadblock on 6 December also failed. By this time the roadblock garrison was down to its last day's rations, and it would soon be out of ammunition. There was nothing for it but to try again.

Malaria was meanwhile claiming more American victims. Losses due to fever had been few at first, but by the end of the first week in December 20 percent of the command had contracted it, and the percentage was rising. On 7 December Major Baetcke and Zeeff both came down with malaria and had to be evacuated. Major Boerem took command of the entire force, which now numbered fewer than 800 men. The 30th Brigade under Brigadier Porter relieved the 16th Brigade that day, and Boerem came under Porter's command.

One of Porter's first acts was to relieve Companies C, D, and L in the front lines near the track junction, and to replace them with his 49 and 55/53 Battalions. Satisfied that none of the Americans could be spared, Porter would go no further. He did not accede to a request by Boerem that the American troops be withdrawn to the rear for rest and reorganization, nor did he authorize the return to the 32d Division of some 350 of them, though this had been promised to General Eichelberger some days before by New Guinea Force. Instead he ordered all of Major Boerem's troops, except those in the roadblock and west of the roadblock, to take up supporting positions immediately to the rear of the 49 and 55/53 Battalions. On the same day he had the two Australian battalions attack frontally toward the road junction in an attempt to break through the roadblock.[17]

The 49 Battalion, Lt. Col. O. A. Kessels commanding, jumped off at 0945 on 7 December after a careful artillery and mortar preparation. By 1400 it was stopped completely with a loss of ninety-nine killed, wounded, and missing. Brigadier Porter then ordered the 55/53 Battalion to pass through the position held by Colonel Kessels' battalion and to resume the attack. The 55/53d, Lt. Col. D. J. H. Lovell commanding, attacked at 1515 with even worse results. Cut down by enemy crossfire, the leading companies of the battalion lost 130 killed, wounded, and missing by the end of the day and gained virtually no ground whatever.

In a few hours of fighting Brigadier Porter had lost 229 men (more men than Major Boerem had had to attack with on 5 December, two days before) and had completely failed to dislodge the enemy. Colonel Tsukamoto's defense was still potent, and it was to be twelve days before the Australians, who now embarked on "a policy of patrolling and edging forward wherever possible," were to try a major attack again.[18]

Nor had things gone well in the roadblock area. A further attempt to break through to the block early that morning was a failure, and the supply party returned in the evening with its supplies undelivered. The Japanese were blocking the trail, in strength, the men reported, and they had not been able to get through.

[16] 3d Bn, 126th Inf, Jnl, Ser 1, 5 Dec 42; Jnl, Co I, 126th Inf, 5 Dec 42; Memo, Maj Dal Ponte for author, 16 Jul 50.

[17] 3d Bn, 126th Inf, Jnl, Ser 5, 6 Dec 42; Sers 1, 2, 4, 7 Dec 42; Msg, NGF to Col Merle H. Howe, G–3, 32d Div, Ser 2466, 7 Dec 42; Tel Msg, Maj Boerem to Col Howe, Ser 2467, 7 Dec 42. Both Msgs in 32d Div G–3 Jnl. ALF Daily Opns Rpts Nos. 256, 257, 6, 7 Dec 42; Jnl, Maj Boerem's Det, 6, 7 Dec 42.
[18] McCarthy, op. cit., Ch. 17.

Lieutenant Dal Ponte at once volunteered to take the supplies through. Taking command of the same force that had failed to get through the day before, he moved out early the next morning. About 300 yards from the roadblock, at nearly the same spot where the Japanese had held up Dal Ponte three days before, the supply party was halted and pinned down by machine gun fire from hidden enemy positions on either side of the trail. Dal Ponte knew what to do. Deliberately exposing himself to draw fire, he located first one enemy position and then the other and personally led infiltrating parties which either silenced the enemy or caused him to withdraw. Though repeatedly attacked the rest of the way, the supply party successfully fought its way into the roadblock and Dal Ponte immediately took command of the garrison. Huggins, who had been carrying on despite his wounds, was evacuated to the rear that night when the supply party returned to the position held by Company K and the Cannon Company to the west of the block.[19]

After arriving at the rear with the supply party, Captain Huggins gave a discouraging report on conditions in the roadblock. He described it as about 200 yards square, with the command post and aid station near the center, "all in elliptical pattern." Fevers were raging, he said, and food, ammunition, and medical supplies were running low. The men had to live in holes, and the disposal of wastes presented a difficult problem. Of the

225 men left in the garrison, he thought that perhaps 125 were in condition to fight.[20]

As Dal Ponte was to recall the matter:

. . . water was procured from a hole dug about 3 feet deep, . . . chlorinated for drinking by administering individual tablets. Another source of water supply was that which the men would catch in their pouches from the downpour during the previous night. . . . The disposal of wastes and the burying of dead had to be accomplished within [the] area. . . . Rations were very meager because the ration parties concentrated on ammunition. . . . Chocolate bars, bully beef, and instant coffee were the main items of food when provided. . . . The weather was almost without [exception] rain at night and boiling hot sun during the day. . . . The men were able to get hot coffee by using canned heat that they had saved from previous ration issues or by an expedient consisting of sand and the gasoline taken from the captured trucks. . . . [21]

On 10 December, with communications again out, a second ration party led by 1st Lt. Zina Carter was able to get through to the roadblock. Lieutenant Carter brought back a message from Lieutenant Dal Ponte that fevers, foot ailments, and ringworm were increasing daily, and that while the spirit of the men was good they were worn out and desperately needed relief.

Life at the roadblock was hard. Although the troops were hungry, feverish, and in need of sleep, they were on an almost perpetual alert. Crouched low in their muddy foxholes, their feet going bad, they repelled attack after attack. Sometimes the Japanese got so close to their slit trenches that the troops were able to grab them by the ankles and pull them in. Several Japanese officers were caught and killed in this way.[22]

---

[19] 3d Bn, 126th Inf, Jnl, Ser 17, 4 Dec 42, Ser 1, 5 Dec 42, Sers 1, 4, 8 Dec 42; Tel Msg, Maj Boerem to Col Howe, Ser 2467, 7 Dec 42, in 32d Div G-3 Jnl; Jnls Cos I and K, 126th Inf, 7, 8 Dec 42; Jnl, Maj Boerem's Force, 7, 8 Dec 42; 126th Inf CT AAR, Papuan Campaign. Both Dal Ponte and Huggins were later awarded the Distinguished Service Cross. The citations are in Hq USAFFE GO No. 28, 24 May 43.

[20] Jnl, Maj Boerem's Force, 8 Dec 42.
[21] Memo, Maj Dal Ponte for author, 16 Jul 50.
[22] 3d Bn, 126th Inf, Jnl, Ser 4, 9 Dec 42, Ser 3, 10 Dec 42; ALF Daily Opns Rpts No. 238, 8 Dec 42, No. 242, 12 Dec 42; Jnl, Co I, 126th Inf, 8 Dec 42.

Deep in the swamp to the west Company K and the Cannon Company were little better off than the troops in the roadblock. On 30 November, the day the block was established, the journal of Company K noted: "We have been living in holes for the last six days. Between mosquitoes, Japs, heat, bad water, and short rations, it has sure been hell on the men." Four days later, the entry was: "In position, but the men are getting weaker from lack of food and the hot sun is baking hell out of them." It rained the following two nights, and, as the journal put it: "Did we ever get wet." But, "Hell," it continued, "we've been wet ever since we got to New Guinea." By 9 December, things were definitely worse. "What is left of the company," the journal noted, "is a pretty sick bunch of boys. It rained again last night, men all wet, and sleeping in mud and water." A day later, on the 10th, things looked up a bit. The troops had something to be happy about: they received hot coffee. The entry for the day reads: "The men haven't washed for a month, or had any dry clothing, but we did get some canned heat and a hot cup of coffee. Sure helps a lot. Boy, was it wonderful." [23]

Communications between the supply base to the west and the troops in the roadblock were poor. The radios in use, the SCR–195 and SCR–288, proved very unreliable. Not only did the Japanese frequently cut the wire laid to the roadblock, but they apparently made a practice of tapping it frequently. Extreme care was therefore observed in telephone conversations. As an additional precaution, frequent use was made of Dutch, a language familiar to many Michigan troops whose forebears had come from the Netherlands.

The condition of the troops south of the track junction was no less bad. Despite double doses of quinine, man after man of Companies C, D, and L was coming down with malaria. More than a quarter of the command had fallen ill or had been evacuated with fever, and the percentage was climbing steadily. Casualty figures had assumed the aspect of a nightmare. By 10 December Boerem had but 635 men fit for duty. Two days later he had only 551, and each day saw the effective strength of his command shrink still further.

On 12 December, after several attempts the day before had failed to reach the roadblock, Major Boerem asked Brigadier Porter to relieve the garrison as well as Company K and the Cannon Company, but without success. Heavy rain and fierce enemy opposition defeated all attempts to supply the roadblock on the 13th. All efforts to establish radio or telephone contact with the garrison that day also failed; even runners were unable to get through. [24]

---

[23] Jnl, Co K, 126th Inf, 30 Nov 42, 4, 9, 10 Dec 42. This journal is an informal affair, apparently carried in someone's pocket for a long time. Despite the lapse of years, it still smells of the jungle.

[24] Jnl, Maj Boerem's Force, 10, 12, 13 Dec 42; 3d Bn, 126th Inf, Jnl, Ser 1, 12 Dec 42; Jnl, Co K, 126th Inf, 13 Dec 42; Memo, Maj Dal Ponte for author, 16 Jul 50. Major Boerem faced other problems. Major Baetcke had radioed a requisition for 81-mm. heavy mortar shells, .50-caliber machine guns, a .37-mm. gun, and medical supplies from Port Moresby. Because he could not keep track of all the personnel losses that were taking place, Baetcke had closed his message with the words, "Send Todish"—meaning CWO Frank O. Todish, a warrant officer skilled in personnel matters. The decoding clerk at Port Moresby, thinking Todish a garble, jumped to the conclusion that what Baetcke meant was, "Send to FISH"—the code name for Pongani. The result was that the supplies for which Boerem was anxiously waiting never reached him. They came in on 10 December to Pongani and were later delivered to Warren Force, which, while grateful for their arrival, had no idea who requisitioned them. Maj Boerem's Force, Jnl, 10 Dec 42; Interv with Col Baetcke, 17 Nov 50.

Things went better on the 14th. A party of fifty-five men fought its way into the roadblock early that morning with rations, ammunition, and medical supplies. It broke through just in time, for the garrison was low on food and was about to run out of ammunition.[25]

Unable to get anywhere with Brigadier Porter in the matter of the relief of his troops, Major Boerem saw General Vasey early on the 14th. As the detachment journal notes: "No doubt the Major emerged a bit victorious, for there was a gleam of accomplishment in his eye upon his return to the C. P." That same afternoon, Company K and the Cannon Company packed up and moved to the rear for a well-earned rest. Their place was taken by Australian troops.[26]

The Relief of the Dal Ponte Force

The relief of the troops in the Huggins Block was to take longer. On 15 December the 2/7 Australian Cavalry Regiment began arriving at Soputa. Three hundred and fifty men, the regiment's advance element, fought their way into the roadblock at 1530 on the 18th. Led by their commander, Lt. Col. Edgar P. Logan, the cavalrymen dug themselves in at once beside Lieutenant Dal Ponte's troops. The 49 Battalion, operating southeast of the roadblock, was held up nearly all day, and the 36 and 55/53 Bat-

talions, attacking frontally, made only negligible progress.

Colonel Logan's instructions were to attack northward the next morning, the 19th, in concert with attacks on the track junction by the 30th Brigade. The Dal Ponte force would be relieved as soon as the 39 Battalion, which had been mopping up east of the Amboga River, could reach the Soputa–Sanananda track.

Action flared up everywhere on the front on the 19th. Early in the morning, while the 2/16 and 2/27 Battalions began relieving the 39 Battalion in the Napapo–Danawatu area, the main body of the cavalry unit moved out of the roadblock and attacked north. The 30th Brigade, joined by the newly arrived 36 Battalion, Lt. Col. O. C. Isaachsen commanding, mounted an all-out attack on the Japanese positions in the track junction. The 36 and 55/53 Battalions attacked frontally, the 49 Battalion attacked east of the track, and Major Boerem's troops executed a holding attack by fire.[27]

Cutting to the left around heavy Japanese opposition immediately northeast of Huggins, the cavalry troops advanced several hundred yards and held their gains. The 36 and 55/53 Battalions breached several Japanese positions in the track junction area, and the 49 Battalion pushed forward to a point just outside the roadblock. A strong attack on Huggins was repulsed, and the 2/7 Cavalry pocketed and mopped up a Japanese force 300 yards northeast of the roadblock. There the cavalrymen set up a new perimeter, which they named Kano. In

[25] Jnl, Co K, 126th Inf, 13–15 Dec 42; Jnl, Maj Boerem's Force, 9–15 Dec 42; 3d Bn, 126th Inf, Jnl, Ser 1, 11 Dec 42, Ser 1, 12 Dec 42; Memo, Maj Dal Ponte for author, 16 Jul 50. Only about 1½ day's rations were brought in, since the shortages of ammunitions and medical supplies were even more acute than the shortage of food.

[26] Jnl, Maj Boerem's Force, 14 Dec 42; Jnl, Co K, 126th Inf, 14 Dec 42; 3d Bn, 126th Inf, Jnl, Sers 2, 4, 14 Dec 42; ALF Daily Opns Rpt No. 244, 14 Dec 42.

[27] ALF Daily Opns Rpts, Nos. 245–251, 15–21 Dec 42; G–3 Opns Rpts, No. 254, 16–17 Dec 42, No. 256, 18–19 Dec 42; Jnl, Maj Boerem's Force, 15 Dec 42; NGF, Notes on Opns in New Guinea, Ser 3.

the day's fighting, they lost their commander, Colonel Logan, who was killed in action.

Some progress was registered on 20 and 21 December. The 36th and 55/53 Battalions reduced several more enemy pockets in front of the track junction. The 49 Battalion, which by this time had fought its way into Huggins, began policing a supply route to it from the southeast. The 2/7 Cavalry consolidated at Kano and probed toward Sanananda.

On 22 December Brigadier Dougherty, 21st Brigade Headquarters, and the 39 Battalion reached Soputa from Gona. They moved directly to the roadblock, where Brigadier Dougherty set up his headquarters. Dougherty took over command of the 49 Battalion, of the 2/7 Cavalry, and of the American troops in the roadblock the same day. Brigadier Porter, who was to mop up the remaining enemy pockets in the track junction area, was left in command of the 36 Battalion, the 55/53 Battalion, and the remaining elements of Major Boerem's command.

At 1500 that day Brigadier Dougherty assigned to the 49 Battalion the role of protecting the line of communications from the southeast (which being over better terrain than that from the southwest was the supply route used thereafter). He ordered the 2/7 Cavalry to continue its attacks northward, and the 39 Battalion to relieve the garrison and hold the roadblock.[28]

The relief was effected that afternoon. At 1750, after checking with Major Boerem, Lieutenant Dal Ponte assembled his command and marched it out of the roadblock. After twenty-two days of continuous fighting against heavy odds, the 126th Infantry troops in the roadblock had finally been relieved. They were dazed, sick, and exhausted, and their feet were in such bad shape that they could scarcely use them. Their spirit, nevertheless, was high,[29] for their defense of the roadblock had been superb.

Stalemate on the Sanananda Front

For the Australian units now in the roadblock area, things went little better than before. It was discovered that the Japanese had a very strong defensive position between Huggins and Kano, and an even stronger position north of Kano. Brigadier Dougherty was able to make only slight and very costly progress in his attacks to the northward. Nor did Brigadier Porter's mopping-up operations in the track junction area go much better. Though a portion of their outer line had been breached, Colonel Tsukamoto's troops, with equally strong defenses to the rear, continued to fight with the same ferocity that had characterized the defenders of Gona. There was a difference, however: most of the Japanese at Gona had been service and construction troops with little combat experience; those defending the track junction were battle-tested infantry

---

[28] ALF Daily Opns Rpts, Nos. 249–254, 19–24 Dec 42; G–2 Daily Summaries Enemy Intel, Nos. 272–275, 20–23 Dec 42; Jnl, Co I, 126th Inf, 19 Dec 42; Jnl, Maj Boerem's Force, 19 Dec 42; NGF, Notes on Opns in New Guinea, Ser 3; *18th Army Opns I*, 26.

[29] Jnl, Co I, 126th Inf, 22 Dec 42; Jnl, Maj Boerem's Force, 22 Dec 42; 126th Inf CT AAR, Papuan Campaign. As an evidence of that spirit, consider two entries in the journal of Company I. On the 15th, with communications out, food short, and only mud to sleep in, the main entry for the day reads, "Wentzloff needs a bath." On the 23d, the day after the relief, the journal contains this entry: "Wentzloff finally took a bath." Alfred R. Wentzloff, it will be remembered, was Company I's 1st sergeant.

troops, probably as good as any the Japanese Army had.

Rooting out the enemy continued to be a slow and costly business. The 30th Brigade attacked west of the track, with the 55/53 Battalion on the left and the 36 Battalion, less one company, on the right. Major Boerem attacked east of the brigade with the company of the 36 Battalion on his right. The American front-line troops, then under command of Captain Wildey of Company M, made slow progress in their sector, and the Australians on either side of them did little better in theirs.[30]

Tsukamoto's troops were by no means passive in their defense. On 24 December, American troops on the right-hand side of the track cleared out an enemy trench and machine gun position with hand grenades.[31] To hold it, however, they had to beat off repeated Japanese counterattacks. On the night of 28–29 December forty Japanese, armed with light machine guns, rifles, and explosive charges, infiltrated the Allied rear and blew up a 25-pounder. Thirteen Japanese were killed and one was taken prisoner,

but the enemy had traded blow for blow.[32]

The Japanese struck again on the night of 30–31 December. A Japanese raiding party succeeded in infiltrating the headquarters perimeter of the Australian company on the American right. Surprise was complete. The company commander and several others were killed, but only a few of the Japanese were accounted for. The rest got away safely in the dark.[33]

Hacking a way through the Japanese defenses, which were in depth for a distance of at least three-quarters of a mile, continued to be grueling work, in which progress was measured in terms of a few yards, and the capture of a single enemy pillbox or trench was a significant gain. The story was the same in Brigadier Dougherty's area as in Brigadier Porter's. Fighting was bitter, and progress slow. Except for minor gains, the entire front was at a stalemate.

The Plight of the American Troops

The conditions under which the troops lived were almost indescribably bad. Colonel Boerem, then Major Boerem, recalls them in these words:

Fighting for weeks . . . with the prevailing wind in our faces continually carrying the stink of rotting bodies to us [raised] a difficult morale problem . . . Most of my time was spent going from one soldier to another in an endeavor to raise morale. After taking one position, one hundred and sixty (160) Aus-

---

[30] 3d Bn, 126th Inf, Jnl, Ser 1, 24 Dec 42, Ser 2, 25 Dec 42, Sers 3, 6, 7, 9, 26 Dec 42, Sers 8, 10, 13, 16, 27 Dec 42, Sers 7, 13, 20 Dec 42, Ser 4, 1 Jan 43; ALF Daily Opns Rpts, Nos. 256–262, 26 Dec 42–2 Jan 43.

[31] Five men were later awarded the Distinguished Service Cross for making the attack possible: Sgt. Chester C. Funk of the Cannon Company; Cpl. Orrin C. Sutton and Pfc. Edward R. Rossman of Company L; and Pvts. Lawrence B. Marion and Harold R. Pederson of Company M. A sap had been dug to within fifteen feet of the enemy trench. Despite repeated enemy attacks Funk, though wounded, held the sap through the night with hand grenades. At dawn the other four men crawled forward from the sap, got a foothold in the trench, and held long enough for the rest of the force to arrive and clear it out completely. The citations of Sutton, Rossman, Marion, and Pederson are in Hq USAFFE, GO No. 32, 15 Jun 43; Funk's is in GO No. 45, 8 Aug 42.

[32] Jnl, Maj Boerem's Force, 23, 24 Dec 42; 3d Bn, 126th Inf, Jnl, Sers 1, 4, 29 Dec 42; 30th Bde, Notes on the Japanese New Year, copy in OCMH files. Of this enemy coup, an American officer remarked, "The Japs apparently used solidified picric, and sufficient was found in the vicinity to blow up Lansing, Michigan." Tel Conv, Warren Force with 7th Div, Ser 4583, 29 Dec 42, in 32d Div G–3 Jnl.

[33] 3d Bn, 126th Inf, Jnl, Ser 14, 31 Dec 42; Jnl, Maj Boerem's Force, 31 Dec 42; 18th Army Opns I, 331.

BOATLOAD OF RATIONS *is brought up the Girua River, December 1942. (Collapsible assault boat.)*

tralian and American dead were counted in all stages of decomposition. We made no attempt to count the Japs.

Boerem did his best to rest the men but was able to relieve "only one or two at a time to go to the rear, bathe in the river, get some clean clothes and return." Food consisted principally of the C ration "put up in Australia with mutton substituted for the beef component." The only supplement was bully beef and D ration bars of hard, concentrated chocolate—a diet, Boerem observes gravely, no one could stomach for very long.[34]

[34] Ltr, Col Richard D. Boerem to author, 2 Nov 51.

To add to his other troubles, Boerem was beginning to experience the greatest difficulty in finding enough troops to man the American part of the line. On Christmas Day he had only a little more than 400 men left in condition to fight. A few days later he had less than 300, and the number was constantly shrinking. To provide troops for the front and to guard the Australian artillery and headquarters perimeter, it became necessary to institute a round-robin system of relief whereby the available troops were rotated between the front line, the headquarters perimeter, and the artillery guard. The time came when, despite the most rigorous screening to catch all possible troops for front-line duty, there were not enough men left with whom to attack.

By the year's end, even the seemingly indestructible Major Boerem was worn out and needed to be spelled off. General Eichelberger sent Maj. Francis L. Irwin to replace him. Boerem nevertheless stayed on with the troops at the front for more than a week longer. There was little left of the American force when Major Irwin arrived. On 31 December, the day he took command, effective American strength west of the Girua River was little more than a company, and the situation in the American sector was grim indeed.

Captain Wildey in command on the front line had been wounded on 26 December. He had been succeeded by 1st Lt. John J. Filarski, 1st Battalion S–4, who had been Lieutenant Dal Ponte's executive in the roadblock. When Filarski was evacuated on 29 December, totally exhausted, Dal Ponte took command of a force that consisted in all of seventy-eight men from ten different companies. All that the troops could do was to hold their lines and support the Australians on right and left by fire.[35] "Our tactics during this period," Dal Ponte recalls, "consisted primarily of holding our sector, pinpointing targets of opportunity, delivering mortar and artillery fire on these targets, and patrolling the flanks and rear of our position . . . ."[36] There were not enough men left to do more.

On 10 December, three days after Major Boerem took over from Major Baetcke, the effective American strength west of the Girua was 635; on 13 December it was 547. By 19 December Boerem had 510 effectives; by Christmas Eve the number had gone down to 417. On New Year's Day, the day after Major Irwin took command, the Americans had suffered 979 casualties—73 killed, 234 wounded, 84 missing, and 588 evacuated sick—and there were only 244 men left in condition to fight.

Companies K and L had entered the battle on 22 November at full strength; on Christmas Day they were down to sixty-one and thirty-six men respectively. A week later Company K had twenty-eight men left, Company L had seventeen, and the other companies had suffered proportionately.[37]

The condition of the effectives is well expressed in the informal journal kept by Company K. The entry for Christmas Day noted that the men were sick and feverish, and that the situation was getting worse all the time. Three days later, it read: "The men are getting sicker. Their nerves are cracking. They are praying for relief. [They] must have it soon."[38] But it was to be some time before the men could be relieved. Brigadier Porter had no troops with which to replace them. Until he did, they would have to remain where they were, despite their steadily worsening physical condition.

[35] 3d Bn, 126th Inf, Jnl, Sers 3, 4, 9, 26 Dec 42, Ser 3, 27 Dec 42, Ser 10, 20 Dec 42, Sers 11, 14, 31 Dec 42, Ser 4, 1 Jan 43, Sers 9, 10, 2 Jan 43; Jnl, Maj Boerem's Force, 26 Dec 42—2 Jan 43; Memo, Dal Ponte for author, 16 Jul 50; Ltr, Boerem to author, 2 Nov 51; Ltr, Dal Ponte to author, 17 Jan 52.
[36] Memo, Dal Ponte for author, 16 Jul 50.

[37] 3d Bn, 126th Inf, Jnl, Ser 1, 25 Dec 42, Ser 1, 1 Jan 43, Ser 9, 2 Jan 43; Jnl, Maj Boerem's Force, 10 Dec 42, 24 Dec 42, 25 Dec 42, 1 Jan 43; Jnl, Co K, 126th Inf, 25 Dec 42, 31 Dec 42; Jnl, Co I, 126th Inf, 1 Jan 43; 126th Inf CT AAR, Papuan Campaign.
[38] Jnl, Co K, 126th Inf, 25, 28 Dec 42.

*The Japanese Reinforce
the Beachhead*

The Enemy Situation

Attacking northward from Huggins and
Kano, Brigadier Dougherty continued to
find the going exceedingly difficult. His
troops were at grips with the Japanese intermediate defense line, a line seemingly as
strong as that on which Brigadier Porter was
working lower down on the track. This line,
which had come under General Oda's command upon his arrival at Giruwa on 21
December, included a forward and a rear
position. The forward position was at the
junction of the Sanananda track and the
subsidiary trail leading to Cape Killerton.
It consisted of two independent perimeters,
one on either side of the track. The rear
position cut across the track and the trail 500
yards farther to the northeast and was about
1,500 yards long. Its main defenses consisted of three interconnected perimeters
straddling the east-west stretch of the
track—two north of it and one south.

Oda commanded a sizable force: the
troops of the *41st Infantry* who had come
in from the Kumusi with Colonel Yazawa;
the remainder of the *144th Infantry* replacements who had arrived from Rabaul
on 23 November; approximately 300 men
of the *15th Independent Engineer Regiment;* the remaining strength of the *47th
Field Antiaircraft Artillery Battalion;* a
battery of the *55th Mountain Artillery;*
and a number of walking wounded. His
troops were not only strongly entrenched
in bunkers, but they could also be reinforced at will from troops in reserve at
Sanananda and Giruwa.[39] Theoretically at

least, Oda was in as favorable a position to
hold the second line of defense as Colonel
Tsukamoto had been to hold the first.

Fortunately for the Allies, the enemy supply situation was desperate. The Japanese,
especially Colonel Tsukamoto's troops in
the track junction, were short of food, weapons, grenades, and all types of ammunition.
Colonel Tsukamoto's troops had to depend
on the dribbles of food that could be supplied them via the Killerton trail, and they
were on the verge of starvation. General
Oda's troops were not much better off. They
were down to a handful of rice a day and
were eating roots, grass, crabs, snakes, or
whatever else they could find in the area
that was edible.[40]

The hospital at Giruwa was a scene of un-
mitigated horror. There was no medicine
and no food. The wards were under water;
most of the medical personnel were dead
and those who remained were themselves
patients.[41]

On 11 December, Colonel Yokoyama
tried to give Rabaul some intimation of how
bad conditions really were. The picture was
so black that General Adachi's operations
officer, Lt. Col. Shigeru Sugiyama, replied
that he doubted that things had really
reached such a pass. "It is hard to believe,"

---

[39] *18th Army* Opns I, 20, 21, 26.

[40] *Yokoyama Det* Bul, 2 Dec 42; *Yokoyama Det*
Orders No. A–17, 5 Dec 42. Both in ATIS CT 18,
No. 229. Diary, Sgt Wada Kiyoshi, *3d Bn, 144th
Inf;* Diary, Sgt Hiroshi Kasahara, *41st Inf.* Both in
32d Div Interrogations and Translations File. *18th
Army* Opns I, 25, 26, 33.
[41] *Yokoyama Det* Bul, Giruwa; Msg, Col Tomita
to CofS *17th Army,* 23 Nov 42. Both in ATIS EP 29.
Interr, Lt Sawatari, *Med Off, 144th Inf,* in 32d Div
Interrogations and Translations File; *18th Army*
Opns I, 25.

Sugiyama wrote, "that the situation is as difficult as stated." [42]

Rabaul was probably more worried about the situation at the beachhead than it cared to admit. It had planned to establish a major supply base at the mouth of the Mambare River, with a secondary base at the mouth of the Kumusi. Submarines would bring in the supplies from Rabaul to the base in Mambare Bay where they would be unloaded. Later, they would be reloaded on large cargo-carrying landing craft, and the landing craft traveling at night would bring them forward by stages to Giruwa.

The plan, well conceived and carefully worked out, had already broken down. For no sooner would the submarines bring in supplies than Lieutenant Noakes, the coast watcher in the area, would find out where they were stored and radio the information to Port Moresby. A few hours later, the air force would reach the scene, blow up the enemy dumps, and usually account for some of the landing craft as well. [43]

To add to the enemy's difficulties, a U. S. motor torpedo boat squadron, Task Force 50.1, based at Tufi since 20 December, was ranging the coast west of Gona to intercept Japanese coastwise shipping. On Christmas Eve, the squadron sank the *I–18*, a 344-foot, 3,180-ton submarine just off the mouth of the Mambare. Later the same night, it destroyed two large Japanese barges filled with troops, fifteen or twenty miles east of Mambare Bay. The troops were part of the rear echelon of the *1st Battalion, 170th Infantry*, which had finally received sufficient landing craft to get it through to the Amboga River area. This was the only mishap the troops were to suffer in transit. The rest of them reached their destination safely that night and reported to General Yamagata. [44]

Yamagata is Ordered Forward

General Adachi had apparently decided to hold the rest of the *170th Infantry* at Rabaul until the supply situation at the beachhead had clarified itself. On 26 December he ordered Yamagata to get his troops to Giruwa immediately. Yamagata complied at once by ordering a 430-man advance echelon to the beachhead the following day. The echelon, which included elements of the *1st Battalion, 170 Infantry*, the *1st Battalion, 41st Infantry*, the brigade engineer unit, the regimental gun company, and the regimental signal unit, began leaving for Giruwa that night by barge. The movement went so smoothly, and was so well-executed, that all the troops got through without being detected by either the Air Force, Task Force 50.1, or the Australian patrols operating along the coast.

General Yamagata himself arrived at Giruwa on 29 December with part of the *3d Battalion, 170th Infantry*. Only a rear guard made up of elements of the *1st Bat-*

---

[42] Msg, Col Yokoyama to CofS *18th Army*, 11 Dec 42, with reply from Lt Col Shigeru Sugiyama, in ATIS CT 26, No. 314.

[43] Allied Air Forces Opns Rpt, 26, 27, 28, 30 Dec 42; *18th Army* Opns I, 34; Feldt, *The Coast Watchers*, p. 196. The Japanese finally had to give up trying to establish bases either at the Mambare or the Kumusi. Noakes was later awarded the Legion of Merit. The citation is in WDGO No. 15, 7 Mar 45.

[44] Comdr Robert J. Bulkley, USNR, A History of Motor Torpedo Boats in the U.S. Navy, copy in Office of Nav Hist; *18th Army* Opns I, 25, 26.

talion, *170 Infantry*, and the *3d Battalion, 170th Infantry*, remained in the Amboga River area, with the mission of engaging the Australians as long as possible. The rest of Yamagata's troops reached Giruwa by the 31st. The 21st Brigade, which was mopping up along the banks of the Amboga, knew nothing of the move. Between 700 and

800 men had successfully reached Giruwa,[45] the last reinforcements the Japanese were to receive.

[45] ALF Daily Opns Rpts No. 259, 29 Dec 42, No. 262, 1 Jan 43; Interr, Superior Pvt Toshio Furukawa, *1st Bn, 41st Inf;* Interr, Sgt Jinsaburo Hirose, *1st Bn, 170th Inf.* Both in 32d Div Interrogations and Translations Files. Diary, Maj Nojiri; Diary, Lt Hikoshige Jin, *3d Bn, 170th Inf,* in ATIS CT 28, No. 339; *18th Army* Opns I, 25, 26.

CHAPTER XIII

Buna: The Second Two Weeks

The 32d Division's supply situation, hopelessly inadequate in late November, began to improve in early December. There were many reasons for the improvement. Airdrops and emergency movements by sea had staved off disaster, and the arrival of supplies which General Harding had requisitioned some time before helped the division to overcome the most pressing of its logistical difficulties. The opening of additional airfields at Dobodura and Popondetta, the completion of the Dobodura–Simemi jeep track and other tracks, the arrival of a new flotilla of luggers to replace those which had been destroyed in November, the establishment of a separate service organization at Dobodura known as ALMA Force, General Eichelberger's efforts, the efforts of Col. George DeGraaf, his quartermaster officer, and the continuing efforts of the division's supply officers—all these things helped to improve the situation, and, for the first time since operations began, the pipeline began to fill.[1]

---

[1] Msg, Gen Harding to Comdr Sinclair, ANF, Ser 186, 1 Dec 42; Msg, Maj Milton F. Ziebell, S–3, 128th Inf, to Maj Chester M. Beaver, Ser 1833, 1 Dec 42; Msg, 5th Air Force to Gen Harding, Ser 1892, 2 Dec 42; Msg, Gen Eichelberger to GOC NGF, Ser 1990, 3 Dec 42; Msg, NGF to NOIC, Porlock Harbor, Ser 2122, 3 Dec 42; Msg, Maj Hall, 2/1 Aust Fld Rgt, to Brig L. E. S. Barker, Comdr Royal Australian Arty, 7th Aust Div, Ser 2035, 3 Dec 42; Msg, NGF to 32d Div, Ser 2069, 3 Dec 42; Interv with Lt Col Carroll K. Moffatt, formerly CO Port Det E, COSC, Buna, 30 Oct 49; Hist 114th Engr Bn (C); Rpt, CG Buna Forces, pp. 17, 21, 23; Eichelberger, *Our Jungle Road to Tokyo*, pp. 26, 34–36.

The Attack of 5 December

Regrouping the Troops

On both the Warren and Urbana fronts the inspection of 2 December found the Allied units, in the words of General Eichelberger, "scrambled like eggs." He at once ordered them regrouped and reorganized. On the Warren front, Company I, 128th Infantry, which had been operating under Colonel Carrier's command off the southwest end of the strip, was returned to Colonel Miller, and Company A, 126th Infantry, which had been under Colonel McCoy's command off the southeast end of the strip, was returned to Colonel Carrier. Colonel Miller's 3d Battalion, 128th Infantry, was disposed to the right of the strip and took up position in an arc extending from the sea to a point just below the dispersal bays at the eastern end of the strip. Colonel McCoy's 1st Battalion, 128th Infantry, moved in on Miller's left, just below (south of) the strip, and Major Harcourt's 2/6 Independent Company covered the gap between Carrier and McCoy. Warren Force had no reserve, but each battalion held small reserve elements out of the line.

On the Urbana front, units of the 2d Battalion, 126th Infantry, which had been outposting Entrance Creek north of the Coconut Grove rejoined their battalion and the Cannon Company, 128th Infantry, in front of Buna Village. The 2d Battalion,

128th Infantry, took over the sector following the west bank of Entrance Creek. Company F, 128th Infantry, continued as before to hold the blocking positions between the Girua River and Siwori Creek.[2]

During the previous week the average daily ration for troops on both fronts had consisted of a single can of meat component and an emergency bar of concentrated chocolate, just enough to subsist on. Though the stockpile of rations was still short, the men ate their first full meal in some time on 3 December, and preparations began for a scheduled attack the next day.[3]

The New Commanders Take Over

When Colonel Martin went forward to the Warren front early on 3 December to take command, he discovered first of all that the troops "had little in the nature of weapons and equipment of what was normally considered necessary to dislodge an enemy from a dug in, concealed position."[4] His forward CP, he found, was "a single shelter half suspended horizontally about five feet from the ground, under which the CP telephone rested against a log on the ground." Maj. Milton F. Ziebell, the regimental S–3, had with him, Martin remembers, a printed map "inaccurate for artillery fire," and "half of a small writing tablet, the kind selling in ten cent stores for a dime, and a pencil." When Martin asked the adjutant

for his files, the latter "patted the pocket of his denim jacket which was a shade of black from the swamp mud, and said that he was keeping what he could there."

Colonel Martin set himself to improve conditions, despite the prevailing "lack of almost everything with which to operate." One of the first things he did upon taking command was to call an officers' meeting at which he told his officers that the men "would be required to do all they could to better their conditions, their personal appearance, and their equipment." Sanitation would be improved. More attention would be paid to the care of equipment, and officers would cease commiserating with the troops and abetting them in the "feeling sorry for ourselves attitude" that he had noticed during his inspection the day before.

The command was to be informed, he said further, that there would be no relief until "after Buna was taken." Martin knew that this news would come as a shock, "but I was certain," he adds, "that after the shock was over, the troops knowing their task would fight better than those just hanging on and continually looking over their shoulders for relief to come."[5]

Unlike Colonel Martin, Colonel Grose had little opportunity to inspect his forces before he took command. He came in by air from Australia on the morning of 3 December and made a hurried inspection of the Urbana front that afternoon. Next day when he took command, he found Colonel McCreary supervising a reorganization of the positions, and he asked General Eichelberger to postpone the attack for a day. General Eichelberger granted the request, though with considerable reluctance, and

---

[2] Msg, Gen Waldron to NGF, Ser 2032, 3 Dec 42: Rpt, CG Buna Forces, p. 20, with accompanying situation maps, 2, 3, and 4 Dec 42: Ltr, Col MacNab to Gen Ward, 7 Mar 51.

[3] Ltr, Gen Eichelberger to Gen Sutherland, 3 Dec 42: Ltr, Gen Eichelberger to Gen MacArthur, 12 Jan 43. Copies of both in OCMH files. Rpt, CG Buna Forces, pp. 92, 93.

[4] Ltr, Col Martin to Gen Ward, 6 Mar 51.

[5] *Ibid.*

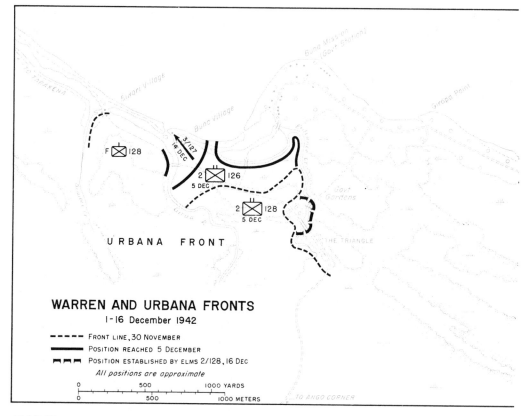

MAP 12

the attack there and on the Warren front was set for 5 December.[6]

The Arrival of the Bren Carriers

Late on the evening of 3 December a section of five Bren gun carriers arrived by boat from Porlock Harbor. The rest of the cargo included forty tons of food and ammunition, a shipment that was particularly welcome inasmuch as Warren Force had run out of rations that day. The carriers were quickly unloaded and given to Colonel

⁶ Col Grose's Diary, 3 Dec 42, 4 Dec 42; Interv with Col Grose, 15 Nov 50; Ltr, Col Grose to Gen Ward, 26 Feb 51.

Martin for use on the 5th in the attack on the Japanese positions in the Duropa Plantation. As soon as they could, Colonel Martin and Colonel MacNab gave Lt. T. St. D. Fergusson, who commanded the carriers, a briefing on the terrain. They stressed the likelihood that his carriers might be "bellied" by stumps and other obstacles in the plantation area. The next day, MacNab sent Fergusson and 1st Lt. David Anderson, commanding officer of the regimental Reconnaissance Platoon, to make a daylight reconnaissance of the area. Though under no illusions about the risk of the attack, Fergusson reported that he believed his carriers could negotiate the ground. To provide

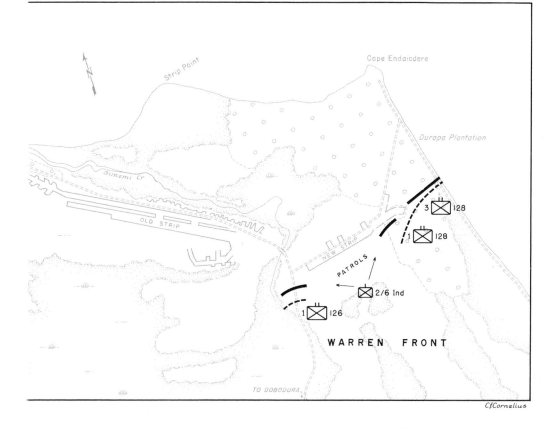

WARREN FRONT

CfCornelius

insurance against unforeseen contingencies he requested additional automatic weapons for his men, and was promptly given all the weapons he asked for.[7]

Sending the thin-skinned vehicles, open at the top and unarmored below, against the formidable enemy positions in the plantation area was a desperate venture at best. The least the Americans could do was to give the Australian crews, who were to spearhead the attack, all the weapons they could use.

Reorganization and regrouping were completed on 4 December. Fortified by an unwonted and much-needed two-day rest, the troops received rations and ammunition and prepared to resume operations under their new commanders.

Colonel Yamamoto's forces and those of Captain Yasuda were ready. Yamamoto had the bulk of his relatively fresh *144th* and *229th Infantry* troops in the plantation and at the northeast end of the New Strip. The rest were holding the bridge between the strips, together with the troops of the *15th Independent Engineer Regiment* and of the *47th Field Antiaircraft Battalion* orig-

---

[7] 3d Bn, 128th Inf, Jnl, 1430, 4 Dec 42; 128th Inf Jnl, Ser 34, 4 Dec 42; Msg, Col Martin to Gen Waldron, Ser 2033, 3 Dec 42; Ltr, Col MacNab to author, 15 Aug 50.

inally assigned there.⁵ Captain Yasuda had his *Yokosuka 5th* and *Sasebo 5th Special Naval Landing* troops, supported by naval pioneer units in the village, the Triangle, and the mission. The Japanese had thrown back every attack thus far, and they were ready to continue doing so.

The plan for the American-Australian attack scheduled for 5 December was embodied in a field order drawn up the day before by General Waldron. Warren Force and the five Bren gun carriers, supported by elements of the Fifth Air Force and the artillery, were to attack the Japanese positions in the Duropa Plantation–Buna Strips area at 0830. Their objective encompassed the entire area east of a line drawn along the coast southwest from Strip Point and extending inland to the Old Strip. Urbana Force, also supported by artillery and air bombardment, was to jump off at 1000 with the mission of taking Buna Village. Both attacking forces were to make an all-out effort.⁹ (*Map 12*)

The Attack on the Right

On the Warren front Colonel Miller's battalion was to be on the right, nearest the sea. Colonel McCoy's battalion was to be on Miller's left, and Colonel Carrier was to be on the far left, with the 2/6 Independent Company intervening between him and McCoy. Company L and the Bren carriers were to attack straight up the coast on a 200-yard front. Company I was to follow

in column on Company L's left rear, and machine gun crews of Company M were to be disposed along the line of departure and immediately to the rear to clean out snipers in trees and give direct support to the advance. Colonel McCoy's leading unit, Company A, 128th Infantry, was to move in on Company L's left and attempt to cross the eastern end of the New Strip. Colonel Carrier's 1st Battalion, 126th Infantry, was to advance northward against the bridge between the strips. Patrols of the Australian Independent Company were to make whatever gains they could in the area between Carrier and McCoy.¹⁰

Between 0820 and 0835 on the morning of 5 December, six A–20's bombed and strafed the area between the Old Strip and Cape Endaiadere. The artillery began to fire at 0830. Supported by mortar and machine gun fire from Company M, the Bren carriers and Company L left the line of departure at 0842. They immediately ran into heavy fire from a barricade near the coast, and from concealed positions on their left front and left. As had been feared, the Bren carriers bellied up badly on the uneven stump-filled ground and their progress was slow. As they rose high in the air to clear stumps and other obstacles, they were easy targets for enemy machine gunners. To complete the job, the Japanese tossed hand grenades over the sides, threw "sticky" bombs that clung to the superstructures, and scored several direct hits with an antitank gun. Within twenty minutes they had knocked out all five vehicles—three just outside the Allied lines and two within their own. The carrier crews suffered heavily. Lieutenant Fergusson was wounded, and thirteen of

⁸ *Yokoyama Det Orders*, 16 Nov 42, in ATIS EP 29; *18th Army Opns I*, pp. 20–21. The *144th* and *229th Infantry* troops under Yamamoto's command came in with him from Rabaul on 17 November, and were thus fresher than any of their attackers.
⁹ 32d Div FO No. 2, 4 Dec 42; Ltr, Gen Eichelberger to Gen Sutherland, 4 Dec 42, copy in OCMH files.

¹⁰ Msg, Maj Ziebell to Col MacNab, Ser 2137, 4 Dec 42; 3d Bn, 128th Inf, Jnl, 1300, 1430, 1635, 1700, 4 Dec 42.

DISABLED BREN GUN CARRIERS *in the Duropa Plantation.*

the twenty others in the carriers were killed, wounded, or missing.

Fergusson's second-in-command, Lt. Ian Walker, heard of the disaster shortly after it happened. From his post at the rear where he had been attending to the housekeeping needs of the platoon, he left for the front on the run, accompanied by a single enlisted man of his command. Covered by fire from Company L, 128th Infantry, the two men methodically removed the guns and ammunition from the three closest carriers. Walker then ordered the enlisted man back, took up a submachine gun, and went forward alone toward the two remaining carriers intending to recover their guns as well. Before he could

reach the nearer of the two carriers, he fell mortally wounded. The Japanese succeeded in stripping the gutted hulks of the two carriers that night before a patrol of Warren Force sent out to recover the guns could get to them.[11]

In attempting to support the Bren carriers in their disastrous attack, Capt. Samuel M. Horton's Company L, 128th Infantry, had also been hit hard. The center platoon

[11] 32d Div G-3 Jnl File, Ser 2357, 5 Dec 42; 128th Inf Jnl, Sers 7, 11, 13, 27, 30, 51, 60, 5 Dec 42; 3d Bn, 128th Inf, Jnl, 0820, 0830, 0835, 0842, 1515, 1712, 1840, 5 Dec 42; Rpt, CG Buna Forces, p. 21. Walker was posthumously awarded the Distinguished Service Cross. The citation is in GHQ SWPA GO No. 7, 15 Jan 43.

suffered so many casualties during the first half-hour of the fighting that it had to have help from the left platoon, which was itself under heavy fire. A platoon of Company I had to plug the resulting gap on the left before the attack could continue.

The men tried to push forward but were unable to. They were blocked, not only by the heavy fire that came from behind the still-unreduced log barricade a few yards in from the coast and from the hidden and carefully sited strongpoints in the plantation, but by the intense heat of the morning. Man after man of Colonel Miller's battalion gave way to heat prostration. By 1010 the battalion had gained less than forty yards, and it could make no further advance that day.[12]

A few minutes after the 3d Battalion attack, the 1st Battalion, 128th Infantry began its move. At 0855 the eighty-three men of Company A, under 1st Lt. Samuel J. Scott, pushed off in the Y-shaped dispersal area at the eastern end of the New Strip. Company B was on Scott's left rear, waiting to go in. Company D was disposed along the line of departure, supporting the advance by fire. Scott's troops moved slowly and cautiously through the tall grass. Despite the heat and heavy casualties from enemy fire, they made good progress at first, and by 1100 most of them were across the lower arm of the Y. There they were halted by rifle grenade, mortar, and machine gun fire from three directions. By noon Japanese action and heat prostration had cut deep into Company A's strength, and Company B, under 1st Lt. Milan J.

Bloecher, had to be ordered in on its left to relieve the pressure.[13]

Company B reached the southeastern end of the strip two hours later at a point just west of the dispersal area occupied by Company A. Setting up light machine guns on the left to cover the strip, Bloecher tried to move his men across, but without success. As the men crawled out of the sheltering tall grass into the heat-ridden strip, heavy enemy fire from bunkers and hidden firing positions in the area immobilized them. Those who managed to get halfway across the strip could move neither forward nor back. Since further advance was impossible, the company began to consolidate at the eastern end of the strip.

Company A was meanwhile having an even rougher time than in the morning. At the center of the Y the troops encountered almost point-blank fire that came at them from three directions. All attempts to cross the northern prong of the Y failed. Men who tried to advance were caught in the enemy's crossfire and either wounded or killed. By late afternoon the situation was seen to be hopeless, and Colonel Martin ordered the company to pull back as soon as it could. That evening he relieved it.[14]

At the western end of the strip Colonel Carrier's battalion did little better. The two companies in attack—A on the right and C on the left—moved out against the bridge between the strips at 0850 and at first reported good progress. Aided by the mortars and the detachment's 37-mm. gun, they succeeded in knocking out seven enemy

---

[12] 128th Inf Jnl, Sers 24, 27, 30, 36, 46, 72, 5 Dec 42; 3d Bn, 128th Inf, Jnl, 0935, 0938, 1010, 1035, 1120, 1640, 5 Dec 42.

[13] 128th Inf Jnl, Sers 67, 5 Dec 42; 1st Bn, 128th Inf, Jnl, Sers 11, 33, 34, 37, 40, 44, 60, 5 Dec 42.
[14] Msg, Maj Ziebell to 32d Div, Ser 2357, 5 Dec 42; 128th Inf Jnl, Sers 21, 40, 43, 67, 70, 73, 108, 113, 5 Dec 42; 1st Bn, 128th Inf, Jnl, Sers 52, 58, 60, 67, 70, 5 Dec 42.

pillboxes during the first two hours of fighting. With the enemy fire from the pillboxes suppressed, the troops began to close on the bridge, only to be halted by heavy fire from front and left when they were only 150 yards from their objective. Artillery fire was called for, but it proved ineffective. The Japanese fire only increased in intensity.

Colonel Carrier's troops, suffering from the heat like the companies on the right, made repeated attempts to advance, but the enemy fire was too heavy. Frontal attack was abandoned; Company B relieved Company A, and an attempt was made to cross Simemi Creek in the hope of flanking the bridge. The attempt was given up because there was quicksand reported in the crossing area and the creek was too deep. At the end of the day's fighting the Japanese still held the bridge between the strips, and Colonel Carrier's troops were dug in about 200 yards south of it.[15]

The "all-out" attack of Warren Force had failed all along the line, and Colonel Yamamoto had the situation in hand.[16] As Colonel Martin put it in a phone call to General Byers that night: "We have hit them and bounced off." [17]

Bottcher's Break-Through

On 4 December Colonel Tomlinson and 126th Infantry headquarters moved from Sanananda to the Urbana front, and advance parties of the 127th Infantry—which was also to be committed to the Urbana front—began reaching Dobodura.[18] By this time the troops in the line—the 2d Battalion, 126th Infantry, the 2d Battalion, 128th Infantry, and the Cannon Company, 128th Infantry—had had a little rest. They would now have another chance to finish the job that they had not been quite able to complete on the 2d.

The plan of attack called for the Cannon Company, 128th Infantry, and the 2d Battalion, 126th Infantry, to attack at specified points on the perimeter of Buna Village. Having suffered very heavy losses during previous attacks, Company F would be in reserve. The Cannon Company would remain on the left of the 126th Infantry and continue as before to support its operations. Colonel Smith's 2d Battalion, 128th Infantry, on Major Smith's right would complete the investiture of the left bank of Entrance Creek. Air and artillery bombardment would support the attacks. From positions behind the large grassy strip west of Entrance Creek, eight 81-mm. mortars would fire on the village. The troops of Company F, 128th Infantry, from their positions on the west side of the Girua River, would fire upon it with two 81-mm. mortars, a 37-mm. gun, and an assortment of light and heavy machine guns.

Colonel Grose went to the front early on the morning of 5 December. After getting the men into line and making a final check of their positions, he returned to his CP about 1015 to find both General Eichelberger and General Waldron there. A number of other officers were present including

---

[15] 128th Inf Jnl, Sers 23, 39, 47, 61, 77, 93, 5 Dec 42; 1st Bn 126th Inf, Jnl, Sers 506, 508, 510, 518, 526, 530, 532, 5 Dec 42.

[16] Tel Msg, Capt Manning, RAA, to 32d Div, Ser 2013, 3 Dec 42; Msg, 32d Div to NGF, Ser 2057, 3 Dec 42; 1st Bn, 128th Inf, Jnl, Ser 31, 35, 3 Dec 42; 2d Bn, 128th Inf, Jnl, 1515, 3 Dec 42. On 3 December Japanese bombers, escorted by Zeros, had parachuted food and ammunition onto the northern end of the Old Strip for Yamamoto's troops.

[17] 128th Inf Jnl, Ser 128, 5 Dec 42.

[18] Msg, Adv NGF to 32d Div, Ser 2086, 3 Dec 42; Msg, NGF to G-2, I Corps, Ser 2090, 4 Dec 42; 2d Bn, 126th Inf, Jnl, 1400, 4 Dec 42; 127th Inf, The Battle for Buna.

Colonel DeGraaf, Colonel Rogers, Colonel McCreary, Colonel Tomlinson, Lt. Col. Merle H. Howe, the division G–3, and General Eichelberger's aide, Captain Edwards. The attack had opened at 1000 with a raid on the mission by nine B–25's. Eichelberger and his party were briefed on how the action was progressing and then went forward to observe the fighting.

After the B–25's hit the target area, the artillery and the mortars began firing on the village. At 1030 the fire ceased, and the infantry moved forward. The Cannon Company, 128th Infantry, attacked along the east bank of the Girua River. On its right Companies E and G attacked abreast, with Company H supporting the attack with fire. Pivoting short from the line of departure, the units fanned out against the enemy perimeter, and Companies E and G in the center hit directly against the village.[19]

The Japanese commander in the area, Navy Captain Yosuda, had a few hundred men in the village—enough for his immediate purpose. With the help of the bunkers, barricades, and trenches available to his men, he could count on holding the village for some time, even though it was his least defensible position.[20]

The attack met strong opposition. On the far left the Cannon Company ran into heavy fire when it emerged onto an open space south of the village. The company sent out

patrols to flank the enemy, the mortar men on the west side of the Girua River began firing on the village to relieve the pressure, and a platoon of Company F, 126th Infantry, under 1st Lt. Paul L. Schwartz, moved in to reinforce the Cannon Company. None of these measures worked. The enemy fire continued, and the company could not advance.

Late in the afternoon Maj. Chester M. Beaver of the divisional staff took over command of the company. Organizing a patrol with Lieutenant Schwartz as his second-in-command, Beaver managed to clear out the enemy positions immediately to the front and then crawled through muck to bring his patrol to a point just outside the village. Beaver and Schwartz had to withdraw when night fell, but by the following morning the Cannon Company and the Company F platoon were on the outskirts of the village, the position they had tried in vain to reach the day before.[21]

Company E, under Captain Schultz, also met tough opposition from the intrenched enemy. By dint of hard fighting, the line moved forward until it reached the Japanese main line of resistance about fifty yards from the village. There the advance was stopped completely, and the troops had to dig in.

That the company pushed even that far in the face of the heavy enemy fire was due principally to the able leadership of two platoon leaders, 1st Lt. Thomas E. Knode and 1st Sgt. Paul R. Lutjens, who were severely wounded as they led their men in

[19] 2d Bn, 126th Inf, Jnl, 1400, 1550, 4 Dec 42, 0730, 1008, 1030, 1100, 5 Dec 42; 2d Bn, 128th Inf, Jnl, 1930, 5 Dec 42; Allied Air Forces Opns Rpt, 5 Dec 42; Msg, Adv NGF to 32d Div, Ser 2180, 5 Dec 42; Rpt, CG Buna Forces, p. 21, with Situation Map, Urbana Force, 5 Dec 42; Eichelberger, *Our Jungle Road to Tokyo*, p. 28.
[20] Interr, Yoshiteru Toyashima, *15th Naval Pioneer Unit*, in 32d Div G–2 Interrogations and Translations File; 127th Inf Tact Hist, Papuan Campaign.

[21] 2d Bn, 126th Inf, Jnl, 1105, 1115, 1117, 1345, 1410, 1554, 1730, 5 Dec 42. Both Beaver and Schwartz were later awarded the Distinguished Service Cross. The citations are in GHQ SWPA, GO No. 1, 1 Jan 43.

the day's fighting. The combat performance of a member of Lutjens' platoon, Sgt. Harold E. Graber, had also helped to push the line forward. When the platoon was pinned down, Sergeant Graber leaped to his feet, fired his light machine gun from the hip, and cleaned out a main Japanese strongpoint which had been holding up the advance—an act that cost him his life.[22]

Company G, under Captain Bailey, was also finding it difficult to make any progress. Disappointed that the attack had bogged down just outside the village, General Eichelberger took direct control of operations. He called Grose forward to the observation post and sent Colonel Tomlinson back to the command post. Then he ordered Company F to pass through Company E and take the village. Colonel Grose immediately protested the order. Instead of committing Company F, his last reserve, to the center of the line, Grose had hoped to use it at a more propitious moment on the left. He told General Eichelberger that there was nothing to be gained by hurrying the attack, that it was the kind of attack that might take "a day or two," but General Eichelberger had apparently set his heart on taking Buna Village that day and overruled his protest.[23]

Summoned to the observation post, 1st Lt. Robert H. Odell, who had taken command of Company F a few days before, was, as he put it, "surprised to see a couple of generals—one a three star—in addition to the usual array of majors and colonels." To continue in Odell's own words,

The Lieutenant General explained what he wanted, and after a brief delay, I brought up the company and deployed accordingly. Pravda [1st Sgt. George Pravda] was to take half the company up one side of the trail, and I the other half on the other side. We were given ten minutes to make our reconnaissance and to gather information from the most forward troops which we were to pass. It was intended that we finish the job—actually take the Village—and [it was thought] that we needed little more than our bayonets to do it. Well, off we went, and within a few minutes our rush forward had been definitely and completely halted. Of the 40 men who started with me, 4 had been (known) killed, and 18 were lying wounded. We were within a few yards of the village, but with . . . no chance of going a step further. . . . [Pravda] was among the wounded, and casualties were about as heavy on his side.[24]

Scarcely had Company F's attack in the center been brought to a halt when electrifying news was received from Captain Bailey on the right. Instead of continuing the profitless attack directly on the village, a platoon of Company H under S. Sgt. Herman J. F. Bottcher, which had been attached to Company G, had pushed north from its position on the far right. Knocking out several pillboxes en route, Bottcher had successfully crossed a creek under enemy fire and by late afternoon had reached the beach with eighteen men and one machine gun. Bottcher, an experienced soldier who had served with the Loyalists in the Spanish Civil War, ordered his men to dig in at once on the edge of the beach. Attacks followed

[22] 2d Bn, 126th Inf, Jnl, 1330, 1345, 5 Dec 42; Kahn, "The Terrible Days of Company E," *The Saturday Evening Post*, 15 Jan 44. Knode, Lutjens, and Graber were all later awarded the Distinguished Service Cross, and Lutjens was commissioned a 2d lieutenant. The citations for Knode and Lutjens are in GHQ SWPA GO No. 64, 28 Dec 42. Graber's posthumous award is in GO No. 1, 1 Jan 43.

[23] Col Grose's Diary, 5 Dec 42; Interv with Col Grose, 15 Nov 50.

[24] Odell, Buna.

from both the village and the mission, but Bottcher and his riflemen, with Bottcher himself at the machine gun, made short work of the enemy. The beach on either side of Bottcher's Corner (as the position came to be known) was soon piled with Japanese corpses, whom neither friend nor foe could immediately bury.[25]

Bottcher's break-through completed the isolation of the village. The Cannon Company, 128th Infantry, and the 2d Battalion, 126th Infantry, less Bottcher's platoon, were now pressed tightly against its inner defenses, and the troops at Bottcher's Corner made its reinforcement from the mission extremely difficult, if not impossible.

Colonel Smith's 2d Battalion, 128th Infantry had meanwhile invested the entire west bank of Entrance Creek except for the Coconut Grove. It was now in position to reduce the grove as well. With the village cut off and Entrance Creek outposted along its entire length, the early fall of the village was assured, provided the Japanese did not in the meantime succeed in their attempts to evict the attackers, particularly those at Bottcher's Corner.[26]

With Colonel Howe, his G–3, General Waldron had been pushing the assault personally in the right center of the line. During

Company F's attack he received a shoulder wound and had to be evacuated. On General Eichelberger's orders, General Byers, his chief of staff, succeeded Waldron as commander of the troops at the front.[27] Colonel Bradley, whom General Waldron had chosen to be his chief of staff, continued to serve in the same capacity under General Byers. Colonel McCreary, for two days commander of Urbana Force, and before that deputy to General Waldron when the latter was division artillery commander, took command of the artillery and mortars on the Urbana front.[28]

General Eichelberger and his party departed for the rear about 1800, less Captain Edwards who had been wounded and evacuated earlier in the day. Colonel Grose was left to reorganize. While he had not taken kindly to the way General Eichelberger had thrown Company F into the battle against his protest, Grose had nothing but praise for the way the troops had performed. "The battalion's men," he wrote that night in his diary, "have been courageous and willing, but they have been pushed almost beyond the limit of human endurance." They were, he continued, "courageous, fine

[25] Tel Msg, Col McCreary to Gen Waldron, Ser 2207, 5 Dec 42; 2d Bn, 126th Inf, Jnl, 1330, 5 Dec 42; Interv, 1st Lt. Kenneth Hechler with Gen Waldron, Washington, D. C., 11 Mar 44; Ltr, Lt Col Herbert M. Smith to Gen Ward, 9 Mar 51; Rpt, CG Buna Forces, p. 2; Odell, Buna; Eichelberger, *Our Jungle Road to Tokyo*, pp. 31, 32. Bottcher was later awarded the Distinguished Service Cross and given a direct battlefield commission as a captain. His citation for the DSC is in GHQ SWPA GO No. 64, 28 Dec 42.

[26] Rpt, CG Buna Forces, p. 21, with Situation Map, 5 Dec 42.

[27] Byers did not take command of the 32d Division, since Brig. Gen. Frayne Baker, commander of the division's rear echelon in Australia and, after Waldron, senior officer of the division, became division commander when Waldron was wounded and evacuated. Ltr, Gen Eichelberger to Gen Sutherland, 18 Dec 42, copy in OCMH files; Ltr, Gen Sutherland to Gen Ward, 6 April 51. Both Waldron and Howe were later awarded the Distinguished Service Cross. Waldron's citation is in GHQ SWPA GO No. 60, 18 Dec 42; Howe's, in GO No. 64, 28 Dec. 42.

[28] Msg, Urbana Force to G–3, Buna Force, Ser 2244, 5 Dec 42; Msgs, Gen Byers to Gen Eichelberger, Sers 2253, 2254, 5 Dec 42; Ltr, Col McCreary to Col Handy, GHQ AGF, Washington, 11 Mar 43, copy in OCMH files.

men," and all of them had given him "the utmost cooperation."[29]

Although the troops had not taken the village, General Eichelberger, who, with members of his staff, had taken a personal hand in the battle, had revised the opinion he expressed on 2 December that they lacked fight. Writing to General Sutherland the next day, Eichelberger noted that the troops had fought hard, that morale had been high, and that there had been "much to be proud of during the day's operations." General Herring, he said, had praised the bravery of the 32d Division highly. As far as he personally was concerned, Eichelberger went on, General MacArthur could begin to stop worrying about its conduct in battle.[30]

Colonel Martin Softens Up the Enemy Line

The New Tactics

The complete failure on 5 December of the attack on the Warren front had satisfied General Eichelberger that the enemy line was too strong to be breached by frontal assault. In the course of a conversation held two days earlier with General Herring at Dobodura, he had learned that he could very shortly expect the arrival of tanks and fresh Australian troops for action on his side of the river. He decided therefore to try no more all-out frontal assaults on the Warren front until he had received the tanks and the promised reinforcements. Mean-

while he intended to do everything possible to weaken the enemy line.[31]

General Herring had suggested late on 5 December that Eichelberger try pushing forward on the Warren front by concentrating on the destruction of individual pillboxes and machine gun nests which lay in the way. This job, General Eichelberger assured Port Moresby the next day, he had "already decided to do." Since the Japanese line on that front had been found to be very strong, he added, he would make the main effort for the time being on the left, "while containing the Japanese on [the] right." [32] Instead of making frontal infantry assaults, which had gotten Warren Force nowhere, the troops now were to soften up the enemy line by attrition and infiltration, and to make the final break-through with the tanks when they arrived.

General Eichelberger's orders to Colonel Martin were therefore to have his men begin vigorous patrolling in order to locate and pinpoint the individual enemy positions. As soon as they located an enemy strongpoint, they were to destroy it. The troops were to move forward by infiltration, and not by frontal assault. On 7 December Colonel Martin explained the new tactics to his battalion commanders. There were to be no more all-out attacks. Instead there was to be constant patrolling by small groups. After the artillery had worked over the enemy emplacements, the patrols were to knock them out one at a time, with mortar, grenade, and rifle. They were to subject the enemy line to constant probing. Instead of rushing ahead, they were to feel their way forward. Every

---

[29] Col Grose's Diary, 5 Dec 42; Eichelberger, *Our Jungle Road to Tokyo,* pp. 30, 31. Col George DeGraaf, Colonel Rogers, and Captain Edwards, who intervened briefly in the fighting in the center, were all later awarded the Distinguished Service Cross. The citations are in GHQ SWPA GO No. 60, 18 Dec 42.

[30] Ltr, Gen Eichelberger to Gen Sutherland, 6 Dec 42, copy in OCMH files.

[31] Ltr, Gen Eichelberger to Gen Sutherland, 6 Dec 42; Intervs with Gen Eichelberger, 6 Feb 50, 26 Apr 50; Eichelberger, *Our Jungle Road to Tokyo,* p. 44.

[32] Ltr, Gen Eichelberger to Gen Sutherland, 6 Dec 42.

effort was to be made meanwhile to make the men comfortable. They were to be given their pack rolls if they wanted them, fed hot food, and allowed to rest.[33]

Intense patrolling became the order of the day on the Warren front. The 37-mm. guns and mortars fired on the bunkers as they were located, and the artillery, aided by Wirraways now based at Dobodura, joined in. But the 37-mm. guns and the mortars were too light to have much effect on the bunkers, and the 3.7-inch mountain howitzers and the 25-pounders using high-explosive shells with superquick fuse proved little more effective. Because it had a higher angle of fire and its shells had delay fuses, the 105-mm. howitzer was much better suited to the task, and soon proved itself to be the only weapon on the front which was effective against the enemy bunkers. By comparison, the 25-pounder with its flatter trajectory had only a limited usefulness. Not only was it often unable to clear the trees, but it could not drop its projectiles on the bunkers as could the 105.[34] General Waldron put the matter in a sentence. "The 25 pounders," he said, "annoyed the Japanese, and that's about all." [35]

The 105-mm. howitzer could have been even more effective had it been properly supplied with ammunition. But shells for it were very slow in coming forward. After having fired the initial few hundred rounds with which it reached the front, the 105 had to remain silent for days. On 6 December the I Corps ordnance officer at Port Moresby wrote to the front as follows: "I've been burning the air waves since 2 December to have 800 rounds of 105-mm. ammunition flown [to you]. The stuff has been at Brisbane airdrome since the night of 3 December. . . . The General asked for 100 rounds per day for 10 days starting 5 December, and there isn't a single damned round here." [36]

Ammunition for the 105 finally began reaching the front during the second week in December, and then (apparently because of the priority situation) only in small amounts. Thus, for much of the time when it could have done most good, the 105 stood useless while artillery pieces less suited to the task tried vainly to deal with the Japanese bunker defenses.[37]

Colonel Martin wanted to move up a few of the artillery pieces for direct fire on the bunkers, but Warren Force had too few guns on hand to risk any of them so far forward. The arrival by sea on 8 December of two more 25-pounders then made it possible to shift the pieces. The two 25-pounders were emplaced just north of Hariko, and the O'Hare Troop (the three 3.7-inch howitzers of the 1st Australian Mountain Battery at Hariko) took up a new position about one mile below the bridge between the strips, completing the move on 11 December. Even though the howitzers at once

---

[33] 1st Bn, 128th Inf, Jnl, Ser 20, 6 Dec 42, Sers 3, 6, 7, 17, 7 Dec 42; 3d Bn, 128th Inf, Jnl, 1213, 6 Dec 42; 128th Inf Jnl, Sers 4, 65, 6 Dec 42, Sers 9, 13, 44, 7 Dec 42.

[34] Tel Msg, Warren Force to 32d Div, Ser 2361, 6 Dec 42; Tel Msgs, Maj Ziebell to 32d Div, Ser 2454, 7 Dec 42, Ser 2693, 9 Dec 42; 1st Bn, 126th Inf, Jnl, Ser 541, 6 Dec 42, Sers 580, 582, 10 Dec 42, Sers 592, 595, 11 Dec 42; 128th Inf Jnl, Ser 24, 10 Dec 42; Ltr, Col Frank S. Bowen, Jr., G–3, I Corps, to Lt Col E. G. Smith, Rear Echelon, I Corps, 11 Jan 43, in I Corps Correspondence File; Gen Waldron, The Buna Campaign, copy in OCMH files.

[35] Interv, Lt Hechler with Gen Waldron, 11 Mar 44.

[36] Ltr, Col Marshall Darby, Ord Off, I Corps, Moresby, to Col William E. McCreight, G–4, I Corps, 6 Dec 42, in I Corps Correspondence File.

[37] Rpt, CG Buna Forces, p. 75; Hist Buna Forces, I Corps Adv Echelon, in I Corps Correspondence File.

began hitting Japanese positions behind both strips with greater effect than before, they were still able to make no apparent impression on the Japanese line, so well was the enemy entrenched.[38]

Throughout the battle the enemy had been achieving excellent results with grenade launchers. Impressed by their effectiveness the troops on the Warren front found time during this period of attritional warfare to experiment with rifle grenades. The experiments were conducted with Australian grenades since no American grenades were available. Using Australian rifles the men found the few grenades on hand very effective. The small supply soon ran out, however, and they received no more during the campaign.[39]

The situation on Colonel Carrier's front during this period was one of unrelieved hardship.

The positions occupied by the 1st Battalion, 126th Infantry [General Martin recalls], were almost unbearably hot in the day time as the tropical sun broiled down, the grass shut off all air, and held in the steaming heat. Due to enemy observation any daylight movement among the forward positions had to be by crawling which added to the misery from the heat. There were cases of heat exhaustion daily, and some of the company commanders strongly urged the battalion commander to permit the troops to withdraw about 300 yards in daytime to positions where there was shade, and reoccupy the froward positions at night.

Martin overruled these requests. He felt that to allow daily withdrawals would contribute nothing to the harassing and softening up of the enemy, "would be psycho-logically bad" for the troops, and "would hurt the rebuilding of their offensive spirit."[40]

The infantry attackers made few gains anywhere along the Warren front. Colonel Carrier's troops met repeated setbacks in their efforts to cross the bridge between the strips, and the forces under Colonel Miller and Colonel McCoy moved ahead only a few yards.[41] The fighting had settled down to a siege.

With the fall of Gona, it became clear that the enemy's beachhead garrison could no longer be supplied easily by sea. But the Japanese could still use the air lanes. On 10 December twenty medium naval bombers flew nonstop from Rabaul and dropped food and ammunition onto the Old Strip. This flight was the second—and last—air supply mission ordered by the enemy head-quarters at Rabaul.[42]

On the same day, the 10th, Major Harcourt's 2/6 Independent Company was returned to the 7th Division, and there were other changes on the Warren front. The three battalion commanders had begun showing signs of wear. When Colonel Carrier, who was suffering from angina pectoris, had to be evacuated on 13 December, General Eichelberger decided the time had come to change the other battalion commanders. Major Beaver replaced Colonel Carrier in command of the 1st Battalion, 126th Infantry. Maj. Gordon Clarkson of I Corps took

---

[38] 1st Bn, 126th Inf, Jnl, Ser 601, 11 Dec 42, Ser 626, 13 Dec 42, Ser 646, 14 Dec 42; Rpt, CG Buna Forces, p. 76a.

[39] 1st Bn, 126th Inf, Jnl, Sers 580, 583, 10 Dec 42, Ser 595, 11 Dec 42; 1st Bn, 128th Inf, Jnl, Ser 33, 10 Dec 42, Ser 6, 11 Dec 42; 3d Bn, 128th Inf, Jnl, 1630, 10 Dec 42, 2030, 11 Dec 42.

[40] Ltr, Gen Martin to Gen Ward, 6 Mar 51.

[41] Sitrep, Warren Force to 32d Div, Ser 2693, 9 Dec 42; Msg, Warren Force S–2 to 32d Div, Ser 2769, 10 Dec 42.

[42] Tel Msg, Maj Ziebell to Gen Byers, Ser 2767, 10 Dec 42; 1st Bn, 128th Inf, Jnl, Ser 25, 10 Dec 42; 2d Bn, 126th Inf, Jnl, 1000, 10 Dec 42; G–2 Hist Sec, GHQ FEC, Interv of Col Kazuyoshi Obata, Supply Staff Officer, *18th Army,* Nov 42–Apr 44, copy in OCMH files; *18th Army* Opns I, p. 46; Rpt, CG Buna Forces, p. 84.

command of the 1st Battalion, 128th Infantry, in place of Colonel McCoy, who returned to division headquarters. Colonel
MacNab, executive officer of Warren Force
under General MacNider, Colonel Hale,
and Colonel Martin, successively, changed
places with Colonel Miller to take command
of the 3d Battalion, 128th Infantry, and
Miller became executive officer to Colonel
Martin.[43]

The attritional type of warfare ordered on
the Warren front did not advance the line
much, but the relentless pounding by the
mortars and artillery and the sharp probing
forays of the infantry were having exactly
the effect intended by General Eichelberger—wearing the enemy down physically
and softening up his defenses for the final
knockout blow.

Urbana Force Makes Its First Gains

The Capture of Buna Village

Though relative quiet had descended on
the Warren front, bitter fighting had continued almost without cease on the Urbana
front. The Japanese in the village were
virtually surrounded. Fire was hitting them
frontally and from across Buna Creek, but
they held their positions with extreme

tenacity, and it began to look as if it would
be necessary to root them out of their
bunkers individually as had been the case at
Gona.

The 2d Battalion, 126th Infantry, was
reorganized on 6 December. Colonel Grose
had been promised command of the 127th
Infantry, which was then on its way to the
front, and left the reorganization to Colonel
Tomlinson and Major Smith. He himself
attended to supply matters and to the re-
adjustment of the positions held by the 2d
Battalion, 128th Infantry, on the right. Feeling that it was really Colonel Tomlinson's
command and that there was no use in
having two regimental commanders at the
front, Colonel Grose asked General Byers
when the latter visited him that afternoon
that Colonel Tomlinson be given the command. Byers agreed. Grose returned to the
rear, and Tomlinson (who formally took
command the next day) went on with preparations for an attack scheduled to be
launched the next morning.[44]

The attack was to have better artillery
support than before, with all the guns east
of the river scheduled to go into action,[45]
and the mortars also were to be used more
effectively than before. Finding that the infantry could not control their mortar fire
in the dense jungle, Colonel McCreary
adopted an innovation in the use of mortars,
based on artillery practice. He consolidated
the seventeen available 81-mm. mortars
on his front into one unit, made a fire-
direction chart from a vertical photograph,
and by observation and mathematical cal-
culation fixed the position of the mortars in
relation to the Japanese positions. He
formed the mortars into three batteries, two

[43] Msg, 128th Inf to G–3, 32d Div, Ser 2751, 10
Dec 42; 128th Inf Jnl, Ser 20, 10 Dec 42; 1st Bn,
126th Inf, Jnl, Ser 637, 13 Dec 42, Ser 650, 14 Dec
42; 1st Bn, 128th Inf, Jnl, Ser 15, 14 Dec 42; 128th
Inf, Jnl, 1900, 1915, 13 Dec 42, 1300, 14 Dec 42.
"I am changing some of my leaders on the right
flank" General Eichelberger told Port Moresby on
the night of 13 December. "Young Clarkson," he
continued, "who only left the military academy in
1938 is going to take one of the battalions on the
right flank and Carrier is being relieved by Major
Beaver. I know Clarkson well, for I raised him from
a pup. . . . He is full of fight and will do what
I tell him." Ltr, Gen Eichelberger to Gen Sutherland, 13 Dec 42, copy in OCMH files.

[44] Col Grose's Diary, 6 Dec 42; Ltr, Col Grose to
Gen Ward, 26 Feb 51; Rpt, CG Buna Forces, p. 23.
[45] 126th Inf Jnl, entries 6–7 Dec 42.

of six guns, and one of five guns. After adjusting the mortars and training the crews in artillery methods, he spent "the next two days 60 feet up in a tree less than 200 yards from the Jap forward elements, throwing hammer blow after hammer blow (all guns firing at once fairly concentrated) on the strong localities, searching through Buna Village." [46]

The attack was to be mounted by the 2d Battalion, 126th Infantry, less the troops at Bottcher's Corner. Companies E and G were to attack on right and left, and the weapons crews of Company H, would support the attack by fire from a position to the right of Company G. The troops at Bottcher's Corner would hold where they were, and Company F would be available as required for the reinforcement of the other companies. The Cannon Company, 128th Infantry, now in regimental reserve, would take up a holding position in the area immediately below Musita Island, and the 2d Battalion, 128th Infantry, would continue to hold on the 126th Infantry's right.

The strike against the village was to be in the early afternoon of 7 December, but the Japanese moved first. At 0600 in the morning, they attacked the troops at Bottcher's Corner from both the village and the mission, but Bottcher's machine gun and the rifle fire of his troops (reinforced by a fresh platoon from Company H) broke up the attack. [47] Urbana Force telephoned the following description of the action: "Bottcher

opened fire on the Buna Mission force first, stopping that attack. He then turned his gun on the Buna Village force, and stopped that attack. During the attack, Bottcher was shot in the hand. He was given first aid treatment, and is now commanding his gun." [48]

The story might have had a different ending had it not been for the alertness of Cpl. Harold L. Mitchell of Company H, who had joined Bottcher's little force the previous day. Acting as a forward outpost, Mitchell detected the enemy force from the village while it was creeping forward under cover of the jungle. Just as it was about to launch its attack, he charged at the Japanese suddenly with a loud yell and bayonet fixed. Mitchell so surprised and dumbfounded them that instead of continuing with the attack they hesitated and momentarily fell back. His yell alerted the rest of the force, with the result that when the Japanese finally did attack they were cut down. Mitchell escaped without a scratch. [49]

The flurry at Bottcher's Corner over, Companies E and G jumped off at 1335 after a fifteen-minute artillery and mortar preparation. They met heavy opposition and made little headway against an enemy that held with fanatic determination. To encourage his troops in their attempts to advance, Major Smith moved to the most exposed forward positions. Less than an hour after the attack began he was severely wounded. Captain Boice, the regimental S-2, who had made the first reconnaissance

---

[46] Ltr, Col McCreary to Col Handy, GHQ AGF, 11 Mar 43. In describing his method, McCreary, using the technical language of the artillerist, wrote that he had "restituted a vertical photograph to a 1/10,000 fire direction chart," and "tied the mortars and our zone of action to the ground by survey and observed fire."

[47] 2d Bn, 126th Inf, Jnl, 0640, 7 Dec 42; Tel Msg, Urbana Force to Gen Byers, Ser 2422, 7 Dec 42.

[48] Tel Msg, Urbana Force to CG, 32d Div, Ser 2422, 7 Dec 42.

[49] 2d Bn, 126th Inf, Jnl, 0640, 7 Dec 42; 1334, 9 Dec 42. Mitchell distinguished himself further on 9 December by bringing in a prisoner for questioning. He was later awarded the Distinguished Service Cross. The citation is in GHQ SWPA GO No. 3, 6 Jan 43.

of the trail to Jaure, immediately replaced him as battalion commander.[50]

The attack made no progress whatever. At 1430 Company F was committed in support of Company E and Company G, and the remaining platoon under Lieutenant Odell was ordered to Bottcher's Corner. The line still did not move forward, and the only successs of the day—a very modest one—was registered by Odell's platoon.[51]

Odell's orders had been to move onto the fire-swept beach and clear out two suspected enemy outposts: one northwest of Bottcher's Corner; the other closer to the village. The first outpost gave no trouble—the enemy troops in it were either dead or dying. The second was a different matter. Odell's platoon, down to a dozen men, began closing in on the objective, when it found itself faced with about fifteen Japanese in a hastily dug trench. As the platoon edged forward, one of the Japanese called out in English that he and his fellows would surrender if the Americans came over to them first. The men (as the battalion journal notes) treated the offer as a "gag." They stormed the trench and mopped up the Japanese, but heavy fire from the village ultimately drove them back to the Corner.[52]

The Japanese kept on trying. An attempt that evening by Captain Yasuda to send boats through to the village from his headquarters in the mission was frustrated when Sergeant Bottcher detected the leading barge and set it on fire with his machine gun. The barge was pulled back to the mission, a blazing hulk. After that rebuff the Japanese made no further attempts to send boats to the village.[53]

On 8 December the companies attacked again. Artillery, mortars, and machine guns opened up at 1400, and the troops started moving forward at 1415. Colonel Mc-Creary's mortars laid down fire as close as fifty yards to the front of the battalion's advance elements, but the Japanese line still held, and the attack was beaten off once again.

The day was marked by a futile attempt to burn out a main Japanese bunker position on the southern edge of the village which had resisted capture for several days. The bunker was on the corner of a kunai flat, with dense jungle and swamp to the rear. It could neither be taken by frontal assault nor flanked. Two primitive flame throwers had reached the front that day, and one of them was immediately pressed into use. Covered by the fire of twenty men, the operator managed to get within thirty feet of the enemy without being detected. Then he stepped into the open and turned on his machine. All that came out of it was a ten or fifteen-foot dribble of flame which set the grass on fire and did not even come near the Japanese position. The operator, two of the men covering him, as well as the chemical officer in charge, were killed. The operation, as reported to Port Moresby that night, had been a complete "fizzle."[54]

The same evening Captain Yasuda made his last diversion in favor of the beleaguered troops in the village. While the Japanese in the village counterattacked on the left with about forty men, a second force of between seventy-five and a hundred men

---

[50] 2d Bn, 126th Inf, Jnl, 1335, 1405, 7 Dec 42. For the heroic example he set his men, Major Smith was later awarded the Distinguished Service Cross. The citation is in Hq USAFFE GO No. 36, 1 Jul 43.

[51] 2d Bn, 126th Inf, Jnl, 1430, 7 Dec 42.

[52] 2d Bn, 126th Inf, Jnl, 1405, 1805, 1910, 7 Dec 42; Odell, Buna.

[53] 2d Bn, 126th Inf, Jnl, 1910, 7 Dec 42; 32d Div Sitrep, No. 89, 8 Dec 42; F. Tillman Durdin, The New York Times, 11 Dec 42.

[54] 32d Div Sitrep, No. 91, 9 Dec 42; 32d Div Chem Sec AAR, Papuan Campaign.

moved from the mission by way of the island and hit the right flank of the 2d Battalion, 126th Infantry. The force from the mission advanced to the attack screaming and yelling, but the battalion's mortars and machine guns beat it off in short order. "Our heavy weapons quieted them down rather fast," was the way the battalion journal described the action.[55]

Colonel McCreary continued his "hammer blows" against the village next day, but the Japanese still held their positions. During the afternoon, 1st Lt. James G. Downer, now commanding Company E, led a patrol against the same bunker position that the flame throwers had failed to reduce the day before. Covered by fire from the rest of the patrol, Downer moved out against the enemy positions alone but was killed by a hidden sniper just before reaching it. Downer's body was recovered and the fight for the bunker went on. Enemy fire slackened by evening and the bunker finally fell after costing the attackers heavy casualties and several days of effort.[56]

By this time the 2d Battalion, 126th Infantry, had launched twelve futile attacks on the village. Its companies had become so understrength that they could do little more than hold their positions. Companies E and F each had less than fifty effectives left, and the whole battalion totaled about 250 men. Its relief had long been overdue, and the task of delivering the final attack on the village went therefore to the fresh 3d Battalion, 127th Infantry, which together with regimental headquarters had completed its

movement to the forward area by air on 9 December.

Colonel Grose, as he had been promised earlier, took over command of the regiment the same day, and Lt. Col. Edwin J. Schmidt, the regimental commander, became his executive officer. On 11 December, Companies I and K, 127th Infantry, relieved Companies E and G, 126th Infantry. Company I took up a position at Bottcher's Corner between the village and the mission, and the 2d Battalion, 126th Infantry, moved into a reserve area along the supply trail.[57]

Companies I and K began probing the Japanese line at once. They made small gains on the 12th and consolidated them. On the 13th the village was subjected to heavy fire from the 25-pounders at Ango, and a heavy mortar concentration was laid down in preparation for a final assault the next day. The Japanese—by that time down to about 100 men—apparently had a premonition of what was coming. They evacuated the village that night and made for Giruwa. Most of them appear to have gotten through.[58]

Early the next morning, 14 December, a

---

[55] 2d Bn, 126th Inf, Jnl, 2045, 8 Dec 42; G-3 Opns Rpt, No. 245, 8 Dec 42.

[56] 2d Bn, 126th Inf, Jnl, 0950, 8 Dec 42, 1400, 9 Dec 42; 32d Div Sitreps, Nos. 91, 92, 9 Dec. 42. Downer was posthumously awarded the Distinguished Service Cross. The citation is in GHQ SWPA GO No. 7, 15 Jan 43.

[57] 2d Bn, 128th Inf, Jnl, 1345, 8 Dec 42; 2d Bn, 126th Inf, Jnl, 0908, 1305, 11 Dec 42; 127th Inf Tact Hist, Papuan Campaign, 9, 10, 11 Dec 42. Rpt, CG Buna Force, p. 24. On 10 December, just as the 2d Battalion was about to be relieved, Pfc. Walter A. Bajdek, of Battalion Headquarters Company, made a dash under heavy enemy fire to re-establish communication with an advanced observation post overlooking the enemy positions. Bajdek was later awarded the Distinguished Service Cross. The citation is in Hq USAFFE, GO No. 32, 15 Jun 43.

[58] Entry, M Sgt A. K. Ushiro, 22 Jan 43, in 32d Div G-2 Interrogations and Translations File. On the 13th, while the Japanese were still holding, Sgt. Samuel G. Winzenreid of Company I, 127th Infantry, acting on his own initiative, single-handedly reduced a strongly held enemy bunker with hand grenades. Winzenreid was later awarded the Distinguished Service Cross. The citation is in Hq USAFFE GO No. 32, 15 Jun 43.

thorough preparation by 25-pounders and mortars was put down on the village. Leaving a small holding force at the corner, Company K moved forward against the village at 0700. Company I was in support on Company K's left flank, and one of its platoons covered Company K's left rear. The advance continued steadily and cautiously. There was no opposition. By 1000 the entire area was overrun. Moving slowly and warily because they feared a trap, the troops soon discovered that none existed. They found no Japanese anywhere in the village. After all the bitter fighting that had raged on the outskirts, the village had fallen without the firing of a single enemy shot.[59]

The village was a mass of wreckage. Its few huts had been blown to bits; the coconut palms in the area were splintered and broken by shellfire; and there were craters and shell holes everywhere. The bunkers still stood, despite evidence of numerous direct hits registered upon them by the artillery. The Japanese had left little equipment and food behind: a few guns, some discarded clothing, a supply of canned goods, and a store of medical supplies.[60]

Thus anticlimactically had Urbana Force taken its first objective. The Coconut Grove remained as the only position on the left bank of Entrance Creek still in Japanese hands. This labyrinth of trenches and bunkers was next.

The Reduction of the Coconut Grove

Lt. Col. Herbert A. Smith, commanding officer of the 2d Battalion, 128th Infantry,

[59] 127th Inf Tact Hist, Papuan Campaign, 12, 13, 14 Dec 42.

[60] Msg, Col Tomlinson to Col Howe, Ser 3096, 14 Dec 42, 127th Inf CT Tact Hist, Papuan Campaign, 14 Dec 42; Durdin, *The New York Times*, 17 Dec 42.

had been told by General Byers a few days before that he would be called upon to take the Coconut Grove when Buna Village fell. Smith and his executive officer, Maj. Roy F. Zinser, lost no time therefore in preparing a plan for its reduction. Since the jungle fronting the grove was split by an open grassy area, the plan called for one company of the battalion to attack on the right under Smith and a second company to attack on the left under Zinser, whose unit was to make the main effort.

About 1300 on 15 December General Byers came to Colonel Smith's CP, west of the grove, and told him he was to attack at once. Smith's battalion numbered about 350 men at the time, but they were scattered along a 1,750-yard front all the way from the apex of the Triangle and along the left bank of Entrance Creek to a point just below Musita Island. Not counting a platoon of heavy machine guns from Company H which was to play a supporting role, Smith had less than 100 men immediately available for the attack: about 40 men from Company E; about 20 men from a Company F platoon; 15 or 20 men from Battalion Headquarters Company; and about 15 men from the Regimental Cannon Company who happened to be in the immediate area. Smith requested more troops, and specifically asked for the rest of Company F, which was then in the Siwori Village area protecting the left flank. General Byers found it impossible to give Smith the men he asked for, and the attack was ordered to begin at 1500 with those he had available.

Smith divided his available strength in half. He gave Zinser the platoon of Company F, most of the troops from Battalion Headquarters Company, and a few men from the Cannon Company detachment. He himself took Company E and a few men from each of the other units. The two forces moved out quickly to their respective points of departure. At 1510, with the troops in position and ready to go, Colonel Mc-Creary's mortars opened up on the grove.[61]

The mortar preparation, about 100 rounds in all, hit the target area but had little effect. As one who was there recalls, it merely "blew a little dirt from the Japanese emplacements." At 1520 the mortars ceased firing, and the troops moved out on right and left with the help of fire from the platoon of Company H.[62]

The Japanese had the approaches to the grove covered and laid down heavy fire on the attackers. Progress was slow, but Colonel Smith's forces were pressed up tight against their objective by nightfall. A heavy rain fell during the night, drenching the troops and filling their foxholes with water.[63]

Zinser's force took the initiative next morning. Running into a particularly troublesome bunker, it pressed into use a flame thrower of the same type that had worked so badly the week before in front of Buna Village. The result was the same: the flame thrower "fizzed out and Japanese shot it up." [64]

After reducing this position with grenades and small arms fire, the troops on the left discovered a very large bunker which commanded the American approaches to the grove. Since the enemy strongpoint was accessible to both of them, the two forces began converging on it from right and left, clearing out intermediate obstacles as they

went. In this fighting Major Zinser demonstrated conspicuous leadership, but it fell to two men of Company E on the right—Cpl. Daniel F. Rini and Pvt. Bernardino Y. Estrada—to clear out the main position. Rini and Estrada, members of the same squad, had been in the forefront of the company's advance. The climax came when Rini, covered by Estrada's BAR, got close enough to the main bunker to jump on top and knock it out.

That morning Colonel Smith had been watching Rini and Estrada from a position thirty or forty yards behind them, occasionally helping them with fire. Just as Rini reached the bunker, Smith was called to the phone tied to a tree about twenty-five yards to the rear to talk to Colonel Tomlinson. He had scarcely lifted the receiver when he heard shouting from the direction of the main bunker.

I sensed [he recalls] that this was probably the break we were looking for, so I told Colonel Tomlinson that I must get forward and see what was happening. I arrived just in time to see Corporal Rini on top of the big bunker and the rest of the squad closing in on it. Later I learned that Rini, after working up as close as he could, had suddenly made a dash, jumped on top of the bunker, and leaning over had pushed hand grenades through the firing slits.[65]

Realizing that he would have to move fast to take full advantage of this turn in the fighting, Colonel Smith ordered all-out attacks on the remaining enemy positions. Charging at the head of a squad, Smith cleared out a bunker in the center, and Capt. Joseph M. Stehling of Company E did the same in an attack on his right. The bunkers fell in quick succession, but Corporal Rini and Private Estrada were both

---

[61] 2d Bn, 128th Inf, Jnl, 1510, 15 Dec 42; Ltr, Col Herbert A. Smith to author, 23 Mar 50; Ltr, Gen Byers to Lt Col Roy F. Zinser, 20 Feb 51; Ltr, Col Zinser to Gen Byers, 1 Mar 51. Copies of last two in OCMH files.

[62] Ltr, Col Zinser to Gen Byers, 1 Mar 51.

[63] Ltr, Col Herbert A. Smith to author, 23 Mar 50; Rpt, CG Buna Forces, p. 26.

[64] Ltr, Col Zinser to Gen Byers, 1 Mar 51.

[65] Ltr, Col Herbert A. Smith to Gen Ward, 20 Mar 51.

killed in the mop-up which their valor had
made possible. Rini was shot by a wounded
Japanese to whom he was trying to admin-
ister first aid, and Estrada fell not long after
while helping to clear the last enemy position in the grove.[66]

The fighting was over by noon. Thirty-
seven Japanese were buried by the following
day, and more were found and buried subsequently. The cost to the 2d Battalion,
128th Infantry, was four killed and thirteen
wounded.

Booty included 2,000 pounds of rice and
oatmeal, a number of kegs of malt and bar-
ley, a quantity of small arms, several light
machine guns, and a hut full of ammunition. One wounded Japanese sergeant was
taken prisoner.[67]

As soon as the grove was captured, Colonel Smith sent patrols over a footbridge
built by the Japanese across Entrance Creek
and the Ango–Buna track bridge. Though
the latter span lacked flooring, its piling and
stringers were still intact. The patrols met
no opposition, and two heavy machine guns
were immediately emplaced covering the
approaches to the bridges. Late in the afternoon, while the engineers were repairing the
track bridge, an enemy attempt to mass
troops in the Government Gardens, presumably for an attack on the newly won
beachhead east of Entrance Creek, was frustrated by fire from the heavy machine guns
both east and west of the creek.[68]

General Eichelberger wrote General Sutherland that night that he was "delighted"
with the way Colonel Smith's battalion had
performed in the day's fighting. The battalion was now "high" in his favor, Colonel
Smith had "developed into quite a fighter,"
and the men had "a high morale." "As a
matter of fact," he added, "the boys are
coming to life all along the line." [69]

The Scene Brightens

The Situation: Mid-December

General Eichelberger was right. Despite
considerable losses, widespread sickness, and
severe physical discomforts, the troops were
giving an increasingly good account of themselves. By 11 December, after having been
been in action for only twenty-one days, the
two task forces east of the Girua River had
lost 667 killed, wounded, and missing, and
1,260 evacuated sick.[70] Troop morale had
touched bottom during the first week in December and had stayed there for a few days
after. By mid-month, however, a distinct
improvement had become manifest. A report on morale in the 3d Battalion, 128th
Infantry, submitted to Colonel Martin on
13 December, noted that the men were tired
and feverish, that their physical co-ordination was poor, that they complained of the

[66] Ibid; 2d Bn, 128th Inf, Jnl, 0820, 1140, 1200,
1410, 16 Dec 42; 32d Div Sitrep, No. 106, 16 Dec
42. Zinser, Rini, and Estrada were later awarded
the Distinguished Service Cross; Smith and Stehling, the Silver Star. Zinser's citation is in Hq
USAFFE GO No. 2, 11 Jan 44; Rini's and Estrada's
posthumous awards are cited in GHQ SWPA GO
No. 9, 19 Jan 43. The Silver Star citations are in
Hq 32d Div GO No. 54, 14 Jan 43, and in GO
No. 28, 6 Apr 43, of the same headquarters.
[67] Tel Msg, Col Howe to Col Tomlinson, Ser
3488, 17 Dec 42; 32d Div Sitreps, No. 106, 16 Dec
42, No. 108, 17 Dec 42; 127th Inf CT Tact Hist,
Papuan Campaign, 16 Dec 42.

[68] 32d Div Sitrep, No. 106, 16 Dec 42; Msg,
NGF to 32d Div, Ser 3587, 17 Dec 42; Ltr, Col
Herbert A. Smith to author, 23 Mar 50; Ltr, Col
Zinser to Gen Byers, 1 Mar 51.
[69] Ltr, Gen Eichelberger to Gen Sutherland, 16
Dec 42.
[70] 32d Div Strength Rpt to Col Joseph S. Bradley,
CofS, 32d Div, Ser 2932, 11 Dec 42, in 32d Div G–3
Jnl. The detailed figures are: KIA, 113; WIA, 490;
MIA, 64. Warren Force sustained 422 of these cas-
ualties; Urbana Force, 245.

food and of the difficulty of getting rest at night. The same report nevertheless commented that their "spirits" had "livened-up" considerably during the preceding few days.[71]

There were good reasons for the upswing in morale. The fact that the troops had by this time learned their business had a great deal to do with it. More food and rest, the arrival of the 127th Infantry, the victories on the Urbana front, the receipt of mail for the first time since the campaign began, and the knowledge that tanks and fresh Australian troops were coming had boosted morale still further.

The supply situation was improving. More luggers were becoming available, and General Johns of the Combined Operational Service Command (COSC) had already decided to send large freighters into Oro Bay. The airlift was beginning to bring in truly impressive tonnages. On 14 December, for example, the air force in seventy-four individual flights between Port Moresby and the airfields at Dobodura and Popondetta brought in 178 tons of high-priority matériel. This was a maximum effort that was never equaled during the rest of the campaign, but it indicated what the air force could do when it extended itself and the weather was favorable.[72]

The rapidly growing airlift, the opening of a fourth field at Dobodura, regular nightly deliveries by the luggers, and the completion by the engineers of additional jeep trails to the front had done more than merely make good the supply shortages that had so long afflicted the 32d Division. They had made it possible for the first time to begin stockpiling food and ammunition for a sustained offensive effort.[73]

There were other improvements. The sound-power telephone, pressed into use at this time for fire control purposes, was proving itself highly efficient within a two-mile range, and the introduction of the new 4-inch-to-1-mile Buna Map, in place of the improvised Buna Target Plan No. 24, was already paying the troops dividends. With a more accurate base map, improved communications with the forward observers, and observation from the air, the artillery was beginning to give an even better account of itself. From time to time, it was executing fire missions on bunkers adjacent to the bridge between the strips, and on those flanking the dispersal bays off the northeastern end of the New Strip. It was laying down harassing fire on the enemy front and rear. Direct hits were chipping away at the bunkers, but except in the case of the 105-mm. howitzer, using shells with delayed fuses, artillery had little effect on the enemy bunker positions.[74]

On the more strongly defended Warren front what was needed, in addition to more effective artillery support, was special equipment for the reduction of bunkers. Such equipment—routine later on—was simply

---

[71] 3d Bn, 128th Inf, Jnl, 1100, 13 Dec 42.
[72] 32d Div G–4 Sec, Record of Air Shipments, Rear Echelon, Port Moresby, Papuan Campaign; Interv with Col Moffatt, 30 Oct 49.

[73] 128th Inf Jnl, 0230, 0450, 1232, 8 Dec 42; 0500, 9 Dec 42; 0825, 1838, 1925, 11 Dec 42; Msg, Gen Byers to NGF, Ser 2710, 10 Dec 42; Msg, Gen Eichelberger to Gen Kenney, Ser 3039, 13 Dec 42; 32d Div G–4 Sec, Record of Air Shipments, Rear Echelon, Port Moresby, Papuan Campaign.
[74] Msg, NGF to 32d Div, Ser 2775, 10 Dec 42; Msg NGF to Adv NGF, Ser 3630, 18 Dec 42; 128th Inf Jnl, Ser 24, 11 Dec 42; Ser 13, 12 Dec 42; Ltr, Col Horace Harding to Lt Col James F. Collins, 4 Jan 43, in I Corps Correspondence File; Memo, Col Irwin, 6th Aust Div, for Brig Wootten, 4 Jan 43, sub: Japanese Strongpoints—Expedients in Assisting Attack, copy in OCMH files.

not to be had at Buna. It was expected that the tanks, when they finally reached the front, would make up for these deficiencies.

The Arrival of the Australians

Early on 7 December General Herring and his chief of staff, Brig. R. N. L. Hopkins, visited General Eichelberger's headquarters at Henahamburi to make arrangements for the reception of the Australian troops and tanks that General Eichelberger had been promised on 3 December. General Blamey had chosen Brig. George F. Wootten of the 18th Brigade (then still at Milne Bay) to command the incoming Australian force. General Eichelberger at once offered to put Wootten in command of Warren Force with Colonel Martin as second-in-command—an offer which General Herring promptly accepted.[75]

General Blamey had discussed the matter with General MacArthur the day before. The two commanders had agreed that the operation would require at least a battalion of troops from Milne Bay and a suitable number of tanks from Port Moresby. Since General Blamey did not have enough small ships to move the battalion, he asked General MacArthur to prevail upon the Navy (which up to that time had been unwilling to send its ships into the waters around Buna) to provide corvettes or destroyers to get the troops forward. On 8 December— the same day that Brigadier Wootten was ordered to report to General Blamey at Port Moresby—the Navy agreed to provide three corvettes for the purpose, and New Guinea

Force issued its first orders relating to the movement the following day.[76]

The orders provided that one troop (four tanks) of the 2/6 Australian Armored Regiment at Port Moresby, and the 2/9 Australian Infantry Battalion at Milne Bay, were to be sent to Buna. The tanks were to go forward in the Dutch ship *Karsik*, a 3,300-ton, four-hatch freighter of the K. P. M. line; the Australian corvettes *Colac, Ballarat,* and *Broome* were to carry the troops. The *Karsik* was to pick up supplies and ammunition at Milne Bay before moving on to Oro Bay where it was to be unloaded on the night of 11–12 December. The three corvettes would touch at Milne Bay on the 12th. After taking on brigade headquarters and the 2/9 Battalion, they would make a speedy run northward and rendezvous the same night off Soena Plantation just below Cape Sudest with landing craft from Porlock Harbor which were to ferry the troops and their equipment ashore.[77]

Brigadier Wootten reported to General Blamey on 10 December and received his instructions. Blamey had decided by that time to send another troop of tanks and another infantry battalion to Buna. Of Brigadier Wootten's two remaining battalions, the 2/10th was at Wanigela and Porlock Harbor, and the 2/12th was at Goodenough Island. Blamey therefore intended to draw the additional battalion from the 7th Brigade, which was still at

[75] Rpt, CG Buna Force, pp. 23, 27, 28; Interv with Gen Eichelberger, 6 Feb 50; Eichelberger, *Our Jungle Road to Tokyo,* p. 44.

[76] Ltr, Gen Blamey to Gen MacArthur, 8 Dec 42, in G–3 Jnl, GHQ SWPA; NGF OI No. 49, 9 Dec 42; Rpt on Opns 18th Bde Gp at Cape Endaiadere and Giropa Point.

[77] NGF OI No. 49, 9 Dec 42; Interv with Col Moffatt, 2 Mar 50; The *Koninklijke Paktevaart Maatschapij* (K.P.M. Line) and the War in the Southwest Pacific Area.

Milne Bay. However, at Brigadier Wootten's request, the 2/10 Battalion, the 18th Brigade unit at Wanigela and Porlock Harbor, was substituted. This change in plan made it necessary to move the battalion of the 7th Brigade to Wanigela and Porlock Harbor before the 2/10 Battalion could be sent forward to Buna. The change-over began immediately in order to permit the 2/10 Battalion to reach Buna by the night of 17–18 December.[78]

Brigadier Wootten flew to Popondetta at dawn the next morning, 11 December. After conferring with General Herring and Brigadier Hopkins, he and Hopkins flew to Dobodura where they met General Eichelberger. Wootten spent the afternoon reconnoitering the Warren front, and that night, while he slept at General Eichelberger's headquarters, the *Karsik* came into Oro Bay.

The *Karsik* had in its hold four light American M3 tanks (General Stuarts) belonging to the 2/6 Australian Armored Regiment. It carried also a seven-day level of supply for the 2/9 Battalion. Maj. Carroll K. Moffatt, an American infantry officer serving with the COSC, supervised the unloading. He had just reached the area from Milne Bay with six Higgins boats (LCVP's) and two Australian barges, the first Allied landing craft to reach the combat zone. The actual unloading was done by troops of the 287th U. S. Port Battalion who had come in on the *Karsik*. They did the job quickly, and, the ship got away safely before daylight. The tanks were transferred to specially constructed barges (which had reached the area a few days before), towed to shore, unloaded, and hidden in the jungle. They were reloaded on the barges the next night and then towed by luggers to Boreo. There they were landed, run into the jungle, and hidden at a tank lying-up point a few hundred yards north of the village.

Brigade headquarters, the 2/9 Battalion, and the commanding officer of the 2/10 Battalion (who had flown in from Wanigela the night before) left in the *Colac, Broome,* and *Ballarat* early on 12 December. Traveling at high speed, the ships reached the rendezvous point off Cape Sudest late that night to find Major Moffatt and the eight landing craft waiting for them.

Unloading began at once, but scarcely had the first seventy-five men, including the two battalion commanders, stepped into the two leading LCVP's when the captain of the *Ballarat,* the senior officer in charge of the corvettes, learned that a "large" Japanese naval force, was moving on Buna from Rabaul. He immediately pulled the corvettes back to Porlock Harbor with the rest of the troops still aboard.[79]

The two loaded landing craft let the troops off at Boreo, and all eight craft made for the Oro Bay area, their hiding place during the day. Just before they reached it, they were bombed by patrolling Australian aircraft, which mistook them for Japanese—an understandable error since the pilots had not been told to look out for Allied landing craft, and the Allies had up to that time had no landing craft of any

---

[78] NGF OI No. 51, 11 Dec 42; Rpt on Opns 18th Inf Bde Gp at Cape Endaiadere and Giropa Point. Since Wanigela and Porlock Harbor were only a short distance from Buna, the transfer of the 2/10th to the front by corvette could be made quickly once it had been relieved by the battalion of the 7th Brigade.

[79] Rpt on Opns 18th Inf Bde Gp at Cape Endaiadere and Giropa Point; Interv with Col Moffatt, 30 Oct 49. The enemy force was the one bearing General Oda and the *1st Battalion, 170th Infantry,* which was to reach the mouth of the Mambare the following morning.

THREE GENERALS CONVALESCING *in an Australian hospital, December 1942.*
Left to right, Generals MacNider, Waldron, and Byers.

kind in the area. One LCVP was sunk, and
another had to be beached, a total loss.
Nine crew members were wounded, and
one died before he could reach a hospital.[80]

The corvettes returned the following
night. Instead of rendezvousing with the

landing craft off Cape Sudest as planned,
the corvettes landed the troops at Oro Bay,
a full day's march away. The Japanese naval force was still in the area and unac-
counted for, and the corvettes had no intention of running into it, especially with troops
aboard.

The Australian troops reached Hariko
the following night. The next morning—15
December—they moved up to their permanent bivouac area about a mile north of
Boreo and a quarter-mile inland. That night
the *Karsik* came in again to Oro Bay, with
100 tons of cargo and a second troop of
tanks. As in the case of the first tank move-

[80] Rpt on Opns 18th Inf Bde Gp at Cape Endaiadere and Giropa Point; Interv with Col Moffatt, 30
Oct 49; Kenney, *General Kenney Reports*, pp. 165,
166. General Kenney's story of the bombing is inaccurate in that he says that no one was hurt, and
fails to mention that, in addition to the one craft
sunk, a second was rendered useless and had to be
abandoned. The figures given are from records kept
by Colonel Moffatt, who was in charge of the landing craft.

ment, the four tanks were put aboard barges, towed to Boreo, unloaded, and moved up the beach to the tank park. With the first four tanks they were organized into a composite unit: X Squadron of the 2/6 Armored Regiment.[81]

On 16 December Advance New Guinea Force moved to Dobodura from Popondetta. General Byers was wounded while in the front lines during the attack on the Coconut Grove, and General Eichelberger, as the only U.S. general officer present, took command of the American forces at the front.[82] The next day, 17 December, after consulting with General Eichelberger, Brigadier Wootten took over command of the Warren front, and Buna Force set 18 December as D Day.[83]

General MacArthur had been urging General Eichelberger to speed his preparations,[84] and Eichelberger had done his best to comply. The attack General MacArthur had asked for was now ready. Warren Force was to move out on the 18th with tanks; its successive objectives were Duropa Plantation and Cape Endaiadere (including a bridgehead across the mouth of Simemi Creek), the New Strip, and the Old Strip. Urbana Force was to attack on the 19th— D plus 1. It was to storm the Triangle, cut through to the coast, and seize the track junction between Buna Mission and Giropa Point, thereby isolating the one from the other, and exposing both to attack on their inward flanks.[85] Captain Yasuda and Colonel Yamamoto were now each faced with a double envelopment, and both were about to be caught in a pincers from which there was no escape.

---

[81] Rpt of Opns 18th Inf Bde Gp at Cape Endaiadere and Giropa Point; Interv with Gen Eichelberger, 6 Feb 50; Interv with Col Moffatt, 30 Oct 49; Hist Port Det E, COSC, Buna.

[82] Rpt, CG Buna Force, p. 27; Eichelberger, *Our Jungle Road to Tokyo*, p. 41. Byers, who was wounded immediately after his troops jumped off, was awarded the Distinguished Service Cross nine days later. The citation is in GHQ SWPA GO No. 63, 24 Dec 42.

[83] Tel Msg, Brig Hopkins to 32d Div, Ser 3227, 15 Dec 42; Tel Msg, 18th Bde to 32d Div, Ser 3426, 17 Dec 42; Rpt on Opns 18th Inf Bde Gp at Cape Endaiadere and Giropa Point.

[84] Ltr, Gen MacArthur to Gen Eichelberger, 13 Dec 42, copy in OCMH files.

[85] NGF OI No. 53, 16 Dec 42; Buna Force FO No. 3, 17 Dec 42; 18th Aust Bde Gp Opns Orders No. 1, 17 Dec 42.

CHAPTER XIV

Warren Force Takes the Initiative

On 18 December, the day appointed for the tank-infantry attack in the Duropa Plantation–New Strip area, New Guinea Force ordered the construction of a road from Oro Bay to the airfields at Dobodura. Engineer troops to build the road and port detachment troops to operate the port left Gili Gili for Oro Bay the same day in the K. P. M. ship *Japara*.[1] Such a road, in conjunction with the port, would make it possible to base bomber and fighter aircraft north of the Owen Stanley Range for the first time. It would serve to seal off Port Moresby from attack and help write the doom of the Japanese garrisons in the Huon Peninsula. The establishment of the port and the construction of the road—prerequisites to the enjoyment by the Southwest Pacific Area of the fruits of victory at Buna—were, in short, being undertaken even as the victory was being won. With tanks finally on hand for the reduction of the Japanese positions in the Duropa Plantation and behind the New Strip, that victory could not be far off.

The Advance to Simemi Creek

Preparing the Tank Attack

As General Harding had concluded in November when he first asked for tanks, the

[1] NGF OI No. 54, 18 Dec 42; Interv with Col Moffatt, 30 Oct 49; Hist Port Det E, COSC, Buna, abstract in OCMH files.

Australian tank men found the plantation area and the New Strip entirely suitable for tank action. The plan of attack on the Warren front therefore called for the main body of the tank squadron, closely followed by two companies of the 2/9 Battalion, to attack in the Duropa Plantation, straight up the coast to Cape Endaiadere. The 3d Battalion, 128th Infantry, was to mop up immediately to the rear. After taking the cape, the attackers would then wheel west to the line of Simemi Creek and emerge on the enemy's rear by securing a bridgehead across the creek near its mouth. The New Strip would be attacked simultaneously from south and east. The 1st Battalion, 126th Infantry, was to move on the bridge between the strips from its position immediately to the south of it. Preceded by the rest of the tanks and supported by the 1st Battalion, 128th Infantry, another company from the 2/9 Battalion would meanwhile attack at the eastern end of the strip, cut through the dispersal bays, and advance on the bridge between the strips via the northern edge of the New Strip. (*Map 13*)

A heavy artillery and mortar preparation was to precede the attack. Augmenting the 105-mm. howitzer south of Ango, the 25-pounders on either flank, and the two 3.7-inch mountain guns just below the western end of the New Strip, at least one 25-pounder was to be moved up close to the dispersal bays at its eastern end in order to bring the bunkers in that area under direct fire. The 2/10 Battalion (which was expected to arrive on the night of D Day) was to take over the 2/9 Battalion's bivouac area and be committed to action upon order from Brigadier Wootten.[2]

At 1800 on the night of the 17th, X Squadron—seven tanks, less one tank in reserve—began moving up to the line of departure. The sound of aircraft was to have covered the rumble of the tanks as they moved up to the starting line, but the planes did not materialize. Instead, the 1st and 3d Battalions, 128th Infantry, laid down a mortar barrage to drown out the roar of the motors and the clank of the treads. The expedient was successful. Even though the Japanese had patrols very close to the area in which the tanks were arriving, no alarm was aroused.[3]

The American troops were then pressed up tight against the Japanese line, in most cases less than fifty yards from the nearest enemy bunker. They were to withdraw about 300 yards to the rear, just behind the Australian line of departure that was marked that night with white tape. Thus the attacking Australians and supporting American troops would not be endangered by the

close-in artillery and mortar preparation, and both the infantry and the tanks would gain maneuver space in the attack.[4]

The First Day

The attack went off as planned. Early the following morning between 0600 and 0645 the 1st and 3d Battalions, 128th Infantry, withdrew quietly 300 yards to their appointed positions. At 0650 Allied air began bombing and strafing, and every artillery piece and mortar on the front opened up on the enemy positions. During this ten-minute preparation the 2/9 Battalion under its commander, Lt. Col. Clement J. Cummings, passed through Colonel MacNab's and Major Clarkson's troops and arrived at the taped-out line of departure just forward of the Americans. At 0700 the artillery and mortar barrage ceased, the planes stopped bombing, and the Australians with tanks in the lead moved out.

Three companies of the 2/9th—A, D, and C—were committed to the attack; the remaining company—Company B—was left in reserve. Companies A and D, and five tanks pushed straight north up the coast, on a two-company front. After jumping off with the other companies, Company C spearheaded by two tanks wheeled northwestward and attacked the enemy bunkers in the area off the eastern end of the New Strip. As soon as the Australians had left the line of departure, Colonel MacNab's and Major Clarkson's troops began moving forward north and west in support of the attacking Australians. Major Beaver meanwhile kept up a steady pressure on the bridge area at the other end of the strip, supported by fire from

---

[2] Buna Force, Instructions to Warren Force in Projected Opns, 15 Dec 42, Ser 3226, in 32d Div G–3 Jnl; NGF OI No. 53, 16 Dec 42; 18th Bde Gp OI No. 1, 17 Dec 42; 1st Bn, 126th Inf, Jnl, Ser 685, 17 Dec 42; 1st Bn, 128th Inf, Jnl, Sers 13, 14, 17 Dec 42; 3d Bn, 128th Inf, Jnl, 1300, 17 Dec 42; Rpt on Opns 18th Bde Gp at Cape Endaiadere and Giropa Point.

[3] Tel Msg, Gen Eichelberger to Adv NGF, Ser 3451, 17 Dec 42, in 32d Div G–3 Jnl; 1st Bn, 128th Inf, Jnl, 1554, 1853, 17 Dec 42; 3d Bn, 128th Inf, Jnl, 1554, 1853, 17 Dec 42; 128th Inf Jnl, 1815, 1840, 1900, 2103, 17 Dec 42; Rpt on Opns 18th Bde Gp at Cape Endaiadere and Giropa Point.

[4] Ltr, Gen Martin to Gen Ward, 6 Mar 51.

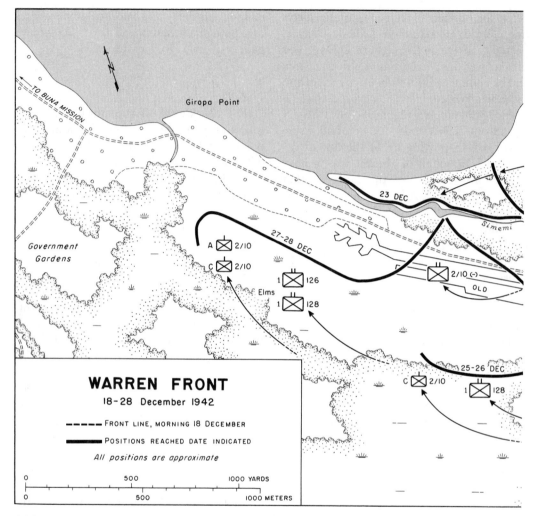

MAP 13

the 3.7-inch mountain guns of the O'Hare Troop.[5]

Even though the heavy artillery and mortar preparation failed to destroy the enemy bunkers, the coastal attack on Cape Endai-

[5] Tel Msgs, 18th Bde to 32d Div, Sers 3529, 3563, 3609, 18 Dec 42, in 32d Div G–3 Jnl; 1st Bn, 126th Inf, Jnl, Sers 685, 686, 17 Dec 42; 1st Bn, 128th Inf, Jnl, Sers 11, 13, 14, 17 Dec 42, Sers 2, 4, 6, 10, 16, 18 Dec 42; 32d Div Sitrep, No. 110, 18 Dec 42.

adere was a brilliant success. Taking Colonel Yamamoto's *144th* and *229th Infantry* troops completely by surprise, the tanks and the fresh Australian troops advancing behind them made short work of the Japanese positions in the plantation which had so long held up the attack on the coastal flank.

As Colonel MacNab, who was on the scene waiting to go in with his battalion, described it,

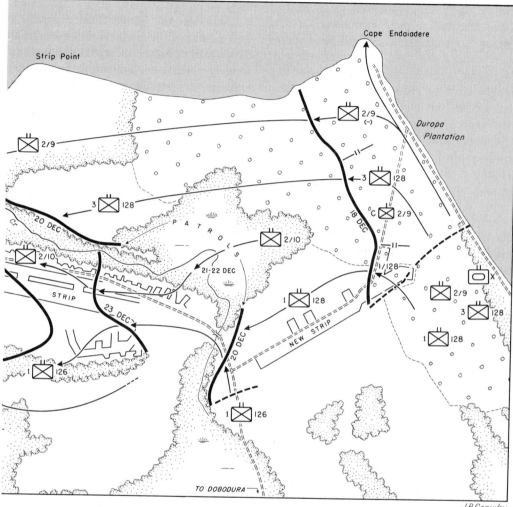

Cape Endaiadere

Strip Point

2/9 (-)

Duropa Plantation

2/9

3 ← 128

3 ← 128 C 2/9

20 DEC

P A T R O L S

18 DEC

2/10

2/10

21-22 DEC

2/9

STRIP

23 DEC

1 128

1 128 3 128

20 DEC

NEW STRIP

1 128

1 126

20 DEC

1 126

TO DOBODURA →

J.R.Crowley

The tanks really did that job. They apparently completely demoralized the Japs . . . [who] fought like cornered rats when they were forced into the open [as a result of] having their fires masked when the tanks broke through their final protective line. . . . There were few holes knocked in the bunkers except where the tanks stood off and blasted them at short range with their 37-mm. guns.[6]

[6] Ltr, Col MacNab to author, 25 Nov 49.

The two Australian companies took heavy casualties as they overran the successive Japanese positions. Two tanks were lost—one to a Molotov cocktail, and the other when its motor failed as it skirted a burning enemy dump, but so well did the attack go that the Australians had reached the cape within the hour. Without delay they headed west and began moving on the next objective, Strip Point, with the three remaining tanks. About 500 yards west of Cape Endaiadere they encountered a new enemy line whose bunkers and blockhouses had escaped the artillery bombardment. Here they again met stiff resistance. They fought hard to reduce this new Japanese strongpoint but could advance no farther that day.

Colonel MacNab's battalion had meanwhile pushed forward. There were more Japanese left in the coastal area than expected, and the opposition was relatively heavy. The battalion finished mopping up by evening and established an all-around defense perimeter in the plantation extending from its former front line to a point just below Cape Endaiadere.

The attack on the enemy positions off the eastern end of the New Strip had not gone as well as that on Cape Endaiadere. Company C, 2/9 Battalion, and the two tanks were stopped in their tracks only a short distance from the line of departure. Reserves were called for. Company B, 2/9 Battalion—Colonel Cummings' reserve company—was brought up, and the 1st Battalion, 128th Infantry, was ordered in on both flanks. Despite these reinforcements, the Japanese still held to their positions, and soon put one of the tanks temporarily out of action by damaging its vision slits with machine gun fire.

At 1600 the three tanks from the north flank and the tank that had been in reserve were committed to the action. Again the two Australian companies attacked, supported as before by Major Clarkson's battalion. After two hours of bitter fighting, they finally overran the strongpoint. It was found to be made up of twenty pillboxes, several of them of concrete and steel construction. Pulling back just in time, the enemy troops less a small rear guard with-

drew along the northern edge of the strip to bunkers near the bridge. Their position, as well as that of the engineer and antiaircraft troops whom they reinforced, was now extremely precarious. The whole bridge area and the few still-unreduced bunkers south of the bridge had been under heavy fire during the day from Major Beaver's mortars, the mountain guns of the O'Hare Troop, and the 105-mm. howitzer south of Ango, which for the first time in the campaign had ammunition to spare.[7]

The 2/9 Battalion lost 160 men in the day's fighting—49 killed and 111 wounded—and the tank squadron lost two of its seven tanks, but the day's gains had been decisive. The enemy's line in the Duropa Plantation–New Strip area had been broken, and his defenses had been overcome in the area east of Simemi Creek.

As the mopping up proceeded and the construction of the enemy bunkers in the area was examined, it became apparent that infantry, with the weapons and support that the 32d Division had, could probably never have reduced the enemy line alone. General Eichelberger put his finger squarely on the difficulty in a letter to General Sutherland. "I know General MacArthur will be glad to know," he wrote, "that we found concrete pillboxes with steel doors, interlocked in such a way that it would have been almost impossible for [infantry] unassisted to get across." Two days later he made his meaning plainer when, in the course of praising Brigadier Wootten for doing a fine

---

[7] Msgs, 18th Bde to 32d Div, Sers 3539, 3563, 3566, 3579, 3591, 3601, 3609, 18 Dec 42, in 32d Div G–3 Jnl; 1st Bn, 126th Inf, Jnl, Sers 692, 693, 697, 709, 712, 714, 18 Dec 42; 1st Bn, 128th Inf, Jnl, Sers 38, 48, 49, 73, 18 Dec 42; 3d Bn, 128th Inf, Jnl, 0840, 0930, 1250, 18 Dec 42; 128th Inf, Jnl, Sers 24, 28, 41, 55, 57, 59, 85, 18 Dec 42; Rpt on Opns 18th Inf Bde at Cape Endaiadere and Giropa Point.

GENERAL STUART LIGHT TANKS M3 *manned by the 2/6 Australian Armored Regiment, December 1942.*

job, ne added, "I am glad he has the tanks to help him. I do not believe he or anyone else would have gone very far without them." [8]

The Push Westward

On the evening of 18 December Brigadier Wootten was given permission to use the next day for regrouping his troops, and later the same night the 2/10 Battalion, less two

companies, came in from Porlock Harbor by corvette. The incoming troops took over the bivouac area previously occupied by the 2/9 Battalion, and went into brigade reserve. [9]

The 19th was comparatively quiet. Two Australian 4.5-inch howitzers (the Stokes Troop), which had been flown in on the 18th, went into action south of the O'Hare Troop below the bridge, and several con-

---

[8] Ltrs, Gen Eichelberger to Gen Sutherland, 18 Dec 42, 20 Dec 42, copies in OCMH files.

[9] Ltr, Gen Eichelberger to Gen Sutherland, 18 Dec 42; Rpt on Opns 18th Bde Gp at Cape Endaiadere and Giropa Point.

centrations were fired during the morning on newly located bunkers in the bridge area.[10] The two Australian companies that had been operating off the eastern end of the strip moved north to join the rest of the 2/9 Battalion in front of Strip Point. Then, as Major Clarkson's troops moved forward along the northern edge of the strip to join Beaver's men in front of the bridge, the 3d Battalion, 128th Infantry, faced west, and began moving with the 2/9 toward Simemi Creek, its right flank in contact with the Australian left.[11]

The corvettes brought in the rest of the 2/10 Battalion from Porlock Harbor that night, and the *Japara* came into Oro Bay the same night with U.S. troops and cargo. Troop commander on the *Japara* was Col. Collin S. Myers, who upon arrival became Commander COSC, Oro Bay. The ship carried 750 tons of cargo. Also on board were additional port battalion troops and an advance echelon of the 43d U.S. Engineers, the unit which was to build the road between Oro Bay and Dobodura.

The *Japara* had brought in a number of Australian ponton barges for use in unloading operations. The barges were quickly lowered over the side, piled high with cargo,

and pushed to shore, where they were subsequently used as a floating dock. Unloading was accomplished in record time, and the *Japara* was out of harm's way before daylight.[12]

Early on 20 December, following a heavy artillery preparation, the 2/9 Battalion with four tanks attacked the enemy positions east of Strip Point. After a fight that lasted all day, the enemy opposition was overcome, and the 2/9 Battalion and units of the 3d Battalion, 128th Infantry, operating immediately to the south, began moving forward to the right bank of Simemi Creek. Company I, on the far left, ran into a sizable Japanese force before it reached the river bank. A heavy fire fight ensued, but the company, with the aid of Company C, 2/9 Battalion, on its right, cleared out the enemy pocket and pushed on to the bank of the creek. By the end of the day only a small finger of land, extending into the mouth of the creek, remained in enemy hands.

Thus far, the M3 tanks had performed well. West of Strip Point, however, the terrain turned very marshy, and the tanks, fourteen tons dead-weight and never noted for their tractive power, began to bog down. One had to be abandoned, and a second was mired so badly it could not be extricated until the following day when the attack on the Japanese in the finger at the mouth of the creek was resumed.

In the New Strip area the last pocket of Japanese resistance was mopped up on 20 December. The Clarkson and Beaver forces made contact early in the morning and by noon had succeeded in clearing out the last of the enemy bunkers in front of the bridge.

Fighting a skillful delaying action, Col-

---

[10] Msg, Adv NGF to NGF, Ser 3630, 18 Dec 42; Tel Conv, Col Bowen, G–3 Buna Force, to Lt Col G. A. Bertram, Adv NGF, Ser 3760, in 32d Div G–3 Jnl; Rpt, CG Buna Forces, pp. 74, 75, 76A; 32d Div Rpt of Arty, Papuan Campaign.

[11] Tel Msg, 18th Bde to 32d Div, Ser 3737, 19 Dec 42; Tel Msg, 32d Div to Adv NGF, Ser 3760, 20 Dec 42, in 32d Div G–3 Jnl; 1st Bn, 126th Inf, Jnl, Sers 723, 733, 19 Dec 42; 1st Bn, 128th Inf, Jnl, Sers 14, 15, 22, 19 Dec 42; Buna Forces Sitrep, G–3, 19 Dec 42; Rpt on Opns 18th Bde Gp at Cape Endaiadere and Giropa Point. Company K, 128th Infantry, had lost so many men by this time that it was attached as a platoon to Company I. Ltr, Col MacNab to Gen Ward, 7 Mar 51.

[12] Hist Port Det E, COSC, Buna; Interv with Col Moffatt, 30 Oct 49.

onel Yamamoto had by this time managed to get the bulk of his remaining troops, mostly from the *229th Infantry,* across the creek. They had made the crossing at two principal points. Those who had fought in the New Strip area used the bridge, and those who had survived the Duropa Plantation–Strip Point fighting forded the shallows at the mouth of the creek. Colonel Yamamoto took great pains to guard this crossing, for it was the only place along the entire length of the creek where troops could readily wade over. A Japanese strongpoint on a tiny island at the mouth of the creek was heavily reinforced, and emplacements sited to fire across the shallows were set up on the west bank of the creek to deal with any attempt by the Allies to cross at that point.[13]

Crossing the Creek

The Problem

It was not immediately clear how the Allies were to cross the creek. Tanks could not negotiate the shallows, and an attempt to have troops attack in that area would cost many lives. An assault across the bridge, which was 125 feet long and spanned not

only the creek but heavy swamp on either side of it, seemed the best solution. But this too presented difficulties since the Japanese had blown a large gap in the bridge and were covering it with several machine guns and forty or fifty riflemen.[14]

A patrol of the 1st Battalion, 128th Infantry, attempted to cross the bridge just before noon on 20 December. Intense fire drove it off before it could even reach the eastern end.[15] Later in the day, a few men of the Ammunition and Pioneer platoon of the 1st Battalion, 126th Infantry, under their commanding officer, 1st Lt. John E. Sweet, tried to put down a catwalk across the hole in the bridge, under cover of smoke shells from two 37-mm. guns. With two of his men, Sweet moved out in the face of the enemy fire and started laying the catwalk, only to find that it had been cut about six inches too short.[16]

Seeing the failure of the attempt to close the gap in the bridge, Colonel Martin at once proposed a second attempt, this time

---

[13] 1st Bn, 126th Inf, Jnl, Sers 749, 757, 760, 764, 765, 767, 20 Dec 42, Sers 785, 787, 788, 21 Dec 42; 3d Bn, 128th Inf, Jnl, 0857, 1315, 1747, 1817, 1205, 1210, 20 Dec 42; Buna Force G-3 Daily Periodic Rpt, 20 Dec 42; Rpt on Opns 18th Bde Gp at Cape Endaiadere and Giropa Point; *18th Army* Opns I, 21, 29; Ltr, Col MacNab to author, 18 Apr 50. There are no figures as to the number of men Colonel Yamamoto had left when he began crossing the creek. However, I Corps overlays identify all four companies of the *3d Battalion, 229th Infantry,* and *Battalion Headquarters* as being on the Old Strip, and the subsequent fighting on the strip would seem to indicate that Yamamoto had managed to get a substantial part of his command across the creek.

[14] 1st Bn, 126th Inf, Jnl, Sers 760, 764, 767, 768, 20 Dec 42, Sers 787, 788, 21 Dec 42; 3d Bn, 128th Inf, Jnl, 1315, 1330, 20 Dec 42, 0210, 21 Dec 42; Rpt on Opns 18th Bde Gp at Cape Endaiadere and Giropa Point; Hist 114th Engr Bn (C), Papuan Campaign.

[15] 128th Inf Jnl, 1150, 20 Dec 42. During the withdrawal, a member of the patrol was seriously wounded and fell directly in the enemy's line of fire. A second member of the patrol, Pvt. Steve W. Parks, turned back and braved the bullets to carry the wounded man to safety. Parks was later awarded the Distinguished Service Cross. The citation is in Hq USAFFE GO No. 36, 1 Jul 43.

[16] 1st Bn, 126th Inf, Jnl, Sers 772, 774, 20 Dec 42; 128th Inf Jnl, 1230, 1315, 1320, 1813, 20 Dec 42; Hist 114th Engr Bn (C), Papuan Campaign; Interv with Lt Col Clifton P. Hannum, 18 Jan 51. Hannum, then a lieutenant and Major Beaver's S-3, witnessed the abortive attempt to bridge the gap in the bridge. Sweet was later awarded the Distinguished Service Cross. The citation is in Hq USAFFE GO No. 32, 15 Jun 43.

SIMEMI CREEK AREA *west of the New Strip. Note swampy terrain and water-filled shell holes.*

with the aid of one of Brigadier Wootten's tanks. While the troops were laying the catwalk, Martin suggested, the tank would suddenly engage the enemy bunkers at the other end of the bridge and draw their fire. Brigadier Wootten had other plans for the tanks and the idea was dropped.[17]

Only one practicable alternative remained: to have troops cross the creek on foot and neutralize the enemy forces at the western end of the bridge when they got there. At best, this would be a difficult feat, since the creek, except at its mouth, was very deep, and the approaches to it were through

[17] Ltr, Col Martin to Gen Ward, 5 Mar 51.

heavy swamp, full of prickly, closely spaced sago palms eighteen to twenty feet high.[18]

Ordered by Colonel Martin to find a crossing, Major Beaver sent a patrol into the creek late that afternoon. The men tried crossing at a point just north of the bridge. Japanese fire almost blew them out of the water and forced them back to their own side of the creek. Beaver tried again late that night, this time picking a spot south of the bridge. Company B, 126th Infantry, was chosen to make the crossing, but its attempt also failed. The water was too deep and the enemy too alert. At dawn Colonel

[18] Hist 114th Engr Bn (C), Papuan Campaign; Interv with Col Teesdale-Smith, 10 Mar 50.

BRIDGE OVER SIMEMI CREEK. *New Strip in the background. (Photograph taken after bridge was repaired by the 114th Engineers.)*

Martin called the whole thing off. It was clear that there was no crossing to be found in the bridge area.[19]

The Australians Find a Crossing

Strong efforts to find a crossing were being made downstream. Brigadier Wootten had assigned Company C, 2/10 Battalion, to Colonel Cummings on the 19th, partly to carry out that task and partly to make up

---

[19] Tel Msg, Warren Force to Buna Force, Ser 3812, 21 Dec 42, in 32d Div G–3 Jnl; 1st Bn, 126th Inf, Jnl, Sers 765, 767, 782, 20 Dec 42, Sers 785, 787, 788, 793, 796, 810, 21 Dec 42; 128th Inf Jnl, 0210, 21 Dec 42; Rpt on Opns 18th Bde Gp at Cape Endaiadere and Giropa Point.

for the heavy casualties Cumming's battalion had suffered the day before. Wootten had also ordered Colonel MacNab to look for a crossing in his area, but his troops tried hard and failed. The 2/10 Battalion, less the company with the 2/9 Battalion, moved up to the front at noon on 20 December, and its commander, Lt. Col. James G. Dobbs, immediately gave his troops the task of finding a way across. At 1500 the following day, after the most difficult kind of reconnoitering during which the men were sometimes forced to move in water up to their necks, a patrol of Company A, 2/10 Battalion, found a practicable crossing at a stream bend about 400 yards north of the

SWAMP EAST OF THE BRIDGE *between New and Old Strips. (Photograph taken on 26 December 1942.)*

bridge. Moving cautiously through the creek and the treacherous swamp beyond, the troops emerged on the other side at a point just below the lower (or eastern) end of the Old Strip, and there they consolidated. Except for a few strands of barbed wire, no signs of the Japanese were found in the area.[20]

[20] 3d Bn, 128th Inf, Jnl, 1315, 1330, 20 Dec 42, 0823, 1000, 1510, 1900, 2300, 21 Dec 42; Rpt on Opns 18th Bde Gp at Cape Endaiadere and Giropa Point; Interv with Col Teesdale-Smith, 10 Mar 50. Colonel Teesdale-Smith, then intelligence officer of the 2/10 Battalion and a captain, was among the first to make the crossing.

The rest of the battalion began crossing at once, using as a marker a galvanized iron hut on legs, which the Japanese had apparently used as a control tower. By the following morning most of the battalion's riflemen were across the creek. Except for a few mortar shells that fell in the crossing area from time to time, they met no opposition from the Japanese.

The crossing by the 2/10 Battalion continued through 22 December. By then the 2/9 Battalion, the attached company of the 2/10 Battalion, and four tanks had finished the task of clearing the Japanese from the east bank of Simemi Creek. Several enemy machine guns were still active on the island at the mouth of the creek, but, since they were difficult to get at and had only a nuisance value, Brigadier Wootten decided to ignore them for the moment.[21]

The Repair of the Bridge

Final preparations for repair of the bridge were completed during the 22d. The engineer platoon charged with its repair—the 3d Platoon, Company C, 114th Engineer Battalion—had finished gathering and hauling the needed timbers and other materials to the bridge site. The timbers, mostly coconut logs, were to be put in place, and the bridge secured for the passage next day not only of troops but also of tanks. Major Beaver's troops and those of Major Clarkson were standing by ready to cross, and four tanks of the 2/6 Armored Regiment were moving toward the bridge to be in position to cross as soon as it was repaired.[22]

By first light the next morning, 23 December, the 2/10 Battalion, except for Company C which was still with the 2/9 Battalion, was across the creek. Colonel Dobbs, whose troops were now to the rear of the Japanese in the bridge area, at once sent two companies southward to clear them out. Appar-

ently warned in time of the Australian approach, most of the Japanese pulled out of their bunkers before the Australians arrived. By noon the few that were found had been killed, and the Australians were able to report "the bridge and 300 yards north neutralized." The bridge was still under fire from emplacements on the southwest side of the Old Strip, but these could be dealt with later when the repairs to the bridge were completed, and the Americans and the tanks crossed.[23]

The platoon of the 114th Engineer Battalion had begun working on the bridge as soon as it turned light. Despite heavy enemy fire, first from the bunkers at the other end of the bridge and then from the Old Strip when the Australians cleared the enemy out of the bridge area, the work proceeded speedily and efficiently under the able direction of 2d Lt. James G. Doughtie, the engineer officer in charge. Cool and imperturbable under fire, Doughtie was everywhere, directing, encouraging, and steadying his men. By noon the repair of the bridge was well advanced. Half an hour later Doughtie had a catwalk down, and in ten minutes the leading platoon of Company B, 126th Infantry was on the other side of the creek. It was quickly joined by the rest of the battalion. The 1st Battalion 128th Infantry, was to cross later in the afternoon; the four tanks, as soon as the bridge was completed and found capable of bearing their weight. The 2/9 Battalion and the 3d Battalion, 128th Infantry, were to remain in position and hold the coast. It was understood that Com-

---

[21] Msgs, 18th Bde to 32d Div, Ser 3914, 22 Dec 42, Ser 4030, 23 Dec 42, in 32d Div G–3 Jnl; Rpt on Opns 18th Bde Gp at Cape Endaiadere and Giropa Point; Interv with Col Teesdale-Smith, 10 Mar 50.

[22] Tel Msg, Gen Eichelberger to 2d Lt James G. Doughtie, 114th Engr Bn, Ser 3759, 20 Dec 42; Tel Msg, Lt Winkler to Col Howe, Ser 4031, 23 Dec 42. Both in 32d Div G–3 Jnl. 1st Bn, 126th Inf, Jnl, Sers 840, 858, 23 Dec 42; 1st Bn, 128th Inf, Jnl, Ser 4, 23 Dec 42; Hist 114th Engr Bn (C), Papuan Campaign. The bridge is described in the engineer history as having been of "pile bent construction" requiring the replacement of "one bent, new bracing, and decking throughout its entire length."

[23] 1st Bn, 126th Inf, Jnl, Sers 840, 845, 23 Dec 42; Ltr, Gen Eichelberger to Gen Sutherland, 24 Dec 42, copy in OCMH files; Interv with Col Teesdale-Smith, 10 Mar 50; Hist 114th Engr Bn (C), Papuan Campaign; Rpt on Opns 18th Bde Gp at Cape Endaiadere and Giropa Point.

pany C, 2/10 Battalion, would be returned to Colonel Dobbs' command when the mop-up east of the creek was completed.[24]

The Fight for the Old Strip

The Situation on the Eve of the Attack

As soon as they crossed the bridge, Major Beaver's troops began moving toward the strip. Enemy fire from flat-trajectory weapons and mortars was heavy, and progress was slow. Colonel Martin joined the troops at 1530. They tied in on Colonel Dobbs' left at 1745 and took up a position along the southern edge of the strip. The last drift-pin was driven into the bridge an hour later, and Major Clarkson's battalion was across the creek and had moved up on Major Beaver's left by 1920. The plan now was to have the tanks cross the bridge and join the infantry early the next morning. Upon their arrival, the 2/10 Battalion, with the two American battalions in support would attack straight up the strip. The force would jump off from a line drawn perpendicularly across the strip from the galvanized iron hut or control tower where the Australians had established their first bridgehead on 21 December.

Colonel Yamamoto had had time to man the prepared positions in the Old Strip area and appeared to be holding them in consid-

erable strength. The area was a warren of trenches and bunkers. The Japanese had dug several lines of trenches across the width of the strip and their trench system extended from the swamp to Simemi Creek. There were bunkers in the dispersal bays north of the strip, in the area south of it on the strip itself, and in a grove of coconut trees off its northwestern end.

Nor did Yamamoto lack weapons. He was well provided with machine guns and mortars, and he had at least two 75-mm. guns, two 37-mm. guns, and, at the northwest end of the strip, several 25-mm. dual and triple pompoms—a type of multiple barrel automatic cannon much favored by the Japanese. Near the northwest end of the strip and several hundred yards to the southeast he had in position several 3-inch naval guns in triangular pattern connecting with bunkers and fire trenches. With still another 3-inch gun north of the strip, Yamamoto was in an excellent position to sweep the strip with fire provided his ammunition held out.

It had been known for some time that the Japanese had 3-inch guns on the strip, but the artillery believed that they had been knocked out. The fact that the air force had not received any antiaircraft fire from the strip for several days seemed to confirm this belief. To be on the safe side, it was decided to commit only three of the four tanks. The fourth tank would be kept in reserve until the situation clarified itself.[25]

---

[24] Tel Msg, Brig Wootten to 32d Div, Ser 1014, 23 Dec 42, in 32d Div G–3 Jnl; 1st Bn, 126th Inf, Jnl, Sers 840, 849, 850, 854, 856, 858, 861, 23 Dec 42; 1st Bn, 128th Inf, Jnl, Sers 2, 4, 5, 18, 26, 34, 23 Dec 42; 3d Bn, 128th Inf, Jnl, 1135, 1430, 23 Dec 42; 128th Inf Jnl, 0915, 1304, 1450, 1530, 1615, 1723, 23 Dec 42; Rpt on Opns 18th Bde Gp at Cape Endaiadere and Giropa Point. Doughtie was later awarded the Distinguished Service Cross. The citation is in GHQ SWPA GO No. 4, 10 Jan 43.

[25] Tel Msg, Maj Ziebell to Col Howe, Ser 4023, 23 Dec 42; Tel Msgs, Lt Winkler to Col Howe, Sers 4031, 4051, 23 Dec 42; Tel Msg, Lt Hannum to Col Howe, Ser 4033, 23 Dec 42; 3d Bn, 128th Inf, Jnl, 1135, 1430, 23 Dec 42; 128th Inf, Jnl, 1450, 1512, 1723, 1745, 1910, 1920, 23 Dec 42; 32d Div Sitrep, No. 120, 23 Dec 42; Rpt on Opns 18th Bde Gp at Cape Endaiadere and Giropa Point; Interv with Col Teesdale-Smith, 3 Mar 50.

At dusk of the same night, 23 December, two armed Japanese motor-torpedo-type boats—which may have been the same boats that brought General Oda to Giruwa the night before—rounded Cape Endaiadere and sank the *Eva*, an ammunition-laden barge at Hariko, as it was being unloaded by the troops of the Service Company, 128th Infantry. The two Japanese boats then machine-gunned the beach at 2250 with .50-caliber tracer ammunition. The Service Company answered with small arms fire from positions just off the beach, but the boats got away before heavier weapons could be brought to bear upon them. Taking no chances, Colonel MacNab at once began strengthening his beach defenses lest the Japanese try something of the same sort again.[26]

While the Japanese were shooting up Hariko with little result, further down the coast at Oro Bay the *Bantam*, a K.P.M. ship of the same class as the *Karsik* and the *Japara*, came in with two more M3 tanks, and 420 tons of supplies. The ship was quickly unloaded and returned safely to Porlock Harbor before daybreak.[27]

The Attack Opens

Early on 24 December the tanks crossed the bridge and moved up to the Australian area on the northern side of the strip from which the main attack was to be launched. After an artillery preparation with smoke, the troops jumped off at 0950 from a line of departure approximately 200 yards up the strip. The tanks and two companies of the 2/10 Battalion were on the far right,

one company of the 2/10th was on the strip itself, the 1st Battalion, 126th Infantry, under Major Beaver, was immediately to the left, and the 1st Battalion, 128th Infantry, under Major Clarkson, was on the far left. Beaver's mission was to protect the Australian flank; Clarkson's to comb the swamp for Japanese and destroy them.

During the first hour the attack went well, but it ran into serious trouble just before 1100. The dual purpose 3-inch guns opened up on the thinly armored M3's and quickly knocked out two of them. The third tank went the way of the first two when it turned over in a shell hole a few moments later and was rendered useless by enemy shellfire.

With the tanks out of the way, the enemy guns and pompoms began firing down the center of the strip. Company A, 2/10 Battalion, had to move from its position on the strip in the center of the Allied line to the Australian side of the runway. For the next two days no Allied troops could use the strip itself.

Forward observers located one of the enemy's 3-inch guns on the left shortly after it had fired on the tanks, and the artillery promptly knocked it out. Because the observers were unable to locate the remaining guns, Brigadier Wootten decided to commit no more M3's to the attack until he knew definitely that all the enemy's 3-inch guns were out of action. Without tanks the attack moved slowly against enemy machine gun, mortar, and pompom fire.

A light rain during the afternoon further retarded the fighting. Urged on by Colonel Martin and Major Beaver the latter's troops pulled abreast of Colonel Dobb's force by nightfall. The Allies had gained about 450 yards in the day's operations and were about 650 yards up the strip on either side of it. On the far left Major Clarkson's troops had

[26] 3d Bn, 128th Inf, Jnl, 2250, 2320, 23 Dec 42; 128th Inf Jnl, 2225, 23 Dec 42, 1105, 24 Dec 42.
[27] Interv with Col Moffatt, 30 Oct 49; Hist Port Det E, COSC, Buna.

met no Japanese, but heavy swamp crippled their movement early in the action. They were then ordered out of the swamp and put in line along the southern edge of the strip, immediately to the rear of Major Beaver's force. Clarkson's men were to follow Beaver's, mop up behind them, and ultimately take their place in the front line.[28]

On the east side of the creek relative tranquillity had descended. The last vestiges of Japanese opposition were overcome on 23 December, though not before Colonel Cummings had been wounded in the breast and arm by a shell fragment from the other side of the creek. Colonel MacNab, whose CP was just below Cape Endaiadere, took command of the sector. Because Company C, 2/10 Battalion, was no longer needed in the area, it was detached from the 2/9 Battalion and ordered across the creek to rejoin its parent battalion.

The 2/9 Battalion and the 3d Battalion, 128th Infantry, improved their Cape Endaiadere defensive positions. The Australian battalion occupied the east bank of the creek and the shore from its mouth to Strip Point; the American battalion took over defense of the coast line from Strip Point around Cape Endaiadere and south to Boreo. With no fighting to do for the moment, the troops in this sector took time to clean up. Those along the coast were permitted to swim. Some of the soldiers even

began amusing themselves by catching fish, using Mills bombs to subdue them.[29]

The Fighting on the Old Strip

On the Old Strip, meanwhile, there was the bitterest kind of fighting. Attempts by patrols of the 2/10 Battalion to take ground from the Japanese during the night were unsuccessful. The enemy troops in foxholes forward of the bunkers were too alert and determined.

At 0515, Christmas morning, Company C, 2/10 Battalion, reverted to Colonel Dobbs' command and, on Brigadier Wootten's order, was sent to the far left of the

---

[28] Tel Msg, Capt R. J. C. O'Loan, ALO, to G-2, 32d Div, Ser 4120, 24 Dec 42; Msg, 18th Bde to 32d Div, Ser 4136, 24 Dec 42; Tel Msg, Brig Wootten to 32d Div, Ser 4137, 24 Dec 42. All in 32d Div G-3 Jnl. 1st Bn, 126th Inf, Jnl, Sers 879, 882, 883, 884, 891, 893, 895, 24 Dec 42; 1st Bn, 128th Inf, Jnl, Sers 1, 4, 8, 10, 11, 14, 16, 19, 24 Dec 42; 128th Inf Jnl, 0920, 1130, 1225, 1331, 1352, 1405, 1407, 24 Dec 42; 32d Div Sitrep, No. 122, 24 Dec 42; Rpt on Opns 18th Bde Gp at Cape Endaiadere and Giropa Point.

[29] Msg, 18th Bde to 32d Div, Ser 4136, 24 Dec 42; Tel Msg, Capt Khail, S-2, 3d Bn, 128th Inf, to G-2, 32d Div, Ser 4195, 25 Dec 42; 3d Bn, 128th Inf, Jnl, 1738, 2135, 24 Dec 42, 1430, 25 Dec 42; Rpt on Opns 18th Bde Gp at Cape Endaiadere and Giropa Point. Colonel MacNab tells two stories illustrative of the comradeship between his troops and the Australians. On the afternoon of the 24th Colonel MacNab visited the 2/9 Battalion, which was then under his command. On his way back he wished a couple of Australian soldiers a Merry Christmas. Thereupon, in Colonel MacNab's words, "An older corporal replied, 'I sie Colonel, where shall I hang me bloody sock?' I replied, 'well away from your foxhole—the Nip may play Santa Claus.' Sure enough, the Jap bombed us . . . that night. The next morning when I was going up this same group [intercepted] me. The same corporal reported, 'Colonel, you were too right, see where I hung my sock?' He pointed to a sock hanging on a bush over a new bomb crater about fifty yards away. We had a good laugh. I am reasonably sure the sock was hung there that morning."

The American troops had gotten their Red Cross Christmas boxes on time, but, as Colonel MacNab tells it, "the Aussie boxes, furnished by a volunteer ladies organization in Australia did not arrive. Our men were very solicitous to share their delicacies with the Australians. Later, when the Australian boxes arrived, the woods were full of raucous Aussies looking for 'that Yank bastard who gave me most of his Christmas.' During both occasions, I never saw a man eating his stuff alone." Ltr, Col MacNab to author, 18 Apr 50.

AMERICAN AND AUSTRALIAN CASUALTIES, *to be moved to the rear by natives,* *wait on litters in the Cape Endaiadere area.*

Allied line. Its instructions were to move through the swamp and threaten the enemy's right flank while the Americans and the rest of the 2/10 Battalion continued their efforts to push forward frontally. Brigadier Wootten also ordered two platoons of the 2/9 Battalion to the bridge, where they were to be available when needed for action on the strip.[30]

The Allies attacked at 0700 after a ten-minute artillery smoke barrage. Throughout the day Company C, 2/10 Battalion, made very slow progress in the swamp, and the American and Australian companies farther to the right had little success against the well-manned enemy bunker and trench positions. Company C, 126th Infantry, Major Beaver's leading unit, had scarcely left the line of departure when it was stopped by a hidden enemy strongpoint somewhere to its front, and Major Clarkson's battalion on Beaver's left had the same experience.

Colonel Martin, who was still in the front lines lending a hand personally in the conduct of operations, at once ordered a patrol of the 1st Battalion, 128th Infantry, into the swamp with orders to come in on the enemy's rear. The patrol returned with a report that the swamp was impenetrable. Convinced that troops could get through the swamp if they had the will to do so, Martin asked Clarkson for an officer with "guts" to take the assignment. Clarkson picked 2d Lt. George J. Hess of Company A for the task. Hess left the battalion CP about 0900 with fifteen men. Swinging to the left, he and his men worked their way through the swamp,

sometimes sinking waist deep in mud. Colonel Martin went about halfway with them, gave his final instructions, and returned to the American line. By early afternoon, the patrol had cut its way around the Japanese right flank and established itself on dry ground on the Japanese left rear without being observed by the enemy.

Colonel Martin spent the rest of the afternoon in the front lines trying to get troops through to the position held by Hess but was not immediately able to do so.[31] Heavy fighting developed all along the front, but there was little change in dispositions except for the flanking movements on the left. By late afternoon the Allied line was a shallow V, with the runway still open and the point of the V east of the area where Yamamoto had most of his 3-inch guns emplaced.

The Japanese had meanwhile discovered that there were American troops in the dense undergrowth on their right rear. They started sending mortar and small arms fire in that direction, but were slow in organizing a force to drive them out. Company C, 128th Infantry, under 1st Lt. Donald A. Foss reached Hess' position before nightfall. Except for intermittent area fire, the unit met no opposition from the enemy. Colonel Martin, who was with the incoming troops, ordered Foss to launch an attack the next morning on the nearest enemy

---

[30] Tel Msg, 18th Bde to 32d Div, Sers 4218, 4245, 25 Dec 42; Rpt on Opns 18th Bde Gp at Cape Endaiadere and Giropa Point.

[31] Martin spent as much time as he possibly could in the front lines. At one point in the day's fighting he climbed a tall tree that overlooked the Japanese positions in order to get a better bead on enemy troops lurking in the tall grass immediately to his front. From this vantage point he killed several of them with a rifle. He was later awarded the Distinguished Service Cross. The citation, which covers the period 3 December 1942 to 5 January 1943, is in GHQ SWPA GO No. 2, 30 Mar 43.

emplacement about 100 yards to the northeast.[32]

By the following morning, 26 December, after a very difficult march through the swamp, Company C, 2/10 Battalion, was in position on Lieutenant Foss's left. After a ten-minute artillery preparation, the two companies attacked the enemy from the flank at 0702, in concert with the troops attacking from the front. After close-in fighting, two Japanese guns were taken, one by the American company and the other by the Australian company. The guns, installed on concrete bases, were sited so that they could command all approaches from south and east. Each was surrounded by a 4½-foot-high circular earth embankment, so overgrown with grass that it was impossible to distinguish it from the surrounding kunai grass except at very close range. Bunkers and flanking trenches connected with it, but the enemy guns had run out of ammunition.

Because the left-flank operations gave more promise of success than frontal assault up the strip, Brigadier Wootten decided to reinforce his left. Company A, 2/10 Battalion, crossed the runway and took up a position in the left center of the line on Major Beaver's right, leaving Companies D and B to deal with the opposition to the right of the strip. Company C, 2/10 Battalion, thereupon flanked farther to the left

to deal with an especially formidable concentration of bunkers on up the strip. Company A, 2/10 Battalion, and the two American battalions with it, were left to overcome the strong enemy positions south of the strip.[33]

Except for this movement on the left flank, little change occurred on the front. The center of the line was still about 650 yards up the strip. The line itself had the appearance of a sickle: the Australian troops on the far right formed the handle; the Australian and American troops in the center and left center, the blade; and Company C, 2/10 Battalion, on the far left and thrusting northward, the hook.[34]

Late that night, while the Japanese on the Old Strip unsuccessfully counterattacked Company D, 2/10 Battalion, on the far right, the *Japara* came into Oro Bay for the second time. It brought in another troop of M3 tanks, the remainder of the men who were to operate the port, and the rest of the engineer troops who were to build the Oro Bay–Dobodura road. Unloading proceeded rapidly, and the ship left before daylight.[35]

[32] Tel Msg, Maj Beaver to Col Howe, Ser 4208, 25 Dec 42; Tel Msg, Maj Ziebell to 32d Div, Ser 4217, 25 Dec 42; Tel Msg, Brig Wootten to 32d Div, Sers 4281, 4245, 25 Dec 42; Tel Msg, Lt Winkler to 32d Div, Ser 4274, 25 Dec 42; 1st Bn, 126th Inf, Jnl, Sers 908, 909, 910, 912, 918, 25 Dec 42; 1st Bn, 128th Inf, Jnl, Sers 1, 3 through 7, 25 Dec 42; 128th Inf Jnl, 0800, 0950, 1012, 1108, 1230, 1440, 1902, 25 Dec 42; 32d Div Sitrep, No. 124, 25 Dec 42; Rpt on Opns 18th Bde Gp at Cape Endaiadere and Giropa Point; Ltr, Gen Martin to Gen Ward, 6 Mar 51. Hess was later awarded the Silver Star. The citation is in GO No. 37, Hq USAFFE, 12 May 44.

[33] Msgs, Lt Winkler to 32d Div, Sers 4269, 4321, 26 Dec 42; Tel Msgs, Maj Beaver to Col Howe, Sers 4288, 4306, 26 Dec 42; Msgs, 18th Bde to 32d Div, Sers 4300, 4307, 4325, 4333, 26 Dec 42; 1st Bn, 126th Inf, Jnl, Sers 923, 924, 925, 935, 944, 26 Dec 42; 32d Div Sitrep, No. 126, 26 Dec 42; Rpt on Opns 18th Bde Gp at Cape Endaiadere and Giropa Point.

[34] Msg, 18th Bde to 32d Div, Sers 4307, 4333, 26 Dec 42; Tel Msg, Lt Winkler to 32d Div, Ser 4321, 26 Dec. 42; 32d Div Sitrep, No. 126, 26 Dec 42; Rpt on Opns 18th Bde Gp at Cape Endaiadere and Giropa Point.

[35] Msg, NGF to 32d Div, Ser 4275, 25 Dec 42; Msg, Col Collin S. Myers to Col Howe, Ser 4484, 28 Dec 42, in 32d Div G-3 Jnl; Hist Port Det E, COSC, Buna; Interv with Col Moffatt, 30 Oct 49; Rpt on Opns 18th Bde Gp at Cape Endaiadere and Giropa Point.

After an unsuccessful raid on Dobodura early on 26 December, fifty-four Rabaul-based Japanese aircraft, staging through Lae, raided Buna again the following morning. The raid netted little. Allied losses on the ground were three killed and eight wounded, but the enemy was intercepted by twenty fighter planes of the Fifth Air Force and lost fourteen aircraft. The Allies lost one P–38.[36]

The 3.7-inch howitzers of the O'Hare Troop below the bridge ran out of ammunition on 26 December and could take no further part in the fighting. However, a 25-pounder of the Hall Troop, emplaced early on 27 December at the southeast end of the strip, more than made up for the loss, for this weapon finally broke the Japanese defense of the Old Strip. The gun had excellent observation of the enemy positions on the strip, bringing observed direct fire upon them. Using armor-piercing projectiles with supercharge at about a 1,000-yard range, the 25-pounder not only knocked out one of the remaining enemy pompoms but, with the 4.5 howitzers of the Stokes Troop, forced enemy troops out of their bunkers by fire alone––a feat that only the 105-mm. howitzer had previously been able to accomplish.[37]

---

[36] 1st Bn, 128th Inf, Jnl, Ser 1, 26 Dec 42, Ser 23, 27 Dec 42; Allied Air Forces Opns Rpt, 27 Dec 42; G–3 Opns Rpt, No. 264, 27 Dec 42; 32d Div Sitrep, No. 128, 27 Dec 42; 18th Army Opns I, 31. These two raids marked the debut in the fighting of the 11th Air Regiment, the first Japanese army air force unit to reach Rabaul.

[37] Msg, 18th Bde to 32d Div, Ser 4433, 28 Dec 42; Msg, NGF to 32d Div, Ser 4536, 28 Dec 42; 32d Div Hist of Arty, Papuan Campaign; Rpt on Opns 18th Bde Gp at Cape Endaiadere and Giropa Point. Another expedient used by the troop commander was to leave in place the small brass protecting caps that came with the fuses, thereby giving the projectiles a slightly delayed action which increased their effectiveness still further. Ltr, Col MacNab to Gen Ward, 7 Mar 51.

Clearing the Strip

Thus by 27 December the fight for the strip was in its last stages. Allied artillery fire and pressure on his right flank forced Colonel Yamamoto to begin withdrawing to the plantation area around Giropa Point, though a desperately fighting rear guard tried to keep the fact of the withdrawal from Warren Force as long as possible. The Australian companies moving on the Japanese positions at the head of the strip from either flank met appreciably less resistance. In the center the Australian and American troops who, up to this time, had been meeting the most fanatical Japanese opposition noted a similar weakening.[38]

The advance went slowly during the morning of the 27th but accelerated during the afternoon as the 25-pounder took its toll of enemy positions. At 1615 Colonel Martin reported that the enemy was on the run. Progress thereafter was rapid. Companies A and D, 2/10 Battalion, and Major Clarkson's battalion, aided by elements of Company C, 2/10 Battalion, had things their own way that afternoon. They squeezed the Japanese out of the last line of trenches across the strip and cleaned out a large bunker as well as an even larger dispersal bay to the rear of the trenches. At nightfall the troops in the center—Company A, 2/10 Battalion, and Company A, 128th Infantry—were working on a main enemy bunker behind the dispersal bay—the last organized enemy position on the runway.[39]

---

[38] 1st Bn, 126th Inf, Jnl, Sers 978, 981, 27 Dec 42; 128th Inf Jnl, 1446, 1750, 27 Dec 42; 18th Army Opns I, 27; Rpt on Opns 18th Bde Gp at Cape Endaiadere and Giropa Point.

[39] Tel Msg, Maj Ziebell to Col Howe, Ser 4404, 27 Dec 42; 1st Bn, 126th Inf, Jnl, Sers 982, 984, 27 Dec 42; 1st Bn, 128th Inf, Jnl, Sers 18, 19, 27 Dec 42; 128th Inf Jnl, 1225, 1446, 1615, 1621, 1750, 2000, 27 Dec 42; Rpt on Opns 18th Bde Gp at Cape Endaiadere and Giropa Point.

The line was rearranged during the evening. The company from the 2/9 Battalion, in brigade reserve, was ordered across the bridge to be available on the strip in case of need. Stretched across the upper third of the strip, the troops were now advancing on an 850-yard front that extended from the edge of the swamp on the left to Simemi Creek on the right. The men were abreast—Australian and American units alternating. From left to right the line was held by Company C, 2/10 Battalion, Company B, 128th Infantry, and Companies D and B, 2/10 Battalion, with the other tired and depleted units in close support.[40]

That night the Australian freighter *Mulcra* came in to Oro Bay with a troop of M3 tanks and 400 tons of cargo. As it unloaded and got away, the Japanese in the dispersal bays at the head of the strip again counterattacked Company D, 2/10 Battalion, on the far right. The Japanese fought hard but, as had been the case the night before, were repulsed with heavy loss.[41]

Although Brigadier Wootten still had four tanks on hand, and seven more were on their way from Oro Bay, he no longer needed tanks for the reduction of the Old Strip. Heavy fire of all kinds was still coming from the dispersal bays at the head of the strip, and still heavier fire from the enemy positions in the Government Plantation immediately to the rear, but in the area through which the Old Strip ran and on the strip itself, there was little but sporadic rifle fire. Organized resistance in the area collapsed

by noon of 28 December and the troops began mopping up.

It was a bloody business. The remaining Japanese, cornered and hopeless, fought to the end. Hand grenades tossed into their holes would be tossed back, and the Allied troops always had to be on the alert for frenzied suicide rushes with sword or bayonet. Some of the bypassed enemy troops had taken refuge in trees. In at least one instance, three Japanese were shot out of a single tree. In another case half a dozen Japanese troops were cut down carrying M1's and wearing American helmets and fatigues. A few Japanese on the far left tried to escape by taking to the swamp; they were picked off one by one by troops ordered by Major Clarkson into the swamp for that purpose.[42]

The Allied troops stabilized their line by noon, 28 December, with Company C, 2/10 Battalion, on the far left, within 200 or 300 yards of the belt of coconut palms forward of the point. The other companies made only slight gains as they came under extremely heavy fire from the dispersal bays and enemy emplacements among the trees of the plantation. A further attack late in the afternoon by Company C, 2/10 Battalion, though supported by artillery, failed. As evening fell, the Japanese began counterattacking. They struck against the center of the line at 1940, while Company C, 128th Infantry, was in the process of relieving Company A, 2/10 Battalion. Joint action by both companies repulsed the attack, and the Australian company took up a new position on the left.

---

[40] 1st Bn, 128th Inf, Jnl, Ser 28, 27 Dec 42; 128th Inf Jnl, 1446, 1621, 1854, 1930, 27 Dec 42; Tel Msg, Col Martin to 32d Div, Ser 4454, 28 Dec 42; 32d Div Sitrep, No. 129, 28 Dec 42.

[41] Msg, Col Myers to Col Howe, Ser 4484, 28 Dec 42; Tel Msg, 18th Bde to 32d Div, Ser 4446, 28 Dec 42; Hist Port Det E, COSC, Buna; Interv with Col Moffatt, 30 Oct 49.

[42] Msg, NGF to 32d Div, Ser 4537, 28 Dec 42; 1st Bn, 128th Inf, Jnl, Sers 4, 16, 36, 48, 49, 51, 59, 60, 65, 73, 76, 28 Dec 42; Rpt on Opns 18th Bde Gp at Cape Endaiadere and Giropa Point; F. Tillman Durdin, *The New York Times*, 1 Jan 43.

WARREN FORCE MEN AFTER THE ATTACK *on Cape Endaiadere, 22 December.*

At 2300 the Japanese in the dispersal bays at the head of the strip unleashed their third blow in three nights at Company D, 2/10 Battalion, on the far right. Once again they were repulsed. About twenty Japanese, who had apparently been caught inside the Allied lines, managed to reach the command post of Company C, 128th Infantry, at 0400 the next morning without being detected. They attacked in the dark with grenades and bayonets, some yelling, "Medic, Medic," the call used by American wounded. Several men who were asleep in the command post area were bayoneted by the enemy, and other Americans, mostly without weapons, were killed in hand-to-hand encounters. By the time the Japanese were driven off they had killed fifteen men

and wounded twelve, including Lieutenant Foss, Company C's fifth commander in the five weeks since the fighting began. Since Foss was the company's only remaining officer, 1st Lt. Sheldon M. Dannelly, commanding officer of Company A, 128th Infantry, which was on C's right, took command of Company C. Only five of the raiding Japanese were killed.[43]

The enemy's counterattacks had gained him no ground. The Old Strip was firmly

---

[43] Tel Msgs, 18th Bde to 32d Div, Ser 4446, 28 Dec 42, Ser 4527, 29 Dec 42; Tel Msg, Capt Khail to Maj Hawkins, Ser 4533, 29 Dec 42; 1st Bn, 126th Inf, Jnl, Ser 1001, 28 Dec 42; 1st Bn, 128th Inf, Jnl, Sers 70, 72, 75, 28 Dec 42, Sers 3, 13, 29 Dec 42; 128th Inf Jnl, 1405, 1914, 2135, 28 Dec 42; 32d Div Sitrep, No. 132, 29 Dec 42; Rpt on Opns 18th Bde Gp at Cape Endaiadere and Giropa Point; Durdin, *The New York Times,* 1 Jan 43.

in Allied hands. Warren Force was within easy striking distance of Giropa Point, the last enemy stronghold on the Warren front. The next step would be to take the point and clear the area between it and the west bank of Simemi Creek. This step—a climactic one which would put the entire shore between Giropa Point and Cape Endaiadere in Allied hands—Brigadier Wootten was to lose no time in taking.

CHAPTER XV

Urbana Force Closes on the Mission

On 16 December, in compliance with orders of Advance New Guinea Force, Colonel Tomlinson, then in command of Urbana Force, ordered a platoon of Company F, 126th Infantry, led by Lieutenant Schwartz to Tarakena, a point about one mile northwest of Siwori Village. The move was taken to prevent the Japanese in the Giruwa area from reinforcing their hard-pressed brethren east of the river. Buna Force issued orders the next day for the capture of the island and Triangle. The island was to be taken on 18 December, the day of the tank attack on the Warren front; the Triangle, one day later. An element of the 127th Infantry would take the island; what was left of the 126th Infantry, the Triangle.[1] (*Map 14*)

The Search for an Axis of Attack

The Situation: 18 December

Capture of Buna Village had narrowed down the ground still held by the Japanese on the Urbana front, but the main objective, Buna Mission, was still in Japanese hands, and seemingly as hard to get at as ever. The problem was to find a practicable axis of

---

[1] NGF OI No. 53, 16 Dec 42; 2d Bn, 126th Inf, Jnl, 1335, 16 Dec 42; Buna Force FO No. 3, 17 Dec 42; Tel Msg, Urbana Force to Col Howe, Ser 3522, 18 Dec 42.

attack, and this the projected operations were designed to provide. Seizure of the island would not only make it possible to bring the mission under close-in fire but might supply a jumping-off point for a direct attack upon it from the south. The Triangle, in turn, would furnish an excellent line of departure for an advance through Government Gardens to the sea, a necessary preliminary to an attack on the mission from the southeast.

The fresh 127th Infantry would be available in its entirety for these operations. The 3d Battalion was already in the line and had been for several days. After consolidating at Ango, the 2d Battalion had just begun moving to the front. Companies E and F were on their way there, and Headquarters Company and Companies G and H were moving forward. The 1st Battalion was still being flown in and would come forward as soon as its air movement was completed.

With the 127th Infantry moving up steadily, Colonel Tomlinson reshuffled his line. Company I, 127th Infantry, took the place of the 2d Battalion, 128th Infantry, in the area between the island and the Coconut Grove. The battalion, less the mortar platoon of Company H, which remained behind, was ordered to Simemi for a well-earned rest. The 2d Battalion, 126th Infantry, took over in the Coconut Grove and moved troops into position above and

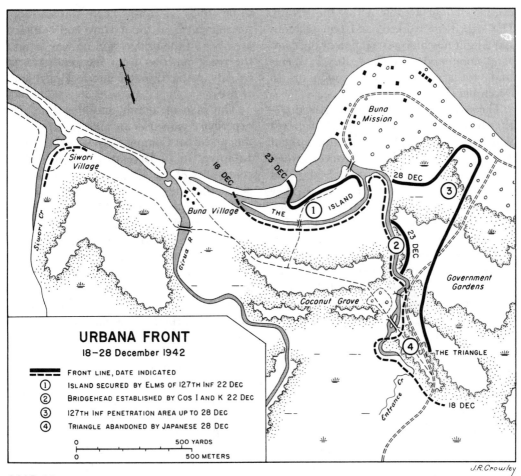

URBANA FRONT
18–28 December 1942

▬▬▬ FRONT LINE, DATE INDICATED
① ISLAND SECURED BY ELMS OF 127TH INF 22 DEC
② BRIDGEHEAD ESTABLISHED BY COS I AND K 22 DEC
③ 127TH INF PENETRATION AREA UP TO 28 DEC
④ TRIANGLE ABANDONED BY JAPANESE 28 DEC

J.R. Crowley

MAP 14

below the Triangle. Companies E and F, 127th Infantry, meanwhile reached the front and went into reserve. A mixed platoon of the 126th Infantry under 1st Lt. Alfred Kirchenbauer began moving to Siwori Village to replace the 128th Infantry troops there, and the Schwartz patrol of 15 men started out for Tarakena.[2]

---

[2] 2d Bn, 126th Inf, Jnl, 1245, 1800, 2200, 18 Dec 42; Tel Msg, Col Bowen to Cols Grose and Tomlinson, Ser 3634, 19 Dec 42; 2d Bn, 128th Inf, Jnl, 0700, 1400, 19 Dec 42.

The First Try at the Island

On 17 December Colonel Tomlinson gave Company L, 127th Infantry, orders to take the island the next morning. This was to be no easy task, for the footbridge to the island had been destroyed and the creek was a tidal stream, unfordable even at low tide. The troops had no bridge-building equipment, and the distance from one bank to the other was too great to be bridged by felling trees. One alternative remained: to have swimmers drag a cable across the stream. This expedient worked, and two platoons and a light machine gun section of the company, commanded by Capt. Roy F. Wentland, got across just before noon on 18 December.

The two platoons, joined shortly thereafter by a third, moved cautiously forward along the eastern half of the island without meeting any opposition. However, when they started moving toward the bridge that connected the island with the mission, they ran into very heavy fire from concealed enemy positions. In the fire fight that followed, five men, including Captain Wentland, where killed and six were wounded. The heavy enemy fire continued, and the troops, under the impression that they were heavily outnumbered, pulled back to the mainland that night, leaving the island still in enemy hands.[3]

The 126th Infantry
Attacks the Triangle

The attack on the island had failed. The attack on the Triangle was next. This narrow, jungle-covered tongue of land set in the midst of a swamp, and covering the only good track to Buna Mission, was in effect a natural fortress. Improving upon nature, the Japanese had hidden bunkers and fire trenches on either arm of the Triangle and in the track junction itself. To try to storm the junction from the south meant taking prohibitive losses. To try taking it from the north by advancing into its mouth by way of the bridge over Entrance Creek was likely

to be almost as costly. There was no room for maneuver in the narrow and confined area east of the bridge, and no way to take the track junction from the south except by advancing through interlocking bands of fire.

The plan of assault, profiting from the experience gained in an abortive attack on the place by Companies E and G, 128th Infantry, on 17 December, called for two companies of the 126th Infantry to attack across the bridge from the Coconut Grove, and a third company to block the position from the south. The jump-off would be preceded by an air strike on the mission and a preparation on the Triangle itself by Colonel McCreary's seventeen 81-mm. mortars, which were in battery about 300 yards south of the bridge to the island. Since the Triangle was narrow and inaccessible, neither air nor artillery would be used in direct support of the troops lest they be hit by friendly fire.

Some 100 men from Companies E and G, plus the attached weapons crews of Company H, were to mount the attack. They crossed the bridge over Entrance Creek and moved into the bridgehead area at the mouth of the Triangle at 2200, 18 December. Shortly thereafter, the thirty-six men of Company F, the holding force, went into position in the area below the track junction.[4]

Beginning at 0650 the following morning, nine B–25's dropped 100-pound and 500-pound demolitions on the mission. They were followed at 0715 by thirteen A–20's which bombed and strafed the coastal track between the mission and Giropa Point. The

[3] Tel Msg, Col Howe to Buna Force, Ser 3553, 18 Dec 42; Tel Msg, Col Howe to Col Bowen, Ser 3568, 18 Dec 42; Tel Msg, Capt Oliver O. Dixon, S–3 Urbana Force, to G–3 Buna Force, Ser 3580, 18 Dec 42; Tel Msg, Col Tomlinson to Col Bowen, Ser 3582, 18 Dec 42; 2d Bn, 128th Inf, Jnl, 1150, 18 Dec 42; 127th Inf Tact Hist, 18, 19 Dec 42.

[4] Buna Force No. 3, 17 Dec 42; Tel Msgs, Col Howe to Col Bowen, Sers 3568, 3647, 19 Dec 42; Tel Msg, Capt Dixon to Col Bradley, Ser 3631, 19 Dec 42; Tel Msg, Col Bowen to Col Tomlinson, Ser 3634, 19 Dec 42.

A–20's dropped 475 twenty-pound parachute and cluster fragmentation bombs and fired more than 21,000 rounds of .30-caliber and .50-caliber ammunition during the attack. They probably did the enemy a great deal of damage, but their accuracy left much to be desired. A stick of four bombs was dropped within fifty yards of a bivouac area occupied by the 127th Infantry, and a chaplain visiting the troops at Buna Village was hit by bullets meant for the Japanese at Giropa Point.[5]

At 0730 Colonel McCreary's mortars, which were so disposed that they could drop their shells on any point in the Triangle, began firing their preparation. Fifteen minutes later Companies E and G attacked straight south under cover of a rolling mortar barrage. The barrage did the attacking troops little good. They were stopped by enemy crossfire just after they left the line of departure. In the forefront of the attack, Captain Boice did everything he could to get things moving again, but the crossfire proved impenetrable. Every attempt by the troops to slip through it only added to the toll of casualties. At 0945 Boice was mortally wounded by mortar fire and died shortly afterward. He was succeeded as battalion commander by Capt. John J. Sullivan, who had just come up from the rear with a handful of replacements.[6]

On General Eichelberger's orders the mortars laid down a concentration of white phosphorous smoke in the Triangle at 1415, and the attack was resumed. The troops gained a few yards with the help of the smoke, but were again stopped by enemy crossfire. At 1600 a third attack was mounted. This time the mortars fired a 700-round preparation—some forty rounds per mortar—but the result was the same; the men found it impossible to break through the murderous enemy crossfire. When night fell and the utterly spent troops dug in, they had lost forty killed and wounded out of the 107 men who had begun the attack.[7]

Obviously in no condition to continue the attack, the two companies were relieved early the following morning by Company E, 127th Infantry, and went into reserve with the rest of the 2d Battalion, 126th Infantry. Except for Company F, which continued for the time being at the tip of the Triangle, the troops in the Siwori Village–Tarakena area, the whole battalion, now 240 men all told, was in reserve. The main burden of operations henceforward would be on the 127th Infantry.[8]

The 127th Infantry Takes Over the Attack

The attack on the Japanese positions in the Triangle was resumed on 20 December. The plan was prepared the night before. Since it provided for an artillery prepara-

---

[5] Tel Msg, Col Bradley to Col Howe, Ser 3771, 20 Dec 42; Allied Air Forces Opns Rpts, 19 Dec 42, 20 Dec 42, in G–3 Jnl, GHQ SWPA; Ltr, Gen Eichelberger to Gen Sutherland, 22 Dec 42, copy in OCMH files.

[6] Tel Msg, Urbana Force to 32d Div, Ser 3700, 19 Dec 42; 2d Bn, 126th Inf, Jnl, 0715, 0745, 0945, 1250, 19 Dec 42; 126th Inf, Jnl, Ser 20, 19 Dec 42; Ltr, Gen Eichelberger to Gen Sutherland, 19 Dec 42, copy in OCMH files; Rpt, CG Buna Forces, p. 29. Captain Boice, who was at the very head of his troops when he met his death, was posthumously awarded the Distinguished Service Cross. The citation is in GHQ SWPA GO No. 3, 6 Jan 43.

[7] Tel Msg, Urbana Force to 32d Div, Ser 3700, 19 Dec 42; 2d Bn, 126th Inf, Jnl, 0715, 0730, 0745, 0945, 1250, 1600, 19 Dec 42; 126th Inf Jnl, Ser 35, 19 Dec 42; Ltr, Gen Eichelberger to Gen Sutherland, 19 Dec 42; 126th Inf CT AAR, Papuan Campaign.

[8] 32d Div Sitrep, No. 111, 19 Dec 42; 2d Bn, 126th Inf, Jnl, 0200, 0700, 1700, 20 Dec 42; 126th Inf Jnl, Ser 20, 20 Dec 42; 127th Inf Tact Hist, 20 Dec 42.

tion, safeguards were taken to ensure that the artillery did not hit the attacking troops. Company E, 127th Infantry, which was to deliver the blow was ordered into the Coconut Grove at daybreak. Its instructions were to remain there under cover until ordered across the creek, over which a second footbridge had been built a short distance from the first. Company F, 126th Infantry, still in place below the Triangle, was ordered to pull back about 300 yards in order to permit the artillery to use the track junction as its registration point.

After registering on the junction, the Manning battery of 25-pounders and the 105-mm. howitzer, both using smoke, were to fire on the enemy positions in the track junction for five minutes at the rate of two rounds per gun per minute. A second five-minute preparation was to follow at a somewhat faster rate. As soon as the registration was over and the first five-minute preparation began, Company E, covered by smoke from the artillery and the mortars, would dash across the two bridges, form up on the east bank of the stream at a position south of the original crossing, and wait out the artillery fire there. When the artillery fire ceased, the mortars, firing a salvo every minute, were to place a concentration of forty rounds of white phosphorus on the target. When the first smoke shell from the mortars went down, Company E was to rush forward, get within close range of the bunkers under cover of the smoke, and clear out the enemy with hand grenades.[9]

The artillery registered in at 0845. As soon as it began firing its first preparation, the troops dashed across the creek "in a cloud of smoke." Though General Eichelberger confessed to General Sutherland that night that he had been very much worried that some of them might be hit, "as this is very thick country and our troops are in close to the junction," not a man was hit by the artillery. Just as everything seemed to be going well, some "trigger-happy" machine gunners on the west bank of the creek, to the rear of the line of departure, spoiled everything by opening fire prematurely. This unauthorized firing from the rear threw the inexperienced troops along the line of departure into great confusion. When the troops finally attacked at 1000, they found the enemy alert and ready for them. In an hour and a half of action Company E was unable to get within even grenade distance of the enemy.[10]

The attack was called off at 1130. Capt. James L. Alford, the company commander, thereupon proposed a new attempt. Alford's proposal was that a reinforced platoon, led by 1st Lt. Paul Whittaker, with 2d Lt. Donald W. Feury as second-in-command, infiltrate the low-lying area in the center of the Triangle with the help of fire from the rest of the company. When the platoon was as close as it could get to the enemy bunkers, it would charge and clean them out with hand grenades. Colonel Tomlinson sanctioned the plan, but General Eichelberger, who was present, vetoed it immediately as reckless and likely only to cause useless casualties. On Captain Alford's assurance that the two lieutenants and the men who were to make the attack were confident of its success, the general let the attack proceed.[11]

---

[9] Tel Msg, Col Bowen to Col Tomlinson, Ser 3711, 19 Dec 42; 126th Inf Jnl, Ser 36, 19 Dec 42.

[10] 126th Inf Jnl, Ser 2, 20 Dec 42; Ltr, Gen Eichelberger to Gen Sutherland, 20 Dec 42, copy in OCMH files; 127th Inf Tact Hist, 20 Dec 42.

[11] 127th Inf Tact Hist, 20 Dec 42.

127TH REGIMENTAL HEADQUARTERS COMMAND POST. *Colonel Grose, seated, studies plans for the next attack.*

General Eichelberger's original misgivings were quickly justified. With S.Sgt. John F. Rehak, Jr., leading the way, the platoon managed to get within grenade distance of the bunkers and charged. The Japanese had meanwhile pulled out of the bunkers apparently in anticipation of just such a move. They caught the platoon with enfilading fire and nearly wiped it out with a few bursts of their automatic weapons. Seven men, including Lieutenant Feury, Lieutenant Whittaker, and Sergeant Rehak, were killed, and twenty were wounded. The two attacks had gained nothing, and they had cost Company E thirty-nine casualties—better than 40 per-cent of its strength—in its first day of combat.[12]

Colonel Tomlinson called off the attack at 1335, and a badly rattled Company E spent the next few hours getting its dead and wounded out of the Triangle—a perilous business because the Japanese, taking full advantage of the situation, were laying down heavy fire on the rescue parties. When the

[12] 126th Inf Jnl, Ser 13, 20 Dec 42; Ltr, Gen Eichelberger to Gen Sutherland, 20 Dec 42; 127th Inf Tact Hist, 20 Dec 42. Rehak was posthumously awarded the Distinguished Service Cross, and the two lieutenants, the Silver Star. Rehak's citation is in GHQ SWPA GO No. 4, 10 Jan 43; Feury's and Whittaker's in GO No. 14, 30 Jan 43.

job was done, the company, less outposts in the mouth of the Triangle, withdrew to the Coconut Grove where the men were made as comfortable as the circumstances would permit.[13]

At 1410 Colonel Tomlinson, who was physically exhausted, suggested to Colonel Grose that he take over command of Urbana Force inasmuch as the 127th Infantry now made up the great bulk of the troops in the line. Grose's reply was that it was not within his authority to assume command. He told Tomlinson that he could take over only if ordered to do so by General Eichelberger. At 1522 Tomlinson called Eichelberger and asked to be relieved of command of Urbana Force. Realizing that Tomlinson had been under strain for too long a time, General Eichelberger relieved him at once and ordered Colonel Grose to take his place. Grose assumed command of Urbana Force at 1700, and all elements of the 127th Infantry not already there were immediately ordered to the front.[14]

The Attack Moves North

The Plan To Bypass the Triangle

It had become perfectly clear by this time that the reduction of the Triangle would be an extremely difficult task. Not only did the troops have no room to maneuver, but the enemy's fire permitted not a single man

to get through alive. It became a question therefore of whether it might not be wiser to break off the fight and try to find a better line of departure elsewhere for the projected drive across the gardens to the coast.[15]

General Eichelberger had made such a suggestion to General Herring on 19 December. Herring saw the point and authorized Eichelberger to bypass the Triangle if the next day's attack upon it also failed.[16]

When the attempt on the 20th did fail, General Eichelberger began immediately to plan for a new axis of attack across the gardens. As he explained the situation to General Sutherland that night: "General Herring is very anxious for me to take the track junction, and I am most willing, but the enemy is . . . strong there and is able to reinforce his position at will. I am going to pour in artillery on him . . . and I am going to continue that tomorrow morning. Then I am going to find a weak spot across Government Gardens."[17]

The next morning General Eichelberger ordered Company E, 127th Infantry, to contain the Triangle from the north and Company F, 126th Infantry, to continue blocking it from the south. He then tried a ruse to lead the Japanese into believing that another infantry attack on the Triangle was imminent. To that end, the program of artillery and mortar fire executed the day before was repeated exactly. There were the same five-minute intervals of artillery fire and the same salvos of smoke from the mor-

---

[13] 126th Inf Jnl, Sers 8, 9, 13, 18, 20 Dec 42; 127th Inf Tact Hist, 20 Dec 42.

[14] 126th Inf Jnl, Sers 17, 21, 20 Dec 42; 127th Inf Jnl, 1700, 20 Dec 42; 127th Inf Tact Hist, 20 Dec 42. Though no longer commander of Urbana Force, Tomlinson continued as commander of the 126th Infantry. Reporting the change to General Sutherland that night, General Eichelberger wrote, "I am going to bring Tomlinson in here for a day or so to rest him up." Ltr, Gen Eichelberger to Gen Sutherland, 20 Dec 42.

[15] Ltr, Gen Eichelberger to Gen Sutherland, 20 Dec 42; Interv with Gen Eichelberger, 26 Apr 50.

[16] Tel Msg, Brig Hopkins to Col Bowen, Scr 3791, 20 Dec 42; Msg, Adv NGF to CG Buna Force, Scr 3808, 20 Dec 42, in 32d Div G-3 Jnl; Ltr, Gen Eichelberger to Gen MacArthur, 26 Dec 42, copy in OCMH files.

[17] Ltr, Gen Eichelberger to Gen Sutherland, 20 Dec 42.

tars. Company E dashed across the bridge at exactly the same time and in exactly the same way as the day before, and, as the first smoke shell went down, the men fixed bayonets as if to attack, and cheered loudly for two minutes. The Japanese had pulled out of their bunkers as usual and were in their trenches braced for the expected infantry charge. This time, however, there was no attack. Instead, the infantrymen held their positions and the artillery and mortars poured everything they had into the smoke-enveloped track junction.[18]

General Eichelberger reported that evening that he was sure he had killed a large number of the enemy with his "phony attack of artillery and smoke followed by the fixing of bayonets and a cheer." But he had to admit that despite all the artillery and mortar fire that had been laid down on the Japanese positions in the Triangle, and the heavy losses that had been sustained in trying to take it, "our attempts to get the road junction have all failed."[19] The failure to take the Triangle was no great setback since General Eichelberger had already decided upon a more promising axis of attack across Entrance Creek in the area north of the Coconut Grove and the Triangle.

The Crossing of Entrance Creek

Where to establish the initial bridgehead on the other side of the creek was the problem. After studying available maps, General Eichelberger concluded that the best place for it lay in a fringe of woods just off the northwest end of the gardens where there seemed to be better cover and less enemy fire than elsewhere. He therefore issued orders late on the night of 20–21 December that the bridgehead be established there the next day.[20]

Colonel Grose chose Companies I and K for the task and early the next morning began to make his dispositions for the crossing. He ordered Company L to move from its position below the island to the right of Company I, which was already deployed in the area immediately north of the Coconut Grove. Company K, which had previously been to the rear of Company I, was ordered to go in on Company L's left and to extend along the west bank of the creek almost to its mouth. The move brought Company K directly across the creek from the prescribed bridgehead area and in position to cross.[21]

From the beginning it was recognized that Company K's crossing would be more difficult than Company I's. The swift tidal stream that had to be crossed was less than twenty-five yards wide in Company I's sector, and the engineers had only that morning finished building a small footbridge there improvised from a few saplings and a captured enemy boat anchored in the center of the stream. In Company K's sector, on the other hand, the creek was at least fifty yards wide at the point of crossing and seven or eight feet deep. Colonel Grose went down to Company K's sector to look things over and did not like what he saw. Thinking that there was a possibility that Company K, crossing in Company I's sector, might be

---

[18] Tel Msg, Col Bowen to Col Grose, Ser 3793, 20 Dec 42; Ltr, Gen Eichelberger to Gen Sutherland, 21 Dec 42, copy in OCMH files; 127th Inf Tact Hist, 22 Dec 42.

[19] Ltr, Gen Eichelberger to Gen Sutherland, 21 Dec 42.

[20] Ltr, Gen Eichelberger to Gen Sutherland, 20 Dec 42; 127th Inf Jnl, 0800, 21 Dec 42; Interv with Col Grose, 15 Nov 50; Ltr, Gen Eichelberger to author, 15 Jan 52.

[21] 127th Inf Jnl, 0800, 21 Dec 42; 127th Inf Tact Hist, 21 Dec 42; Ltr, Col Grose to Gen Ward, 26 Feb 51; Ltr, [Capt] Alfred E. Meyer to author, 13 Mar 51.

able to work its way under the bank to the bridgehead area and establish itself there, he telephoned General Eichelberger and asked for more time. In the heat of the moment, he apparently failed to make clear to the general the reason for his request. In any event, Grose recalls, Eichelberger was impatient of any suggestion for postponement. He refused to give him more time, and Grose at once called in Capt. Alfred E. Meyer, the Company K commander, and ordered him to proceed with the crossing.[22]

At 1600 that afternoon Meyer sent troops into the creek to see if it could be forded. Not only could they find no crossing; they were nearly "blown out of the water" by enemy fire from the other side of the stream. Greatly perturbed at being ordered to make what he considered a suicidal crossing, Meyer pleaded with Grose to let him cross over the bridge in Company I's area. If that permission was impossible to grant, Meyer requested that he be allowed to cross at night with the aid of ropes, pontons, or whatever equipment was available. Colonel Grose, who had already asked for more time without being able to get it, told Meyer that he was to start crossing immediately even if the men had to swim across.[23]

Captain Meyer went back to his company and made several attempts to get men across in daylight, but the enemy fire from the other side of the creek proved too heavy. By nightfall the company finally located a heavy rope, and the attempts to cross were renewed.

Unbidden, 1st Lt. Edward M. Greene, Jr., picked up one end of the rope, and with several enlisted men started swimming for the opposite shore. Greene was killed almost instantly by enemy fire, and his body was swept away by the current. A few minutes later one of the enlisted men lost his hold on the rope and was swept away. One of the swimmers finally got the rope across the river, and the rest of the night was spent in getting the heavily weighted troops over in the face of the continuing enemy fire. By about 0200 forty-seven men were on the other side of the creek, and when daylight came the total was seventy-five. Company K suffered fifty-four casualties that night—six killed or drowned in the crossing, and eight killed and forty wounded in the fighting at the bridgehead area.

Early on the morning of 22 December, while Company K engaged the enemy frontally in the bridgehead area and Company M's heavy weapons covered it with fire from the west bank, Company I, under Capt. Michael F. Ustruck, crossed on the footbridge. Finding, as Colonel Grose had surmised, that there was a safe and easy approach to the bridgehead under the bank, the company went into position on Company K's right by 1235 without losing a man.[24]

Bodies of troops of Company K who had been drowned in the crossing on the night of 21–22 December were to be seen the next day bobbing in the stream,[25] but the cross-

---

[22] Col Grose's Diary, 21 Dec 42; Intervs with Col Grose, 15 Nov 50, 1 Feb 51; Ltr, Gen Eichelberger to author, 15 Jan 52.

[23] Ltr, Capt Meyer to author, 13 Mar 51; Interv with Col Grose, 18 Nov 50; Ltr, Col Grose to Gen Ward, 2 Feb 51.

[24] 127th Inf Jnl, 2130, 21 Dec 42, 0630, 22 Dec 42; 127th Inf Tact Hist, 22 Dec 42; Tel Conv, Col Bowen with Col Grose, Ser 3911, 22 Dec 42; Col Grose's Diary, 22 Dec 42; Interv with Col Grose, 15 Nov 50; Ltr, Meyer to author, 13 Mar 51.

[25] Ltr, Maj Robert P. McCampbell to author, 18 Jan 51; "A Case History," Time, 4 Dec 44, p. 68.

ing had been accomplished, and there was a strong bridgehead on the other side of the creek. It had been a difficult and frustrating operation. As General Eichelberger put it two days later, "When we put K Company across an unfordable stream in the dark against heavy fire the other night we did something that would be a Leavenworth nightmare." [26]

The Subsidiary Operations

The Situation on the Left Flank

While these operations were progressing, there had been a flurry of activity on the left flank. On 18 and 19 December the Schwartz patrol had clashed with enemy patrols west of Siwori Village. On 20 December, upon the insistence of General Herring that the left flank be better secured, Schwartz was reinforced with another twenty men of the 2d Battalion, 126th Infantry, which was in reserve at the time below Buna Village. Schwartz's force, now numbering thirty-five, began moving on its objective, Tarakena, a small village on the west bank of Konombi Creek, about a mile northwest of Siwori Village.

The men reached Tarakena early on 20 December, only to be thrown out of the place by a superior Japanese force. Col. Frank S. Bowen, Jr., G–3, Buna Force, immediately ordered forward another mixed unit of thirty-two men from the 2d Battalion, 126th Infantry. Schwartz got the reinforcements late in the afternoon and moved on Tarakena at dusk with his sixty-

seven men to stage, as he said, "a heckling party" for the enemy's benefit.[27]

The patrol succeeded in retaking a corner of the village during the night, but the enemy, much stronger than had been anticipated, counterattacked and forced it back across the creek. The patrol suffered fifteen casualties during the encounter, including Schwartz who was wounded. Command of the patrol fell to 1st Lt. James R. Griffith. He was wounded the same afternoon, and 1st Lt. Louis A. Chagnon of Headquarters Company, 127th Infantry, took over, bringing with him members of Headquarters Company and the Service Company. Since he was obviously outnumbered, Chagnon took up a defensive position a few hundred yards southeast of Tarakena and awaited the enemy's next move.[28]

The Capture of the Island

By 22 December the engineers, meeting no enemy interference, had repaired the south bridge between the mainland and the island. That afternoon, as soon as the bridge was down, a patrol of Company L, 127th Infantry, moved over it and crossed the island without opposition. As the men approached the north bridge between the island and the mission, they began receiving heavy fire. Two platoons of Company F

---

[26] Ltr, Gen Eichelberger to Gen Sutherland, 24 Dec 42, copy in OCMH files. The reference is to the Command and General Staff College at Fort Leavenworth, Kansas.

[27] Tel Msg, Urbana Force to G–3 32d Div, Ser 3577, 18 Dec 42; Tel Msg, Col Howe to Col Bowen, Ser 3647, 19 Dec 42; Tel Msg, Brig R. N. L. Hopkins, CofS, Adv NGF, to Col Bowen, Ser 3791, 20 Dec 42; Msg, Adv NGF to Buna Force, Ser 3808, 20 Dec 42; Tel Msg, Urbana Force to G–3 Buna Force, Ser 3837, 20 Dec 42; Tel Msg, Col Grose to Col Howe, Ser 3833, 21 Dec 42; 127th Inf Jnl, 0815, 1550, 21 Dec 42.

[28] 2d Bn, 126th Inf, Jnl, 22 Dec 42; 127th Inf Jnl, 0800, 0940, 0945, 1805, 2010, 2020, 22 Dec 42, 0800, 23 Dec 42; 127th Inf Tact Hist, 22 Dec 42, 23 Dec 42.

FOOTBRIDGE OVER ENTRANCE CREEK *to Musita Island.*

and a machine gun section of Company M, under Lt. Col. Benjamin R. Farrar, then serving as S–3 of the 127th Infantry, moved in to meet the situation. By 1115 the next morning, the last Japanese to be found on the island had been overcome, and Company F, its work done, pulled back to the mainland.

Company H thereupon moved onto the island, bringing with it, in addition to its heavy weapons, a 37-mm. gun "with plenty of canister." A platoon of Company E, 127th Infantry, on the village spit (the small peninsula east of Buna Village) also had a 37-mm. gun firing canister. From their separate points of vantage the two units began bring-

ing down close-in harassing fire on the mission and continued to do so day and night.[29]

Now that the island had fallen, General Eichelberger had a new axis of advance for an attack on the mission. All that remained was to get troops across the north bridge between the island and the mission and to establish a beachhead on the opposite shore. "Maybe I can get a toehold there," General Eichelberger mused in a letter to General Sutherland. "It might prove easier," he

[29] Tel Msg, Col Bradley to Col Howe, Sers 3942, 3945, 22 Dec 42; Tel Msg, Col Howe to Col Grose, Ser 3949, 22 Dec 42; 127th Inf Tact Hist, 22 Dec 42; 127th Inf Jnl, 1015, 23 Dec 42.

added, "than where I now plan to go across."[30]

The Corridor to the Coast

The Attack in the Gardens

On the evening of 23 December, with the bridgehead at the northwest end of Government Gardens firmly secured, General Eichelberger ordered Colonel Grose to attack in an easterly direction across the gardens the following morning. Grose had five companies of the 127th Infantry for the attack. The plan called for the 3d Battalion rifle units to launch the attack, supported by the heavy weapons crews of Company M disposed along Entrance Creek to the rear of the line of departure, with some of the men in trees. Company G would be in reserve and would go into action upon orders from Colonel Grose.

There would be no direct air support because the troops were too close to the enemy. The artillery at Ango and Colonel McCreary's massed mortars south of the island were to lay down a heavy preparation before the troops jumped off, and were to follow it with a rolling barrage when the advance got under way. The troops on the island and on the village spit would make a maximum effort to saturate the mission with fire, in order to deceive the enemy as to the direction of the attack and to prevent the reinforcement of his positions in the gardens.[31]

The troops on the island and on the vil-lage spit laid down heavy fire on the mission during the night, as did the 25-pounders and the 105-mm. howitzer at Ango. The Japanese, in turn, kept the bridgehead under continual harassment, using mountain guns, heavy mortars, and antiaircraft guns depressed for flat-trajectory fire. All along the line of departure the companies remained on the alert throughout the night, but the Japanese made no move either to counterattack or to infiltrate the American lines.

At dawn of 24 December Company G crossed the creek, and the heavy weapons crew of Company M took up supporting positions along the bank of the stream. Company L replaced Company I on the left, Company I extended to the right, and Company K, shaken by its experience of the night before, went into reserve. Shortly thereafter, the two assault companies, I and L, each reinforced by weapons crews of Company M, moved into position along the line of departure. At 0600 the artillery and mortars began firing their preparation, and Company H on the island opened up on the mission with all its weapons. Covered by the rolling barrage, the troops jumped off fifteen minutes later on a 400-yard front.[32]

The drive across the gardens to the sea had about 800 yards to go. Neglected and overgrown with thick clumps of shoulder-high kunai grass, the gardens extended for some 400 yards to a swamp about 100 yards wide. On the other side of the swamp, looking out on the sea, was a coconut plantation, about 300 yards across, through which ran

---

[30] Ltr, Gen Eichelberger to Gen Sutherland, 22 Dec 42.

[31] Ltrs, Gen Eichelberger to Gen MacArthur, 23 Dec 42, 24 Dec 42, copies in OCMH files; 127th Inf Tact Hist, 23 Dec 42, 24 Dec 42; 127th Inf Jnl, 0956, 24 Dec 42; Ltr, Col Grose to Gen Ward, 26 Feb 51.

[32] 127th Inf Tact Hist, 23 Dec 42, 24 Dec 42; 127th Inf Jnl, 0956, 24 Dec 42; G–3 Sitrep Buna Force, 23 Dec 42; 32d Div Sitrep No. 121, 24 Dec 42; Ltrs, Gen Eichelberger to Gen MacArthur, 24 Dec 42, 25 Dec 42, copies in OCMH files; Rpt, CG Buna Forces, p. 31.

the coastal track between Buna Mission and Giropa Point.

Captain Yasuda had the area well prepared for defense and could cover nearly every foot of it with both observed and unobserved fire. The track through the gardens was covered by bunkers, and on either side of it, echeloned in depth to the rear and hidden by the kunai grass, were numerous individual foxholes and firing pits, most of them with overhead cover. In the surrounding swamp, north and east of the gardens, were strong bunker positions, and even stronger fortifications were to be found in the plantation and along the shore.[33]

For an attacking force, the gardens would have presented great difficulties even had there been no bunkers. One who was there recalls the situation in these words:

There was very little cover on the eastward side of Entrance Creek which forced troops to be heavily bunched during the staging period of an attack. The gardens themselves were very flat, covered by a substantial growth of Kunai grass, and accordingly provided excellent cover for the Japanese as well as a good field of fire. The surrounding swamp areas were infested with snipers in trees. All of which made operations across the Government Gardens a very difficult maneuver.[34]

As the two companies left the line of departure and began moving through the kunai grass they were met by heavy fire and both were held up. The fire was particularly heavy on Company I's front. The company cleaned out an isolated enemy bunker just forward of the line of departure, but its attempts to infiltrate and knock out a main Japanese strongpoint immediately to the rear met with no success whatever. Making

full use of the many hidden positions at their disposal, the Japanese successfully countered the unit's every attempt to move forward.[35]

The fighting was bitter and at close quarters. While the company was pinned down in front of the strongpoint, its 1st sergeant, Elmer J. Burr, saw an enemy grenade strike close to Captain Ustruck, who was out in front with his men. The sergeant threw himself on the grenade and smothered the explosion with his body. Burr was posthumously awarded the Medal of Honor—the first man to receive the award during the campaign.[36]

Though Colonel Grose had a temporary forward CP close to the line of departure—so close in fact that Colonel Farrar was wounded that morning by small arms fire while in the CP area—he could not see why Company I was not moving forward. Maj. Harold M. Hootman, the regimental S–4, who was in the CP with him, asked permission to go to Company I and try to find out what was happening. Grose recalls that he was "a bit flabbergasted" at the request, "because it seemed to be the desire of so many to find a good reason for going to the rear," but he gave Hootman permission to go and asked him to report his findings to him when he got back. That was the last time he saw the man alive. Hootman's body

---

[33] 32d Div Overlay, 24 Dec 42, in 32d Div Overlays, Papuan Campaign; Buna Defense Plan, Japanese, in Rpt, CG Buna Forces; Interv with General Eichelberger, 26 Apr 50; Ltr, Col Gordon B. Rogers to author, 26 Jun 50.

[34] Ltr, Maj McCampbell to author, 26 Aug 50.

[35] G–3 Sitrep, Buna Force, 23–24 Dec; Tel Msg, Urbana Force to G–3 Buna Force, Ser 4112, 24 Dec 42; 127th Inf Tact Hist, 24 Dec 42.

[36] WD GO No. 66, 11 Oct 43. On the same day, 24 December 1942, another member of the company, Pfc. Albert L. Fisher, who had been evacuated for treatment of his wounds to a point just behind the front line, saw two men of his unit lying wounded in an area swept by enemy fire. Disregarding his wounds and the continuing enemy fire, Fisher crawled into the open and dragged both men to safety. He was later awarded the Distinguished Service Cross. The citation is in Hq USAFFE GO No. 36, 1 Jul 43.

JAPANESE-BUILT BRIDGE *to Buna Mission over Entrance Creek.*

was later recovered, rifle in hand, not far from a Japanese bunker under circumstances which suggested that he fell while trying to take it singlehanded.[37]

Hootman had scarcely left the CP when news came back that Company I had suffered heavy casualties and become disorganized. Colonel Grose finally went out to the company himself and what he saw confirmed the news. He ordered the unit to the rear to reorganize and, at 0950, sent in

Company G in its place. Within the hour, Company G reported that the enemy had been cleared out of a three-bunker strongpoint which had previously held up the advance. Despite this promising start, Company G did not get much farther that day. Setting up his command post in the most forward of the captured bunkers, the company commander, Capt. William H. Dames, continued with the task of rooting the enemy out of his remaining bunker positions. Under an unusually aggressive commander, the fresh company cut through to the track and straddled it but, try as it

[37] 127th Inf Jnl, 0610, 24 Dec 42; Col Grose's Diary, 24 Dec 42; Ltr, Col Grose to Gen Ward, 26 Feb 51.

would, could not move forward immediately because of the intense fire from the enemy's hidden bunker positions.[38]

The real disappointment of the day, however, came on the far left, where Company L was to have made the main penetration. Under 1st Lt. Marcelles P. Fahres, Captain Wentland's successor, Company L was given all the aid that was available. The automatic weapons of Company M along Entrance Creek fired heavily in its support, as did the massed 81-mm. mortars south of the island, first under Colonel McCreary, and when McCreary was wounded that day, under Col. Horace Harding, General Eichelberger's artillery officer who was acting as division artillery commander. Nevertheless, the company, after making small initial gains, did not move forward.[39]

Aware of the situation, Colonel Grose at 1028 ordered a platoon of twenty men from Company A to cross over to the mission from the island by way of the north bridge and hold there as long as possible. The Japanese were so busy in the gardens that the troops actually got across the bridge, which though rickety was still standing. Unopposed at first, the platoon was soon set upon by the Japanese, who killed eight of its members and forced the rest back across the bridge.[40]

The diversion appears to have succeeded better than was at first realized. Captain Yasuda's troops by this time were spread thin, and he was apparently forced to transfer troops from the strongpoint at the northwest end of the gardens to the mission in order to meet the new threat there. Feeling the pressure upon it ease, Company L's left platoon, under 2d Lts. Fred W. Matz and Charles A. Middendorf, began pushing ahead. Meeting little opposition, the platoon started racing forward alone through the tall grass, unnoticed by the rest of the company. The company commander did not see the men go and did not miss them until some time later. Within a short while, the platoon was through the gardens and on the outskirts of the Coconut Plantation. There the men ran into two well-manned enemy bunk-

---

[38] Tel Msgs, Col Bradley to Col Howe, Ser No. 4088, 24 Dec 42, Ser 4090, 24 Dec 42, Ser 4093, 24 Dec 42, Ser 4099, 24 Dec 42; 127th Inf Jnl, 0950, 24 Dec 42; 127th Inf Tact Hist, 24 Dec 42. Eichelberger, *Our Jungle Road to Tokyo*, p. 42. Actually it was a sergeant from Company I, Sgt. Francis J. Vondracek, with the help of members of Company G, who cleared out the strongpoint. When Company G took over from Company I, Vondracek, an acting platoon leader of Company I, remained behind at his own request. Covered by rifle fire from Company G, he knocked out the three bunkers in quick succession by flinging hand grenades through their firing apertures. Vondracek was later awarded the Distinguished Service Cross. The citation is in Hq USAFFE GO No. 34, 21 Jun 43.

[39] Rpt, CG Buna Forces, p. 31; 127th Inf Tact Hist, 24 Dec 42. Colonel McCreary directed the fire of the mortars personally most of the day from a coconut tree about fifty yards from the enemy lines—the only good observation post he could find. Though wounded in the back by a shell fragment, he strapped himself in his tree and continued to direct the mortars until he lapsed into unconsciousness from loss of blood and had to be evacuated. Colonel Harding, who was at the front inspecting the artillery, thereupon took over direction of the mortar fire using the same tree Colonel McCreary had just vacated. Both colonels were later awarded the Distinguished Service Cross. McCreary's citation is in GHQ SWPA GO No. 2, 2 Jan 43; Harding's, in GO No. 4, 10 Jan 43.

[40] 127th Inf Jnl, 1028, 1430, 1442, 24 Dec 42; Interv with Col Grose, 15 Nov 50; Ltr, Col Grose to Gen Ward, 26 Feb 51. Neither Colonel Grose nor General Eichelberger knew of his presence, but Brig. Gen. Spencer B. Akin, General MacArthur's signal officer, was on the island for a few minutes during the forenoon. Before he left, he saw American troops walking erect in the mission area. Shortly thereafter, General Eichelberger began receiving congratulations on having taken the mission. Exceedingly wroth, Eichelberger not only refused to accept the congratulations but demanded an immediate explanation of the matter from Colonel Grose, who, until he learned that General Akin had been present on the island, was at a loss to understand what General Eichelberger was talking about.

ers which stood directly in the way of their advance. Sgt. Kenneth E. Gruennert, in the lead, undertook to knock them out. Covered by fire from the rest of the platoon, he crawled forward alone against the first bunker and killed everyone in it by throwing grenades through one of its firing slits. Although severely wounded in the shoulder while doing so, Gruennert refused to return to the rear. He bandaged the wound himself and moved out against the second bunker. Hurling his grenades with great precision despite his bad shoulder, Gruennert forced the enemy out of the second bunker as well but was himself shot down by an enemy sniper. Gruennert was posthumously awarded the Medal of Honor—the second to be conferred on a 127th Infantry soldier for the day's action.[41]

Completely out of touch with its company and the rest of Urbana Force the platoon consolidated and pushed on. By noon it was within sight of the sea, and there its troubles really began. The Japanese started closing in, and the artillery at Ango, unaware that friendly troops were so far forward, shelled the area with great thoroughness, killing Lieutenant Middendorf and wounding Lieutenant Matz slightly.

One of the eight men left with Matz was badly wounded and unable to march. The lieutenant decided to stay with him and ordered the rest of the troops to withdraw. They got back safely to their own lines two

days later after a difficult march, most of it through hip-deep swamp. Matz and the enlisted man, who would have died had the lieutenant not stayed with him, remained hidden behind the enemy lines until Urbana Force overran the area eight days later.[42]

Colonel Grose did not learn of the platoon's break-through until just before noon when a runner got back with the news. He at once ordered Company I back into the line to the right of Company G and sent Company K to the far left with orders to go to the platoon's assistance. The company attacked in the direction it was believed the platoon had followed. Captain Yasuda had meanwhile plugged the hole in his defenses, and it was only after heavy fighting that 1st Lt. Paul M. Krasne and eight men of the company finally broke through. They raced to the beach, found no trace of the Matz patrol, and promptly withdrew lest they be cut off.

Seeing that the line did not move, Colonel Grose ordered Company F to attack on Company L's right at 1511. The result was the same. The line remained where it was and by evening was no more than 150 yards from the line of departure.[43]

Colonel Grose asked General Eichelberger for time to reorganize but the request was refused, and he was ordered

[41] Tel Msg, Urbana Force to Col Bowen, Ser 4112, 24 Dec 42; Tel Msg, Col Bradley to Col Bowen, Ser 4125, 24 Dec 42; 127th Inf Tact Hist, 24 Dec 42; Col Grose's Diary, 24 Dec 42; Ltr, Gen Eichelberger to Gen MacArthur, 25 Dec 42; Ltr, Col Grose to Gen Ward, 26 Feb 51. Gruennert's citation for the Medal of Honor is in WD GO No. 66, 11 Oct 43.

[42] Tel Msg, Col Bowen to 32d Div, Ser 4124, 24 Dec 42; 127th Inf Tact Hist, 24 Dec 42; 127th Inf Jnl, 1400, 26 Dec 42; Ltr, Meyer to author, 13 Mar 51. Matz was later awarded the Distinguished Service Cross. The citation is in Hq USAFFE GO No. 34, 21 Jun 43.

[43] Tel Msg, Col Bowen to Col Howe, Ser 4124, 24 Dec 42; Tel Msg, Col Bradley to Col Bowen, Ser 4125, 24 Dec 42; 127th Inf Tact Hist, 24 Dec 42; Ltrs, Gen Eichelberger to Gen MacArthur, 24 Dec 42, 25 Dec 42; Col Grose's Diary, 24 Dec 42; Interv with Col Grose, 18 Nov 50; Rpt, CG Buna Forces, p. 31.

instead to resume the attack early Christmas morning. Eichelberger, who had been at the front all day, taking an active part in the conduct of operations, reported the refusal to General MacArthur the next day, adding in words charged with emotion, that seeing the attack fail had been the "all time low" of his life.[44]

The Attack on Christmas Day

Colonel Grose now had eight companies of the 127th Infantry at the front—A, C, F, G, I, K, L, and M. His plan was to have Companies A and F attack on the far left and push through to the coast. Companies K and L, in the center of the line, would push forward in their sector in concert with the companies on the left. Companies I and G would concentrate on reducing the bunkers that covered the trail through the gardens and would be aided in that endeavor by a diversionary attack in the afternoon on the Japanese positions in the Triangle. Company C would be in reserve.

Companies A and F were to launch their attack on the far left without mortar or artillery preparation of any kind. Instead, there would first be the pretense of a full-scale attack on the mission from the island, in the hope that the enemy would weaken his dispositions in the gardens in order to meet the new threat. As soon as it became evident that the enemy had swallowed the bait, Companies A and F would suddenly attack in the gardens. It was hoped that the enemy would be taken completely by surprise by this maneuver.[45]

On Christmas morning, the mortars and artillery in a thunderous barrage gave the mission a thorough working over, and Company H, on the island, made a great show of being about to attack the mission across the north bridge, a makeshift structure that miraculously still stood. At 1135, while the commotion on the island was at its height, Companies A and F attacked across the gardens without preparation of any kind. The ruse worked. Company A (less two platoons which had not yet arrived) was held up, but Company F, which had found it impossible to move forward the day before, found the going relatively easy. Led by Capt. Byron B. Bradford, the company cut its way through the gardens and the swamp and reached the Coconut Plantation by 1345. Obviously caught off base, the Japanese rallied, surrounded the company, and began a counterattack. After beating off the attack with very heavy losses to itself, the company established an all-around perimeter in a triangular cluster of shell holes just outside the plantation. The position was about 200 yards west of the track junction, about 250 from the sea, and 600 from the mission.

An advance detachment of Company A, under its commanding officer, Capt. Horace N. Harger, broke through to F's position at 1620, but its weapons platoon was ambushed and destroyed by the enemy just as it was on the point of going through. The rest of Company A reached the front late in the afternoon but was unable to get through. As night fell, its leading elements and those of Companies K and L were at least 350

---

[44] Ltr, Gen Eichelberger to Gen MacArthur, 25 Dec 42.

[45] Tel Msg, Col Grose to Col Bowen, Ser 4146, 24 Dec 42; Tel Msg, Col Bowen to Col Grose, Ser 4148, 24 Dec 42; 127th Inf Tact Hist, 25 Dec 42.

yards from the beleaguered companies near the coast.[46]

The diversionary attack on the enemy bunker positions in the Triangle to help Companies G and I on the right was mounted late in the afternoon. A platoon of Company E was to advance into the mouth of the Triangle and engage the enemy with fire while a platoon of Company C, with the support of heavy weapons crews of Company D, launched the main effort from the south. Although the attack, led by Capt. James W. Workman, commanding officer of Company C, was carefully planned and prepared, it failed, as had all previous efforts to take this position. The attack was finally called off toward evening after Captain Workman was killed while charging an enemy bunker at the head of his troops.[47]

For all its cost, the diversion had done little to ease the pressure on Companies G and I. After fighting hard all day, the two units had made only slight gains. The enemy bunkers were too well defended and too cleverly concealed. Captain Dames and Lieutenant Fahres tried digging saps toward them, but at the end of the day, the enemy bunkers still stood, seemingly as impregnable as ever.[48]

Urbana Force had not been able to make contact with Companies A and F since morning because their radios were wet and would not work. Three men of Headquarters Company, 127th Infantry—Pvt. Gordon W. Eoff, Pfc. William Balza, and Sgt. William Fale—distinguished themselves while attempting to get telephone wire forward, but all efforts to regain communications with the two companies that day failed.[49]

Establishing the Corridor

Late in the afternoon Colonel Grose redisposed his command, in accordance with his practice of rotating "the units so that they could get out of the lines and have a few days rest." Pulling Companies I and K out of the line, he ordered Company C (less one platoon, which was holding the area below the Triangle) in on the far left. Company I returned to the other side of the creek, Company K went into reserve, and Company L, extending itself to the right, tied in on Company G's left.[50]

---

[46] Tel Msgs, Col Bradley to Col Howe, Ser 4205, 25 Dec 42, Ser 4220, 25 Dec 42; Tel Msg, Col Grose to Col Howe, Ser 4228, 25 Dec 42; Tel Msg, Capt Stephen Hewitt, S–2, 127th Inf, to Maj Hawkins, G–2, 32d Div, Ser 4270, 26 Dec 42; 127th Inf Jnl, 1110, 1130, 1135, 25 Dec 42; 127th Inf Tact Hist, 26 Dec 42, 27 Dec 42; 32d Div Sitrep, No. 124, 25 Dec 42.

[47] Tel Msg, Col Bradley to 32d Div, Ser 4220, 25 Dec 42; 32d Div Sitrep, No. 124, 25 Dec 42. Workman was posthumously awarded the Distinguished Service Cross. The citation is in Hq USAFFE GO No. 32, 15 Jan 43.

[48] 127th Inf Tact Hist, 25 Dec 42; 32d Div Overlays, Papuan Campaign, 25 Dec 42; Col Grose's Diary, 25 Dec 42.

[49] 127th Inf Tact Hist, 25 Dec 42; Tel Msg, Col Bradley to Col Howe, Ser 4316, 26 Dec 42. Eoff, Balza, and Fale were later awarded the Distinguished Service Cross. Eoff's citation is in Hq USAFFE GO No. 36, 1 Jul 42; Balza's in GO No. 34, 21 Jun 43; Fale's, in GHQ SWPA GO No. 29, 30 Mar 42.

[50] Ltr, Col Grose to Gen Ward, 26 Feb 51; 32d Div Overlays, Papuan Campaign, 26 Dec 42. There were no facilities for resting the troops. "It was difficult," Colonel Grose recalls, "to find a dry spot for this purpose, and since there were no tents or other shelter, the men were quite often wet from rain even when resting. The relief from the tensions of the front was a help. I found that this system worked, and continued to use it all the way through, despite the fact that there were those in the higher echelons who insisted that all the men needed was proper leadership."

Company C's instructions for 26 December were to break through to the companies near the coast, and link up with them to form a corridor from Entrance Creek to the sea. Maj. Edmund R. Schroeder, commander of the 1st Battalion, who reported to Colonel Grose that evening, would take personal charge of the attack.[51]

Things went somewhat better on the 26th. Assisted by Company I, Company G knocked out several bunkers on the right along the trail during the morning and began working on those that remained. On the far left, however, the enemy was still resisting stubbornly, and Company C made no progress all morning.

The Japanese were obviously reinforcing their positions north of the gardens directly from the mission. To discourage this activity, the artillery put down a ten-minute concentration on the southwest corner of the mission at noon that day. Major Schroeder ordered an element of Company C, split into patrols, into the swamp north of the gardens to deal with the Japanese there. The rest of the company, joined during the afternoon by Company B, commanded by 1st Lt. John B. Lewis, continued to attack frontally.[52]

The attack made little progress, and it became apparent during the early afternoon that Company C was not going to break through. Colonel Grose ordered Colonel Bradley, now chief of staff of the 32d Division, to go to the beleaguered companies and bring back a report on their condition. Bradley, who at Grose's request was also acting as executive officer of the 127th Infantry, was to be accompanied by Major Schroeder, 1st Lt. Robert P. McCampbell, S-2 of the 2d Battalion, and a platoon of Company C, led by 1st Lt. Ted C. Johnson. The patrol set out at once, carrying with it wire, ammunition, and food. After some sharp skirmishing with the enemy the patrol reached its destination at 1745 that afternoon.[53]

The two companies were in very bad condition when the patrol reached them. Major McCampbell, or Lieutenant McCampbell as he then was, recalls the matter in these words:

The condition of the companies on our arrival was deplorable. The dead had not been buried. Wounded, bunched together, had been given only a modicum of care, and the troops were demoralized. Major Schroeder did a wonderful job of reorganizing the position and helping the wounded. The dead were covered with earth . . . the entire tactical position of the companies were reorganized and [they were] placed in a strong defensive position. . . .[54]

That evening Colonel Bradley, accompanied by a small patrol, returned from the perimeter with a complete report. Major Schroeder and Lieutenant McCampbell re-

---

[51] Tel Msgs, Col Bradley to 32d Div, Ser 4205, 25 Dec 42, Ser 4220, 25 Dec 42; Tel Msg, Urbana Force to Col Bowen, Ser 4260, 26 Dec 42; 32d Div Overlays, Papuan Campaign, 26 Dec 42.

[52] 127th Inf Jnl, 1113, 1145, 1205, 1215, 1230, 1245, 26 Dec 42; 127th Inf Tact Hist, 26 Dec 42; Ltr, Col Grose to Gen Ward, 26 Feb 51.

[53] 127th Inf Jnl, 1745, 26 Dec 42; Ltr, Maj McCampbell to author, 26 Aug 50; Ltr, Col Grose to Gen Ward, 26 Feb 51. Bradley, Schroeder, and McCampbell were all later decorated for getting through to the surrounded companies: Schroeder and McCampbell with the Distinguished Service Cross; Bradley with the Silver Star. Schroeder's citation is in GHQ SWPA GO No. 14, 30 Jan 43; McCampbell's is in Hq USAFFE GO No. 34, 21 Jun 43; Bradley's is in Hq U.S. Forces Buna Area GO No. 7, 14 Jan 43.

[54] Ltr, Maj McCampbell to author, 26 Aug 50.

mained behind to continue with the reorganization of the troops.[55]

The attack was resumed early on 27 December, with Colonel Bradley, on Colonel Grose's orders, in command of Companies B and C and the detachment of Company A. Company C and the detachment of Captain Harger's company were held up by the bunkers north of the gardens, but Company B on their right made good progress all day. A grass fire set in the gardens by the enemy during the afternoon caused only slight interruption in its advance. By 1700 Lieutenant Lewis had moved through to Schroeder's position with his entire company.[56]

By the morning of 28 December Major Schroeder had the forward perimeter well organized for action. The telephone was operating without interruption, ammunition and food were going through, the walking wounded had been successfully evacu-

ated to the rear, and the troops were being organized for attack.[57]

Early that morning Colonel Grose ordered Company L out of the line to rest and clean up. He expected the break-through to the beleaguered companies to come momentarily. This expectation was quickly realized. Just before noon Company C on the left and Company G on the right broke through to the position held by Companies F and B and the detachment of Company A. The rest of Company A moved in soon after and the result was a broad corridor from Entrance Creek to the Coconut Plantation. Major Schroeder reported the establishment of the corridor the minute Companies C and G got through and, with a flourish characteristic of the man, asked Colonel Grose over the telephone, "Do you need any help in the rear areas?" [58]

It was obvious that the Japanese could not hope to hold the Triangle once they lost control of the gardens for the position was now outflanked and cut off. No one knew this better than the Japanese commander, Captain Yasuda, who had apparently lost no time in ordering it evacuated. When a volunteer party of Company E, 127th Infantry, led by Sgt. Charles E. Wagner, with Pfc. James G. Greene as his second-in-command, pushed its way cautiously into the Triangle that evening, it found that the Japanese had pulled out of the area some time before and that the fourteen bunkers

---

[55] Tel Msg, Col Bradley to Col Howe, Ser 4361, 26 Dec 42; Interv with Col Grose, 18 Nov 50. In a letter he wrote to General Sutherland and then decided not to send, General Eichelberger noted the situation as Colonel Bradley reported it to him personally. It was to the effect that Company F had been "practically wiped out," and that the detachment of Company A had received "numerous casualties." "I must be frank, however, and tell you," he continued, "that the first two companies have taken tremendous losses, and everyone on the Urbana front has recommended that we reorganize and substitute two fresh companies of [them]." "I believe," he added, "that the greater part of the Japanese strength has been on our two forward companies." Ltr, Gen Eichelberger to Gen Sutherland, 27 Dec 42, marked "not sent," copy in OCMH files.
[56] 127th Inf Jnl, 0200, 0830, 1500, 1525, 27 Dec 42, 0826, 28 Dec 42; 127th Inf Tact Hist, 27 Dec 42, 28 Dec 42; 32d Div Overlay, Papuan Campaign, 27 Dec 42, 28 Dec 42. Capt. Millard G. Gray, General Eichelberger's new aide-de-camp, who was in command of Company C between 24 December and 1 January, was later awarded the Distinguished Service Cross. The citation is in Hq USAFFE GO No. 51, 30 Aug 43.

[57] Ltr, Maj McCampbell to author, 26 Aug 50.
[58] 127th Inf Jnl, 0750, 1131, 28 Dec 42; 127th Inf Tact Hist, 28 Dec 42; Interv with Col Grose, 18 Nov 50. Colonel Bradley, who had been in the front lines with Company C all morning directing the advance and urging the men forward, was later awarded the Distinguished Service Cross. The citation is in Hq USAFFE GO No. 36, 1 Jul 43.

GENERAL EICHELBERGER AND MEMBERS OF HIS STAFF *look over newly taken ground in the Triangle area.*

and innumerable trenches making up the position were empty.[59]

There was every indication that the Japanese had left their positions in the Triangle in a great hurry. Pieces of equipment and quantities of small arms ammunition were strewn about in the bunkers and fire trenches, and two 20-mm., gas operated, cart-mounted antiaircraft guns, together with large quantities of antiaircraft ammunition, had been left behind. The entire area was pockmarked with shell holes, and there

was mute evidence that some of the enemy had not long ago been caught in the open by Allied artillery fire.[60]

In evacuating the Triangle the Japanese had given up an immensely strong position that Urbana Force, despite many costly attempts, had found it impossible to take. Going over the ground a day later, General Eichelberger reported to General Sutherland: "I walked along there and found it terrifically strong. It is a mass of bunkers and

---

[59] 127th Inf Tact Hist, 28 Dec 42.

[60] 127th Inf Jnl, 1755, 28 Dec 42; 127th Inf Tact Hist, 28 Dec 42.

entrenchments surrounded by swamp. It is easy to see how they held us off so long." [61]

By the evening of the 28th Urbana Force was able to use the trail through the gardens as far as the Coconut Grove and also controlled the track junction along the coast. Major Schroeder's force was deep in the Coconut Plantation, and Company B, its forward element, was only 120 yards from the sea.[62] The corridor from Entrance Creek to the coast had finally been established. Split off from Giropa Point, the mission now lay open to assault.

[61] Ltr, Gen Eichelberger to Gen Sutherland, 29 Dec 42, copy in OCMH files.

[62] Tel Msg, Gen Eichelberger to Col Howe, Ser 4487, 28 Dec 42; 32d Div G-3 Daily Periodic Rpt, 28 Dec 42.

CHAPTER XVI

The Fall of Buna

With Warren Force poised to attack Giropa Point, and Urbana Force moving to envelop Buna Mission along the newly established corridor from Entrance Creek to the coast, the reduction of the enemy positions on the Buna side of the Girua River was finally at hand. This was to be no easy task. The enemy at Buna was heavily outnumbered and almost completely surrounded, but he was fighting with the utmost ferocity and was to be cleared out of his remaining positions at Buna only after some of the bitterest fighting of the campaign.

The Advance to Giropa Point

The Abortive Attack
of 29 December

Warren Force had completed the reduction of the Old Strip on the 28th. Just before midnight of the same day the 2/12 Battalion, thirty officers and 570 other ranks under Lt. Col. A. S. W. Arnold, reached Oro Bay from Goodenough Island by corvette. The battalion and its gear were landed safely during the night, and the troops who were to begin moving forward to the front the next day went into bivouac in the brigade area near Boreo.[1]

Brigadier Wootten devoted the next morning to regrouping and reorganization. Company A, 2/10 Battalion, moved to the left flank and took up a position on the right of Company C, 2/10 Battalion, which continued on the far left as the main assault company. Companies B and D, 2/10 Battalion, continued as before on the far right, with D on the outside and B on D's left flank. Companies C and A, 128th Infantry, and Company C, 126th Infantry, with Company A, 126th Infantry, in support, were in the center of the line. Company B, 126th Infantry, Company B, 128th Infantry, and a composite company of the 2/9 Battalion were in reserve. Four tanks in position at the bridge between the strips were ready to go, and seven others, which had just reached Boreo from Oro Bay, were in reserve, as was the 2/12 Battalion, which began moving to the front that morning.[2]

At 1235 Wootten gave verbal orders for an attack on the area between Giropa Point and the mouth of Simemi Creek. The attack, which was to be in a northeasterly direction toward the coast, was to be mounted after 1400 with the four available tanks. Company C, 2/10 Battalion, was to follow the tanks and in general make the main

---

[1] Tel Msg, Col Myers to Col Howe, Ser 4540, 29 Dec 42; 3d Bn, 128th Inf, Jnl, 2257, 29 Dec 42; Rpt on Opns 18th Bde Gp at Cape Endaiadere and Giropa Point. The 18th Brigade was replaced on Goodenough Island by the 7th Brigade from Milne Bay—the 2/12 Battalion, for instance, being replaced there by the 25 Battalion.

[2] Tel Msg, Lt Winkler to Maj Hawkins, Ser 4541, 29 Dec 42; Buna Force G–3 Sitrep, 29 Dec 42; Overlay, Buna Force Dispositions, 1700, 29 Dec 42; Rpt on Opns 18th Bde Gp at Cape Endaiadere and Giropa Point.

effort, but the companies on its right were to take advantage of every opportunity to advance provided they did not unnecessarily expose their flanks.[3]

Colonel Dobbs fixed zero hour at 1600. The tanks were delayed, and the attack did not get under way until 1715, following an artillery preparation with smoke. In an effort apparently to make up for lost time, the tanks moved at high speed and came in obliquely across the line of departure. Without waiting for the slower-moving infantry to close in behind them, they moved north without moderating their speed. The infantry as a result had to attack independently of the tanks, and the tanks, far in front of the infantry, had to move on the enemy bunkers without infantry support.

As the tanks hit the first line of bunkers, the Japanese, with no Allied infantry at hand to stop them, pulled back to their second bunker line. When the tanks finally discovered what had happened and began working on the second line, the Japanese filtered back into the first line, in plenty of time to stop the foot soldiers who had meanwhile managed to fight their way into the grove. At 1845 the attack had to be called off. The tanks by that time had expended all their ammunition, and the infantrymen were met by such intense fire from hidden enemy bunker positions that they had to pull back to the edge of the Coconut Plantation and consolidate.[4]

The 2/12 Battalion is Committed

The fresh 2/12 Battalion reached the front that night, 29 December. Early the following morning Brigadier Wootten ordered it to take over on the left in place of the 2/10 Battalion, which had seen a great deal of action and needed rest. The day was devoted to regrouping and reorganization. Colonel Arnold went forward to reconnoiter the front his battalion was to take over. Major Beaver's 126th Infantry troops, who were also in need of rest, exchanged places with Colonel MacNab's battalion, the 3d Battalion, 128th Infantry, which after a week of rest in the Cape Endaiadere area was again ready to attack.

The redisposition of the troops was completed next day. By evening of 31 December the battalions were in place: the 2/12 Battalion on the left, the 3d Battalion, 128th Infantry in the center, and the 2/10 Battalion on the right. The 2/12 Battalion and the 3d Battalion, 128th Infantry, were on an 1,100-yard east-west front and faced the coast. The 2/10 Battalion, with a holding mission, was drawn up across the head of the strip on a 500-yard front at right angles to them, its left tied in on the 3d Battalion, 128th Infantry, and its right on Simemi Creek. Major Clarkson's 1st Battalion, 128th Infantry, was on the 2/12 Battalion's left rear; Company A, 2/9 Battalion, was in reserve.[5] (*Map 15*)

---

[3] Tel Msg, 18th Bde to 32d Div, Ser 4554, 29 Dec 42.

[4] Tel Msg, Maj Ziebell to Col Howe, Ser 4565, 29 Dec 42; Tel Msg, Capt Conley to Col Howe, Ser 4577, 29 Dec 42; Tel Msg, 18th Bde to 32d Div, Ser 4579, 29 Dec 42; 128th Inf Jnl, 1715, 1750, 29 Dec 42; Rpt on Opns 18th Bde Gp at Cape Endaiadere and Giropa Point.

[5] 1st Bn, 126th Inf, Jnl, Sers 1027, 1034, 30 Dec 42; 3d Bn, 128th Inf, Jnl, 0831, 1033, 1300, 1500, 1730, 30 Dec 42; 32d Div Sitreps No. 134, 30 Dec 42, No. 136, 31 Dec 42; Buna Force G-3 Sitrep, 31 Dec 42; 32d Div Overlays, 31 Dec 42; Rpt on Opns 18th Bde Gp at Cape Endaiadere and Giropa Point.

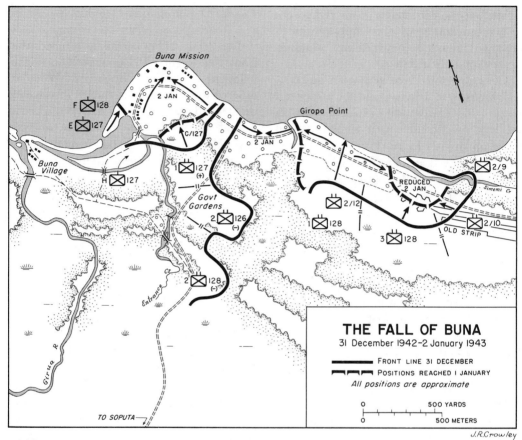

Buna Mission

F 128
E 127
2 JAN

C/127

Giropa Point

2 JAN

REDUCED
2 JAN

2/9

Simemi Cr

Buna
Village

H 127

1 127
(+)

Govt
Gardens

2 126
(-)

2/12

128

2/10

OLD STRIP

3 128

Entrance Cr

2 128
(-)

Girua R.

THE FALL OF BUNA
31 December 1942-2 January 1943

———— FRONT LINE 31 DECEMBER
▭▭▭ POSITIONS REACHED I JANUARY
All positions are approximate

0 ————————— 500 YARDS
0 ————————— 500 METERS

TO SOPUTA →

J.R.Crowley

MAP 15

At 1535 Brigadier Wootten issued a carefully drawn plan for the reduction the next day of Giropa Point and the area between it and the Old Strip. The attack would be supported by the mortars of the 2/10 Battalion, the 25-pounders of the Manning and Hall Troops, and the 4.5-inch howitzers of the Stokes Troop. Of the eleven tanks of X Squadron, 2/6 Armored Regiment, nine would be committed to the attack: six immediately, and the remaining three as they were needed.

The operation was to be in two phases. In Phase One the 2/12 Battalion and the tanks, with the 1st Battalion, 128th Infantry, as left-flank guard, were to attack in a northeasterly direction, break through to the coast, and turn southeast, thereby completing the enemy's encirclement. In Phase Two, the 2/12 Battalion was to herd the encircled Japanese toward the companies advancing on the right and, with their help, destroy them.[6]

That night, while the troops snatched what rest they could before the next day's attack, the K.P.M. ship *Bath* and the Austral-

[6] 18th Aust Inf Bde Gp Opns Order No. 2, 31 Dec 42; 1st Bn, 128th Inf, Jnl, Ser 6, 31 Dec 42.

ian freighter *Comara* came into Oro Bay with 350 and 500 tons of cargo, respectively, unloaded, and departed before daybreak. The arrival of the *Bath* and the *Comara* marked a logistical milestone in the campaign. Since the night of 11–12 December, when the *Karsik* made the first pioneering trip to Oro Bay, six freighters making nine individual trips had brought in roughly 4,000 tons of cargo. This was more than three times the 1,252 tons that the Air Force had flown in to the 32d Division during the same period, and 1,550 more than the 2,450 tons that it was to fly in for the 32d Division's use during the entire period that the division was in combat. Between the freighters and the luggers, an average of 200 tons of cargo was now coming into Oro Bay daily and had been since 20 December.[7] Supply at Buna, in short, had ceased to be a problem just as the fight for the place was coming to an end.

The Attack on New Year's Day

After a heavy artillery and mortar preparation, the troops on the right and left moved out for the attack at 0800, New Year's Day. On the left, Companies A and D, 2/12 Battalion, and the six tanks cut northeast through the plantation toward the coast. The 1st Battalion, 128th Infantry, followed

them. Facing north, Companies I, K, and L, 128th Infantry, moved on the dispersal bays off the northwest end from below (south), and the 2/10 Battalion, facing west, remained in position on the Old Strip.

Without tanks to support it, the attack by the 3d Battalion, 128th Infantry, went slowly. The Japanese in the dispersal bays were well entrenched and fighting hard. On the left, the attack made excellent progress from the start. Closely followed by the infantry, the tanks made short work of the enemy defenses in the Giropa Plantation. The leading tank reached the coastal track below Giropa Point at 0830. A half-hour later all the tanks and most of the infantry had reached the coast. The 1st Battalion, 128th Infantry, moved forward, mopping up pockets of enemy resistance that the Australians had overlooked or bypassed. Company A, 2/12 Battalion, with Company D immediately behind it, anchored its left flank on Giropa Creek, just west of Giropa Point, and began to consolidate on a 400-yard front along the shore. Companies B and C, 2/12 Battalion, which had been operating to the rear of Companies A and D, began moving eastward and southeastward with the tanks to complete the second phase of the attack.

Against the stiffest kind of opposition, the tanks and the Australian infantry following them moved steadily forward. By evening Companies C and D had cleared out the beach as far as the mouth of Simemi Creek. The 2/12 Battalion lost 62 killed, 128 wounded, and one missing in the day's fighting, but the Japanese on the Warren front were finished. All that remained was to deliver the *coup de grâce*.[8]

---

[7] Hist Port Det E, COSC, Buna; 32d Div G-4 Sec, Rear Echelon, Record of Air Shipments, 13 Nov 42–23 Jan 43; 32d Div AAR, Papuan Campaign; 32d Div QM Det, Rpt on Activities, Papuan Campaign; Interv with Col Moffatt, 23 Feb 50. The tonnage brought in by the freighters during the twenty-day period in question included 3,100 tons of general cargo and an estimated 900 tons of tanks, vehicles, and road-building equipment for which no precise figures are available. The six freighters were the *Karsik*, the *Japara*, the *Bantam*, the *Mulcra*, the *Bath*, and the *Comara*. The *Karsik* made three individual trips during this period; the *Japara*, two; the rest, one each.

[8] 1st Bn, 128th Inf, Jnl, Sers 2, 3, 5, 12, 1 Jan 43; 3d Bn, 128th Inf, Jnl, 1445, 1645, 2230, 1 Jan 43; No. 138, 32d Div Sitrep, 1 Jan 43; Rpt on Opns 18th Bde Gp at Cape Endaiadere and Giropa Point.

FIRING A 60-MM. MORTAR *into the enemy lines at Buna Mission.*

The Australians had pressed into use that day for the first time a blast bomb of their own invention consisting essentially of a Mills bomb screwed into a two-pound can of ammonal explosive. As Colonel MacNab recalls, it was used in the following manner: "A tank would knock a corner off the enemy bunker, and while this hole was 'buttoned up' by automatic or rifle fire, a volunteer would creep up to the side of the bunker, heave in the bomb, and duck. The explosion would rock the bunker and stupefy the Japanese inside. Then a can of Jap aviation gasoline would be tossed in, ignited by tracers, and the bunker would be burned out." [9]

The end came the next morning. Major Clarkson's 1st Battalion, 128th Infantry, finished clearing out the last pocket of enemy resistance on the left; details of the 2/9 and 2/10 Battalions finally cleaned out the enemy emplacements on the island at the mouth of Simemi Creek; and Companies C and B, 2/12 Battalion, the 3d Battalion,

---

[9] Ltr, Col MacNab to author, 25 Nov 49. The explosive ammonal consists of a mixture of ammonium nitrate, powdered aluminum, and charcoal, and is noted for its powerful blast properties.

128th Infantry, and eight tanks attacked the Japanese in the dispersal bays. The 2/10 Battalion, with Allied fire coming in its direction, stayed down out of harm's way.[10]

The attacks by Colonel Arnold and Colonel MacNab, the one attacking from the west and the other from the south, were soon over. As the fire slackened, the officers and men of the 2/10 Battalion rose out of their holes in the Old Strip area and watched the last Japanese positions being overrun.[11]

This was the last organized attack delivered by Warren Force. After taking Giropa Point and the area immediately to the eastward, the troops had little left to do but mop up. Orders were issued that day to the 2/12 Battalion and the 3d Battalion, 128th Infantry, to begin moving westward toward Buna Mission in the morning. The orders were revoked a few hours later, when

---

[10] Tel Msg, Lt Winkler to Col Howe, Ser 4862, 2 Jan 43; Tel Msg, 18th Bde to 32d Div, Ser 4878, 2 Jan 43; Tel Msg, 18th Bde to Adv NGF, Ser 4918, 2 Jan 43; 32d Div Sitrep, No. 140, 2 Jan 43; Buna Force G–3 Sitrep, 2 Jan 43; Rpt on Opns 18th Bde Gp at Cape Endaiadere and Giropa Point; Ltr, Col MacNab to Gen Ward, 7 Mar 51.

[11] Ltr, Col MacNab to Gen Ward, 7 Mar 51. Colonel MacNab recalls the attack in these words: "Arnold and I took our outfits in with a sort of old-time flourish. . . . Arnold and I had been in view of each other almost continuously during this period, each in the front line of his troops. . . . When he had gotten fairly close to the line of bunkers (we were coming in on their rear and flank) he yelled to my troops, 'Where is the American commander?' I replied . . ., 'you know damn well where I am, you've been trying to get abreast for an hour.' He yelled 'Let's get the bastards,' and I yelled at my Company L and one platoon of Company K in the front wave, 'Come on you grease balls.' (Never before or since have I ever called a man that.) We all, Aussies and Yanks, went in on the run. There were not many Japs left. We killed them in the grass with bayonets, and . . . when we couldn't reach them [with fire]." Ltr, Col MacNab to author, 18 Apr 50. MacNab was later awarded the Distinguished Service Cross. The citation is in Hq USAFFE GO No. 34, 21 Jun 43.

it was found that contact had been made with Urbana Force, and that that force was already proceeding with the envelopment of Buna Mission.[12]

The Capture of Buna Mission

The Failure To Cross the North Bridge

At 1330, 28 December, while Urbana Force was tidying up its corridor from Entrance Creek to the coast and preparing to move forward to the sea, General Eichelberger, accompanied by General Sutherland, Colonel Bowen, Colonel Rogers, and Colonel Harding, arrived at Colonel Grose's CP from Buna Force headquarters. Asked for a report on the situation, Grose gave Eichelberger a résumé of how things stood. Among other things, Grose told Eichelberger that he had just taken the 3d Battalion out of the line for a much-needed rest. At 1428, without discussing the matter further with Grose, Eichelberger ordered that the 3d Battalion, split into two elements, launch an immediate attack on Buna Mission. One element was to advance on the mission from the island by way of the north bridge; the other element, starting from the southern side of the island, was to move upon it in five Australian assault boats which had reached the front the day before.

Eichelberger and Grose had discussed this plan and several others some days before, but had never worked out the details. Grose recalls that he was so startled by the sudden order to commit the tired battalion to such an attack that it took him a few

---

[12] 3d Bn, 128th Inf, Jnl, 1930, 2 Jan 43, 0723, 0810, 3 Jan 43; Rpt on Opns 18th Bde Gp at Cape Endaiadere and Giropa Point.

minutes to organize the maneuvers in his mind.[13]

Aside from the weariness of his troops, there was another even greater difficulty. The enemy had a line of bunkers just off the northern end of the bridge, and the bridge itself, a narrow, makeshift structure forty feet long and a couple of feet wide, had a fifteen-foot gap at its northern end—the result of a recent Allied artillery hit.[14]

As soon as I had my thoughts collected [Grose recalls], I called for volunteers among the officers present to do certain things. Colonel Bowen volunteered to get the engineers and collect the necessary timbers to fix the bridge, Colonel Rogers to reconnoiter the position on the island and see that the troops were conducted thereto, and Colonel Harding to coordinate and control the mortar and artillery fire. I ordered Captain Stephen Hewitt, my S-2, to make the reconnaissance of the route the boats were to take . . . and Captain Leonard E. Garret, my S-3, to arrange for and coordinate the fires of Company H from the island and the troops on the finger, both of which were to fire on the mission preceding the attack.[15]

Colonel Grose quickly worked out the details of the plan. The attack was to open with fifteen minutes of artillery and mortar fire on the mission and the bunkers facing the bridge. Guided by directions given them by Captain Hewitt as a result of his reconnaissance, forty men of Company K in the

five assault boats were to round the eastern end of the island just as the preparatory fire began lifting. They were to land east of the bridge and establish a bridgehead. Supported by fire from Company H on the island and from a platoon of Company E at the tip of the village finger, they were to engage the enemy with fire, thereby masking the bridge and permitting the planks required to make it usable to be laid in safety. As soon as the planks were down, the rest of Company K would dash across the bridge in single file, and would be followed by Company I and Company L, in that order. When all three companies were across, they would attack north in concert with Major Schroeder's force on the coast, which would attack from the southeast.[16]

The preliminary tasks were completed in short order. Captain Hewitt, who had gone out in one of the assault boats, returned with the results of his reconnaissance. Six enlisted men volunteered to lay in place the three heavy timbers that would span the gap at the northern end of the bridge. Commanding the assault boats, 1st Lt. Clarence Riggs of the 3d Battalion's Ammunition and Pioneer Platoon quickly moved them into position in some heavy foliage off the southern side of the island. The rest of the 3d Battalion, guided by Colonel Rogers, began moving forward to the bridge area from the center of the island. Having been told only a little while before that they were to be given a rest, the troops of the battalion were slow in moving forward, and Colonel Rogers was unable to get them into position south of the bridge until the first salvo of the artillery preparation hit the mission.

The time was 1720. As the first artillery salvo went down, the boats pushed off from

[13] Col Grose's Diary, 28 Dec 42; Intervs with Col Grose, 18 Nov 50, 1 Feb 51; Ltr, Col Grose to Gen Ward, 26 Feb 51.
[14] Tel Msg, Capt Hewitt, Ser 4474, 28 Dec 42; 127th Inf Jnl, 1428, 28 Dec 42; Col Bowen, Certificate, 3 Jan 43, copy in OCMH files; Rpt, CG Buna Forces, p. 3.
[15] Ltr, Col Grose to Gen Ward, 26 Feb 51. This finger was a narrow spit of land projecting from the vicinity of Buna Village to the mouth of Entrance Creek. It will be called hereafter the village finger. The finger on the other side of the mouth of Entrance Creek will be called the mission finger.
[16] 127th Inf Jnl, 1428, 1538, 28 Dec 42; 127th Inf Tact Hist, 28 Dec 42.

their hidden position. The troops had been misdirected by Captain Hewitt, however. Instead of going around the island and landing on the east side of Entrance Creek, they tried to land on the mission finger. The platoon of Company E on the village finger mistook them for the enemy and opened fire on them, as did the Japanese. Lieutenant Riggs' boat, in the lead, swamped and sank. Although Riggs could not swim, he somehow reached shore and managed to stop the firing from the village finger, but it was too late: most of the boats had already been sunk in the shallows. Fortunately no one was killed or drowned.[17]

Things had also miscarried at the bridge. The six men to volunteer—Pvts. Arthur Melanson and Earl Mittelberger, T/5's Charles H. Gray and Bart McDonough of Company A, 114th Engineer Battalion, and Pvts. Elmer R. Hangarten and Edward G. Squires of Company H—had advanced across the bridge, two men to a timber. Amid heavy fire from the opposite shore, they dropped the three timbers in place, and all except Mittelberger, who was killed on the bridge, lived to tell the tale. As soon as the timbers were in place, Company K started crossing. Scarcely had the first two men reached the northern end of the bridge, when the newly laid planks fell into the stream because of the weakness of the pilings at the other end of the bridge. The two men, one of them wounded and neither

able to swim, hid under the bank on the other side of the stream, only their heads showing. They were rescued the following night by 1st Lt. William H. Bragg, Jr., commanding officer of the mortar platoon of Company H, and three enlisted men of the company, who swam across the creek to save them.[18]

The New Plan

On the night of 28–29 December ammunition and pioneer troops of the 127th Infantry finished digging a 2½-foot-deep trench across the northwest end of the gardens. The trench, which they had begun the night before, was the idea of Capt. W. A. Larson, Major Hootman's successor as regimental S–4. Early on 29 December it went into use as a route by which supplies were brought forward and the wounded were carried back. It was an immediate success and proved as useful in the transfer of troops as in evacuation and supply.[19]

Later the same morning the original Urbana Force—the 2d Battalion, 126th

---

[17] 127th Inf Jnl, 1515, 1538, 1720, 1735, 28 Dec 42; 127th Inf Tact Hist, 28 Dec 42; Col Grose's Diary, 28 Dec 42; Col Bowen, Certificate, 3 Jan 4; Interv with Col Grose, 18 Nov 50; Ltr, Col Rogers to author, 26 Jun 50; Ltr, Maj Philip A. Jenson to author, 24 Jun 51; Ltr, Col Grose to Gen Ward, 26 Feb 51. S. Sgt. Milan J. Miljativich of Company K took command when Lieutenant Riggs' boat sank and tried desperately to redirect the rest of the boats to the mission. He was later awarded the Distinguished Service Cross. The citation is in Hq USAFFE GO No. 34, 21 Jun 43.

[18] 127th Inf Jnl, 1735, 28 Dec 42, 2215, 29 Dec 42; 127th Inf Tact Hist, 27 Dec 42, 28 Dec 42; Ltr, Col Rogers to author, 26 Jun 50; Ltr, Col Grose to Gen Ward, 26 Feb 51; Ltr, Col Herbert A. Smith to Gen Ward, 20 Mar 51. The six volunteers were later awarded the Distinguished Service Cross. Their citations are in GHQ SWPA GO No. 11, 22 Jan 43. Colonel Bowen and Colonel Rogers, who were both active at the southern end of the bridge trying to get the attack started, were also awarded the Distinguished Service Cross. For Colonel Rogers, who was twice wounded that afternoon, it was the second time in the campaign that he was to be so decorated. Colonel Bowen's citation for the Distinguished Service Cross is in GHQ SWPA GO No. 4, 10 Jan 43; Colonel Roger's citation for the Oak Leaf Cluster to the Distinguished Service Cross is in GHQ SWPA GO No. 7, 15 Jan 43.

[19] 127th Inf Jnl, 1850, 27 Dec 42; Col Grose's Diary, 27 Dec 42; Interv with Col Grose, 18 Nov 50; Ltr, Lt Col W. A. Larson to author, 23 Jan 51.

Infantry, and the 2d Battalion, 128th Infantry—went back into the line. The 2d
Battalion, 126th Infantry, less the troops at
Tarakena and Siwori Village, took up a
holding position at the southeast end of the
Government Gardens, and the 2d Battalion,
128th Infantry, moved into the Triangle to
take over its defense. Just after the two battalions began moving forward from their
rest areas, Company B, 127th Infantry,
from its position along the coast southeast
of the mission, pushed forward to the sea
and established a 200-foot frontage along
the shore.[20]

Major Schroeder's line now extended
from Entrance Creek to the sea, but the
troops on the island were still held up by
fire from the northern end of the bridge.
An apparent solution to the problem was
found that night. Just before midnight a
patrol of Company H, 127th Infantry,
under 1st Lt. Allan W. Simms, waded across
from the village sandspit to the spit projecting from the mission. The patrol remained
on the mission side of the creek for half an
hour, without receiving any fire or finding
any Japanese in the area. On the basis of
this evidence of enemy weakness, a new
plan to envelop the mission was drawn on
30 December.

Under the new plan, Company E, 127th
Infantry, and Company F, 128th Infantry,
the 127th Infantry troops leading, would
cross the shallows between the village and
the mission. Company E was to turn right
and establish a bridgehead. Company F
crossing behind it would move northeast
along the coast directly on the mission as
soon as Company E had knocked out the
bunkers and the bridge was repaired. Com-

pany H, 127th Infantry, and Company G,
128th Infantry, would cross over from the
island, tie in on Company F's right along
the coast, and attack. Major Schroeder's
1st Battalion, 127th Infantry, reinforced
by elements of the 2d and 3d Battalions,
would meanwhile be moving on the mission
from the southeast. The result would be a
double envelopment of the mission with
separate columns converging upon it simultaneously from the front and from both
flanks. This final, multipronged attack was
to open at dawn the following morning,
31 December.[21]

The Attack of 31 December

Preparations for the attacks from the village spit were completed in good time on the
30th. Early in the morning, while Company
G, 127th Infantry, under Captain Dames,
moved into the Coconut Grove for a well-
earned rest, Company F, 128th Infantry,
under Capt. Jefferson R. Cronk, went into
bivouac at Buna Village, and was joined
there by Company E, 127th Infantry (less
the platoon on the finger). Company E, low
in morale after its heavy losses in the Triangle, was under the command of Lieutenant Bragg of Company H, who had volunteered to lead it in the attack across the
shallows.[22]

Major Schroeder had meanwhile been
attacking toward the mission. The Japanese
were still holding strongly along the coast,
and he made little progress. There was no
cause for concern, however, for Schroeder's
position was secure. Facing Buna Mission,

[20] Tel Msg, Col Bowen to Col Howe, Ser 4539, 29
Dec 42; 2d Bn, 126th Inf, Jnl, 0935, 1200, 1220,
29 Dec 42; 127th Inf Jnl, 0750, 1320, 29 Dec 42;
32d Div G–3 Daily Periodic Rpt, 29 Dec 42.

[21] Urbana Force FO No. 1, 30 Dec 42, FO No. 2,
30 Dec 42; 127th Inf Jnl, 1700, 30 Dec 42; 127th
Inf Tact Hist, 30 Dec 42; Ltr, Col Herbert A. Smith
to Gen Ward, 20 Mar 51.
[22] 127th Inf Jnl, 0625, 30 Dec 42; 127th Inf Tact
Hist, 30 Dec 42.

the line was held by Companies F, A, K, and L. Elements of Company M and Company B in platoon strength were in place in the gardens on both sides of the corridor; Companies C and I were in the center of the corridor; Company D was to the east of it facing Giropa Point.[23] It was clear that the enemy for all his tenacity would not be able to hold on the coast when the attacks from the village and the island got under way.

At 0430 the following morning, while it was still dark, Company E, 127th Infantry, and Company F, 128th Infantry, started moving in single file across the shallows between the finger and the mission. Company E was in the lead, with Lieutenant Bragg at the head of the column. The plan was to launch a surprise attack on the enemy positions opposite the bridge at daybreak. The men were under orders to make as little noise as possible and had been warned not to fire their weapons until told to do so. Company E gained the spit on the mission side without alerting the enemy, turned right, and began to move inland. Just as the leading elements of the company reached the spit, some of the men to the rear, unable to resist the temptation, threw grenades into a couple of landing barges that were stranded on the beach. At once the whole area broke into an uproar, the beach lit up with flares, and the troops were assailed with hand grenades, rifle grenades, and automatic weapons.[24]

The Japanese reaction threw the troops into a panic. Their plight became even worse when Lieutenant Bragg, who in General Eichelberger's words was to have been "the spark plug of the whole affair," was shot in the legs during the first few moments of the firing and, in the confusion of the moment, was reported missing.[25]

Colonel Grose waited on the village spit to hear news of the attack. He had a man with sound-powered telephone and a roll of wire following the action and reporting on its progress. The first information Grose heard on the phone was that the lieutenant who had taken command when Bragg fell was "running to the rear," and that there were others with him.

I told the man [Colonel Grose recalls] to stop them and send them back. He replied that he couldn't because they were already past him. Then the man said, 'The whole company is following them.' So I placed myself on the trail over which I knew they would have to come, and, pistol in hand, I stopped the lieutenant and all those following him. I directed the lieutenant to return and he said he couldn't. I then asked him if he knew what that meant and he said he did. The first sergeant was wounded, and I therefore let him proceed to the dressing station. I designated a sergeant nearby to take the men back and he did so. I then sent the lieutenant to the rear in arrest and under guard.[26]

Although Company E, in its flight, passed through Company F, 128th Infantry, which had been moving forward immediately to its rear, Captain Cronk's company was not affected by Company E's disorganization. Cronk himself, Colonel Grose recalls, was as calm and collected as if he were on the drill

[23] 127th Inf Jnl, 0710, 1320, 29 Dec 42, 0815, 1035, 1050, 1120, 1220, 1330, 1630, 30 Dec 42; 32d Div G–3 Daily Periodic Rpt, 29 Dec 42; 127th Inf Tact Hist, 29 Dec 42, 30 Dec 42; 32d Div Overlays, Papuan Campaign, 30 Dec 42.

[24] 127th Inf Jnl, 0430, 0505, 31 Dec 42; 2d Bn, 128th Inf, Jnl, 0700, 31 Dec 42; 127th Inf Tact Hist, 31 Dec 42; Col Grose, Affidavit, 7 Apr 44, in 450.4, I Corps File, in AGO RAC Files; Memo, Col Grose, Comments on the Buna–Sanananda Operation, 20 Feb 46, copy in OCMH files; Ltr, Col Grose to Gen Ward, 26 Feb 51.

[25] Col Grose's Diary, 31 Dec 42; Ltr, Gen Eichelberger to Gen Sutherland, 31 Dec 42, copy in OCMH files; Ltr, Col Grose to Gen Ward, 26 Feb 51.

[26] Ltr, Col Grose to Gen Ward, 26 Feb 51.

field. The 128th Infantry troops moved forward steadily and, by the time they were finally joined by Company E, had established a strong position on the spit and were holding their own. On Colonel Grose's orders Captain Cronk took command of Company E, and the two companies began attacking toward the bunkers in the area north of the bridge. They met stiff resistance, and, in a full day's fighting, Cronk could report only a small advance, though he hoped to do better the next day.[27]

The steadiness under fire of Captain Cronk's company had saved the day. General Eichelberger finally had his long-sought toe hold on the mission, and Captain Yasuda's troops, under attack for the first time from two directions, faced annihilation.

Yasuda had received some rations and ammunition by submarine on the night of the 25th and continued to fight stoutly for the mission with his remaining troops.[28] The fighting was particularly bitter along the coast southeast of the mission and in the swamp north of the gardens, where elements of Company C were still busy cleaning out pockets of enemy resistance. Although Companies E, F, and H, 126th Infantry, under Captain Sullivan, advanced 300 yards in the area east of the right fork of the Triangle, thus completing the capture of the gardens, the day's gains along the coast

and in the swamp north of the gardens were disappointing.[29]

The enemy was resisting fanatically, but he was obviously nearing the end of his powers. For several days artillery overs from the Warren front had been troubling the troops on the Urbana front, and the troops on the Warren front were, in turn, receiving fire that could have come only from Urbana Force. Not only were the two forces moving closer together, but a patrol of the 2d Battalion, 126th Infantry, had made contact that morning with a patrol of Warren Force at the southwest end of the gardens.[30]

Since Warren Force was to mount its final attack on Giropa Point in the morning, Company B, 127th Infantry, was ordered to attack eastward the next day to link up with Warren Force and assist it in the cleanup. General Eichelberger wrote to General Sutherland that night that he hoped the attack would "go through in fine shape." "If it did," he added, "it will then be just a matter of cleaning up Buna Mission."[31]

---

[27] 127th Inf Jnl, 0505, 0610, 0635, 31 Dec 42; 127th Inf Tact Hist, 21 Dec 42; Ltr, Gen Eichelberger to Gen Sutherland, 31 Dec 42; 32d Div G-3 Daily Periodic Rpt, 31 Dec 42; Col Grose, Affidavit, 7 Apr 44; Col Grose, Comments on the Buna-Sanananda Operation, 20 Feb 46.

[28] Statement of unnamed POW, in 1st Bn, 128th Inf, Jnl, 1232, 1 Jan 43. The submarine, which had surfaced and shelled the shore the same night, got away safely. 127th Inf Tact Hist, 25 Dec 42; 32d Div Hist of Arty, Papuan Campaign.

[29] 2d Bn, 126th Inf, Jnl, 31 Dec 42; 127th Inf Jnl, 0818, 31 Dec 42; 32d Div G-3 Daily Periodic Rpt, 31 Dec 42; 127th Inf Tact Hist, 31 Dec 42; Ltr, Gen Eichelberger to Gen Sutherland, 31 Dec 42; Rpt, CG Buna Forces, p. 36. Pvt. Earl Johnson and Pfc. Herman Bender of Company M, 127th Infantry—both killed that day—greatly distinguished themselves in the fighting along the coast. Johnson was killed while covering the withdrawal of his squad from a dangerously advanced position where it had been pinned down by enemy fire; Bender met his death as the result of a bold dash through an open field swept by enemy fire to find the flank of a neighboring unit with which all contact had been lost. Both men were posthumously awarded the Distinguished Service Cross. The citations are in Hq USAFFE GO No. 32, 15 Jun 43.

[30] Tel Msg, Brig Wootten to Col Howe, Ser 4486, 28 Dec 42; Tel Msg, Maj Henry G. Nulton to Col Bowen, Ser 4680, 31 Dec 42; 32d Div G-3 Daily Periodic Rpt, 31 Dec 42.

[31] Ltr, Gen Eichelberger to Gen Sutherland, 31 Dec 42.

General Eichelberger described the situation "as it is at present" in these words:

On the right, the Australians with their tanks have moved up to the mouth of Simemi Creek, [and] the entire area of the two strips is in our hands. Martin's men have extended to the left from the Old Strip for several hundred yards so that the forces of the Urbana and Warren fronts are now only about 600 yards apart. On the left, we have established a corridor between Giropa Point and Buna Mission, and have moved enough men in there to make it hold. The famous "Triangle" which held us up so long, was finally taken, and our men also occupy the island south of Buna Village. Today, we are moving on Buna Mission from both directions, and I sincerely hope we will be able to knock it off.

After noting that there had hitherto been many disappointments in the campaign, he went on to say, "Little by little we are getting those devils penned in and perhaps we shall be able to finish them shortly." [32]

Colonel Yazawa's Mission

At Rabual, meanwhile, the impending collapse at Buna was causing *18th Army* headquarters the deepest concern. On 26 December General Adachi ordered General Yamagata (whose headquarters, it will be recalled, was then at Danawatu, north of Gona) to move all his troops by sea to Giruwa. He was to use them first to rescue the Buna garrison. If the rescue failed, he was to divert them to the defense of Giruwa and hold it to the last. Two days later, Adachi ordered Buna evacuated. Its defenders were to fight their way to Giruwa with the help of a special force which would be under command of Colonel Yazawa, who was to proceed to Buna Mission from

Giruwa by way of the beach and attack the American left flank. After cutting his way through to the beleaguered Japanese Army and Navy troops holding the mission, he was to withdraw with them to Giruwa. [33]

It was a desperate plan, but not necessarily an impracticable one. The Japanese must have known from clashing with Lieutenant Chagnon's fifty-two men near Tarakena that the American flank covering Buna was virtually undefended. They may have thought, therefore, that Colonel Yazawa's raiding party might still save the defenders of Buna Mission—only about two miles from Tarakena by beach—by launching a sudden surprise attack, advancing swiftly, and making a quick withdrawal.

General Yamagata lost no time in complying with General Adachi's orders. On 27 December he ordered 430 men from Danawatu to Giruwa, with orders to report to Colonel Yazawa. Yazawa, who had led his regiment across the Owen Stanleys and back, was perhaps the most experienced and resourceful commander the Japanese had at Giruwa. The fact that he was detailed to the task of rescuing the Buna garrison was an indication of the importance Rabaul attached to his mission.

General Yamagata arrived at Giruwa on 29 December and, two days later, gave Colonel Yazawa his orders. The rescue operation, the orders read, was to be directly under Yamagata's command. It was to be undertaken as soon as a suitable concentration of forces reached Giruwa from Danawatu. [34] The move came too late. Even as

[32] Ltr, Gen Eichelberger to Col Rex Chandler, DCofS, I Corps, Rockhampton, 31 Dec 42, in 312, I Corps File, in ORB RAC, AGO.

[33] *Buna Shitai* Opns Orders No. 44, North Giruwa, 31 Dec 42, in ATIS CT 29, No. 350; *18th Army* Opns I, pp. 27, 28.
[34] *18th Army* Opns I, pp. 27, 28; *Buna Shitai* Opns Orders No. A–39, 27 Dec 42, in ATIS CT 29, No. 350.

Yazawa began assembling troops for the thrust eastward, the fall of Buna Mission was imminent, and most of its defenders had only a few hours to live.

The Envelopment

On New Year's day, while Warren Force and its tanks were reducing Giropa Point, Urbana Force launched what it hoped would be the final assault on Buna Mission. Early in the morning, while Company B attacked eastward toward Giropa Point, the artillery and mortars laid down a heavy barrage on the mission and the rest of Urbana Force struck at the Japanese line around the mission. Captain Cronk attacked from the mission spit, and Major Schroeder's troops, pivoting on Entrance Creek, moved on the mission from the southeast. Some Company B men could already see the tanks on Giropa Point, but the unit was still held up by very strong enemy resistance. Company F, 128th Infantry, left alone on the spit when Colonel Grose withdrew Company E, 127th Infantry, for reorganization, also found itself unable to move forward. In the swamp Company C, supported on the right by Company M, moved forward 150 yards, and the remaining companies to the right of M—F, A, and L, with I and D immediately to the rear—made some progress.

The enemy had thus far fought with the greatest tenacity, but evidence of his disintegration was not lacking. On the evening of 1 January while Colonel Smith of the 2d Battalion, 128th Infantry, and Major Clarkson of the 1st Battalion, 128th Infantry, established a joint Urbana Force-Warren Force outpost in the no man's land between their two fronts, Japanese troops were sighted for the first time trying to swim from

the mission—an unmistakable sign that the mission's defense was on the point of collapse.[35]

Urbana Force made careful preparations for the next day's attack. The main effort was to be along the coast. It was to be spearheaded by two relatively rested units, Company G, 127th Infantry, and Company G, 128th Infantry, which had gone into reserve when the troops on the mission spit failed to knock out the bunkers facing the north bridge. Company H, 127th Infantry, would cross over from the island as soon as either Company F, 128th Infantry, advancing from the mission spit, or Company C, 127th Infantry, moving up through the swamp north of the gardens, took over the area north of the bridge and made repair of the bridge possible.[36]

The Japanese continued their desperate attempts to escape. Just before dawn of the next day, Saturday, twenty enemy soldiers carrying heavy packs and led by a lieutenant made a break for the beached landing barges on the mission spit. They had three machine guns with them and their packs were loaded with food, medicine, and personal effects, as if for a quick getaway. Captain Cronk's company turned its machine guns and rifles on them and cut them down to a man. At daylight, observers all the way from Buna Village to Tarakena caught sight of large numbers of Japanese in the water. Some

[35] 127th Inf Jnl, 1600, 1850, 1900, 1 Jan 43; G–3 Daily Periodic Rpt, Buna Force, 1 Jan 43; Ltr, Gen Eichelberger to Gen Sutherland, 1 Jan 43, copy in OCMH files. During this day's action Pvt. Robert H. Campbell of Company M, 127th Infantry, crawled to the rescue of a wounded member of the company, who was lying in the open in the direct line of fire of an enemy machine gun. Campbell was later awarded the Distinguished Service Cross. The citation is in Hq USAFFE GO No. 34, 21 Jun 43.
[36] 127th Inf Jnl, 1300, 1 Jan 43; Ltr, Gen Eichelberger to Gen Sutherland, 1 Jan 43.

were swimming, others were clinging to boxes, rafts, and logs; still others were trying to escape in small boats. Artillery and machine gun fire was immediately laid down on the troops in the water, and, at 1000, the air force began systematically strafing them with B–25's, P–39's, and Wirraways.[37]

The two top Japanese commanders at Buna had chosen to die at their posts. Realizing that the end was near, Captain Yasuda and Colonel Yamamoto met at a central point the same day, Saturday, and killed themselves in the traditional Japanese fashion by cutting open their bellies.[38]

Despite the fact that the mission was already partly evacuated, there were still enough Japanese left in the mission and along its approaches to give Urbana Force (in General Eichelberger's phrase) "the darndest fight" all day.[39] At 1000, just as the attack was about to open, Major Schroeder, who was in a forward observation post at the time, was struck and mortally wounded by a Japanese bullet which penetrated his skull. Capt. Donald F. Runnoe, a member of Schroeder's staff, at once took over command of Schroeder's battalion, and Colonel Grose came up and took personal charge of the coastal drive.[40]

A heavy artillery barrage and white phosphorous smoke shells hit the enemy before the troops finally jumped off at 1015. Captain Cronk's company on the spit attacked southeast. Company C in the swamp, with

Company M still on its right, attacked toward the north bridge between the island and the mission. The two G Companies— Company G, 128th Infantry, and Company G, 127th Infantry, with the latter unit under Captain Dames leading—passed through the lines of Companies I, L, and M and advanced through the Coconut Plantation to attack the mission from the southeast. The attack went smoothly from the first. The phosphorous shells set fire to the grass and trees at several points in the mission area and, in one instance, exposed a whole line of enemy bunkers to Allied fire. Attempts by the Japanese to flee these exposed positions were met by machine gun fire from the troops on the island and on the mission spit. As the phosphorous shells exploded in trees, they also set afire several of the huts in the mission. When enemy troops in dugouts beneath the burning huts tried to escape, they ran into bursts of Allied fire which killed most of them.

The remaining Japanese continued their dogged last-ditch resistance and had to be rooted out of each dugout and bunker by grenade, machine gun, and submachine gun fire. Company C, 127th Infantry, on the left, and Company G, 127th Infantry, on the right, made excellent progress, but Company F, 128th Infantry, on the mission spit was held up, as was Company B, 127th Infantry, which had meanwhile resumed its attack to the eastward.[41]

[37] 127th Inf Jnl, 0545, 0600, 0706, 0745, 0800, 0815, 0905, 0930, 1010, 1040, 2 Jan 43; 127th Inf Tact Hist, 2 Jan 43; G–3 Daily Periodic Rpt, Buna Force, 2 Jan 43; Ltr, Gen Eichelberger to Gen Sutherland, 2 Jan 43, copy in OCMH files.
[38] 18th Army Opns I, p. 29.
[39] Ltr, Gen Eichelberger to Gen Sutherland, 2 Jan 43.
[40] 127th Inf Tact Hist, 2 Jan 43; Ltr, Gen Eichelberger to Gen Sutherland, 3 Jan 43, copy in OCMH files.

[41] 127th Inf Jnl, 1315, 1523, 1627, 2 Jan 43; 127th Inf Tact Hist, 2 Jan 43; Ltr, Gen Eichelberger to Gen Sutherland, 2 Jan 43; F. Tillman Durdin, The New York Times, 8 Jan 43; Rpt, CG Buna Forces, p. 36; Col Grose, Comments on the Buna–Sanananda Opn, 2 Feb 46. For their performance in the day's fighting, Colonel Grose and Captain Runnoe were later awarded the Distinguished Service Cross. Grose's citation is in GHQ SWPA GO No. 4, 10 Jan 43; Runnoe's, in Hq USAFFE GO No. 34, 21 Jun 43.

37-MM. ANTITANK GUN *in position to fire at the enemy in Buna Mission.*

At 1400 Company C was in sight of the bunkers covering the north bridge. An hour and a half later Company G, 127th Infantry, reached the point of the mission with Company G, 128th Infantry, hard on its heels. Only scattered rifle fire met the troops, and they quickly took their first prisoners—a dozen Chinese laborers, naked except for breechcloths.

Ten minutes later Company C came up, followed by Company M, and in a few more minutes Companies I, L, and A reached the scene. The engineers had meanwhile been repairing the north bridge. By 1620 Com-

pany H was across it, thus finally completing the envelopment.

The mission was overrun by 1632. The remaining enemy troops in the area were either flushed out of their hiding places and killed, or entombed in them. By 1700 the fighting was over except in a few pockets of resistance near the beach. There a handful of Japanese held out stubbornly and were left to be dealt with the next day.

The mission was a scene of utter desolation. All through the area the ground was pitted with shell holes. The trees were broken and bedraggled. Abandoned weapons and derelict landing craft littered the beach, and Japanese dead were everywhere.[42]

In its attack toward Giropa Point, Company B had been held up by a line of enemy bunkers in the road junction near the coast, which had been bypassed in the coastal advance. As soon as he could, General Eichelberger pulled Company C out of the mission area and sent it to the assistance of Company B. The two companies launched a concerted attack late that afternoon, cleared out the bunkers, and by 1930 had made contact with the 2/12 Battalion. With the 2/10 Battalion and the 1st and 3d Battalions, 128th Infantry, the 2/12th had finished clearing out the area between Giropa Point and the west bank of Simemi Creek earlier in the day.[43] After more than six weeks of fighting, the Buna area in its entirety was finally in Allied hands.

The End at Buna

Cleaning Out the Pockets

Mopping up of isolated pockets of resistance on both Warren and Urbana fronts continued for several days until the last of the enemy troops were accounted for. An observer describes the scene on 3 January, a Sunday, as follows:

[By] Sunday, the . . . front from the shattered palms of Buna Village to Cape Endaiadere was almost peaceful. It was pos-

sible to walk its entire length and hear only a few scattered shots and occasional bursts of mortar fire. In the . . . swamp . . . a few Japanese snipers still held out, in a patch of jungle . . . a bunker or two still resisted, but great stretches of the front were scenes of quiet desolation. . . . The only considerable fighting during the day occurred in the jungle area southwest of Giropa Point, where a small group of laborers, estimated as high as a hundred, fled when the point was captured. Their intention perhaps was to try to escape through the swamps and jungles, and scatter into the interior. . . .

Americans and Australians however drew a line around them from all sides and made contact along the beach between Buna Mission and Giropa Point, and methodically mopped up the enemy pocket.

Americans quelled the last resistance to Buna Mission by Sunday noon in a little thicket on the beach where a few Japanese held out in bunkers. Routed from the bunkers, some scurried behind a wrecked barge on the beach and continued to fire. They were finally killed by a high explosive charge that blew the barge and the Japanese to bits.

By noon, the Americans had counted roughly 150 Japanese dead in the Buna Mission area.

Small squads finished the job of eliminating the last fighting Japanese. Some Americans [went swimming in] the sea. Some washed out their clothing for the first time in weeks, some simply slept the deep sleep of exhaustion, curled up under shell-shattered trees or in sandy foxholes. By Tuesday, the only Japanese left in the area extending from Buna Village through Cape Endaiadere were roving groups and individuals . . . who were hiding out in jungle and sago swamp, and who by now had become desperately hungry. These Japanese were trying to keep under cover during the day [to prowl] at night through moonless blackness in American-Australian lines seeking something to eat.[44]

Some 190 Japanese were finally buried at Buna Mission, and 300 at Giropa Point.

---

[42] Tel Msg, Capt Hewitt to Col Howe, Ser 4892, 2 Jan 43; Msg, Gen Eichelberger to Adv NGF, Ser 4897, 2 Jan 43, in 32d Div G–3 Jnl. 127th Inf Jnl, 1550, 1554, 1600, 1627, 1712, 2 Jan 43; 127th Inf Tact Hist, 2 Jan 43; Durdin, *The New York Times*, 8 Jan 43; Col Grose, Comments on the Buna–Sanananda Operation, 20 Feb 46.

[43] 127th Inf Jnl, 1930, 2 Jan 43; Buna Force G–3 Sitrep, 2 Jan 43; Ltr, Gen Eichelberger to Gen Sutherland, 2 Jan 43; Rpt, CG Buna Forces, p. 37.

[44] Durdin, *The New York Times*, 8 Jan 43.

32D DIVISION TROOPS EXAMINE BOOTY *after taking Buna Mission.*

Fifty prisoners were taken. Warren Force took twenty-one horribly emaciated Koreans and one Japanese soldier. Urbana Force took twenty-eight prisoners, mainly Chinese and Koreans. Of the few Japanese among them most were captured near Siwori Village and Tarakena when they were caught naked and unarmed as they swam in from the sea.[45]

Booty was heavy on both fronts. On the

Warren front it included, in addition to the three-inch naval guns and the pompoms, rifles, machine guns, radio equipment, several 37-mm. guns, two 75-mm. mountain guns on wheels, nine unserviceable trucks, some of American make, and a number of smashed fighter aircraft, two of them Zero-type planes that were found on the Old Strip and looked as if they could be repaired. Booty taken by Urbana Force, besides the weapons taken in the Triangle and several antiaircraft guns captured in the Government Gardens, included a 75-mm. gun and miscellaneous items of equipment. Hardly

[45] Tel Msg, 18th Bde to 32d Div, Ser 4869, 2 Jan 43; Tel Msg, Capt George E. Aurell to G–2, 32d Div, Ser 4889, 2 Jan 43; Tel Msg, 18th Bde to Adv NGF, Ser 4918, 2 Jan 43; Ltr, Gen Eichelberger to Gen Sutherland, 7 Dec 42, copy in OCMH files.

EMACIATED PRISONERS BEING LED TO THE REAR AREA *for questioning.*

any food or ammunition was found on either front.[46]

The Congratulatory Messages

By 3 January it was obvious that all organized resistance on the Buna side of the Girua River was over. In a special memorandum issued at noon that day, General Eichelberger told American troops who had taken part in the fighting that they had had their baptism of fire and were now veterans. The lessons they had learned at Buna, he added, would serve to reduce losses in the future and bring further victories.[47]

Later that day General Blamey sent a message of congratulations to Brigadier Wootten and the troops serving under him on the successful conclusion of the fighting on the Warren Front. Their operations, he said, had been marked "by the greatest thoroughness in planning," by "constant

[46] Rpt on Opns 18th Bde Gp at Cape Endaiadere and Giropa Point; 127th Inf Tact Hist, 2 Jan 43; Ltr, Gen Eichelberger to Gen Sutherland, 7 Jan 43; Rpt, CG Buna Forces, p. 42.

[47] Memo, Gen Eichelberger for American troops in the Buna Area, 3 Jan 43, Ser 4649, in 32d Div G-3 Jnl.

GENERAL BLAMEY TOURING THE BATTLE AREA *with General Eichelberger.*

steadiness in control," and by "valor and determination in execution." [48]

General Herring in turn, issued a special order of the day in which he expressed to Australians and Americans alike his appreciation of "their magnificent and prolonged effort." He dwelt on the strength of the enemy's defenses, his tenacious resistance, the hardships that the men had borne, and the fortitude with which they had borne them. He complimented all concerned on their steadfastness and determination and

said, "You have done a job of which both our countries should indeed be proud." [49]

General Marshall sent General MacArthur his congratulations the next day. MacArthur thanked Marshall for his congratulatory message, and added, "However unwarranted it may be, the impression prevailed that this area's efforts were belittled and disparaged at home, and despite all my efforts to the contrary the effect was de-

---

[48] Msg, Gen Blamey to Brig Wootten, Ser 4988, 3 Jan 43, in 32d Div G–3 Jnl.

[49] Lt Gen Edmund F. Herring, GOC New Guinea Force, Order of the Day, 3 Jan 43, copy in OCMH files.

pressing. Your tributes have had a tonic effect." [50]

Buna's Cost

Battle Losses

There were 1,400 Japanese buried at Buna—500 west of Giropa Point and 900 east of it.[51] On the Allied side, 620 were killed, 2,065 wounded, and 132 missing. The 32d Division sustained 1,954 of these casualties—353 killed, 1,508 wounded, and 93 missing; [52] the 18th Brigade had 863 casualties—267 killed, 557 wounded, and 39 missing.[53]

The total casualties were thus 2,817 killed, wounded, and missing—a figure considerably in excess of the 2,200 men the Japanese were estimated to have had at Buna when the 32d Division launched its first attacks upon them there.[54]

Losses Due to Sickness and Disease

The troops had been plagued unceasingly by all manner of chiggers, mites, and insects, exposed to debilitating tropical infections, fevers, and diseases, and forced most of the time to eat cold and inadequate rations, sleep in water-filled foxholes, and go for days on end without being dry. Their gaunt and haggard faces, knobby knees and elbows that poked through ragged uniforms attested to what the men had been through.[55]

Some of the hazards that faced them were revealed vividly in a letter written on 10 January by Maj. E. Mansfield Gunn, a medical officer on General Eichelberger's staff:

. . . Be sure to rinse the dyed jungle equipment over and over again in cold water, otherwise it will ruin everything [and] make everything stink. . . . Furthermore, we are not sure [the dye] is not absorbed by the body, and then excreted in the urine, because some of the urine would indicate [that was the case]. . . . Tablets for individual chlorination of water in the canteen would be of the greatest value for all; two pairs of shoes are definitely needed [because] everything dries very slowly. A chigger repellent for each individual is needed for there are millions of the little fellows. . . .

[There] is a growing incidence of scrub typhus here. . . . The inoculations we all received were designed to prevent the European typhus, and hence there is nothing to do but hope. There are some tremendous rats in the area, and no doubt the fleas on same are carrying the infection from the dead Japanese to our soldiers. One medical officer just died of the disease and another one is in very poor shape today. There has been an awful lot of work to do with these units, and under existing travel conditions, it is the toughest situation any of us have ever been in. . . . Sickness of all sorts, particularly of the various tropical

---

[50] Msg, Gen MacArthur to Gen Marshall, No. C–43, CM–IN 2047, 5 Jan 43. Marshall's message is No. 91, CM–OUT 1193, 4 Jan 43.

[51] Ltr, Gen Eichelberger to Gen Sutherland, 7 Jan 43; Rpt, CG Buna Forces, p. 42. The above figure includes only the counted dead. It does not include Japanese dead who could not be counted because their bunkers had caved in or had been sealed up during the fighting.

[52] Rad, Gen Eichelberger to Lt Col G. C. Sherman, G–1 Rear Echelon, 32d Div, Ser 5298, 9 Jan 43, in 32d Div G–3 Jnl; Rad, Col Sherman to CG Buna Forces, 1455, 10 Jan 43, in 32d Div G–1 Jnl. These figures are of 6 January, and thus include casualties sustained in the mop-up. They do not include a figure for those who were wounded before 6 January and died of their wounds after that date. It should be noted that the figures are for Buna only. They do not include the casualties sustained by the 1st and 3d Battalions, and attached troops, of the 126th Infantry on the Sanananda front, who as of 6 January had suffered 394 casualties—76 killed, 235 wounded, and 83 missing. Jnl, Maj Boerem's Det, 6 Jan 43.

[53] Rpt on Opns 18th Bde Gp at Cape Endaiadere and Giropa Point. Of the 267 Australians killed, 230 were killed in action, and 37 died of wounds.

[54] Rpt, CG Buna Forces, p. 42.

[55] Durdin, *The New York Times,* 8 Jan 43; Interv with Col Moffatt, 24 Feb 50; Interv with Col Teesdale-Smith, 10 Mar 50; Interv with Col Grose, 18 Nov 50; Interv with Maj Odell, 14 Dec 50.

fevers is on the increase also, so I expect that almost everyone in the division will come out of here either wounded or sick. I do not intend to paint a depressing picture, but that is the truth as things stand today. The figures will be appalling to you when you see them.[56]

As late as mid-January Colonel Warmenhoven, then the division surgeon, was urging that all troops be compelled to take quinine daily, but the difficulty was that the medicine was still in short supply. He cited the case of a battalion in the 128th Infantry that had gone for several days entirely without it. Warmenhoven found also that the drinking water was often polluted and sometimes insufficiently chlorinated. There were now field ranges at most of the jeepheads, and some of the men had canned heat and primus stoves, but the division surgeon nevertheless noted that rations were still inadequate and that the troops were still eating them cold most of the time.[57]

The cost of sickness and disease at Buna was to reach staggering proportions. In a check of the health of the 32d Division undertaken shortly after the Buna mop-up was completed, the temperature of 675 soldiers, representing a cross section of the division's three combat teams, was taken. Colonel Warmenhoven reported that "53 percent of this group of soldiers were running a temperature ranging between 99 degrees to 104.6 degrees. . . . In order of prevalence, the cause of the rise in temperature is due to the following: Malaria, Exhaustive States, Gastro-Enteritis, Dengue Fever, Acute Upper Respiratory Infection, and Typhus (scrub)." The average normal sick-call rate of a command, the colonel pointed out, was 3.8 percent of its strength. The sick-call rate of the 32d Division was 24 percent, and going higher. Some 2,952 men (more than three quarters of them from Buna where the division had made its primary effort) were already hospitalized because of disease and fever, and fifty to one hundred were being evacuated from Buna to Port Moresby daily for the same cause.[58]

The Situation to the Westward

Colonel Yazawa Scatters the Tarakena Patrol

Ordered on 31 December to rescue the troops at Buna Mission, Colonel Yazawa had been unable to leave Giruwa until the evening of 2 January and then with only 250 men, most of them from the *1st Battalion, 170th Infantry.*[59] Shortly after he left Giruwa he learned that Buna Mission had already fallen. His energies thereafter were devoted to picking up as many of the survivors as possible. The success of his rescue mission required that the spit off Tarakena (on which many of the swimmers were landing, after hiding out during the day from Allied planes and patrols) be in Japanese

---

[56] Ltr, Maj E. Mansfield Gunn, MC, I Corps, to 1st Lt. C. A. Farish, I Corps Rear Echelon, Rockhampton, 10 Jan 43, in I Corps Corr File.

[57] Memo, Col Warmenhoven for CG 32d Div, 16 Jan 43, incl to 1st Ind, 32d Div Hq to Regimental Combat Teams of 32d Div, 114th Engr Bn, and Hq Co, 32d Div, 16 Jan 43, copy in OCMH files; 32d Div Hist of Medical Activities, Papuan Campaign, in Surgeon General's Hist File.

[58] Ltr, Col Warmenhoven to CG Buna Forces, 15 Jan 43, sub: Health of the Command: Final Report, copy in OCMH files.

[59] Diary, Maj Nojiri, CO *1st Bn, 170th Inf,* in ATIS CT 29, No. 350; *18th Army Opns I,* p. 27. The reason for the delay was a shortage of gasoline for the motor launches which were to bring the men in from the Amboga River area. Yazawa waited as long as he dared for the troops to arrive. Unable to wait any longer, he left for Buna Mission the evening it fell with the men already at hand.

hands. Ordering a careful reconnaissance of Lieutenant Chagnon's position, he attacked it at dusk on 4 January with the bulk of his force.[60]

Lieutenant Chagnon had been reinforced that afternoon by twenty-one men of Company E, 126th Infantry. When attacked, he had under his command seventy-three soldiers from seven different companies—including men from the Headquarters and Service Companies of the 127th Infantry—a 60-mm. mortar, and three light machine guns. The force was short of ammunition and grenades, and the attack came as a complete surprise. Hit from the front, rear, and left, Chagnon's men fought as best they could until all their ammunition was gone and they had no recourse but to swim for it. The lieutenant, who retrieved one of the machine guns under fire and continued operating it until it jammed, was the last man out. Members of Chagnon's patrol kept straggling into Siwori Village all that night. By the following day all but four had come in—a small loss in view of the fact that Yazawa's attack had been made in overwhelming strength.[61]

Having cleared Chagnon's position on the spit and mainland, Yazawa proceeded with his rescue work. He was soon able to report that he had picked up some 190 survivors of the Buna garrison. Most of them had swum from the mission and had had the good sense to keep out of sight during the day.[62]

Colonel Grose meanwhile had not been idle. By the early morning of 5 January he had part of Company F, 127th Infantry, across Siwori Creek. The crossing was unopposed. The men quickly re-established themselves on the other side of the creek and began moving northwestward.[63]

The Stalemate at Sanananda

Buna had fallen, and the bridgehead across Siwori Creek had been re-established. The campaign, however, was far from over. West of the Girua River on the Sanananda front things were at a stalemate, and had been for some time. In his order of the day of 3 January General Herring had told the troops that the battle for Buna was "but a step on the way." They still had, he said, the difficult job ahead of them of cleaning the enemy out of the Sanananda area, a job that would "not be any easier than Buna." [64]

It was a timely reminder. As Col. Leslie M. Skerry, General Eichelberger's G–1, put the matter: "While we were engaged in the Buna area, we did not have much opportunity to think about what was going on elsewhere. But after getting rid of the Japanese here, we awoke to the fact that there was another most difficult situation existing in the Sanananda area next door." There,

---

[60] 127th Inf Jnl, 1830, 1910, 4 Jan 42; 127th Inf Tact Hist, 4 Jan 42; 18th Army Opns I, pp. 28, 29.

[61] Tel Msgs, Capt Hewitt to Buna Force, Ser 5047, 4 Jan 43, Ser 5051, 4 Jan 43, Ser 5106, 5 Jan 43, Ser 5108, 5 Jan 43; 127th Inf Jnl, 1100, 1900, 4 Jan 43, 1430, 5 Jan 43; 127th Inf Tact Hist, 4 Jan 43. Capt Louis A. Chagnon, The Actions of a Left Flank Security Patrol During the Operations of the 32d Division at Buna, 16 December 1942–4 January 1943, Infantry School Monograph, in TIS Files. As a result of his reconnaissance, Yazawa set the strength of Chagnon's force when he scattered it on the 4th as about 100 men—a remarkably close estimate.

[62] Maj Nojiri's Diary, in ATIS CT 29, No. 350; 18th Army Opns I, pp. 28, 29.

[63] Col Grose's Diary, 4 Dec 42; Col Grose, Comments on the Buna–Sanananda Operation, 20 Feb 46.

[64] Gen Herring, Order of the Day, 3 Jan 43.

WEARY SOLDIER SLEEPS *after the battle is over.*

Skerry noted, "a state of semi-siege has been going on . . . with little progress being made." [65]

---

[65] Ltr, Col Leslie M. Skerry, I Corps Adv Echelon, to Col M. J. Conway, Adj Gen, I Corps Rear Echelon, Rockhampton, 15 Jan 43, in I Corps Corr File.

With the 127th Infantry in position to move on Tarakena, and the 18th Brigade, the tanks, and most of the guns in use at Buna available for use on the other side of the river, the time had come to move on the enemy's Sanananda–Giruwa position in force.

CHAPTER XVII

Clearing the Track Junction

The offensive on the Sanananda front had indeed bogged down. By the end of December the Allies had established roadblocks at Huggins and Kano, and made the first breaches in the formidable enemy perimeter which covered the track junction south of Huggins. These, however, were only interim victories. The Japanese were still fighting desperately in the track junction area south of Huggins; they were well entrenched in the area between Huggins and Kano; and they were holding strong positions north of Kano. The tactical situation, especially on the Motor Transport or M. T. Road, as the Soputa–Sanananda track was sometimes known, was to say the least unusual. As one observer, in describing it, remarked, "At first glance, the situation map was simply startling. Along the M. T. Road Red and Blue alternated like beads on a string." [1] The task was to squeeze out the Red—a supremely difficult task in the existing terrain.

General Herring Calls a Conference

The Arrival of the 163d Infantry

There were actually three fronts on the western side of the river at this time. The first was south of the track junction; the second was in the roadblock area at Huggins and Kano; the third was in the Napapo–Amboga River area north of Gona. Brigadier Porter of the 30th Brigade, in charge of track junction operations, had under his command the 36 and 55/53 Battalions and what was left of the 126th Infantry troops fighting west of the river, then about 200 men. Brigadier Dougherty with his 21st Brigade headquarters was operating from the two roadblocks and had under his command the 39 and 49 Battalions and the 2/7 Cavalry Regiment. His battalions, the 2/14th, 2/16th, and 2/27th, normally a part of the 21st Brigade, were mopping up in the Amboga River area.

These battalions of the 21st Brigade had suffered extremely heavy casualties in this, their second tour of duty during the campaign. By late December they were down to less than company strength. The 2/27 Battalion, for instance, numbered 55 men and the 2/16 Battalion was down to 89. It was clear that if the brigade was to fight again it would have to be relieved quickly. [2]

Relief was already on the way. As planned by General Herring, a fresh headquarters, that of the 14th Brigade at Port Moresby, was to take over in the Gona area, and the 163d Infantry Regiment of the 41st

---

[1] 163d Inf, The Battle of Sanananda.

[2] Ltr, Gen Blamey to Gen MacArthur, 27 Dec 42.

Infantry Division in the roadblock area.[3] The arrival at the front of the 163d Infantry would release troops for action in the Gona area, make possible the immediate relief of the 21st Brigade's battalions, and permit intensification of the attack both north and south of Huggins.

The 163d Infantry Regimental Combat Team, consisting of the 163d Infantry Regiment and 550 attached divisional troops, less artillery, arrived at Port Moresby on 27 December, 3,820 strong, under Col. Jens A. Doe.[4] Though it looked for a time as if

the regiment might be sent to the Urbana front, the final decision was to have it proceed, as General Herring had planned, to Sanananda rather than Buna.

On 27 December, the very day the 163d Infantry reached Port Moresby, General MacArthur had conveyed orders to General Blamey (through General Sutherland who was then visiting the front) that the regiment was to be sent to Buna to help in the reduction of Buna Mission, rather than as previously planned to the Sanananda front. General Blamey immediately protested this change of plan. He pointed out that General Eichelberger had sufficient troops to take Buna. He insisted that it was imperative that the 21st Brigade be relieved immediately, if it was to continue as a fighting force, and expressed his regret that General MacArthur had taken it upon himself to interfere in the matter. Blamey wrote that while he did not "for one moment question the right of the Commander-in-Chief to give such orders as he may think fit," he nevertheless gave it as his belief that nothing could be "more contrary to sound principles of command than that the Commander-in-Chief . . . should [personally] take over the direction of a portion of the battle."[5] General MacArthur apparently saw the point, and General Herring's decision to use the 163d Infantry on the Sanananda front was permitted to stand.

The 163d Infantry, the unit which had engendered this high-level contention, was by this time well-trained, and the men, fresh, ably led, and in superb physical condition,

---

[3] Msg, Gen MacArthur to Gen Chamberlin, No. P–481, 4 Dec 42; Ltr, Gen Blamey to Gen MacArthur, 27 Dec 42; 163d Inf, The Battle of Sanananda; ALF, Rpt on New Guinea Opns; 23 Sep 42–23 Jan 43; NGF, Notes on Opns in New Guinea, Ser 3.

The history of the 163d Infantry goes back to 1887 when the unit was first organized as the 1st Battalion, Montana National Guard. In 1898 and 1899, it served in the Philippine Islands as the 1st Montana Volunteer Infantry. In 1916 it saw service on the Mexican border as the 2d Infantry, Montana National Guard. It was mustered into the federal service in March 1917 as the 163d Infantry, 41st Division. In December 1917 it arrived in France where it was used as a replacement and training organization. In 1924 the 2d Infantry, Montana National Guard, was reorganized as the 163d Infantry. In September 1940 the regiment was inducted into the federal service with other National Guard elements from Washington, Oregon, and Idaho, as part of the 41st Infantry Division. It reached Australia on 6 April 1942, one of the first American infantry units to do so. Memo, Brig Gen Oliver L. Spaulding, Chief Hist Sec, AGO, for Opns Br AGO, 11 May 43, copy in OCMH files; AGF, Fact Sheet on the 41st Div, in DRB HRS, AGO.

[4] Eichelberger, *Our Jungle Road to Tokyo*, pp. 59, 60. The following divisional units were attached to the regiment: Company E, 116th Engineer Battalion; Company E, 116th Medical Battalion; one platoon of the Clearing Company, 116th Medical Battalion; the 7th, 11th, and 12th Portable Hospitals; detachments of the 41st Signal Company, the 41st Ordnance Company, and the 116th Quartermaster Company. There was also a detachment of military police. Ten units of fire for all weapons,

thirty days' supply of all classes, and complete organizational equipment, except for motor transport, arrived at Port Moresby with the troops. Msg, Gen MacArthur to Gen Chamberlin, No. P–481, 14 Dec 42; 163d Inf, The Battle of Sanananda.

[5] Ltr, Gen Blamey to Gen MacArthur, 27 Dec 42.

were ready for combat.[6] It was at once arranged that they would be flown to the front, the 1st Battalion leading. The 2d and 3d Battalions, which were to come in later, would follow in that order.

Early on 30 December the 1st Battalion and regimental headquarters were flown over the mountains, part to Dobodura and the rest to Popondetta. Lt. Col. Charles R. Dawley, Colonel Doe's executive officer, who was with the echelon that landed at Dobodura, immediately reported to Advance New Guinea Force, General Herring's headquarters, at Dobodura. Shortly thereafter Colonel Doe flew in from Popondetta, and he and Dawley had a conference with General Herring, Maj. Gen. F. H. Berryman, General Blamey's chief of staff, and General Vasey, who had meanwhile come in from Soputa. During the course of the conference, Doe and Dawley were told that the 163d Infantry would fight west of the Girua—the first direct intimation they had had of what the regiment's role would be. They then went with Berryman and Vasey to see General Eichelberger.[7]

The four officers reached Eichelberger's headquarters about 1030, and were offered tea. General Eichelberger seemed to be under the impression that he was to get the 163d Infantry for action on his side of the river, and this, as General Doe recalls, is what followed: "While tea was being pre-

pared, General Eichelberger explained the situation to us and told me he would take me up front after lunch to show me where the 163d Infantry was to go. Generals Vasey and Berryman sat silent, and when they did not speak up, I told General Eichelberger I had been informed the 163d was to go to the Sanananda front." "Plainly surprised," it was now General Eichelberger's turn to remain silent.[8]

When tea was over, Doe and Dawley went on to 7th Division headquarters at Soputa with General Vasey. Vasey went over the situation with them and told them that they were to take over in the roadblock area as soon as possible. On 31 December, while the 1st Battalion assembled at Soputa, General Vasey, Colonel Doe, and the regimental staff went forward to Huggins and reconnoitered the area. On 1 January, while Doe and Dawley were busy establishing a supply base for the regiment, the commander of the 1st Battalion, Lt. Col. Harold M. Lindstrom, and his staff went forward to Huggins and made arrangements to relieve Brigadier Dougherty's forces. On 2 January, the day that Buna Mission fell, the 1st Battalion took over at Huggins and Kano, and Colonel Doe took command of the area from Brigadier Dougherty the next day.[9] (Map 16)

General Vasey at once reshuffled his command. He ordered the 39 Battalion, which had been holding the roadblock, the 49 Battalion, which had been guarding the supply trail, and the 2/7 Cavalry Regiment, which had been operating from Kano, to replace the 36 and 55/53 Battalions south of the

---

[6] Interv with Gen Eichelberger, 26 Apr 50. The regiments of the 41st Division, General Eichelberger kept stressing, would enter combat much better trained than those of the 32d. "For four months," he wrote, "we were able to supervise their work, and insisted upon a lot of scouting and patrolling, individual, and squad combat firing with ammunition, etc." Ltr, Gen Eichelberger to Gen MacArthur, 12 Jan 43, copy in OCMH files.

[7] Ltr, Maj Gen Jens A. Doe to Gen Ward, 3 Mar 51; Ltr, Col Charles A. Dawley to Gen Ward, 7 Mar 51, with incls; 163d Inf, The Battle of Sanananda.

[8] Ltr, Gen Doe to Gen Ward, 3 Mar 51. General Eichelberger later commented, "He [Doe] is right in saying that I was surprised that the 163d Infantry would not come to the Buna side." Ltr, Gen Eichelberger to author, 19 Dec 51.

[9] Ltr, Gen Doe to Gen Ward, 3 Mar 51; Ltr, Col Dawley to Gen Ward, 7 Mar 51.

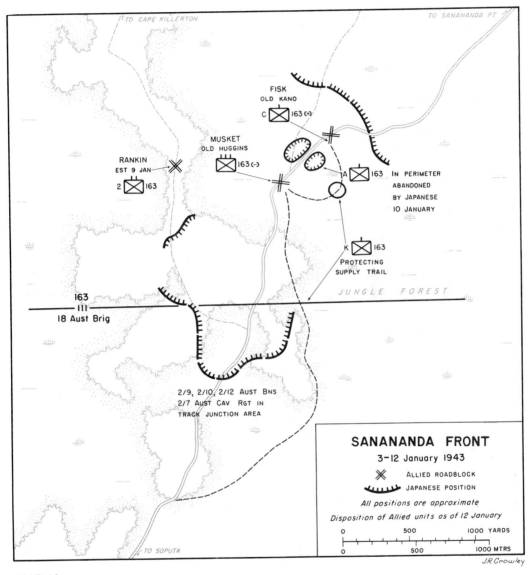

MAP 16

track junction. Upon their relief, the latter two battalions would move to Gona, where they would relieve the depleted battalions of the 21st Brigade, and come under command of 14th Brigade headquarters which had then just reached the Gona area. The relief of what was left of the 126th Infantry would be accomplished as soon as the 18th Brigade could be redeployed from Buna to the Sanananda side of the river.[10]

[10] Msg, 7th Div to Adv NGF, Ser 4900, 4911, 2 Jan 43; Msgs, 7th Div to 32d Div, Ser 4849, 2 Jan 43, Ser 4978, 3 Jan 43, in 32d Div G–3 Jnl; ALF Daily Opns Rpts No. 262, 1 Jan 43, No. 264, 3 Jan 43; ALF, Rpt on New Guinea Opns.

GENERAL HERRING, *Commander, Advanced New Guinea Force (left), and General Eichelberger.*

The Conference of 4 January

General Herring had ordered on 29 December that, when Buna fell, the 18th Brigade and the bulk of the guns and tanks in use east of the river be redeployed to the Sanananda front.[11] On 2 January, with all organized resistance at Buna at an end, he ordered that two troops of 25-pounder artillery previously in use at Buna be assigned to the Sanananda front. The next day he ordered a portion of the tanks to Soputa. On 4 January Herring met at his headquarters with General Eichelberger, General Berryman, General Vasey, and Brigadier Wootten, to work out a final,

comprehensive plan for the reduction of the enemy positions west of the river.[12]

Although the conferees had met to devise a plan to destroy the enemy, they discovered that they had very little knowledge of his strength and dispositions, especially those north of Kano. It was supposed that he had plenty of weapons and ammunition but was short of food; his strength, however, was anyone's guess. In describing the conference several days later General Eichelberger wrote, "We decided that we did not know whether there were one thousand Japs at Sanananda or five thousand." [13]

Despite the lack of any definite knowledge about the enemy's strength, the Allied commanders, acting on the assumption that there were still several thousand Japanese effectives in the area, quickly agreed upon a basic plan of action. As soon as the 2d and 3d Battalions, 163d Infantry, and 800 replacements for the 18th Brigade reached the front, the 18th Brigade, the 163d Infantry, and the 127th Infantry would launch a double envelopment of the enemy's Sanananda–Giruwa position. The first two units, under command of General Vasey, would move on Sanananda by way of the Cape Killerton trail and the M.T. Road respectively. The 127th Infantry would complete the envelopment by moving on Sanananda by way of Tarakena and Giruwa.

The main attack was to follow a number of essential preliminary operations. These would begin with the capture of Tarakena

---

[11] NGF OI No. 57, 29 Dec 42.

[12] Msgs, Adv NGF to Buna Force, Ser 4920, 2 Jan 43, Ser 4924, 2 Jan 43, Ser 4929, 2 Jan 43, Ser 4948, 3 Jan 43, in 32d Div G–3 Jnl; Ltr, Gen Eichelberger to Gen Sutherland, 3, 4 Jan 43, copies in OCMH files.

[13] Ltr, Gen Eichelberger to Gen Sutherland, 9 Jan 42, copy in OCMH files.

by the 127th Infantry and the clearing of the area between Huggins and Kano by the 1st Battalion, 163d Infantry. The 2d Battalion, 163d Infantry, meanwhile, would capture a position astride the Cape Killerton trail, just west of Huggins. Then the 18th Brigade would clear out all enemy opposition south of Huggins. As soon as these preliminaries were completed, the general advance would begin, with the 127th Infantry attacking westward along the coastal track, and the 163d Infantry and the 18th Brigade, northward, along the M.T. Road and the Cape Killerton trail.[14]

The 18th Brigade Reaches Soputa

The first elements of the 18th Brigade—brigade headquarters and the 2/9 Battalion—reached Soputa on 5 January, as did one troop (four tanks) of B Squadron, 2/6 Australian Armored Regiment. The tanks left Buna just in time, for extremely heavy rains had made the road net between the Old Strip, Dobodura, and Soputa impassable to vehicular traffic, and no more tanks or artillery were able to get through for days. The 2/10 Battalion arrived at Soputa on the 6th, and the 2/12 Battalion joined it a day later. The rest of the tanks and the two 25-pounder troops, which had been assigned to General Vasey upon the fall of Buna, had to remain where they were on the eastern side of the river because of the wretched state of the roads.

The weather had not only cost General Vasey the use of most of the tanks allotted to his front, but it had also made it impossible for him to make the best use of the additional artillery he had gained as a result of the fall of Buna. Because of the close quarters at which the battle was being fought, the two batteries in question, the Manning and Hall Troops, had no choice but to fire obliquely across the front, and to take special precautions not to hit friendly troops.[15] The guns were useful, but they would have been much more useful had it been possible to get them across the river.

The weather had done General Vasey another disservice by temporarily dislocating the flow of supply. The rains were so heavy and the tracks so muddy that even jeeps could not use them. To compound the difficulties, the "all-weather" airstrips at Dobodura and Popondetta became so mired that they remained unserviceable for days. Fortunately for the Allied offensive effort, there was already enough matériel stockpiled at the front to tide the troops over until the weather changed.[16]

By 7 January the 18th Brigade troops from the other side of the river were all at Soputa. General Vasey ordered Brigadier Wootten to take command of the 2/7 Cavalry and to relieve Brigadier Porter's remaining troops—the 39 and 49 Battalions and the remnants of the 126th Infantry. The orders provided that the 39 and 49 Battalions would go into divisional reserve near Soputa; that the 21st Brigade, whose shrunken battalions had by this time come in from Gona, would be returned forthwith to Port Moresby; and that the remaining

---

[14] NGF OI No. 58, 4 Jan 43; 7th Div OI No. 21, 7 Jan 43; Ltr, Gen Eichelberger to Gen Sutherland, 7 Jan 43, copy in OCMH files.

[15] Tel Msgs, Adv NGF to Buna Force, Ser 4924, 2 Jan 43, Ser 4989, 3 Jan 43, Ser 4995, 3 Jan 43; Tel Msg, Adv NGF to 7th Div, Ser 5000, 4 Jan 43; Msgs, 7th Div to 32d Div, Ser 5157, 6 Jan 43, Ser 5227, 7 Jan 43. All in 32d Div G-3 Jnl. Rpt on Opns 18th Bde Gp at Sanananda.

[16] Msgs, 7th Div to 32d Div, Ser 4952, 4990, 3 Jan 43, Ser 5017, 5038, 4 Jan 43; Buna Force G-4 Rpt, Ser 5022, 4 Jan 43; Tel Msg, Adv NGF to 32d Div, Ser 4995, 4 Jan 43; 32d Div AAR, Papuan Campaign.

SANANANDA POINT. *M. T. Road, lower left, joins the coastal Cape Killerton trail. Note enemy barges along the coast. (Photograph taken in October 1942.)*

126th Infantry troops, under command of Major Irwin, would be returned to their regiment at Buna as quickly as possible.[17]

The Relief of the 126th Infantry

The relief of the 126th Infantry troops was completed by the early afternoon of 9 January, and Major Boerem, who had been acting as Major Irwin's executive officer, returned to Buna the same day to prepare for their reception.[18] The Australians were not

unmindful of the gallantry with which the American troops had fought, and of the heavy losses that they had sustained. On the 8th, Brigadier Porter issued orders adjuring them and his other troops to "march out in as soldierly a manner as possible, . . . in keeping with the pride and quality of their past service." [19] In a letter which he gave to Major Boerem to deliver to General Eichelberger, Porter wrote:

I am taking the opportunity offered by Major Boerem's return to you to express my appreciation of what the men of your divi-

[17] 7th Aust Inf Div OI No. 21, 7 Jan 43.
[18] 3d Bn, 126th Inf, Jnl, Ser 59, 8 Jan 43, Ser 61, 9 Jan 43.

[19] 30th Aust Inf Bde GO No. 14, 8 Jan 43.

sion who have been under my command have done to assist our efforts on the Sanananda Road.

By now it is realized that greater difficulties presented themselves here than were foreseen, and the men of your division probably bore most of them. . . . Your men are worthy comrades and stout hearts. I trust that they will have the opportunity to rebuild their depleted ranks in the very near future. With their present fund of experience they will rebuild into a formidable force. . . .[20]

When the troops had gone into action during the third week of November, they were 1,400 strong. Sixty-five men of regimental headquarters had transferred to Buna in early December, and there had been no other transfers. On 9 January, the day of their relief, the troops numbered only 165 men, nearly all of them in such poor physical shape as to be scarcely able to walk.[21]

Three days later, with the fighting strength of the unit down to 158 men, the troops began marching to Buna. Major Irwin was at their head, with Captain Dal Ponte, as he now was, as his second-in-command. After reaching their bivouac at Simemi in the afternoon, the men shaved and cleaned up as best they could and were issued some sorely needed shelter halves and

mosquito nets. Two days later, 14 January, General Eichelberger had a little ceremony of welcome for them.[22] "I received the troops," he recalls, "with band music, and with what might well be described as a martial welcome. Actually, it was, whatever face could be put upon it, a melancholy homecoming. Sickness, death, and wounds had taken an appalling toll. . . . [The men] were so ragged and so pitiful when I greeted them my eyes were wet." [23]

The Preliminary Operations

Tarakena and Konombi Creek

The general plan of operations formulated on 4 January at General Herring's headquarters provided that, until the 163d Infantry and the 18th Brigade were completely in place and ready to move on Sanananda, the enemy was to be deceived into thinking that the coastal drive on Tarakena and across Konombi Creek was "the main push." [24] (*See Map IV.*) General Eichelberger laid his plans accordingly. Urbana Force, now principally the 127th Infantry

[20] Ltr, Brig Porter to Gen Eichelberger, 9 Jan 43, copy in OCMH files.
[21] Ltr, Gen Eichelberger to Gen MacArthur, 14 Jan 43; 3d Bn, 126th Inf, Jnl, Ser 59, 8 Jan 43, Ser 60, 61, 9 Jan 43; Jnl, Maj Boerem's Det, 9 Jan 43; Memo, Maj Dal Ponte for author, 12 Jul 50. The casualties as of 9 January were: KIA, 91, WIA, 237, MIA, 70; evacuated sick, 711. The bodies of most of the missing were later recovered and their number was added to the list of those killed in action. The total number of casualties, including the evacuated sick, but excluding 88 men on the sick list who had not yet been evacuated, amounted to 1,109

[22] Tel Msg, 7th Div to 32d Div, Ser 6114, 11 Jan 43; Tel Msg, Col Tomlinson to 32d Div, Ser 6147, 12 Jan 43; Memo, Maj Dal Ponte for author, 12 Jul 50; 3d Bn, 126th Inf, Jnl, Ser 64, 12 Jan 43; Jnl, Maj Boerem's Det, 14 Jan 43.
[23] Eichelberger, *Our Jungle Road to Tokyo,* pp. 56, 57. Reporting to General MacArthur that night, General Eichelberger wrote, "Today I talked to men of the 126th who returned from the Sanananda track and are now near my C. P. . . . The strange thing is that they looked good to me, General. They had been cleaned up, and I can see hopes for the future in them far beyond anything that they imagine." Ltr, Gen Eichelberger to Gen MacArthur, 14 Jan 43, copy in OCMH files.
[24] Ltr, Gen Eichelberger to Gen Sutherland, 7 Jan 43.

(with elements of the 126th and 128th Infantries in reserve), would mount the push westward; Warren Force, principally the 128th Infantry, would remain in place and occupy itself with the beach defense.

Colonel Yazawa's scattering of the Chagnon patrol from its position near Tarakena on the evening of 4 January made it necessary for Colonel Grose to order forward a fresh force to retrieve the lost beachhead on the other side of Siwori Creek. Artillery fire was laid down on the area during the night to make it untenable for the Japanese until the troops got there. Early on the 5th, Company G, 127th Infantry, under command of Lieutenant McCampbell, crossed Siwori Creek, followed shortly afterward by Company F, under 1st Lt. James T. Coker. The crossing was slow, for the creek was broad and Colonel Grose had only two small boats (one a black rubber affair captured from the Japanese) with which to ferry the troops and their supplies across. The troops finished crossing by 0900 and began moving westward—Company G along the narrow, exposed coastal track and Company F, in the swamp, covering it from the left.

Colonel Yazawa's troops, principally elements of the *1st Battalion, 170th Infantry,* the so-called *Nojiri Battalion,* were still in the area. During the 5th and 6th they made several stubborn stands, retreating only when the Americans were on the point of overrunning their positions. By the 7th the two companies were within 500 yards of the village, and there the enemy again made a stand. Company E, under 1st Lt. Powell A. Fraser, meanwhile moved onto the sandspit with a 37-mm. gun, and began to enfilade the Japanese with canister. With this support the two companies again pushed the enemy back on the evening of the 7th.

They captured five machine guns, including two lost by the Chagnon patrol.[25]

The next day Company G again moved forward. As before Company E was on the right supporting its advance by fire, and Company F in the swamp covered it from the left. The numerous enemy troops in the swamp and the swamp itself made it difficult for Company F to keep up.[26] Spurred on by Lieutenant Coker, the company commander, and S. Sgt. Herman T. Shaw, in command of the leading platoon,[27] the company drew abreast of Company G and kept its position there for the rest of the day.

At 1600 Company G attacked again. It reached the outskirts of Tarakena village within the hour and captured three enemy machine guns, an enemy mortar, and the remaining machine gun lost by the Chagnon patrol. Two fresh companies of the 1st Battalion, Companies C and A, ordered forward earlier in the day by Colonel Grose, had just come up, and reduction of the village was left to them. The two companies passed through Company G, Company C leading, and launched the attack that evening. The attack gained its objective quickly. Company C was inside the village

[25] Msg, Capt Hewitt to Col Howe, Ser 5155, 6 Jan 43, in 32d Div G–3 Jnl; 127th Inf Jnl, 0630, 0854, 5 Jan 43, 0835, 0940, 1105, 1107, 1110, 1320, 6 Jan 43; 32d Div Sitreps, No. 146, 5 Jan 43, No. 148, 6 Jan 43, No. 150, 7 Jan 43; 127th Inf Tact Hist, 5, 6, 7 Jan 43; Diary, Maj Nojiri, in ATIS CT 29, No. 350; Interv with Col Grose, 15 Nov 50.
[26] Tel Msg, Capt Hewitt to Col Howe, Ser 5256, 8 Jan 43; 127th Inf Tact Hist, 8 Jan 43; Ltr, Gen Eichelberger to Gen Sutherland, 9 Jan 43, copy in OCMH files. Company E by this time also had a .50-caliber machine gun which it was using with excellent effect on the Japanese in the village.
[27] Coker and Shaw were both later awarded the Distinguished Service Cross. The award in the case of Shaw, who was killed late in the day, was posthumous. The citations are in Hq USAFFE GO No. 29, 30 Mar 43.

COLLAPSIBLE ASSAULT BOATS *being used by 127th Infantrymen to cross the Siwori Creek. Note guide rope across the creek.*

by 1830 and the fighting was over by 2130.[28] Forty-two Japanese were killed, and a quantity of Japanese ordnance was captured. The 127th Infantry sustained nineteen casualties in the day's fighting—two killed, sixteen wounded, and one missing.[29]

By this time the three companies that had launched the attack were much below strength. Company F had only 72 men left; Company A, 81; Company C, 89. Morale, however, was good. As General Eichelberger, who had gone forward to the sandspit that morning to see how things were going, reported to General MacArthur the next day, "Now that the men are living where the Japanese lived, they look entirely different. The swamp rats who lived in the water now have their place in the sun and I even heard some singing yesterday for the first time."[30]

[28] Tel Msg, Capt Hewitt to Col Howe, Ser 5256, 8 Jan 43; Msg, 1st Lt. Robert A. Dix to Col Rogers, Ser 5266, 8 Jan 43, in 32d Div G–3 Jnl; 127th Inf Jnl, 1650, 1700, 1710, 1730, 1740, 1754, 1930, 8 Jan 43; 32d Div Sitrep, No. 152, 8 Jan 43; 32d Div G–3 Periodic Rpt, 8 Jan 43.

[29] Ltr, Gen Eichelberger to Gen Sutherland, 10 Jan 43, copy in OCMH files.

[30] Ltr, Gen Eichelberger to Gen MacArthur, 9 Jan 43.

The village in hand, the next step was to cross Konombi Creek, a tidal stream about forty feet across. A suspension bridge over the creek was badly damaged, and attempts on 9 January to cross it were met by fire from hidden enemy emplacements on the opposite shore. Colonel Grose's plan was therefore to flank the enemy positions by sending an element of Company C across the creek that night in the two available boats. The company commander, 1st Lt. Tally D. Fulmer, was put in charge of the crossing.

The troops embarked at 0240 on the 10th. The swift current started taking the boats out to sea, but the danger was perceived in time, and the men reached shore before any harm was done.

There was only one thing left to do: secure a guy wire to the opposite shore. Two volunteers, S. Sgt. Robert Thompson of Company C and Pfc. Jack K. Cunningham of Company E, swam across the creek in the dark and, just before daylight, had a wire in place on the other side. It broke when the leading boat caught on a sand bar, and the crossing had to be made in daylight.

In late afternoon Sergeant Thompson again swam the creek, followed this time by four volunteers from Company C—Pfc. Raymond Milby and Pvts. Raymond R. Judd, Marvin M. Petersen, and Lawrence F. Sprague. To cover the crossing, Lieutenant Fraser of Company E emplaced his mortars and his 37-mm. gun on the east bank of the creek. As the men began swimming across, armed only with pistols and hand grenades, Fraser and his weapons crews engaged the enemy on the opposite shore with fire. The enemy replied in kind, but Fraser and his men held their position along the river bank, and all five men got safely across the creek.

By 1740 the wire was in place, and Lieutenant Fulmer and a platoon of Company C began crossing. The boat made the trip safely, covered by fire from Lieutenant Fraser's mortars and 37-mm. gun, which quickly reduced the enemy emplacements commanding the bridge. Thereafter the crossing went swiftly. Company C was across by 1755, followed closely by Company A. By evening the two companies, disposed in depth, held a 200-yard bridgehead on the other side of the creek.[31]

On the other side of the creek the advancing troops ran into terrain difficulties. No trails could be found branching southward from the coast, and the coast line, a narrow strip of sand bounded by a tidal swamp which came almost to the shore, was frequently under water at high tide.[32] Since the enemy was present in the area in strength, it seemed to be the better part of wisdom to hold up the 127th Infantry advance until the concerted offensive on the Sanananda front got under way and eased the enemy pressure.

General Eichelberger explained the situation to General MacArthur on the 12th. "On their side of the Girua," he wrote, "we have a fine bridgehead established across [Konombi] Creek, but now comes a section where the mangrove swamp comes down to the sea. At high tide the ocean is right in the swamp. . . ." It would not be wise, he thought, for Grose to extend too far until

---

[31] Msg, Adv NGF to NGF, Ser 6098, 11 Jan 43; Tel Msg, Capt Hewitt to Col Rogers, Ser 6101, 11 Jan 43, in 32d Div G–3 Jnl; 32d Div Sitrep, No. 158, 11 Jan 43; 32d Div G–3 Periodic Rpt, 11 Jan 43; 127th Inf Tact Hist, 11, 12 Jan 43; Interv with Col Grose, 15 Nov 50. Lieutenants Fraser and Fulmer, Sergeant Thompson and Privates Milby, Judd, Petersen, and Sprague were all later awarded the Distinguished Service Cross. The citations are in Hq USAFFE GO No. 34, 21 Jun 43.
[32] 32d Div Sitrep, No. 160, 12 Jan 43.

there had been "developments across the Girua." [33] The coastal advance, in short, would mark time until the 163d Infantry and the 18th Brigade began driving directly on Sanananda.

The Attacks Between Musket and Kano

The scheduled operations on the M. T. Road preliminary to the concerted advance on Sanananda had meanwhile been proceeding. The 1st Battalion, 163d Infantry, and regimental headquarters took over complete responsibility for the roadblock area on 3 January. Colonel Doe, who had immediately given Huggins the regimental code name, Musket, had deployed Company C and a platoon of Company D at Kano. Regimental headquarters, battalion headquarters, Company B, and Company D, less the platoon at Kano, were in place at Musket. Company A (less one platoon at Moore, a perimeter about 400 yards east of Musket) covered the supply trail east of the M. T. Road.

By this time Musket (or Old Huggins as it was also known) was a well-developed position. It consisted essentially of an inner and outer perimeter, with rifle and automatic weapons squads in square or circular formation on the periphery of each perimeter, and field kitchens (which had finally come up) in the center. The squads, each with its own straddle trench and water seep, were spaced about fifteen yards apart. Within the inner perimeter were regimental and battalion headquarters, switchboard, aid station, ammunition dump, and the 81-mm. mortars. Between the two perimeters were company headquarters and for-

ward dumps. The entire area was crisscrossed with trenches, and the scene, when newly arrived troops were moving into or through the position, put one observer in mind of "a crowded seal rock." [34]

Upon taking over from the Australians, the troops had been troubled by fire from riflemen in the tall jungle trees that overlooked the perimeter. Though experienced intermittently throughout the entire twenty-four hours, the fire was particularly intense at mealtimes. The troops were also bothered at night by individual enemy riflemen or small patrols. These would harass the flanks and the southern end or rear of the perimeter with short bursts of rifle or automatic weapons fire. Colonel Doe lost no time in devising means to abate these nuisances. He established two-man sniper-observer posts in slit trenches along the forward edge of the perimeter, and in trees on the flanks and rear. Using ladders made of telephone wire with stout wooden rungs, the troops in the trees made it their business to fire systematically on all trees thought to harbor snipers, and were particularly active during such times as the Japanese were firing. As soon as the posts in the trees were established, small countersniping patrols of two or three men, covered by the troops in the trees, began to pick off the Japanese tree marksmen from the ground. To stop Japanese sniping at night from the flanks and rear, the countersniping patrols set out booby traps, consisting usually of two grenades tied to adjoining trees with the pins connected by a cord.

These measures got results quickly. The enemy marksmen were thinned out and forced back. Soon the only reminder that there were still tree snipers in the area was

---

[33] Ltr, Gen Eichelberger to Gen MacArthur, 12 Jan 43, copy in OCMH files.

[34] 163d Inf, The Battle of Sanananda.

SETTING UP A FIELD SWITCHBOARD

distant, ineffective fire, delivered as a rule only at mealtimes.[35]

With the perimeter more or less secure, Musket's role became principally that of a regimental bivouac area, and stringent security measures were observed in the area, especially at night. The men took to their slit trenches at dusk and stayed in them till daylight. Movement through the area during the night was strictly forbidden, and front-line troops on the outer perimeter were under orders to use only hand grenades against suspicious noises or movements in order to avoid disclosing weapons positions to the enemy.

The delivery of supplies, haphazard in Captain Huggins' and Lieutenant Dal Ponte's time, had by now become a routine operation. Natives working in shifts brought the supplies forward to specified points behind the firing line and carried back the wounded. A water purification unit was installed, and the individual water seeps were filled in. Additional mortars and two 37-mm. guns, firing canister, were emplaced to advantage within the perimeter.

Pending the arrival of the rest of the regiment, the 1st Battalion gave the enemy line a thorough probing. It did not take long to find that the Japanese had two strong perimeters between Musket and Kano, about 200 yards north of Musket and roughly the same distance south of Kano. The perimeters were abreast on either side of the road, with the one on the west about twice the size of the one on the east. Since the two positions were on relatively dry ground in a swampy jungle area, dominated like Musket by tall trees, they could be reached only from the track or through the swamp.

The 2d Battalion, led by Maj. Walter R. Rankin, reached the front on the 7th. Colonel Doe disposed the battalion along the supply trail east of the M.T. Road and ordered the 1st Battalion to reduce the two enemy perimeters between Musket and Kano the next day. If the attack proved succesful, the battalion would move into Kano, and Major Rankin's battalion would take over at Musket.

The plan of attack called for Companies B and C to attack from either flank—Company B, the larger perimeter west of the road, and Company C, the smaller perimeter east of it. Company B would move out of Musket and, after circling west and north, hit the larger perimeter from the west; Company C, advancing from a position between Moore and Kano, was to hit the smaller perimeter east of the track from the northeast. The 25-pounders of Hanson Troop and the machine guns and mortars of the rest of the battalion would be available to support the attack.[36]

Just before noon on 8 January, the Hanson Troop put down a fifteen-minute concentration on both perimeters. The troop now had only shells with delayed fuse, and these, as General Doe recalls, "simply buried themselves in the muck or exploded under the ground surface." Although the two companies were covered by all the mortars and machine guns the battalion could muster, neither attack was successful. Hanson Troop, firing from the southeast, could not lay down supporting fire for Company B's flank attack. The result was that the company, forced to attack frontally, not only ran into fire from both perimeters, but also hit the larger perimeter at its strongest point. The company recoiled and was finally forced to dig in that night about thirty yards short of its objective.

Company C had even worse luck. It had rained heavily the day before, and the company, attacking in a southwesterly direction, ran into what had become, since the previous day, a waist-deep swamp. The troops tried to cut through the swamp under heavy fire, but the swamp was too deep and the fire too heavy. After losing one of its officers, 1st Lt. Harold R. Fisk, whose body could not immediately be recovered, the company returned to its original position at Kano, which it renamed Fisk a day or two later. Company B, in slit trenches forward of Musket which were waist-deep in water, was relieved that night by Company E. The next morning, after Company B's troops had had some sleep and some hot food, they took over their former positions, and Company E rejoined its battalion, still in place along the supply trail.[37]

The Establishment of Rankin

On 7 January, with the 2d Battalion, 163d Infantry, and Brigadier Wootten's

---

[36] 163d Inf, The Battle of Sanananda.

[37] 163d Inf Jnl, 0830, 0840, 9 Jan 43. Ltr, Gen Doe to Gen Ward, 3 Mar 51; 163d Inf, The Battle of Sanananda. Lieutenant Fisk was later posthumously awarded the Silver Star. The citation is in Hq 41st Div GO No. 5, 7 Feb 43.

first 400 replacements at hand, General
Vasey issued the divisional plan of attack.
The attack would be in four stages. In Stage
I, the 2d Battalion, 163d Infantry, would
cut off the enemy in the track junction by
getting astride the Killerton trail; in Stage
II, the 18th Brigade, the 2/7 Cavalry, and
the tanks would destroy the Japanese in the
track junction, and clear out the area south
of Musket; in Stage III, the 163d Infantry
would move on Sanananda Point by way
of the M.T. Road, and the 18th Brigade
would do so by first moving north along
the Killerton trail and then turning east
to complete the envelopment. Stage IV
would be the mop-up.

Stage I, the blocking of the Killerton
trail, would secure two main advantages.
It would prevent the rapidly failing Japanese in the track junction from using it as
an escape route, and would provide the 18th
Brigade with a jumping-off point for its
advance on Sanananda when it had completed clearing out the track junction.

Early on 9 January, after being briefed
on its role by Colonel Doe, the 2d Battalion,
under its commander, Major Rankin,
moved out from its position along the supply trail, passed through Musket, and began marching on the Killerton trail a half
mile away. The march was in a southwesterly direction, and during its course telephone wire was payed out to maintain
communications.

The first enemy opposition was encountered at 1030, just as the battalion was
approaching a narrow, corridorlike, north-
south clearing through which the Killerton
trail ran. Major Rankin ordered a platoon
of Company G to the edge of the jungle
at the southern end of the corridor to act
as cover for the battalion's left flank. The
platoon began receiving heavy rifle and

mortar fire from a cluster of enemy positions enfilading the corridor from the south.
Company headquarters, a second platoon,
and half of the company's weapons platoon
crossed the clearing before heavy machine
gun and rifle fire stopped further crossing.
Under Capt. William C. Benson, the rest
of the company finally advanced through
the clearing and across the trail via a sap
dug through the clearing. The main body
of the company set up a perimeter on the
west side of the trail, and the covering platoon remained in place to the east of it.
There it was strongly engaged by the Japanese who were in position only a few yards
away.

The rest of the battalion, under Capt.
Paul G. Hollister, the battalion S–3, had
meanwhile turned north. After following
the edge of the jungle for about 250 yards,
the troops crossed over and, against only
light opposition, established themselves
astride the trail. The new perimeter, which
was almost due west of Musket, was named
Rankin after the battalion commander.

The day's operations had cost the 2d
Battalion four killed and seven wounded,
and the battalion was to suffer other losses
during the succeeding few days in maintaining its position,[38] but the first stages of
the divisional plan for the advance on
Sanananda had been completed. The last
possible escape route of Colonel Tsukamoto's troops in the track junction was
closed.

The 1st Battalion had meanwhile continued to attack the area between Musket
and Fisk (Kano). On 10 January the 3d
Battalion, under Maj. Leonard A. Wing,

[38] 163d Inf Jnl, 1740, 9 Jan 43; Ltr, Gen Doe to
Gen Ward, 3 Mar 51; Ltr, Col Paul G. Hollister to
author, 11 Apr 51; 163d Inf, The Battle of
Sanananda.

reached the front with Brigadier Wootten's last 400 replacements. Cpl. Paul H. Knight, a member of the regimental Antitank Company, noticed that the enemy was not firing from the smaller perimeter east of the track. Reconnoitering the position on his own initiative, he discovered that the enemy had for some unaccountable reason abandoned it. Colonel Doe lost no time in exploiting the windfall. A platoon of Company A took over the position immediately, and it was joined there the next morning by the rest of the company. Company K took Company A's place on the supply trail, and Companies I, L, and M moved forward to Musket to relieve Company B, which went into reserve.

The Japanese left behind considerable matériel when they evacuated the perimeter. Included were a water-cooled, .50-caliber machine gun, two mortars, some hand grenades, a quantity of small arms ammunition, and a cache of rifles. The enemy troops had obviously been very hungry when they abandoned the perimeter, and there was gruesome evidence that some of them had been reduced to cannibalism.[39]

The Attack on the Track Junction

Satisfied by this time that the tactical situation no longer required his presence, General MacArthur returned to Brisbane on 8 January,[40] and General Blamey followed him there several days later. Upon General Blamey's return to Australia, General Herring again became commander of New Guinea Force and returned to Port Moresby on 11 January. Two days later, General Eichelberger took command of all Australian and American troops at the front as Commander, Advance New Guinea Force, and General Berryman became his chief of staff.[41]

On the 11th, two days after the establishment of Rankin, Brigadier Wootten called a conference of his subordinate commanders to discuss his plan for the reduction next day of the area south of Musket. The discussion revealed that artillery would be of only limited usefulness because the Australian front line was by this time within fifty yards of the enemy. The main reliance therefore would have to be on armor even though, because of the marshy nature of the terrain, the tanks would have to attack straight up the M.T. Road.

As finally put down on paper the same day, the plan of attack called for the 2/9 Battalion to attack on the right and the 2/12

[39] 163d Inf Jnl, 1700, 1737, 1750, 10 Jan 43; Col Doe, The Battle of Sanananda; Ltr, Col Dawley to author, 13 Nov 50. The extremity to which the Japanese had been reduced by this time is well evidenced by an enemy diary captured in the Sanananda–Giruwa area. Under the date 10 January it contains the following entry: "No medicine for malaria, no food for the company for a week. . . . Went to collect the bodies of enemy dead. Ate human flesh for the first time. It tastes comparatively good." Diary, member *3d Bn, 144th Inf,* in ATIS CT 25, Bul Notes No. 183.

[40] The next day, the 9th, General MacArthur issued a special order of the day in which he announced the award of the Distinguished Service Cross (among others) to the following—General Blamey, General Kenney, General Eichelberger, General Sutherland, General Casey, General Willoughby, General Whitehead, Brigadier Eather, and Brigadier Wootten. The order, in apparent anticipation of an early end to the campaign, ended with these words: "To Almighty God I give thanks for that guidance which has brought us this success in our great crusade. His is the honor, the power and the glory forever, Amen." Msg, Gen MacArthur to Gen Marshall, No. C–128, 9 Jan 43. The orders are to be found also in *The New York Times,* 9 Jan 43.

[41] Ltr, Gen Eichelberger to Gen Herring, Port Moresby, 13 Jan 43, copy in OCMH files; Rpt, CG Buna Forces, p. 40; Eichelberger, *Our Jungle Road to Tokyo,* p. 59.

GENERAL MacARTHUR WITH GENERAL KENNEY *arriving in Australia from New Guinea, 8 January 1943.*

Battalion, its left flank anchored on the M.T. Road, to attack on the left. They were to be supported by the mortars of both battalions, brigaded together. Supported by a company of the 2/10 Battalion, the 2/9th would move off to the northeast, circle the enemy's left flank, and try to come in behind the track junction. The main attack would be generally to the right of the M.T. Road. It would be launched by the 2/12 Battalion, a company of the 2/10 Battalion, and three of the four available tanks. The 2/7 Cavalry and the remaining two companies of the 2/10 Battalion would be in reserve to the

left and rear of the 2/12 Battalion, ready to go in at a moment's notice. The troops at Musket would lend direct support to the operations of the 2/9 Battalion on the right, and those at Rankin would aid operations generally by exerting pressure to the south on the enemy's right rear.[42]

At 0800 the next morning, while the 163d Infantry executed feints from Musket and Rankin, the two battalions of the 18th Brigade attacked the Japanese positions

---

[42] 18th Bde Gp Opns Order No. 3, 11 Jan 43; Rpt on Opns, 18th Bde Gp at Sanananda.

covering the junction. After a heavy artillery concentration from south and east, principally on the enemy's rear areas, the 2/9 Battalion moved off to the northeast on a two-company front, with Company K, 163d Infantry, covering its right flank. The 2/12 Battalion, with one company and three tanks on the road, and two companies to the right of the road, moved off on the left. Preceded by the tanks, the company on the road attacked straight up the track, and the companies on the right, which were a short distance forward, attacked obliquely toward the road.

The tank attack miscarried. It had been assumed in drawing up the plan that the tanks would receive no antitank fire, since the Japanese had fired neither field guns nor antitank guns on this front since 23 December. The assumption was a mistake. Colonel Tsukamoto had not only mined the road but he also had some antitank shells that he apparently had been hoarding for just such an emergency. As the tanks advanced up the narrow road in column, a 3-inch antitank shell pierced the leading tank and destroyed its radio set. The troop commander, who was inside, got the tank off the road but was unable to warn the tanks behind him that they were facing short-range antitank fire. As a result, each of the other two tanks was hit as it came forward. The first tank bogged down when it left the road but managed finally to withdraw. The second tank went out of control when hit and, after careening wildly along the track, was finally knocked out by the Japanese. The third tank, though disabled by both antitank shells and land mines, was subsequently recovered.

Left without tank support, the 2/12 Battalion nonetheless fought on doggedly, killing a great many Japanese and reducing a number of enemy positions. The little ground that it gained, however, was mostly on the right side of the road. The 2/9 Battalion on the right flank met less opposition and gained more ground, but it still faced a number of unreduced enemy positions at the end of the day.[43]

Though the 18th Brigade had lost 142 men in the day's fighting—34 killed, 66 wounded, and 51 missing (some of whom were later recovered)—the Japanese line, as far as could be ascertained, was intact. General Eichelberger reported the prevailing feeling to General MacArthur that night when he wrote: "The attack on that darned area was not successful. The advance went through where there were no Japanese and bogged down where the Japanese were."[44]

The next morning, at General Vasey's request, General Eichelberger flew across the river to see what could be done. He reported the situation to General Herring that night as follows:

It had been my intention to move down to your old headquarters today but General Vasey after an attack yesterday wanted to discuss his plans so I decided to go over there instead. General Vasey, General Berryman and Brigadier Wootten are all agreed that any more all-out attacks on that Japanese area will be abortive. The best plan would seem to be to surround the area and cut off all supplies, accompanied by plenty of mortar fire and constant harassing. This seemed to me very slow work, but I realize that any other decision may result in tremendous loss of personnel without commensurate gains. For the immediate present, I have asked General Vasey to have a survey made to see if it is possible for troops to live in these swamps.

---

[43] ALF Daily Opns Rpt, No. 274, 13 Jan 43, in G-3 Jnl, GHQ SWPA; Rpt on Opns, 18th Bde Gp at Sanananda; 163d Inf, The Battle of Sanananda.
[44] Ltr, Gen Eichelberger to Gen MacArthur, 12 Jan 43, copy in OCMH files.

The Japanese naturally have settled on the only high sandy ground.[45]

The Allies had misread the situation. The attack of 12 January had succeeded better than they realized. There were still plenty of unreduced bunkers standing which appeared to be even stronger and better camouflaged than those at Buna,[46] but the enemy had had enough. Surrounded, his supply line completely cut, Colonel Tsukamoto had already ordered his troops to begin evacuating the track junction area.[47]

Tokyo Decides To Withdraw

General Yamagata's Position

Despite the fact that they were still fighting hard, and had up to this point succeeded in imposing a stalemate on the Sanananda front, the situation of the Japanese there was hopeless. They had worked hard to establish a base at the mouth of the Mambare to supply Giruwa, using submarines and high-speed launches, but the vigilance of the coast watchers and the air force had defeated the plan. The result for the Japanese was catastrophic. General Yamagata had some 5,000 troops at the beachhead (including the sick and wounded), but the men had almost nothing to eat and every Japanese in the area faced death by starvation.[48]

The food situation could not have been more critical. The standard daily issue of rice to Japanese troops at this time was about

twenty-eight ounces. At the end of December the ration on the Sanananda front was ten ounces. It was down to two ounces by the first week in January. By 12 January there was no rice left for issue to the troops.[49]

The Japanese were not only starving, they were critically short of medicine and medical supplies. At the hospital at Giruwa there had been no medicine for over a month, the wards were under water, and nearly all the medical personnel were either dead or themselves patients. The troops were short of rifles, hand grenades, and rifle grenades, and mortar shells and rifle ammunition were being strictly rationed, since stocks of both had already begun to run out.[50]

Upon his arrival at Giruwa on 22 December General Oda had professed great optimism about the future. He told the troops that they would be reinforced in good time and assured them that, whatever else happened, the homeland would never let Giruwa fall.[51] General Yamagata had been under no such illusions about the situation. In an operations order which he issued while still at the Amboga River, he wrote, "It appears we are now in the final stages." [52] He was right, and Tokyo by that time was of the same opinion.

The Orders of 4 and 13 January

Things had gone as badly for the Japanese on Guadalcanal. The main difficulty there as on the New Guinea front was supply. After preliminary discussion of the matter in late December, *Imperial General*

---

[45] Ltr, Gen Eichelberger to Gen Herring, 13 Jan 43, copy in OCMH files.
[46] Msg, Adv NGF to NGF, Ser 6139, 12 Jan 43; Msg, 7th Aust Div to 32d Div, Ser 6165, 12 Jan 43. Both in 32d Div G–3 Jnl. ALF Daily Opns Rpt, No. 275, 14 Jan 43, in G–3 Jnl, GHQ SWPA.
[47] *18th Army* Opns I, 30.
[48] Diary, Sgt Kiyoshi; *18th Army* Opns I, 33, 34, 43, 45, 48.

[49] *18th Army* Opns I, 33.
[50] Rad, Col Tomita to CofS *17th Army*, 23 Nov 42; Interr, Lt Sawatari; *18th Army* Opns I, 29, 30.
[51] Diary, Sgt Kiyoshi.
[52] *Buna Shitai* Opns Orders No. A–39, 27 Dec 42, in ATIS CT 29, No. 350.

Headquarters decided on 4 January that, because of a critical lack of shipping and the virtual impossibility of supplying either Guadalcanal or Buna effectively, all thoughts of recapturing the one or holding the other would have to be abandoned. It gave orders therefore that the forces on Guadalcanal would evacuate the island gradually by night and take up defensive positions in the northern Solomons. The troops at Sanananda and Giruwa, in turn, would be evacuated to Lae and Salamaua after fresh troops from Rabaul reinforced the latter two points.[53]

The orders of 4 January were immediately transmitted to the *8th Area Army* at Rabaul. Its commander, General Imamura, left the timing and the manner of withdrawal at Buna to General Adachi. A *51st Division* unit, the *102d Infantry, Reinforced*, was already on board ship waiting to move to Lae, and General Adachi ordered it forward at once. The ships left Rabaul the next day and, despite determined attempts by the air force to stop them, reached Lae safely on the 7th.[54]

---

[53] Miller, *Guadalcanal: The First Offensive*, pp. 336–38; Hist Rec *Army Section Imperial General Headquarters*, pp. 67, 71, 72; Hist *8th Area Army*, p. 7; *Southeast Area* Naval Opns I, 54, 59.

[54] Allied Air Forces Opns Rpts, 7 Jan 43, 8 Jan 43, in G–3 Jnl, GHQ SWPA; Msg, NGF to Adv NGF, Ser 5272, 8 Jan 43, in 32 Div G–3 Jnl; *18th Army* Opns I, 32; Hist *8th Area Army*, p. 7. The convoy consisted of four transports, escorted by five destroyers, and had very strong air cover. Although Allied planes were unable to stop the convoy, they did succeed in sinking two of the four transports while the ships were unloading in the harbor, and in destroying a large number of enemy planes. Allied Air Forces Opns Rpt, 8–9 Jan 43, in G–3 Jnl, GHQ SWPA; Msg, Adv NGF to 32d Div, Ser 5271, 8 Jan 43, in 32d Div G–3 Jnl; *Southeast Area* Naval Opns I, 60; Msg, Gen MacArthur to Gen Marshall, No. C–93, CM–IN 5153, 11 Jan 43.

General Adachi Finally Orders the Withdrawal

Five days went by without orders from General Adachi. On 12 January, the day that the broken remnants of Colonel Tsukamoto's troops began evacuating the track junction, General Oda, from his headquarters at Sanananda Village, sent the chief of staff of the *18th Army* an urgent message.

Most of the men [Oda wrote] are stricken with dysentery. Those not . . . in bed with illness are without food and too weak for hand-to-hand fighting. . . . Starvation is taking many lives, and it is weakening our already extended lines. We are doomed. In several days, we are bound to meet the same fate that overtook Basabua and Buna. . . . Our duty will have been accomplished if we fight and lay down our lives here on the field. However, [since] this would mean that our foothold in [eastern] New Guinea would be lost and the sacrifices of our fellow soldiers during the past six months will have been in vain . . . [I] urge that reinforcements be landed near Gona at once.[55]

The next day General Adachi finally gave General Yamagata permission to begin evacuating Sanananda and Giruwa. According to a plan drawn by Adachi himself, the troops would withdraw to the mouths of the Kumusi and Mambare Rivers, and from there they would either march or be taken by sea to Lae and Salamaua. As many of the troops as possible would be evacuated in motor launches, but the rest would have to make their way westward to the Japanese-held area on the other side of Gona by slipping through the Allied lines. Evacuation by launch of the sick and wounded would begin at once and would continue nightly until those not in

---

[55] Rad, Gen Oda to CofS, *18th Army*, 12 Jan 43, in *18th Army* Opns I, 29, 36.

condition to fight were completely evacuated. Because of the favorable moon, the attempt to reach the area west of Gona overland would begin on 25 January and be completed by the 29th.[56] How Sanananda and Giruwa were to be held until the 25th in the desperate circumstances outlined by General Oda in his message of the 12th was not made clear.

The Clean-up South of Musket

After the supposed failure of the attack on 12 January, General Vasey, on General Eichelberger's suggestion, ordered intensive patrolling of the entire track junction area. The 2/9 and 2/12 Battalions kept the Japanese positions to their front under steady pressure, and the 163d Infantry at Musket sent patrols south to find out how far north the enemy positions in the junction extended, an endeavor which was to be richly rewarded.

On the 14th, shortly after daybreak, a 163d Infantry patrol came upon a sick Japanese lying in some bushes just south of Musket. Taken prisoner and interrogated, the Japanese revealed that the orders of the 12th had called for the withdrawal of all able-bodied troops from the junction area. He had left with the rest, he told his captors, but had been too sick to keep up and had collapsed on the trail.[57]

That was all General Vasey needed to know. He immediately ordered the 18th Brigade to launch a general offensive and the 163d Infantry to send all available troops southward to block off all possible escape

routes along the M.T. Road and the Killerton trail. Company K, 163d Infantry, which had been operating to the east of the road on the right flank of the 2/9 Battalion, was joined by Company B from Musket, and the two companies moved southward along the M.T. Road to meet the oncoming Australians. On the Killerton trail Companies E and G moved out of Rankin. Aided by Hanson Troop and the battalion's mortars, the units led by Major Rankin, the battalion commander, reduced the three enemy perimeters on their southern flank. At least a hundred Japanese were killed in the attack, many of them apparently escapees from the track junction. Machine guns, rifles, and ammunition were the principal booty taken.[58]

The 18th Brigade, with the 2/7 Cavalry under its command, made short work of the Japanese who were still to be found in the track junction area. By early afternoon the Australian troops had swept completely through the area and had joined hands with the 163d Infantry units on both the M.T. Road and the Killerton track. Enemy equipment taken by the Australians included a 3-inch antiaircraft gun, six grenade launchers, forty machine guns (including thirteen Brens), 120 rifles (thirty of them Australian 303's), and a quantity of hand grenades, but their bag of the enemy was small—152 Japanese killed and six prisoners of war.[59]

---

[56] 18th Army Opns Orders MO No. A-72, 13 Jan 43, in 18th Army Opns I, 36.

[57] Msg, 7th Div to 32d Div, Ser 6237, 14 Jan 43; Msg, NGF to 32d Div, Ser 6253, 14 Jan 43, in 32d Div G-3 Jnl; Rpt on Opns, 18th Inf Bde Gp at Sanananda; 163d Inf, The Battle of Sanananda.

[58] Rpt on Opns, 18th Inf Bde Gp at Sanananda; 163d Inf, the Battle of Sanananda. During the attack, Major Rankin himself reconnoitered the area ahead of his troops and personally directed the fire of the mortars and the artillery from an exposed position within a few yards of the enemy. He was later awarded the Distinguished Service Cross. The citation is in USAFFE GO No. 37, 7 Jul 43.

[59] Msg, 7th Div to 32d Div, Ser 6237, 14 Jan 43; Msg, NGF to 32d Div, Ser 6378, 14 Jan 43. Both in 32d Div G-3 Jnl. Rpt on Opns, 18th Inf Bde Gp at Sanananda.

It was clear by this time that the Australians had really won the victory two days before. The dramatic way in which the situation had changed on the 14th did not escape General Eichelberger. He wrote to General Sutherland the next day:

The day before yesterday I went over to Sanananda at General Vasey's request, accompanied by Berryman. Wootten and all were certain it was impossible to take out the Japanese pocket by direct attack and recommended that we surround the area and hammer it to pieces as well as starve the Japanese out. The only decision I made was that the whole area be patrolled with a view to finding out the condition of the swamps, etc. These patrols ran into signs the Japanese were evacuating the pocket and an attack was ordered. As a result a lot of Japanese were killed and a lot of valuable materiel captured.

Today, all is optimism. Vasey, from pessimism, has changed 100% and he now feels the Japanese have gotten out. Berryman and I are not at all sure. . . . Nevertheless the elimination of the pocket has improved the situation immeasurably.[60]

It had indeed. The way was clear at last for the general advance on Sanananda.

---

[60] Ltr, Gen Eichelberger to Gen Sutherland, 15 Jan 43, copy in OCMH files.

CHAPTER XVIII

The Final Offensive

With the clearing of the area south of Musket, the fighting on the Sanananda front entered its last phase. The Japanese were about to be enveloped by the 18th Brigade, the 163d Infantry, and the 127th Infantry from the west, the south, and the east. The end could not be far off.

The Three-Way Push

The Preparations in General Vasey's Area

On the evening of 14 January the mop-up in the track junction was turned over to the 2/7 Cavalry and the 39 and 49 Battalions, and the 18th Brigade began moving to Rankin, the 2/10 Battalion leading. After spending the night in the area, the troops passed through Rankin and moved up to a coconut plantation a mile and a half north. One company of 2/12 Battalion thereupon moved to secure a track junction 500 yards east of the plantation, the 2/9 Battalion and the rest of the 2/12 Battalion went into bivouac in the plantation area, and the 2/10 Battalion and brigade headquarters moved a mile and a quarter farther north where they secured a track junction about 900 yards from the coast. Toward evening the 2d Battalion, 163d Infantry, took over the junction east of the plantation secured earlier by the 2/12 Battalion, and Company B of the 2/10 Battalion began

moving east to occupy Killerton Village, about 1,000 yards south of Cape Killerton.[1] (*Map 17*)

No opposition had been met during the day, and the brigade was now poised to move on Cape Killerton, Wye Point, and Sanananda. It could attack south to the M.T. Road from Killerton Village, and north to the coast from the village and the junction secured by the 2/10 Battalion. The 2d Battalion, 163d Infantry, was also in position and was preparing to attack eastward toward the M.T. Road as the rest of the 163d Infantry attacked northward from Fisk.[2]

The 163d Infantry at Musket and Fisk also had progress to report at the end of the day. The alertness of Company A, which had been operating out of the captured perimeter between Musket and Fisk, was largely responsible for the day's successes. At 0730 that morning a platoon of the company crossed the M.T. Road and sneaked into the large Japanese perimeter on the other side from the north without being detected by its defenders. Under the company commander, 1st Lt. Howard McKinney,

[1] Msg, 18th Inf Bde to 2/9, 2/10, 2/12 Bns, No. 0.120, 14 Jan 43, copy in OCMH files; Tel Msgs, 7th Div to 32d Div, Ser 6252, 15 Jan 43, Ser 6263, 15 Jan 43; Msgs, Adv NGF to 32d Div, Ser 6258, 15 Jan 43, Ser 6379, 15 Jan 43, in 32d Div G–3 Jnl; Rpt on Opns 18th Inf Bde Gp at Sanananda.

[2] Tel Msg, 7th Div to 32d Div, Ser 6252, 15 Jan 43; 163d Inf, The Battle of Sanananda; Rpt on Opns 18th Inf Bde Gp at Sanananda.

the rest of the company moved in at once and began to attack. The perimeter, about 300 yards long and 150 wide, consisted of a labyrinth of interconnected bunkers and fire trenches, and the enemy, though taken by surprise, resisted fiercely. Colonel Doe lost no time in ordering a platoon of Company C from Fisk to attack the perimeter from the east and Company B (which with Companies E, G, and K, had by this time completed its part in the mop-up south of Musket) to attack from the west. The encirclement was complete, but so strong was the Japanese bunker line and so desperate the Japanese defense that it quickly became apparent that the perimeter was not going to be reduced that day.[3]

Just before noon that day, 15 January, General Vasey came up to Colonel Doe's command post to give him his instructions for an all-out attack the following morning on the Japanese line north of Fisk. The 2d Battalion was already committed to the attack eastward from the coconut plantation to the M.T. Road, and Colonel Doe chose the 1st Battalion, by this time his most experienced unit, for the northward attack. The 3d Battalion's role would be to complete the reduction of the Japanese pocket between Musket and Fisk and to support the attack with its heavy weapons and those of the rest of the battalion massed in Musket.

The decision to use the 1st Battalion in the attack north of Fisk made it necessary for Colonel Doe to regroup. Company I took over from Company C at Moore and Fisk, and Companies K and L relieved Companies A and B and the platoon of Company C which had been working on the Japanese pocket between Musket and Fisk. For the first time since its arrival at the front, all of the 1st Battalion was under the direct control of Colonel Lindstrom, the battalion commander.[4]

The plan of attack was carefully drawn. Fifteen 81-mm. mortars from Musket, and the 25-pounders of the Manning and Hall Troops from the other side of the river would give support. The 2/6 Armored Regiment's remaining two tanks would stand by southwest of Fisk to be used at Colonel Lindstrom's discretion. After harassing artillery fire during the night and a fifteen-minute preparation in the morning, the battalion would attack from the woods west of Fisk. It would envelop the enemy's right flank and rear west of the road, effect a junction with the 2d Battalion as it came in from the west, and move forward with it to the M.T. Road.[5]

The Situation on the Right

From its bridgehead on the west bank of Konombi Creek the 127th Infantry had meanwhile been patrolling toward Giruwa, which was now only a mile away. An advance under enemy fire along a track five or six feet wide over which the waves broke at high tide and innudated the mangrove swamp on the other side was no easy matter. But with the 18th Brigade and the 163d Infantry in position for an all-out attack on 16 January the time had come for the 127th Infantry to begin moving forward again.

On 14 January General Eichelberger had put Colonel Howe, 32d Division G–3, in

---

[3] 163d Inf, The Battle of Sanananda. During the morning's fighting, S. Sgt. Paul Ziegele of Company A crept up to a Japanese bunker containing a .50-caliber machine gun, and in the face of strong enemy fire killed four of the bunker's five occupants with his M1. He later received the Distinguished Service Cross. The citation is in Hq, USAFFE GO No. 41, 25 Jul 43.

[4] 163d Inf Jnl, 1710, 15 Jan 43; 163d Inf, The Battle of Sanananda.

[5] 163d Inf FO No. 4, 15 Jan 43.

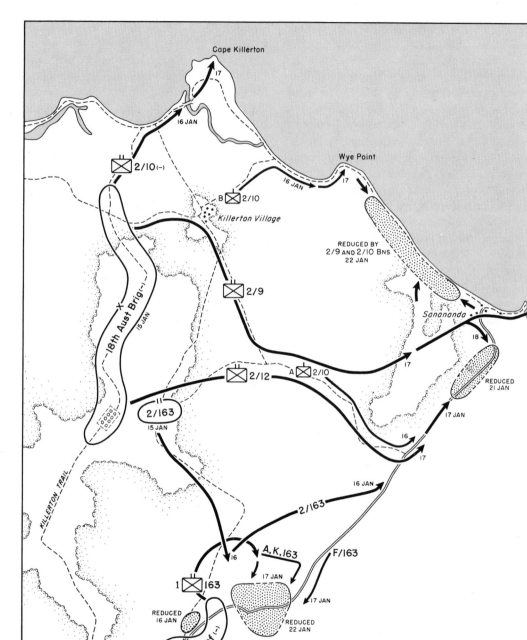

Cape Killerton

17

16 JAN

Wye Point

2/10 (-)

16 JAN

17

B 2/10

Killerton Village

REDUCED BY
2/9 AND 2/10 BNS
22 JAN

2/9

18th Aust Brig (-)

15 JAN

Sanananda

18

17

2/12   A 2/10

17

2/163

15 JAN

REDUCED
21 JAN

17 JAN

16

17

KILLERTON TRAIL

16 JAN

2/163

2/163

A, K, 163   F/163

16

1 163

17 JAN

17 JAN

REDUCED
16 JAN

REDUCED
22 JAN

163d Inf (-)

15 JAN

TO SOPUTA

MAP 17

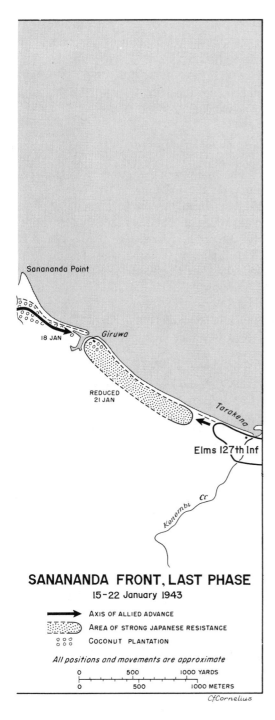

SANANANDA FRONT, LAST PHASE

15-22 January 1943

➤ AXIS OF ALLIED ADVANCE

▨ AREA OF STRONG JAPANESE RESISTANCE

○ COCONUT PLANTATION

All positions and movements are approximate

0   500   1000 YARDS

0   500   1000 METERS

CfCornelius

Sanananda Point

18 JAN

Giruwa

REDUCED
21 JAN

Tarakena

Elms 127th Inf

Konombi Cr

command of Urbana Force. Colonel Grose returned to headquarters, and Boerem, now a lieutenant colonel, became Colonel Howe's executive officer. The next day, General Eichelberger ordered Howe to begin moving on Giruwa in the morning.[6]

On the 15th, the day he assumed command, Howe ordered Company B to try moving up the coast. The artillery and the mortars gave the known enemy positions in the area a complete going over before the troops moved forward, but when the company was a few hundred yards out the Japanese opened up with a machine gun at almost point-blank range, killing two and wounding five. The artillery and the mortars thereupon went over the area even more carefully than before, and the company again tried to advance, only to have a second machine gun open up on it from a new position. A squad moved into the swamp to find the enemy guns and outflank them but ran into the fire of another machine gun. Another squad ordered in from another point on the track ran into such dense swamp growth that it was unable to hack its way through.

Describing the situation for Colonel Bradley over the phone that evening, Colonel Howe had this to say:

This damn swamp up here consists of big mangrove trees, not small ones like they have in Australia, but great big ones. Their knees stick up in the air . . . as much as six or eight feet above the ground, and where a big tree grows it is right on top of a clay knoll.

[6] Tel Conv, Col Bradley with Col Howe, Ser 6277, 15 Jan 43. Reporting to General Sutherland that night, General Eichelberger wrote: "Howe will take command of the left flank and the 127th Infantry. Howe is very competent. I will be glad to see him there for he is not a regular officer and I do not want to give the impression that I favor the regular army." Ltr, Gen Eichelberger to Gen Sutherland, 15 Jan 43, copy in OCMH files.

A man or possibly two men can . . . dig in a little bit, but in no place do they have an adequate dug-in position. The rest of this area is swamp that stinks like hell. You step into it and go up to your knees. That's the whole damn area, except for the narrow strip on the beach. I waded over the whole thing myself to make sure I saw it all. . . . There is no place along that beach that would not be under water when the tide comes in. . . .

To make matters worse, there seemed to be Japanese to the southward who could have got there from Sanananda only by a trail unknown to the 127th Infantry. Colonel Howe reported that one of his patrols (which the enemy tried unsuccessfully to ambush before it left the area) had discovered a whole series of Japanese defensive positions, a five-ton hoist, a small jetty, and a rubber boat along the bank of a branch stream running into Konombi Creek. In these circumstances, Howe wanted to know whether "the Old Man" still wanted "to go on with this thing." "It will take a whole regiment," he added, "if we do." [7]

Late that night Colonel Bradley telephoned Colonel Howe that General Eichelberger was releasing the entire regiment to him except for Companies D, H, and M, the heavy weapons units, which would be left in the Buna Mission–Giropa Point area for beach defense. He told him further that, except for the remnant of the 126th Infantry which was in no circumstances to be touched, he could in an emergency count on the support of Colonel Martin's troops as well.[8]

The forces for the envelopment of Sanananda were in place and the attack was ready to go. The weather, so long adverse, had finally turned favorable. The rains had stopped on the 13th, and for the first time in weeks the track was dry.[9]

The Troops Jump Off

The many-pronged attack was launched early on the morning of 16 January. On the left, from the track junction near the coast where he had his headquarters, Brigadier Wootten ordered Companies C and D, 2/10 Battalion, to push to the coast and turn east toward Cape Killerton and Wye Point. Company A, 2/10 Battalion, was to move east and south to a track junction a mile southeast of Killerton Village. From there it was to attack eastward toward the M.T. Road. The 2/9 and 2/12 Battalions were left for the time being in reserve.

On Colonel Doe's front the 2d Battalion, 163d Infantry, pushed off toward the road from the junction east of the plantation and marched southeast to take the enemy troops north of Fisk in the rear. In the center the 1st Battalion, 163d Infantry, attacked the left flank of the enemy line immediately to its front. The 3d Battalion, operating to the rear of the 1st Battalion, continued to work

[7] Tel Msg, Col Howe to Col Bradley, Ser 6267, 15 Jan 43.

[8] Tel Msg, Col Bradley to Col Howe, Ser 6277, 15 Jan 43. The restriction apparently did not apply to Company A, 126th Infantry, which both Colonel Grose and Colonel Howe had been using for reconnaissance missions, though not for combat.

[9] Msg, 7th Div to 32d Div, Ser 6172, 13 Jan 43; Rads, Adv NGF to 32d Div, Ser 6249, 15 Jan 43, Ser 6314, 16 Jan 43, in 32d Div G–3 Jnl. General Eichelberger whimsically claimed some of the credit for the change in weather. He based his claim on a statement that he had made at Brigadier Wootten's headquarters on the 13th. "I made the remark," he wrote, "that I was going to call on my luck to see that there was no more rain for awhile. They looked at me as though I were crazy and yet there hasn't been anything but sunshine since that moment." Ltr, Gen Eichelberger to Gen Herring, 16 Jan 43, copy in OCMH files.

on the Japanese pocket between Musket and Fisk.

On Colonel Howe's front the 127th Infantry moved south and west. Company I moved south to investigate the area where the chain hoist had been found the day before, and Companies A and B attacked west along the coastal track, Company A in the swamp covering Company B from the left.[10]

The Japanese Line Falls Apart

Companies C and D, 2/10 Battalion, reached the coast on the morning of the 16th without encountering any enemy troops. They met strong opposition, however, at a bridge over an unnamed creek just west of Cape Killerton. Brigadier Wootten thereupon ordered Company B (which had just reached Killerton Village after losing its way during the night and bivouacking a mile to the south) to advance from the village northeast to the coast. It was then to turn east and move on Wye Point. As it came out on the coast, the company ran into light opposition and scattered it. Moving east, it hit a strong line of Japanese bunkers on the beach just west of Wye Point and was held up there for the rest of the day. Company A, after a very difficult march through swamp, had meanwhile come out on the M.T. Road, about a mile south of Sanananda and a mile and a half north of the main Japanese defense line on the M.T. Road. Turning northeast toward Sanananda, it was stopped by a secondary Japanese defense line across the road.

Having now felt out the enemy, Brigadier Wootten knew what to do. The 39 Battalion was moving up from the south to cover his rearward communications, and he still had both the 2/9 and 2/12 Battalions in reserve in the plantation area. Leaving the three companies of the 2/10 Battalion on the coast to work on the opposition they had encountered near Cape Killerton and Wye Point, he ordered Colonel Arnold to move forward with his entire battalion to the M.T. Road. As soon as he reached it, he was to take Company A, 2/10 Battalion, under command and move directly on Sanananda.[11]

The 2/12 Battalion joined Company A on the M.T. Road the following afternoon, 17 January. Colonel Arnold attacked at once to the northeastward, but was stopped by heavy enemy opposition. The 2/10 Battalion, under Lt. Col. C. J. Geard, took both Cape Killerton and Wye Point that day. Past Wye Point it met strong opposition and was also stopped. To hasten a decision there and along the M.T. Road, Brigadier Wootten ordered the 2/9 Battalion to march cross-country from its bivouac in the plantation area to a large kunai strip about a mile and a half east. At one point this strip was only a few hundred yards from Sanananda Village. Brigadier Wootten reasoned that the Japanese, relying upon the unfavorable terrain which surrounded the strip, might not have taken the trouble to defend it. The 2/9 Battalion, under Colonel Cummings' successor, Maj. W. N. Parry-Okeden, reached the strip that evening to find that Brigadier Wootten's surmise had been correct. The strip was completely undefended, and all that separated the Australians from the village was a stretch of heavy swamp, no

---

[10] Rpt on Opns 18th Inf Bde Gp at Sanananda; 163d Inf, The Battle of Sanananda; 127th Inf, Tact Hist, 16 Jan 43.

[11] Msgs, 7th Div to 32d Div, Sers 6287, 6298, 6314, 6315, 16 Jan 43; Msg, NGF to 32d Div, Ser 6338, 16 Jan 43. All in 32d Div G-3 Jnl. Rpt on Opns 18th Inf Bde Gp at Sanananda; 163d Inf, The Battle of Sanananda.

worse than others they had already crossed.

After a difficult advance through the swamp, the battalion launched a surprise attack on Sanananda the following morning and took it by 1300. Leaving a platoon to hold Sanananda, the battalion commander ordered one company south to meet the 2/12 Battalion and pushed on eastward along the beach with the rest of his battalion. By evening the 2/9th had overrun Sanananda Point and reached the approaches to Giruwa Village. There the Japanese resistance stiffened, and advance came to a halt. Except for a 1,500-yard strip between Wye Point and Sanananda, the beach from Cape Killerton almost to the outskirts of Giruwa was in Australian hands.[12]

The attack of the 163d Infantry had also gone well. Early on 16 January, after an all-night artillery harassment of the Japanese main line north of Fisk, the 1st Battalion began forming up for the attack on the west side of the road along the edge of a woods west of Fisk. Companies A and C, Lieutenant McKinney and Capt. Jack Van Duyn commanding, were abreast on an 800-yard front, and Company B (Capt. Robert M. Hamilton commanding) was immediately to the rear in battalion reserve. Company A was on the right, and its right flank was anchored on the road. Company C, on the left, extended beyond the Japanese right flank in order to get around it and come in on the Japanese rear.

The attack was well prepared. The artillery opened fire at 0845. The .30-caliber machine guns of Company D started spraying the woods and underbrush on both flanks

of the battalion, while those of Company M, in place east of Fisk, began searching out the area to the south and southeast. At 0857 the fifteen 81-mm. mortars of companies D, H, and M opened up from Musket, and at 0859 the 60-mm. mortars of the 3d Battalion, in battery south of Fisk, opened fire on the Japanese line. At 0900 the artillery and 81-mm. mortars ceased firing, and the troops moved forward. The direction was northeast, roughly parallel to the track.[13]

Fairly heavy fire came from the Japanese positions as the troops crawled out from the line of departure. A strongpoint on the right gave Company A a lot of trouble, especially when riflemen opened up from positions in the tall trees behind it. Light machine guns were brought up to clean out the snipers, and the crawling skirmishers advanced steadily. Company C on the left continued to move forward and around the enemy, but Company A ran into trouble as it neared the enemy strongpoint immediately to its front.

"The assault line [the company commander recalls] got within twenty yards of the Jap bunkers when it was definitely stopped by a combination of flat ground and at least four machine guns. The sun was blazing hot and the heat was terrific. The air in the small open space was dead still. The heat and nervous strain tore at everyone; two officers and eighteen men collapsed and were evacuated . . ."[14]

Worse was in store. The troops used up all their machine gun ammunition. The Japanese tree snipers grew bolder, and it was impossible to use the mortars and artillery because the front line was too close to the Japanese positions. Colonel Lindstrom

[12] Msgs, 7th Div to 32d Div, Sers 6340, 6347, 6358, 6360, 17 Jan 43, Sers 6383, 6385, 6402, 18 Jan 43, in 32d Div G-3 Jnl; ALF Daily Opns Rpts No. 278, 17 Jan 43, No. 279, 18 Jan 43, No. 280, 18 Jan 43; Rpt on Opns 18th Inf Bde Gp at Sanananda.

[13] 41st Inf Div Tng Notes No. 2, 19 May 43, copy in OCMH files; 163d Inf, The Battle of Sanananda.
[14] 41st Inf Div Tng Notes No. 2, 19 May 43.

ordered in a platoon from Company B, but it too was pinned down. By noon the situation was clearly hopeless, and Lindstrom gave the order to withdraw. There had been nine killed and seventeen wounded in the attack.[15]

Company C meanwhile had met only negligible opposition. Seeing that its attack was going through, Colonel Lindstrom had pushed in Company B. The two companies swept around the Japanese right flank and quickly established a perimeter 200 yards behind the Japanese line. The new position, to which the 1st Battalion moved as quickly as it could, was about 400 yards west of the road.[16]

The 2d Battalion was now reaching the area with Companies F and G in the lead. Part of Company H had been left behind at trail junction east of the plantation to cover the battalion's rear. Although the battalion had to cut its way through on a compass course when all traces of the trail it was following disappeared, it came out just south of the 1st Battalion. A patrol of Company B met it and guided it into the 1st Battalion perimeter. After a meal and a short rest, Major Rankin's troops chopped their way east to a point on the M.T. Road about 1,000 yards behind the Japanese line, and there they made contact with the 2/12 Battalion.

Early that afternoon Companies K and L overcame the last enemy resistance in the pocket between Musket and Kano. The entire area south of Fisk was finally clear of the enemy.[17]

The 1st and 2d Battalions were now north of Fisk and behind the main Japanese line. As a result, Colonel Doe was in a position to envelop the remaining enemy troops in the area from the front, flanks, and rear. He first attached Company K to the 1st Battalion to chop a supply trail from a new battalion supply point to the southwest of Fisk. Then, after seeing to it that the troops of the battalion had some rest and food, he proceeded to his task.

On 17 January patrols of Company B located the Japanese stronghold which had balked Company A the day before. The company left the 1st Battalion bivouac, moved southwest, and spent the night about 100 yards from the enemy position. In the morning the men attacked across a fifteen-foot-wide, chest-high stream. In the face of heavy fire from a line of enemy bunkers on the other side of the stream, only one platoon was able to get across. The platoon knocked out one of the bunkers to its front, only to find itself up against a second line of bunkers immediately to the rear. Pinned down by heavy fire, it made no further progress that day. Patrols were sent to the left to look for an easier crossing. When they returned with a report that the double line of bunkers extended as far as the eye could see, Captain Hamilton, the company commander, ordered the company into bivouac for another try at the enemy position in the morning.

Companies A and K had moved out that morning to envelop the enemy position from the M.T. Road. While trying to reach the road, they ran into an enemy strongpoint in a road bend about 250 yards behind the Japanese line and were also halted. Company F, advancing southward along the M. T. Road from the 2d Battalion bivouac, ran into Company K's right flank as it began

[15] 163d Inf, The Battle of Sanananda.

[16] Msg, NGF to 32d Div, Ser 6338, 16 Jan 43, in 32d Div G–3 Jnl; 163d Inf Jnl, 1400, 16 Jan 43; 163d Inf, The Battle of Sanananda.

[17] 163d Inf Jnl, 1400, 16 Jan 43; 163d Inf, The Battle of Sanananda.

approaching the road bend, and moved off to the left to make contact with the enemy positions on the east side of the road. The company soon encountered very strong enemy resistance and began working on it.[18]

The 163d Infantry had accounted for more than 250 of the enemy since the 16th and was now in contact with the remaining Japanese positions in its area. All that remained for Colonel Doe to do was to surround and destroy them.

On Colonel Howe's front gains on the 16th, the opening day of the advance, had been negligible. The area of the chain hoist was investigated and found to be deserted, but an attempt to move forward on Giruwa along the coastal track had made virtually no progress. Although the attack on the coastal track had been preceded by a rolling barrage of both artillery and mortar fire, the 127th Infantry had gained only a few yards in a full day's fighting. Toward evening Companies F and G relieved Companies A and B, and plans were drawn for a stronger and better-supported attack in the morning.[19]

The next morning, 17 January, Companies I and K moved southward along the west bank of Konombi Creek to see whether there were Japanese beyond the place where the chain hoist had been found. Companies G and F, following the usual artillery and mortar barrage, attacked westward. Company G moved forward along the track, and Company F (as in the advance on Tarakena) covered it from the swamp on the left. The going was infinitely more difficult than on the other side of the river. The

swamp was deeper and harder to cut through, and there was no spit from which enfilading fire could be put down on the enemy.

The advance did not go far that day. After Company G had gained a few yards and taken one machine gun, it was stopped by a second machine gun so cleverly sited that the troops were unable to flank it. Companies I and K, operating to the southward, had meanwhile run into an enemy outpost about fifty yards south of the chain hoist. They killed eleven ragged and horribly emaciated Japanese in the encounter.

The coastal attack was resumed on 18 January with Company G still on the right, and Company F, as before, on its left. Companies K and I were on Company F's left rear, and an element of Company L was between K and F. The opposition had perceptibly weakened, and the two lead companies gained 300 yards that day.[20] Although the fantastically difficult terrain in which the 127th Infantry was operating heavily favored the enemy, he was finally on the run on that flank too.

Finishing the Job

The Mop-up Begins

By 19 January operations had definitely entered the mop-up stage. The enemy was fighting to the death, and the opposition continued to be heavy, so heavy in fact, that the companies of the 2/10 Battalion on the coast west of Sanananda and of the 2/9 Battalion on the eastern outskirts of Giruwa were held up that day and the day follow-

---

[18] Ltr, Gen Doe to Gen Ward, 3 Mar 51; 163d Inf, The Battle of Sanananda; 41st Div Tng Notes No. 2, 19 May 43.
[19] Tel Conv, Maj Hawkins with Col Howe, Ser 6304, 16 Jan 43, 127th Inf Jnl, 1200, 1615, 16 Jan 43; 127th Inf Tact Hist, 16 Jan 43.

[20] Tel Msg, Capt Hewitt to Capt M. H. Haag, Ser 6354, 17 Jan 43; 127th Inf Jnl, 1630, 17 Jan 43, 1625 1650, 18 Jan 43; 127th Inf Tact Hist, 17, 18 Jan 43.

ing.[21] The 2/12 Battalion and the company of the 2/9 Battalion that had been working from south and north on the enemy position immediately south of Sanananda were more fortunate. They managed to make contact west of the road on the afternoon on the 19th, although the job was accomplished, as the historian of the 18th Brigade notes, "under the most miserable conditions, the troops . . . never being out of the water and frequently remaining for hours in the water up to their waist." [22] There was still opposition in the area east of the road, and the next day was devoted to reducing it. At nightfall on 20 January the task was almost complete, and Brigadier Wootten had already ordered Colonel Arnold to move north as soon as the last organized enemy opposition in the area was overcome.[23]

Colonel Doe's efforts to reduce the three remaining enemy pockets in his area were intensified on 19 January. The pockets—remnants of the Japanese main line on the M.T. Road immediately northeast of Fisk—were heavily engaged during the day. Company C moved in on the left of Company B at daybreak, and the two companies attacked the westernmost Japanese strongpoint north of the road. Company F, after advancing 250 yards since the day before, attacked the larger perimeter south of the road from the northeast. From the northwest Companies A and K continued their attack on the roadbend perimeter, a few hundred yards to the northeast of the first two.[24]

The plan for the reduction of the west perimeter called for Company B on the right to drive ahead from its shallow penetration of the day before and clear out the Japanese second line, while Company C on the left rolled up the first line. Preparations for the attack were thorough. The four rifle platoons and the 60-mm. mortars were linked up with sound-power telephones on a party line, and the two company commanders, Captain Hamilton of Company B and Captain Van Duyn of Company C, working closely together, took turns at the telephone and in the front lines.

As long as the stream still had to be crossed, the advantage was with the enemy. Enemy fire from the other side of the creek was again very heavy, and Company C, which attacked first, had a hard time crossing. At first, part of only one platoon, under the platoon leader, S. Sgt. John L. Mohl, managed to get across. Mohl, who had only nine men with him, moved out on the enemy bunkers at once with another enlisted man, Cpl. Wilbur H. Rummel. The two men, covered by fire from the other eight, knocked out six bunkers in quick succession, making it a comparatively easy matter for the rest of the company to cross.[25] While the enemy was occupied with Company C, Company B was able to get across without undue trouble. It spent all afternoon working on the second bunker line. Just when its attack seemed on the point of going through, the Japanese pulled out of both the first and second lines into a third line immediately to the rear of the first two and once again blocked further advance.

[21] ALF Daily Opns Rpts, No. 281, 20 Jan 43, No. 282, 21 Jan 43; Rpt on Opns 18th Inf Bde Gp at Sanananda.
[22] Rpt on Opns 18th Inf Bde Gp at Sanananda.
[23] ALF Daily Opns Rpt No. 282, 21 Jan 43; Rpt on Opns 18th Inf Bde Gp at Sanananda.
[24] 163d Inf, The Battle of Sanananda.

[25] 163 Inf, The Battle of Sanananda; 41st Div Tng Notes No. 2, 19 May 43. Both Mohl and Rummel were later awarded the Distinguished Service Cross. The citations are in Hq USAFFE GO No. 37, 7 Jul 43.

.50-CAL. BROWNING MACHINE GUN, *directed at Giruwa Point.*

It had turned dark by this time. Taking up a defensive bivouac in the middle of the Japanese position, the troops had their evening meal and prepared for further action in the morning.

East of the road Company F had also met heavy opposition during the morning. Finding a double line of log and dirt bunkers in its way, it called for the artillery and the 81-mm. mortars. The company commander, Capt. Conway M. Ellers, established an observation post about thirty yards from the Japanese bunker line and was joined there by Major Rankin and an Australian forward observer. The artillery and the 81-mm. mortars ranged in and at 1400 opened up on the bunkers. At 1530 the

preparation ceased and the troops, who had been a short distance to the rear, attacked. They found that the artillery and mortars had done their work well. The bunkers, made of softwood logs and not so well constructed as at Buna, had been demolished, and most of the Japanese inside had been killed.

After advancing 150 yards past the Japanese bunker line, the company found itself wedged between two shoulder-deep streams with Japanese machine guns on front and flank. Five men were killed while trying to clear out one of the machine gun nests, and a flanking move by the support platoon along the bank of one of the streams failed. Because it was growing dark and the company had nearly expended its ammunition, Major Rankin ordered Company E, Capt. James Buckland commanding, to relieve Company F. While the relief was in progress, the Japanese discovered what was going on and counterattacked, but fire from Buckland's company drove them off.

The push of Companies A and K on the road-bend perimeter had been supported by a platoon of heavy machine guns on the right flank, and by their own light machine guns thrust out to the front. Everything went well until the advance masked the fire of the machine guns. Taking advantage of their opportunity, the Japanese counterattacked and halted the movement. From a wounded Japanese who crawled into the perimeter at dusk and gave himself up, the two company commanders, Lieutenant McKinney and 1st Lt. Allen Zimmerman, learned that they were approaching the main Japanese headquarters in the area, presumably that of Colonel Yokoyama.[26]

The next day, 20 January, while Companies B and C continued working on the desperately resisting Japanese in the west perimeter, and Companies A and K on those in the road bend, Company I moved up from the south and launched a strong attack on the south perimeter. Preceded by 250 rounds from the 25-pounders and 750 from the 81-mm. mortars at Musket, the attack had also the support of the machine guns of Company M at Fisk. The heavy weapons crews swept the trees and underbrush in the area thoroughly before the troops jumped off. Just as the company was about to move forward, a mortar shot

killed its commander, Capt. Duncan V. Dupree, and its 1st sergeant, James W. Boland. Seconds later, enemy rifle fire killed one of the platoon leaders. The company faltered just long enough for the Japanese to leave their bunkers, get into firing position, and repulse the attack.[27]

The 163d Infantry had taken heavy toll of the enemy during the preceding two days, but the latter, though encircled and cut off, were still holding their positions. It was obvious they would be unable to do so much longer.

The mop-up on the 127th Infantry's front had gone well. At daybreak on 19 January Company E had started pushing up the beach with Company K on its left. To help Company K overcome continued heavy opposition in the swamp, a .50-caliber machine gun was brought up. It proved very effective against the hastily improvised enemy positions there. The 37-mm. gun which had played so notable a part in the taking of Tarakena was also brought up. Emplaced on the beach to cover Company E's advance, it again proved extremely effective against the enemy.

The next morning Company F joined Company E along the beach, Company C moved in on the left, and Companies I and L began moving forward on the far left. There was little opposition now. Several enemy machine guns were captured, and a number of prisoners were taken, all of them suffering from dysentery and starvation. By 1630 in the afternoon the Americans were in sight of Giruwa and could see the Australians moving forward along the coastal track on the other side of the village.[28]

[26] Msg, 7th Div to 32d Div, Ser 6442, 20 Jan 43, in 32d Div G–3 Jnl; 163d Inf, The Battle of Sanananda; 41st Div Tng Notes No. 2, 19 May 43; Buggy, *Pacific Victory*, p. 213.

[27] 163d Inf, The Battle of Sanananda.
[28] 127th Inf Tact Hist, 19, 20 Jan 43.

General Yamagata Gets Out in Time

By the 18th General Yamagata, with the Sanananda front collapsing about his ears,[29] had seen enough to convince him that his troops could not wait until the 25th to abandon their positions and try to make their way westward through the Allied lines as General Adachi had ordered five days before. He therefore drew up orders at noon on the 18th which advanced the withdrawal five days: from 2000 hours, 25 January, to 2000 hours, 20 January. After slipping through the Allied lines, his troops were to assemble near Bakumbari, a point about seven miles north of Gona, where boats would be waiting to take them to safety. General Yamagata, his staff, and his headquarters would leave the area by motor launch on 19 January—X minus 1.[30]

Early on 19 January Yamagata handed the orders personally to General Oda, who was holding the western approaches to Giruwa, and one of his staff officers delivered them personally to Colonel Yazawa, who was in command of operations east of Giruwa. The orders were sealed, and the two commanders (apparently for morale reasons) were instructed not to open them until 1600. At 2130 Yamagata, his staff, a

section of his headquarters, and 140 sick and wounded left for the mouth of the Kumusi in two large motor launches. Though bombed on the way, they arrived safely at their destination at 0230 the next morning.[31]

That night several Japanese motor boats tried to put in at Giruwa in order to take off all remaining communications equipment and as many as possible of the sick and wounded. Allied artillery drove them off. At the same time General Oda, Colonel Yazawa, and an unknown number of their troops abandoned their positions, east and west of Giruwa and took to the swamp, trying to escape toward Bakumbari as their orders bade them. Some got through, but Oda and Yazawa did not. Both were killed the same night when they apparently ran into Australian outposts that stood in the way.[32]

The End at Last

Along the M.T. Road immediately south of Sanananda, the 2/12 Battalion overcame the last vestiges of enemy opposition in the area. Relieved by the 2d Battalion, 163d Infantry, early on 21 January, Colonel Arnold moved north to take over the Sanananda Point–Giruwa area from the 2/9 Battalion. The relief was completed that afternoon, and the 2/9 Battalion moved out against the Japanese pocket west of Sanananda which had so long held back the 2/10 Battalion.

[29] Yamagata had other troubles. The night before, three of the motor launches with which he was evacuating patients were sunk by a motor torpedo boat of Task Force 50.1 near Douglas Harbor, a few miles from Mambare Bay. To Yamagata, this was a major disaster, for it left him with only five launches with which to make last-minute evacuations of the area. Msg, 7th Div to 32d Div, Ser 6372, 18 Jan 43, in 32d Div G–3 Jnl; Bulkley, A History of Motor Torpedo Boats in the U. S. Navy, p. 236; 18th Army Opns I, 36, 38, 40.
[30] Western Opns Orders No. A–65, Northern Giruwa, 1200, 18 Jan 43, quoted in 18th Army Opns I, 36, 37. A captured copy of these orders is to be found as an appendix to 163d Inf, The Battle of Sanananda.

[31] Msg, 7th Div to 32d Div, Ser 6442, 20 Jan 43, in 32d Div G–3 Jnl; 18th Army Opns I, 36, 37, 38. Yamagata may have made an effort to try to inform the surrounded troops under Colonel Yokoyama of the impending withdrawal, but there is no evidence that such in fact was the case.
[32] Tel Msg, Capt Earl R. Kindig to Col Rogers, Ser 6470, 20 Jan 43; Msg, NGF to 32d Div, Ser 6516, 20 Jan 43, in 32d Div G–3 Jnl; 127th Inf Tact Hist, 20 Jan 43; 18th Army Opns I, 39.

There was to be a three-way envelopment of the pocket. Two companies of the 2/10 Battalion would attack from the northwest, the 2/9 Battalion would attack from the southeast, and Company C of the 2/10 Battalion would attack from the top of the large kunai strip west of Sanananda, and take the Japanese in the center. The Australians moved out that afternoon. They met surprisingly little opposition, and only one man was wounded in the day's fighting. At the end of the day a single enemy pocket remained. It was quickly reduced the next morning with the help of artillery fire from Hanson Troop. The three attacking forces made contact along the beach at 1315, a meeting that marked the end of organized resistance in the area. More than 200 Japanese had been killed in the two-day attack.[33] The enemy position west of Sanananda had finally been reduced.

The reduction of Giruwa was also to prove an easy task. Companies E, C, and A, 127th Infantry, pushed forward along the coastal track early on 21 January with Company E leading. They found the terrain much better now; the track was broader, and there was less swamp. The enemy was no longer trying to hold, and only scattered rifle fire was met. At 1230 Company E, under Lieutenant Fraser, swept through Giruwa Village, meeting virtually no opposition. Forty-five minutes later Fraser and his company joined the Australians on the east bank of the Giruwa lagoon. Soon after,

a patrol of Company E, exploring the area just east of Giruwa, came upon what was left of the *67th Line of Communications Hospital*. The scene was a grisly one. Sick and wounded were scattered through the area, a large number of them in the last stages of starvation. There were many unburied dead, and what the patrol described as "several skeletons walking around." There was evidence too that some of the enemy had been practicing cannibalism. Even in this extremity, the Japanese fought back. Twenty were killed in the hospital area resisting capture; sixty-nine others, too helpless to resist, were taken prisoner.

The Japanese tried to land boats at Giruwa during the night and were again driven off by the artillery. The fighting came to an end early the next morning when the troops mopped up the last resisting Japanese in the area. Giruwa, the main Japanese headquarters west of the river, had fallen after only token resistance.[34]

The heaviest fighting of all developed on the 163d Infantry front where the bulk of the enemy troops still left at the beachhead were penned in. As at Giruwa and the pocket west of Sanananda, the climactic day was the 21st. Colonel Doe was in at the kill, personally directing operations from an exposed position in the front line.[35] The attacks that morning went off well. At 1015, after Companies A and K pulled back 150 yards, the

---

[33] Msgs, NGF to 32d Div, Ser 6516, 20 Jan 43, Ser 6545, 21 Jan 43, Ser 6546, 21 Jan 43, Ser 6547, 22 Jan 43, in 32d Div G-3 Jnl; ALF Daily Opns Rpts No. 282, 21 Jan 43, No. 283, 23 Jan 43; Rpt on Opns 18th Inf Bde Gp at Sanananda. The sudden feebleness of the defense seems to indicate that here, as at Giruwa, a portion of the enemy had pulled out on the night of the 20th and tried to escape westward.

[34] Tel Msg, Col Howe to Col Bradley, Ser 6488, 21 Jan 43; Tel Msg, Capt Hewitt to Col Bradley, Ser 6498, 21 Jan 43; Tel Msg, Col Bradley to Capt Haag, Ser 6520, 22 Jan 43; *18th Army* Opns I, 39. Interrogation of the prisoners revealed that most of the able-bodied troops had pulled out of the area a short time before and that Giruwa's last defenders consisted principally of sick and wounded still able to bear arms. 127th Inf Tact Hist, 21 Jan 43.

[35] Doe was later awarded the Distinguished Service Cross. The citation is in Hq USAFFE GO No. 36, 1 Jul 43.

artillery began firing on the last Japanese bunker line in the road-bend perimeter. When the artillery barrage ceased at 1030, the massed 81-mm. mortars at Musket supplemented by the machine guns, began firing on the position. Five minutes later, just as the last mortar salvo was fired, Companies A and K attacked. Covered by their own assault fire, they caught most of the Japanese still in their shelters or trying to get out of them. The Japanese were killed in droves, and the perimeter was quickly overrun. Company A on the right fanned out and lent some of its fire power to Companies B and C, which were still working on the west perimeter. Feeling the pressure ease, Companies B and C surged forward and quickly cleaned out the enemy position. All four companies thereupon moved south to the M.T. Road, where Companies B and K, the one wheeling right and the other left, joined forces and completed the mop-up. More than 500 enemy dead were counted at the end of the day, the largest single day's destruction of the enemy since Gorari. The 163d Infantry lost one killed and six wounded.

That same day, 1st Lt. John R. Jacobucci, S–2 of the 3d Battalion, personally located the main enemy strongpoint in the east perimeter after several patrols failed to do so. The next morning at 1047, Companies I and L, 1st Lt. Loren E. O'Dell and Capt. Edward L. Reams commanding, attacked the perimeter from the south, concentrating on the strongpoint that Jacobucci had discovered. As before, the troops went in on the run behind the last mortar salvo and again caught the Japanese still in their holes or trying to leave them. The position was overrun by 1152, and the mop-up was completed by 1300 with the

help of Company E, which had been at the northeast end of the perimeter supporting the attack by fire. This attack marked the end of all organized resistance on the M.T. Road. By evening the mop-up on either side of the road was complete.[36] Giruwa and the Japanese pocket west of Sanananda had already been reduced some hours before. The 18th Brigade and the 127th and 163d Infantry Regiments had suffered 828 casualties since being committed to the Sanananda front,[37] but they had finished the job. The Papuan Campaign was over, six months to the day after it had begun.

The Victory at Sanananda

The Cost to the Enemy

The 18th Brigade, the 127th Infantry, and the 163d Infantry at Sanananda, and the 14th Brigade at Gona, captured a great deal of enemy matériel, including rifles, machine guns, mortars, antitank guns, land mines, radio transmitters, signal equipment, medical supplies, tools of all kinds, and a dozen motor vehicles, some with U.S. Army markings. They buried 1,993 of the enemy,

---

[36] Msg, 7th Div to Adv NGF, Ser 6547, 22 Jan 43, in 32d Div G–3 Jnl; Memo, Col Doe for Maj Leonard A. Wing, 22 Jan 43, copy in OCMH files; 163d Inf, The Battle of Sanananda. Jacobucci was later awarded the Distinguished Service Cross. His citation is in Hq USAFFE GO No. 37, 7 Jul 43.

[37] 32d Div Sitrep No. 184, 24 Jan 43; Rpt on Opns 18th Bde Gp at Sanananda; 163d Inf, The Battle of Sanananda, The 18th Brigade sustained 426 casualties—155 killed or died of wounds, 269 wounded, and 2 missing. The 127th and 163d Infantry Regiments had 402 casualties—110 killed or died of wounds, 287 wounded, and 5 missing. Of these casualties, 86 were sustained by the 127th Infantry, and 316 by the 163d Infantry.

ORDER OF THE DAY

On Completion Of

RECAPTURE OF BUNA-GONA AREA

By

Lieutenant-General E. F. HERRING,
C.B.E., D.S.O., M.C., E.D

G.O.C., NEW GUINEA FORCE

Headquarters,

New Guinea Force,

22 January, 1943.

THE campaign we have been engaged in for the recapture of the BUNA-GONA area is now virtually at a close. I desire to express to all Australians and Americans alike who have taken part in this long and tedious campaign my heartfelt congratulations and my appreciation of all you have done.

First to the Infantry I would like to pay a special tribute. Seldom have Infantry been called on to endure greater hardships or discomfort than those provided by the mountains, the swamps, the floods, of tropical NEW GUINEA. All this you have endured with cheerfulness and meantime have outfought a dour and determined enemy on ground of his own choosing in well prepared defences. Your achievements have been such as to earn the admiration and appreciation of all your countrymen.

Secondly, I would thank the Air Forces for their magnificent work, for the shattering blows they have delivered to the air forces of the enemy and his ships, which have tried so often and so vainly to reinforce and supply him. To the air transport service which made this campaign a feasible operation, for your untiring efforts in all weathers, I thank you.

Thirdly, there are all those who have supported so splendidly the Infantry in their fighting, the Armoured Regiment, the Artillery, the Engineers and the Army Co-operation Squadron, and the Medical services who have cared for sick and wounded in most difficult circumstances. You have all done magnificently.

Fourthly, I want to thank all those in the Services who have kept supplies of all kinds going to the forward troops, and also COSC and all its personnel and particularly its small boat section that has braved hazardous waters and enemy action in getting supplies up the coast.

And finally my thanks to the Navy for its assistance in protecting sea routes and clearing the waters round the battle area and further NORTH.

We have won a striking victory but a long and hard road lies ahead. All I ask is that all of you maintain the standard you have set. I know you will.

E.F.Herring

Lieutenant-General,
GOC New Guinea Force.

DOBODURA AIRSTRIP. *41st Division troops arriving from Port Moresby, 4 February 1943.*

and took more than 200 prisoners, including 159 Japanese.[38]

The final count of enemy dead in General Vasey's area since the beginning of operations was 2,537—959 of them killed at Gona and in the area west of Gona.[39] The victory however, was not as complete as could be desired, for a great many of the enemy's ablebodied troops escaped, leaving mostly sick and wounded behind. General Willoughby may have suspected as much when he wrote that the count of enemy dead at Sanananda could not be considered "a true count of effective enemy strength" since it

---

[38] Tel Msg, Capt Hewitt to Col Bradley, Ser 6498, 21 Jan 43; Ltr, Gen Eichelberger to Gen MacArthur, 24 Jan 43, copy in OCMH files; 127th Inf Tact Hist; Rpt on Opns 18th Bde Inf Gp at Sanananda; 163d Inf, The Battle of Sanananda; G–2 Daily Summaries Enemy Intel Nos. 306, 307, 23 Jan 43, 24 Jan 43, in G–3 Jnl, GHQ SWPA; 32d Div. Sitrep No. 184, 24 Jan 43. According to 32d Division figures, the 127th Infantry buried 415 enemy dead and the units under General Vasey's command buried 1,578—1,216 at Sanananda and 362 at Gona. There was apparently a great deal of duplicate counting of enemy killed at the lower levels, for the 18th Brigade and the 163d Infantry in their after action reports claim either to have killed or to have found dead more than

2,000 of the enemy—almost twice the number of enemy dead that the 7th Division gave them credit for. A careful examination of the sources leaves no doubt that the correct figure was that kept by the 7th Division, the responsible headquarters in the area.

[39] Msg, 7th Div to 32d Div, Ser 6578, 24 Jan 43, in 32d Div G–3 Jnl.

DOBODURA AIRSTRIP. *32d Division troops departing for Port Moresby, 4 February 1943.*

included many "sick and wounded who were killed." [40]

The Australians on the ground, especially at Gona, realized that Japanese troops in considerable numbers were slipping past them. Because of the thick and tangled jungle terrain, they were able to intercept only a portion of them. The Australians estimated at the time that about 700 Japanese had succeeded in getting through their lines,[41] but the actual figure was far higher. A total of 1,190 enemy sick and wounded were evacuated by sea between 13 and 20 January, and by the end of the month about 1,000 able-bodied Japanese succeeded in filtering through the Allied lines and reaching safety on the other side of Gona.[42]

The Allied Cost

The cost of the victory had not been light. The Australian troops who fought on the Sanananda side of the river—the 2/7 Cavalry, and the 14th, 16th, 18th, 21st, 25th, and 30th Brigades—sustained some 2,700 casualties.[43] The American units on this

---

[40] G–2 Daily Summary Enemy Intel No. 306, 23 Jan 43.

[41] AMF, The Battle of the Beaches, pp. 115, 116.

[42] *18th Army* Opns I, 40, 41.

[43] Information extracted from AMF, New Guinea Campaign—Battle Casualties, incl to Ltr, The Australian Official War Historian, Canberra, to author, 15 Feb 50, copy to OCMH files.

front—the 127th Infantry, the 163d Infantry, and the detachment of the 126th Infantry—suffered 798.[44] The casualties incurred in clearing the 7th Division area were thus about 3,500, roughly 700 more than at Buna.

The 41st Division Takes Over

With the campaign at an end, the time had come to relieve the worn-out troops of the 7th and 32d Divisions, some of whom had been in the area since early November. The 41st Division, whose remaining regiments had by this time begun reaching the front, was designated for the task, and the reliefs were effected as quickly as possible.

General Fuller took over operational control of all Allied troops in the Oro Bay–Gona area on 25 January, and General Eichelberger and the I Corps staff returned to Port Moresby the same day. Eichelberger was followed there a few days later by General Berryman and a nucleus of Advance New Guinea Force which had remained behind to assist General Fuller with the reliefs.

By prior arrangement the hard-hit 126th Infantry left the combat zone on the 22d, and relief of the remaining troops was completed by the end of the month. As air space became available, the men were flown to Port Moresby and, after a short stay, were returned to Australia by sea.[45]

The victory in Papua had been crushing and decisive. By the end of January all that was left of the enemy troops who had fought there were broken remnants at the mouths of the Kumusi and Mambare Rivers, whom the air force had under constant attack and against whom the 41st Division was already moving.[46]

It was not the only victory. On 7 February, the Japanese finished evacuating Guadalcanal. Two days later the fighting on the island came to a end, as in Papua, exactly six months after it began.[47] The Japanese had been defeated all along the line. The initiative both in New Guinea and in the Solomons was finally in Allied hands.

---

[44] 3d Bn, 163d Inf, Jnl, 11 Jan 43; 32d Div Sitrep No. 184, 24 Jan 43; 163d Inf, The Battle of Sanananda, App. 3. The breakdown is as follows:

	KIA/DofW	WIA	MIA	Total
Det 126th Inf	81	237	78	396
127th Inf	13	72	1	86
163d Inf	97	215	4	316
	191	524	83	798

[45] NGF OI's No. 62, 21 Jan 43, No. 64, 23 Jan 43; Tel Msg, G–4, 32d Div to G–3, 32d Div, Ser 6515, 22 Jan 43; Rad COIC, Moresby, to COIC, Brisbane, No. P–1108, 22 Jan 43; ALF Daily Opns Rpts, No. 287, 26 Jan 43, No. 289, 28 Jan 43, No. 291, 30 Jan 43, in G–3 Jnl, GHQ SWPA.

[46] Allied Air Forces Opns Rpt, 21 through 24 Jan 43; GHQ SWPA G–3 Opns Rpt No. 291, 22–23 Jan 43; ALF Daily Opns Rpt, Nos. 290 through 295, 29 Jan–4 Feb 43. All in G–3 Jnl, GHQ SWPA.

[47] 17th Army Opns II, 49, 50; Miller, Guadalcanal: The First Offensive, 349, 350.

CHAPTER XIX

The Victory

For the student of military history, the Papuan Campaign is most noteworthy for the tactical aspects of its final or beachhead phase, for it was at the Buna-Gona beachhead that the Allies, for the first time in World War II, encountered and reduced an area fortified and defended in depth by the Japanese. Although the attack was from the landward, and succeeding campaigns generally from the sea, the basic tactical situation was the same—the Allies were attacking and the Japanese were defending an elaborately fortified area. The essential difference was thus not that Buna was a land operation while the succeeding operations were amphibious; it was rather that in later campaigns the attacking troops hit the beachhead better prepared and supported, with a variety of tactics and weapons for the speedy reduction of the Japanese positions. In the Buna area, on the other hand, poorly supported Allied infantry attacked again and again in vain; the action took on the aspect of a siege, and starvation was a significant factor in the enemy's final collapse. American conduct of operations was to profit from Buna as from few other campaigns, and the profit was to accrue not only in the negative sense, but in the positive sense as well.

The Campaign in Review

The Time Element

Contrary to the final headquarters press release on the subject, the Papuan Campaign had been neither cheaply won nor conducted on the supposition that there was "no necessity of a hurry attack." [1] In the perspective of succeeding Pacific campaigns, the picture, especially in the final beachhead phase of operations, had been rather one in which the troops suffered heavy casualties while being hastily pressed forward in repeated attacks on prepared enemy positions with little more in the way of weapons than

---

[1] In this press release General MacArthur's headquarters announced that the losses had been low, less than half those of the enemy, battle casualties and sick included. It gave as the reason for this favorable result that there had been no need to hurry the attack because "the time element was in this case of little importance." Communique, United Nations Headquarters, Australia, 28 Jan 43, in *The New York Times*, 29 Jan 1943. General Eichelberger has written: "The statement to the correspondents in Brisbane after Buna that 'losses were small because there was no hurry' was one of the great surprises of my life. As you know, our Allied losses were heavy and as commander in the field, I had been told many times of the necessity for speed." Ltr, Gen Eichelberger to author, 8 Mar 54, OCMH files.

their rifles, machine guns, mortars, and hand grenades.

Throughout the fighting, General Eichelberger had been a man under pressure. Told by General MacArthur on 30 November that "time was of the essence," on 13 December that "time is working desperately against us," and on 25 December that "if results were not achieved shortly the whole picture [might] radically change," General Eichelberger had pushed the attack in every way he could.[2] On 18 December, though able to report progress, he nevertheless made it a point to assure General MacArthur that he "never forgot for a moment that we have not much time. . . ." On 30 December, when General Herring asked him why he did not let his troops "take it easy since the Australians were not going to do anything today or tomorrow," Eichelberger had replied that he had no intention of doing so, for he had always considered that "time was the essential element of the attack."[3] Whether GHQ realized it or not, hurrying the attack had become the leitmotiv of the campaign.

The Losses

During the six months that the Australian ground forces had been in action, they had committed seven infantry brigades and one dismounted cavalry unit of battalion strength.[4] Though there were times when elements of as many as four brigades were in the line, the Australians usually had no more than three brigades (roughly 7,000 to 7,500 men) in contact with the enemy at any one time. Sometimes they had as few as two and, during the opening weeks of the campaign, less than two.

The American ground commitment, dating from mid-November 1942, was four infantry regiments—the 126th, 127th, 128th, and the 163d Infantry Regiments, a total of just under 15,000 men. During most of the period that the Americans were in action, they had at least three regiments at the front, though until the arrival of the 127th Infantry in early December there had been only two. There were almost no replacements, and the strength of the units fell steadily until, in a few instances, they were near the extinction point when relieved.[5]

The campaign cost the Australian ground forces, 5,698 battle casualties—1,731 killed in action, 306 dead of wounds, 128 dead from other causes, and 3,533 wounded in action.[6] American ground casualties were 2,848—687 killed in action, 160 dead of wounds, 17 dead from other causes, 66 missing in action, and 1,918 wounded in action.

Of the 66 Americans missing, the 32d Division lost 62 and the 163d Infantry lost 4. Other losses sustained by the 32d Division but not included as among the killed, wounded, or missing were 211 from shell

---

[2] Ltrs, Gen MacArthur to Gen Eichelberger, 13 Dec 42, 25 Dec 42, copies in OCMH files; Interv with Gen Eichelberger, 31 Mar 50; Eichelberger, *Our Jungle Road to Tokyo,* p. 42.

[3] Ltrs, Gen Eichelberger to Gen Sutherland, 18 Dec 42, 30 Dec 42, copies in OCMH files.

[4] The 7th, 14th, 16th, 18th, 21st, 25th, and 30th Infantry Brigades, and the 2/7 Cavalry Regiment, a total of between 18,000 and 20,000 men.

[5] Average and total American and Australian front-line strengths by unit for the periods indicated can be obtained from the applicable ALF Opns Rpts and G–3 Opns Rpts, both in G–3 Jnl, GHQ SWPA. For the Australians, the figure given is an approximation since no precise figures on actual Australian front-line strength are available. Ltr, John Balfour to author, 21 Dec 51.

[6] Signal, Australian Military Headquarters, Melbourne to the Australian Military Mission, Washington, No. MW–179, 22 Jun 50, abstract in OCMH files. It should be noted that in these figures the missing in action are carried as killed in action, and hence are not listed separately.

shock and concussion, and 287 from battle-field injuries.[7]

American Battle Casualties, Less the Missing

32d Division	KIA	D of W	D of O/C	WIA
126th Inf.	266	34	5	728
127th Inf.	182	29	3	504
128th Inf.	138	25	4	434
Div. Troops	16	0	5	14
	602	88	17	1,680
41st Division				
163d Inf.	85	12	0	238
	687	100	17	1,918

All together 3,095 Australians and Americans lost their lives in the campaign, and 5,451 were wounded. Total battle casualties were 8,546.[8]

Australian losses had been so heavy that brigade after brigade had seen its battalions reduced to company strength and less before it was relieved.[9] But if the Australian units had suffered severe attrition, so had the 32d Division. General Eichelberger put the situation to General MacArthur in a sentence. "Regiments here," he wrote in mid-January, "soon have the strength of battalions and a little later are not much

more than companies." [10] The casualty reports bear out General Eichelberger's observation. Out of their total strength in the combat zone of 10,825, the three combat teams of the 32d Division had suffered 9,688 casualties, including 7,125 sick,[11] a casualty rate of almost 90 percent. The 126th Infantry, hardest-hit of the three, had 131 officers and 3,040 enlisted men when it entered the combat zone in mid-November. When it was evacuated to Port Moresby on 22 January, 32 officers and 579 enlisted men were left—less than a full battalion. The regiment as such had ceased to exist.[12]

A detailed strength report of the 126th Infantry Regiment as of 20 January 1943, two days before it was returned to Port Moresby, was as follows:

Regt	Offrs	EM	2d Bn	Offrs	EM
Hq Co . . .	7	39	Hq Co . . .	2	45
Serv Co . . .	3	12	Co E	1	16
At Co . . .	0	10	Co F	1	22
Can Co . . .	0	14	Co G	1	27
			Co H	1	16
	10	75		6	126
1st Bn			*3d Bn*		
Hq Co . . .	4	86	Hq Co . . .	3	27
Co A	2	69	Co I	0	17
Co B	2	62	Co K	0	18
Co C	2	52	Co L	1	14
Co D	0	17	Co M	2	16
	10	286		6	92

---

[7] Rpt, CG Buna Forces, p. 105; 163d Inf, The Battle of Sanananda.

[8] The figures given are for the entire Papuan Campaign, including the period 22 July through 16 November, in which the Australians lost 2,127 killed, wounded, and missing. Combined Australian-American casualties for the fighting at the beachhead, the last phase of operations, were 6,419 killed, wounded, and missing. There were 2,701 more casualties in the Papuan Campaign than on Guadalcanal, where 1,600 were killed, and 4,245 were wounded, but there, during much of the fighting, the positions were reversed: the Japanese were attacking, and the Americans were holding a fortified position.

[9] Ltr, Gen Blamey to Gen MacArthur, 27 Dec 42, in G–3 Jnl, GHQ SWPA; Ltr, John Balfour to author, 12 Mar 50; Interv with Col Teesdale-Smith, 11 Dec 50; Rpt on Opns 18th Inf Bde Gp at Sanananda; Buggy, *Pacific Victory*, p. 213.

---

[10] Ltr, Gen Eichelberger to Gen MacArthur, 14 Jan 43, copy in OCMH files.

[11] Rpt, CG Buna Forces, p. 106.

[12] Ltr, CG 32d Div to GOC NGF, 14 Nov 42, sub: Strength Rpt, copy in OCMH files; 32d Div Strength Rpt, Ser 6450, 20 Jan 43; Memo, Col Tomlinson for CG 32d Div, Ser 6455, 20 Jan 43; Msg, G–4, 32d Div to G–3 32d Div, Ser 6515, 22 Jan 43. Last three in 32d Div G–3 Jnl. Attached divisional troops flown out on 22 January with the 126th Infantry numbered 20 officer and 141 enlisted men. Thus, as moved that day, the entire regiment with all attachments totaled 52 officers and 720 enlisted men.

The amount of sickness during the campaign had been crushingly heavy. With only a few thousand more troops in action, the Australians had 15,575 cases of infectious disease to the end of 1942 alone, including 9,249 cases of malaria, 3,643 cases of dysentery, 1,186 cases of dengue fever, and 186 cases of scrub typhus.[13] The Americans, out of the 14,646 troops committed in the combat area, had a total of 8,659 during the course of the campaign. There were 5,358 cases of malaria among the almost 11,000 troops of the 32d Division who served in New Guinea—4,000 first attacks, and the rest recurrences. In addition, the medical record showed 17 deaths from scrub typhus, and 2,147 cases of "miscellaneous disease," including dysentery and dengue fever.[14]

When the troops reached Australia, a check of their physical condition revealed that each man had suffered a sharp loss in weight, that 563 were still suffering from diarrhea and dysentery, and that 1,200 had hookworm. Anemia, exhaustion, and malnutrition had taken heavy toll: one out of every five had a low blood count, and one out of every eight had poor hemoglobin.[15]

The diarrheas, the anemias, and the hookworms yielded to treatment, but much of the malaria did not. Neither rest, suppressive drugs, nor special care proved of avail in more than half of the cases treated. The patients got worse instead of better. Relapse followed relapse until finally the men had to be dropped from the division in September as unfit for combat. The total number dropped at the time was 2,334 officers and men,[16] all of them casualties of the campaign just as surely as if they had been wounded in battle.

With the story presumably the same in the case of the Australians, the conclusion is inescapable that the fighting in Papua had been even costlier than had at first been thought, and that the victory there, proportionate to the forces engaged, had been one of the costliest of the Pacific war.

The enemy had suffered much heavier losses. The Japanese committed between 16,000 and 17,000 troops to the campaign. They successfully evacuated 1,300 men from Milne Bay and 300 from Goodenough Island. An estimated 1,000 sick and wounded were returned to Rabaul from Basabua during the period that Japanese ships were still making the run there, and about 2,000 men, including sick and wounded, managed to get out by sea and on foot during the closing days of the campaign. The Japanese had thus successfully evacuated about 4,500 men, and lost approximately 12,000.[17] Of the latter number, the Allies buried 7,000 and took 350 pris-

---

[13] AMF, The New Guinea Campaign, Battle Casualties, incl to Ltr, John Balfour to author, 15 Mar 50.

[14] Rpt, CG Buna Forces, p. 105; 163d Inf, The Battle of Sanananda.

[15] Ltr, Maj Herbert B. Shields MC, Actg Div Surgeon, 32d Div, 4 May 43, sub: Monthly Sanitary Rpt; Col De Pasquale, MC, Surgeon 32d Div, Medical Hist of 32d Div, 1 Jan 43–30 Jun 43; Ltr, Col De Pasquale to TAG, 4 Oct 43, sub: Sanitary Rpt for the Month of September 1943. All in The Surgeon General's Historical File. Rpt, CG Buna Forces, p. 105.

[16] Col De Pasquale, Medical Hist of 32d Div, 1 Oct 43–31 Dec 43, in The Surgeon General's Historical File.

[17] No final figure can be found covering the total Japanese commitment in Papua. The figure given, the total of all known Japanese movements to Papua since 22 July, as developed in the narrative above, agrees closely with contemporary estimates, notably with those contained in AMF, The Battle of the Beaches, p. 116, and Buggy, Pacific Victory, p. 213.

JAPANESE PRISONERS AT DOBODURA *eating canned rations supplied by Australian soldiers. These prisoners were brought in by 163d Infantrymen.*

oners.[18] The Japanese apparently buried the remaining 4,500 or 5,000.

Starvation As a Factor in Operations

Starvation had worn down the enemy troops and had contributed directly to their final defeat. The evidences of cannibalism that the Australians and the 163d Infantry encountered on the Soputa-Sanananda track, and the emaciated enemy remains the 127th Infantry found scattered about in the Giruwa hospital area were indicative of the level to which the Japanese had been reduced during the closing weeks of the campaign. How greatly their resistance was undermined by starvation during the weeks immediately preceding was another matter not so easily determined.

When Gona fell on 9 December, the Australians found some moldy rice and a little ammunition left—enough for only a few more days of fighting. There had still been a little food and ammunition on hand when Buna Village was overrun on 14 December, but very little food and virtually no ammunition was taken when Buna Mission fell on 2 January. The Japanese had received their last two ounces of rice on 12 January, two days after the 163d Infantry had found indisputable evidence that some of them had already been reduced to cannibalism. As each successive position on the front fell, it became evident from the horrible emaciation of the corpses of those who had defended it that they could not have held their positions much longer even had there been no attack.

Maj. Mitsuo Koiwai, commanding officer of the *2d Battalion, 41st Infantry,* the only field grade officer of the *South Seas Detach-*

ment known to have gone all through the campaign and survived it,[19] when interrogated at the end of the war, said, "We lost at Buna because we could not retain air superiority, because we could not supply our troops, and because our navy and air force could not disrupt the enemy supply line." When he was asked about the effectiveness of the Allied attack, he agreed that it had been skillfully conducted and then added an observation which had apparently been in the minds of most of the Japanese at the beachhead: "Tactically the Allied co-ordination of fire power and advance was very skillful. However we were in such a position at Buna that we wondered whether the Americans would by-pass us and leave us to starve." [20] It was clear that starvation had been a potent factor in the final reduction of the beachhead and that, had the Allies not been so determined to reduce it by direct attack, hunger would in due course have accomplished the same thing for them.

Artillery, Air, and Naval Support

The artillery had not played the part of which it was capable in the campaign, mostly because not enough pieces of the right type for the task in hand had been sent forward. Though more artillery was repeatedly and urgently requested by the

---

[18] ALF Daily Opns Rpt, No. 295, 3 Feb 43.

[19] Major Koiwai arrived at Basabua with his battalion on 16 August 1942. He led it across the Owen Stanleys to Ioribaiwa and back. On 28 January 1943, after filtering through the Australian lines, he reached Bakumbari with 150 others of the *41st Infantry.* An aggravated case of malaria, picked up at Buna, caused him to be invalided out of the service, and was probably the main reason why he was available for questioning at the end of the war. *18th Army* Opns I, p. 39; GHQ FEC G–2 Hist Sec, Interv of Maj Mitsuo Koiwai, Tokyo, 11 Aug 47, copy in OCMH files.
[20] GHQ FEC G–2 Hist Sec, Interv of Maj Koiwai.

American commanders on the scene, only one artillery piece at the front had been capable of knocking out a Japanese bunker with a single direct hit. This was the 105-mm. howitzer of the 129th Field Artillery Battalion, commanded by Captain Kobs, but even this piece had had too few shells for more than intermittent firing. Had there been more 105's at the front with enough shells and delay fuses (or, as General Waldron suggests, a few 155's similarly provided), there might have been no need to bring in tanks; countless lives might have been saved, and the campaign might have been appreciably shortened.[21]

The air force had played many roles in the campaign, most of them well. Its transports had moved whole regiments and brigades to the front. In addition to evacuating some 6,000 Australians and American sick and wounded, it had flown out other regiments and brigades that were returning to Port Moresby for rest and rehabilitation. It had delivered 2,450 tons of rations, equipment, and ammunition to the troops at the front. It had carried out some seventy-two support missions, using 568 aircraft, 121 of them in close support of attacking ground troops. Ceaselessly reconnoitering the coasts and searching the sea, it had disrupted repeated attempts by the enemy to reinforce and supply his beleaguered beachhead garrison.[22]

The logistical accomplishment of the air force had been superb. The luggers and the freighters (including the K.P.M. ships) had, it is true, brought in by sea more than three times the tonnage that had come in by air.[23] It was nevertheless a fact that the attack could not have been sustained without the airlift, especially during the critical days in November and early December when seaborne supply had been reduced to the merest trickle because of the destruction of the luggers.

The reconnaissance of the coasts and of the sea, the sustained attacks on enemy convoys seeking to reinforce the beachhead, and the frustration of the enemy's efforts to establish supply bases at the mouth of the Kumusi and Mambare Rivers showed the Fifth Air Force and the Australian air units brigaded with it at their best. Nor was there anything to criticize in the way the air force spotted for the artillery, or intercepted enemy aircraft over the combat zone. Both tasks were done admirably.

The quality of its direct support of ground troops was something else again. Even the statistics of this activity are unimpressive—121 sorties flown, 40 tons of bombs dropped, and 97,000 rounds of .30-caliber and .50-caliber ammunition fired. Though this was light support at best, it brought in its train another difficulty. In far too many instances the pilots bombed and shot up Allied troops instead of the enemy, with grievous repercussions on troop morale.

There were good reasons for these frequent mishaps. The Fifth Air Force had at the time too few planes for all its multifarious activities; many of its pilots were inex-

---

[21] Ltr, Gen Waldron to Gen Ward, 5 Mar 51.

[22] 32d Div, G–4 Rear Echelon, Recapitulation of Air Shipments, 13 Nov 42–23 Jan 43; 32d Div AAR, Papuan Campaign; Craven and Cate, *The Army Air Forces in World War II*, IV, 121, 122, 126, 713, 714.

[23] Interv with Col Moffatt, 30 Oct 49; Hist Port Det E, CO SC Buna; 32d Div AAR, Papuan Campaign; 32d Div QM Section, Rpt on Activities, Papuan Campaign. It will be recalled that by the end of December, the freighters alone had brought in more than 3,000 tons of cargo, exclusive of vehicles and tanks. Between 19 November 1942, the date of the first contact with the enemy, and the end of the campaign, the total tonnage delivered by sea (exclusive of tanks, vehicles, and road building equipment of whose weight no record was kept) was 8,560 tons.

perienced; and the only planes available for air-ground co-operation were in general not suited to do the kind of precision bombing required. Not only were the pilots unable to recognize the Allied front lines from the air, but air-ground liaison was virtually nonexistent. It was indeed so bad that there had not been a single instance during the fighting of a pilot's having successful radio contact with the troops on the ground.[24]

As the fighting went on, and it came to be realized that the available aircraft, while excellent for area bombing and the interception of enemy aircraft, could not be relied on for the pinpoint bombing of enemy positions under attack by the front-line troops, the air force was called upon less and less for direct air support. The decision not to use air for the direct support of the ground troops because of the close quarters at which the battle came to be waged was a source of regret to the ground commanders who could have used the air arm to excellent advantage had it been capable at the time of greater discrimination in its bombing and strafing. "I wish," General Eichelberger wrote in late December, "we had some precision dive bombers that could lay the bombs in a barrel. The greatest weapon we have is our air force and I do not like to see it used so little. I realize we should be willing to take a certain number of losses. If I could be sure nineteen bombs out of twenty would drop on the Japanese I would be willing to have the twentieth come in on our own troops, rather than not use air."[25]

The fact that between 22 December, the date of General Eichelberger's letter, and the end of the campaign not a single request was made by American forces in the field for direct air support[26] was an indication of how much the air force had yet to learn about its direct-support responsibility.

The role of the Allied Naval Forces in support of the beachhead fighting had been small. Admiral Carpender's reluctance to send his ships into the waters around Buna had from the first ruled out the possibility of a more active role. In the end, except for the activity of the motor torpedo boats, the actual naval support of the fighting at the beachhead was restricted to a single mission—the transfer there by corvette of the successive echelons of the 18th Brigade.

What the Campaign Taught

On the tactical level, the most important lesson taught was that existing tactics and techniques would have to be developed to a high point of perfection to reduce the kind of strongpoints planted in jungle terrain with which the Japanese had so long held up the Allied advance. By the end of the campaign, a beginning had been made in developing tactics and techniques which, with good artillery support, usually proved effective. The first step was to have patrols "fix" the position of the bunker. Next, the artillery would drive all the enemy troops in the immediate area into the bunker and perhaps stun them. Just before the artillery fire lifted, the infantry would attack under cover of its own fire so as to catch the enemy troops in the bunker before they could get into firing position. The enemy could then be finished off by grenades or the ammonal

---

[24] Ltr, Col W. J. Paul, Dir, Air University Library, Maxwell Field, to Gen Ward, 5 Apr 51, with incl; 32d Div AAR, Papuan Campaign; Craven and Cate, *The Army Air Forces in World War II,* IV, 124, 125, 126.

[25] Ltr, Gen Eichelberger to Gen Sutherland, 22 Dec 42, copy in OCMH files.

[26] G–3 Daily Periodic Rpt, American Forces Buna Area, 21 Dec 42–23 Jan 43.

blast bomb devised by the Australians, flipped into the bunker. Such devices as satchel charges, effective flame throwers, jellied gasoline (napalm), all used in later Pacific operations, were not available at Buna, but the experience there helped to establish the need for them and undoubtedly hastened their development for use in subsequent operations.

The campaign emphasized other lessons, some as old as warfare itself. It drove home the point that troops should be trained in the kind of warfare they are called upon to fight; that they should be habituated to overhead fire during the training period; that they should enter combat "as hard as nails." Although the amount of artillery that general headquarters provided was always far less than the U.S. commanders on the scene regarded as necessary, the campaign demonstrated the soundness of General Harding's and General Waldron's representations to that headquarters that the artillery could go into the jungle with the infantry and, what was more, could be used effectively in jungle terrain. The campaign established that artillery, provided it was of the right kind, was one of the best weapons a commander could have when faced with bunkers of the type that the Japanese had built in the Buna–Gona area.

The campaign made clear that there would have to be better communication between ground and air, and that to be useful in the jungle walkie-talkie radios would have to be greatly improved. It established the effectiveness of the sound-power telephone at ranges of up to two miles. It demonstrated that the .37-mm. antitank gun with canister was an excellent antipersonnel weapon and that rifle grenades were highly effective against enemy troops in trenches or dugouts. The campaign also established the need of a lighter and simpler weapon than the M–1 rifle in jungle warfare—a need that the carbine, had it been available to the troops at Buna, would have met.

On the medical side, the campaign underlined the need for better distribution to the troops of such items as chlorination pellets, vitamin pills, salt tablets, and the like. It suggested the wisdom (following the successful experience with it on Guadalcanal) of thenceforward using atabrine as a malaria suppressive. But even more important, the campaign instilled in the troops and their commanders an awareness of the necessity for the most thoroughgoing malaria discipline. The rigid malaria control measures, so much a feature of subsequent operations in the Southwest Pacific, were in large measure the fruit of the Papuan experience.

The campaign also drove home the lesson that, as a general rule, field kitchens and sterilizing equipment should go with the troops and that failure to bring them forward might jeopardize the health of the entire command. It reaffirmed the age-old lessons that to be effective in combat the troops could not be allowed to go hungry and that they needed such minimum amenities as occasional hot meals, a little variety in the ration, and a chance to rest and clean up after being too long in action.

Conclusion

On the strategic level, the victory in Papua had been a bitter anticlimax, partaking more of tragedy than of triumph. The Japanese had seized the Buna-Gona beachhead on the night of 21–22 July 1942 before Allied troops could fortify it. A bloody and long drawn out campaign had ensued. When it finally ended on 22 January 1943, the only result, strategically speaking, was that after six months of bitter fighting and some 8,500 casualties, including 3,000 dead, the Southwest Pacific Area was exactly where it would have been the previous July had it been able to secure the beachhead before the Japanese got there.

But whatever the cost, the Southwest Pacific Area had finally broken the Japanese toe hold in Papua; it had added the airfields at Dobodura and the port of Oro Bay to its other bases and could now embark upon a more aggressive phase of operations. The hour of the Japanese garrisons in the Huon Peninsula and in western New Britain had struck.

Bibliographical Note

The Allied Side: Documentary Sources

The Records of Higher Headquarters

War Department Files. The strategic background of this volume was developed for the most part from War Department files. The applicable papers of the U.S. Joint Chiefs (JCS), the Combined Chiefs of Staff (CCS), the Combined Staff Planners (CPS), and the Joint Staff Planners (JPS), were consulted in the files of the Assistant Chief of Staff for Operations, War Department General Staff. Two main collections of joint and combined papers, belonging originally to the Operations Division, War Department General Staff (OPD), were used: the files of the Strategy and Policy Group (the "ABC" Files), now in the Departmental Records Branch, Historical Records Section, Adjutant General's office (DRB HRS, AGO) at Alexandria, Virginia, and those of the Executive Group (the "Exec" File), now temporarily in the custody of the Chief of Military History. In these files, the OPD decimal files, the files of OPD's predecessor, WPD, and the various War Department message files were also found the relevant messages and correspondence passing between General Marshall and Admiral King, between Mr. Roosevelt, Mr. Churchill, and Mr. Curtin, and between Mr. Roosevelt, General Marshall, and General MacArthur.

The Files of GHQ SWPA. The files of General Headquarters, Southwest Pacific Area (GHQ SWPA) include the daily G–3 journal in DRB HRS, AGO, and the numbered decimal files in the Organizational Records Branch, Records Administration Center, Adjutant General's Office (ORB RAC, AGO) at Kansas City. The G–3 journal is without question the most valuable single collection of records kept by GHQ. In addition to current planning papers, movement orders, operating instructions, conference minutes, appreciations by the Australian Chiefs of Staff, and the more important messages, general orders, letters, and periodic intelligence reports, each day's journal usually includes the daily G–3 operations report, the daily situation report, the daily G–2 intelligence summary, and the daily operations reports of the Allied Air Forces, Allied Land Forces, and Allied Naval Forces. In the decimal files, the 314.7 MacArthur file, was an invaluable source as regards General MacArthur's relations with Mr. Curtin, and the 384 and 385 files were extremely useful in operational and planning matters.

The Records of Other Headquarters. The files of other higher headquarters which were of use in the preparation of the volume include the following: the Surgeon General's Historical File, the U. S. Army Forces Pacific (AFPAC) Engineer File, and the I Corps File. The Surgeon General's Historical File, kept in the Surgeon General's Office (SGO) at Washington, D. C., was valuable chiefly for its monthly reports on the physical condition of the troops in the field. The AFPAC Engineer File is the wartime file of Maj. Gen. Hugh J. Casey,

General MacArthur's Engineer Officer. The best single source for the construction of the early bases in the Southwest Pacific Area, it was consulted in the District Engineer's Office, Baltimore, Maryland, its present repository. The I Corps File, kept in ORB RAC, AGO, at Kansas City, was useful for its account of the activities of the corps staff during the campaign.

The Combat Records

American Ground Action. All the official records of Buna Force, I Corps, the 32d Division, the 163d Infantry, and the attached units, located at the time of writing in the DRB HRS, AGO, at Alexandria, and in the ORB RAC, AGO, at Kansas City, were consulted. The G–2, G–3 journals of the 32d Division, filed together during the period 17 September to 30 November, and thereafter (and until the end of the campaign) kept separately—a total of 8,921 separate messages and other entries—were a principal, primary source. The message files and journals of the combat units on the battalion and regimental level were also valuable primary sources. The histories and after action reports (AAR's) of these units, and General Eichelberger's official report, Report of the Commanding General Buna Forces on the Buna Campaign, December 1, 1942–January 25, 1942, were useful secondary sources.

Other sources used included on-the-spot reports of three Army Ground Forces observers—Col. Harry Knight, Col. Herbert B. Laux, and Col. H. F. Handy. The report of Maj. David B. Parker, an engineer observer, who was present at Buna during the early days of the attack, was useful. Materials in the possession of Mr. Hanson W. Baldwin, Military Editor of *The New York*

Times, on the march across the Owen Stanleys of the 2d Battalion, 126th Infantry, obtained by Mr. Baldwin from a participant, were also helpful, as were the dispatches from the field of another staff member of *The New York Times,* Mr. F. Tillman Durdin. Col. Bernd G. Baetcke's letters to GHQ SWPA on the early fighting on the Sanananda track were a useful source, as was an interview by the Historical Section, GHQ SWPA, with Col. J. Tracy Hale, Jr., previously commander of Warren Force. Two Infantry School monographs written by participants—Maj. Alfred Medendorp's study, The March and Operations of the Antitank and Cannon Companies, 126th Infantry, in the Attack on Wairopi, and Capt. Louis A. Chagnon's account of his experiences in the Tarakena area—served to clarify events which otherwise would have remained obscure. The letters passing between Maj. Gen. Clovis E. Byers and Col. Roy F. Zinser helped to clear up certain disputed points on the capture of the Coconut Grove, and the personal experiences of troop commanders of the 163d Infantry at Sanananda, as embodied in the 41st Division training notes filed in DRB HRS, AGO, were of great help in describing the final phases of the Sanananda fighting.

Australian Ground Action. The following were the principal official operational reports used to portray Australian ground action: Allied Land Forces, Report of New Guinea Operations, Buna to Ioribaiwa; Allied Land Forces, Report on New Guinea Operations, 23 September 1942–22 January 1943; Allied Land Forces, Summary of Operations in New Guinea, Owen Stanley, Buna–Gona Areas, 22 July 1942–22 January 1943; Allied Land Forces, Report on New Guinea Operations, Goodenough Island and Milne

Bay; New Guinea Force, Notes on Operations in New Guinea, Serial 3; Commander Milne Force, Report on Operations, 25 August–7 September 1942; 18th Brigade, Report on Operations 18th Australian Infantry Brigade Group at Cape Endaiadere–Giropa Point and Sanananda Area, 14 December 1942–22 January 1943, with appendixes.

Draft chapters in the forthcoming Australian official history by Dudley McCarthy, The Southwest Pacific Area: The First Year, which the author was permitted to see and use, were drawn upon heavily in the discussion of early operations on the Sanananda track, and the fighting at Gona. Brig. S. H. Porter's report on the part played by the 30th Brigade in the Owen Stanleys, and Osmar White's notes on the fighting in the Owen Stanleys (copies of which are to be found in OCMH files) were of help in portraying the desperate fighting along the Kokoda track. Another useful source was Maj. J. W. Dunlop's account of the operations of his battalion, the 2/2d, on the Sanananda track. The daily Allied Land Forces operations report, the daily G–3 report, and the situation reports of the Australian units filed in the 32d Division G–3 Journal were constant stand-bys, and there was always John Balfour of the office of the Official Australian War Historian at Canberra to write to, when a knotty problem arose to which the available Australian documents seemed to give no ready answer.

Air Force and Naval Action. The day-to day stand-by for Allied air operations was the daily Allied Air Forces operations report in the G–3 Journal, GHQ SWPA, and for naval operations in the SWPA, the periodic reports of Allied Naval Forces filed in the same journal. Two Air Forces studies—The

Army Air Forces in Australia to the Summer of 1942, and Air Action in Papua, 21 July 1942–23 January 1943—were useful, as was the History of the 19th Bomb Group (H). Manuscript histories in the Office of Naval History, Washington, which were of value included the History of U.S. Naval Administration in World War II, Commander U.S. Naval Forces, Southwest Pacific, and Comdr. Robert J. Bulkley's History of Motor Torpedo Boats in the U.S. Navy. The three ONI operational studies cited—Early Raids in the Pacific, The Battle of the Coral Sea, and The Battle of Midway—were all useful.

Miscellaneous Records

The following miscellaneous records were used: Allied Geographic Section, Southwest Pacific Area, Terrain Study No. 28, Main Routes Across New Guinea, 18 October 1942; Maj. Gen. Julian F. Barnes, The Organization and Activities of the United States Army Forces in Australia (USAFIA); History of Port Detachment E, Combined Operational Service Command (COSC), Buna, all in OCMH files; War Department, Survey of Australia, 25 February, 1942, in G–2, WDGS files; Report on Australia for the Commander in Chief Allied Forces, 14 March 1942, in G–3 Journal, GHQ SWPA; The *Koninklijke Paktevaart Maatschappij* (K.P.M. Line) and the War in the Southwest Pacific, in the Office of Naval History, Washington.

Information From Participants

Interviews. Except for an interview of Maj. Gen. Albert W. Waldron by 1st Lt. Kenneth Hechler, and one of Lt. Gen.

382

Richard K. Sutherland by Louis Morton, all the interviews used in the preparation of the volume were conducted by the author in Washington, D. C. Individuals interviewed by him there included: Lt. Gen. Stephen J. Chamberlin, Lt. Gen. Robert L. Eichelberger, Maj. Gen. Clovis E. Byers, Maj. Gen. Edwin F. Harding, Col. Bernd G. Baetcke, Col. Julian F. Barnes, Col. John E. Grose, Lt. Col. Clifton P. Hannum, Lt. Col. Carroll K. Moffatt, Lt. Col. Peter S. Teesdale-Smith, AMF, and Maj. Robert H. Odell. Copies of the interviews are in OCMH files.

Letters. Letters replying to the author's inquiries or reviewing the manuscript in draft form were received from the following: Gen. George C. Kenney, Lt. Gen. Robert L. Eichelberger, Lt. Gen. Richard K. Sutherland, Maj. Gen. Joseph S. Bradley, Maj. Gen. Clovis E. Byers, Maj. Gen. Hugh J. Casey, Maj. Gen. Jens A. Doe, Maj. Gen. Edwin F. Harding, Maj. Gen. Clarence A. Martin, Maj. Gen. Albert W. Waldron, Maj. Gen. Charles A. Willoughby, Col. Bernd G. Baetcke, Col. Richard D. Boerem, Col. Charles R. Dawley, Col. John E. Grose, Col. Carl Hanna, MC, Col. Paul G. Hollister, Col. Harold M. Lindstrom, Col. Alexander J. MacNab, Col. Kelsie E. Miller, Col. Gordon B. Rogers, Col. Herbert A. Smith, Col. Clarence M. Tomlinson, Lt. Col. Peter L. Dal Ponte, Lt. Col. Oliver O. Dixon, Lt. Col. Charles W. Hash, Lt. Col. Wilbur A. Larson, Lt. Col. Bevin D. Lee, Lt. Col. Robert P. McCampbell, Lt. Col. Carroll K. Moffatt, Lt. Col. Ewald E. Mietzel, Lt. Col. Herbert M. Smith, Lt. Col. Bert Zeeff, Maj. Robert H. Odell, Maj. Phillip A. Jenson, and Capt. Alfred E. Meyer. Lt. Gen. V. A. H. Sturdee, and Lt. Gen. Sydney F. Rowell, then Chief of Staff

and Vice Chief of Staff respectively of the Australian General Staff, wrote an extremely valuable memorandum for the author's benefit on the deliberations of the Australian Chiefs of Staff during the early days of the war, and General Rowell, by that time Chief of Staff in succession to General Sturdee, reviewed the entire manuscript, and made very valuable comments on it.

Private Papers. General Eichelberger and General Harding each loaned the author his letters and private papers for use in writing the volume, and General Harding loaned his diary. Colonel Grose also gave the author permission to use his diary, and General Waldron put all his papers relating to the campaign at the author's disposal, as did Colonel Dawley and Major Odell. These private papers were of value, not only for the wealth of information they afforded, but also for the insight they gave the author into his other materials.

The Japanese Side: Documentary Sources

The Wartime Records

Captured Documents. Japanese documents captured in the fighting and published by the Allied Translator and Interpreter Section, Southwest Pacific Area (ATIS SWPA), a section of G–2, GHQ SWPA, proved very useful since they included diaries, messages, field orders, headquarters correspondence, and the like. A full set of these documents, divided into two principal groups, Enemy Publications and Current Translations, are on file in the Intelligence Library, War Department General Staff. Relevant materials were found in Enemy Publications 24 through 39, and in Current Translations 1 through 4 and 14 through 29.

Prisoner of War Interrogations. Prisoner of war interrogations are to be found in the 32d Division Interrogation and Translation File, and in the mimeographed publications of the G–2 Section of Buna Force. Generally speaking, these interrogations were of limited usefulness since most of the prisoners taken were either laborers or low-ranking enlisted men, who, except for conditions on their immediate front, knew little of what was going on.

Intelligence Summaries. The G–2 Daily Summary of Enemy Intelligence, and the periodic intelligence summaries of the Allied Air Forces, the Allied Naval Forces, and of the Combined Operational Intelligence Center (COIC) were the best day-to-day sources on what the Allies knew or thought they knew about the enemy. The periodic intelligence summaries put out by the 32d Division and by Buna Force were useful in this respect, as was the current intelligence information radioed or phoned to the 32d Division by New Guinea Force and recorded in the division's G–2, G–3 journals.

Intelligence Studies. The following intelligence studies were particularly useful: Allied Land Forces, History of the Lae-Salamaua Garrison (Japanese), in DRB HRS, AGO; Southeast Asia Translator and Interpreter Section, Historical Bulletin No. 243, History of the Japanese *28th Army,* in G–2, WDGS Files.

The Postwar Records

Japanese Studies in World War II. These studies were prepared under the direction of the Historical Section, G–2 Far East Command (FEC) by former Japanese staff officers from official documents and their own knowledge or personal recollection of the events described. The studies are uneven in quality, but taken together form a valuable summary of Japanese operations in World War II. Studies used in preparation of the volume include the following: No. 35, Japanese Activities in Mopping-Up Operations; No. 36, Central Pacific Operations; No. 39, *17th Army* Operations, Volume I; No. 41, *18th Army* Operations, Volume I; No. 48, *Southeast Area* Naval Operations, Volume I; No. 55, *South Seas Detachment* Operations; No. 72, Historical Record, *Army Section Imperial General Headquarters;* No. 100, Naval Account, Japanese Invasion Eastern New Guinea; No. 109, *South Seas Detachment* Operations, 2d edition.

Postwar Interrogations. The published interrogations of Japanese officials by the Naval Analysis Division of the United States Strategic Bombing Survey referred to elsewhere were of value, especially as to Japanese naval operations and strategic thinking. The interrogation by the G–2 Section, Far East Command, of Maj. Mitsuo Koiwai, a survivor of the *South Seas Detachment,* was an exceedingly valuable source, as was the Australian interrogation at Rabaul of Lt. Gen. Hatazo Adachi, Commanding General, *18th Army,* and members of his staff. The other FEC interrogation cited, that of Col. Kazuyoshi Obata, Adachi's supply officer, was of limited usefulness even as to supply matters.

The ATIS SCAP Documents. The orders of the *Navy Section, Imperial General Headquarters,* used in the volume are from the files of the Allied Translator and Interpreter Section, Supreme Commander Allied Powers (ATIS SCAP), postwar successor to ATIS SWPA

Published Materials

Dispatches

"*ABDACOM*": *An Official Account of Events in the South-West Pacific Command, January–February 1942* (New Delhi, 1942).

Despatch by the Supreme Commander of the ABDA Area to the Combined Chiefs of Staff on the Operations in the South-West Pacific: 15 January 1942 to 25 February 1942 (London, 1948).

Books

Hugh Buggy, *Pacific Victory* (Melbourne, 1945). A popular, semiofficial account of Pacific operations, written for Australians.

Winston S. Churchill, *The Hinge of Fate* (Boston, 1950). Useful for its discussion of Mr. Churchill's relationships with Mr. Curtin.

Wesley F. Craven and James L. Cate, eds., *The Army Air Forces in World War II*, Volume I, *Early Plans and Operations, January 1939 to August 1942* (Chicago, 1948). A well-written, well-documented history.

Wesley F. Craven and James L. Cate, eds., *The Army Air Forces in World War II*, Volume IV, *The Pacific: Guadalcanal to Saipan, August 1942 to July 1944* (Chicago, 1950). Includes a valuable summary of air action at Buna.

Lt. Gen. Robert L. Eichelberger, *Our Jungle Road to Tokyo* (New York, 1950). Useful for its Buna chapters.

Comdr. Eric A. Feldt, RAN, *The Coast Watchers* (Melbourne, 1947). The accomplishments of the Coast Watchers by their wartime chief.

C. Hartley Grattan, ed., *Australia* (Berkeley, 1947). A notable symposium, useful chiefly for Gavin Long's excellent chapter, "Australia in the Second World War."

Frazier Hunt, *MacArthur and the War Against Japan* (New York, 1944). An admiring portrait of General MacArthur by a journalist accredited to his headquarters.

George H. Johnson, *The Toughest Fighting in the World* (New York, 1943). An Australian correspondent describes the New Guinea fighting.

George H. Johnson, *Pacific Partner* (New York, 1944). A vivid picture of Australia in wartime.

E. J. Kahn, Jr., *G. I. Jungle* (New York, 1943). Sketches of Army life in New Guinea by a former warrant officer of the 32d Division.

Gen. George C. Kenney, *General Kenney Reports* (New York, 1944). A vivid memoir useful for Buna operations but occasionally inaccurate as to detail.

John Miller, jr., *Guadalcanal: The First Offensive*, UNITED STATES ARMY IN WORLD WAR II (Washington, 1949). The Guadalcanal campaign by an Army historian.

Samuel Eliot Morison, *History of United States Naval Operations in World War II*, Volume III, *The Rising Sun in the Pacific* (Boston, 1948). The first Pacific volume in this excellent, semiofficial series.

Samuel Eliot Morison, *History of United States Naval Operations in World War II*, Volume IV, *Coral Sea, Midway, and Submarine Actions* (Boston, 1949). The best account to date of the Coral Sea and Midway actions.

Office of the Chief Engineer, U. S. Army Forces Pacific, *Engineers in Theater Operations*, Volume I (Washington, 1949). The accomplishments of the Corps of Engineers in General MacArthur's theater.

U. S. Army Air Forces, *The Army Air Forces in the War Against Japan 1941–1942* (Washington, 1945). A useful, well-written summary by the wartime historical section of the Army Air Forces.

United States Strategic Bombing Survey, *The Allied Campaign Against Rabaul* (Washington, 1946). An excellent piece of work, based in large part on postwar interrogations at Rabaul.

United States Strategic Bombing Survey, *The Campaigns of the Pacific War* (Washington, 1946). A good, one-volume treatment of the naval side of the Pacific war by the Naval Analysis Division of the Bomb Survey.

United States Strategic Bombing Survey, *Interrogations of Japanese Officials* (Washington, n.d.). A useful compilation chiefly concerned with Japanese strategic thinking and naval operations.

Roger W. Shugg and Harvey A. De-Weerd, *The World at War: 1939–1944* (Washington, 1945). A useful reference work.

Roland E. Walker, *The Australian Economy in War and Reconstruction* (New York, 1947). A scholarly study.

Osmar White, *Green Armor* (New York, 1945). The fighting in the Southwest Pacific, as witnessed by a noted Australian correspondent.

Pamphlets

Australian Military Forces, *The Battle of Wau* (Melbourne, 1943). A popular account of the fighting in the Bulolo Valley.

Australian Military Forces, *The Battle of the Beaches* (Melbourne, 1944). The fighting at the Buna–Gona beachhead, written for Australians.

Military Intelligence Division, War Department General Staff, *Papuan Campaign, The Buna-Sanananda Operation, 16 November 1942–23 January 1943*. AMERICAN FORCES IN ACTION SERIES (Washington, 1944). A brief, well-written preliminary study designed at the time it was written for the information of wounded veterans of the campaign.

United States Strategic Bombing Survey, *The Fifth Air Force in the War Against Japan* (Washington, 1947). A useful summary.

Office of Naval Intelligence, *The Japanese Story of the Battle of Midway* (Washington, 1947). Midway through Japanese eyes.

Articles

Hanson W. Baldwin, "Doughboy's March a High Point in the War," *The New York Times*, 7 May 1944. The march of the 2d Battalion, 126th Infantry, to Jaure based on an eyewitness account.

Lt. Gen. George H. Brett, "The MacArthur I Knew," *True*, October 1947. General Brett's relations with General MacArthur.

F. Tillman Durdin, "The Grim Hide and Seek of Jungle Warfare," *The New York Times Magazine*, 7 March 1943. A thoughtful, well-presented analysis.

E. J. Kahn, Jr., "The Terrible Days of Company E," *The Saturday Evening Post*, Part I, 8 January 1944; Part II, 15 January 1944. A vivid account of the march across the Owen Stanleys developed from diaries and the recollection of participants.

Walton L. Robinson, "AKAGI, Famous Japanese Carrier," in *U.S. Naval Institute Proceedings*, May 1948. The AKAGI in action.

Glossary

AAA	Airborne Antiaircraft Artillery
AAF	Army Air Forces
A&P	Ammunition and Pioneer, as in A&P platoon
AAR	After Action Report
ABDA Area	An Allied strategic area extending from the Bay of Bengal through Burma and the Netherlands Indies to northwest Australia
ABDACOM	The American-British-Dutch-Australian command operating in the ABDA area
ACH	Area Combined Headquarters, as in ACH Townsville
ACofS	Assistant Chief of Staff
Actn	Action
Adv	Advance
AF	Air Force
AFPAC	U.S. Army Forces, Pacific
AG	Adjutant General
AGF	Army Ground Forces
AGO	Adjutant General's Office
AGS	Allied Geographic Section, Southwest Pacific Area
AIF	Australian Imperial Forces
Airintel	Air Intelligence
ALF	Allied Land Forces
ALO	Air Liaison Officer
AMF	Australian Military Forces
ANF	Allied Naval Forces
ANGAU	The Australia-New Guinea Administrative Unit
ANZAC Area	An Allied strategic command covering principally the ocean areas east and northeast of Australia
ANZAC Force	The naval force operating in the ANZAC area.
App	Appendix
Arty	Artillery
ATIS	Allied Translator and Interpreter Section
Aust	Australian
BAR	Browning Automatic Rifle
Bde	Brigade
Bde Gp	Brigade Group
Bn	Battalion

BOLERO	The build-up of troops and supplies in the United Kingdom in preparation for a cross-channel attack
BOSTON	The Abau-Mullins Harbor area in southeast New Guinea
Br	Branch
Brig	Brigadier
Bul	Bulletin
Bur	Bureau
Butai	Japanese for force, usually of battalion strength or above
Ca.	*Circa,* about
CAV	Cavalry
CCS	Combined Chiefs of Staff
CE	Corps of Engineers
CG	Commanding General
CGS	Chief of the General Staff
CinC	Commander in Chief
CINCPAC	Commander in Chief U. S. Pacific Fleet
CINCSWPA	Commander in Chief Southwest Pacific Area
CM–IN	Classified Message In
CMF	Citizen Military Forces
CM–OUT	Classified Message Out
COIC	Combined Operational Intelligence Center
COMANZACFOR	Commander of ANZAC Force
COMCRUDIV	Commander Cruiser Division
Comdr	Commander
COMINCH	Commander in Chief U.S. Fleet
COMSOPAC	Commander South Pacific Area
COMSOPACFOR	Commander South Pacific Force
Conf	Conference
COSC	Combined Operational Service Command
CPS	Combined Staff Planners
CT	Combat Team; Current Translations
CWO	Chief Warrant Officer
CWR	Combined War Room
DCGS	Deputy Chief of the General Staff (Australian)
Demob	Demobilization
Dept	Department
Det	Detachment
Dir	Directive
DNI	Director of Naval Intelligence (Australian)
DOI	Director of Intelligence, Allied Air Forces
DRB HRS	Departmental Records Branch, Historical Records Section, AGO
DSC	Distinguished Service Cross

Engr	Engineer
EP	Enemy Publications
Exec	Executive
FA	Field Artillery
FALL RIVER	Milne Bay
FEC	Far East Command
Fld	Field
FO	Field Order
G–1	Personnel Officer of division or higher staff
G–2	Intelligence Officer
G–3	Operations Officer
G–4	Supply Officer
GHQ	General Headquarters
GO	General Orders
G.O.C.	General Officer Commanding
Gp	Group
GS	General Staff
Hist	History or Historical
IMB	Independent Mixed Brigade (Japanese)
Ind	Independent
Instns	Instructions
Intel	Intelligence
Interr	Interrogation
JCS	U.S. Joint Chiefs of Staff
Jnl	Journal
JPS	Joint Staff Planners
KANGA Force	The Australian force in the Bulolo Valley
KIA	Killed in Action
KPM Line	The Royal Steamship Packet Line (Dutch)
Lanops	Allied Land Forces Operations
LCVP	Landing Craft, Vehicle and Personnel
LHQ	Allied Land Headquarters
LILLIPUT	The plan for the supply of Buna following its capture
LMG	Light Machine Gun
MAPLE	Port Moresby
MAROUBRA Force	The Australian force charged with defense of the Kokoda Trail
MC	Medical Corps
Med	Medical
MG	Machine Gun
MIA	Missing in Action
Mil Comd	Military Command
MLR	Main Line of Resistance

Msg	Message
Nankai Shitai	*The South Seas Detachment*
NGF	New Guinea Force
NGVR	New Guinea Volunteer Rifles
NOIC	Naval Officer in Charge
OCE	Office of the Chief Engineer
OCMH	Office of the Chief of Military History
Off	Officer
OI	Operating Instructions
ONI	Office of Naval Intelligence
OPD	Operations Division, War Department General Staff
Opns	Operations
ORB RAC	Organizational Records Branch, Records Administrative Center, AGO
Ord	Ordnance
Pac Strat	Pacific strategy
PETERSBURG	The plan for the evacuation of New Guinea should Guadalcanal fall to the Japanese
PIB	The Papuan Infantry Battalion
Plat	Platoon
POA	Pacific Ocean Area
PROVIDENCE	Allied plan to occupy Buna and establish an airfield in the Buna area
PTO	Pacific Theater of Operations
RAA	Royal Australian Artillery
RAAF	Royal Australian Air Force
Rad	Radio
RAE	Royal Australian Engineers
RAF	Royal Air Force
RAN	Royal Australian Navy
R&R	Records and Routing Sheet
RCT	Regimental Combat Team
Recon	Reconnaissance
S–1	Personnel Officer of regimental or battalion staff
S–2	Intelligence Officer
S–3	Operations Officer
S–4	Supply Officer
S&P	Strategy and Policy Group, OPD
SCAP	Supreme Commander Allied Powers
SCR	Signal Corps Radio
SEATIC	South East Asia Translator and Interpreter Center
Sec	Section
Ser	Serial

Shitai	Japanese for task force
Sig	Signal (radio message)
SIO	Supervising Intelligence Officer, RAN (the head of the Coast Watchers)
Sitrep	Situation Report
SNLF	Japanese Special Naval Landing Force
SOPAC	South Pacific Area
SSUSA	Special Staff, U.S. Army
SWPA	Southwest Pacific Area
Tac	Tactical
TAG	The Adjutant General
Tai	Japanese for a small force, usually of company strength or below
Tng	Training
Tr	Translation
Tulsa	An early SWPA plan for the reduction of Rabaul
USAFFE	U.S. Army Forces in the Far East
USAFIA	U.S. Army Forces in Australia
USASOS	U.S. Army Services of Supply
USFIA	U.S. Forces in Australia
USSBS	U.S. Strategic Bombing Survey
VCGS	Vice Chief of the Australian General Staff
VDC	Volunteer Defense Corps (Australian)
WIA	Wounded in Action

Basic Military Map Symbols*

Symbols within a rectangle indicate a military unit, within a triangle an observation post, and within a circle a supply point.

Military Units—Identification

Antiaircraft Artillery . . . .

Armored Command . . . .

Army Air Forces . . . .

Artillery, except Antiaircraft and Coast Artillery . . . .

Cavalry, Horse . . . .

Cavalry, Mechanized . . . .

Chemical Warfare Service . . . .

Coast Artillery . . . .

Engineers . . . .

Infantry . . . .

Medical Corps . . . .

Ordnance Department . . . .

Quartermaster Corps . . . .

Signal Corps . . . .

Tank Destroyer . . . .

Transportation Corps . . . .

Veterinary Corps . . . .

Airborne units are designated by combining a gull wing symbol with the arm or service symbol:

Airborne Artillery . . . .

Airborne Infantry . . . .

---

*For complete listing of symbols in use during the World War II period, see FM 21–30, dated October 1943, from which these are taken.

Size Symbols

The following symbols placed either in boundary lines or above the rectangle, triangle, or circle inclosing the identifying arm or service symbol indicate the size of military organization:

Squad . . . . ●

Section . . . . ● ●

Platoon . . . . ● ● ●

Company, troop, battery, Air Force flight I

Battalion, cavalry squadron, or Air Force squadron . . . . I I

Regiment or group; combat team (with abbreviation CT following identifying numeral) . . . . I I I

Brigade, Combat Command of Armored Division, or Air Force Wing X

Division or Command of an Air Force XX

Corps or Air Force XXX

Army XXXX

Group of Armies XXXXX

EXAMPLES

The letter or number to the left of the symbol indicates the unit designation; that to the right, the designation of the parent unit to which it belongs. Letters or numbers above or below boundary lines designate the units separated by the lines:

Company A, 137th Infantry . . . . A⊠137

8th Field Artillery Battalion . . . . •|8

Combat Command A, 1st Armored Division . . . . A⬭|I

Observation Post, 23d Infantry . . . . △23

Command Post, 5th Infantry Division . . . . ⊠5

Boundary between 137th and 138th Infantry . . . . —137—III—138

Weapons

Machine gun . . . . •→

Gun . . . . •

Gun battery . . . . ⊔⊔⊔

Howitzer or Mortar . . . . •

Tank . . . . ◇

Self-propelled gun . . . . ⬓

UNITED STATES ARMY IN WORLD WAR II

The following volumes have been published or are in press:

The War Department
  Chief of Staff: Prewar Plans and Preparations
  Washington Command Post: The Operations Division
  Strategic Planning for Coalition Warfare: 1941–1942
  Strategic Planning for Coalition Warfare: 1943–1944
  Global Logistics and Strategy: 1940–1943
  Global Logistics and Strategy: 1943–1945
  The Army and Economic Mobilization
  The Army and Industrial Manpower
The Army Ground Forces
  The Organization of Ground Combat Troops
  The Procurement and Training of Ground Combat Troops
The Army Service Forces
  The Organization and Role of the Army Service Forces
The Western Hemisphere
  The Framework of Hemisphere Defense
  Guarding the United States and Its Outposts
The War in the Pacific
  The Fall of the Philippines
  Guadalcanal: The First Offensive
  Victory in Papua
  CARTWHEEL: The Reduction of Rabaul
  Seizure of the Gilberts and Marshalls
  Campaign in the Marianas
  The Approach to the Philippines
  Leyte: The Return to the Philippines
  Triumph in the Philippines
  Okinawa: The Last Battle
  Strategy and Command: The First Two Years
The Mediterranean Theater of Operations
  Northwest Africa: Seizing the Initiative in the West
  Sicily and the Surrender of Italy
  Salerno to Cassino
  Cassino to the Alps
The European Theater of Operations
  Cross-Channel Attack
  Breakout and Pursuit
  The Lorraine Campaign
  The Siegfried Line Campaign
  The Ardennes: Battle of the Bulge
  The Last Offensive

Index

☆ U.S. GOVERNMENT PRINTING OFFICE: 1988 222–407